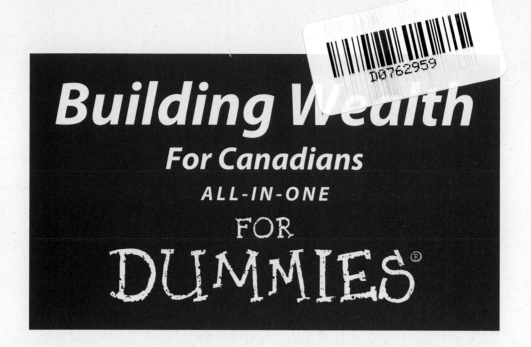

Building Wealth

For Canadians

ALL-IN-ONE

FOR

DUMMIES®

by Bryan Borzykowski, Andrew Bell, Christopher Cottier, BSc, MBA, Andrew Dagys, CMA, Matthew Elder, Lita Epstein, Douglas Gray, LLB, Michael Griffis, Ann C. Logue, MBA, Peter Mitham & Paul Mladjenovic, CFP

John Wiley & Sons Canada, Ltd.

Building Wealth For Canadians All-in-One For Dummies®

Published by
John Wiley & Sons Canada, Ltd.
6045 Freemont Boulevard
Mississauga, Ontario, L5R 4J3
www.wiley.com

Copyright © 2012 by John Wiley & Sons Canada, Ltd.

Published by John Wiley & Sons Canada. Ltd.

For general information on John Wiley & Sons Canada, Ltd., including all books published by John Wiley & Sons, Inc., please call our warehouse, Tel 1-800-567-4797. For reseller information, including discounts and premium sales, please call our sales department, Tel 416-646-7992. For press review copies, author interviews, or other publicity information, please contact our marketing department, Tel 416-646-4584, Fax 416-236-4448.

For technical support, please visit www.wiley.com/techsupport.

Wiley also publishes its books in a variety of electronic formats and by print-on-demand. Not all content that is available in standard print versions of this book may appear or be packaged in all book formats. If you have purchased a version of this book that did not include media that is referenced by or accompanies a standard print version, you may request this media by visiting http://booksupport.wiley.com. For more information about Wiley products, visit us at www.wiley.com.

Library and Archives Canada Cataloguing in Publication

Building wealth for Canadians all-in-one for dummies / Bryan Borzykowski ... [et al.].

Includes index.

Issued also in electronic formats.

ISBN 978-1-118-18106-5 (pbk.)

  1. Investments—Canada. 2. Finance, Personal—Canada.

I. Borzykowski, Bryan

HG5152.B85 2012   332.6'0971   C2011-907867-8

E-ISBNs: 978-1-118-22393-2, 978-1-118-22396-3, 978-1-118-22399-4

Printed in the United States of America

1 2 3 4 5 RRD 16 15 14 13 12

WILEY

About the Authors

Bryan Borzykowski is an award-winning financial journalist, who writes mostly about investing, personal finance and small business. He's the co-author of *Day Trading For Canadians For Dummies* and contributes to the *Globe and Mail*, *Business* magazine, the *Toronto Star*, *MoneySense* and other leading Canadian publications. You can find Bryan at www. bryanborzykowski.com or on Twitter @bborzyko.

Andrew Bell was an investment reporter and editor with *The Globe and Mail* for 12 years. He joined Business News Network as a reporter in 2001. Bell, an import from Dublin, Ireland, was for 10 years the main compiler of Stars & Dogs in Saturday's Globe. The roundup of hot and damp stocks and mutual funds was an invaluable therapeutic aid in relieving his own myriad jealousies, regrets, and resentments. He has also taken to the stage, where he practises a demanding "method" that involves getting the audience and other performers as off-balance and upset as possible. He lives in Cabbagetown, Toronto, with his wife and daughter.

Christopher Cottier, BSc, MBA, is a senior investment advisor based in British Columbia. In 1982, he left the world of banking to join the investment industry in Vancouver so he could continue to pursue his love of rugby. More than twenty five years later, he's still managing money and playing rugby. With Betty Jane Wylie, Christopher is the co-author of *The Best Is Yet to Come: Enjoying a Financially Secure Retirement* (Key Porter). Christopher was ably assisted by Daniel Quon, BA, who has been awarded the Queen Elizabeth 11 Golden Jubilee Medal.

Andrew Dagys, CMA, is a best-selling author who has written and coauthored several books, including *Stocking Investing For Canadians For Dummies* and *Investing Online For Canadians For Dummies*. He has appeared on Canada AM and several popular CBC broadcasts to offer his insights on the Canadian and world investment landscapes. Andrew has contributed columns to *CanadianLiving, Forever Young,* and other publications. He has appeared on Canada AM and several popular CBC broadcasts to offer his insights on the Canadian and world investment landscapes.

Matthew Elder is a writer and communications consultant based in Toronto. Previously he was vice-president, content and editorial, of *Morningstar Canada*. A Montreal native, he was a columnist and editor specializing in personal finance with *The Gazette* for 10 years before moving to the *Financial Post* in 1995, where he was mutual funds editor and columnist until joining *Morningstar* in 2000.

Lita Epstein, who earned her MBA from Emory University's Goizueta Business School, enjoys helping people develop good financial, investing, and tax planning skills. She designs and teaches online courses and has written more than 20 books, including *Bookkeeping For Dummies* and *Reading Financial Reports For Dummies*, both published by Wiley.

Douglas Gray, B.A., LL.B., formerly a practicing lawyer, has extensive experience in all aspects of real estate and mortgage financing. He has acted on behalf of buyers, sellers, developers, investors, lenders and borrowers. In addition, he has over 35 years of personal experience investing in real estate. He is the author of 26 best-selling real estate, business and personal finance books, as well as a consultant and columnist.

Mr. Gray gives seminars on real estate throughout Canada to the public, as well as for professional-development programs for the real estate industry. He has presented to more than 250,000 people and is frequently interviewed by the media as an authority on real estate and small business entrepreneurship. Mr. Gray is president of the Canadian Enterprise Development Group Inc. and lives in Vancouver, BC. His website is www.homebuyer.ca.

Michael Griffis became an active trader in the mid 1980s. He first traded commodities and precious metals after taking a commodities trading class as part of his MBA program at Rollins College. He became a stockbroker in 1992, where he helped businesses and individuals manage investments in stocks, bonds, mutual funds, retirement plans, 401(k) employee-savings plans, and asset management programs. Michael is an author and business owner and has written about stock trading for online audiences.

Ann C. Logue, MBA, is the author of *Day Trading For Dummies* and *Emerging Markets For Dummies*. She has written for Barron's, The New York Times, Newsweek Japan, Wealth Manager, and the International Monetary Fund. She is a lecturer at the Liautaud Graduate School of Business at the University of Illinois at Chicago. Her current career follows 12 years of experience as an investment analyst. She has a B.A. from Northwestern University and an M.B.A. from the University of Chicago, and she holds the Chartered Financial Analyst (CFA) designation.

Peter Mitham has written on Canadian real estate for publications in Canada and abroad. He contributes a weekly column of real estate news for *Business in Vancouver* and writes regularly for *Western Investor*, a sister publication focused on real estate investment opportunities in Western Canada, as well as *Canadian Real Estate Magazine.* He has also collaborated with Douglas Gray on *The Canadian Landlord's Guide: Expert Advice for the Profitable Real Estate Investor* (Wiley).

Paul Mladjenovic, CFP is a certified financial planner practitioner, writer, and public speaker. His business, PM Financial Services, has helped people with financial and business concerns since 1981. He is the author of *Stock Investing For Dummies* (Wiley) and has accurately forecast many economic events, such as the rise of gold, the decline of the U.S. dollar, and the housing crisis. Paul's personal website can be found at www.mladjenovic.com.

Publisher's Acknowledgments

We're proud of this book; please send us your comments at http://dummies.custhelp.com. For other comments, please contact our Customer Care Department within the U.S. at 877-762-2974, outside the U.S. at 317-572-3993 or fax 317-572-4002.

Some of the people who helped bring this book to market include the following:

Acquisitions and Editorial

Editor: Anam Ahmed

Production Editor: Pauline Ricablanca

Editorial Assistant: Kathy Deady

Technical Editor: Christopher Cottier

Cover Photo: © iStock / Feng Yu

Cartoons: Rich Tennant
(www.the5thwave.com)

Composition Services

Project Coordinator: Kristie Rees

Layout and Graphics: Sennett Vaughan Johnson, Lavonne Roberts

Proofreaders: Rebecca Denoncour, Lisa Young Stiers

Indexer: BIM Indexing & Proofreading Services

John Wiley & Sons Canada, Ltd.

Deborah Barton, Vice President and Director of Operations

Jennifer Smith, Publisher, Professional and Trade Division

Alison Maclean, Managing Editor

Publishing and Editorial for Consumer Dummies

Kristin Ferguson-Wagstaffe, Product Development Director, Consumer Dummies

Ensley Eikenburg, Associate Publisher, Travel

Kelly Regan, Editorial Director, Travel

Publishing for Technology Dummies

Andy Cummings, Vice President and Publisher

Composition Services

Debbie Stailey, Director of Composition Services

Contents at a Glance

Table of Contents

Book II: Making Money with Mutual Funds 53

Introduction

Long gone are the good old days, when the stock market was producing solid returns and worries about retirement savings were non-existent. As bad as the recent financial crisis was — and it was gruesome, with the Canadian stock market falling about 36 percent in 2008 — there was plenty good that came out of it, including a renewed conversation on how people can build wealth.

Today, you can't read the news without landing on a money saving tip or some investment advice and that's a good thing — it means people are taking a greater interest in their financial futures. And that's where we come in. Building wealth is still possible. People retire with healthy bank accounts every day and, despite what you may read, Canadians will continue to live out their dreams long after their working lives are over. The difference between today and years gone by, though, is that now you have to know what you're doing. Canadians can't just put their money in any investment and watch it grow. You need to understand the way stocks and mutual funds work, be able to read an annual report, and get a sense of how professional traders play the markets.

Building Wealth All-in-One For Canadians For Dummies will help you gain that knowledge and more. From understanding the concept of guaranteed investment certificates to the fast-paced world of day trading, we'll help you find out everything you need to know about building wealth and growing your portfolios. When you're done with this book, you should be well on your way to building that nest egg you've always wanted.

About This Book

You already know that financial issues are a hot topic these days — otherwise you wouldn't be reading this paragraph. If you're in your local bookstore, look around — you probably see a tonne of tomes on building wealth, portfolio management, investing, trading, and more. No one has time to read everything, which is why we put together *Building Wealth For Canadians All-in-One For Dummies*. This is your starting point. In nearly 700 pages we tackle everything from understanding your net worth and mutual fund basics to choosing the rights stocks and making currency trades.

Yes, that's a lot of pages, but not only is it better than reading myriad books on each topic, but you can also use this as a reference. Keep it in your desk, stash it next to your computer, or take it with you on a long flight. Every time you have a question about bonds, stocks, or funds, or if you need to remember how to calculate a net worth statement, open this up and you'll likely find your answer.

Ultimately, we don't care how you choose to grow your wealth, we just want you to grow it and build it properly. That's why we present numerous different wealth-building options for every kind of investor.

It's always a good idea to read as much as you can — so go ahead and buy other books that speak to some of these topics — but keep this one handy; we promise you'll come back to it again and again.

Conventions Used in This Book

Because some information in this book really deserves to stand out, you'll find certain conventions that apply to the following situations:

Website addresses appear in `this font`.

Terms and phrases that may be unfamiliar to you appear in *italics*. You'll find an appropriate definition of the term or phrase nearby.

Bolded words or phrases highlight the action parts of numbered steps or keywords in bulleted lists.

The occasional sidebar (a shaded grey box) has information that's interesting to know but not necessarily critical to your understanding of a particular wealth-building topic.

Throughout this book, you'll find cross-references to other sections that have information that adds to or supplements the content you're perusing. If a cross-reference directs you to a section in the same Book, you'll read something like, "Check out Chapter 3 for more information." If the cross-reference is to a different Book, look for something like, "Find out more in Book II, Chapter 2."

Foolish Assumptions

You'll be happy to know that, when it comes to this book, all our reader assumptions are thrown out the window. Well, almost all. We do assume that you want to grow your bank account and, ultimately, retire with more than a few Shekels in your pocket. Whether you've opened your first bank account or are a bona fide number cruncher, you'll find something useful here. You just need a desire to save, invest, and learn. That's really it.

We start with net worth–building basics and then get into more complex trading strategies, so while we suggest starting at Book I, Chapter 1, you can also flip through to the section that best suits your investing level.

How This Book Is Organized

Building Wealth For Canadians All-in-One For Dummies is sorted into six parts so that you can find what you need to know quickly.

Book 1: The Basics of Building Wealth

We know you're anxious to get your money growing, but before you jump into the stock market you need to understand just what it takes to build wealth. That means paying down debt, investing in an RRSP, and more. Get a good grasp of the basics and you'll be well on your way.

Book II: Making Money with Mutual Funds

Canadians love mutual funds. And it's not hard to understand why. These products hold numerous securities, so they're well diversified, and with professional management you don't have to worry about picking stocks. But like with any investment, you need to know what you're buying. This book explains everything you need to know about mutual funds, from the different types to the returns you can expect and how fund fees affect returns.

Book III: The Skinny on Stocks

Some investors like to be a little more hands-on with their wealth building. That's where stocks come in. Pick the right one and your net worth could soar. Of course, choose a dud and you could be in trouble. In this book we reveal how stock investing can help grow a portfolio and what you need to do to make sure you're buying the right companies.

Book IV: Trials and Tribulations of Trading

Trading — short-term buying and selling — isn't for everyone, but do it right and you can add some serious wealth to your portfolio. Not only does this book explain how to make short-term trades, but you'll learn about things like short selling and leverage too. The book isn't just for traders — long-term investors also will learn a tonne about the markets.

Book V: Delving into Day Trading

Day trading has come in and out of fashion over the years, but one thing's for certain: if you love the markets, have a lot of time on your hands, and can keep your emotions in check, this type of trading may be the ideal wealth building method for you. This book digs deep into technical analysis, but we also talk about how taxes and regulation affect investors.

Book VI: Reviewing Real Estate Investing

For some Canadians, investing in the market isn't enough. Real estate typically provides investors regular income and asset appreciation, and with property values continuing to skyrocket returns can be better than what you'd find in equities. But real estate investing comes with its own rules and challenges. This book walks you through all that — we explain what to look for in a rental property, how to buy and sell real estate, the differences between owning residential and commercial spaces, and more.

Icons Used in This Book

You'll see various icons scattered around the margins of the text. Each icon points out a certain type of information, most of which you should know or may find interesting. They go as follows:

This icon notes something you should highlight, write down, or just file away in the back of your brain. It may refer to something that is covered elsewhere in the book, or it may highlight something you need to remember for future wealth-building decisions.

Tip information tells you how to build your wealth a little better, a little smarter, a little more efficiently. Tips can help you make better investing decisions or ask better questions of people who want to sell you funds, stocks, or advice.

Nothing in this book can cause death or bodily harm, as far as we can figure out, but there are plenty of ways investors and savers can harm their portfolios. These points help you avoid big problems.

We put the boring (but sometimes helpful) academic stuff here. By reading this material, you get the detailed information behind the various theories and techniques discussed in the book.

This icon — judiciously used — denotes a product or particular fund that does a good job and offers you benefits. But watch out — funds have an annoying habit of dropping to the bottom of the performance table right after writers recommend them. In part that's because the type of investments the fund buys have already shot up in value.

If you haven't noticed, this book is nearly 700 pages long. Even so, you won't find the answers to all your questions here. This icon indicates some suggestions of where you may want to look for additional information.

When you see this icon, know we're discussing higher-end, more technical material for the experienced trader.

Where to Go from Here

Well, open up the book and get going! We suggest starting with Book I, Chapter 1, which gives you some basic information on building wealth. Before you can start investing, you need to know how debt affects net worth, so it's a good idea to figure that out. If you already make it a priority to pay down debt, then you can start with Book II to get a handle on investing. The entire book offers up interesting investing advice, so even if you just want to trade a few stocks, or park your cash in a mutual fund, it's a good idea to read the other chapters to learn as much as you can about growing your wealth.

However, if you're an adrenaline junkie looking to trade stocks on a more frequent basis, you could start with Book IV or Book V, where we talk, more specifically, about swing and day trading.

Finally, if you're itching to investing in real estate, flip to Book VI, where we talk, in depth, on how to invest in more tangible assets.

Book I

The Basics of Building Wealth

Contents at a Glance

Chapter 1: The Basics of Building Wealth

In This Chapter

- **Developing a net worth statement**
- **Distinguishing bad debt from good debt**
- **Understanding risk and reward**
- **Harnessing the power of compounding**

The Road to Building Wealth Starts Here. . .

Many Canadians assume that the only way to build wealth is to score some high stock market returns. But if we've learned anything since the 2008 financial crisis, it's that markets alone won't get you rich. After seeing your portfolio fall during the recession, you may be wondering how one can possibly build wealth in an unpredictable economic environment — but you can. Many people still retire wealthy every day.

Although investing remains an important component of wealth building, Canadians need to devote even more of their attention to other things like paying down debt, saving money, developing a net worth statement, and more like taxes.

This chapter will dutifully delve into many of the basic tenets of building wealth. When you're done here, you'll be ready to dig into the details.

The Net Worth Statement

If you want to retire wealthy tomorrow, you need to find out where you stand financially today. That's why many experts say that the best way to get a handle on your financial situation is to develop a net worth statement. When you know how much you're worth, you'll be able to compare it to where you want to be.

You may think of what you own and what you owe as the most important parts of your financial life, but the combination of the two is what truly matters. If you have $1 million in assets, that sounds like a lot. But what if you also owe $930,000 in mortgages, student loans, and credit card debt? The difference between your assets and your liabilities is your *net worth,* which is what gives you stability in times of financial uncertainty.

Think of your current net worth statement as the You Are Here sticker on your financial map. Your net worth statement summarizes what you own, what you owe, and what would be left if you paid off all debt. *Assets* include money, investments, the fair market value of your house and furniture, your car, other real estate, and anything else you own. *Liabilities* include mortgages, car loans, credit card debt, and any other amounts owing like taxes. Here's how to determine your net worth:

Net worth = Assets – Liabilities

To meet many of your financial goals, you need to increase your net worth, either by increasing the amount of assets you have or by reducing your liabilities. A regular review of your net worth statement tells you a lot about how you're progressing. For example, you'll be able to see the following:

✦ Whether you're increasing your assets through saving or decreasing your assets through spending

✦ Whether your invested assets are growing at the rate you expect

✦ How you're doing in your quest to eliminate your debt and taxes

✦ Whether you're drawing down your assets too quickly during retirement or you can afford to take that month-long European cruise after all

Preparing the net worth statement isn't difficult; it just takes a bit of time and access to your financial statements. If you use personal finance software like Quicken or the online money management site Mint.com, much of your net worth statement is available to you already. You can also try out the various online net worth calculators offered by bank websites.

Use the Net Worth Statement to Reach Your Goals

Tracking your net worth over a period of time can help you keep a cool head as you work toward building your wealth. By looking at the big picture, you don't get as discouraged when an investment stumbles, as long as other investments are still gaining in value. Knowing that hitting a bump in the road doesn't mean you'll fall short of your destination can help get you back on track to meet your long-term financial goals.

How does this work? Don't simply complete one net worth statement and call it a day. Here's how to look at your net worth:

1. **Commit to calculating your net worth periodically.**

This can be quarterly, semiannually, or annually. More frequently than quarterly is overkill; less frequently than annually may put you way off course when you do review your position.

2. **Calculate your initial net worth.**

3. **Re-calculate your net worth at the next calculation period.**

4. **Compare the changes in assets, liabilities, and overall net worth.**

Are you getting closer to your goals or farther away from them? Make a point of understanding the general direction of each category. Are your assets lower now because your investments are down with the market? Or are your investments down while the market is up? Are you spending more than you're earning and depleting your assets to cover your living expenses?

5. **Identify where you have control over improving your financial direction.**

6. **Plan actions to increase your net worth before the next review period.**

Tracking your net worth periodically through the ups and downs in the economic cycle can prevent you from losing sight of your financial progress.

Think of your lifetime income and earnings as a pipeline that flows from when you start making money to the last day of your life. Along the way, various faucets in the pipeline open and divert money to pay for needs (such as living expenses, a home purchase, taxes, education, furniture, and transportation) and wants (like big-screen TVs, vacations, a fishing boat, and more). For items you buy using debt — mortgages, loans, credit card purchases — the faucet opens wider and runs longer because you're paying not only for the item but also for interest. The result is that you have to either work longer to earn more money to repay the debt or scale back on your goals.

Avoid Bad Debt

The first step to building wealth is to avoid unnecessary debt. Not only does setting aside money for future expenses save you the cost of debt interest payments, but it can also earn money for you if you invest your saved cash in an interest-bearing account. As you save, you help fill your pipeline instead of draining it!

Putting off purchases until you've saved enough also gives you an additional reserve beyond your emergency fund. For example, if you're saving money for a new barbecue, you can instead use those funds to replace a clothes dryer that tumbled its last towel or any other unanticipated expense that exceeds your emergency fund.

But like most people, you can't afford to pay cash for everything. Buying your home most likely required a mortgage. Buying cars, furniture, and appliances may involve financing. When you can't pay cash for high-cost items, you need to borrow at least some of the purchase amount.

Four criteria determine whether debt is good or bad. Before taking on debt, ask yourself the following questions. If the answer to *all* four questions is yes, you're signing up for good debt:

✦ **Is it a need?** If dependable transportation is a requirement for your job, buying a car to replace one that's on its last legs is clearly a need. But if your TV works and those ads for big-screen flat-panel models are making your mouth water, that's a want — which leads to bad debt.

   Note: Where you live is important for your quality of life, so although you can live in an apartment, you may choose to buy a home to provide a more desirable environment, which would qualify as a *need* on the scorecard.

✦ **Do you need to buy it before you can save up for it?** Consider the timing. You're looking at good debt if your car is beyond repair and you need dependable transportation to keep your job. If the big-screen TV is on sale this weekend, you can wait. It'll almost certainly be cheaper six months down the line.

✦ **Can you afford the payment?** If the payment fits your budget, you won't have to cut back on other needs. That's good debt. If you can't afford it, you'll have to cut back on some newly defined extras — like gas, food, and braces for the kids.

✦ **Are the financing terms okay?** Check the

   • Rate

   • Terms

   • Prepayment penalties (which, ideally, are none)

With good debt, you may have checked with your bank, credit union, or trust company, so you know the interest rate is competitive and the length of the car loan isn't longer than 48 months. You're into bad debt if you use the in-store financing to buy that new couch. The danger: If you don't pay off your purchase within the allotted time, the finance company generally applies interest retroactively, effective from the date of purchase at rates as high as 35 percent! So that $1,000 sofa could suddenly cost you at least $1,350, and interest continues to accumulate until you pay it off.

Saving up for a future expenditure keeps you in control of your money. By signing up for debt, you give away that control. Avoiding bad debt keeps more money in your income pipeline going toward your needs, wants, and other goals.

Dump Debt Sooner

Few things both make you feel good *and* improve your financial situation as much as paying off debt! The sooner you can shut off those debt faucets, the longer your income pipeline will stay filled.

Pay more than the minimum

Expensive credit card debt can eat up your funds quickly. Consider this: If you have a credit card with a balance of $1,500 at an interest rate of 21 percent, you will need over 14 years to repay the balance if you make the minimum monthly payments of 3 percent. That's $1,800 in interest, for a total bill of $3,300. Think a 21 percent interest rate sounds exorbitant? Department store interest rates can run as high as 28 percent!

Reduce your rates

Your first step in dealing with existing debt is working to reduce your interest rates. Here's how:

✦ You may have gotten your home mortgage when rates were much higher — check on the rate you can get by refinancing.

✦ Reconsider reward cards. Rates are always sky high and you don't get points on the interest! Use it only when you know you can pay it off in full every month. Also, get in the habit of calling your credit card companies to ask for a lower rate. Tell them about lower-rate offers you've gotten in the mail. Do this at least once a year.

✦ Check with your bank, credit union, or trust company to see whether you can refinance your car loan at a lower rate. Consider the cost of refinancing and whether it's worth the lower payment you may get.

When checking on lower-rate refinancing, ask the same questions about terms and prepayment penalties that you would when looking for good debt.

Accelerate your payments

As soon as you're paying the lowest rates available, you want to start accelerating debt payments to get out of debt sooner. Whether it's bad debt or good debt, the less interest you pay, the better. The order in which you eliminate your debts depends on the type of account and how the interest is calculated.

Here's the usual priority order for paying off debt:

1. Credit cards and other revolving consumer accounts

2. Auto, furniture, and appliance loans

3. Boat and RV loans

4. Home equity loans

5. Home equity lines of credit (HELOC)

6. Student loans

7. Home mortgages

You can pay off your debts most efficiently by applying any extra cash to just one account at a time (usually the one with the highest interest rate and smallest balance). As soon as that first account is paid off, accelerate payments on account number 2 by applying the full amount you'd been paying on account number 1 (basic payment plus the extra amount). As each debt is paid off, keep rolling the full amount being paid to the next debt account.

Free online debt-reduction calculators can help you see how much interest you'll save and help you choose which debt to pay off first. (Try one out here: `http://cgi.money.cnn.com/tools/debtplanner/debt planner.jsp`.)

Don't bury your head in the sand. If you're having debt problems, contact a *free* credit counselling service in your community. These nonprofit agencies can help you come up with a realistic budget. In some cases, they even contact creditors for you to negotiate a break on interest. To find one in your area, do an Internet search or check the Yellow Pages under "credit & debt counselling" and the name of your city or province.

As soon as a credit card account is paid off, don't close it — just cut up the card. Closing an account you've paid off hurts your credit score by reducing the total amount of credit you have available.

Start Saving

After you ditch your debt, you can start saving, building up funds to invest. You can find as many ways to save as you can to spend your money. And no matter how much your paycheque increases, you'll probably have no trouble finding more things to buy with the extra money.

So what's a hard-working gal or guy to do? Follow these two rules:

✦ Rule #1: Just do it.

✦ Rule #2: Pay yourself first.

You can't spend what you don't have. That's why you set aside a portion of your paycheque each month and then spend what's left. If you find this concept painful, play a game with yourself. Tell yourself that you'll just try it for a month or two.

Some folks call this strategy, "Set it and forget it." First you set it, and then you forget it. Soon you'll be on your way to feeling smug about that tidy sum in the bank.

If you automate your savings, you spend less than you make without having to think about it.

Perhaps you're still insisting that you can't budget for savings. Well, take a look at what you spend on things that aren't absolutely essential, that don't match your life goals, or that don't give your life pleasure. Keep track of your spending for several weeks. Carry a little log book in your pocket and write down everything you spend. After a few weeks, pull out the log book and your regular monthly bills. Look at where your money goes. (During this exercise, having a glass of wine or a mug of your favourite tea by your side is helpful.)

Ponder these questions:

✦ Do you need a landline *and* a cellphone?

✦ Do you need to buy books or is the library a better choice?

✦ Are you an impulse shopper at the supermarket? Try planning a weekly menu and make a shopping list of ingredients. Stick to the list, and you'll cut out expensive impulse buys.

✦ Can you host a potluck instead of meeting at a restaurant?

✦ Can you (heaven forbid!) make your own coffee at home and invest in a travel mug?

✦ Could you live in a modest home?

✦ Could you buy a used car rather than the latest new model? Or better yet, join a car co-op like www.zipcar.com.

✦ Do you have subscriptions to magazines you never read or health club memberships you never use?

✦ Can you make your own wine or beer?

The idea is not to feel deprived, but rather to make conscious spending decisions. Looking closely at where your money goes can help you decide where to cut, so that you can free up enough savings for the emergency fund without feeling bereft.

Hey, you may find that the joy of watching your savings grow far exceeds the momentary pleasure of an impulse purchase!

If you need a little boost, try this: The next time you pay something off, whether it's a small credit card balance or a car payment, continue making the payment. Only now, make the payment to that rainy-day account. You likely won't notice anything other than the size of the pay-yourself-first account increasing.

To further inspire yourself, post a bar graph on your refrigerator to track your progress. Pat yourself on the back every day.

Understanding Risk and Reward

What has drawn you to investing? Maybe the turmoil we've seen in the stock market recently has you wondering if bargains are to be had. Perhaps you're enticed by the idea that you can put your money to work for you by investing it.

Although the benefits of investing are often made clear in success story after success story in advertisements, magazines, newspapers, and websites devoted to investing, it's important to remember that no gain comes without potential pain. That means that when you invest your money, you can lose part or all of it.

Actually, rewards and risks are usually closely related. The greater an investment's potential for reward, the greater the potential for risk and actual loss. The high-flying stock that earned a 100 percent return last month is probably the very same stock that will tumble (and tumble hard) in the months and years ahead. The same goes for growth mutual funds and, potentially, even real estate.

You must take on some risk in order to reap the benefits of investing. That's the bad news. The good news is that usually, over time, a decent investment will bounce back, paying off in the end.

What's the worst-case scenario?

Recent history has left many investors gun-shy about the market. If you look at returns on some stock investments, you can understand why.

Canada's benchmark stock index — the S&P/TSX Composite — lost about 35 percent of its value in 2008 — the biggest drop since the Great Depression. The year's worst-performing TSX sector was information technology, which declined by 50 percent. That means if you invested $1,000 in information technology stocks at the beginning of the year, you would have seen your investment reduced to $500 by the end. On top of that, financial services stocks dropped by 39 percent, and energy stocks fell 38 percent. Anyone with a 100-percent-stocks portfolio needed nerves of steel to hang on during the dizzying market dips.

You can lose all of your money in an investment if a company declares bankruptcy.

What's the best I can hope for?

The best you can hope to achieve with an investment depends on the nature of the investment. Some investments — such as savings accounts and guaranteed investment certificates (GICs) (see Chapter 2 for more on GICs) — offer stable, secure returns. Other investments — such as stocks, bonds, and mutual funds — depend entirely on market conditions. A *return* is an investment's performance over time. It's easy to calculate the best-case scenario with vehicles such as savings accounts, Canada Savings Bonds (CSBs), and GICs. On the other hand, you can never predict with 100 percent accuracy what kind of return you will get with more volatile investments such as stocks and mutual funds.

As a rule, however, stocks have delivered returns that beat GICs and bonds. Even after the stock market bloodbath of 2008, investors who held Canada's most popular exchange-traded fund, the iShares Cdn LargeCap 60 Index Fund, made an average annual return of 7.6 percent for the previous five years.

What's a realistic course?

The good news is that if you try to choose your investments carefully — and subsequent chapters of this book give you the tools to do this — you should be able to minimize your losses. Ideally, your losses from any one investment may even be offset by the successes of your other investments.

Of course, if you're completely uncomfortable with the prospect of losing money, or if you need your money within five years, then investment vehicles such as stocks and bonds aren't for you. You're better off putting your money into safer, more liquid places such as bank accounts and guaranteed investments, discussed in Chapter 2.

Realizing Gains through Compounding

Starting out as a first-time investor doesn't require a whole lot of money, which means that you don't need to wait until you've accumulated a large reserve of ready cash. You may ask: Why the big rush to start investing?

The answer is simple: You want to begin earning *compound growth* as soon as you can. Compound growth is actually the growth you earn on your interest. For example, if you invested $10,000 and earned 3 percent growth in the next year, your growth income would be $300 and you'd have a total of $10,300. If you earned 3 percent again the following year, the $9 you would earn on the $300 (in growth you earned in the current year) would be considered compound growth. Over time, compound growth builds up, even when returns are low.

Compounding is a compelling reason to start and keep investing for the long term because money left untouched reaps the greatest reward from compounding.

Table 1–1 shows you the power of compounding and how quickly even $100 saved or invested each month can grow under different interest-rate scenarios. The first row is the amount you'd have if you invested $100 a year for five, 10, 15 years, and so on with no growth. The rest of the chart shows what that base amount would be after returns.

Table 1–1	The Beauty of Compound Growth				
% Return	**5 years**	**10 years**	**15 years**	**20 years**	**30 years**
0%	$6,000	$12,000	$18,000	$24,000	$36,000
1.5%	$6,227	$12,938	$20,172	$27,968	$39,316
3%	$6,562	$14,169	$22,988	$33,211	$58,803
5%	$6,829	$15,592	$26,840	$41,275	$83,573

To calculate how many years it will take to double your money as a result of compounding, use the *Rule of 72*. Just follow these steps:

1. Determine what interest rate you think your money will earn.

2. Divide 72 by that interest rate.

The number you get is the number of years it will take to double your money.

For example, suppose that you believe you'll earn 5 percent annually in the coming years. If you divide 72 by 5, you can see that doubling your money will take a little more than 14 years.

Focusing on a Goal

You can take the first step toward creating your investment plan by asking yourself a simple question: What do I want to accomplish? Actually, this step is your single most important move toward ensuring that your investment plan has a sound foundation. After all, these goals are the reason that you're launching a personal investment plan. So don't shirk this exercise. Dream away.

Perhaps you've always wanted to travel around the world or build a beach-front chalet. Or maybe you are interested in going back to school or starting your own business. Write down your goals. Your list of goals can serve as a constant reminder that you're on the course to success.

Don't forget the necessities, either. If you have kids who plan to go to college or university, you need to start preparing for that expenditure now. Your retirement plans fall into this category as well — now is the time to start planning for it.

Separate your goals into long-, mid-, and short-term time frames based on when you expect or need to achieve the goal. For example:

✦ Buying a vacation home or retiring 10 or more years from now is a long-term goal.

✦ Sending your child to college or university in 5 to 8 years is a mid-term goal.

✦ Buying a car in the next 1 to 4 years because you know your current model is likely to be on its last legs is a short-term goal.

As you jot down your goals, also write down their costs. Use your best "guesstimate"; or, if you're not sure, search the newspaper for, say, the cost of a beachfront home that approximates the one you want to purchase. Leave the "Time and Monthly Investment" category alone for now — that column represents the next step, which we tell you about shortly.

Okay, now for the tricky part. How much do you need to invest each month, and over what period of time, to achieve your goals?

Of course, you need to know an approximate rate of return before you can plan. Your rate of return will differ depending on the sort of investment you choose. Research can help you accurately estimate your rate of return. (Chapters 2 and 3 tell you how to go about getting this information for different types of investments.)

As an example, Table 1–2 shows you roughly what you need to invest each month to earn $100,000 over different periods of time. Need $10,000 instead? Divide the monthly investment amount shown in Table 1–2 by 10. Want to save a million dollars instead? Simply multiply the amount by 10.

Table 1–2	Monthly Investments to Earn $100,000 at Varying Rates of Growth			
Years	*1.5%*	*3%*	*5%*	*8%*
5	$1,650	$1,600	$1,480	$1,350
10	$800	$716	$640	$540
15	$500	$450	$370	$290
20	$360	$320	$240	$170

If you're older, in retirement, or just plain more conservative (and like keeping a good bit of your money in accounts or investments that earn lower rate of return), you may want to use a lower estimated rate of return in your calculations to reflect your situation.

Or you may be investing in another type of asset — real estate, for example. In this case a real estate agent can tell you the appreciation rate or the annual rate of return for properties in your area. You can use that rate as a rough gauge to estimate what you're likely to earn in future years.

For determining how much you need to sock away annually to meet your goals over a specific period of time, using a scientific calculator is easiest.

Starting Your Savings Now

Throughout the rest of this book, we tell you about different types of investments that match your investment goals. To start out with any sort of investment, you need a cash reserve — and the amount varies, depending on your investment choice.

As you're doing your research and deciding which investments match your goals, start putting away $100 a month in an account earmarked for investment. By the time you determine the investing opportunities that best fit your needs, you should be well on your way to affording your investment.

Watching your dollars multiply can serve as motivation in itself: Your investment accounts may become as (or more) important to you as some of the other expenses that have eaten up your money in the past.

If you're the type who's been saving gobs of cash in a bureau drawer for a long time and now want to start earning real returns, you're one step ahead of the pack. You have the discipline. Now what you need is the knowledge and the tools.

Starting and Staying with a Diversified Investment Approach

The goal of diversification is to minimize risk. Instead of putting your eggs in one basket by investing every dime you have in one stock, one bond, or one mutual fund, you should diversify.

Diversification is a strategy for investing in a wide array of investments that ideally move slightly out of step with each other. For example, an investment in an international mutual fund might be doing poorly while an investment in a Canadian equity mutual fund is doing well. By investing in different sectors of the investment markets, you create a balanced portfolio. Parts of that portfolio should zig when other sections zag.

Think back to the 2000–2002 technology implosion and market collapse for a good example of how diversification can save your bacon. Although stocks took a beating, the losses were offset by gains in real estate investment trusts, commodities, and bonds. Of course, it didn't work quite so efficiently in 2008 and 2009, when the real estate and credit crises created a perfect storm. We saw virtually all asset classes, in all nations, get pushed down at the same time, except the price of gold.

The sad fact is: to be properly diversified, you need to own assets that historically don't earn as much as stocks do. Consider the protection bonds offer: For the 10 years leading up to January 2009, the Dow Jones Moderately Conservative Portfolio Index, a passively run global benchmark that's rebalanced monthly and holds 40 percent stocks with the remainder in bonds and cash, posted a 3.9 percent annualized total return. Over the same period, the S&P 500 lost an annual 2.7 percent.

It's important to determine the percentage of stocks, bonds, and cash you want in your portfolio. In the stock and bond categories (or mutual funds that invest in these assets), it's also important not to load up on any one sector of the economy. So steer clear of the temptation to invest in three technology mutual funds, four Internet stocks, or six junk bonds — even if they're paying more than other investments.

The saying "no pain, no gain" also applies to the investment experience. You can avoid the prospect of experiencing any pain at all by investing only in Canada Savings Bonds and GICs that are federally or provincially insured. The price to be paid for that strategy: You may never lose money in the traditional sense, but you never gain much either, which means that you can still fall behind. You also run the risk of falling behind because of inflation and income tax, which eats up about 1 to 3 percent of your purchasing power each year. If you earn only 2 or 3 percent a year on your savings or investments, you'll have a hard time preserving the capital you have, let alone growing it.

Developing a Dollar Cost Averaging Plan

No one can afford to have an investing plan forgotten or relegated to the back burner. You need to set up a plan for making set, regular investments. This way, you ensure your money is working for you even when your best intentions are diverted.

Dollar cost averaging is a way to ensure that you make fixed investments every month or quarter, regardless of other distractions in your life. Dollar cost averaging is a simple concept: You invest a specified dollar amount each month without concern about the price per share or cost of the bond. The market is *fluid* — the price of your investment moves up and down — so you end up buying some shares when they're inexpensive, some when they're expensive, and some when they're somewhere in between. Because of the commission cost to buy small amounts of stocks or bonds, dollar cost averaging is better suited for buying zero commission mutual funds.

In addition to helping you overcome procrastination about saving for investments, dollar cost averaging can help you sidestep some of the anxiety many first-time investors feel about starting to invest in a market that can seem dangerously volatile. With set purchases each month or quarter, you buy shares of your chosen investments regardless of how the market is doing.

Dollar cost averaging isn't statistically the most lucrative way to invest. Because markets rise more often than they decline, you're better off saving up your money and buying stocks, bonds, or mutual funds when they hit rock bottom. But dollar cost averaging is the most disciplined and reliable way to invest. Consider this: If you set up a dollar cost averaging plan now, then in 10, 20, or 30 years you'll have invested every month in between — and accumulated a pretty penny in the interim.

Chapter 2: Playing It Safe

In This Chapter

- ✔ Sticking with the tried-and-true: savings accounts
- ✔ Tacking on more interest with tiered accounts
- ✔ Discovering GICs
- ✔ Exploring bonds

This chapter is about vehicles (investment options) that are appropriate for money you don't want to put at great risk — for example, money that you have earmarked for emergency funds, or money that you're saving to buy a car, furniture, or a home within the next few years. By keeping your short-term money somewhere safe and convenient, you may feel more comfortable putting your long-term money at somewhat greater risk.

Although they may not be the most exciting investments you'll ever make, savings accounts, tiered accounts, guaranteed investment certificates (GICs) and some — but not all — bonds are worthwhile considerations for novice investors. Everyone should have some money in stable, safe investment vehicles. Savings accounts, tiered accounts, GICs, and Government of Canada bonds are basic savings tools and are the first step on your path to investing. These tools can help you build up the money you need in order to start investing in other ways.

As you learn about vehicles for building wealth through this book, you find out which ones are good for short-term investments and which are best for the long haul. How you invest your money depends largely on two factors: how long the money can remain out of your reach (time); and how much of it you can afford to lose (risk). Some investments are a lot riskier than others.

In this chapter, we tell you about the safest investments for short-term money that you can't afford to lose, and we also discuss what you need to know before you throw your hard-earned dollars into the pot.

Starting with Savings Accounts

Savings accounts are a form of investment — a very safe form. Although many banks don't pay interest on traditional chequing accounts, they may pay at least a small amount of interest on traditional savings accounts. Most banks will offer a variety of accounts — some that combine an interest-bearing savings account with limited cheque-writing privileges.

It pays to shop around for higher interest rates on a savings account. The conventional banks tend to pay nothing on savings account balances below $5,000. But increasingly popular online banks, such as ING Direct, Ally, or PC Financial, pay interest on all accounts — as much as 2 percent at the time of writing.

The problem with savings accounts is that, after you've paid taxes on your earnings and taken inflation into account, with the very low rates seen in the past few years you might end up with no return at all.

Still, consider opening a savings account, for several reasons. First, if you are a truly novice investor, a savings account can be the beginning of your learning process. You'll gain confidence when shopping around for the best possible interest rate, and again when you deal with the financial institution directly while opening the account.

Second, and more importantly, the money you invest in a savings account comes with an ironclad guarantee. Why? If the institution has Canadian Deposit Insurance Corporation (CDIC) insurance, your savings account is backed by the full strength and credit of the federal government. If the institution fails, the feds see that you automatically get your savings back — up to $100,000 per person, per institution, subject to some restrictions. As with any other insurance, you may sleep better knowing that it's there in the worst-case scenario.

Although putting your money in a savings account has serious limitations if it's your one and only investment strategy, having some of your money in a cash reserve makes sense. But as investments go, you wouldn't want to rely wholeheartedly on a savings account because the return on your investment is so low. Of course, factors such as fluctuating interest rates and the rate of inflation play a major role in how well your money does in this type of investment vehicle.

The big banks generally have special no-fee accounts for young and old and low-fee accounts for students. For the rest of us, flat-fee accounts exist that include a set number of transactions.

The Financial Consumer Agency of Canada (www.fcac-acfc.gc.ca) has an interactive Cost of Banking Guide that provides a list of packages or accounts that best fit your banking profile. Just enter your typical minimum monthly balance and the numbers of each kind of transaction you do (i.e., in-branch withdrawals, ABM transfers, writing cheques), and the guide suggests packages that would be cheapest for each kind of account. The FCAC's Banking Package Selector Tool also publishes a list of interest rates at major

Canadian financial institutions including banks, credit unions, and trust companies for easy comparison.

Tiered Accounts

Some banks offer savings accounts with the added incentive of earning additional interest if your account balance remains consistently above a specified amount. This amount is usually at least $1,000, and frequently it's higher.

These types of accounts are often referred to as *tiered,* or as using *deposit interest tiers.* For example, according to the most recent interest rate structure, TD Bank's high-interest savings account offers customers no interest rate with balances under $5,000. Between $5,000 and $5 million you earn 1.2 percent. Interestingly, if for some reason you keep more than $5 million in the account, the interest rate falls back to zero. You'll find the highest interest rates at the online banks, but even conventional banks pay a bit more for higher balances. Scotiabank's Moneymaster Savings Account, for example, pays .25 percent on balances above $5,000 and .15 percent on balances below that amount.

As the TD Bank example illustrates, some tiered accounts pay no interest at all on balances below a certain threshold, often $5,000. Find out whether that's a realistic sum for you before opening this type of account. Also, be sure to find out if the higher rates of interest apply to your entire balance or just the portion above the minimum needed to receive that rate. Finally, keep in mind that transaction fees for tiered accounts can be considerably heftier than you would face with a traditional savings account, although online banks tend to keep these fees low.

Diving in to Savings Accounts

Rather than "taking the plunge," opening a savings account is more like dipping your toe into the water. But we've all got to start somewhere, and this is where many people start out. Opening a savings account can be the first step to a lifetime of good savings habits.

As we mention in Chapter 1, the first rule of savings is "pay yourself first." That doesn't mean give yourself some cash so that you can go shopping. When you sit down to pay bills, write the first cheque to a savings or investment account. It doesn't matter if you start with a very small amount, just make savings a habit. And when you get bonuses and raises, you can increase those cheques you write to yourself.

When you shop for a bank, credit union, or trust where you can open a savings account, make sure to ask the following questions:

✦ **Is there a required minimum balance for a savings account?** Some institutions charge a fee if your balance falls below a required minimum.

✦ **What are your fees for savings accounts?** You can expect to be charged either a monthly or quarterly maintenance fee. The institution may also charge you a fee if you close the account before a specified period of time.

✦ **How much interest will I get on my savings?** Expect less than 1 percent interest, and often no interest at all.

✦ **Is the account federally insured?** Ask specifically whether the institution has Canada Deposit Insurance Corporation (CDIC) insurance or provincial insurance. If it does, then you can get up to $100,000 of your savings back if the bank fails.

✦ **What services do you offer?** Banks now offer banking by telephone and the Internet.

✦ **Does the bank use a tiered account system?** A tiered account system allows you to earn higher interest if your account balance is consistently over an amount specified by the bank.

✦ **Does the bank pay higher interest on the entire balance in a tiered account?** Some banks pay you the higher rate only on the amount above the minimum needed to receive that rate.

Call around to at least three different institutions — banks, trusts, and/ or credit unions — to compare their offerings. You can also call brokerage firms, which offer GICs, to find out their minimums and fees.

If the answers to all of these questions come out about equal, choose the institution that's most convenient for you and offers the best service, the most automated teller machines (ATMs), convenient hours, friendly staff — whatever suits your banking habits best. Savings accounts come in several types, including:

✦ **Basic savings account:** These usually require a minimum opening deposit of $100.

✦ **Tiered savings account:** These often require a higher minimum opening balance and pay a higher yield than basic accounts, although in today's low-interest-rate environment, you still won't get much. For example, you might earn 0 percent interest with an account balance below $5,000, but as much as .75 percent interest or more with a balance over $5,000.

✦ **Package deal:** These new-age savings accounts may permit extra privileges, like cheque-writing.

✦ **Online banks:** You'll find higher rates of interest and lower fees with so-called virtual banks that have no bricks-and-mortar locations and therefore are able to keep overhead costs low. Remember: you must be able to use an ATM if you want to access your money without incurring extra fees. Make sure the online bank has an ATM, or enough of them, in your city before you sign up.

The Financial Consumer Agency of Canada (www.fcac-acfc.gc.ca) has a good banking package selector tool to help you compare offerings from both online and bricks-and-mortar banks and trust companies.

Considering Guaranteed Investment Certificates

If your savings grow to the point where you have more money than you think you need anytime soon, congratulations! One of the places you can consider depositing some of the balance is a guaranteed investment certificate (GIC).

A GIC is a receipt for a deposit of funds in a financial institution. Like savings accounts and money market accounts, GICs are investments for security.

With a GIC, you agree to lend your money to the financial institution for a number of months or years. You can't touch that money for the specified period of time without being penalized.

Why would a financial institution need you to loan it money? Typically, institutions use the deposits they take in to fund loans or other investments. If an institution primarily issues car loans, for example, it's apt to pay attractive rates to lure money to four-year or five-year GICs, the typical car-loan term.

Generally, the longer you agree to lend your money, the higher the interest rate you receive. The most popular GICs are for one year, two years, three years, four years, or five years; some institutions also offer a 30-day GIC. No fee exists for buying a GIC.

By depositing the money (a minimum of $500 at most institutions) for the specified amount of time, the financial institution pays you a higher rate of interest than if you put your money in a savings or chequing account that offers immediate access to your money. When your GIC matures (comes due), the institution returns your deposit to you, plus interest.

The institution notifies you of your GIC's maturation by mail or phone and usually offers the option to roll the GIC over into another GIC. When your GIC matures, you can call your institution to find out the current rates and roll the money into another GIC, or transfer your funds into another type of account.

Some institutions give you a grace period, ten days or so, to decide what to do with your money when the GIC matures. In most cases, though, you can specify in advance what should happen to the money by giving your bank *instructions for maturation* when you buy the GIC. At a CDIC-insured financial institution, your investment is guaranteed to be there when the GIC matures.

You may have heard about investment vehicles called *term deposits*. Depending on the financial institution, term deposits function in almost exactly the same way as GICs. In some cases, these names are used interchangeably.

Financial advisers say that GICs make the most sense when you know that you can invest your money for one year, after which you'll need the money for some purchase you expect to make. The main reward of investing in GICs is that you know for sure what your return will amount to and can plan around it. That's because GIC rates are usually set for the term of the certificate. Be sure to check on the interest-rate terms though, because some institutions change their rate weekly.

For example, after buying a house in early fall, our imaginary friend Mark made plans to have the exterior repainted the following year (a short-term goal). In October, he received a nice $4,000 bonus from work. Knowing that he might be tempted to spend that money on dinners and movies, Mark invested the $4,000 in a one-year guaranteed investment certificate with a 2 percent interest rate. When spring rolled around, his GIC matured, and he received $4,080. That amount he gained in interest may not sound like a lot, but he would have received nothing had he deposited the money in a typical savings account.

GICs are most useful as an investment when interest rates are high, as they were back in the 1980s. These days, consistently low interest rates mean Canadians should at least consider other types of investments that are both safe and will probably earn more money over the same period of time.

The interest rates paid on GICs are contingent on many factors. Although they do tend to reflect prevailing interest rates in the general market, GICs have *administered rates,* meaning financial institutions use discretion when setting them. For example, banks may increase rates during RRSP contribution season to attract investors. This also means rates are negotiable, depending on the size of the deposit and the relationship between the bank and the client.

Because of this flexibility, it pays to shop around for GIC specials to get the best interest rate. Remember to check out the rates at credit unions too.

A good place to shop around for the best rates on GICs is www.ratesuper market.ca/gic_rates. This site lets you compare GIC rates on many different financial products.

If you want your money back before the end of the GIC's term, you will be heavily penalized, usually with the loss of several months' worth of interest. A second drawback is that whatever interest you earn on your principal (including earnings from the market-linked GICs we discuss below) must be claimed as income, and is fully taxable on an annual basis. That means your financial institution will report the interest you earned during each tax year to Canada Revenue Agency. You will pay tax on that amount annually — despite the fact that you won't see the interest until the GIC matures.

If rates are low, you may want to purchase shorter-term GICs and wait for rates to rise. This way, you won't be tying up your funds for long periods of time while rates might be climbing.

Before you buy a traditional GIC or term deposit, ask about the *market-linked* GICs being offered by many of Canada's big financial institutions. Market-linked GICs are tied to the performance of the stock market. Like GICs, your principal is guaranteed. You won't lose any of your original investment, no matter how much the stock market fluctuates. But with a market-linked GIC, instead of receiving a fixed rate of interest, your return depends on the value of the stock market during the term of your deposit. If the stock market performs well, this will probably give you a bigger return than you could get with a traditional GIC — although most financial institutions will impose a maximum cap. If the market plummets, however, you might end up with the same amount you invested in the first place, *sans* the interest income you'd earn on a traditional GIC.

The downside of market-linked GICs is that they generally pay no interest until maturity, meaning you don't get the benefit of the interest on your interest (compounding) over time. In addition, your earnings are considered interest income instead of capital gains, so they're taxed at a higher rate.

See Table 2–1 for some suggested uses for entry-level investments.

Table 2–1	The Uses for Entry-Level Investments
Type of Investment	*Suggested Use*
Savings Account or Tiered Account	Tuck away some money in a traditional or tiered chequing or savings account to allow you to access it quickly for emergencies, such as car repairs or dentist bills.
Guaranteed Investment Certificate (GIC) or Term Deposit	GICs and term deposits are good investments if you are saving for larger-ticket items such as a down payment on a car or a major appliance—items you don't intend to purchase for at least a year.

Comparing GICs

As with the other investments we discuss in this chapter, talk to at least three different institutions before you invest in GICs. When you shop around for a GIC, ask the following questions:

+ **What's the minimum deposit to open the account?** Usually this amount is $500.

+ **What's the interest rate?** What is the compounded annual yield? Interest is the percentage that the bank pays you for allowing them to keep your money. The rate of interest is also called *yield*. Compounded annual yield comes into play if a bank is paying interest monthly, for example. After the first month's interest is credited to your account, that interest starts earning interest, too, meaning that the compounded annual yield is slightly higher than the interest rate.

+ **How often is the interest compounded?** Remember, the more frequently it's compounded, the better it is for you. Continuous compounding is best.

+ **Is the interest rate fixed or variable?** Make sure that the institution offers you a way to get current interest rates quickly and easily — by phone, for example.

+ **Can you add to your fund at a higher interest rate if the rate goes up while your money is invested?** If the rate goes up substantially, and you can add to your fund, then you can significantly increase your yield.

+ **What's the penalty for early withdrawal?** These penalties can wipe out any interest you earn.

+ **What happens to the deposit when the GIC matures?** Does the institution roll a matured GIC into a new one of a similar term? Does it mail a cheque? Credit your chequing account?

+ **Do they offer market-linked GICs?** Market-linked GICs are indexed (or tied) to the performance of the stock market. Be sure to ask what formula the bank will use to determine performance.

Checking up on savings accounts and GICs

Unlike other wealth-building vehicles, these accounts don't require nearly as much monitoring. That said, it does pay to keep an eye on them. In this section, we give you some tips on what to watch for.

Traditional savings accounts and tiered accounts

Monitoring your savings account or tiered account is a lot like monitoring your chequing account. You receive statements from the institution (like your bank or credit union) that tell you your balance including accrued interest. Many institutions also have a telephone number — often toll-free —

that allows you to access balance information by using your account number and your personal code number. In addition, most financial institutions have online banking, which allows you to access your account information from your computer.

GICs

When you invest in a GIC, you receive an actual document that indicates the principal you invested, the interest rate, the length of time of the investment, and the final amount you will receive. Some institutions include your balance information on the statements you receive from other accounts you have with them, but not all do that.

The most important question with a GIC is what will happen to your money (both the principal and the interest you earn) when the GIC matures. This is your decision. Keep in mind that with GICs you've agreed to lock in your principal as well as the interest for a specified amount of time. What happens to that money after the term of the GIC is entirely up to you.

Banks and credit unions will generally ask for your *instructions for maturity* when you buy the GIC. You can instruct them to reinvest the money into another GIC, move it into a different investment, place it in a bank account, or have it returned to you.

Most institutions send out a notice a few weeks before your GIC matures. If you want to change your instructions for maturity at that time (or any time before the maturation date), call your financial institution and let them know.

Learning about Bond Basics

A bond is basically an IOU. When you purchase a bond, you are lending money to a government, municipality, corporation, crown corporation, or other entity. In return for the loan, the entity promises to pay you a specified rate of interest during the life of the bond and to repay the *face value* (the *principal*) of the bond when it matures (or comes due).

When you buy a new bond from the original *issuer* (the entity to whom you're lending your money), you will purchase it at face value, also called *par value*, and you will be promised a specific rate of interest, called the *coupon*. If you buy a bond that's already been resold before maturity (from what's called the *secondary market*, where existing bonds are bought and sold), you may buy it at a *discount* (less than par) or at a *premium* (above par).

Bonds aren't like stocks. You are not buying part ownership in a company or government when you purchase a bond. Instead, what you're actually buying — or betting on — is the issuer's ability to pay you back with interest.

Understanding how bonds work

You have a number of important variables to consider when you invest in bonds, including the stability of the issuer, the bond's maturity or due date, interest rate, price, yield, tax status, and risk. As with any investment, ensuring that all these variables match up with your own investment goals is key to making the right choice for your money.

Be sure to buy a bond with a maturity date that tracks with your financial plans. For instance, if you have a child's post-secondary education to fund 15 years from now and you want to invest part of his or her education fund in bonds, you need to select vehicles that have maturities that match that need. If you have to sell a bond before its due date, you receive the prevailing market price, which may be more or less than the price you paid.

In general, because they often specify the yield you'll be paid, bonds can't make you a millionaire overnight like a stock can. What can you expect to earn? That depends on a number of factors, including the type of bond you buy and market conditions, like prevailing interest rates. What can you expect to lose? That depends on how safe the issuer is.

In low-interest-rate environments, buying long-term bonds could be the wrong way to go. When interest rates rise bond prices fall and yields climb. If you hold a 10-year bond and rates climb, your bond's worth could fall dramatically. Of course it only matters if you need to sell it before the decade's up. Another thing to consider is that when rates rise, yields go up. If you own a short-term bond that matures, say, between one and five years, you'll then be able to buy another fixed income instrument at a higher yield.

Recognizing different types of bonds

Bonds come in all shapes and sizes, and they enable you to choose one that meets your needs in terms of your investment time horizon, risk profile, and income needs. First, here is a look at the different types of Government of Canada securities available:

✦ **Treasury bills:** T-bills are offered in 3-month, 6-month, and 12-month maturities. These short-term government securities do not pay current interest, but instead are always sold at a discount price, which is lower than par value. The difference between the discount price and the par value received is considered interest (and is taxed as income). For example, if you pay the discount price of $950 for a $1,000 T-bill, you pay 5 percent less than you actually get back when the bill matures. Par is considered to be $100 worth of a bond (which, although selling for a $1,000 minimum, is always expressed in a $100 measure for the purpose of valuation). The minimum investment for T-bills is $5,000, but you can subsequently purchase them in $1,000 increments.

✦ **Government of Canada bonds:** Unlike T-bills, Government of Canada bonds have fixed coupons that pay a specific interest at regular intervals (every six months). These bonds are longer-term offerings than T-bills, with maturities of between 1 and 30 years. Typically, the longer the term, the higher the interest paid. The minimum investment is the same as T-bills, $5,000. But they are also issued in larger denominations. The interest you earn on Government of Canada bonds is considered income and taxed as such. If the market value of your bond accrues, this is considered a capital gain.

✦ **Strip or zero-coupon bonds:** Strip bonds, so named because the coupon has been "stripped" from the bond's principal, work almost like T-bills. They are sold at a steep discount, and interest accrues (builds up) during the life of the bond. At maturity, the investor receives all the accrued interest plus the original investment. Strip bonds are guaranteed by the federal and provincial governments, as well as corporations, and can be sold anytime. As with T-bills, the difference between the discounted price you pay for a strip bond and the value at maturity is considered interest income, and is fully taxed.

✦ **Canada Savings Bonds (CSBs):** These have long been a fall investment ritual for Canadians. You purchase Canada Savings Bonds from your bank, trust, credit union, or investment dealer during the annual selling season. As of 2010 the season, which was once between October and April, was shortened to two months — October and November. The bond is registered to you and is non-transferable. The value of the bond itself never changes and federal rules prevent CSBs from being traded.

Quite simply, by buying a Canada Savings Bond you are lending your money to the federal government in return for interest. With a regular-interest CSB, that interest is paid out once a year, on November 1, and is taxable as income. With compound-interest CSBs, your interest is reinvested until maturity, thereby compounding your interest, but you still have to claim it as income each year. For more zest, the government also offers an indexed CSB, which takes into account rising interest rates. The bond's yield is based on the inflation rate plus a fixed rate of return. For more information on CSBs, visit the federal government's Canada Investment and Savings website at www.csb.gc.ca.

Although Government of Canada bonds are some of the safest investment bets around — because they're guaranteed by the strength of the federal government — remember that risk and reward are tradeoffs you need to look at in tandem. As with all investments, the safer the investment the less you're likely to earn or lose!

The following are other types of available bonds:

✦ **Provincial bonds:** Provincial governments issue both T-bills and bonds (short-, medium-, and long-term), much like the federal government. Although these are safe investments, bonds issued by provinces facing economic uncertainty are considered slightly more risky by investors. In return for the added risk, they usually pay a higher yield.

✦ **Municipal bonds:** These are loans you make to a local government, whether it's in your city or town.

✦ **Commercial paper:** These are short-term debt instruments employed by both publicly owned Crown corporations (referred to as Government Guaranteed Commercial Paper) and private-sector corporations. Like T-bills and strip bonds, they are sold at a discount, but yields tend to be higher.

✦ **Corporate bonds:** A growing area in Canada, these are issued by companies that need to raise money, including public utilities and transportation companies, industrial corporations and manufacturers, and financial service companies.

Corporate bonds can be riskier than either Canadian government bonds or provincial bonds because companies can go bankrupt. So a company's credit risk is an important tool for evaluating the safety of a corporate bond. Even if an organization doesn't throw in the towel, its risk factor can be enough to cause credit rating analysts to downgrade the company's overall rating. If that happens, you may find it more difficult to sell the bond early.

✦ **Junk bonds:** Junk bonds pay high yields because the issuer may be in financial trouble, may have a poor credit rating, and may be likely to have a difficult time finding buyers. Although you may decide that junk bonds or junk bond mutual funds have a place in your portfolio, if you're a conservative investor, make sure that spot is small because these bonds carry high risk.

Although junk bonds may look particularly attractive at times, think twice before you buy. They don't call them junk for nothing. You could potentially suffer a total loss if the issuer declares bankruptcy.

Identifying potential bond investments

Some items you need to evaluate before investing in bonds include the following:

✦ **Issuer stability:** This is also known as *credit quality,* which assesses an issuer's ability to pay back its debts, including the interest and principal it owes its bond holders, in full and on time. Although many corporations, the Canadian government, and the provinces have never defaulted on a bond, you can expect that some issuers can and will be unable to repay.

✦ **Maturity:** A bond's maturity refers to the specific future date when you can expect your principal to be repaid. Bond maturities can range from as short as one day all the way up to 50 years. Make sure that the bond you select has a maturity date that works with your needs. T-bills and strip bonds pay interest at maturity. All other bonds pay interest twice yearly or quarterly. Most investors buy bonds in order to have a steady flow of income (from interest).

The longer the maturity in a bond, the more risk associated with it — that is, the greater the fluctuation in bond value based upon changes in interest rates.

✦ **Interest rate:** Bonds pay interest that can be fixed-rate, floating, or payable at maturity. Most bond rates are fixed until maturity, and the amount is based on a percentage of the face or principal amount.

✦ **Face value:** This is the stated value of a bond. The bond is selling at a *premium* when the price is above its face value; pricing below its face value means that it's selling at a *discount*.

✦ **Price:** The price you pay for a bond is based on an array of different factors, including credit rating, current interest rates, supply and demand, and maturity.

✦ **Current yield:** This is the annual percentage rate of return earned on a bond. You can find a bond's current yield by dividing the bond's annual interest payment by its purchase price. For example, assume that a particular bond is trading at par, or 100 cents on the dollar, and that it pays a coupon rate of 3 percent. The bond's current yield will also be 3 percent (see below).

```
CY = 3 / 100 = 3.00%
```

Now let's say that the same bond is trading at a discount to its par value — perhaps the investor can purchase it for 95 cents on the dollar. Even though the bond will still be paying a 3 percent coupon, its current yield will be slightly higher (see below):

```
CY = 3 / 95 = 3.16%
```

✦ **Yield to maturity (YTM):** This tells you the total return you can expect to receive if you hold a bond until it matures. Its calculation takes into account the bond's face value, interest rates, its current price, and the years left until the bond matures. The calculation is an elaborate one, but the broker you're buying a bond from should be able to give you its YTM. The YTM also enables you to compare bonds with different maturities and yields.

Don't buy a bond on current yield alone. Ask the bank or brokerage firm from whom you're buying the bond to provide a YTM figure so that you can have a clear idea about the bond's real value to your portfolio. You can also access the bond yield calculator at www.moneychimp.com. Just click on "Calculator" on the main menu and then "Bond Yield."

✦ **Tax status:** Outside your RRSP, the interest you earn on bonds is fully taxable as interest income. The difference between what you paid for a discounted bond and the value at maturity is also considered income. Gains you make on the value of a bond if you sell it before maturity are considered a capital gain. You will be taxed on 50 percent of your capital gains in the year you realize your capital gains.

If you sell a Government of Canada, provincial, municipal, or corporate bond for more than you paid for it, you'll pay tax on the difference, which is considered a capital gain. Canada Revenue Agency will tax you on 50 percent of that gain.

Purchasing Bonds

Buying bonds is a lot like buying stocks (see Book II, Chapter 1). You just get in touch with your broker, set up an account, and place your order. If you already have an account with a broker, whether in person or online, you shouldn't have to fill out any additional paperwork to buy a bond. The one account should allow you to purchase stocks, bonds, and mutual funds as well. Unless you are going to concentrate most of your investment money in bonds, usually no need exists to select a broker who specializes in this kind of security.

You do, of course, have to pay for any bonds that you purchase. You pay in the same way and time frame as with stocks (within three business days of placing the buying order). Fortunately, you don't get charged much in the way of miscellaneous fees when you buy bonds. These fees vary with the brokerage, but in almost all cases they are very small (sometimes less than $1 per transaction).

Commissions on bonds are usually lower than fees on stocks, because full-service brokers have huge bond inventories. Still, fees vary depending on whether you buy bonds from an advisor or from a discount broker.

The Internet doesn't have as many websites devoted to information about investing in bonds as it does sites about the stock market. However, a couple of outstanding Canadian sites more than make up for the lack of numbers. Try www.pfin.ca/canadianfixedincome for access to the price and yield information from CBID, Canada's only electronic, multi-dealer fixed-income market. For information on yields for all types of Government of Canada bonds, check out Canada Investment and Savings at www.cis-pec.gc.ca; for strip bonds, go to http://stripbonds.info. For information about bond ratings, go to the Dominion Bond Rating Service at www.dbrs.com. Although specific to the U.S. bond market, general information on buying bonds and answers to frequently asked questions about the industry can be had at The Securities Industry and Financial Markets Association Website: www.investinginbonds.com.

Bonds trade on a type of OTC (over-the-counter) market, and most trade without the securities symbols you see on an organized stock exchange, like the Toronto Stock Exchange. Therefore, the investor has to tell the broker the type, how long (time) the investor will hold the bond, and state the investor's risk parameters. Most brokerages (discount and full-service) maintain a bond-trading department in order to meet varied customer needs and preferences.

Looking at Bond Performance: The Indices

An *index* is a statistical yardstick used to gauge the performance of a particular market or group of investments. By tracking average prices or the movement of prices of a group of similar investments, such as bonds, an index produces a benchmark measure against which you can assess an individual investment's performance.

Think of using an index the same way that you may use a list of comparable home sales when you shop for a house in a neighbourhood. If the list of comparable homes shows you that the average three-bedroom colonial sells for $325,000, you can't expect to buy a similar house for too much less than that. You also don't want to pay too much more. In the same respect, the benchmarks produced by an index show you a reasonable performance target.

A *return* is an investment's performance over time. If you're looking at performance for a period of time, say five years, look for an average annual return. If the same mutual fund returned 7 percent over the course of those five years, its average annual return would be 7 percent.

If an investment's performance over the course of a year is vastly superior or inferior to the appropriate index's return, you'll want to know why. Your investment may be outpacing its peers because it's a lot riskier. A mutual fund, for example, may invest in stocks or bonds that are far riskier than other funds it may resemble. On the other hand, an investment may be lagging its peers simply because it's a poor performer. Bear in mind, however, that you have to build a performance history over time to determine the character of a particular investment.

Checking out the DEX

If you're invested in the Canadian bond market, you won't be able to track the performance of your investments using a stock index like the S&P/TSX Composite. You have to consult an index designed specifically to track bonds. In Canada, the DEX index tracks a combination of investment-grade Canadian bonds, including federal, provincial, municipal, and corporate bonds that mature in more than one year. It pretty much represents the entire Canadian bond market.

Until 2007, the DEX fixed-income indices were known as the Scotia Capital indices. The indices' owner, the Toronto Stock Exchange, changed the name after it began taking fixed-income data from multiple dealers, not just Scotia. You'll find the DEX bond indices reported in daily newspapers alongside the major stock indices. The bond indices are similarly calculated to reflect both number and percentage changes.

Coping with poor performance

If a bond is doing poorly, maybe because interest rates have risen (bond prices move in reverse of interest rates), ask yourself what cost you can expect from hanging on to the bond until maturity. Compare that expense with what it will cost you to sell the bond. If interest rates jump substantially, say, to 8 percent, and you're hanging on to a bond paying 1.5 percent, you might well be better off selling the older issue and buying a new bond.

Chapter 3: Mind your Rs and Ts: RRSPs and TFSAs

In This Chapter

✔ Finding out about RRSPs

✔ Getting acquainted with the Tax-Free Savings Account

✔ Putting RESPs to work

✔ Understanding the tax implications

The investments discussed in this chapter are some of the most popular with Canadians — and the most useful. Although in some cases your initial contribution isn't guaranteed the way it is in a savings account, the potential for growing your money is far superior.

Investing in RRSPs

Established in 1957, RRSPs, or Registered Retirement Savings Plans, were designed by the federal government to help Canadians invest for retirement. Anyone who earns income (as defined by the government) can invest in an RRSP, and probably should.

You set up your RRSP on your own, with a bank, mutual fund company or dealer, brokerage firm, credit union, trust company, insurance company, or financial adviser. And you can invest your RRSP money in almost anything you can think of, from aggressive-growth stocks to conservative GICs.

Remember that long-term investments like those within an RRSP take advantage of long-term growth potential. That means the earlier you start making contributions, the better. When you're in your 20s and 30s, retirement may seem impossibly far off — so far off, in fact, that it's hard to imagine planning for it now. However, if you want to retire in comfort, you have to think ahead.

Table 3–1 shows how financially beneficial it is to invest in an RRSP as early as possible. The first column shows how many years before retirement the contributor started investing. The second column shows the accumulated balance at retirement, assuming annual contributions of $4,000 and a 6 percent annual return on investment.

Table 3–1	Investing Early for Retirement
Number of Years to Retirement	*Accumulated Savings at Retirement*
40 years	$656,191
30 years	$335,207
20 years	$155,971
10 years	$55,887
5 years	$23,901

Deciding not to contribute to an RRSP because you don't want to cut back on your take-home pay, or are telling yourself retirement is a long way off, may prove to be a big mistake. Ultimately, you won't be paying yourself, and could risk ending up without enough money after you retire.

The key benefits of RRSPs

If you invest in an RRSP, your contributions offer two powerful, tangible benefits: First, you receive an immediate tax deduction for the amount you've invested; second, you get tax protection (a shelter) for the returns you will accrue on those investments within the RRSP until you withdraw the money at retirement.

Let's say, for example, that you earned $45,000 of taxable income this year, but made a $3,000 contribution to your RRSP. If your *marginal tax rate* (the highest rate of combined federal and provincial income tax you pay on the money you earn in a given year) is 30 percent, you will achieve an immediate tax savings of $900 for this year, bringing your tax bill down from $13,500 to $12,600. That's money you will now be able to spend — or, even better, invest.

How much you can contribute

Your RRSP contribution limit depends on your earned income. You are allowed to contribute a percentage of that income every year, up to a maximum limit. As of 2012, the federal government allows you to contribute 18 percent of the tax year's earned income up to $22,970. The limit can be greater if you have a *carry-forward*, meaning that you contributed less than your limit in previous years. The limit goes down if you are also contributing to a company pension plan or participating in a deferred profit sharing plan.

Deciding where to put your RRSP money

A very broad range of investment vehicles is eligible to go into your RRSP, including the following:

✦ Deposits in savings or tiered savings accounts

✦ GICs and term deposits

✦ Stocks

✦ Bonds

✦ Mutual funds

✦ Mortgages

Depending on your risk tolerance, you can buy RRSPs that focus on different types of investments. *Guaranteed plans* invest in vehicles that guarantee you won't lose your principal, like GICs and CDIC-insured savings accounts. With a guaranteed plan, you will know ahead of time exactly how much and how fast your money will grow. *Variable-rate plans* don't necessarily guarantee your initial investment, but can be very safe and offer far better returns. Those returns will fluctuate, however, because you can't predict the performance of the investment vehicles, like mutual funds or stocks. Keep in mind that with stocks and mutual funds you have the added option of investing in a variety of fund types whose risk ranges from conservative to aggressive.

You don't have to choose just one kind of investment for your RRSP. In fact, unless your research tells you otherwise, you should invest only a certain percentage of your money in a high-risk investment, such as stocks. To determine what percentage of your money to invest in stocks, many financial advisers recommend that you subtract your age from 100. For example, if you're 25, you should invest 75 percent of your money in stocks; at 55, you'd invest 45 percent in stocks.

When considering an overall investment portfolio, some financial planners advise using RRSPs for more conservative investments. The thinking here is that the tax-deferring power of your RRSP will compensate for lower returns. In other words, why jeopardize your retirement savings with high-risk investments when the real return on a more conservative RRSP investment may be only slightly lower? As well, safer investments such as GICs usually pay interest, which is taxed at a higher rate than the capital gains earned on stocks, so you're better off keeping them in your RRSP.

Self-directed RRSPs

Most Canadians set up their RRSPs through a financial institution like a bank or mutual fund company. The institution puts your money into RRSP-eligible investment vehicles for you. Novice investors often choose this type of RRSP because they don't feel confident enough to do otherwise.

However, for those who want more control over their investment choices, you can set up what's called a *self-directed RRSP,* which allows you to pick and choose investment vehicles from wherever you want. Think of a self-directed RRSP as a shopping cart for the savvy investment consumer. When you've chosen a particular investment, you place it in your cart to take advantage of the RRSP benefits discussed earlier.

You can register your self-directed RRSP with a financial institution or brokerage house, which becomes a trustee of the RRSP. In exchange, you may have to pay a yearly fee of about $100 to $150, although many firms will dispense with the fee if you have enough money in your account.

If you decide to set up a self-directed RRSP, you can transfer into it money you've already placed inside other RRSPs to create a single RRSP. To do so, you will have to fill out a special form provided by the federal government and pay a fee.

Even the savviest investment consumer needs advice. People with self-directed RRSPs may wish to take advantage of the professional insights of a qualified financial planner to guide their strategy.

Income splitting and spousal RRSPs

Making contributions to a spousal RRSP used to make a great deal of sense for couples who had one high earner and another earner who made little or no money. The higher earner would make a contribution for the lower earner with the result that the higher earner got a much-needed tax deduction and the lower earning spouse got a separate stream of income in retirement — a strategy that generally results in tax savings.

In 2007, however, the government announced a major change to how pension income can be split in retirement. Spouses receiving pension income can now shift up to 50 percent of this income from one to the other to minimize the overall taxes they pay. This includes income from:

✦ Pension plans

✦ Registered retirement income funds (RRIFs)

✦ Life income funds (LIFs)

✦ Locked-in retirement income funds (LRIFs)

✦ Annuities purchased from RRSPs

✦ Deferred profit sharing plans

You might think the spousal RRSP no longer has a role, but you'd be wrong. A spousal RRSP can still be an effective tool in four circumstances:

✦ **You plan on taking early retirement.** That's because your ability to split income before age 65 is limited to income from a registered pension plan. That means if you retire at age 60, and you're relying on income from a RRIF – a Registered Retirement Income Fund – for example, you won't be able to split that income with a spouse until you reach age 65. It makes sense to contribute to a spousal RRSP now so that you can split income in the five years before you're able to take advantage of the new income-splitting rules.

✦ **You have a lot of income from non-RRSP sources that can't be split.** Perhaps you have a lot of investment, rental, or non-pension income in retirement that will be attributed back to you. In that case, you can transfer as much as 100 percent of your RRSP contributions to your spouse, boosting his or her income in retirement and reducing your taxes now.

✦ **You're over age 71 and can no longer have an RRSP in your own name.** You can continue to contribute to a younger spouse's RRSP until the year that person turns 71, when an RRSP converts into a RRIF and you're forced to withdraw savings every year.

✦ **A spousal RRSP equates to pre-paid alimony.** Sad but true.

Contributing to a spousal RRSP does not preclude you from investing in your own RRSP, as long as the combined contribution does not exceed your allowable limit for that year.

Foreign content inside RRSPs

The Canadian economy is among the most stable in the world and has stood up relatively well during the recent downturn. But it still represents only about 3 percent of the world economy. By limiting yourself to domestic investments, you are ensuring that your portfolio is not geographically diversified and limiting your ability to profit from more powerful economies. Fortunately, in 2005 the government scrapped the rules limiting foreign content in RRSPs to 30 percent of your holdings. You now have *carte blanche* to invest where you wish.

Borrowing from your RRSPs for a home or education

If you take money out of your RRSP, you pay income tax upfront. However, the government lets you borrow from your RRSP tax-free and interest-free in two instances:

✦ **The Home Buyers' Plan (HBP):** First-time home buyers (as defined by the federal government) can borrow up to $25,000 from their RRSP to finance their purchase through the HBP. This amount may double if you have a spouse with her or his own RRSP. However, the government has strict rules governing repayment, which must be completed within 15 years. Keep in mind, your HBP loan does affect the future gains you will miss out on for the period of time the money is outside your sheltered RRSP.

✦ **The Lifelong Learning Plan (LLP):** Using the LLP, people who want to go back to school full-time to finish their education can borrow up to $10,000 per year to a maximum of $20,000 over four years from their RRSP. The loan must be paid back within 10 years. Like the HBP, your loan is interest-free and tax-free. But again, consider seriously the fact that the money you borrow will no longer be compounding inside your RRSP.

Cashing in your RRSPs — and the benefits of RRIFs

Unless they are locked into an illiquid investment, you can withdraw funds from your RRSP anytime. The government imposes no penalty for withdrawal other than taxes for which you are liable, unless, as we explain above, you are participating in the government's Home Buyers' Plan or Lifelong Learning Plan.

The government extracts the income tax on withdrawals upfront through a withholding tax (simply the government's means of collecting the income tax right away).

All RRSPs mature the year you turn 71. You have three options when you *convert,* or dismantle, your RRSP. They are:

✦ **Convert your RRSP into a lump-sum cash payout.** By the end of the calendar year following your 71st birthday, unless you've made other arrangements, your RRSP funds must all be withdrawn and face combined federal and provincial income tax. This tax will be levied upfront through the withholding tax, and can be very steep because it varies upward depending on the size of the withdrawal.

✦ **Convert your RRSP into an annuity.** People who want the security of knowing they will have a stream of income for the rest of their lives can choose to use their RRSP funds to buy a life *annuity.* Sold by insurance companies, many annuities pay regular installments of fixed income for life. Annuities are not like investments that can grow or shrink. The payments are fixed and can pose problems because they are inflexible to factors like inflation and enhancing your estate.

✦ **Convert your RRSP into a Registered Retirement Income Fund (RRIF).** This allows you to bypass some of the problems faced when choosing either of the preceding options. First, a RRIF will extend the benefit of the tax shelter by allowing you to withdraw your funds over time rather than in a highly taxed lump sum. Second, a RRIF gives you flexibility because you maintain your investments, which can continue to grow — possibly earning you more money for the times in your retirement when you might need more. With a RRIF, you are required to withdraw a minimum amount each year.

Borrowing for your RRSP

Although conservative investors may feel nervous about borrowing to put away money for their retirement, borrowing to make an RRSP contribution can be a smart option. Many lending institutions eager to attract clients to their investment products will offer loans for very low interest rates. Also, because your RRSP contribution is tax-deductible, you will probably be eligible for a tax refund that can then be used to pay off a portion of your loan. As a rule of thumb, don't borrow more money than you can pay off within a year.

The interest you pay on an RRSP loan is not, unfortunately, tax-deductible.

What Is a Tax-Free Savings Account?

Canada Revenue Agency (CRA) has added to the average Canadian's bag of retirement planning tools by offering up the new Tax-Free Savings Account (TFSA). As of January 2009, you can shelter up to $5,000 a year in investments in a TFSA. Although you won't get a tax deduction for the money you invest, as you would with an RRSP, you can withdraw money from your TFSA tax-free at any time and then replace it the following year.

The TFSA rules

Like all government-implemented tax shelters, TFSAs have rules. Keep in mind the following points:

✦ You can begin to contribute to a TFSA at 18 — all you need is a Social Insurance Number (SIN).

✦ TFSA contribution room accumulates even if you don't open an account.

✦ Overcontributions are subject to a penalty tax of 1 percent per month.

✦ Eligible investments in a TFSA run the gamut from daily interest savings accounts to stocks, mutual funds, bonds, GICs, and, in some cases, shares in small business corporations.

✦ Income earned in a TFSA, including interest, dividends, or capital gains, isn't taxable.

✦ Unlike any other tax-advantaged savings vehicle, you will recover contribution room the year after you make a withdrawal.

✦ If you die, the fair market value of your TFSA goes into your estate tax-free but any gain or income that builds up afterward is taxable.

Just like contributing to a spousal RRSP, you can make contributions for your spouse to a TFSA. You can also contribute for an adult child or other relative, even a friend, so that they too can reach their own annual contribution limit. You won't get a tax deduction for your contribution, but the income earned on the money won't be attributed back to you.

The TFSA vs. the RRSP

Ideally, you should maximize both your RRSP and your TFSA contributions to fund a comfortable retirement. But realistically, you may have to focus on one investment or the other. You might assume that you're always better off investing in an RRSP because of the tax deduction you get on contributions. In the following situations, however, you'd be better off maximizing contributions to your TFSA first.

✦ Expecting an inheritance? Or perhaps you've just been a spectacular saver or have an iron-clad pension. At any rate, if you firmly believe you'll have even more money in retirement than when you were working, you might be better off investing in a TFSA. With a TFSA, you can withdraw as much money as you want, when you want. It doesn't add to your income and therefore you won't have to pay tax on it at your top marginal tax rate.

✦ If you've got almost no savings, you would certainly be better off putting what money you *do* manage to set aside in a TFSA. Why? Because government benefits like Old Age Security and the Guaranteed Income Supplement are "income tested" — meaning they begin to be clawed back as your retirement income level rises. Because withdrawals from TFSAs will not be considered income, they won't count against any benefits or income-tested tax credits that you would be eligible for from the federal government. Withdrawals from RRSPs or RRIFs, by contrast, *do* count as income.

If, like most people, you expect your income in retirement to be marginally lower than your income from working, you should probably choose an RRSP as your primary savings vehicle. Consider this: if you live in Alberta, and your taxable income totals more than about $38,832, you'll get at least a 32 percent tax refund on your RRSP contribution.

Later on, when you've retired, you can roll that RRSP money you've saved over into a RRIF and, assuming that your post-retirement income will be below $41,544, you'll pay tax on withdrawals at about 25 percent. So you get tax relief today and you pay tax later at a lower rate in the long run. What's not to like?

Mother's (and Father's) Little Helper: The RESP

With university tuition costing more and more every year, it's as important to save money for your children's education as it is to save for yourself. Although you're not building wealth in the truest sense — in other words, saving for university tuition won't get you rich — having to pay for post-secondary school at the last minute surely will put a major dent in your retirement savings. Plus, if you start saving today, compound interest means that by the time your child is 18 you'll have more money saved than you put in over the years.

Using a Registered Education Savings Plan (RESP) is the best and most popular way to save for education costs. Here's why:

✦ **You can get a government grant of up to $500 a year — or 20 percent of your contribution — toward your child's education.** To get the full grant, you'd have to contribute $2,500 a year (per child). A lifetime grant limit of $7,200 does exist: if you invest the maximum amount, you'll reach it in your 15th year of contributing.

✦ **You don't have to pay tax on the investment earnings accumulating in the plan.** When you turn the money over to your university-aged sons or daughters to cover school expenses, they'll be students (and hence broke), so they're not likely to pay any tax at all.

Comparing pooled and open RESPs

Two basic kinds of RESPs are available:

✦ **Pooled plans:** These plans are often referred to as scholarship trusts. You pay a set amount monthly and the plan administrator invests it, usually conservatively, and doles it out to the beneficiaries according to its own rules. If you drop out of the plan, you forfeit your earnings to the plan, so others benefit.

✦ **Self-directed plans:** These plans are available through investment dealers, banks, and mutual fund companies. You contribute what and when you wish, choose the investments yourself, and dole out cash as you will so long as it's within 25 years of opening the account. If your child doesn't go to university, you can roll the earnings over into your RRSP if you have the contribution room.

Most financial advisers favour self-directed plans because of their flexibility.

Considering the disadvantage of RESPs

The main disadvantage of any kind of RESP is that you can name one or more beneficiaries but if none of them enroll full-time in a university, college, CEGEP, or designated post-secondary school by the time they're 21 you have to give the government grant money back to the government.

Transferring RESP funds into an RRSP

You can get your original contributions back, and you can transfer as much as $50,000 of the earnings on those contributions to your own RRSP, providing that

+ Your plan allows for that option.

+ You've been paying into the plan for at least ten years.

+ You have enough unused contribution room. Whatever you can't transfer becomes taxable income, and you get charged a 20 percent penalty tax on top of that (30 percent in Quebec).

Investing with Your Eye on Taxes

Unfortunately, with investing, as with just about any other activity that generates income, gains are taxable as well as dividend and interest income. The federal government collects all income tax for itself and on behalf of the provinces, except in Quebec, where the provincial government collects its own income tax. As a rule, provincial income tax is calculated as a percentage of your federal income tax rate.

The fact that you will pay combined federal and provincial income tax on your investment returns should not deter you from trying to invest successfully. A good investor will come out ahead in the end. But you should realize now that you will pay taxes on investment gains. Consider the following tax implications for investments *outside* your RRSP.

Savings accounts

Interest on simple savings accounts and tiered savings accounts are taxed as income. Banks and financial institutions report this interest income to Canada Revenue Agency, just as all investment returns are reported.

GICs

The interest you earn on GICs (guaranteed investment certificates) must be declared as taxable income, and will be fully taxed on an annual basis. If, for example, your GIC is locked in for five years, that means you will pay tax each of those years — even if you haven't yet received any of the interest.

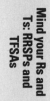

Mutual funds

With mutual funds, unfortunately, you have to pay tax each year on the dividends, interest, and capital gains that the fund distributes to each of its shareholders. You also have to pay taxes on your own gains when you sell shares — another reason for adopting a long-term buy-and-hold strategy.

Bonds

Price appreciation (if any) on a bond — whether it is a government or corporate bond — is taxable when the bond matures as a capital gain (you will pay tax on 50 percent of your capital gains annually). If your bond loses value, that loss is deemed a *capital gains loss.* You can apply that loss against other capital gains you report to Canada Revenue Agency.

The interest you earn on a bond is fully taxable annually. That rule applies even to compounded Canada Savings Bonds, where the interest is reinvested yearly, meaning you'll pay tax on interest you haven't yet received.

Stocks

With stocks, you don't pay taxes on your gains until you sell your shares — a feature that fans of stock investing say is a clear advantage in the long run. The downside, however, is that when you do cash in shares down the road, your tax bracket or the tax rate may have increased.

Tax-deferred investing with RRSPs

Maxing out your contributions to your RRSP really does boil down to a choice of paying yourself or paying Canada Revenue Agency.

As we discuss above, the benefits of investing within an RRSP are twofold: First, all the contributions you make within your RRSP are tax-deductible — in other words, these contributions, up to the allowable limit, become an immediate deduction from your taxable income. Second, the government defers the tax bill for any gains you make on those investments, be they interest, capital gains, or dividends, until you cash in your RRSP.

Even after you turn 71, the tax deferral power of your RRSP will keep working for you. How? You will have to convert your RRSP into a registered retirement income fund (RRIF) and withdraw your funds over time rather than in a lump sum. You'll pay less this way, because the government charges less upfront income tax (called withholding tax) on smaller withdrawals. On top of that, the government gives you a *pension income credit* up to $1,000 annually (when using a RRIF), which reduces the amount of tax you owe for income you receive from qualifying pension income, including RRSP funds.

Because interest-bearing investments are fully taxed at your *marginal tax rate* (the rate at which you are taxed on your last earned dollar of a given tax year), many investment advisers suggest these as your first choice to go inside an RRSP. Because capital gains are taxed at a lower rate (only 50 percent of the gain is added to your overall taxable income), these might be investments to keep outside your RRSP. Dividend-bearing investments from shares in Canadian equities are also taxed at a lower rate. That's because dividends represent a corporation's after-tax profits. To avoid double taxation, the federal government provides some tax relief in the form of a *dividend tax credit,* which reduces the rate at which your dividends from Canadian corporations will be taxed.

Calculating the dividend tax credit is a bit confusing (especially for residents of Quebec, who follow a different formula). If you received a dividend after 2005, the type of credit depends on what kind of corporation made the payout. Most Canadian stock exchange-listed corporations are eligible for the enhanced dividend tax credit, which is why they're called eligible dividends. Those dividends that don't qualify because, for some reason, the corporation that issues them is not paying tax at the general corporate income tax rate are called *non-eligible dividends.*

Prior to the 2006 tax year, you would have paid tax at a rate of about 31 percent on all dividends, based on the top marginal tax rate in Ontario. But that meant dividends were being taxed twice. The corporation paying the dividend had already paid tax on its profits and the individual receiving the dividend then had to pay tax again. So, beginning in 2006, the federal government reduced the total tax paid on eligible dividends by Canadians, prompting many provinces to follow suit. The result, in Ontario, is that the tax on eligible dividends dropped from 31 percent to 25 percent. The dividend tax rate has been creeping back up — in 2011, the rate for Canadians with taxable income over $128,800 was 28.19 percent. The percentage is lower in other provinces, such Alberta and British Columbia.

The (tax) price you pay for tapping your retirement accounts early

Do not take money out of your RRSP on a whim — say, when you're changing jobs or feel the need for an extravagant vacation. The money is considered income and is taxed as such by Canada Revenue Agency at your marginal tax rate. You'll also lose the tax-sheltered earning potential that the money bought you inside the plan.

Income tax on RRSP withdrawals is levied immediately when you take the money out. This way, the government gets its money upfront, rather than waiting for you to file your tax return. This manner of extracting income tax is called a withholding tax, and is based on the amount you withdraw. As of the 2011 tax year, if you take $5,000 out of your RRSP you'll be charged 10 percent withholding tax (unless you live in Quebec, where you'll have to pay more — 21 percent — because the province levies its own withholding tax). Between $5,000 and $15,000, that tax jumps to 20 percent (26 percent for residents of Quebec), and again to 30 percent for withdrawals over $15,000 (31 percent for residents of Quebec).

Because the withholding tax may not match the amount of tax you actually owe on the money you've withdrawn, you will still have to reckon with Canada Revenue Agency at tax time. Depending on your tax bracket, that will either mean paying more when you file your tax return, or, in some cases, getting a rebate for overpayment.

Book II

Making Money with Mutual Funds

The 5th Wave   By Rich Tennant

"The first thing we should do is get you two
into a good mutual fund. Let me get out the
'Magic 8 Ball' and we'll run some options."

Contents at a Glance

Chapter 1: Understanding Mutual Funds

In This Chapter

✔ Grasping the basics of mutual funds

✔ Looking at how funds can make you money

✔ Identifying the four types of mutual funds

✔ Understanding the pros and cons of mutual funds

✔ Choosing between load and no-load funds

For many, many years, people have been building their wealth by investing in mutual funds. To some, the mutual fund world seems overwhelming — with so many to choose from, it feels impossible to get started. Some people just buy the first thing their banker or financial planner suggests, which all too often leaves Canadians disappointed with their funds' performance. Others are sold funds that either are unsuitable or carry pricy management fees that make a major dent in returns. It's a shame, because building a portfolio of excellent funds is easy when you follow a few simple rules and use your own common sense. This stuff isn't complicated — a mutual fund is just a money-management service that operates under clear rules.

The fund industry is competitive and sophisticated, which means plenty of good choices exist. In this chapter, we show you how funds can make you money — especially when you leave your investment in place for several years. We also touch on the different types of funds available, look at the pros and cons of investing in funds, and fill you in on the difference between load and no-load funds.

Mutual Fund Basics

A *mutual fund* is a pool of money that a company gets from investors like you and divides up into equally priced *units*. Each unit is a tiny slice of the fund. When you put money into the fund or take it out again, you either buy or sell units. For example, say a fund has *total assets* — that is, money held in trust for investors — of $10 million and investors have been sold a total of 1 million units. Then each unit is worth $10. If you put money into the fund, you're simply sold units at that day's value. If you take money out, the fund buys units back from you at the same price for that day. (Handling purchase and sale transactions in units makes it far simpler to do the paperwork.) And the system has another huge advantage: As long as you know how many units you own, you can simply check their current price to find out how much your total investment is worth. For example, if you hold 475 units of a fund whose current unit price is $15.20, then you know your holding has a value of 475 times $15.20, or $7,220.

Owning units of a mutual fund makes you — you guessed it — a *unitholder.* In fact, you and the other unitholders are the legal owners of the fund. But the fund is run by a company that's legally known as the *fund manager* — the firm that handles the investing and also deals with the fund's administration. The terminology gets confusing here because the person (usually an employee of the fund manager) who chooses which stocks, bonds, or other investments the fund should buy is also usually called the fund manager. To make things clear, we refer to the company that sells and administers the fund as the *management company* or *fund sponsor.* We use the term *fund manager* for the person who picks the stocks and bonds. His or her skill is one of the main benefits you get from a mutual fund. Obviously, the fund manager should be experienced and not too reckless — after all, you're trusting him or her with your money.

Under professional management, the fund invests in stocks and bonds, increasing the pool of money for the investors and boosting the value of the individual units. For example, if you bought units at $10 each and the fund manager managed to pick investments that doubled in value, your units would grow to $20. In return, the management company slices off fees and expenses. (In the world of mutual funds, just like almost everywhere else, you don't get something for nothing.) Fees and expenses usually come to between 0.3 percent and 3 percent of the fund's assets each year — though the average fee is around 2 percent of assets. Some specialized funds charge much more.

Confused? Don't be, it isn't rocket science. This example should help. Units in one of Canada's biggest mutual funds, Investors Dividend Fund — run by the country's largest fund company, Investors Group — were bought from and sold to people like you and me at $20.94 each on October 31, 2011. So if you invested $1,000 in the fund that day, you owned 47.8 units ($1,000 divided by $20.94). The price you pay for each unit is known as the fund's *net asset value* per unit. The net asset value is the fund's assets minus its liabilities, hence the "net" (which means after costs and debts are taken away), divided by the number of units outstanding.

So a fund company buys and sells the units to the public at their net asset value. This value increases or decreases proportionally as the value of the fund's investments rises or falls. Let's say in March you pay $10 each for 100 units in a fund that invests in oil and gas shares, always a smelly and risky game. Now by, say, July, the value of the shares the fund holds has dropped by one-fifth. Then your units are worth just $8 each. So your original $1,000 investment is now worth only $800. But that August, a bunch of companies in which the fund has invested strike oil in Alberta. That sends the value of their shares soaring and lifts the fund's units to $15 each. The value of your investment has now grown to $1,500.

Where can you go from here? You've made a tidy profit after a bit of a let-down, but what happens next? Well, that depends on you. You can hang in there and see if more oil's in them there hills, or you can cash out. With most funds, you can simply buy or sell units at that day's net asset value. That flexibility is one of the great beauties of mutual funds. Funds that let you come and go as you please in this way are known as *open-end funds,* as though they had a giant door that's never locked. Think of a raucous Viking banquet where guests are free to come and go at will because the wall at one end of the dining hall has been removed.

Book II
Chapter 1

Understanding
Mutual Funds

That means most mutual funds are marvellously flexible and convenient. The managers allow you to put money into the fund on any business day by buying units, and you take money out again at will by selling your units back to the fund. In other words, an investment in a mutual fund is a *liquid asset.* A liquid asset is either cash or it's an investment that can be sold and turned into good old cash at a moment's notice. The idea is that cash and close-to-cash investments, just like water, are adaptable and useful in all sorts of situations. The ability to get your cash back at any time is called *liquidity* in investment jargon, and professionals prize it above all else — more than they prize red Porsches with very loud sound systems or crystal goblets in lovely velvet-lined boxes with their initials engraved in gold.

The other type of fund is a *closed-end fund.* Investors in these funds often are sold their units when the fund is launched, but to get their money back they must find another investor to buy the units on the stock market like a share, often at a loss. The fund usually won't buy the units back, or may buy only a portion. You can make money in closed-end funds, but it's very tricky. As craven investment analysts sometimes say when they hate a stock but can't pluck up the courage to tell investors to sell it: "Avoid."

The Nitty Gritty: How a Fund Makes You Money

We'll stick with the example of Investors Dividend, a huge and well-run fund generally available only through Investors Group agents across the country. Investors Dividend's $12.8 billion in assets as of October 2011 made it Canada's biggest mutual fund. That's $1 million 12,800 times over, or about $427 for each of the approximately 30 million people living in Canada. The fund, which dates to 1962, invests in shares of large Canadian banks and blue-chip companies. This behemoth lumbers along in the middle of the performance pack of similar funds. Like other mutual fund companies, Investors Group, based in Winnipeg, sells units of Investors Dividend to the public every business day and buys them back from other investors at the same price.

With most companies' funds you're free to come and go as you please, but companies often impose a small levy on investors who sell their units within 90 days of buying them. That's because constant trading raises expenses for the other unitholders and makes the fund manager's job harder. The charge (which should go to the fund, and usually does) is generally 2 percent of the units sold, but it can be more. Check this out before you invest, especially if you're thinking of moving your cash around shortly after you buy.

Returns — What's in it for you?

The main reason why people buy mutual funds is to earn a *return*. A return is simply the profit you get in exchange for either investing in a business (by buying its shares) or for lending money to a government or company (by buying its bonds). It's money you get as a reward for letting other people use your cash — and for putting your money at risk. Mutual fund buyers earn the same sorts of profits but they make them indirectly because they're using a fund manager to pick their investments for them. The fund itself earns the profits, which are either paid out to the unitholders or retained within the fund itself, increasing the value of each of its units.

When you invest money, you nearly always hope to get:

✦ **Trading profits** or *capital gains* (the two mean nearly the same thing) when the value of your holdings goes up. Capital is just the money you've tied up in an investment, and a capital gain is simply an increase in its value. For example, say you buy gold bars at $100 each and their price rises to $150. You've earned a capital gain of $50 when you sell.

✦ **Income** in the form of interest on a bond or loan, or dividends from a company. *Interest* is the regular payment you get in return for lending your money, and *dividends* are a portion of a company's revenue, hopefully from profits paid out to its shareowners. For example, say you deposit $1,000 at a bank at an annual interest rate of 5 percent; each year you'll get interest of $50 (or 5 percent of the money you deposited). Dividends are usually paid out by companies on a per-share basis. Say, for example, you own 10,000 shares and the company's directors decide to pay a dividend of 50 cents per share. You'll get a cheque for $5,000.

You also hope to get the money you originally invest back at the end of the day, which doesn't always happen. That's part of the risk you assume with almost any investment. Companies can lose money, sending the value of their shares tumbling. Or inflation can rise, which nearly always makes the value of both shares and bonds drop rapidly. That's because inflation eats away at the value of the money, which makes it less attractive to have the money tied up in such long-term investments where it's vulnerable to steady erosion.

Here's an example to illustrate the difference between earning capital gains and dividend income. Say you buy 100 shares of a company — a Costa Rican crocodile farm, for example — for $115 each and hold them for an entire year. Also, say you get $50 in dividend income during the year because the company has a policy of paying four quarterly dividends of 12.5 cents, or 50 cents per share, annually (that is, 50 cents times the 100 shares you own — $50 right into your pocket).

Now imagine the price of the share rises in the open market by $12, from $115 to $127. The value of your 100 shares rises from $11,500 to $12,700, for a total capital gain of $1,200.

REMEMBER

Your capital gain is only on paper unless you actually sell your holdings at that price.

Add up your gains and income, and that's your total return — $50 in dividends plus a capital gain of $1,200, for a total of $1,250.

Another example should make this crystal clear. Back in April of 2007 — before the financial crisis hit — Investors Dividend units were sold to the public at $24.77 and rose to $25.48 by the end of May. Things weren't so good the rest of the year: The unit price went up and down until October, when it began a prolonged fall, to $21.83 by the end of March 2008. (It fell even further between March and July 2009.) That was a loss of 2.9 cents on every unit an investor held.

The fund also paid out a quarterly *distribution,* a special or scheduled payment to unitholders, of 14.5 cents per unit at the end of June and September 2007; 15.2 cents at the end of December 2007; and 16.0 cents at the end of March 2008, for a total distribution of 58.7 cents. Distributions are made when a fund has earned capital gains, interest, or dividends from its investments.

So what was the investor's return during the year? On a per-unit basis, she started with $24.77 at risk and during the following 12 months suffered a capital loss of $2.94 if she sold her units. However, thanks to the 58.7 cents of distributions, this loss was trimmed to about $2.44 a unit. That represented about 9.8 percent of the starting figure of $24.77, so the *percentage return,* the amount she earned or lost by being invested, was a loss of 9.8 percent. Calculating the return is actually a little more complicated than that because most investors would have simply reinvested the quarterly distribution in more units immediately after being paid out. In fact, returns for mutual funds always assume that all distributions are reinvested in more units. Investors Dividend's official return for the year ended March 31, 2008, was a loss of 9.5 percent but only if units were sold.

Returns as a percentage

Returns on mutual funds, and nearly all other investments, are usually expressed as a percentage of the capital the investor originally put up. That way you can easily compare returns and work out whether or not you did well.

After all, if you tied up $10 million in an investment to earn only $1,000, you wouldn't be using your cash very smartly. That's why the return on any investment is nearly always stated in percentages by expressing the return as a proportion of the original investment. In the example of the crocodile farm, the return was $50 in dividends plus $1,200 in *capital appreciation,* which is just a fancy term for an increase in the value of your capital, for a total of $1,250. At the beginning of the year you put $11,500 into the shares by buying 100 of them at $115 each. To get your *percentage return* (the amount your money grew expressed as a percentage of your initial investment), divide your total return by the amount you initially invested and then multiply the answer by 100. The return of $1,250 represented 10.9 percent of $11,500, so your percentage return during the year was 10.9 percent. It's the return produced by an investment over several years, however, that people are usually interested in. Yes, it's often useful to look at the return in each individual year — for example, a loss of 10 percent in Year 1, a gain of 15 percent in Year 2, and so on. But that's a long-winded way of expressing things. It's handy to be able to state the return in just one number that represents the average yearly return over a set period. It makes it much easier, for instance, to compare the performance of two different funds. The math can start getting complex here, but don't worry — we stick to the basic method used by the fund industry.

Fund returns are expressed, in percentages, as an *average annual compound return.* That sounds like a mouthful, but the concept is simple. Say you invested $1,000 in a fund for three years. In the first year, the value of your investment dropped by 10 percent, or one-tenth, leaving you with $900. In Year 2, the fund earned a return of 20 percent, leaving you with $1,080. And in Year 3, the fund produced a return of 10 percent, leaving you with $1,188. So, over the three years, you earned a total of $188, or 18.8 percent of your initial $1,000 investment. When mutual fund companies convert that return to an "average annual" number, they invariably express the number as a "compound" figure. That simply means the return in Year 2 is added (or compounded) onto the return in Year 1, and the return in Year 3 is then compounded onto the new higher total, and so on. A return of 18.8 percent over three years works out to an average annual compound return of about 5.9 percent.

As the example demonstrates, the actual value of the investment fluctuated over the three years, but say it actually grew steadily at 5.9 percent. After one year, the $1,000 would be worth $1,059. After two years, it would be worth $1,121.48. And after three years, it would be worth $1,187.65. The total differs from $1,188 by a few cents because we rounded off the average annual return to one decimal place, instead of fiddling around with hundredths of a percentage point.

Remember these important points when looking at an average annual compound return:

✦ **Average:** That innocuous-looking average usually smooths out some mighty rough periods. Mutual funds can easily lose money for years on end — it happened, for example, when the world economy was hurt by inflation and recession in the 1970s and the recent recession saw the returns of many funds nosedive.

✦ **Annual:** Obviously, this means per year. And mutual funds should be thought of as long-term holdings to be owned for several years. The general rule in the industry is that you shouldn't buy an equity fund — one that invests in shares — unless you plan to own it for five years. That's because stocks can drop sharply, often for a year or more, and you'd be silly to risk money you might need in the short term (to buy a home, say) in an investment that might be down from its purchase value when you go to cash it in. With money you'll need in the near future, you're better off to stick to a super-stable, short-term bond or money market fund that will lose little or no money.

Of course, mutual fund companies sometimes use the old "long-term investing" mantra as an excuse. If their funds are down, they claim it's a long-term game and that investors should give their miraculous strategy time to work. But if the funds are up, the managers run ads screaming about the short-term returns.

✦ **Compound:** This little word, which means "added" or "combined" in this context, is the plutonium trigger at the heart of investing. It's the device that makes the whole thing go. It simply means that to really build your nest egg, you have to leave your profits or interest in place and working for you so you can start earning income on income. After a while, of course, you start earning income on the income you've earned, until it becomes a very nicely furnished hall of mirrors.

Another example will help. Mr. Simple and Ms. Compound each have $1,000 to invest, and the bank's offering 10 percent a year. (If only!) Now, let's say Mr. Simple puts his money into the bank, but each year he takes the interest earned and hides it under his mattress. Simple-minded, huh? After ten years, he'll have his original $1,000 plus the ten annual interest payments of $100 each under his futon, for a total of $2,000. But canny Ms. Compound leaves her money in the account, so each year the interest is added to the pile and the next year's interest is calculated on the higher amount. In other words, at the end of the first year, the bank adds her $100 in interest to her $1,000 initial deposit and then calculates the 10 percent interest for the following year on the higher base of $1,100, which earns her $110. Depending on how the interest is calculated and timed, she'll end the ten years with about $2,594, or $594 more than Mr. Simple. That extra $594 is compound interest earned on interest.

How funds can make you rich

The real beauty of mutual funds is the way they can grow your money over many years. "Letting your money ride" in a casino — by just leaving it on the odd numbers in roulette, for example — is a dumb strategy. The house will eventually win it from you because the odds are stacked in the casino operator's favour. But letting your money ride in a mutual fund over a decade or more can make you rich.

An investment in Investors Dividend Fund from its launch in 1962 through the end of October 2011 produced an annual average compound return of 7.55 percent. If your granny had been prescient enough to put $10,000 into the fund when it was launched, instead of blowing all her dough on sports cars and wild men, it would have been worth $353,924 by autumn 2011.

The main reason why Canadians had more than $748 billion in mutual funds at the end of 2011 is that funds let you make money in the stock and bond markets almost effortlessly. By the way, that $748 billion figure, which works out to an incredible $22,195 or so for everyone in the country, doesn't even include billions more sitting in *segregated* funds, which are mutual fund–like products sold by life insurance companies. (They're called segregated because they're kept separate from the life insurer's regular assets.)

Of course, no law says you have to buy mutual funds in order to invest. You might make more money investing on your own behalf, either in stocks or exchange-traded funds (see below), and lots of people from all walks of life do. But for less savvy investors, do-it-yourself investing can be tricky and dangerous. So millions of Canadians too busy or scared to learn the ropes themselves have found that funds are a wonderfully handy and reasonably cheap alternative. The Canadian fund industry association, the Investment Funds Institute of Canada, reports the public had more than 44 million accounts with its member firms at the end of 2011. Buying funds is like going out to a restaurant compared with buying food, cooking a meal, and cleaning up afterward. Yes, eating out is expensive, but it sure is nice not to have to face those cold pots in the sink covered in slowly congealing mustard sauce.

What mutual funds buy

Mutual funds and other investors put their money into just two long-term investments:

✦ **Stocks and shares:** Tiny slices of companies that trade in a big, sometimes chaotic but reasonably well-run electronic vortex called, yes, the stock market.

✦ **Bonds:** Loans made to governments or companies, which are packaged up so that investors can trade them to one another.

Types of Funds

Mutual funds fall into four main categories:

✦ **Equity funds:** By far the most popular type of fund on the market, equity funds hold stocks and shares. Stocks are often called "equity" because every share is supposed to entitle its owner to an equal portion of the company. In mid-2008, Canadians had $178 billion in Canadian stock funds, $93 billion in global stock funds, and another $20 billion in U.S. equity funds. These funds represent an investment in raw capitalism — ownership of businesses. We look at the range of equity funds available to you in Chapter 3.

✦ **Balanced funds:** The next biggest category is balanced funds. They generally hold a mixture of just about everything — from Canadian and foreign stocks to bonds from all around the world, as well as very short-term bonds that are almost as safe as cash.

✦ **Bond funds:** These beauties, also referred to as "fixed-income" funds, essentially lend money to governments and big companies, collecting regular interest each year and (nearly always) getting the cash back in the end.

✦ **Money market funds:** They hold the least volatile and most stable of all investments — very short-term bonds issued by governments and large companies that usually provide the lowest returns. These funds are basically savings vehicles for money you can't afford to take any risks with. They can also act as the safe little cushion of cash found in nearly all well-run portfolios. Read *Mutual Fund Investing For Canadians For Dummies* for more on money market funds. We give details on other types of funds in Chapter 3.

Reasons to Buy Funds

Here we give you some specific, significant reasons to make mutual funds a big part of your financial plan.

Offering safety in numbers: Public scrutiny and accountability

Perhaps the best thing about mutual funds is that their performance is public knowledge. When you own a fund, you're in the same boat as thousands of other unitholders, meaning the fund company is pressured to keep up the performance. If the fund lags its rivals for too long, unitholders will start *redeeming,* or cashing in, their units, which is the sort of thing that makes a manager stare at the ceiling at 4 a.m. Each fund sends unitholders clear annual *financial statements* of the fund's operations. These statements are tables of figures showing what the fund owns at the end of the year, what expenses and fees it paid to the management company, and how well it performed. Statements are audited (that is, checked) by big accounting firms. The management company must also at least offer to send you the semi-annual statements, showing how the fund was doing halfway through the year. (Make a note of looking for this information on the fund company's website.)

A lot of the information in the statements is hard to understand and not particularly useful, but always check one thing: Look at the fund's main holdings. If you bought what you thought was a conservative Canadian stock, for example, then you want to see lots of bank stocks and other companies you've at least heard of.

Don't confuse the *financial statements* — which describe how the fund is doing — with your own individual *account statement.* Your account statements are personal mailings that show how many units you own, how many you've bought and sold, and how much your holdings are worth. Companies usually must send you personal account statements at least twice a year. Some fund sellers, such as banks, send quarterly statements, and discount brokers often mail them monthly as do all full-service investment advisers. Fund companies also have Internet-based and telephone-based services that let you verify the amount of money in your account every day.

The next section helps you decipher price and performance figures. When you know what to look for, you can accurately track your funds' performance. We're not saying your fund manager won't give you the straight story, but getting a second opinion is never a bad plan, especially when it comes to your cash.

Finding and reading price tables

Time was you could check a mutual fund's unit price, or net asset value per share, in most daily newspapers. But daily tables are now virtually extinct, and the few that remain are on the endangered species list. Although the two national dailies, *The Globe and Mail* and the *National Post,* still publish weekly price summary tables, these include only a handful of the larger, more popular funds. It takes a lot of news-page space to print more than 7,000 fund prices, so the newspaper industry now uses the Internet to provide this information. If you're Internet-savvy, you also can look up fund prices on individual fund company websites.

Most mutual funds calculate and publish a value for their units every day that stock and bond markets are open. Some small or very specialized funds do this only monthly or weekly, and some take a day or two getting the information out, but unit prices for most widely available funds are provided the next day on fund information websites and, to a limited extent, in major newspapers. The listing also usually shows the change in unit price from the previous day.

Checking and reading mutual fund performance

Newspapers' monthly fund performance reports have gone the way of the dodo bird. This is unfortunate if you liked to open up those broad pages full of wide tables and highlight and circle things. Checking fund performance is now strictly an Internet operation. Assuming you are comfortable online, this is a very good thing. Apart from saving countless trees that used to be chopped up into newsprint pulp, you can get more immediate information and easily compare a fund against its peers and other investments.

Because mutual fund investing is primarily a longer-term undertaking, performance statistics should command more of your attention than daily prices do. How often should you check your fund's performance? Unfortunately, this question has no easy answer. But it's a good idea to look every three months or so to see how your manager is doing. Even if you bought your funds through a financial planner or other investment adviser — who's supposed to be looking out for your interests — it never hurts to keep an eye on how well the recommendations are turning out.

**Book II
Chapter 1**

Understanding Mutual Funds

Funds that buy the same sorts of investments are listed together, by category. Determining how a fund is categorized isn't easy nowadays, because data providers, who are members of the Canadian Investment Funds Standards Committee, use more than 40 asset categories. Your first step, then, is to enter the name of a fund in a website's general fund search tool, and then check its category on the page that appears.

Making sense of the numbers

What can you do with this jumble of numbers? The unit price is useful information, because by multiplying the price by the number of units you own you can work out the value of your holdings. You can also make sure the unit price in the newspaper matches the price shown on the statement you get from your broker or fund company, in order to double-check their bookkeeping. Keep the newspaper's mutual fund reports for June 30 and December 31 in your little sequined satchel until you've done your checking, because you'll be getting reports from your fund company showing the value of your holdings as of those dates.

The unit price is also handy if you're hazy on which fund you actually own. Don't laugh — a lot of smart people aren't always sure. With more than 7,000 funds, versions of funds, and fund-like products available in Canada, it's easy to get confused. Often, several different versions of a particular fund are on sale, depending on how you buy it (such as a front-end or back-end load) and other factors such as investment guarantees. If your account statement shows you own a fund with a unit price of $10.95, for instance, and the newspaper reports the same price, chances are you're talking about the same fund. However, you might have to go so far as to check your statements for the precise name of the fund, including the series or class letter — or even check the fund sales code, which is used by fund salespeople when making transactions.

The difference between the average and the median

Sometimes figuring out whether a fund has done better than other funds in its group is harder than it looks. When you look at a newspaper fund report, you'll come across two terms used to describe the typical fund's performance: The *average* and the *median*. The average and the median are both numbers that attempt to show how funds in a particular category have done. That way, if you're interested in a fund you can compare its performance with that of its rivals. For example, if you're considering buying your bank's U.S. equity fund, it's a good idea to see how it has done compared with other funds in the U.S. equity category. However, sometimes the average can be distorted upward or downward by a few extreme cases, so the median acts as a middle point, giving a good idea of what the typical return for funds was. Here's how it works:

✔ The **average** is calculated by simply adding up the return figures for all funds for a particular period and then dividing by the number of funds involved.

✔ The **median** is the halfway mark. Half of the funds were below that point and half were above.

Normally, the two numbers are very similar, but a sprinkling of very high or low returns in the sample can pull them apart. An "average" figure can be a misleading comparative, because it gives equal weight to each and every member of that group — regardless of the significance of each member. To be truly useful, an average must be "weighted" according to, in the case of a fund category, each individual fund's assets.

The meat of the subject is contained in the performance numbers. These returns are after the fund's fees and expenses have been deducted. Some exceptions to this practice exist in the monthly report — that is, funds that levy extra charges that reduce the performance shown — but the returns for all of the biggest companies are after charges. The companies that deduct fees and expenses *after* the returns shown in such tables are generally fund companies that sell funds as part of a comprehensive financial package. Clients get a customized statement that lists their fees separately, instead of lumping in the charges with the fund's overall return. Always check whether the returns you're being shown are before or after the deduction of all charges and costs.

Putting your eggs in many baskets

Another good reason to buy mutual funds is the fact that they instantly mitigate your risk by letting you own lots of stocks and bonds, ideally in many different markets. *Diversification,* spreading your dollars around, is the cornerstone of successful investing. Diversifying means you won't be slaughtered by a collapse in the price of one or two shares.

Some people learn about diversification the hard way. Investors think they've lucked into the next big thing, hand over their entire fortune, and then lose it all in a cruel market correction. Pinning your hopes on just one stock or handful of stocks is never a wise move, so don't let this happen to you.

Mutual funds let ordinary investors buy into faraway markets and assets. It would be difficult and expensive for most ordinary people to purchase shares in Asia or Europe, or bonds issued by Latin American governments (go easy on those, though), if they couldn't buy them through mutual funds. Although events of global impact such as terrorist activity, sovereign debt problems, natural disasters, and the volatile price of oil have an impact on markets worldwide, some respond positively to developments, and others respond negatively. It's tough to keep track of it all and predict which markets will be affected and by how much. So, we ask: Why even try? History demonstrates that a portfolio with lots of different and varied asset classes will tend to suffer fewer speed bumps.

Most equity mutual funds own shares in at least 50 companies — fund managers who try to go with more "concentrated" portfolios have been known to get their fingers burned. In fact, academic research suggests that only seven stocks may be enough to provide adequate diversification for an investor, but seeing dozens of names in a portfolio offers a lot more reassurance.

Getting good returns from professional management

One of the most entertaining and informative books ever written on the subject of investing is *A Fool and His Money: The Odyssey of an Average Investor* by John Rothchild. First published in 1988, the book describes Mr. Rothchild's own abject failure in the market and includes his observation that most amateur investors are less than frank about how they've actually done. Even if they've had their heads handed to them, they tend to claim they ended up "about even." The moral of the story: Even if your relatives and pals claim to have made a fortune in the market, treat their boasts with a goodly dose of skepticism.

Yes, bad funds abound. But chances are you'll do better in a mutual fund than you would investing on your own. Usually, people running funds readily dump a stock when it turns sour, instead of hanging on like grim death, as we amateurs tend to do. But the opposite is true too. During the financial crisis, when do-it-yourself investors were liquidating entire portfolios, the good fund managers were hanging on, and riding out the storm. They were also buying stock when the market was at its lowest, which many regular investing folk were too scared to do.

Investing without breaking the bank

The typical Canadian stock fund rakes off about 2.3 percent of your money each year in fees and costs. That's a hefty charge, but the fund company also relieves you of a lot of drudgery and tiresome paperwork in return. Funds offer a lot of convenience. The fund company keeps your money safe and handles the recordkeeping for your savings. It all leaves you free and clear to get on with your first love, naked samba dancing.

In fact, mutual funds are a positive bargain when you're just starting to invest. Quite a few companies will let you put as little as $500 into their funds, and you can often open up a regular investment plan — where the money is simply taken out of your bank account — for as little as $50 a month. That's a pretty good deal when you realize that fund companies actually lose money on small accounts. If an investor has, say, $1,000 in an equity fund with a management expense ratio (MER) of 2.3 percent, then the company is collecting only $23 in fees and expenses, barely enough to cover postage and administration costs let alone turn a profit.

The costs of a mutual fund investment are buried in the management expense ratio (MER) and the relatively incomprehensible statement of operations, but at least you can work them out with a bit of digging. Try asking traditional full-service investment advisers for a clear explanation of their commission rates. You'll get a lot of mumbling and long sentences containing the phrase "it depends," but thank goodness more clear answers are forthcoming these days. Note that the costs of operating a mutual fund are the same, regardless of it being sold by a discount broker, investment adviser, or financial planner.

Watching over your investment

Mutual fund companies are pretty closely watched, not only by overworked provincial securities regulators, but also, believe it or not, by rival companies. Competing companies don't want a rotten peach spoiling the reputation of the whole barrel. The Investment Funds Institute of Canada (IFIC), the industry lobby group, is a mouthpiece for the companies, naturally. But it also generally keeps an eye on things. Yes, greed abounds. Despite some improvements in recent years, fees are still too high, unitholder reports are often difficult to decipher, salespeople are given goodies, and funds are sometimes used as horns of plenty when managers divert their trading, and the resulting flow of commissions, to their investment buddies. The good news is most companies are simply making too much money honestly to risk it all by running scams.

The stocks, bonds, and other securities a fund buys with your money don't even stay in the coffers of the fund company: Under provincial securities laws, the actual assets of the fund must be held by a separate "custodian," usually a big bank or similar institution. You're most likely to get swindled by your salesperson; *Mutual Fund Investing For Canadians For Dummies* sets out some of the best ways to protect yourself. Just stick with regular mutual funds, those that come with a document called a "simplified prospectus" and are managed by widely known companies, and you should be okay.

Cashing out — Getting your money if you need it

If you decide to move your hard-earned cash out of a fund, your fund company will normally get your money to you within three business days. So keep that in mind when you sell – if you need the money in an hour, you may need to dip into your bank account or line of credit.

Don't forget that lots of other investments, including guaranteed investment certificates, hit you with a penalty if you take your cash out early. Selling a stock invariably costs you a commission with no guarantee you'll get a decent price for your shares if you choose to sell illiquid shares during a bear market. Sell a bond and you're often at the mercy of your dealer, who could pluck a price out of the air — though they're no longer allowed to rip you off.

Perils and Pitfalls of Funds

So now that you're convinced funds are the right place to be, we're going to throw you for a bit of a loop. It's important to realize that funds aren't perfect. None of these disadvantages mean you shouldn't buy mutual funds. But keeping them in mind will help you stay out of overpriced and unsuitable investments.

Excessive costs

When you start amassing serious money in mutual funds, your costs can get outrageous. For example, if you invest $100,000 in a set of typical equity funds with a management expense ratio of 2.3 percent, the fund company is siphoning off $2,300 of your money every year. The math gets truly chilling when you extrapolate the cost of management fees over long periods. Over 20 years, at an MER of 2.3 percent, the fund company will end up with an incredible 50 percent or so of the total accumulated capital. How so? Simply by slicing that little 2.3 percent off the top each year.

In theory, that's what it costs to pay a fund manager to actively invest on your behalf. But if you're content to accept whatever return — good or bad — the overall market can achieve, then you can save a bundle by owning *index funds* or, better still, *exchange-traded funds (ETFs)*. Index funds are funds with low expenses that simply track the whole stock or bond market by producing a return in line with a market index, such as the S&P/TSX Composite Index of approximately 300 large capitalization companies. An ETF is similar to an index fund except it trades on a stock exchange. They don't have a portfolio manager as they simply own all of the stocks in an index. A typical index fund, such as RBC Canadian Index, has expenses of 0.7 percent, and the main Canadian market ETF, iShares Canadian Composite Index, charges just 0.25 percent.

Another problem with charging so much to operate a mutual fund is that research has proven, time and time again, that actively managed funds — such as mutual funds — rarely beat the benchmark. Blame it on the fees. Even if a fund manager does his or her job and ends the year with a better return than the S&P/TSX Composite Index, the fees could eat into that positive return and make it negative. These days, even equity returns can be low, so if you're getting dinged 2 percent it could impact your portfolio pretty significantly. Keep that in mind when you're investing — if you think there's no hope the manager will outperform the market, or that the fees could put your returns into negative territory, you might want to consider buying an exchange-traded fund.

When bad managers attack

They may be smart and they may be professionals, but fund managers sure can blow it, leaving behind nothing but a lot of little scraps of grey polyester and a bunch of ugly minus signs in front of their returns. Put down whatever you're eating — what you're about to see would make a 400-pound wild boar queasy — and have a look at Table 1–1. It shows some of the worst-performing Canadian equity funds during the past decade, with assets over $100 million. If you hung around with any of these lads for the whole of the decade, you missed out on a lot of fun.

Table 1–1	Slow Lane: Canadian Equity Underperformers in the Ten Years to November 2011 % Returns		
1-Year	*5-Year Annual*	*10-Year Annual Fund Name*	*Return*
CIBC Canadian Equity Value	−5.87%	− 0.04%	2.48%
National Bank Canadian Equity	− 8.21%	− 1.79%	3.15%
Scotia Canadian Blue Chip	− 7.19%	− 1.28%	3.38%
CIBC Canadian Equity	− 3.25%	− 1.60%	3.62%
Manulife Canadian Equity	− 10.45%	− 2.25%	4.35%
HSBC Equity Inv	− 6.85	0.02%	4.38%
Altamira Canadian Equity Growth	− 9.58%	0.27%	4.48%
TD Canadian Value	− 11.78%	− 1.66%	4.61%
IA Clarington Canadian Leaders	− 14.53%	1.84%	5.34%
S&P/TSX Composite Index	− 3.35%	− 0.15%	8.5%

It's very rarely as terrifying as that, though. Companies usually replace managers of big funds after just a couple years of bad performance. Having a decent Canadian equity fund, in particular, is a marquee attraction for a company. It's the fund category carrying the most prestige, partly because it wins the most attention from the media. You can be sure that just about every manager running a large equity or balanced fund, Canadian or global, is working his or her silk socks off trying to top the performance league. Every so often, companies get in bidding wars for managers with a great reputation. So everyone running a fund is trying to get public notice for earning hot returns, because it increases his or her market value.

Can't see the forest for the funds

By the end of 2011, Canada had an unbelievable 11,000 or so funds and fund-like products, counting segregated funds, U.S.–dollar editions, different versions with varying sales charges, and "guaranteed" funds with endlessly changing small print. This ridiculous profusion of products exists for several reasons:

✦ Fund companies have learned the folly of relying too much on just one or two funds. The danger, for them, is that if performance goes in the tank then investors head for the door, pulling out tens of millions of dollars.

✦ Running a mutual fund is profitable. When a fund company can get its assets above $100 million or so, it's difficult to lose money because those 2 percent management fees keep rolling in. And all sorts of newcomers have been coming into the fund industry, including insurance companies and even financial planning chains. But they love to offer their own house-brand funds because they get to keep all the fees instead of splitting the take with a separate name-brand fund company.

✦ In fairness to the industry, some of the new funds are meant to satisfy consumers' demands. Investors' thirst for income-producing investments in recent years brought a raft of funds that invest in income trusts and other income-generating securities. Although income trusts no longer exist (not counting real estate income trusts), income-producing investments remain a popular tool for many boomer-age and older investors.

Vague explanations of poor performance

No matter how badly a fund did, the analysis given to investors is frequently a languid description of the stock or bond market and a few of the manager's choice reflections on the future of civilization.

What unitholders deserve, but too often are denied, is an honest discussion of whether their fund kept up with the market and its peers. Securities regulators are putting the squeeze on companies to improve their reports, but it'll take time.

In the meantime, if your fund lags the market and other funds in the same category, ask for a clear explanation from your broker or financial planner if you got advice when buying funds. If you bought a no-load fund, look for a written set of reasons in the company's regular mailings to unitholders. Because no-load companies deal directly with their investors — instead of going through a salesperson — their reports are often clearer than the information provided by companies that market their funds through advisers.

Another big problem in the reporting of performance is that all too often it's not at all clear who is actually running your fund and how long they've been doing it. Fund companies rarely, if ever, print the length of a manager's tenure, and they usually don't warn investors in a timely way if he or she quits or is fired. Rather than worry about finding a genius to pick your stocks, you're much better off looking at the fund itself. Make your decision about investing with an eye to how the fund has performed and what it currently holds, rather than trying to figure out who is in the top spot.

Prospectuses that don't say enough

It's often hard to tell from a company's website, promotional handouts, and even official reports to unitholders whether the returns from its funds have been any good. That's because most companies, incredibly, still don't show their performance against an appropriate market benchmark, such as the S&P/TSX Composite Index for Canadian equity funds or the MSCI World Index for global equity funds. However, things have gotten better since the fund industry began producing *prospectuses* that are fairly easy to understand. A prospectus is the document that must be given to the purchasers of a fund, describing its rules and risks. A prospectus must provide performance numbers that compare a fund to a benchmark, such as the S&P/TSX for Canadian equity funds. Prospectuses also give the fund's returns on a year-by-year calendar basis, which is invaluable for checking whether unitholders have enjoyed steady returns or suffered through insane swings.

However, prospectuses are still of only limited usefulness because they don't say *why* the fund has lagged or outperformed its benchmark. Fortunately, a fairly new, additional document, the *management report of fund performance,* has taken a big step toward providing useful comparative data and explanations of a fund's recent performance.

Too many funds and too few long-term results

Fund managers love to talk about how investing is a long-term game — especially when they're losing money — but have you noticed how many ads you see touting performance over periods as short as one year? And companies seem unable to resist launching new funds that invest in the hottest new asset class — just in time to lose money for investors when the bubble bursts. It happened with science and technology funds in the early 2000s. At the beginning of the decade, the number of funds in this category had multiplied to more than 120, but the group then tanked with huge losses in 2001 and 2002. Today, almost no science and technology funds are in existence.

It's easy to get dizzy amid the flashing lights and loud music, and jump aboard the fund industry's carousel of new products. But steer clear of the fancy stuff and stick to plain old conservative equity and bond funds with your serious long-term money, and you'll end up ahead.

Load versus No-Load — The Great Divide

You can buy mutual funds in two main ways:

Book II
Chapter 1

**Understanding
Mutual Funds**

✦ **Through a professional seller:** You can get a salesperson such as an investment adviser, discount broker or financial planner to help. The adviser has to earn a living, so you'll almost certainly end up buying load funds — a load is a sales charge or commission that's paid to the adviser, either by you or by the fund company.

✦ **Going it alone:** You can pick your funds on your own, with perhaps some advice from a bank staffer or mutual fund employee. In that case, you'll often end up buying *no-load* funds, which don't levy a sales commission.

Grey areas abound. You can buy *load* funds on your own and pay no commissions (through a discount broker, which will provide little or no advice). Some advisers will sell you no-load funds or load funds on which they waive commissions. And banks can fall in between the two stools. But those are the two essential methods.

Load funds — The comfort zone

Most mutual funds in Canada are sold to investors by a salesperson who is in turn paid by way of a sales commission. Millions of people love the feeling of having an advocate and adviser who seems to know his or her way through the jungle of investing. And why not hire a professional? After all, you probably don't fix your plumbing yourself or remove your own appendix (too hard to get the stains out of the kitchen tiles).

Your adviser might work for an investment dealer, a financial planning firm, or an insurance company — or he or she might be self-employed. But the important point is this: If you buy funds through a salesperson, your primary relationship is with them, not with the fund company.

Any fund company should be able to answer your questions about your account. Always make sure you get a regular account statement from the fund company itself (unless you're with one of the big investment dealers who usually handle all of the recordkeeping). But load companies, such as CI

Financial, Invesco Trimark, and Fidelity Investments Canada, won't even sell you funds directly. You have to open an account with an investment adviser or planner, who will then put the order through for you. The companies' systems and much of their marketing are designed to deal with salespeople, not members of the public, so your buy and sell orders must come from your discount broker or investment adviser.

Decoding sales commissions

Sales commissions on load funds come in a bewildering number of variations and forms. And discount brokers have dreamed up even more ways to make the whole thing even more complicated (see *Mutual Fund Investing For Canadians For Dummies* for details). But when you buy a load fund from an investment adviser, discount broker, or planner, you have three basic options.

You can negotiate and pay an upfront commission — known as a *sales charge* or *front load* — to the salesperson. Savvy investors usually pay 2 percent or less. That entitles you to sell the fund at any time with no further charges, and it sometimes gets you lower annual expenses.

Alternately, you can buy funds on a "low-load" basis. Some firms refer to this as "no-load," even though you must buy them through an adviser. There's no free lunch, of course, as a low-load fund generally will have higher annual expenses than the front-end version of the same fund.

Finally, you can buy funds with a *back-end load* deferred sales charge (DSC) or *redemption charge*. In that case, the fund company itself pays the commission to the broker — usually 5 percent in the case of an equity fund or a balanced fund and less for a bond fund. However, you, the investor, are on the hook for a declining "redemption charge" if you sell the fund within a set number of years.

The redemption charge is based either on the original purchase cost of the units you're redeeming or their value at the time you sell. The policy varies by company. For example, Investors Group charges it on the value at the time of redemption, while Fidelity bases this fee on the value at the time of purchase. The first option is slightly better for you because, presumably, the value of your units will have increased by the time you redeem. For example, say you invest $10,000 in a fund on a back-end-load basis and the fund gains 20 percent, leaving you with $12,000. Say you decide to redeem half of your holding, incurring a 4.5 percent back-end load. If the redemption charge is based on your original investment, you pay $225 (which is 4.5 percent of $5,000), but if it's based on the current market value, you pay $270 (4.5 percent of $6,000).

But a difficulty exists for the fund industry with back-end loads. If the adviser doesn't have to wangle a commission out of the client every time he or she buys a fund, more of a temptation exists for advisers and planners to switch customers from fund to fund, collecting commissions from the fund companies along the way. So the fund industry borrowed a technique from the life insurers, who have been dealing with salespeople's naughty tricks for generations, and introduced the *trailer fee*. Trailers are essentially yet another commission — usually between 0.5 percent and 1 percent of the value of the client's holding annually — that's paid by the company to the salesperson each year as long as his or her customer stays in the fund. It's a payment for loyalty. You can almost think of it as a storage fee. If you store your money in that mutual fund, your adviser gets paid a fee. The trailer comes out of the management fee, not out of your account, so you never see it.

Many load companies pay a higher trailer to salespeople when they sell the fund on a front-load basis, getting their sales commission directly from the investor. That's because the company itself hasn't had to pay the charge. So on front-load fund sales, where the investor negotiates and pays the commission, a company might pay a trailer of 1 percent of the client's holding of equity funds each year; but on deferred-load sales, where a company paid the original sales commission, the trailer might be only 0.5 percent. It all gets pretty confusing — and it gets more complicated as you go further in — but that's the basis of the commission structure in mutual funds.

No-load funds — The direct approach

The other great branch of the fund industry is the no-load sector — funds that sell directly to the public with no sales commissions. Here, life is much simpler. A no-load shop will open an account for you when you contact them; you do this without the involvement of a discount broker, planner, or any other kind of adviser. You're not charged to buy or sell a fund, although remember that to discourage in-and-out trading you often face a penalty of 2 percent or so if you dump a fund within three months of buying.

The banks dominate the no-load fund business through their vast customer bases, discount brokerage arms, and branch networks. Until recently they had difficulty building a strong record, and big market share, in equity funds. However, the Big Five banks have made gains in this area through improved performance and marketing through their branch networks, which has helped propel them to the top rungs of the fund-asset rankings.

Because no-load funds usually don't pay sales commissions to advisers — although they sometimes pay trailer fees to persuade advisers to sell their funds — their annual expenses and fees should be much lower than those of load funds. Should be, but aren't. Bankers aren't known for cutting fees where they can get away with keeping them high, and most no-load funds in Canada are only slightly cheaper than adviser-sold funds. In other words, you can expect to part with more than 2 percent of your assets each year when you invest in most equity or balanced funds, no matter where you buy them. Some bank-run equity funds charge less than 2 percent — mostly income-oriented dividend funds, which generally are less complicated to manage than more aggressive stock funds.

The banks and a few other no-load-fund sellers also are the place to find index funds, which have ultra-low expenses — mostly less than 1 percent. An index fund costs very little to manage because its portfolio simply tracks the whole market by mimicking an index. These are known as passively managed funds, with no investment decisions necessary on the part of the managers. Because index funds generate such small management fees, load companies can't afford to sell them and also pay commissions to advisers. See Chapter 3 for more about index funds — and even less expensive passive investments known as exchange-traded funds, or ETFs.

No-load fund sellers' main bread and butter, like other fund companies, are actively managed funds — some of which also have relatively low expenses. An example is Phillips, Hager & North Ltd. of Vancouver (now owned by RBC), which has numerous "actively managed" funds with expenses of less than 2 percent. Actively managed funds, unlike index funds, buy and sell particular stocks in an attempt to beat the market and other managers. However, no-load shops' bargain funds often have relatively high minimum investments in order to keep costs low (servicing tiny accounts isn't profitable, remember). PH&N requires a minimum account size of $25,000 with the company.

Chapter 2: Figuring Out Fees — Discount or Full-Service Brokers?

In This Chapter

✔ Recognizing discount brokers and how they can save you money

✔ Getting the details on the various types of advisers

✔ Understanding how the financial pros get paid

✔ Identifying direct sellers and knowing when you should consider one

Want to know a surefire way to build up your wealth? Don't spend a fortune on fees. Management fees can make a serious dent in returns over time. That's why exchange-traded funds — funds that track an index's performance and don't use professional management — are growing in popularity. Although mutual funds continue to be the preferred investment choice for Canadian investors, you don't have to pay an arm and a leg to own one.

In this chapter we explain some of the ways to buy funds cheap. We walk you through the joys (and headaches) of using a discount broker and delve into the complex world of full-service investment advisers. You might think full-service is better — after all, someone else is doing all the heavy lifting for you — but there are many different types of people who are offering their help, from financial planners to investment advisers, and they all charge different fees.

We'll also talk about using your bank versus an independent mutual fund company, and touch on ways you can make sure your adviser is legit.

In the end, you should be able to decide if you want to work with a pro or go the do-it-yourself route — and how both options will affect your returns.

What Are Discount Brokers?

A *discount broker* is a true broker in the sense that it's a firm set up simply to act as an agent. It collects a *commission* — that is, a transaction fee — when you buy or sell stocks, bonds, funds, and other investments. Yes, financial planners, insurance agents, and traditional investment advisers also take your orders in this way, but they also bill themselves as advisers and experts who get a fee for helping out. Nothing wrong with that as such, but their fees eat into your returns. A Canadian discount brokerage firm is often an arm of a big bank, taking most orders over the Internet or over the telephone, but numerous non-bank discount brokerages now do too. In the United States, discounters execute your share-buying transactions for as little as US$7.99. In Canada, minimum charges for a single trade are generally $20 and up for smaller accounts and between $6.99 and $9.99 for larger ones, although you can trade for even less through some discount brokerages.

Discounters, then, essentially offer a simple service. They employ a bunch of youngsters who are paid a wage for covering the phone and who don't traditionally get extra pay for persuading customers to buy things. In return for charging low commissions, discounters hope to attract enough business to turn a profit. That's why they're so keen to turn as much of their business as possible over to the Internet, where it can be automated.

In the past, discounters were subject to the provincial securities rule that obliges brokers to ensure trades are suitable for the client. Like other people in the investment business who accept your money, they were supposed to follow the Know Your Client rule. However, in recent years, securities regulators in Canada have relaxed the requirement that trades through a discount broker be vetted to see if they fit with the customer's risk tolerance and investment knowledge. That was after lobbying by the discounters, who claimed that having a human being check every trade slowed up the process too much. The message, for those who may have missed it, is this: When investing through a discounter, you're on your own.

Considering the savings

How much cheaper are the discounters? Well, their commissions for trading stocks are usually a small fraction of the fees levied by traditional investment advisers, or even less, for trades of all sizes. And, unlike full-service advisers, discounters publish their rates openly. For example:

✦ At a bank-owned, full-service adviser, trading 100 shares priced at $25 each could cost as much as $150, the minimum fee, but in many cases this would be discounted to $100 or less.

✦ The same trade at that bank's discount brokerage arm would cost less than $30 if the trade were placed online, and approximately $60 if placed over the phone with one of the discounter's agents.

In both cases, more active traders and individual large transactions would be eligible for much lower commissions.

Getting set up with a discounter

Setting up an account with a discount broker is simplicity itself. You don't have to sit through a sales spiel or show that you have thousands to invest — just go online or telephone them, complete a few forms, open an account, and put in some money. Here's more about how to get set up:

✦ Visit the website of the discount broker you picked and print out an account application form or an RRSP application form.

✦ Notice the dense pages of conditions they make you sign. Guess what? They're not in your favour. But just about all discount brokers impose these convoluted terms — which essentially say that in the event of a disagreement the broker is always right — so you can't really escape.

✦ A discounter will pretty well accept your business no matter how poor you are. But you'll have to have the necessary cash in your account, Jack, before you make the first trade. For a fund, the minimum buy is nearly always $1,000.

✦ You never have to meet anyone face to face. The anonymity is relaxing, although you'll almost certainly get put on hold for a good stretch when problems occur in your account. And you'll get used to shouting at dazed employees in a harsh barking tone.

✦ After you're set up, just enter your orders at the firm's website, or phone them in. Ensure you have fast access to the trade-confirmation slip, and check it against the order you placed.

You can access your password-protected, discount-brokerage account on the Internet. You also can opt to receive periodic statements by mail. Either way, check the account information against your own records.

Using a discount broker is investing for grownups. No one is around to hold your tiny hand or coo into your tight little rosebud of an ear that "the market always comes back." In return for the low commissions they charge, discounters are geared to provide little or no personal service.

Weighing the Advantages of a Discount Broker

If you're confident about making investment decisions yourself, a discount broker is the best place to buy and hold mutual funds. Discounters let you buy certain mutual funds for no upfront charge when other advisers might demand a commission. They also carry a vast selection of hundreds of mutual funds (more than most investment dealers), lots of bonds, and just about any stock you care to name. That means you can hold funds from a multitude of different companies — including some low-cost, no-load funds that are hard to buy from an investment adviser or financial planner. And a discount brokerage account also lets you combine funds with your other investments, such as stocks or guaranteed investment certificates, so that all your holdings show up on one convenient statement. This is also true of investment advisers but not of financial planners.

Discounters are the perfect source for mutual funds because the choice is so huge and the charges are so low. Here's a rundown of the other main reasons to strongly consider leaving your money with a discounter.

Your one-stop shop — Convenience

Discount brokers are just extremely convenient. You can be on top of a mountain in Nepal, or in a jail cell in Ballydehob (say hello to Liam but don't let him "arm wrestle" you), but as long as you can get access to the Internet or a telephone you should be able to sell or buy funds, stocks, and bonds in your discount brokerage account. By contrast, a full-service adviser may be out of the office, ill, or busy, creating a delay if the backup person is slow.

Another reason to love discounters: They've embraced the Internet wholeheartedly, with many letting you look at your account, and place orders, at any time over the Web. So if you enjoy surfing the Web, then a discounter is the place for you. With a discounter, you have control over what happens in your account. No salespeople are there to interfere or offer advice that may be tainted by the desire to earn sales commissions or — by orders from higher-up, brutal Stalinist-style commands that blare from a cracked loudspeaker inches from the poor adviser's ear — to push a particular stock or fund.

Access to a broad selection of options

Wide selection is a powerful reason to go with a discount broker, because discounters sell just about everything. A bank branch or no-load fund company can generally sell you only its own funds, and an adviser is likely to have a "select list" of funds with which he or she is most familiar. But a discount broker will let you buy hundreds of funds, as well as thousands of stocks and bonds, in North America and often on overseas markets as well. Advisers can offer you a much bigger menu of stocks and bonds around the world but perhaps not every mutual fund in the world. That means you can have the luxury of just one central portfolio that holds all your investments, instead of spreading them all around town.

Discounters have to carry every major fund because otherwise their competitors will beat them on selection. Having every fund available can be very useful for you if you want to leave an underperforming fund. It means you have somewhere to move the money. If you're with an adviser who doesn't sell the funds you want to switch to, however, you're in trouble.

The big banks in Canada own most of the discounters as well as most of the investment advisers. So if you don't get what you want at the end of the bank's counter, then go to the other end.

Many firms proclaim that they carry hundreds of funds, and in fact they probably do. But you'll find that some low-cost funds from independent providers come with high minimum purchases of $5,000 and up. Always ask if the fund you're interested in is available and find out about any conditions.

A wealth of investing information

Finally, discount brokers can be useful channels for getting hold of investing information. Check out their websites and you'll find fee calculators and other useful online tools. Some may have offers of investment newsletters and books at cut-rate prices. A few discounters sell research reports from stock analysts at full-service investment dealers — usually the brokerage owned by the discounter's parent — namely, one of Canada's big five banks.

Research shows that most investment newsletters fail to beat the market over time. And analysts are notorious for seeing the world through rose-coloured glasses; they rarely say a stock is a Sell because that's certain to enrage the company's management. Angry corporate managers are likely to cut the critical analyst off from information and may even blacklist his or her firm in the future when it comes to picking investment dealers to handle a stock issue or other deal.

Book II
Chapter 2

Figuring Out
Fees — Discount
or Full-Service
Brokers?

A break on costs

One of the big pluses with discounters is the fact that most let you buy funds on a *front-load* basis at no initial cost to you. Front-load means that the fund buyer pays an upfront commission directly to the broker or financial planner at the time of purchase — the exact rate is negotiable, but it's usually 3 percent or less these days, and sometimes as little as 1 percent. The advantage to paying a front load is that the funds can then be sold at any time with no further charges.

The discounters aren't being particularly generous with their zero-load offer on front-load funds, mind you. Fund companies love it when their wares are sold zero because they don't have to pay any commission to the discount broker. So they pay an especially generous annual *trailer commission* — typically 1 percent of the client's holding in an equity fund — to the broker that sold the fund when it was bought on a zero load basis. Trailer commissions are ongoing commissions that a salesperson or his or her firm gets as long as the client stays in the fund or funds sold by the manager. Paid by the fund company itself, trailer commissions ultimately come out of the management fee your fund is charged. Big fat trailers on mutual funds sold on a zero load basis (when the investor actually paid no load) are the reason why discounters are happy to let you have front-load funds at what looks like no charge — they're often indirectly collecting 1 percent of your money each year from the fund company.

Investigating the Disadvantages of Discounters

The major problem with discounters, especially for investors who are just getting going, is that they do not provide advice on your personal financial situation or help you create a financial plan. A discounter is essentially a tool for doing transactions — but buying and selling investments is only part of getting rich.

Discounters leave you on your own to make all the decisions, but freedom can bring problems. Some research seems to show that retail investors who work without an adviser don't do well because they're prone to buying high and selling low. That is, they euphorically buy shares and equity funds when the market has soared and then dump them when prices have already crashed. That may be true or just a self-serving myth fostered by the investment industry. But a good fund salesperson can impose valuable discipline in two ways: by getting you to save money in the first place and by persuading you to hang on when things look bleak.

So if you're a nervous or impulsive type, holding your stocks and funds at a discount broker might be a recipe for panic selling and hysterical buying. Perhaps you'd be better off with a planner or old-style investment adviser.

Picking a Discounter

Don't get in a lather comparing the discounters' commissions and totting up their special offers. Seeing people in the investment business offering to cut their prices is wonderful, but over the long term, saving $100 on a one-off basis doesn't amount to much. If you plan to simply buy and hold high-quality funds and stocks, it doesn't make a lot of difference if you've spent $100 or $200 in commissions building the portfolio. Yes, cheaper is always better, but fast and polite responses to your orders or questions, and investments that suit your needs, are just as important as low rates.

Getting a feel for the service

The important thing is efficient, accurate, and prompt service — something that, sadly, discounters seem to have had a problem providing in the past. After a debacle in the hectic stock market of early 2000, when some clients said they were left on the phone for up to a week, the discount firms embarked on a hiring frenzy aimed at ensuring they had enough staff to handle soaring demand. Service levels are better now — although lots of the credit goes to the fact that much of discount trading happens online nowadays, with no human intervention required.

Back-end-load rebates and bonuses: As if life wasn't complicated enough

We're sorry to keep burdening you with all this commission stuff. And by now you're probably wondering: Why is everyone in the fund industry obsessed with sales charges? Why do they create myriad different classes of the same fund, each sold with a different commission, and drape them with incomprehensible conditions, rules, and names? Well, the bottom line is that selling expenses — particularly the cost of paying commissions to advisers and financial planners — are an enormous cost of business for mutual fund companies. Let's look at this example: Equity-fund salespeople, as a general rule, get 1 percent of the client's assets each year, either upfront or payable as an annual "trailer" commission. Well, the median Canadian equity fund charges an annual MER of 2.1 percent, so about half of the management fee revenue is going to the adviser or financial planner who sold the fund.

Just one more commission complication before we leave the subject. Some discount brokers have tried taking the 5 percent commission they get from the company for selling a deferred-load fund and "rebating" some of it to the customer in the form of a bonus. For example, if you invest $10,000 in a fund on a back-end-load basis, and the discounter pays you a 2 percent bonus, then $10,200 would immediately show up in your account. Seems like you're getting money for nothing. These rear-load rebates have ranged from 2 to almost 3 percent depending on which broker you're dealing with — as long as you meet their many conditions.

Getting a bonus straight off the top like that sounds like a great deal, but it hasn't proved popular with discount brokerage customers. That's because with a deferred-load fund, you're "locked in" by the commission you must pay to the fund company if you cash out within about six years. Rather than pay the required fee to abandon your chosen mutual fund company, most wise investors will simply switch to another fund in that family of funds for free. This way you can wait out the deferred fee schedule if you so choose. Discount brokerage customers are independent souls who don't like having their hands tied in any way. So they have steered clear of rear-end-load funds carrying rebates, even if the funds looked like a real bargain at first glance.

The bottom line? Sure, take advantage of a rebate if you're certain you want to stay in the fund for several years (until the deferred load no longer applies), but don't lose dollars just to save cents. If you think a possibility exists that you'll want to sell the fund again while the back-end load is still in effect, then go with the front-load version to keep life simple and your investment strategy unencumbered.

**Book II
Chapter 2**

**Figuring Out
Fees — Discount
or Full-Service
Brokers?**

TIP

If you've got the time and energy, you could pick a firm by first opening two or even three separate accounts at different discounters — signing up as a client generally doesn't cost a cent. After a year or so, you'll get a good feel for which discounter is most reliable and the easiest to use and you can transfer all your assets there.

Apart from commissions, the fee you're most likely to face at a discount broker is an annual administration fee of roughly $40 to $100, although some no-charge brokerages do exist. In any event, some firms will waive RRSP fees if you have assets of $15,000 to $25,000 or more in the account.

Finding the right discounter for you

A good source of information on discount brokers (and low-cost investing in general) is the Stingy Investor website, at www.ndir.com. Run by avid number-cruncher Norman Rothery of Toronto, it offers a rundown of discounters' rates. (Before deciding to use a particular firm, however, be sure to double-check fees with the brokerages you are considering.)

Don't become obsessed with commission rates when choosing a discounter. Some have decided to market themselves as cut-price providers, offering minimum commissions for a stock trade that can run $25 or even less. That's a tremendous deal for investors, but remember that if you don't plan to trade stocks frequently, it's only of limited value. Look at the whole picture — including mutual fund commissions, service standards, and special options — before you make your choice.

Try calling the company a couple of times with questions. If you can't seem to get decent answers, then consider going somewhere else.

Considering a mutual fund discount broker

Apart from the true discount brokers, which are licensed to deal in stocks and bonds as well as funds, investors also can choose from among dozens of "no-load" or "discount" mutual fund dealers that sell only mutual funds. These companies, which are often happy to buy and sell funds over the telephone, usually charge no commission on front-load funds, living off the rich trailer payment instead. Individual investment advisers and financial planners also frequently offer to sell funds with no load as well as offer discount trading on your stocks and bonds.

Discount fund dealers will clearly save you money, and if you're happy with the level of service available and the selection of funds, then go with one. But, once again, don't let cost be the only deciding factor. Saving yourself a one-off expense of 2 percent is pointless if the dealer subsequently doesn't give you enough advice and choice of products.

From our perspective, if we were looking to save money we'd stick to a regular discount broker who's able to sell us shares and bonds as well as funds while also offering low commissions. Call us scaredy-cats, but we'd rather deal with a discounter that's a large multi-billion-dollar organization. That way, we know the systems are in place to administer our accounts properly.

Buying Where You Bank

Banks and credit unions are the very simplest place to buy mutual funds: Just walk in (virtually or to a branch) and put your money into a selection of the house brands. But don't assume they're the best choice. A bank is a great place to start out buying funds, but certainly do take a long, hard look at what they can and can't offer.

Providing one-stop shopping

Even if you don't have an account with a bank, you can still walk into a branch, hand over a cheque, and sign up for a mutual fund account. Okay, it might take a couple of days to arrange an appointment with a *registered representative,* a bank employee who is licensed to sell funds, but after that the process should be painless. Most banks have telephone services for buying and selling funds after you've opened a fund account, and nearly all offer telephone and Internet services that let you check your account balance and recent transactions. In fact, most banks will let you open a mutual fund investing account online, as part of your banking account access. (In some cases you might have to set up an online account in person at a branch.)

Banks sell their own funds on a no-load basis — no commissions or sales loads. That means all your money goes to work for you right away, and you can cash out at any time with no penalty (although companies impose a short-term trading penalty, typically 2 percent, on those who sell a fund within 30 to 90 days, depending on the specific fund).

You can set up a fairly decent mutual fund RRSP (Registered Retirement Savings Plan), a tax-sheltered account of retirement money, at a bank in half an hour flat by simply buying one of their pre-selected fund packages. Staff are trained to sell these mixtures, and questionnaires are designed to slot you into the right one so you're likely to get a reasonable fit. See Chapter 3 in Book 1 for more on using RRSPs.

Keeping it together

Most likely you have your mortgage, line of credit, and chequing account at a bank or credit union. So buying mutual funds from the company that already holds the mortgage on your house means you can take care of everything in one place, be it a branch, at the credit union or bank's Internet site, or on the phone.

Offering to move your mutual fund business to a bank can radically improve your bargaining power when seeking a loan or mortgage. Bank employees get little chocolate soccer balls as rewards when their customers bring their investment portfolios to the branch. Use this to your advantage when looking to extend your credit, take a plunge into the real estate market, or buy a

**Book II
Chapter 2**

**Figuring Out
Fees — Discount
or Full-Service
Brokers?**

car. In today's competitive banking environment, an investor with a portfolio is a sought-after prize.

Offering appealing options

The employees you deal with at a bank branch or on the telephone are paid wages, so they're not commission-driven jackals. But they usually sell only the house brand. And yes, they receive incentives to attract business, and yes, the banks tend to be vague on exactly what bonuses are paid. Credit unions pay bonuses to their owners who are also their customers and to their communities.

For the most part, you'll find that banks are happy to sell you *index funds* — low-expense funds that simply track the stock- or bond-market index or benchmark. Index funds are such a good deal they should be part of every investor's arsenal, although we suggest you also have between one-third and one-half of your stock market investments in traditional *actively managed funds,* featuring a person who buys and sells investments in search of trading profits.

Banks, unlike mutual fund companies that market their products through commission-paid salespeople, are able to make money from running index funds because they don't have to pay out those big commissions. Most offer index funds with low expenses — around 1 percent or less — compared with 2.5 percent on, for example, the median Canadian equity mutual fund. If you were to simply walk into a branch and open up a mutual fund account full of index funds like that, chances are you'd do better than millions of mutual fund investors. For that matter, almost all of the banks' actively managed (non-index-based) mutual funds have expenses that are less than the category medians.

Fighting for the right to serve you

The banks are hungry for your mutual fund business and they're willing to cut prices and improve service to get it. The fantastic growth of the Canadian mutual fund industry, with assets soaring to more than $773 billion in October 2011 from less than $30 billion in 1990, has represented a migration of cash from bank savings accounts and guaranteed investment certificates into funds. The banks have been working very hard to hold on to as much of that money as they can.

Another reason why the banks are fund-mad: Mutual funds are a wonderfully profitable and low-risk business. The management company just keeps raking in those fees no matter how well or badly the fund does. That must be a great comfort to Canadians invested in U.S. equity funds; the median U.S. stock fund lost more than 22 percent in 2008.

Lending money, banks' traditional way of making a profit, is more risky than selling mutual funds because borrowers can default and interest rates can jump, leaving the banks stuck with a pile of underpriced loans. So the banks have reinvented themselves as "wealth management" companies, and mutual funds are key players in that ballgame.

Buyer Beware: Shortfalls in Bank Offerings

Nobody's perfect, and buying funds at a bank — online, on the phone, or in person — has its drawbacks. Here, for your viewing pleasure, are the drawbacks of lining the pockets of nasal, power-hungry guys from Quebec and New Brunswick, the sort who become bank chairpersons.

One tactic of revenge is for you to invest in shares of the bank that has you in their grip. You will receive nice dividend cheques every three months and your shares will rise as the bank's profits rise.

Few options

The big problem is lack of choice: The banks have been in no hurry to market other companies' funds because a banker likes sharing fees like a lobster enjoys taking a hot bath. That means customers are often stuck with the bank's line of products, which isn't always the strongest. More and more bank employees have personal finance training, but most aren't specialists in the field. To get a full analysis of your situation, you may still have to go to a planner or investment adviser working for an independent firm.

The narrow selection of funds at many branches is the biggest problem with buying from a bank. Most of the big banks offer a full range of funds under their own brand name, but that doesn't necessarily mean that their Canadian equity or global equity funds will be any good. And even if you try to build a diversified fund portfolio by buying the bank's index funds and actively managed funds as well, you run a risk you're leaving too much money with just one investment team. Let's say a particular coterie usually tends to get excited about flashy technology stocks — then you're likely to lose money when other investors get tired of such high-priced, science fiction tales. You can get around this lack of *diversification* — the annoying word for spreading out your investments — by opening an account elsewhere as well, perhaps with another bank. Or you can at least increase your diversification by buying several of the bank's actively managed funds.

Overworked and underpaid: Not just you, some bankers too

With the rapid growth in online banking and investing, it's getting harder and harder to talk to an actual human being unless you've got a whopping balance in your account. That's a drag, and it's a disadvantage of going to a bank if you'd rather deal with a person than peck at the keyboard of a machine (what's wrong with you, anyway?). Banks may be losing their traditional advantage of owning huge networks of physical branches, because all their competitors are as easily accessed online as they are. Well, almost, because you likely visit your banking website every week anyway.

Lack of pressure to perform

Customers who buy funds from a bank are isolated in the sense that the fund managers don't have brokers and other salespeople breathing in a damp, hot way down their necks, insisting on good returns. If a broker-sold fund's performance goes into the tank, salespeople get angry and embarrassed because they have to face the clients they put into the loser. That's never a fun session. The sales force demands explanations from the manager. So the presence of salespeople probably serves to impose some discipline on fund companies. With bank funds where no brokers are involved, terrible performance used to drag on for years with little publicity or outcry.

Banks now take funds more seriously, meaning that problems get fixed fairly quickly, but bank fund unitholders arguably still don't have anyone looking out for their interests. Nearly all mutual funds have "trustees" who, some might say, should be on the side of investors, but, really, they're merely hired to provide the safekeeping and number-crunching for the assets owned by your mutual fund. Most unitholders wouldn't know where to look for the trustees' names and no wonder — you have to dig deep into a financial report to find them. However, this search is less onerous now that fund companies are obligated to produce a management report of fund performance twice a year. You no longer have to plow through a fund's obscure "annual information form" to identify the trustees.

Another problem with buying funds from your bank is that, well, you're forced to deal with a bank. The Internet has made this a lot easier, but if you need to reach them by phone, your calls may get routed to on-hold hell or voice-mail purgatory before they end up in the bottomless pit of general delivery, with Tats in shipping. Increasingly, bank customers are being asked to telephone a central information line or go to an Internet site (which saves the bank a packet). This is intended to relieve some of the pressure on branch staff, who usually have to deal with all the other services and products the bank delivers. So you might not get the sort of personal attention and time that a good financial planner or even investment adviser delivers.

Alphabet Soup: Figuring Out All Those Titles

You could spend a good month or two crafting a long list of all the elaborate titles financial advisers give themselves. You could then have a couple of gloomy women in leotards read it out on a darkened stage at the Toronto Fringe Festival, to the accompaniment of randomly played cymbals and flutes. Probably be a huge hit — better than the usual dreary one-person show about a failed actor, anyway — but it wouldn't help people much with their financial planning. So how do you wade through all the options and get down to what's best for you and your money? That's the key — your first challenge should be figuring out exactly what kind of financial planning you want rather than trying to decode their titles. In other words, do you need a fast once-over or a harrowing session of soul-searching?

After you've decided you need some help drawing up a financial plan and picking the right mutual funds, ask yourself two questions:

**Book II
Chapter 2**

Figuring Out
Fees — Discount
or Full-Service
Brokers?

+ **Do I want just a quick solution or a complete financial plan?** If you're reasonably comfortable with your money arrangements as they stand and you just want someone who'll suggest a few funds, then you can keep things simple by going to a storefront mutual fund dealer, an investment adviser, or a bank. They can recommend a package of funds and set up the account for you. If, however, you want help planning your fiscal future, make sure you deal with someone who has had some formal financial planning training (more on that later) and is also genuinely interested in the subject. And the best choice of all is to go with an unbiased planner who charges you a separate fee for his or her expertise, instead of selling you mutual funds that pay them a commission.

+ **How much money will I be investing?** Don't expect miracles. If you're planning to put $5,000 a year into your fund portfolio, the chairman of CIBC World Markets Inc. won't be asking you out to golf. It can be a good idea to tell the adviser upfront how much you think you're likely to save each year. You'll often be able to tell from his or her reaction whether you're likely to get much in the way of attention or advice.

Here's a great way to find out if a fund salesperson is likely to be of much use in drawing up a financial plan: Don't just ask about investing. Also bring up subjects such as buying disability and life insurance, estate planning, and minimizing taxes. If the answers are superficial or unsatisfactory, then this person probably isn't the best adviser to help you build a successful plan.

Drawing up a comprehensive financial plan is a complicated process, covering the client's taxes, income, spending, estate planning, powers of attorney, and retirement plans. Choosing investments is only a small part of that, but many advisers are paid just for selling life insurance or mutual funds, so saving and investing become all they want to talk about. In fact, as we outline in Book I, every competent investment adviser or financial planner worth his or her salt should emphasize getting rid of high-interest debt as your first step toward sound money management especially if the interest expense on your debt is not tax deductible If they don't look at your whole financial picture, look elsewhere for help. So beware of commission-paid salespeople who encourage you to go ahead and buy funds even though you already have huge credit card debt. This is no way to build a sound financial plan or invest for profit because you'll be going two steps forward and three steps backwards just for someone to earn a commission.

Be sure a financial planner is qualified. The Institute of Advanced Financial Planners (IAFP) has some good guidelines. Check out the Consumer Guide section of the IAFP website at www.iafp.ca. Advocis also has excellent information in its Consumer Info section at www.advocis.ca.

Advisers can be divided into several main groups according to how they earn their living: You'll find advisers who

✦ Get paid a commission for selling you investments.

✦ Charge a one-time fee for producing a financial plan, without specific investment advice.

✦ Charge you a separate fee for designing an investment portfolio.

✦ Earn a salary from an organization such as a bank that markets its own line of investments.

Commissioned advisers

The vast majority of Canadians choose to go with an investment adviser who gets paid by an investment dealer for selling investment "products" such as stocks, bonds, mutual funds, treasury bills, RRSPs, RESPs, TFSAs, etc. In part that could be a reflection of the nation's thrifty Scottish psyche. Unlike many Americans, a lot of Canadians seem to prefer mutual funds thus having the expense of investing advice hidden from them, buried in the fee of a mutual fund or the cost of insurance. That way, it seems so much less painful than having to cut the adviser a cheque.

An obvious example of a commission-paid salesperson is the traditional investment adviser, who makes money when you buy and sell stocks, bonds, or funds. The adviser gets a transaction fee, or *commission,* almost each time you put an order through.

✦ With stocks, the commission is added onto the cost when you buy or is deducted from the proceeds when you sell — and your transaction confirmation should clearly show how much was charged. For example, when you buy or sell $10,000 worth of shares, you can expect to pay a commission of about $300.

✦ With bonds, the "commission" is normally a profit margin that's hidden in the price, just like buying a pair of jeans at the Gap. That's because advisers usually sell to their clients bonds that they already own themselves. No separate commission is charged or shown on your confirmation slip because the adviser has already taken a markup. You must always examine the yield on your bond then you'll know how much the bond price was padded by the built-in commission.

✦ With funds, things get more complicated. But the essence of the system is that the adviser (or financial planner or insurance salesperson) is paid by the fund company. The fund company, remember, charges an annual management fee — which is deducted from the assets of the fund — and pays roughly half of that out to the salesperson.

Commission-paid salespeople also include life insurance salespeople, whether independent or tied to a particular insurance company. In addition to life insurance, these agents are often licensed to sell mutual funds or the insurance industry's version of mutual funds, some of which are known as segregated funds. Segregated funds — so-called because their assets must be kept separate from those of the insurance company — sometimes carry guarantees to refund up to 100 percent of an investor's initial outlay.

Finally, Canada is home to thousands of *financial planners,* either in franchises, chains of stores, or small independent offices, whose bread and butter is the mutual fund — and mostly the dreaded rear-load deferred sales charge form of mutual fund.

**Book II
Chapter 2**

**Figuring Out
Fees — Discount
or Full-Service
Brokers?**

Fee-only financial planners

The next group is far smaller but represents an excellent choice for those who don't mind signing a cheque to get advice. They're *fee-only* financial planners who aren't interested in selling products. In fact, they are not all licensed to sell products. More and more full-service investment advisers are managing money with a fee-only rather than commission-based service. Fee-only planners will draw up a financial plan that addresses your entire money situation and sets personal financial goals, both near term and far. A good financial plan helps you set broad investing goals but does not discuss specific investments, or even market sectors. Rather, it points you in the right investing direction based on your present lifestyle needs, tax situation, insurance needs, and estate planning goals, among other factors. You must go to a licensed investment adviser, commissioned or fee-based, to construct and maintain an investment portfolio.

A properly executed, custom financial plan will cost $1,000 or more, although some acceptable — but less customized — financial plans are available for a few hundred dollars. These plans are created by planners who use off-the-shelf computer software.

A fee-only financial planner might produce a plan and then refer you to a commission-charging dealer — or even collect commissions on funds you buy under the table. First, such practices are illegal. Second, that kind of double-charging adds another layer of complexity and fees, and it might not be the best deal for you. If the adviser is simply putting you into funds that pay commissions to salespeople, then why did you pay a fee for advice?

Fee-based investment advisers

Unlike fee-only financial planners, fee-based investment advisers are licensed investment salespeople who can be affiliated with a traditional investment dealer firm, a mutual fund dealer, or a financial planning firm. The drawback of going with a fee-based adviser is the pain of paying the freight, which can be substantial. It might be a fee based on assets under management — a percentage of your investments (typically 1 or 2 percent) — or it can be a charge that ranges from $100 an hour to a few hundred, depending on the complexity of your affairs.

With a fee-charging planner, you may have to make more choices about the investments you buy and the strategy you adopt. That's because the financial plan produced for each client is different, reflecting individual needs and wants, whereas commission-paid salespeople are often happiest suggesting a predesigned and relatively fixed package of funds that leaves you with few decisions to make.

Investors with substantial assets — say, approaching $1 million — should strongly consider going with a fee-charging planner or investment adviser. Your accountant or lawyer may offer the service or may be willing to recommend someone. The fee will often run into several hundred dollars, but that's a bargain compared with the hidden cost of high mutual fund management fees levied by fund companies that sell through commissioned advisers.

Salaried advisers

Thousands of financial advisers are being trained by the banks to take over the "wealth-management" needs of the aging baby boomers. They're generally on salary — plus bonuses if they can persuade you to put your savings into one of the bank's products, usually mutual funds or some other kind of managed-money program.

These bank employees are often limited in the products they can offer, and their training may not be as full as that of advisers or specialized financial planners. That means their advice should always be taken with a pinch of salt: They're employed to push the bank's products or sell funds that pay the bank a fat commission. Still, especially for investors with relatively simple needs and clear financial goals, the bank can be a great place to start off investing. Compared with the hard-driving world of advisers or financial planners, little sales pressure occurs. The product choices are simple, and having all your money in one place makes for easy recordkeeping.

But don't forget you're doing the bank a favour by handing over your savings. That means you're entitled to a helpful and experienced bank employee, not some rookie or sleepyhead. And don't get railroaded into buying one of the fixed arrangements of funds the banks love to pitch (it makes their administration much easier, for one thing). If you feel that none of the pre-selected packages meets your needs, insist on a custom mixture of funds.

In general, the bank is the perfect first stop for starting-out investors who have only a few thousand dollars at their disposal. The banks are equipped to deal with small accounts and they have handy automated systems that allow you to check your account balance and transactions without waiting for someone to get back to you.

And banks' employee training in investment advice is getting better all the time as the wealth-management business becomes vital to their future profit growth. Some banks even have qualified advisers available in the branch who can sell you a range of stocks and bonds or funds from nearly every company.

**Book II
Chapter 2**

Figuring Out
Fees — Discount
or Full-Service
Brokers?

The blurred distinctions among all these types of commission-paid advisers make the whole business of looking for help confusing. But at least you have one thing going for you: Remember that if you buy mutual funds, your money is reasonably safe because it goes to the fund company instead of staying with the adviser or dealer. So if you decide to dump your salesperson and his or her firm, you can simply shift the account elsewhere, after some whinging and delays on the part of the former salesperson. Your money is doubly safe because even the fund company itself has to leave the fund's assets with a separate custodian for safekeeping.

Make sure you'll be receiving a statement at least twice a year from the fund company (ask to see a sample) so you can be certain you're on the fund company's books. And make your cheque out to the fund company, not to the salesperson. Finally, get transaction confirmations for your purchases from the company — alternatively, you can call the fund company itself to double-check that they have a record of your investment.

Deciding Whether to Pay a Fee or a Commission

Your first decision when selecting an adviser is this: Do you want to pay a fee to a fee-based adviser, or are you happy with a commission-collecting salesperson? Don't rush your decision and just take the easy way out by refusing to pay a fee upfront. For example, you could go to a tax accountant, agree to pay a couple of hundred dollars to have the accountant look over your taxes and file your return. You could get back a much bigger refund than you would have on your own, and it feels great to have a professional working for you. And because you pay the accountant a fee, you know what was motivating him.

Paying fees

The first step in hiring an adviser is to look for fee transparency. A fee-only planner or fee-based adviser charges by the hour or by the project (say, producing a financial plan). A fee-based adviser is licensed and may charge by the hour or by assets under management, and/or earn commission for product sales. A commissioned adviser depends entirely on product sales to cover the cost of doing planning work.

In any case, insist on an "engagement letter" stating what the adviser will be doing for you and how you will be paying for it. That way, you've separated or "unbundled" the advice from the sale of the investment product.

Be realistic. If you have only a few thousand dollars to invest, the commissions are not going to cover much. If you want planning, you'll have to pay extra. Competent professionals don't come cheap. Fee-only planners and accountants will almost certainly charge from several hundred to several thousand dollars to produce anything more than a "quickie" plan. Be aware that a fee-only adviser might not be licensed to provide specific investment advice, so you still have to find someone to help purchase and manage your investments.

Going with a commission-paid adviser

You often indirectly pay hundreds of dollars to invest in mutual funds. Frequently, commissioned advisers are able and willing to provide significant planning in return for your investment business.

Fee-charging advisers who'll also help with investing are easier to find in Canada than was the case a few years ago, although you'll have to ask around. Canadians by the millions use commission-paid salespeople. After all, such advisers offer a handy one-stop solution: a financial roadmap of sorts and the glitz and comfort of a mutual fund from a familiar name — all backed up by gorgeous brochures and torrents of advertising in the press and on television, and increasingly on Internet sites. Most of them do a reasonable job for clients, putting them into solid (if overpriced) funds and getting them to save money, the first step in wealth accumulation.

Imagine a confusing, tangled jungle where every plant, animal, and weird fungus is grey. Well, that's kind of like the financial planning scene in Canada, where investors are confronted by competing trade associations, duelling regulators, and rival professional qualifications. Except in Quebec and British Columbia, just about anyone can call himself or herself a financial planner — even with no training.

Progress has occurred on the self-regulatory front, however. Many financial planners are members of Advocis, a national umbrella group formed in 2002 through the merger of the Canadian Association of Insurance and

Financial Advisors (CAIFA) and the Canadian Association of Financial Planners (CAFP). The much smaller Institute of Advanced Financial Planners (IAFP) was formed by a group of financial planners who saw a need to promote the former CAFP's professional designation, the RFP or Registered Financial Planner. Also significant was the creation of the Financial Planners Standards Council (FPSC) in 1995 by Advocis, groups representing the three accounting professions, and the credit unions. The FPSC is the official administrator of the Certified Financial Planner (CFP) designation in Canada. Although not legally required, the CFP is regarded as the minimum qualification for a Canadian financial planner. The IAFP believes its RFP designation is superior, but of course that falls into the category of debate.

Commission-paid salespeople and advisers usually fit into one of these three groups:

**Book II
Chapter 2**

**Figuring Out
Fees — Discount
or Full-Service
Brokers?**

✦ **Investment advisors:** They often like to be known by more touchy-feely names such as "investment adviser" and are at the top of the food chain. They used to be known as stockbrokers until they started selling bonds, treasury bills, and mutual funds as well as stocks of course. They work for fairly tightly regulated traditional firms known as investment dealers, the biggest of which are owned by the major banks. Examples include RBC Dominion Securities, CIBC Wood Gundy, and BMO Nesbitt Burns. Because investment firms generally are geared to dealing with relatively wealthy clients, an adviser usually won't give you too much time unless you have $100,000 or so to invest. He or she may take you on as a client if you have less money than that, but don't expect fawning attention, just a meeting or two per year at most. For those with enough money, advisers can be an excellent choice because they can sell anything — including stocks, bonds, funds, and a range of more exotic investments. Another plus: Their training and in-house support are fairly good.

On the negative side, be aware that many brokers are obligated to promote stocks and other securities that are underwritten by their firm's investment bankers.

Investment dealers are self-regulated by the Investment Industry Regulatory Organization of Canada (IIROC), and are members of one or more stock exchanges. Find out more about IIROC online at www. iiroc.ca.

✦ **Financial planners:** They are usually licensed to deal only in mutual funds or guaranteed investment certificates. They may work independently or as part of a large chain, and their quality varies greatly. Some are professional, smart, and dedicated, and many are little more than part-timers who can sell you a fund and that's about it. To deal in funds, they must register with the provincial securities commission, but regulation of the profession has been patchy. The creation of the Mutual Fund Dealers Association of Canada (MFDA) in 1998 has provided a self-regulatory framework for fund dealers. It was set up to catch mutual fund dealers who "fall through the cracks" with no industry-run body to keep an eye on them. The MFDA is affiliated with IIROC and governs all mutual fund dealers who aren't already covered by IIROC or a similar body. It will admit members, check that they're complying with the rules, and publicly discipline offenders, imposing fines, suspension, or termination of membership. Learn more about the MFDA online at `www.mfda.ca`.

✦ **Insurance agents and brokers:** They will sell you insurance, but an agent usually deals with numerous insurance companies while some agents generally have a relationship with just one. The lines have blurred to an extent between financial institutions, due to ownership of fund companies by insurance companies and other relationships between the two. As a result, some insurance salespeople now are registered to sell mutual funds. Moreover, life insurers, which once had a lock on the retirement planning market, in some cases have launched their own mutual fund families to hang on to customers' money. They've also made their traditional *segregated funds* more innovative and have spruced up their marketing. Seg funds are mutual fund–like products that usually promise to refund your invested capital if you hold them long enough. In general, pick an insurance agent to help you with financial planning if they are able to sell mutual funds as well as insurance products. If the salesperson is limited to insurance, you're narrowing your options.

Considering and Finding the Right Adviser or Planner

We've all got hectic lives, so it can be a nice feeling to have someone take us by the hand and deal with our investing dilemmas. The stock and bond markets are confusing, scary places, and millions of people find it reassuring to have an ally looking out for them.

Advisers or planners, especially if they're experienced, will usually know some neat tricks and handy shortcuts when it comes to investing. For example, they may suggest ways of minimizing your tax liability by setting up a simple trust for your children or grandchildren.

A good adviser imposes discipline on his or her clients by inducing them to save money — and should prevent them from making rash decisions, such as selling after the market turns down sharply. Without an arm's-length person imposing some sort of structure on your finances, it's easy to let debts mount up and your money problems drift.

To fix yourself up with a well-trained and professional planner, make sure he or she meets one of the following tests:

✦ **Membership in Advocis:** This national association and lobby group for financial planners, also known as the Financial Advisors Association of Canada, had more than 11,000 members as of late 2011. To join, a planner must complete some fairly tough planning courses or have a professional designation such as Chartered Accountant. The requirement to take courses probably discourages complete incompetents from becoming members of Advocis. The group has a code of ethics — although no guarantee exists you won't end up with a bad apple — and it imposes follow-up "education" on members each year. Contact Advocis at www. advocis.ca.

✦ **Membership in the Institute of Advanced Financial Planners:** The IAFP was set up in 2002 by a group of RFPs to promote, as the organization's name suggests, a higher level of financial planning than is promised by the FPSC and its presumably more basic CFP designation. The group claims its requirements for admission (including the RFP exam) and continuing education are more stringent. Contact IAFP at www.iafp.ca.

✦ **Completion of a recognized industry course:** These include courses that lead to the Certified Financial Planner (CFP) and Registered Financial Planner (RFP) designations. You can confirm that an individual has one of these designations by contacting the FPSC or IAFP, respectively; both organizations' websites have look-up tools.

✦ **Employment by a chartered bank or by an investment dealer who is a member of IIROC:** If the person works for a bank, you can be sure of some supervision, although take nothing for granted. The banks have set up their own personal finance training system, but no guarantee exists the person you get is particularly knowledgeable. If the adviser works for an IIROC investment dealer, he or she could be incompetent or greedy, but at least you know he or she has passed the courses required to become an Investment Adviser, the official term that describes an IIROC-member adviser.

The core IIROC-qualifying course is the Canadian Securities Course, which covers an impressive range of investing and industry-related information. Members of the public are also welcome to take this and other excellent courses offered by IIROC's educational arm, Canadian Securities Institute (CSI). Contact the CSI at www.csi.ca. IIROC is a lobby group and disciplinary body for investment dealers. If the person who wants to sell you mutual funds doesn't work for an IIROC firm, then check the Mutual Fund Dealers Association.

✦ **Employment by a member of the Mutual Fund Dealers Association (MFDA):** This provides protection to mutual fund investors similar to that offered by its affiliate, IIROC. See the section "Going with a commission-paid adviser" in this chapter for more on MFDA.

**Book II
Chapter 2**

**Figuring Out
Fees — Discount
or Full-Service
Brokers?**

✦ **In Quebec, membership in the Institut québécois de planification financière:** Quebec regulates financial planners based in that province, requiring an exam and offering its own designation, the Financial Planner (F.Pl., or *planificateur financier* in French). A financial planner practising in Quebec also must either have a certificate issued by the Autorité des marchés financiers, the Quebec government body that regulates securities markets in that province, or hold one of several professional designations. Contact the IQFP at www.iqpf.org.

Unfortunately, you can easily come across bad planners, discount brokers, and advisers who have impressive qualifications or reputable employers. But at least you know that if they've gone to the trouble of getting trained, or they're under some kind of supervision from a large organization, you're less likely to be stuck with a complete turkey.

The right way to pick an adviser

Finding an adviser is like picking a building contractor or nanny: Word of mouth and your own gut instincts are among the best methods to use. So your first move should be to ask friends and relatives what they've done and whether they're happy with their advisers. Then go see several candidates. Apart from qualifications and membership in a professional association, also check out a few more things.

Does the adviser seem curious about you and willing to answer questions frankly?

A good adviser will ask you questions about your income, life history, assets, financial goals, health, marital status, pension, and investment knowledge. If that doesn't happen, you could be dealing with a sales-driven hotshot who's just looking to make commissions quickly. Shop elsewhere. And ask about sales commissions as well as the adviser's experience and training. Vague answers are a bad sign.

Does the adviser work for a firm with an adequate back office for client recordkeeping and supervision?

Jargon alert — having an adequate "back office" is just a fancy way of saying they are set up to administer clients' accounts and orders. Ask to see a typical client statement and ensure that the firm has a *compliance officer,* an employee who keeps an eye on the salespeople and the way they treat clients.

Does the adviser sell a broad range of products?

A planner who wants to talk about funds from just one or two companies is probably lazy. Nobody can be familiar with the products from every company, but you want someone with a good idea of what's out there. You also want an adviser who's knowledgeable about life insurance, or who can at least hook you up with an insurance expert.

Are the adviser's office, grooming, and general image professional?

Nobody's looking for Armani or marble halls, but sloppy-looking premises or a scruffy appearance are signs of someone who hasn't been able to attract many clients.

The wrong way to pick an adviser

Unfortunately, a lot of what passes for investor education is just a giant sales pitch. So-called "seminars" that purport to enlighten you on a particular topic such as preparing a will or taking early retirement are really just a way of getting lots of sales targets into a room. Wandering around a glitzy "exhibition" or "forum" for investors may be fun and even informative, but these events are also a lure for getting "prospects" — potential customers — into a nice concentrated bunch where they can be picked off easily. In fact, be careful about attending seminars if you're the excitable or gullible type. The colourful celebrity speakers who work the investment circuit are often masters of making their audience both greedy and afraid — and easy targets for the inevitable sales spiel from the salespeople who paid for the event.

If the phone rings with an adviser or planner offering to help, decline politely and hang up. Always. Such "cold calls" are a time-honoured method of drumming up business for advisers. The salesperson calling may be perfectly legitimate, but responding to a random phone call out of the blue is an awful way of picking someone who's supposed to help you manage your money — such an important aspect of your life.

The telephone is still a favourite tool of those creatures that occasionally crawl out from under the rocks — the dishonest salespeople pushing "unlisted" and "over-the-counter" stocks or other "unregistered" investments that promise fantastic returns. Do yourself a favour and have some fun. Rent any of three wonderful movies about these crooked sales reptiles: *Glengarry Glen Ross,* based on David Mamet's play about sleazy real estate marketers, and *Boiler Room,* which tells the tale of some Long Island junkstock pushers. Then there's *Margin Call* released in autumn of 2011 which deals with Wall Street dumping toxic rubbish on investors during 2008. Scary stuff. After watching those great films, you'll be better equipped to deal with telephone sales pitches.

**Book II
Chapter 2**

Figuring Out
Fees — Discount
or Full-Service
Brokers?

Minding your ABCs — And T's

Glance down the mutual fund listings and you'll notice that quite a few adviser-sold fund families market their funds in different *classes* or *series,* often listed as A or B and even C through F. Not to mention I's and T's. Alternatively, some, such as Guardian Group of Funds, sell funds labelled "classic mutual" or "adviser."

What do these labels mean to you, the potential unitholder? In most cases, the difference is in the management expense ratio (MER) — the fee charged to the fund to cover sales commissions, portfolio management, and other management costs. In most cases, the MER difference is purely due to the type of sales loads (front- or back-end). Sometimes it is because investors in that class of units have paid the sales charge themselves or because they bought the fund directly from the company, bypassing the salesperson. The difference in annual expenses is usually between 0.5 percent and 1 percent per year. We offer a few examples here:

- Invesco Trimark (formerly AIM Trimark) has for years sold its funds in two basic versions. Its original funds, such as the Trimark Fund SC and the Trimark Canadian Fund SC, can be bought only on a front-load or "sales charge" basis (hence the SC). Its "Select" versions can be bought with a back-end load. The back-end load is expensive for the company to finance — because it must dish out the sales commissions to the salespeople itself — so the Select funds carry higher expenses. Just to make things even more confusing, the original SC funds can also be bought with a back-end load — and higher expenses for the investor.

- Several fund companies, including RBC, have introduced T-class funds, in which the T stands for "tax." These funds pay distributions to unitholders in the form of return of investment capital rather than dividends, interest, or capital gains. The latter remain within your fund investment, while the return on capital is paid out to you tax-free. As part of your original investment capital, it is not taxable income.

- Many F-class funds now exist. These have very small MERs, as they are sold only through advisers who charge management fees directly to their clients. In effect, the MER represents only the fund's portfolio management fee.

It's all pretty bewildering, but treating investors differently according to how they buy a fund is arguably fair. That's because the front-load buyers have saved the company a lot of money by paying the load themselves, so they deserve a break on the management fee.

If you're buying a fund that comes in more than one class, do everything you can to get the one with the lowest management fee, especially if you plan to invest for a long time. Sometimes even paying a small sales load is a good idea — but remember that with a front-load fund your adviser often gets a bigger trailer, so don't put up with any whining at the bargaining table. Over the years, a difference of only 0.5 percent in management fees really adds up. For example, say you put $10,000 into a deferred-load fund that produced an average annual compound return of 10 percent over a decade: You'd end up with $25,937. But say the fund was also available in a front-load version with a management fee that was 0.5 percentage points lower. The fund would be likely to give you an annual return of 10.5 percent instead of 10 percent. If you managed to buy that version of the fund with no sales load, your $10,000 would grow to $27,141 — or $1,200 more! Even if you had to pay an upfront sales load of 2 percent, reducing your initial investment to only $9,800, you would still end up with $26,598, or $661 more than an investor who chose the rear-load version.

Getting Started with Direct Sellers

Your other option for buying mutual funds is to buy them directly. Setting yourself up with an independent no-load company is easy:

1. **Check out the investing philosophy and fund lineups of the independent no-load companies on the Internet.** You can consult both the companies' own websites (which we list in Table 2–1) and third-party information sources such as Globefund.com and Morningstar.ca.

2. **Download the company's application forms (if available online) and then call them to open an account.**

Table 2–1 lists the biggest no-load fund companies on the Canadian scene, their website addresses, and their phone numbers.

Table 2–1	No-Load Direct Sellers in Canada	
Company	*Website*	*Toll-free Phone*
Beutel Goodman	www.beutel-can.com	800-461-4551
Pembroke Management Ltd.	www.pml.ca	800-667-0716
Leith Wheeler	www.leithwheeler.com	888-292-1122
Mawer	www.mawer.com	1–800–889–6248
McLean Budden	www.mcleanbudden.com	877-343-0322
Fiera Sceptre	www.fierasceptre.ca	514-954-3300

No-load fund managers treat you rather like discount brokers do. They have an accessible telephone-answering staff that will handle your orders, but they don't know much about you. All you have to do to invest is call their number (often toll-free) and transfer some money or send a cheque. Some companies have forms on their websites that you can download and fill out in advance, before you call to set up the account. You won't face any wheedling, pawing salesperson in the shape of a broker, planner, or insurance agent, which means you needn't worry about any fiddly and costly commissions.

No-load companies are generally fairly big businesses, and they can usually be relied on to send pretty reliable statements of your account. Sounds perfect, doesn't it? It is — except you'll have to put up with a narrow selection and a higher minimum investment.

Paying to play

Expect to face stiff minimum investments of $5,000 or more with some companies that sell directly to the public. The fees they charge are low, so they can't afford to fool around with tiny accounts. By contrast, most banks and fund companies that sell through advisers let you invest as little as $100.

Direct sellers impose these high minimum purchases because they have pretty small mutual fund operations. Their main business is usually managing money for institutions such as pension funds. These companies are not equipped to deal with thousands of unitholders, so to avoid attracting lots of small and unprofitable accounts, they often impose the required minimum investments.

Take Calgary-based Mawer Investment Management Ltd., for example. It sells its no-load funds directly to the public in several provinces, although they also can be purchased through salespeople such as financial planners. Mawer requires a minimum investment of $5,000 in its funds if acquired through an adviser, and $50,000 minimum if bought directly. So an investor who wants to buy direct but is just getting started may have to build up a pile of cash elsewhere before transferring money to the company.

Considering whether a direct seller is right for you

Many Canadians are still in love with their banks and advisers, not independent no-load fund companies. They continue to seek out the reassurance of a salesperson or the comforting embrace of a giant institution. That means no-load direct sellers have yet to really catch on in this country. That said, direct sellers are an excellent choice for investors who like to follow their investments closely or seek out funds with low costs.

If you can belly up to the bar with the minimum required investment and don't mind the lack of a personal touch, take a good look at this chapter to see if you're really a fit with this type of investing. Direct sellers of no-load funds are best suited for:

✦ **Investors looking for simplicity:** People who are very keen to get a simple solution, with all of their investments on one clear account statement. Direct sellers are easy to deal with because you can simply call up and ask questions or make changes to your account without having to go through a discount broker or other adviser. The same advantages apply to holding your funds at a bank — but direct sellers are much smaller than banks, so they're easier to talk to.

✦ **Savvy market trackers:** People who are interested in investing and want to follow the process closely. Such savvy investors love the low annual expenses and often excellent performance that no-load fund sellers offer. Many choose to leave a portion of their money in an account with a direct seller while investing the rest elsewhere. People who enjoy watching the markets often find that the information given to investors in direct-sold funds is more complete — that's because no-load companies deal directly with the investor and see him or her as the customer; fund salespeople won't muddy the picture. And the simplicity of a no-load account held at a fund company, instead of through an adviser, makes it easy to move money from fund to fund. Active investors who closely track the markets often do more switching around.

The Advantages of Dealing with an Independent No-Load Company

Book II
Chapter 2

Figuring Out
Fees — Discount
or Full-Service
Brokers?

Using a no-load company that sells to the public is a halfway house between the lonely course of picking your own funds at a discount broker on the one hand and the comfy warm blanket of getting help from a bank employee or an investment adviser who earns commissions on the other. When you go to such a salesperson or a bank, you get lots of help — but you usually pay for the advice in the form of higher annual costs imposed on your fund. And the selection that a bank or commission-paid salesperson carries is often limited to only a few hundred funds. At a no-load company, the people answering the phone will offer some advice, and the expenses on their funds may be low. But the selection of funds on offer is once again limited to the company's own products, and that might be just a handful of funds. Discount brokers, whoopee, have lots of funds on their sales lists. They're the amusement park of funds. But you'll be riding that roller coaster alone, because you'll get hardly any help.

When you contact any fund company, no matter how it sells its products, ignore all of the marketing blather and ask for an application form and prospectus. In many cases, these are available online. Those two usually set out the stuff you need to know, such as minimum investment and annual costs. You can always slip 'em in the recycling bin later. Or toss them in that old rusty oil drum you use to burn garbage. (Don't the people next door complain about the choking greasy plume of smoke, by the way?)

Putting more money in your pocket

If you want a hassle-free solution to buying your mutual funds, going with a no-load, direct fund seller offers some important advantages. In this section, we discuss the main ones.

The biggest plus of buying from a no-load company is the fact that you cut out the intermediary. No-load companies can charge you lower fees — although they don't always choose to do so. Because they don't have to pay an army of advisers — or cover the expense of running a sprawling network of bank branches — some direct sellers' domestic equity funds have annual expenses of 1.3 percent or less. That's much cheaper than most domestic equity mutual funds, which have total annual costs and fees closer to 2.5 percent. The more expensive fund is taking an extra 1 percent annually out of your mottled hide — over ten years, that difference adds up to 10 percent of your money.

If you were to invest $10,000 and earn a tax-free average annual return of 9 percent for a decade, you'd end up with $23,674. But the same $10,000 invested at a 10 percent rate of return, because the expenses were one percentage point lower, would grow to nearly $26,000 (see Table 2–2). That's why it's better to have a fund with a significantly lower annual expense ratio.

Table 2–2	**Think 1 Percent Doesn't Matter?** **That'll Be $2,263 Please**	
Year	*Value at 9 Percent Return*	*Value at 10 Percent Return*
Initial investment	$10,000	$10,000
1st	$10,900	$11,000
2nd	$11,881	$12,100
3rd	$12,950	$3,310
4th	$14,116	$14,641
5th	$15,386	$16,105
6th	$16,771	$17,716
7th	$18,280	$19,487
8th	$19,926	$21,436
9th	$21,719	$23,579
10th	$23,674	$25,937

Offering advice for adults

Another advantage of going directly to a fund company is that you're treated like an adult rather than simply as a faceless consumer of the fund product. In other words, the company's website and mailings to investors often are more candid about performance. That's because many of the investors who use no-load companies tend to be independent souls who relish the low costs and are happy with the lower level of advice. They're the sort to demand complete reporting of performance.

If you're not satisfied with the performance of your no-load funds, or if you have queries, it's simple to just pick up the phone and call. You may not get the errant fund manager or a senior executive, but the representative who answers the phone will probably be able to give you some answers.

And, best of all, buying no-load doesn't mean you have to give up getting advice altogether. Unlike discount brokerages, for a fee, most direct sellers have staff who can advise you on choosing funds and even help you shape your overall investment strategy, but don't expect too much as their licences to extend advice are often very limited.

Keeping things simple

Dealing with a fund company directly is simpler than buying a fund through a salesperson. You're not forced to relay your order or request via someone else, potentially causing confusion or delay. You can call up the company and buy and sell funds in your account right over the phone, as well as ask for forms or other administrative help. Your relationship as a customer is clearly with the fund seller, not with an intermediary like a discount broker. That's great for you because

✦ You have just one company to deal with and complain to if a mistake occurs in your account. Or did you say you enjoyed muttering endlessly into voice mail?

✦ You get just one annual and quarterly statement of account.

✦ If you own several funds, it's handy to be able to check on their performance if they're all included in one company's mailings.

✦ You can switch money easily from fund to fund as your needs or assets change.

**Book II
Chapter 2**

**Figuring Out
Fees — Discount
or Full-Service
Brokers?**

Allowing frequent trades

Moving your money frequently from fund to fund in an attempt to catch rising stock markets and avoid falling ones is often tempting. Naturally, frequent traders love using no-load companies because they don't charge investors to switch their money in and out. That makes a no-load fund company the perfect choice if you fancy yourself someone with the ability to time movements in stock and bond prices — for example, every time the Canadian stock market goes up 20 percent in a year, you might decide to pull out of stocks. But no-load fund companies don't appreciate it when customers move their money around constantly, because it greatly increases the company's administration costs (all of those transfers must be accounted for). So they'll eventually crack down on you by limiting your trades. And you'll often get slapped with a charge of 2 percent of your money if you switch out of a fund within three months of buying it.

Switching into and out of no-load funds through a discount broker can in fact cost you commissions, because discounters often impose small fees of $25 or more each time you sell a no-load fund. A conventional adviser won't welcome your business if you plan to chop and change your portfolio all the time, because of all the troublesome paperwork you create. (In fact, if you bring a portfolio containing no-load funds to a full-service broker, expect these funds to be sold eventually because they pay no fees or commissions.)

A 2 percent penalty for trading early seems small, but it reduces your return. Imagine you invest in the Canadian stock market ahead of an oil boom. (As the past few years have reminded us, foreign investors see us as resource producers in toques, so they tend to buy into our market when prices for commodities, such as lumber, energy, and metals, are going up.) Say you put $10,000 into a no-load company's Canadian *equity fund,* a fund that invests in stocks and shares (which in turn are a tiny slice of ownership of companies). The Canadian market goes up 10 percent in two weeks and your fund matches the rise in the broad market, boosting your investment to $11,000 — at which point you sell half of your holding in the fund, or $5,500. If the company slaps a 2 percent fee on investors who leave a fund after less than 90 days, then you'll receive a cheque for just $5,390, which is $5,500 minus 2 percent. Of course, your other $5,500 is still sitting in the fund.

Knowing when to hold 'em

How many trades are too many? Well, research seems to show that almost any level of chopping and changing reduces overall returns because most investors let emotion distort their judgment, leading them to do things at the wrong time. People sell when the market has slumped and is about to bounce back. And they buy after it has already shot up and is about to go on the slide.

Over time, share prices may tend to rise remorselessly as good companies thrive and the world economy grows, but the stock market also advances in sudden starts. If, following the dictates of your brilliant, can't-lose trading strategy, you happen to have sold your equity funds just before one of those days, then you miss out on the profits.

Knowing when to walk away

Moving money out of a fund can be sensible at times, and holding the fund directly at a no-load company makes the process easier. Good times to move money include when

✦ The fund has gone up so much that it now represents a huge portion of your portfolio. For example, if you've decided to keep just half of your money in shares, but one or more of your equity funds have produced a 100 percent return over the past year, then you probably have too much money riding on equities. Time to sell some of those stock funds.

✦ You've been foolhardy enough to bet on a *specialty* fund that invests in just one narrow section of the market, such as South Korea or financial-services shares, and were lucky enough to score a big profit. Such one-flavour funds tend to post huge crashes soon after their big wins — as investors go cool on the kind of stocks they hold. So think strongly about selling at least some of your units in a specialty fund as soon as it has a good year. No, don't just think about it: Pick up the phone and do it immediately.

✦ Your reason for holding the fund no longer applies. For example, a fund manager you like may have quit, or the fund may have changed its investment style.

Check your portfolio once or twice a year, and if it's out of line with your ideal mix of investments, then readjust it by moving money from one fund to another. For example, say you've decided you want one-third of your $10,000 mutual fund collection in sure-and-steady government bonds — investments issued by the government that pay interest and can be cashed in again at the issue price after a set number of years or sold at any time. The other two-thirds is in lucrative-but-dangerous stocks, those tiny pieces of ownership in companies.

Book II
Chapter 2

Figuring Out
Fees — Discount
or Full-Service
Brokers?

So your setup is

$3,300 bond funds	33 percent of portfolio
$6,700 stock funds	67 percent of portfolio
$10,000 total portfolio	100 percent of portfolio

Say the bonds hold their value over the next year, remaining at $3,300, but the stocks rise 30 percent to $8,710, which gives you a mix of:

$3,300 bond funds	27 percent of portfolio
$8,710 stock funds	73 percent of portfolio
$12,010 total portfolio	100 percent of portfolio

This means you have too much riding on the stock market in relation to your original plan — almost three-quarters of the total pile. You can fix it easily by moving $663 out of stock funds and into bond funds, leaving you with a portfolio that looks like this:

$3,963 bond funds	33 percent of portfolio
$8,047 stock funds	67 percent of portfolio
$12,010 total portfolio	100 percent of portfolio

If you hold a super-volatile fund that invests in a narrow sector or region, such as a technology company or Latin America, it's a good strategy to move some money out of the fund if it shoots up in value. That way, you lock some profits before the inevitable crash. Holding such funds forever is of dubious benefit because they're at risk of losing money for long periods.

Weighing the Drawbacks of Going Direct

Most no-load mutual fund companies offer too few funds to really give you a diversified portfolio — that means an account with many different types of investment. Here are the main drawbacks to using a direct seller.

Significant levels of cash required

As we mention at the beginning of this chapter, not everyone can go direct. As attractive as it seems to investors who are serious minimalists in terms of their need for guidance and their interest in paying fees to invest, you need a minimum amount of cash to play — in one case, as much as $100,000. This is obviously not the case with novice investors, or those in the process of building their portfolio. Although this type of investing may not be the right choice for you now, it is something to keep an eye on as your investing savvy and your portfolio grow.

Lack of choice

The main problem with direct purchase of funds is the narrow selection. Few direct sellers have more than one or two funds, so if you leave all your money with one company, you're at risk of seeing the market turn against that particular investment style.

You can avoid this lack-of-choice drawback by buying the direct seller's funds through a discount broker instead, if they're available. That lets you use the no-load seller's funds, with their nice low expenses, in combination with index funds or funds from other companies. However, your discount broker may not even carry a low-expense company's funds (because the discounter gets little or nothing in sales commissions or in trailer or storage fees).

Chapter 3: Surveying Your Fund Options

In This Chapter

⮕ **Choosing the right fund**

⮕ **Finding funds based on region**

⮕ **Understanding the difference between equity and balanced funds**

⮕ **Knowing why index funds and ETFs might be the better option**

⮕ **Earning money through dividend funds**

*E*quity mutual funds, which buy stocks, are one way — a good way! — to build wealth. They're attractive because they hold shares in a huge variety of usually great companies (or that's at least what they're supposed to do). So wide is the selection of holdings in most equity funds that if some of the businesses fail or stagnate, the fund often has enough winners to pull you through.

Long-term investors — people who usually hold equities for at least five years — sometimes favour mutual funds rather than selecting their own equities. Despite what happened during the recession, and the years since, the economy will grow over time, and so will your portfolio. If you want to earn decent returns on your cash over the long term, and you've decided to buy mutual funds, you're pretty well forced to buy equity funds. That's because they're the only type of fund likely to produce decent returns over the long haul.

Yes, the stock market and the funds that invest in it can drop sharply, sometimes for years — we provide some scary examples in this chapter. So make sure you have a good chunk of your own bonds or bond funds in your holdings as well. But strong evidence exists that equity markets pretty well always rise over periods of ten years or more (even if your tenth year is during a major recession, like we saw in 2008), so equity funds are a relatively safe bet for buyers who are sure they can hold on for a long time without needing the money back at short notice.

In this chapter we give you a crash course on how the stock market works and explain why funds are a great way to profit from it. We show why you're best off buying equity funds that invest in big and stable companies, especially businesses that sell their wares all over the world. We also make clear why it's a good idea to hold six or seven equity funds — three Canadian and three or four global — and we give you simple tips for selecting great funds.

Why Investing in Stocks Is Simple

Making money in the stock market is easy — in theory. You just buy *shares* — tiny slices of ownership — in well-managed companies and then hold on to them for years. As the businesses you've invested in thrive, so do their owners, and that includes you as a *shareholder*. But when you actually try to select wonderful companies, things get complicated. For one thing, it's hard to tell which companies have genuinely bright prospects, because the managers of just about every corporation do a great job of blowing their little brass horns and making everything look wonderful in their garden. And, like everything else, the stock market is subject to the whims of fashion. When investors decide they love a particular company or industry, the shares usually go to fantastic heights. At that point, buying stocks turns into a risky game — no point buying a great business if you pay several times what it's really worth.

Being fallible human beings, we constantly sabotage ourselves in the stock market. When everything is going well and shares are climbing to record highs, we feel all warm, fuzzy, and enthusiastic — and we stumble into the market just in time for the crash. And when the economy or the stock market is slumping, we get all depressed and sell our shares at bargain-basement prices — just when we should be grabbing more. But perhaps the biggest problem with investors is our innate belief that we're smarter than everybody else. Everybody thinks the same thing, which means that lots of us are going to end up losers. Don't let us stop you: You can try to make pots of money buying speculative technology companies or penny mining stocks or companies consolidating the pallet industry, but that's really gambling. True investing in stock markets is simply buying well-established, well-run businesses and holding the shares and collecting their dividends, ideally for years.

The real kicker in stock market investing is figuring out whether a company is genuinely good — a quality outfit worth putting money into — and whether the price you're being asked to pay for shares is too high. Unfortunately, though, there may be no such thing as a true value for a company, because the numbers all vary so wildly according to the assumptions you make about the future. In that case, a stock is simply worth what people decide to pay for it on any given day. And that may not be very much: Stocks can dive for no apparent reason. But ordinary people saving for the future should care about the crazy volatile stock market for one reason: Good companies thrive, their profits go up, they pay dividends, and their stocks gain value over the long term.

Sometimes, selecting a good company to invest in can be almost embarrassingly simple. Take the iPod, everyone's favourite music listening toy, and its smarter and handsomer sibling the iPhone. From the day these minuscule but versatile little computers appeared in electronic stores, they became a must-have addition to daily life. Innovation, good design, and clever marketing are no accident — it requires talented people, and they don't stay long with badly run companies. Sure enough, an investor who bought shares of Apple, or AAPL, on October 23, 2001, the day the company released the iPod, would see their investment grow by an incredible 4193 percent over the next decade. That's a spectacular case, but once in a while Apple-like success stories come along.

The ABCs of Picking a Fund

If you've been worrying about which equity fund among the 3,000-plus on sale in Canada has the best chance of beating the market, forget it. You're better off looking for UFOs in the evening sky. No point trying to pick a fund that'll beat the market, because only a tiny group of managers are likely to do so consistently, based on experience over several decades.

Even if a brochure, ad, or salesperson tells you (or at least implies) a fund is the sure road to riches, always make sure you kick the tires yourself. (We explain just how to kick those tires later in this section.) The people who design and run mutual funds are master marketers and they often sincerely believe their fund is a magic lamp that will reliably outperform the market. If you go to a discount broker, investment adviser, financial planner, or insurance agent to buy your funds, they too will trot out the same line. It will be an honest adviser who suggests you invest in shares of any public mutual fund manager while you own their mutual funds. If you drink lots of milk, buy a piece of the cow!

These people are salesmen and saleswomen and, to do a good job, they have almost certainly convinced themselves the fund they're selling you is a world-beater. They'll use reassuring phrases and labels such as "conservative" or "growth at a reasonable price" to convince you their fund is a way to achieve that impossible dream: Big returns at almost no risk. They'll even talk about the fund's "black box" (a cynical expression used in the investment industry) in the shape of some impressive-sounding formula or method that purports to maximize returns while reducing the danger of losses. Think of witch doctors brandishing painted bones and you'll get the idea. Yes, you might get lucky and seize on a manager who outperforms the pack for a while, but they always fall to Earth.

Of the nearly 600 funds broadly classified as Canadian equity with a five-year track record as of October 2011, 361 managed to beat the −0.15 percent return from the S&P/TSX index during that period. It was worse for the three-year period, when 385 among the more than 780 funds that had been in

**Book II
Chapter 3**

**Surveying Your
Fund Options**

existence for three years on that date beat the benchmark. And around half of the nearly 1,000 funds managed this feat for the one-year period. It's tough to beat the index, apparently.

So instead of using complicated criteria to choose a fund you hope will be a world-beater, we recommend that you follow three basic rules, what we call the ABCs of selecting a great equity fund:

1. Look for a fund that's full of companies from **A**ll industries — and, in the case of global funds, **A**ll major regions of the world.

2. Insist that your fund holds lots of big, stable, and conservative companies — the type that investors call **B**lue-chip (because the blue chip is traditionally the most valuable in poker).

3. Look for a fund that has a habit of producing **C**onsistent returns over the years that aren't out of line with the market or with its rival funds. Later in this chapter, we show you how to do that.

Select from all industries

A fund should hold companies from all, or nearly all, major industries, in order to spread risk — and to give unitholders a chance to profit if the stock market suddenly falls in love with a particular type of company. Here is one way to break down the industry groups:

✦ Banks and other financial companies, such as Citigroup, Royal Bank of Canada, or Deutsche Bank.

✦ Natural resource processors, such as Imperial Oil, Rio Tinto Alcan, or Canfor.

✦ Technology companies, such as Microsoft, Intel, or Research In Motion.

✦ Telecom businesses, such as Rogers, BCE, or Telus.

✦ Manufacturers of industrial and consumer products, such as drug maker Pfizer or General Electric.

✦ Dull but steady utility and pipeline companies such as Alberta power generator TransAlta or pipeline system TransCanada PipeLines.

✦ Retail and consumer service companies such as Canadian Tire and Walmart.

Not every group has to be represented in the top holdings of every fund, but a portfolio without at least one resource stock, financial services giant, or technology player among its biggest ten investments might represent a dangerous gamble. Why? Because of the ever-present chance that share prices in that missing sector will suddenly and unpredictably take off, leaving your fund in the dust. Avoid funds making bets like that.

Hold blue-chip winners

Glossy mutual fund brochures often promise the Sun, Moon, and stars . . . but just look at the fund's top holdings. Whether the fund is Canadian, U.S., or international, at least two-thirds of its ten biggest investments should be big, blue-chip companies that you or someone you trust has at least heard of. A list of the top stocks in any fund is readily available on the Internet. Look in the fund's marketing material or in the reports and documents given to unit-holders. What you're looking for are big and stable firms, the type that offer the best prospect of increasing their shareholders' wealth over the years.

Talk is cheap and fund managers love to drone on about how conservative they are. But managers of supposedly careful funds can sometimes quietly take risks: They put big portions of the fund into weird stuff like resource stocks or Latin America to jazz up their returns and attract more investors. The list of top holdings is one of the most valuable pieces of information an investor has about a fund because it can't be faked or fudged (ruling out pure fraudulent reporting). If you don't see at least a few giant names in the fund's list of its biggest holdings, then the fund manager may be taking undue risks, fooling around with small or obscure companies.

Check out past performance, with caution

After you've satisfied the first two of these conditions, look at the fund's past performance. Begin by filtering out funds that have been around for fewer than five years, unless it's quite clear someone with a record you can check has been running the money. Then look for consistent returns that aren't too much above or below the market. We all want to make lots of money, so leaving past returns until last may seem crazy, and exactly opposite to one's natural inclination. But it's the way sophisticated professionals do it. If the people in charge of a multi-billion-dollar pension fund are interviewing new money-management firms, for example, they'll ask first about the expenses and fees the money managers charge and also about the style and method the firms use to select stocks and bonds (more on that topic later). Only then do the pros examine the past record of the managers — it's just assumed they'll be near the average.

Judging whether past performance will repeat itself is almost as impossible as determining the true value of a company's stock — it depends entirely on complex and varying assumptions and conditions. Betting too heavily on yesterday's hot performers, hoping they'll outrun the pack again tomorrow, is a good way to end up in a dud fund.

Who's running your fund? Managers on the move

Equity funds offer endless sources of amusement. One of the fun games you can play with a fund is figuring out who exactly is running it. This is often so difficult that investors shouldn't get too worried about it when they start buying funds. It's impossible with some companies that use a vague "team" to pick stocks. And remember that a superstar manager is extra likely to go cold because he or she gets too much money to manage wisely. Remember that what is actually in the portfolio is far more important than any amount of talk of wizards running your money.

If you get more interested in mutual funds, you'll no doubt start wondering: Why not just put my money with guys and gals who have been successful in the past? One problem is that managers move around so much. As soon as a stock picker builds a strong reputation, all too often he or she jumps ship to another fund that offers a fat signing bonus. And remember the warning that we've been repeating endlessly, in a smug nasal drone: Star managers invariably fall to Earth. Sometimes, they go inside themselves and sometimes they seem to . . . well, they always go inside themselves. Don't get excited about the past history of the manager running your fund. And pay even less attention to fawning newspaper articles proclaiming them a genius. Just look at the fund's main holdings and its track record. If these meet the ABC tests outlined above, then it's probably a high-quality fund.

Find out what a fund's past performance has been and, above all, compare it with that of rival funds and the market as a whole. You can find this information on the Internet — the leading sites for Canadian mutual fund investors and investment advisers are Morningstar.ca, Globefund.com and the Financial Post's Fund Centre (`http://www.financialpost.com/markets/funds/index.html`). Morningstar.ca is run by the Canadian unit of Chicago-based Morningstar, Inc., and Globefund.com is owned by *The Globe and Mail.* (Advisers also rely on desktop computer software sold by these organizations.)

Remember to stick to funds that have been around for at least five years. Compare a fund's numbers against those of its peers — those within the same category — and also against the median returns for all funds in the category.

Globefund.com and Morningstar.ca supply the annual compound returns for every fund as well as for the average fund in its category and for the market as a whole. If you're interested in a fund, its compound returns should be above the average for its group, but if they're way above — for example, an annual return of 15 percent over five years while the average fund made less than 10 percent — then the manager is probably a risk-taker. Above all, though, be wary of funds whose returns over five and ten years are below those of the average fund: Such pooches have a dispiriting habit of continuing to bark and dig holes in the garden.

Also check whether the fund has been near the top or bottom in each individual calendar year, to detect big swings in performance over time.

How Many Equity Funds Do You Need?

Building a great portfolio of mutual funds is simple. All you have to do is make two decisions:

✦ How much risk you want to take — in other words, how much you want riding on equity funds.

✦ How much you like Canada's long-term economic prospects.

We wish we could tell you simply to buy one stock market fund, using the techniques we suggest, and forget about it. Some salespeople will even insist you're safe with a single wonderful fund. But that course is just too dangerous.

How many funds should you buy to ensure you've assembled an adequately varied collection? Before we answer that, look at the only two types of funds to consider for your serious long-term money:

✦ **Global equity funds** buy stocks and shares everywhere, from Taiwan to Tupelo. In practice, they usually end up investing in large companies in the rich economies of the world because, to paraphrase the bank robber, that's where the money is. In other words, giant corporations have proven to be just about the most profitable and most stable investments you can make.

✦ **Canadian equity funds,** not surprisingly, buy Canadian stocks. A number of individual categories exist under the Canadian equity umbrella. Some funds concentrate on the very largest corporations, such as the big banks or other blue-chip companies like communications giant Telus Corp., and others are more specialized, such as *small-cap funds,* which buy only smaller companies with supposedly bigger growth prospects. In practice, Canadian equity funds end up holding pretty well the same companies because the Canadian market offers a limited selection, although it offers a little more variety among small-cap funds.

Deciding how much to put into equity funds

All of us as investors fall into one of three groups:

✦ **Savers,** who need to use their money in the next couple of years, shouldn't own any equity funds. The risk of loss in the short term is too great, so savers should just buy investments that pay regular interest.

✦ **Balanced investors,** who want only modest drops in the value of their funds in any one year, often put 45 percent or slightly more (up to about 60 percent) into equity funds. With the rest they buy bond funds, which invest in loans to governments and corporations, leaving a small portion of their money sitting in cash or cash-like investments. Or they buy special balanced funds, which consist of a mixture of stocks and bonds.

✦ **Growth investors,** who want the maximum return on their money and plan to let it ride the ups and downs of funds for five years or more, often put about 75 percent of their money into equity funds. If you're investing for periods of ten years or more, and definitely don't mind big slumps in the value of your mutual fund portfolio along the way, you might want to put even more into the stock market with its allure of higher returns.

Dividing your money between Canadian and foreign equity funds

Should you be patriotic and keep your money in Canada, or look abroad for your investments? No definite answer exists, but the prevailing advice has been to keep the majority of your stock market money outside Canada. The world offers many wonderful opportunities and the Canadian stock market represents a tiny fraction of the world's overall stock market value. For example, few Canadian companies have the might of Japan's Sony Corp., Royal Dutch Shell of the Netherlands, or U.S.–based Microsoft Corp.

However, most experts would also advise keeping at least some of your money in Canada if you plan to go on living in this country, because you'll need to have assets in Canadian dollars to pay for your expenses here. Plus our market has fared pretty well during the past decade or so. But if you're convinced that Canada's in trouble, then you may want to move 80 percent or more of your mutual fund money, including equity funds, into non-Canadian stocks and bonds.

How do you split your money among equity funds?

It's a good idea to put one-half to two-thirds of your stock market money into *index funds* or *exchange-traded funds,* funds that simply track the entire market at low cost to the investor instead of trying to pick the stocks that will go up the most. Keep reading for more on index funds and ETFs. Their reliability and low expenses make them one of the best deals out there for investors.

Canadian stock market index funds and ETFs track the S&P/TSX Composite Index or the S&P/TSX 60 Index (a more focused collection of the biggest companies listed on the TSX). Global index funds used to be rare, so you had to buy a combo: a U.S. index fund that gives you the same return each year as a list of giant U.S. companies such as the S&P 500 stock index, and an international index fund that tracks all the major global markets except for the United States and Canada. That's no longer the case and now there are as many global index funds as there are global stock markets. Put a U.S. index fund and an international index fund together, and you've got a pretty good global equity index fund. So all you need to buy is a Canadian, a U.S., and an international index fund from the many choices now available.

Two categories of funds invest broadly in foreign stock markets:

✦ Global equity

✦ International equity

Here's the difference. *Global equity funds* are free to invest anywhere, including the United States, but *international equity funds* stay outside Canada and the United States. The idea behind international funds is that many investors already have plenty of money in the States by owning stocks or other funds, so some fund companies offer funds that stay out of the U.S. market. That's logical thinking, but in keeping with the ABC rules, we believe that when picking your non-Canadian stock funds you're better off sticking with a fund that's free to go anywhere the manager anticipates getting the best return.

With the rest of your equity fund money, buy just four equity funds — two global and two Canadian — that have a person or team trying to select winning shares. Those are called *actively managed* funds because they buy and sell holdings in an attempt to beat the market and other fund managers instead of just trying to keep up with a market benchmark. The managers, in other words, are trying to pick the few stocks that go up the most.

Often, though, managers fail. But if you buy a few actively managed funds as well as index funds, you at least have a portfolio that isn't tied to just one market benchmark. It has enough variety to ensure that one of your funds is probably doing relatively well, even if the others are sagging — as long as the whole stock market isn't crashing. In the event of a wholesale decline in stocks — like we saw in 2008 — just about all equity funds, both Canadian and global, will be losers anyway.

**Book II
Chapter 3**

**Surveying Your
Fund Options**

Global Equity Funds: Meet Faraway People and Exploit Them

Global equities are the Boeing 747s of the mutual fund world, huge magic carpets that offer the best chance of steady, high returns on your savings over many years. They should make up about two-thirds of the money you're putting into the stock market — unless you're convinced the Canadian stock market will outperform for the long-term.

Global equity funds have, for the most part, earned steady, attractive returns over the years, which makes them the very best type of fund to own. Put most of your money here because

✦ They tend to own multinational blue-chip companies, the best growth asset of all.

✦ They invest all over the world, spreading your risk and smoothing out your ups and downs — when one country is up, another is often down.

✦ The executives running multinational corporations sometimes foul up (remember "new Coke"?), but the companies are usually large enough and sufficiently sophisticated to recover from errors.

✦ Your mutual fund company is just one of dozens of big international money managers owning shares in these firms — between them, all those sharp lassies wearing Prada and those lads in Armani keep an eye on the companies. When their hangovers aren't too bad, that is.

Many of Canada's biggest mutual funds fall into the global equity class, and some large ones have produced excellent results over the years. Global equity funds are hugely profitable for the companies that run them, so the managers are intensely motivated not to let the performance slip too much. Most global equity funds hold high-quality, blue-chip companies and they spread their risk over numerous industries and countries, so they also meet our ABC test.

Buy at least two global equity funds, because an individual fund can go into a slump for a year or more. Different managers are hot and cold at different times.

Be sure to apply the ABC rules when selecting a global equity fund. (If you've forgotten the rules, flip back a few pages.)

Investors who just go to a bank branch to buy their funds or who deal with another company that sells funds directly to the public will have a problem: The bank or company may offer just one suitable global equity fund. And you may not be able to buy index funds. No easy way around this problem exists. If you can't or don't want to go somewhere with a wider selection of funds, just buy the global fund with half of the money you've earmarked for global stocks and then hedge your bets by putting the rest into one or two narrower funds that invest in a single region, such as Europe or Asia.

Also, check any global equity fund you buy to make sure it offers plenty of variety. If the top holdings contain no European stocks, for example, or they seem to be all technology companies, then look elsewhere.

Canadian Equity Funds: Making Maple-Syrup-Flavoured Money

Your first move when picking Canadian equity funds for the core of your portfolio is to make sure they're classified in one of the Canadian equity categories. These include:

✦ **Canadian equity:** These funds must have 90 percent of their holdings in Canadian-based companies; the fund's average market capitalization must be above $2.9 billion (for 2011).

✦ **Canadian focused equity:** The criteria are identical to the Canadian equity category, except funds need be only 50 percent or more in Canada.

✦ **Canadian small/mid-cap equity:** These funds must be 90 percent in Canadian stocks with an average market cap below $2.9 billion (again, for 2011).

✦ **Canadian focused small/mid-cap equity:** The same as Canadian small/mid-cap equity, except funds need be only 50 percent or more in Canada.

✦ **Canadian dividend and income equity:** These funds must have a stated mandate to invest primarily in income-generating securities, and 90 percent of their equity holdings must be Canadian.

Book II
Chapter 3

Surveying Your
Fund Options

If the company where you hold your mutual fund account offers only one conventional actively managed Canadian stock fund, then use it for half of your Canadian stock money and put the rest into a Canadian index fund or ETF. If no index fund or ETF is available (and one should be), then open an account elsewhere for at least part of your money.

Keep it simple and don't worry about which equity fund manager is going to thrash the competition. Canada's tiny stock market, which accounts for just 3 percent of the world's publicly traded shares, offers a limited number of companies. In fact, for a big-company fund, only a few suitable names exist outside of the S&P/TSX 60 Index. So most Canadian equity funds tend to be pretty similar.

Small and Mid-Sized Company Funds: Spotty Little Fellows

On the face of it, funds in the Canadian small/mid-cap equity category look mighty enticing. The median Canadian small/mid-cap equity fund had produced an impressive 20-year compound annual return of 12.1 percent as of October 2011. But these funds have benefitted enormously from the success of the Canadian resource industry, in which much of the big money is made when a small resource player strikes it rich. Actually attaining that return, though, is entirely another matter. Small/mid-cap equity funds are a volatile bunch of funds.

Hitting highs and lows

If you had bought Front Street Growth (Series B) in late 1991 and still owned it 20 years later, you would have been bragging about owning the top-performing Canadian small/mid-cap fund. The fund achieved an impressive 18.6 percent annualized return over that period. But "if" is the operative term here. Even more impressive than your profit — more than $303,000 if you'd invested $10,000 back then — would have been your staying power. You'd have weathered some pretty big swings during that time, including a 173.3 percent gain in 1993 and a 52.3 percent loss in 2008. Most investors would have figured, in the early 90s, that a triple-digit return was completely too good to be true and sell out. But then they would have missed the many more years of 50-percent-plus performances.

Who's to know, though? The important thing to note here is that, had you taken the much, much safer middle ground and invested in large-cap Canadian equity funds, you'd have still done well. The median fund in the Canadian equity category achieved a 7 percent compound annual return over those same 20 years.

Picking a winning fund

Long before you worry about having the nerve to stick with a winning small-cap fund, the first challenge is to pick that fund in the first place. The problem is similar to what confronts the guy who's investing directly in small-cap stocks. Guessing which ones are going to "pop" — market talk for getting their stocks to go up — is a tough game. But never fear; investors have a willing ally in the executives and main shareholders of a company. In fact, they're sometimes *only too happy* for their share price to shoot up. *Cling!* — is that a stock option bulb lighting up? (*Stock options* are shares that company management can buy at a fixed low price — and that become nicer and nicer to have when the market price of the shares goes up.) But what's left in a hot stock for everybody else after the corporate management and the investment bankers have torn off their giant hunk often wouldn't fill a small McDonald's pop cup that's been lying for days on the ground beside a gasoline pump. There's a great story in Canada about a certain group of employees who were unhappy so they volunteered to take a cut in pay to become happy millionaires. Who were they? Air Canadian pilots who joined Westjet and got stock options.

First, a vital bit of terminology — a company's *stock market capitalization* is the value in money terms that investors are applying to the business. For example, a company with 50 million shares in the hands of its shareholders and a stock price of $5 has a market value, or "market cap," of only $250 million (or 50 million shares times $5), which still makes it quite a small company.

The three most important things to remember about investing in small and medium-sized companies are that:

✦ Shares in small companies move in their own strange cycles, sometimes sliding when blue-chip stocks go up, which can make them a sort of insurance policy for a portfolio.

✦ And yes, when they're hot, small caps can produce rich returns. Of all the wacky fund categories, small-cap funds can best justify their existence. But you don't really need them, either.

✦ Small-company funds can go into long slumps, leaving you with "dead money" that just stagnates — or, worse, saddles you with heavy losses. Most people are better off putting their savings into regular equity funds that buy big companies, a strategy that offers steadier returns.

Understanding the disadvantages

Take any recommendation to buy a small-cap fund with a hefty dose of salt. These are volatile investments best suited to investors who keep a close eye on their holdings. Unpredictable rallies and collapses are the way that small-cap stocks work. You may have some good years, but disappointments are all too frequent.

So remember that small-company funds are marked by moves upward that happen only too rarely, a disadvantage that makes them unsuitable for much of your serious money. The numbers show that small-cap stocks may have their good long-term record only because of periodic crazy bull markets in small-company shares — typically at the end of a great period in the stock market, when investors feel clever and brave enough to start chasing riskier stuff.

If you insist on buying small-company funds, buy at least two or three. That's because the managers of small-cap funds tend to be eccentric individuals who love poring over obscure little businesses and developing their own methods. It's very personality-driven. Even an excellent manager can do terribly if his or her favourite type of stock is out of fashion. And don't forget that the small-cap sector has plenty of walking dead.

Regional Equity Funds: Welcome to Bangkok — Or Hong Kong?

Funds that invest in limited areas of the world may sound like they're a good way to speculate. After all, the median emerging markets fund had a three-year compound annual return of about 11 percent as of October 2011. Regional funds are exciting investments, however, and that brings both the good and the bad. Although emerging-markets mutual funds have produced double-digit returns in a number of years, it's been a pretty uneven ride.

Uneven as in a 19 percent loss in 1998, a 61 percent gain in 1999, and a 27 percent loss in 2000.

Funds that specialize in a particular area suffer from the curse of all narrow investments, whether they invest in European, Asian, or emerging markets, or in individual countries. These markets usually go into slumps, which was amply demonstrated by Japan in 2000–2002, when the median Japanese equity mutual fund suffered losses of 30, 26, and 13 percent during those calendar years. Things haven't been too good lately for these funds, either. The median Japanese equity mutual fund lost around 7 percent between January and October 2011, resulting in a ten-year compound annual loss of 4.2 percent. Investors in the broader region fared better, as Asia–Pacific Rim mutual funds — which are free to lose money anywhere in the region — eked out a tiny profit of 0.6 percent over those ten years, despite the Japan market's woes.

Instead of regional funds, you may be better off with two or three global equity funds that hold assets in countries just about everywhere. Look at the holdings of nearly any big global equity fund and you'll see European and Asian stocks as well as U.S. names.

The pros aren't infallible, though, and they can easily get the mix of countries wrong. That's why it's important with global equity funds to avoid managers who make big bets on a particular region or country, such as China or India.

Sector Funds: Limitations Galore

Funds that buy stocks in just one industry or sector of the economy — for example, technology or resource funds — are bucking broncos, producing wild leaps and sickening plunges. That's because investors have a long-standing habit, as we've seen, of suddenly falling in love with a particular type of industry or market sector and then bidding those companies' shares to ridiculous prices.

The most recent biotech rally was in 2000, when it wasn't unusual to see obscure biotech stocks on the Toronto Stock Exchange jumping fourfold in a couple of weeks. The median healthcare fund jumped 38 percent that year. Then somebody dropped a jar and biotechs went squelch, and the category fell nearly 35 percent over the next two years.

Specialized funds are far more volatile than high-quality diversified equity funds that hold *all industries,* the first of our ABC rules.

The volatility of these funds means they're essentially a gimmick, and not the place for your serious money. Still, they can be fun. Those who enjoy trading can use no-load sector funds as a cheap vehicle for jumping aboard a trend (or what they fondly hope is a trend). And some of the ideas that fund sellers have come up with are impressive: At the end of this section, we talk about some of the weirder sector and specialty funds.

But investors should consider only two types of sector funds:

✦ Resource and precious metals funds may arguably have a place in the portfolios of those who are very worried about inflation.

✦ Technology funds, despite their difficulties in recent years, may be good long-term holdings because at least the companies they own are doing something new (although all too often lately it's dreaming up new ways to entice money out of investors).

Resource funds: Pouring money down a hole

Resource funds invest in companies that are the backbone of Canada's economy: macho, doughnut-eating types that sell oil, forest products, minerals, and basic commodities like aluminum. For complicated reasons to do with oversupply and shifty men meeting in damp hotel rooms in Belgium, the prices for these commodities tend to be extremely volatile, often doubling or falling by half in a matter of months. That means the shares of resource companies are incredibly prone to swings.

Investors in resource companies must get used to living like teenagers in their first week in junior high. One day they're up, everyone loves them and their shares, and profits are rolling in as commodity prices rock. The next day, prices are down and suddenly everyone in the class thinks you're a freak.

Take oil, for example. Periodically since the 1970s — and most spectacularly in the past few years — the producers have been able to get together in one of those Belgian hotel rooms, sip warm beer, and rig prices for a while. Oil company stocks duly rise accordingly. But it's pretty well a mug's game trying to predict when oil booms will come and go, and oil exploration companies have been abysmal at creating long-term wealth for their shareholders. When their shares rise, they tend to flood new share issues into the hot market to grab as much cash from investors as possible while the going is good — sorry, to raise capital for developing new reserves. Eventually, existing shareholders realize that, thanks a lot, they now must give some of the company's profits and dividends to all those scruffy new shareholders. Then oil prices tank again and, presto, oil stocks collapse.

Although natural resource funds have been on a roll since the millennium, if you look farther back in time you'll be reminded of how uneven this market can be. In the second half of the 1990s, resource funds were a rough place to invest, with the average fund in the group posting back-to-back losses in 1997 and 1998, in an era when consecutive yearly losses were still rare.

Resource funds delivered an abysmal annual return of just 3.1 percent during the 1990s. But when tech became long in the tooth, investors began to look elsewhere and turned to natural resources. Many commodity stocks took off — especially in oil and gold, which were lifted by soaring prices for energy and bullion — and resource funds posted strong gains in 1999 and 2000. Their gains cooled somewhat in 2002, but then took off again. As of October 2011, the median natural resource mutual fund had posted a three-year compound annual return of nearly 17 percent.

The rise in precious metals funds, which buy mostly gold miners' stocks, also has been spectacular. The price of gold bullion rose from less than US$260 an ounce in early 2001 to around US$1,800 by fall 2011. Despite a money-losing 2004, the median precious metals mutual fund had a five-year compound annual return of more than 8 percent and a three-year annualized return of 46 percent as of October 2011.

Why has the price of gold shot up? Well, conspiracy theories abound when it comes to precious metals prices (dark mutterings abound of a plot to keep gold down to protect the U.S. dollar), but the simple answer is that gold tends to rise when the world loses confidence in its paper money as a store of value. And the U.S. greenback certainly has had its woes of late, thanks to the credit crisis. Gold is the world's oldest form of money. It soared back in 1980, when investors around the world were scared that geopolitics was spinning out of control (Jimmy Carter had just stumbled through the Iranian hostage situation and the Soviet Union had invaded Afghanistan). Inflation is also great for gold prices because it means paper money is losing its value, which makes timeless and readily portable bullion more valuable. But gold slid during the 1990s, after Communism collapsed and America basked in a low-inflation golden age. The latest rally in gold began as a partial recovery from bullion's slump in the late 1990s — for most of that decade, the yellow metal traded well above US$325 before heading south.

Very conservative investors may wish to put small amounts into a couple of diversified resource funds, perhaps a couple of percent of one's portfolio in each fund, or even a couple of gold funds. That's because resource stocks can act as portfolio insurance — commodity prices move in their own weird cycles, and sometimes in the opposite direction to stocks in general.

Before you rush to buy into resource stocks along with everybody else, or catch the gold bug a little too late, consider a much simpler and somewhat less risky way to invest in these markets: Just buy a Canadian equity fund, large-cap or small. If you do decide to buy resource funds, try to buy two with very different portfolio mixtures of forestry, energy, mining, and other commodities. That way, if one manager crashes and burns, the other might make it. And if you buy into gold funds, make sure you hold at least two, because managers can easily miss out on the very hottest mining stocks that are leading the whole group higher. Remember, with most precious metals funds you now have the choice to be buying mining companies, as well as bullion. There are many new mutual fund, closed fund and ETF investments built around the need for the world's oldest (and some say only) form of money.

Financial services funds: Buying the banks doesn't always pay

Everybody hates the banks — except as investments, it seems. The Canadian financial services sector is dominated by the huge Big Five banks and several mammoth life insurance companies. Indeed, these institutions are almost as big a driver of the Canadian stock market as resource companies. However, most funds in the financial services category invest globally, so you are buying into not just Canadian institutions but U.S. and overseas ones as well. So if you want to buy Canadian financials, stick to the Canadian equity category — which, as we keep preaching, is a better place to be anyway.

Financial services funds have taken a major hit since the financial crisis and many experts are weary of the sector. Because of some big losses since 2008, the median financial services fund produced five- and ten-year compound annual returns of –10.2 percent and –1.2 percent, respectively, as of October 2011 — well below the returns posted by the median Canadian equity fund.

If you insist on focusing on the Canadian financials rather than participating in this sector through a diversified Canadian equity fund, you can buy the iShares S&P/TSX Capped Financials Index ETF. Its five-year compound annual return at October 2011 was flat. You may not have made any money, but you didn't lose 10 percent either.

Understanding Balanced Funds

Balanced funds are for busy people who want a one-decision product they can buy and forget about. (During the 1980s there was even a new fund called the One-Decision Fund if you can believe it!) Imagine your family had a trusted lawyer or accountant who took care of all of your investing needs — the professional, if he or she were at all prudent, would end up putting the money into a judicious blend of bonds and stocks, with a healthy cushion of cash to further reduce risk. That's the essence of a balanced fund — it includes a little bit of everything so that losses can be kept to a minimum if one type of investment falls in value.

Balanced funds, which have been around since the dawn of the fund industry in the 1920s in one form or another, have attracted billions of dollars in recent years as confused investors decide to let someone else pick the right mix for their savings. As of October 2011, more than $335 billion in total assets were in some sort of balanced fund, compared to $273 billion in equity funds. That's a big shift from the start of 2011 when equity funds held

$312 billion of assets versus $307 billion in balanced funds. (These figures courtesy of the Investment Funds Institute of Canada.) Why did balance funds end up outperforming equity funds in 2011? Nervousness. European sovereign debt problems sent people running into safer securities, worried that countries in the region were on the verge of default.

Reviewing the asset mix of balanced funds

For most investors, a balanced fund should be a ready-made cautious investment portfolio. Yes, it might lose money — not much is absolutely safe in investing — but it's unlikely to drop as much as 10 percent in a year (except, of course, when the markets have a massive meltdown). Just check the fund's mix of assets at the fund company's website or in its handouts. If the fund holds plenty of bonds and cash, it's probably safe enough to buy.

Happily, the knowledgeable and practical folks who supervise the classification of Canadian investment funds into various asset categories, the Canadian Investment Funds Standards Committee, several years ago split the unwieldy Canadian balanced and global balanced categories each into three subsets. The following categories help investors immediately identify a fund's asset mix:

✦ **Equity balanced funds** have at least 60 percent of their portfolio in equities.

✦ **Fixed-income balanced funds** have no more than 40 percent of their portfolio in equities.

✦ **Neutral balanced funds** have between 40 and 60 percent of their portfolio in equities.

To keep things simple, in this section we primarily refer to the middle-of-the-road Canadian neutral balanced category.

Remember the old rule that your portfolio's weighting in bonds plus cash should equal your age? If we assume the average Canadian balanced fund has 54 percent in stocks and 46 percent in guaranteed investments like bonds and cash, then most neutral balanced funds are suitable for investors aged about 46. So if you're younger, look for a slightly more aggressive mix in an equity balanced fund, and if you're older, try to find a fixed income balanced fund that appeals to you.

Plodding along profitably

The good news is that Canadian balanced funds have done a pretty good job of avoiding — or at least limiting — losses. In 2002, the last calendar year in which Canadian equity funds lost money, with the median fund falling nearly 13 percent, the median Canadian neutral balanced fund fell about 6 percent. Of course, balanced funds do a decent job of limiting gains, too. As of October 2011, the median Canadian equity fund did nearly twice as well as the median Canadian neutral balanced fund in terms of 10-year compound annual return: 5.7 percent versus 3.8 percent.

In terms of a global balanced fund — a type of fund we really like because it provides as much diversification as possible within a single fund — it's even better. In 2002, the median global equity fund plummeted more than 20 percent while the median global neutral balanced fund fell just 4.4 percent. If you've owned a balance fund over the last few years — during the financial crisis — the annualized returns of your balanced fund have been better than a global equity fund. The five-year compound annual return for the median global neutral balanced fund is 0.8 percent, compared to –3.8 percent for the median global equity fund.

That's not a bad showing considering that many other investments experienced negative five-year annualized returns. But, you may be saying to yourself, "I thought I was losing money in my balanced fund!" That may be right, but double check whether you're in the same fund today as you were a few years ago. The fund industry has a habit of quietly folding underperformers into its stars, cancelling the dogs' years of terrible returns. For example, Fidelity in the mid-1990s took a weak balanced fund and popped it inside its huge Fidelity Canadian Asset Allocation Fund. The old fund's poor returns vanished forever. It's always possible that you'll find yourself stuck in a similar underperformer. To minimize that risk, the best solution of all is to hold two balanced funds so that your entire portfolio doesn't suffer from weakness in one fund. (Morningstar calculates rates of return that overcome this data weakness — known to data geeks and analysts as *survivorship bias* — with its Morningstar fund indices; for more about these indices, see *Mutual Fund Investing For Canadians For Dummies*.)

Don't worry: Despite the broad licence many fund managers have taken in their definition, balanced funds are all about simplicity. Until you make up your mind about your long-term investing plans, you'll almost certainly do fine over three to five years by simply buying a regular balanced fund, or two for more safety, and then forgetting about them.

Retiring with balanced funds

If you really want to adopt a simple approach, use balanced funds in your RRSP — Registered Retirement Savings Plan, a special account in which investment gains add up without being taxed until you take them out, usually at retirement. Balanced funds are a nice cautious mix, just the thing you want for your life savings. Younger investors can be more aggressive, putting nearly all of their money into stocks, but above the age of 35 it's a wise idea to own bonds as well. Nothing is forever. If you decide later that you want something else in your RRSP, maybe because the balanced fund you picked turned out to be a dog, then it should be a simple matter to shift the money to another fund or funds within the same RRSP or to another RRSP account without incurring taxes.

**Book II
Chapter 3**

Surveying Your
Fund Options

So if you just want a simple investment to buy and forget, go for one or two balanced funds. A balanced fund has a single unit value that used to be published daily in the newspapers and on the Internet, making the value of your holdings easy to check. Its return appears in the papers every month and on the Internet every day. And the performance is also published clearly by the fund company, or should be. As with any regular mutual fund, if you've bought a pooch the whole world can see, the fund manager will be under pressure to improve it.

Steering clear of potholes: Consistently strong returns

Balanced fund managers' scaredy-cat caution has served investors well. As stocks slid in the first half of 2002, the average balanced fund escaped with a modest loss of 5.9 percent, less than half as bad as the median Canadian equity fund.

During the last 25 years, the only year in which Canadian equity funds posted a loss that was less severe than that of Canadian neutral balanced funds was in 1994, when the equity funds lost 2.6 percent while the balanced group fell 3.1 percent. But that wasn't really the fault of the balanced fund managers. Interest rates jumped suddenly that year, slashing the value of the bonds they held.

Otherwise, balanced funds have generated nice steady returns, just as they're supposed to. But remember that balanced funds — and all other investors who own bonds — have had a gale at their backs since the early 1990s, because the drop in inflation has made bonds steadily more valuable. (Keep reading for more on bonds.) Then the inflation rate spiked in mid-2008, precipitating a reminder that bonds easily can underperform stocks. The Canadian Consumer Price Index (CPI) doubled to 3.4 percent during the second quarter of 2008. During that period, the median Canadian fixed income fund fell nearly a percentage point, while Canadian equity funds jumped more than 7 percent. Thanks to the sagging bond market, Canadian neutral balanced mutual funds were held to a modest 1.4 percent return during the quarter.

If we move into an era of deflation (that is, falling prices), bonds will almost certainly become increasingly valuable because the value of their steady payouts of cash rises consistently. In that case, which unfortunately could involve a very painful recession, balanced funds could easily outperform stock funds. But whatever happens, the point remains: A balanced fund is a relatively safe spot for your money, leaving you to get on with your life.

Reviewing the Problems with Balanced Funds

Balanced funds, both Canadian and global, have their problems. Their fees and expenses are far too lavish, which scythes into investors' already modest returns. Fund companies have come up with their usual bewildering variety of products and combinations of products, waving magic wands and muttering incantations that invoke the gods of portfolio theory and the "efficient frontier." It may all be true, but one thing's for sure: You're paying for it. All balanced products are basically porridge. Returns from their different investments are mixed together in a gooey mess, so judging exactly how well the manager did on which asset is hard.

High fees and expenses

The costs and fees charged to balanced fund unitholders are just too high. Fund companies already run big equity and bond funds, paying the salaries and expenses of the people who manage them, and they usually get those people to help select the stuff in their balanced funds. How much extra work is involved in that? The bond manager basically just does the same job again with his or her portion of the balanced fund, and the equity manager does the same. Some geezer in a huge black robe and cone-shaped hat decides what the asset mix will be and you're away to the races. The median Canadian neutral balanced fund vacuums up 2 percent of its investors' money each year, almost as bad as the 1.9 percent charged by the average Canadian equity fund.

The long-term annual return from balanced funds may be only about 6 percent, or even less. The long term, incidentally, means the rest of our lives, as economists like to say (it's the only joke they know). So, say inflation and taxes combined take 4 percent out of your annual 6 percent — then your real return is down to around 2 percent. So, for a tax-paying account, most of your real return from a balanced fund like Royal Bank's giant may go into fund expenses and fees.

Bewildering brews of assets

Fund companies know that many of their customers just want simple solutions they can buy and never look at again. So they've come up with a bewildering array of balanced combinations in which you can buy their wares. Many of these arrangements, such as AGF's "Elements" wrap accounts, have their own unit values, making them look very much like mutual funds themselves. By October 2011, nearly 2,000 Canadian and global balanced funds existed, counting different "classes" of fund units as separate funds.

Difficulty judging fund manager performance

A big difficulty with balanced funds, or any kind of casserole that you buy from a fund company, is that you may have a hard time knowing just what the manager did right or wrong. He or she may have blown it in bonds, or struck out in stocks, but you can't work it out from the comfortable-looking (you hope) overall return number that the company publishes. Some fund companies provide a commentary that at least gives you a clue as to what went right and what exploded in the manager's shiny little face. For many customers that's fine, because they couldn't care less what went on inside the fund as long as the return is reasonably good. And that's a perfectly sensible approach to take if you don't have the time or interest to look further into mutual funds. But balanced funds are opaque and mysterious, violating one of the huge virtues of mutual funds — the ability to check on performance easily.

Because checking where balanced funds' profits came from is difficult, picking the right fund is harder than it is to pick funds in other categories. In other words, you won't get a clear answer to this crucial question: How much risk did the manager take? An extreme example of two imaginary funds helps illustrate the point.

Say you're trying to choose between two balanced funds:

✦ The Tasmanian Devil Fund, which made an average 11 percent over the past ten years, enough to turn $10,000 into $28,394

✦ The Mellow Llama Fund, which made 9 percent a year and turned $10,000 into $23,674, or almost $5,000 less than the Tasmanian Devil

What if the Devil Fund made its bigger profits by buying bonds and shares issued by risky little technology companies, whereas the Llama Fund owned shares and bonds from big and stable companies and governments? Most balanced fund investors would choose the second fund, because the danger of it crashing and losing, say, half of its value in a year is so much less.

The Devil Fund, with its volatile but high-profit-potential stocks, may be suitable for an investor who doesn't need the money for years and can afford to take risks now. But it's not the right fund for an investor who may need the money at any time.

A Simple Plan for Picking the Right Canadian Balanced Fund

When selecting a balanced fund, you needn't get all worked up about picking the right one. Like money market and bond funds, many balanced funds resemble one another. They're run cautiously, remember, so you're unlikely to go too far wrong.

Too many investors make one classic mistake that has cost millions of dollars: Failing to think twice before buying a balanced fund run by the people who also manage your stock fund. First, it will almost certainly be skewed toward equities. Second, within the fund's equity section, you'll likely be putting too many eggs in one basket. Naturally, the managers will tend to select the same shares for both funds, and if they get that wrong, then both of your funds will be poor performers.

We frequently refer to the neutral categories in this chapter because we feel these represent the only true, traditional balanced funds — the type that provide the uninspiring but steady performance making these funds so popular and fundamental to the average Canadian investor.

Knowing what to avoid

Be careful with balanced funds that don't include just about every industry in their list of stock holdings. After all, if they are truly "balanced," the balance should extend across industry sectors (and, in the case of bonds, maturity dates). Consider this example from mid-2008, during the financial crisis. The Ivy Growth & Income Fund — which at that time had assets of about $2.3 billion — was very overweight in consumer staples stocks, which took a beating during the first half of that year. ("Overweight" refers to its position relative to that of the benchmark index, the S&P/TSX composite, which had just 2.2 percent of its constituent stocks in the consumer staples group as of mid-2008.) As a result, the fund lost 4 percent during that period, while the median Canadian equity balanced fund slipped 0.4 percent.

Identifying the best funds

Relax: Picking a good-quality Canadian balanced fund is surprisingly easy. Easier, anyway, than getting a cranky, tired child into a snowsuit at 7 a.m. Look for the following:

✦ **A wide asset mix to reduce the fund's risk of loss:** Under the industry's agreed definition, a middle-of-the-road (that is, neutral) balanced fund should have at least 40 percent of its portfolio anchored in cash or bonds or other liquid short-term securities. (*Liquidity* is a measure of how easy it is to sell an investment without suffering a significant loss.)

✦ **Low expenses:** This is important because returns are relatively modest with this type of fund. Try to choose a fund or funds with annual expenses lower than the median 2 percent for Canadian neutral balanced funds.

Global Balanced Funds — As Good as It Gets?

Those who want to chase (possibly) higher returns outside Canada while spreading their wealth over a huge range of investments may want to explore *global balanced funds,* which, like Canadian balanced funds, come in three varieties: equity balanced, neutral balanced, and fixed income balanced. (For definitions of each of those categories, see "Understanding Balanced Funds" in this chapter.)

As always, check the top holdings in the portfolio of a global balanced fund. If they're not mostly stocks and bonds issued by giant companies that you've already heard of, plus bonds from countries such as the United States, Germany, and Japan, then look elsewhere. Why take a risk on low-quality investments?

Like their Canadian counterparts, global balanced funds pull off the trick of buying a bit of everything, but the fact that they do it globally gives you even more diversification and the potential for higher returns.

Insisting on low costs is important with any balanced fund, Canadian or global, because so much of the portfolio is made up of steady-but-dull bonds and cash, and that keeps annual gains down. So if you want to be left with a decent return, you can't pay too much.

The cost of going global

The median global neutral balanced fund hits its investors for 2 percent in expenses each year. That management expense ratio (MER) works out to $100 annually on a $5,000 investment. Some global balanced funds charge well above that, in excess of 3 percent. These include funds with fancy features, such as *segregated funds* — funds that provide guarantees to refund some or all of your original investment after ten years or to pay at least that much to your heirs (those snivelling jellyfish), even if the fund has in fact produced a loss. These guaranteed or "segregated" funds may give you enormous satisfaction in knowing your money is protected. For that reason, thousands of people buy them. But, like the overpriced extended warranty that pushy electronics salespeople try to get you to buy, such guarantees are usually not worth paying for on something as stable as a balanced fund, which rarely loses money.

Few funds of any sort lose money over ten years, and that means the guarantee is of limited value. So to keep costs down and returns up, look for a global balanced fund with an MER lower than the median 2 percent.

Global funds: A near-perfect investment?

If you had to invest money in a single fund for 100 years without ever moving it or looking at it, some kind of global balanced fund with low expenses would make sense. The global balanced fund has finally caught the imagination of Canadian investors, with the number of these funds skyrocketing between mid-2003 and mid-2008. Between 2008 and 2011, total assets in these funds have increased from $90 billion to about $127 billion. The majority of these assets, happily, are in the global neutral balanced category.

Tactical balanced funds: Balanced funds' unruly sibling

Tactical balanced funds, also known as asset allocation funds, are the unruly younger brothers of balanced funds — given the freedom to raise hell by dumping all their bonds or stocks, and to chase hot returns with lopsided portfolios. ("Tactical" simply means that the fund makes short-term bets on moves in the different asset classes every few months. The conventional balanced fund categories, on the other hand, contain funds with *strategic* portfolios, which usually means a manager adheres to a rigid asset-allocation mandate over the years as required by the fund's stated investment mandate.)

These are funds that move between different types of investments and take bigger risks than regular balanced funds, all in an attempt to earn fatter returns. For example, a fund of this type may sell nearly all of its bonds and seek big profits with a portfolio that's made up almost entirely of shares. Or it might even move heavily into a volatile area of the stock market such as technology stocks. The idea is that the manager is smart and lucky enough to anticipate big swings in the prices of financial assets — history shows, though, that very few people can pull off that trick consistently.

Ultimately, these funds basically represent an opportunity to watch someone mess around with your money. That's fine if you trust the company and the warty old wizard or witch mixing up the ingredients in the cauldron, but remember that the less balanced a portfolio, the greater the exposure to loss if the main asset class goes into a slump.

In some ways, the dull old global balanced fund is the perfect mutual fund. Look at the portfolio of any sophisticated, wealthy investor and it'll almost certainly contain stocks all over the world plus bonds, with the safety cushion of a little cash. That's what a global balanced fund provides for the average person. It offers instant access to a professionally chosen mixture of investments that should produce a consistent return on their money while staying clear of market gambles. Nearly every major fund seller sells some sort of global balanced fund, and it's a simple matter of dumping your money in and forgetting about it.

Over the short term — particularly in recent years — relying on a global balanced fund to address all your investing needs might not seem so shrewd. A big risk attached to a global balanced fund, as with any foreign fund, is the possibility that Canada's economy, and with it the loonie, will prosper relative to the United States and other countries. Well, guess what happened during the past few years? Right. A climbing loonie relative to foreign currencies slashed the value of foreign holdings in Canadian-dollar terms, an unpleasant prospect for those who plan to retire in this country. That's why it's almost certainly a good idea to own Canadian assets, too.

Some Great Reasons to Choose Bonds

Almost any sophisticated investor's holdings should include a good leavening of bonds, because betting the whole wad on shares is just too crazy. That's because it bares your entire savings to nasty losses if the stock market turns down. Some fund salespeople and diehard stock market players used to strut and boast that "I've never owned a bond," but they miss out on the advantages bonds offer.

Offering greater security than equities

Although stocks are generally acknowledged to have better long-term performance than bonds, surprisingly, Canadian stocks have an edge of only 1.5 percentage points over domestic bonds over 25 years. The S&P/TSX Composite index's 25-year compound annual return was 8.4 percent as of October 2011, compared with the Morningstar Canadian Fixed Income index's 6.9 percent.

The *DEX Universe Bond index,* which is the main bond benchmark, tracks a combination of investment-grade Canadian bonds, including federal, provincial, municipal, and investment-grade corporate bonds that mature in more than one year. Until 2007, the DEX fixed income indices formerly were known as the Scotia Capital indices. The indices' owner, the Toronto Stock Exchange, changed the name after it began taking fixed income data from multiple dealers, not just Scotia. DEX is a new derivatives exchange being launched by the TSX Group and the International Securities Exchange.

Here's why you must own some bonds or bond funds: Lending your money short-term, by popping it into a bank deposit or account, doesn't pay you enough. Okay, so you can invest most of your money in the stock market, but that's a recipe for losing most of your pile if the market goes into a huge dive. So we all should leave a portion on long-term loan to big, secure governments and companies. And the way to do that is to buy their bonds, which are essentially certificates representing interest-paying loans to the corporations or governments that issued the bonds.

But with inflation and interest rates still with mostly nowhere to go but up (as of fall 2011), bonds may have trouble doing as well in the coming years. If inflation and rates rise, then bond prices will drop, dragging down bond funds.

Sure, equities have always bounced back in the past. But stocks can go into a slump for years, just as they did in the inflation-and-recession-prone 1970s. From February 1966 to August 1982, a stretch of 16 long years, the Dow Jones Industrial Average of blue-chip U.S. stocks fell 22 percent. Yes, America's blue-chip companies paid regular dividends during the period, reducing investors' losses. But it was still a horrible time to be in the market, a depressing and endless era of new lows.

Remember Japan and the way its market hit a euphoric peak in 1989 (just as technology and communication stocks all over the world did in 2000)? Two decades later, the Japanese market is still a volatile, unprofitable place, unless you get extremely lucky playing the dangerous game of market timing.

Or you might lose your job, have legal troubles, or run into some disaster right in the middle of a periodic stock market slump. It would be ugly to be forced to tap into your serious money just after it's been carved up by a stock sell-off. So own some bonds. They serve as a giant, reassuring outrigger for your canoe, producing steady returns while holding their value.

Increasing their value against deflation

Companies and individuals all over the world are getting smarter and more efficient all the time and are producing goods and services at ever-lower prices. Inflation in most wealthy countries fell to less than 2 percent in recent years from double figures in the 1980s. (U.S. and Canadian rates ticked up to around 3 percent in 2011.) While inflation has been on the rise lately, aided in large part by rapidly rising commodities prices, for a while there was genuine concern that we might enter an era of actual falling prices, or *deflation*. If that happened, bonds and cash would be likely to hold their value or even rise in price because the value of money will be rising (*inflation,* the opposite scenario, simply means that money is losing its purchasing power). In other words, deflation is a weird *Through the Looking Glass* world in which cash under the mattress becomes a solid investment that produces a real return.

Does a world of falling prices sound incredible? It's been happening all around us for years in computers, where prices drop and processing power increases every few months. Natural resource prices were in a slump for most of the 1990s as Russia and other poor countries flooded the market in a desperate bid to get U.S. dollars. Granted, an economy-wide slump in prices hasn't happened since the Depression of the 1930s, so nobody knows what it would be like — or what would happen to equity markets. But falling prices squeeze corporate profit margins like a vice, and declining profits are like rat poison for stocks. From September 1929 to July 1932, as the Depression got going, the Dow fell by almost 90 percent. We wish that was a typographical error, but it's not. The Dow dropped to 41 from 381. So own some bonds.

How Much Do I Need in Bonds?

Take the old rule — that your weighting in cash and bonds should equal your age — as a starting point. Sure, leaving a big 40 percent of one's savings in such dull fixed-income stuff will seem pathetically craven to all you racy 40-year-olds out there. So bring it down to 30 percent, or even 25 percent if you insist. But any lower than that and the volatility of your portfolio — a fancy word for the yearly up-and-down changes in the market value of your holdings — starts going off the scale. In other words, if you own only stocks, you're betting a lot of your wealth on swings in just one asset.

The risk of a long-term slump in equities means that if you're in your 20s, it's probably safe to hold one-fifth of your portfolio in bonds; in your 30s, hold one-third or less in fixed income; in your 40s, hold 40 percent in bonds; in your 50s, hold half your dough in cash and bonds; and in your 60s go toward two-thirds of your portfolio in bonds.

Begin with the age rule and then take the cash-plus-bonds weighting up or down depending on your personality.

 If you already have or will have another source of income, such as a company pension fund, then you can afford to be more aggressive with your independent RRSP money because it doesn't represent your only hope. In other words, own more stocks.

Bonds are a guaranteed source of income, a mighty comforting port in the gale if equity markets collapse. If you're a self-employed professional and you definitely have to generate your entire retirement income from your RRSPs and other savings, then the asset mix in your portfolio is of life or death importance for you. You almost certainly already have an accountant helping with your taxes, so get her or him to help you choose the amount of bonds in your portfolio or refer you to another fee-charging professional who's knowledgeable about financial planning (see Chapter 2).

Just about any commission-paid adviser or financial planner will have an off-the-shelf system or software package to help you choose the amount of bonds to hold. Remember, as always, that the results are only as valid as the assumptions the program makes about inflation, interest rates, and the economy. Professional investors routinely get those conditions wrong, so no reason exists why salespeople or their systems should do any better. But just about everybody will tell you to put a portion of your savings into your own bonds or a bond fund.

Picking a Good Bond Fund in 30 Seconds

Selecting a superior bond fund boils down to two simple rules: It should hold plenty of high-quality long-term bonds, and it must have low expenses. And, as always, favour funds with low MERs.

Here's more good news: Own at least two Canadian and two global stock funds, because any equity manager can go into a slump for years. But you'll almost certainly do fine with just one bond fund, as long as it has a low MER and is full of quality bonds. No big fund seller would allow its managers to make weird bets with a mainstream bond fund, such as buying 20-year paper issued by a bankrupt tin mine. The backlash from investors, the media, and possibly even regulators would be too great.

Insisting on affordability

In general, look only at bond funds with MERs of 1 percent or less. Better still examine bond ETFs with even lower MERs. The funds with low expenses will almost all turn out to be no-load products that you buy directly from a bank or direct-selling fund company. That's because fund companies that sell through investment advisers, financial planners, and other advisers have to add on extra charges in order to have something left over to pay the salespeople; expect to pay an extra 0.5 to 0.75 percent annually on most adviser-sold bond funds.

Looking for quality in provincial and federal bonds

Buy a fund with plenty of high-quality, long-term federal government and provincial bonds. A few super-blue-chip company bonds are okay, but remember today's corporate grande-dame could be tomorrow's bag lady. So go easy on the IBMs. If you're a bit nervous that inflation might come back, you want a middle-of-the road solution when it comes to bonds. So just get a bond fund that matches the DEX universe bond index — which pretty well represents the entire Canadian bond market.

If you want a compromise, buy a plain-vanilla bond fund whose average term to maturity is close to the DEX universe index, which includes both short- and long-term bonds. Many fund companies and bond investors use the index as the benchmark with which they compare the performance and holdings of their funds.

Understanding How Inflation Affects Bonds

Although bonds are generally a stable investment, they do have a pair of mortal enemies: rising inflation and his evil henchman, rising interest rates. National banks generally raise interest rates when an economy starts to overheat, or become inflated. Those higher interest rates tend to cool things off. Unfortunately, they also tend to reduce the value of bonds.

Rising interest rates, falling bond prices

A bond falls in value when interest rates rise, because investors are willing to pay less for it. Just think of the same dynamic that happens to house prices when mortgage rates rise. To take a simple example, say you hold an 8 percent bond but interest rates increase so that other comparable investments, with the same term to maturity, are yielding 9 percent. If you try to sell your old 8 percent bond, you'll have to cut the price to get anyone interested. For example, you might have to mark it down to 95 cents per $1 of face value (bonds always mature at face value or "par," which is 100 cents on the dollar). When you offer the bond at 5 percent off, the buyer of your cut-price bond will get the regular 8 percent interest payment but they'll also make an extra kick because they've bought it at the 5 percent discount. When the bond matures at its full face value of $1 per $1 face value, that'll be enough to bring its yield to maturity up to 9 percent.

In 1999, interest rates increased sharply, mainly because the U.S. Federal Reserve was worried about inflation, and rising interest rates always reduce the market value of bonds that are out in the hands of investors. Bond funds were thus obliged to mark down the value of their holdings accordingly. That year, Canadian bond funds produced a modest average loss of 2.5 percent.

Rising inflation makes bondholders and other lenders very, very afraid because they become petrified of seeing the real value of their money wither away. So they demand higher interest rates and bond yields. That means they refuse to buy bonds without getting big discounts, so bond prices fall and you'll make less money on your bond funds.

Falling interest rates, rising bond prices

When interest rates fall, as they've been doing pretty well without a break since the early 1980s, the picture looks brighter for bonds. If rates in the market drop to 7 percent, then your 8 percent bond becomes a hotcake and investors will be willing to buy it from you at a premium. Same as rising house prices when mortgage rates fall.

Interest rates fall when inflation drops because lenders become confident that their money won't lose its value too fast while it's in the hands of the borrowers. So they're prepared to accept lower interest rates. About the only thing that's likely to send bond prices sharply higher in coming years, giving bond funds more good times, will be an era of falling prices or at least growing confidence among investors that inflation is dead for the foreseeable future. In that case, bond buyers are likely to bid bonds up even higher.

Lower inflation makes bond buyers and other lenders feel more comfortable about tying up their money for years, so they'll accept lower interest rates and bond yields. Lower rates and yields mean higher bond prices, which mean extra profits for your bond funds.

The bottom line, though, is that predicting changes in interest rates is a futile exercise akin to forecasting the weather. Just buy a good bond fund and view it as an insurance policy for your entire savings.

Buying the Whole Enchilada: The Ups and Downs of Index Funds

One of the most effective and profitable investing techniques to emerge in recent years is also a huge idea. It's *indexing:* buying a little of every single significant stock or bond in the market and just holding it, as opposed to trying to pick which one will go up and which will go down. The name comes from the fact that portfolios managed using this method aim to track a given market index or benchmark. To do that, they buy each stock or bond in the index. For example, a fund designed to follow the S&P/TSX Composite Index will buy all (or virtually all) of the shares in Canada's main stock index. Mutual funds that use the technique are called *index funds*.

The whole idea behind index and exchange-traded funds — giving up on trying to pick the best stocks and just betting on the whole market — runs counter to human nature, of course. We all want to believe in the hero fund manager, the Druid who can peer into the entrails of the market and decide which stocks will thrive. So the fund companies run huge ads and the news media produce fawning stories about how wonderfully perceptive and percipient these stock wizards are. But it's a myth: Managers who can be relied on to beat the market over many years are as rare as vegetarian leopards. And even if they do exist, determining in advance which ones will succeed is essentially impossible.

Exploring why index funds and ETFs are great for you

People who invest in index funds or ETFs are often passionate about their chosen vehicle, and will loudly espouse their many virtues.

They outperform most actively managed funds

Because few managers fail to beat the market over many years, index funds are an excellent way to go for ordinary investors. With an index or exchange-traded fund, you don't have to worry whether you made the right choice of manager, because all the fund tries to do is match the market. It doesn't buy and sell stocks or bonds in pursuit of profits, but simply buys the shares or bonds that make up a particular index and holds them while they are members of the index club where they belong. Just like Groucho Marx, some shares do get kicked out of their index club if they get too small or they misbehave. Think Nortel. A computer could run the thing. These funds make stock-picking expertise irrelevant. That's great for busy people who don't have the time or knowledge to check a manager's credentials and find out whether his or her track record was achieved through luck or skill.

Making money in the stock market is a gamble. But it's a casino in which your long-term chances are excellent, because good companies grow their profits and share prices over the years. And you improve your odds even more by simply buying an index fund that tracks the whole market — because these big suckers, the successful companies like financial combine harvester Power Corp. of Canada or network empire Cisco Systems, actually *become* the whole market. And it's good to know that with an index fund, you own them.

They're low-cost

Index and exchange-traded funds have another shining virtue: They're cheap for an investor to own. No research is involved in just buying every stock in the market (although to hear some index funds types pontificate, you'd think it was the hardest thing in the world), so most index funds in Canada have a management expense ratio, or MER, of 1 percent or less. In other words, if you have $10,000 sitting in an index fund, you can expect to pay less than $100 (that is, 1 percent of your money) in fees and costs each year. If an index fund's MER is any higher than 1 percent, the concept starts to unravel, because it runs the risk of failing to keep up with the index that gives it its name.

Even cheaper are *exchange-traded funds* (ETFs), which are virtually the same as an index mutual fund except they're traded on a stock exchange rather than bought from and redeemed with a fund company. MERs range from a negligible 0.09 percent for iShares S&P 500 Fund to 0.65 percent for Claymore Financial Monthly Income Fund. Some cost more, but most of the ones you'll want to buy are in that range. We talk more about ETFs in the next section.

Normal non-index mutual funds — which do try to select particular stocks and bonds in an effort to turn a profit — are known as *actively managed funds.* They're far more expensive to own. The MER of the median Canadian equity mutual fund (active and passive funds included) is about 2 percent, which means the typical actively managed fund rakes off considerably more in fees and costs than an index fund. And that extra 1 percentage point is a lot — over 20 years, it adds up to nearly one-third of your money.

They're great for taxable accounts

Index funds expose you to very little in taxation until you cash them in, making them a great way to defer taxation.

Nearly all mutual funds pay *distributions* to their unitholders — cash payments that most people choose to take in the form of more units of the fund (so the investment continues to compound and grow). Funds make the distributions when they have trading profits or interest (and dividend) income that the manager wants to pay out to the fund's investors.

Say you hold 1,000 units of a fund at the end of the year and the unit value is $10, for a total investment of $10,000. The fund manager generated $1 of trading profits per unit during the year and pays this out to the unitholders. The value of each unit drops by $1, reflecting the payment that has been made. You now hold your original 1,000 units, which are worth $9 each, for a total of $9,000. But you've also received $1,000 in the distribution, which you can take in cash or new units, bringing you back to $10,000.

No matter how you receive the units, though, you're liable for tax on the distribution, just as if you had earned it trading stocks on your own. Some funds whose managers trade a lot can make very large distributions. Note, though, that getting distributions isn't a problem if you hold the fund in a tax-deferred account such as an RRSP, which lets you delay paying taxes on the money you earn within the account.

Index funds just buy and hold the stocks in the index and they do very little trading. So they tend to pay out very little in the way of distributions. That makes them especially suitable for *taxable* accounts — money that isn't held in an RRSP or other tax-deferred account.

Delving into the dark side of index funds and ETFs

No magic bullet exists in investing, and index and exchange-traded funds carry their own dangers. The big hazard is that the stock market indexes themselves — those seemingly logical benchmarks that these funds follow — often become dominated by just a few high-priced companies. In turn, that means the funds that track those benchmarks become risky investments because they're tied to the fortunes of just a few companies.

In recent years, stock market indexes have been dominated by high-priced growth stocks such as Nortel Networks Corp. or General Electric Corp. that left the rest of the market behind for a short while. *Growth stocks* are companies whose sales and profits are expanding rapidly. If investors decide that the companies can go on increasing their revenues and earnings for years, then they'll bid the shares up to high prices. But any sign of a slowdown in a company's growth is likely to make its stock price drop like a rock.

At one point Nortel represented more than 30 percent of the S&P/TSX Composite index. That meant an investor in an S&P/TSX index or exchange-traded fund had one-third of his or her portfolio in a single stock — a very risky bet. The same was true, to a lesser extent, of the U.S. market, where a handful of companies such as GE made up a huge chunk of the market. So index and exchange-traded funds inevitably had a huge proportion of their assets in a few soaring giant companies. Many of the index funds, in other words, had turned into high-risk, high-priced investments as opposed to cautious mirrors of the whole market. Then came the tumble. Of course, the potential nightmare that a dominant stock might crash came true, as Nortel's share price collapsed. GE's shares also plummeted.

So, did index funds and ETFs crash and burn compared with regular funds? The short answer is that they often got whacked harder as growth stocks dropped, but their medium-term returns were still respectable. More important, the Nortel debacle prompted the Toronto Stock Exchange, in 2001, to produce *capped indexes,* which limit the impact of any one stock on an index by restricting a stock's percentage position in an index to 10 percent. One-fifth of a portfolio is not as dominant as one-third, true, but it's still quite a bit. So — no matter how good they may sound — don't put all your stock market money into one index fund or ETF. If the handful of giant stocks that dominate an index turn downward suddenly, your portfolio will take a beating. The Toronto Stock Exchange also contracted out the design and maintenance of their own Composite Index to Standard & Poors.

The essence of wise investing is spreading your risk among a wide variety of holdings. Of the money you've set aside for equity funds, at most two-thirds should be in pure index funds or ETFs.

Buying Index Funds and ETFs

Even though index funds supposedly simplify the experience of buying mutual funds, enabling you to skirt selecting the best fund manager, you do have some decisions to make. Which index should you follow? Should you buy an index fund or an ETF? And where should you buy? Read this section, and all will be revealed.

Selecting the right index

The problem of which index an index fund should use is thorny and difficult. On the one hand, if you start guessing which index is the best one to match, then you're getting close to picking stocks again, and this is the antithesis of passive investing. On the other hand, if you just let things go and blindly match a narrow index such as the S&P/TSX 60, which includes only sixty Canadian stocks with very large market capitalizations, or one that's ruled by a few high-fliers, then your index fund has arguably become an aggressive and volatile fund. However, this problem doesn't have a simple answer: Just follow the advice in this book and keep index funds to a maximum of two-thirds of your equity funds. That way, if the big stocks in the index turn out to be bubbles that burst painfully, a good chunk of your money will be in regular funds as well.

In the U.S. market, the safest policy would be to buy a super-broad index fund, one that tracks the huge Dow Jones Wilshire 5000 Total Market Index, which contains just about every stock in America that's worth buying. CIBC's U.S. index fund tracks the Wilshire, so it would be a good choice. But it seems pretty certain that the better-known S&P 500, which is dominated by fewer and larger companies, will remain the main yardstick for the U.S. market for years to come. U.S. equity index funds are as cheap as Canadian ones, for the most part.

Most global equity index funds track the venerable MSCI World Index, while international equity index funds track the MSCI Europe Australasia Far East (EAFE) Index. You'd expect index funds based on overseas indices to have higher MERs than their North American counterparts, but some in fact have very low MERs, such as TD's offerings.

Choosing between index funds and ETFs

At one time, ETFs were favoured by investors who wanted to work with an investment adviser and who tended to have larger portfolios. But today, both index funds and ETFs are for the do-it-yourselfers. Because advisers generally don't make big commissions on these products, many aren't keen to sell them. That is changing. ETFs and index funds should be considered for a portfolio, so make sure your adviser is open to including them. One advantage to ETFs is that they are bought and sold like stocks, so you can get in and out of them a little faster than index funds. But be careful: commissions are payable on each transaction, so they may be less suited than index funds to smaller investors who are building a portfolio and like to make frequent purchases. Don't forget all commissions are usually negotiable, so negotiate. But that's changing, too. In September 2011 Scotia iTrade allowed people to trade 46 ETFs commission free. Qtrade soon followed. When Charles Schwab in the U.S. began offering no-commission ETFs, nearly all other American financial institutions followed — whether they liked it or not. So expect other Canadian banks to offer no-commission ETFs too. The most significant difference between index funds and ETFs, of course, is the latter have lower MERs.

Knowing where to buy

If you want to buy an index fund with a truly low MER, you'll have to go to the banks. (They are also sold by life insurance companies in the segregated fund format, although many of these charge sales fees and, being seg funds, have higher MERs. We talk more about seg funds earlier in the chapter.) Banks sell index funds on a no-load basis directly to the public. Every discount broker should carry at least one family of index funds, with no hassles.

ETFs are available only from investment dealers that are members of the stock exchange on which a particular ETF is listed, but every discount brokerage allows you to buy and sell them. Although their MERs are extremely low, as exchange-traded securities you must pay to buy and sell them. (Again, that may be changing.) Many advisers who do sell ETFs include these transaction costs in a negotiated annual advisory fee based on the value of the investor's assets under administration.

If you're with a financial planner or adviser who doesn't offer index funds or ETFs, nothing's stopping you from opening a separate index fund account at a bank and holding the rest of your money with your adviser. Each of the big bank-owned discount brokers has index funds available, usually from the bank that owns the firm. The simplicity and relatively clear account statements offered by discount brokers as well as investment dealers make them perfect for holding index funds, especially if you can avoid the fees that some discounters impose for buying and selling other companies' no-load funds. If the discounter is bank-owned, then the bank's own index funds will be free of fees.

What Are Dividend and Income Funds?

When a public company earns a profit, it can do only three things with the money: reinvest it in the business or pay all or part of it out as *dividends,* actual cash paid to those who hold shares in the company. That's true for every public company. Traditionally, established blue-chip corporations have lined their shareholders' pockets over the years by regularly paying a nice increasing annual dividend.

We have some good news for you if you buy into a large blue-chip company. The other shareholders include big and assertive professional investors, horse-faced people with loud voices who usually keep management focused. So if you hold shares in big businesses, you can usually be sure the companies' managers and directors are under at least some pressure to look out for the interests of you and the other shareholders. By contrast, if you invest in small companies, they may not be big enough to attract professional investors, so management might find it easier to neglect shareholders' interests.

Many mutual fund companies sell conservative dividend and income funds that simply buy shares in a bunch of blue-chip mega-companies such as BCE Inc. or Royal Bank of Canada and then pass the dividends they collect straight through to their unitholders. This is investing in dividend funds at its very best — clean and simple.

Looking at the upside of dividend funds

Many big dividend and income funds perform well, producing a stream of ready cash for their investors. In other words, they collect the dividends from big companies and pay them out to you. Best of all, the money normally comes from the fund to you as a dividend payment that's lightly taxed (more on that under "The Appealing Tax Implications of Dividends").

Considering the downside

Sounds great so far, doesn't it? You're probably wondering why we're so cranky about dividend and income funds. The problem is that sometimes their complexity and lack of transparency (always a bad sign in the world of investing) make them next to impossible to wrap your brain around. In theory they're great; in action they can be horribly confusing.

It can be hard to tell whether a fund will actually pay you very much in the way of dividends, whether the distributions will actually be dividends or interest income, and whether the manager is really seeking dividend income or is in fact chasing stocks that will go up. But don't worry, in this section we show you a simple way to figure out what the flow of dividends from a dividend and income fund is likely to be — just look at the fund's main holdings and they'll tip you off as to what sort of job the fund will do for you.

Some dividend and income funds boost their flow of monthly payments to unitholders by holding riskier assets. That'll increase the payments you get from the fund — but the stream of payments these investments dish out to the fund (and ultimately to you) could get cut drastically when business conditions turn down.

No matter how attractive those dividends might sound, over time there seems to be no substitute for good old capital gains. (*Capital gains* are trading profits a fund earns by buying assets at a low price and selling them at a better price.)

Figuring out why companies pay, or don't pay, dividends

Companies pay dividends to their shareholders because that's one way the owners of the business are rewarded. A large and well-established business, such as a bank, usually throws off enough profits each year to cover the cost of acquiring new equipment and other assets and still has money left over to pay out as dividends. But some companies — particularly fast-growing technology outfits with huge needs for cash to research and develop new products — don't earn enough cash each year to come up with a dividend. They offer such good prospects for growth in sales and future profits over the medium to long term, however, that investors are happy to buy their shares even though little chance exists of getting a dividend for several years.

Slow-growing companies

Traditionally, boring businesses whose earnings grow slowly have had to pay out up to half of their profits each year in dividends in order to keep investors interested in their shares. Traditionally this has meant shares of one of the big five banks or utilities, such as pipeline operator TransCanada Corp., which as of early 2012 paid a healthy dividend of $1.68 a share. That works out to a fat annual dividend yield of 4.1 percent. In other words, TransCanada's common shares traded at around $41 in late 2011 and the annual dividend per share was $1.68; $1.68 represents 4.1 percent of $41, so the annual yield was 4.1 percent.

Banks are able to increase their profits faster than utilities, partly because they're expanding in profitable areas such as mutual funds. But banks are such big companies already they can't increase their profits as fast as, say, a software company can. So they occupy a sort of middle ground, made up of companies that are likely to increase their earnings at a respectable but not feverish pace in coming years. Banks also pay out a relatively large proportion of their profits as dividends to shareholders. As of October 2011, most big bank stocks yielded between 4 and 6 percent. That might not sound generous, but it wasn't bad when you consider the stocks in the broad S&P/TSX Composite Index as a whole yielded just 2.78 percent.

Blue-chip companies are sometimes forced to cut their dividends when their profits fall unexpectedly. TransCanada did so, to great consternation and dismay among investors, at the end of 1999. Happily for its investors, the company has been raising its dividend ever since. And, for that matter, dividend cuts by established companies are rare because shareholders hate such reductions. They hate 'em like poison. Managers are unlikely to establish an annual dividend rate in the first place, if they know they'll have to take the humiliating step of reducing it. A portfolio that holds at least half a dozen blue-chip stocks — such as the typical dividend and income fund — will spread your risk, reducing the pain if one of them slashes a dividend.

Growth companies

So-called growth companies, whose profits are expected to increase rapidly, can get away with paying little or nothing in dividends, and investors still tend to throw their hat — and their cash — into the ring by buying the companies' shares. Investors are willing to forgo gratification today so the company can use the cash to build its business instead. The idea is that the share price will rise and when the dividends do eventually come, they'll be bigger than if the company had paid out the cash to shareholders earlier in the game.

When the stock market bull is raging, dividend yield is the farthest thing from an investor's mind. In the techno-frenzy of the late 1990s and in 2000, you hardly heard a murmur about dividends. Dude, who cared? Don't-Care was made to care, in this case, as the Canadian stock market tumbled nearly 20 percent in 2001 and 2002. But the median dividend and income fund, typically with a heavy larding of stable stocks that pay dividends, managed to break even during that two-year period.

Hold at least some conservative dividend-paying stocks, even within an RRSP. Because as the popping of the tech stock balloon showed, it's nice to own something that doesn't depend on a weedy teenage software genius staying conscious. But don't worry. You don't have to take special vitamin pills if your diet is rich and varied, including plenty of herrings' backsides. And, by analogy, you don't need to worry about buying a special dividend fund if your portfolio includes some high-quality equity funds. Those funds are bound to hold several dividend-type stocks — and that covers your daily requirement.

Those seemingly insignificant little quarterly dividend cheques are what capitalism and the stock market are all about. Under the law — in the Anglo-Saxon world, at least (and elsewhere, more and more, as the whole world becomes obsessed with investing in stocks *à l'américaine*) — dividends are about the only way that shareholders can legally get any money out of their company. Yes, they get a payoff if the company is taken over at a fat price or if they sell the shares after they've gone up or if the company "spins off" an asset to its shareholders in the form of a special restructuring. But receiving a dividend remains the only fundamental way in which you can actually extract cash from a business (apart from when an executive receives a bloated salary or options package). It's the thing that ultimately gives a share much of its value.

What does this all mean to the mutual fund investor? Just that it's fine to engage in torrid flirtation with a natural resources fund or aggressive growth fund, but limit it to a dalliance using just a tiny part of your money. Your core equity funds should also hold plenty of blue-chip stocks that pay a meaningful and rising dividend. Because when a market crash comes — and they always do — they're the shares that are most likely to fall the least and recover first.

Determining Whether Dividend and Income Funds Are Right for You

A dividend or income fund will suit you best if you meet one or more of the following tests:

✦ **You're a long-termer but you need cash now:** You need the long-term growth prospects offered by shares, but you also need to make regular withdrawals from your portfolio of investments. Many dividend funds are designed to accumulate a steady stream of cash, which they pay out regularly.

✦ **You're in a high tax bracket:** You face a high rate of tax on the income and profits earned by your investments. That might be because you already have a high income or because your investments are held in a taxable account, not a tax-deferred plan such as an RRSP. Remember that Canadian dividends are lightly taxed in the hands of Canadian tax-payers, which makes them a great way to earn investment income for a taxable investor. That means the payments you get from a dividend fund won't be too badly savaged by the government.

✦ **You're not a risk taker:** You're nervous about the stock market and you feel happiest with a stock fund full of conservatively run large companies, the sort that pay lots of dividends.

✦ **You want to grow your assets faster:** Many investors simply reinvest their dividends. That means, with every payout the person buys more units in the fund. It's a good way to grow a portfolio without adding any more of your own money. You own a bigger piece of what you hope is a growing pie.

But dividend funds aren't right for everyone, especially people who don't care if their investments pay out a regular income. Why bother with collecting dividends if it compromises your long-term returns?

If your aim is to build your money over many years, then you'll probably do better in a regular stock fund that's free to buy shares in all sorts of companies, including those that pay hardly anything in dividends. That way, you'll own a balanced mixture of shares that also includes some high-flying technology players and natural resource producers, and not just a portfolio of blue-chip, conservative names.

The Appealing Tax Implications of Dividends

Dividend and income funds — assuming they are among the vast majority that hold mostly dividend-paying stocks — get special treatment when it comes to taxes. They can be one of the best ways of earning a stream of income that doesn't get too badly mutilated by the tax collector. To encourage Canadians to buy shares issued by Canadian corporations (to help the economy grow), dividends are taxed far more lightly than *interest income,* which is the sort of fixed payment you get from a bank account, bond, or fixed-term deposit such as a guaranteed investment certificate (GIC).

Crunching the numbers

As a quick-and-dirty rule, each $1 of dividend income is as good as $1.25 of interest income because the taxes on the interest-income dollar are so much higher. Interest income is fully taxed just like your salary. If you earn $125 in interest and only $100 in dividends, you'll end up with about the same amount after taxes. Dividends are *tax-efficient* or *tax-advantaged* sources of income, because this type of investment actually helps you keep more of your hard-earned income.

You'll know whether any mutual fund you own has paid you distributions in the form of capital gains, dividends, or interest because it'll be indicated on the T3 or T5 statement of investment income you get from your fund company each year to report on your tax return. The calculation for reporting dividends on your tax form is a little laborious and weird, but you soon get used to it (amazing how the prospect of putting more money in one's pocket tends to fire up the old synapses). Essentially the principle is this: You "gross up" the amount of dividends received by increasing them by 25 percent and you report that amount on your tax form. But you then reduce your tax payable by a "tax credit" amounting to 17.72 percent of the dividends actually received. (This is for people in the highest tax bracket. The rate is lower if you report less income.) Don't fret: The tax form provides a step-by-step guide.

Understanding why dividend funds may or may not be good for your RRSP

Fund salespeople have long preached that collecting dividends within a tax-sheltered account such as a registered retirement savings plan isn't that important. That's for two reasons:

✦ All the income earned inside such a plan is tax-deferred anyway. And all withdrawals from the plan are heavily taxed as regular income. That means the dividend tax break is no use within an RRSP, so dividend funds — which are designed to take advantage of the tax law — arguably aren't a good fit.

✦ For your core equity funds in an RRSP, it may be better to buy normal equity funds rather than dividend funds because the managers of regular funds have a freer hand to play the market, rather than trying to maximize their dividend income.

If you have a choice to keep Canadian dividend paying investments outside of a deferred tax plan, that's a good idea. If you don't have a choice, it's usually still a good idea. It's a game of square pegs in round holes.

But because many dividend and income funds hold big familiar companies, they can logically be treated as super-conservative equity funds that are well suited for RRSPs. Remember the 2001–2002 experience, when dividend and income funds outperformed general Canadian equity funds. The bottom line seems to be this: Check the holdings of a dividend fund, and if it's full of regular shares in big companies — as opposed to things like income trusts or other investments that are designed to throw off regular streams of cash — then it can probably be treated as a conservative equity fund.

An instant dividend-paying portfolio

Index funds are one of our favourite ways to invest. And no better way to do so exists than through an exchange-traded fund (ETF). An ETF is a fund that is traded on a stock exchange — as opposed to being sold and redeemed directly by mutual fund companies. Of greater interest is the fact that its portfolio is based on a stock index, such as the S&P/TSX Composite Index.

The ETF market has expanded rapidly in recent years to include funds that are based on some of the Toronto Stock Exchange's specific industry groups. One fund provides an instant portfolio of blue-chip TSX dividend-paying stocks.

The iShares Dow Jones Canada Select Dividend Index Fund holds 30 of the highest yielding dividend-paying companies in the Dow Jones Canada Total Market Index. Analysts at Dow Jones look at companies' dividend growth, yield, and average payout ratio to determine which stocks make the fund's portfolio. Its three biggest holdings in December 2011 were Canadian Imperial Bank of Commerce, Bonterra Energy Corp., and Bank of Montreal.

Like most ETFs, Dow Select Dividend's MER is low, low, low — 0.55 percent, compared with 2.19 percent for the median Canadian dividend and income fund. Even better, its performance beat the median fund in the category. As of October 2011 it had a three-year compound annual return of 10.4 percent, 1.7 percentage points ahead of the median fund.

Selecting a Winning Dividend Fund

Don't just grab the first dividend and income fund you're offered. Make sure the fund you buy comes with a reasonable management expense ratio — certainly less than the category's 2.19 percent median value. Ensure its largest holdings include the sort of shares and trust units you want to own: high-quality stocks or units of companies in sectors that are known to provide reliable dividends and other income.

Put these questions to your salesperson, no-load fund company, or bank employee. If you can't get a straight answer, then consider shopping elsewhere:

✦ What distributions has this fund paid over the past year, and how frequently?

✦ Is there a stated monthly distribution, and how much is it?

✦ Which distributions over the past year counted as dividends from taxable Canadian corporations, entitling the fund's investors to claim the dividend tax credit?

✦ Did any of the distributions include a *return of capital* — a partial refund of the investor's own money — to maintain a stated payout rate? Such returns of capital can be not only potentially misleading, but also horrendous to account for at tax time.

You can find this information easily in a fund's management report of fund performance, or MRFP, which should be available as a download from the fund company's website. The information will be only as current as the most recent MRFP, but because these reports come out every six months that should be current enough to give you a good idea of what you might expect in the way of distribution types and amounts.

Book III

The Skinny on Stocks

The 5th Wave   By Rich Tennant

"Sell."

Contents at a Glance

Chapter 1: Building Wealth through Investing in Stocks

In This Chapter

✔ Knowing the essentials

✔ Doing your own research

✔ Determining your investment style

✔ Reviewing risks versus rewards

You can find plenty of safe places to put your money. All will help build your wealth, but if you really want to grow your nest egg you'll need to invest in something a bit riskier, such as stocks. The next three chapters help you determine which stocks to buy and give you some solid strategies that can help you profit from the market.

Stocks are tools you can use to build your wealth. When used wisely, for the right purpose, and in the right environment, they do a great job. But when improperly applied, they can lead to disaster. In this chapter, we show you how to choose the right types of investments based on your short- and long-term financial goals. We also show you how to decide on your purpose for investing (growth or income investing) and your style of investing (conservative or aggressive).

Understanding the Basics of Stocks

The basics are so basic that few people pay much attention to them. Perhaps the most basic — and therefore most important — thing to grasp is the risk you face whenever you do anything like putting your hard-earned money in an investment like a stock. When you lose track of the basics, you lose track of why you invested to begin with.

When the late comedian Henny Youngman was asked "How is your wife?" he responded, "Compared to what?" This also applies to stocks. When you're asked, "How is your stock?" you can very well respond that it's doing all right, especially when compared to an acceptable yardstick such as a stock index (like the Canadian S&P/TSX Composite Index, or the American S&P 500).

The bottom line in stock investing is that you shouldn't immediately send your money to a brokerage account or go to a website and click "buy stock." The first thing you should do is find out as much as you can about what stocks are, and how and when to use them to achieve your wealth-building goals.

Now is the time to get straight exactly what a stock is. A *stock* (also known as a share) is a type of security that indicates ownership in a corporation and represents a claim on part of that corporation's assets and earnings. The two primary types of stocks are common and preferred. *Common stock* entitles the owner to vote at shareholders' meetings and receive any dividends the company issues. *Preferred shares* don't usually confer voting rights, but it does include some rights that exceed those of common stock. Preferred shareholders, for example, have priority in certain conditions, such as receiving dividends before common stockholders while the corporation is healthy.

Knowing How to Pick Winners

When you get past the basics, you can get to the meat of stock picking. Successful stock picking isn't mysterious, but it does take some time, effort, and analysis. And the effort is worthwhile, because stocks are a convenient and important part of most investors' portfolios.

Recognizing stock value

Imagine that you are buying eggs at the grocery store. In this example, the eggs are like companies, and the prices represent the prices you would pay for the companies' stock. The grocery store is the stock market. What if two brands of eggs are similar, but one costs 50 cents a carton and the other costs 75 cents? Which would you choose? Odds are you'd look at both brands, judge their quality, and — if they're indeed similar — take the cheaper eggs. The eggs at 75 cents are overpriced. The same is true of stocks. What if you compare two companies that are similar in every respect but have different share prices? All things being equal, the cheaper price has greater value for the investor.

But the egg example has another side. What if the quality of the two brands of eggs is significantly different, but their prices are the same? If one brand of eggs is stale, of poor quality, and priced at 50 cents and the other brand is fresh, of superior quality, and also priced at 50 cents, which would you get? We'd take the good brand because they're better eggs. Perhaps the lesser eggs are an acceptable purchase at 10 cents, but they're definitely overpriced at 50 cents. The same example works with stocks. A poorly run company isn't a good choice if you can buy a better company in the marketplace at the same — or a better — price.

Understanding how market capitalization affects stock value

You can determine a company's value (and thus the value of its stock) in many ways. The most basic way is to look at the company's market value, also known as *market capitalization* (or market cap). Market capitalization is simply the value you get when you multiply all the outstanding shares by the current price of a single share.

Calculating the market cap is easy. If a company has 1 million shares outstanding and its share price is $10, the market cap is $10 million.

Small cap, mid cap, and large cap aren't references to headgear; they're references to how large a company is as measured by its market value. The five basic stock categories of market capitalization are:

✦ **Micro cap (under $250 million):** These stocks are the smallest and hence the riskiest available. The A&W Income Fund is a micro cap example.

✦ **Small cap ($250 million to $1 billion):** These stocks fare better than the micro caps and still have plenty of growth potential. The key word here is "potential." Molson Coors and The Brick are considered small cap companies.

✦ **Mid cap ($1 billion to $10 billion):** For many investors, this category offers a good compromise between small caps and large caps. These stocks have some of the safety of large caps while retaining some of the growth potential of small caps. Canadian mid cap examples include Tim Hortons, Canadian Tire, and Shoppers Drug Mart.

✦ **Large cap ($10 billion to $50 billion):** This category is usually best reserved for conservative stock investors who want steady appreciation with greater safety. Stocks in this category are frequently referred to as *blue chips*. Goldcorp, Potash Corp, and Canadian National Railway all fit this market cap size bracket.

✦ **Ultra cap (over $50 billion):** These stocks are also called *mega caps* and obviously refer to companies that are the biggest of the big. Canadian stocks such as Royal Bank, TD Bank, Bank of Nova Scotia, Suncor Energy, and Barrick Gold are all examples.

From a safety point of view, a company's size and market value do matter. All things being equal, large-cap stocks are considered safer than small-cap stocks. That's because larger companies generally have better operational controls than smaller ones, so their risks are more mitigated. However, small-cap stocks have greater potential for growth. These tend to be leaner, meaner, and more responsive to market and customer needs. They often exploit opportunities more quickly.

Book III Chapter 1

Building Wealth through Investing in Stocks

Although market capitalization is important to consider, don't invest (or not invest) based solely on it. It's just one measure of value. As a serious investor, you need to look at numerous factors that can help you determine whether any given stock is a good investment.

Matching Stocks and Strategies with Your Goals

Various stocks are out there, and so are various investment approaches. The key to success in the stock market is matching the right kind of stock with the right kind of investment situation. You have to choose both the stock and the approach that match your goals.

Before investing in a stock, ask yourself, "When do I want to reach my financial goal?" Stocks are a means to an end. Your job is to figure out what that end is — or, more important, *when* it is. Do you want to retire in ten years or next year? Must you pay for your kid's university education next year or 18 years from now? The length of time you have before you need the money you hope to earn from stock investing determines what stocks you buy. Table 1–1 gives some guidelines for choosing the kind of stock that's best suited to the type of investor you are and the goals you have.

Table 1–1   Investor Types, Financial Goals, and Stock Types

Type of Investor	Time Frame for Financial Goals	Type of Stock Most Suitable
Conservative (worries about risk)	Long-term (over 5 years)	Large-cap stocks and mid-cap stocks
Aggressive (high tolerance to risk)	Long-term (over 5 years)	Small-cap stocks and mid-cap stocks
Conservative (worries about risk)	Intermediate-term (2 to 5 years)	Large-cap stocks, preferably with dividends
Aggressive (high tolerance to risk)	Intermediate-term (2 to 5 years)	Small-cap stocks and mid-cap stocks
Occasional	Short-term (2 years or less)	Stocks are typically not suitable for fulfilling short-term goals. Instead, look at vehicles such as savings accounts and money market funds.

Stock market insanity

Have you ever noticed a stock going up even though the company is reporting terrible results? How about seeing a stock nosedive despite the fact that the company is doing well? What gives? Well, judging the direction of a stock in a short-term period — over the next few days or weeks — is almost impossible.

Yes, in the short term, stock investing is irrational. The price of a stock and the value of its company seem disconnected and crazy. The key phrase to remember is "short term." A stock's price and the company's value become more logical over an extended period of time. The longer a stock is in the public's view, the more rational the performance of the stock's price. In other words, a good company continues to draw attention to itself; hence, more people want its stock, and the share price rises to better match the company's value. Conversely, a bad company doesn't hold up to continued scrutiny over time. As more and more people see that the company isn't doing well, the share price declines. Over the long run, a stock's share price and the company's value eventually become equal for the most part. (Some people do make money off of short-term stock movements. But these folks are usually considered traders rather than investors. You can find out more about short-term — or active — trading in Books 4 and 5.)

Dividends are payments made to an owner (unlike interest, which is payments to a creditor or bondholder). Dividends are a great source of income, and companies that issue dividends tend to have more stable stock prices as well.

Investing by Time Frame

Are your goals long-term or short-term? Answering this question is important because individual stocks can be either great or horrible choices, depending on the time period you want to focus on. Generally, the length of time you plan to invest in stocks can be short term, intermediate term, or long term. The following sections outline what kinds of stocks are most appropriate for each term length.

With stock performance history as an indicator, investing in stocks becomes less risky as the time frame lengthens. Stock prices tend to fluctuate on a daily basis, but they have a tendency to trend up over an extended period of time. Even if you invest in a stock that goes down in the short term, you're likely to see it rise — and possibly go above your initial investment — if you have the patience to wait it out and let the stock price appreciate.

Focusing on the short term

Short term generally means one year or less, although some people extend the period to two years or less. You get the point.

Everyone has short-term goals. Some are modest, such as setting aside money for an exciting vacation in Barbados this year or paying for unwelcome car repair bills. Other short-term goals are more ambitious, such as accruing funds for a down payment to purchase a new home within six months. Whatever the expense or purchase, you need a predictable accumulation of cash soon. If this sounds like your situation, stay away from the stock market!

Because stocks can be so unpredictable in the short term, they're a bad choice for short-term considerations. We continue to marvel in disbelief whenever we hear slick market analysts saying things like, "At $25 a share, XYZ is a solid investment, and we feel that its stock should hit our target price of $40 within six to nine months." You just know that someone will hear that and say, "Gee, why bother with 3 percent at the bank when this stock will rise by more than 50 percent? I better call my broker." The stock may indeed hit that target amount (or even surpass it), or it may not. Most of the time, the stock doesn't reach the target price, and then the investor is disappointed. As we saw during the recession, the stock could even go down, and go down by a lot. The reason why target prices are frequently (usually) missed is that the analyst is only one person and it's difficult to figure out what millions of investors will do in the short term. The short term can be irrational because so many investors have so many reasons for buying and selling that it's difficult to analyze. If you want to use the money you invest for an important short-term need, you could lose very important cash quicker than you think.

Short-term stock investing is very unpredictable. You can better serve your short-term goals with stable, interest-bearing investments such as guaranteed investment certificates (GICs) and certificates of deposit (CDs), as well as short-term bonds or treasury bills, available at chartered banks. If you're so inclined to play the market's ups and downs, take a look at Book 5, where we discuss day trading techniques.

During the raging bull market of the late 1990s, investors watched as some high-profile stocks went up 20 to 50 percent in a matter of months. Hey, who needs a savings account earning a measly interest rate when stocks grow like that! Of course, when the economic crisis hit in 2008 and those same stocks fell 35 percent, a savings account earning a measly interest rate suddenly didn't seem so bad.

Stocks — even the best ones — fluctuate in the short term. In a negative environment, they can be very volatile. No one can accurately predict the price movement (unless you have some inside information), so, unless you're willing to take a risk on day trading, stocks are definitely inappropriate for any financial goal that you need to reach within one year. Revisit Table 1–1 for suggestions about your short-term strategies.

Considering intermediate-term goals

Intermediate term refers to financial goals that you plan to reach within five years. If, for example, you want to accumulate funds to put money down for investing in real estate four years from now, some growth-oriented investments may be suitable.

Although some stocks *may* be appropriate for a two- or three-year time period, not all stocks are good intermediate-term investments. Different types and categories of stocks exist. Some stocks are fairly stable and hold their value well, such as the stock of very large or established dividend-paying companies. Other stocks have prices that jump all over the place, such as the stocks of untested companies that haven't been in existence long enough to develop a consistent track record.

If you plan to invest in the stock market to meet intermediate-term goals, consider large, established companies or dividend-paying companies in industries that provide the necessities of life (like the food and beverage industry, banks, pipelines, or electric utilities). In today's economic environment, we very strongly believe that stocks attached to companies that serve basic human needs should have a major presence in most stock portfolios. They're especially well-suited for intermediate investment goals.

Just because a particular stock is labelled as being appropriate for the intermediate term doesn't mean you should get rid of it by the stroke of midnight on this date five years from now. After all, if the company is doing well and going strong, you can continue holding the stock indefinitely. The more time you give a well-positioned, profitable company's stock to grow, the better you'll do.

Preparing for the long term

Stock investing is best suited for making money over a long period of time. When you measure stocks against other investments in terms of five to (preferably) ten or more years, they excel. Even investors who bought stocks during the depths of the Great Depression saw profitable growth in their stock portfolios over a ten-year period.

In fact, if you examine any ten-year period over the past 70 years, you see that stocks almost always beat out other financial investments — such as bonds or bank investments — when measured by total return (taking reinvesting and the compounding of capital gains and dividends into account)! As you can see, long-term patience often allows stocks to shine. Of course, your work doesn't stop at deciding on a long-term investment. You still have to do your homework and choose stocks wisely — because even in good times you can lose money if you invest in companies that go out of business.

Because you can choose between many different types and categories of stocks, virtually any investor with a long-term perspective should add stocks to his or her investment portfolio. Whether you want to save for your child's university fund or for future retirement goals, carefully selected stocks have proven to be a superior long-term investment for multitudes of Canadians.

Investing for a Purpose

We know of a very nice, elderly lady who had a portfolio brimming with aggressive-growth stocks because she had an overbearing broker. Her purpose should've been conservative, and she should've chosen investments that would preserve her wealth rather than grow it. Obviously, the broker's agenda got in the way. Stocks are just a means to an end. Figure out your desired end and then match the means.

Making loads of money quickly: Growth investing

When investors want their money to grow, they look for investments that appreciate in value. *Appreciate* is just another way of saying "grow." If you have a stock that you bought for $8 per share and now its value is $30 per share, your investment has grown by $22 per share — that's appreciation. We know we would appreciate it!

Appreciation (also known as *capital gain*) is probably the number-one reason why people invest in stocks. Few investments have the potential to grow your wealth as conveniently as stocks. If you want the stock market to make you loads of money relatively quickly (and if you can assume some risk), keep reading and pay attention to the parts on growth stocks.

Stocks are a great way to grow your wealth, but they're not the only way. Many investors seek alternative ways to make money, but many of these alternative ways are more aggressive and carry significantly more risk. You may have heard about people who made quick fortunes in areas such as commodities (like wheat, pork bellies, or precious metals), options, and other more sophisticated investment vehicles. Keep in mind that you should limit risky investments to only a small portion of your portfolio, such as 10 percent of your investable funds. Experienced investors, however, can go as high as their level of comfort permits.

Making money steadily: Income investing

Not all investors want to take on the risk that comes with making a killing. (Hey . . . no guts, no glory!) Some people just want to invest in the stock market as a means of providing a steady income. They don't need stock values to go through the ceiling. Instead, they need stocks that perform well consistently.

If your purpose for investing in stocks is to create income, you need to choose stocks that pay dividends. Dividends are typically paid quarterly to shareholders on record.

Distinguishing between dividends and interest

Don't confuse dividends with interest. Most people are familiar with interest, because that's how you grow your money over the years in the credit union or bank. The important difference is that *interest* is paid to creditors, and *dividends* are paid to owners (meaning *shareholders* — and if you own stock, you're a shareholder, because stocks represent shares in a publicly traded company).

When you buy stock, you buy a piece of that company. When you put money in a bank (or when you buy bonds), you basically loan your money. You become a creditor, and the bank or bond issuer is the debtor and, as such, must eventually pay your money back to you and most of the time with interest.

Recognizing the importance of an income stock's yield

When you invest for income, you have to consider your investment's yield and compare it with the alternatives. The *yield* is an investment's annual payout expressed as a percentage of the investment value. Looking at the yield is a way to compare the income you expect to receive from one investment with the expected income from others. Table 1–2 shows some comparative yields.

Table 1–2	Comparing the Yields of Various Investments				
Investment	*Type*	*Value*	*Pay Type*	*Payout*	*Yield*
Smith Co.	Stock	$50/ share	Dividend	$2.50	5.00%
Jones Co.	Stock	$100/ share	Dividend	$4.00	4.00%
Acme Bank	Bank CD	$500	Interest	$25.00	5.00%
Acme Bank	Bank CD	$2,500	Interest	$131.25	5.25%
Acme Bank	Bank CD	$5,000	Interest	$287.50	5.75%
Brown Co.	Bond	$5,000	Interest	$300.00	6.00%

**Book III
Chapter 1**

Building Wealth through Investing in Stocks

To understand how to calculate yield, you need the following formula:

Yield = annual payout ÷ investment value

Yield enables you to compare how much income you would get for a pro-spective investment with the income you would get from other investments. For the sake of simplicity, this exercise is based on an annual percentage yield basis (compounding would increase the yield).

Jones Co. and Smith Co. are both typical dividend-paying stocks; presume in the example presented by Table 1–2 that both companies are similar in most respects except for their differing dividends. How can you tell whether a $50 stock with a $2.50 annual dividend is better (or worse) than a $100 stock with a $4.00 dividend? The yield tells you.

Even though Jones Co. pays a higher dividend ($4.00), Smith Co. has a higher yield (5 percent). Therefore, if you had to choose between those two stocks as an income investor, you would choose Smith Co., if all else is equal between Jones Co. and Smith Co. Of course, if you truly want to maximize your income and don't really need your investment to appreciate a lot, you should probably choose Brown Co.'s bond because it offers a yield of 6 percent. It gets tricky because of tax treatment of Canadian dividends for Canadian taxpayers, but you get the point.

Dividend-paying stocks do have the ability to increase in value. They may not have the same growth potential as growth stocks, but at the very least they have a greater potential for capital gain than GICs or bonds.

Investing for Your Personal Style

Your investing style isn't a blue-jeans-versus-three-piece-suit debate. It refers to your approach to stock investing. Do you want to be conservative or aggressive? Would you rather be the tortoise or the hare? Your invest-ment personality greatly depends on the term over which you're planning to invest and on your purpose (refer to the previous two sections in this chap-ter). The following sections outline the two most general investment styles.

Conservative investing

Conservative investing means that you put your money in something proven, tried, and true. You invest your money in safe and secure places, such as chartered banks, credit unions, and government-backed securities. But how does that apply to stocks? (Table 1–1 gives you suggestions.)

Conservative stock investors want to place their money in companies that exhibit some of the following qualities:

✦ **Proven performance:** You want companies that show increasing sales and earnings year after year. You don't demand anything spectacular, just a strong and steady performance.

✦ **Market size:** Companies should be *large cap.* In other words, they should have a market value exceeding $10 billion in size. Conservative investors surmise that bigger is safer.

✦ **Market leadership:** Companies should be leaders in their industries.

✦ **Perceived staying power:** You want companies with the financial clout and market position to weather uncertain market and economic conditions. It shouldn't matter what happens in the economy or who gets elected as prime minister.

As a conservative investor, you don't mind if the companies' share prices jump (who would?), but you're more concerned with steady growth over the long term.

Aggressive investing

Aggressive investors can plan over the long term or look only to the intermediate term, but in any case they want stocks that resemble Aesop's fabled hare — they show the potential to break out of the pack.

Aggressive stock investors want to invest their money in companies that exhibit some of the following qualities:

✦ **Great potential:** The company must have superior goods, services, ideas, or ways of doing business compared to its competition.

✦ **Capital gains possibility:** You don't even consider dividends. If anything, you dislike dividends. You feel that the money that would've been dispensed in dividend form is better reinvested in the company. This, in turn, can spur greater growth.

✦ **Innovation:** Companies should have technologies, ideas, or innovative methods that make them stand apart from other companies.

Aggressive investors usually seek out small-capitalization stocks, known as *small caps,* because they have plenty of potential for growth. Take a tree-related example, for instance: A giant redwood may be strong but may not grow much more, whereas a brand-new sapling has plenty of growth to look forward to. Why invest in stodgy, big companies when you can invest in smaller enterprises that may become the leaders of tomorrow? Aggressive investors have no problem investing in obscure companies because they hope that such companies will become another Google, Canadian National Railway, or Research In Motion.

Exploring Different Kinds of Risk

Think about all the ways that an investment can lose money. You can list all sorts of possibilities. So many that you may think, "Holy cow! Why invest at all?"

Don't let risk frighten you. After all, life itself is risky. Just make sure that you understand the different kinds of risk that we discuss in the following sections before you start navigating the investment world. Be mindful of risk and find out about the effects of risk on your investments and personal financial goals.

Financial risk

The financial risk of stock investing is that you can lose your money if the company whose stock you purchase loses money or goes belly up. This type of risk is the most obvious, because companies do go bankrupt.

You can greatly enhance the chances of your financial risk paying off by doing an adequate amount of research and choosing your stocks carefully. Financial risk is a real concern even when the economy is doing well. Some diligent research, a little planning, and a dose of common sense help you reduce your financial risk.

In terms of financial risk, the bottom line is . . . well . . . the bottom line! A healthy bottom line means that a company is making money. And if a company is making money, then you can make money by investing in its stock. However, if a company isn't making money, you might not make money if you invest in it. Profit is the lifeblood of any company.

Interest-rate risk

You can lose money in an apparently sound investment because of something that sounds as harmless as "interest rates have changed." Interest-rate risk may sound like an odd type of risk, but in fact it's a common consideration for investors. Be aware that interest rates change on a regular basis, causing some challenging moments. Governments set interest rates, and the primary institutions to watch closely are the Bank of Canada and the Federal Reserve (the Fed) in the United States — these are, in effect, national central banks. Both institutions raise or lower their interest rates, actions that in turn cause banks and credit unions to raise or lower interest rates accordingly. Interest-rate changes affect consumers, businesses, and, of course, investors.

Historically, rising interest rates have had an adverse effect on stock prices. We outline several reasons why in the following sections. Because Canada and especially the United States are top-heavy in debt, rising interest rates are an obvious risk that threatens both stocks and fixed-income securities (such as bonds). This is the same dynamic as the inverse relationship between properties values and mortgage rates: one up = the other down.

Hurting a company's financial condition

Rising interest rates have a negative impact on companies that carry a large current debt load or that need to take on more debt, because when interest rates rise, the cost of borrowing money rises, too. Ultimately, the company's profitability and ability to grow are reduced. When a company's profits (or earnings) drop, its stock becomes less desirable, and its stock price falls.

Affecting a company's customers

A company's success comes when it sells its products or services. But what happens if increased interest rates negatively impact its customers (specifically, other companies that buy from it)? The financial health of its customers directly affects the company's ability to grow sales and earnings.

Affecting investors' decision-making considerations

When interest rates rise, investors start to rethink their investment strategies, resulting in one of two outcomes:

✦ Investors may sell any shares in interest-sensitive stocks that they hold. Interest-sensitive industries include real estate, the debt-saddled automotive sector, and the very sickly U.S. financial sector. Although increased interest rates can hurt these sectors, the reverse is also generally true: Falling interest rates boost the same industries. Keep in mind that interest rate changes affect some industries more than others.

✦ Investors who favour increased current income (versus waiting for the investment to grow in value to sell for a gain later on) are definitely attracted to investment vehicles that offer a higher yield. Higher interest rates can cause investors to switch from common stocks to bonds or GICs or preferred shares.

Hurting stock prices indirectly

High or rising interest rates can have a negative impact on any investor's total financial picture. What happens when an investor struggles with burdensome debt, such as a second mortgage, credit card debt, or *margin debt* (debt from borrowing against stock in a brokerage account)? He may sell some stock to pay off some of his high-interest debt. Selling stock to service debt is a common practice that, when taken collectively, can hurt stock prices.

Market risk

People talk about "the market" and how it goes up or down, making it sound like a monolithic entity instead of what it really is — a group of millions of individuals making daily decisions to buy or sell stock. No matter how modern our society and economic system, you can't escape the laws of supply and demand. When masses of people want to buy a particular stock, it becomes in demand, and its price rises. That price rises higher when the supply is limited. Conversely, if no one's interested in buying a stock, its price falls. Supply and demand is the nature of market risk. The price of the stock you purchase can rise and fall on the fickle whim of market demand.

Millions of investors buying and selling each minute of every trading day affect the share price of your stock. This fact makes it impossible to judge which way your stock will move tomorrow, or next week. This unpredictability and seeming irrationality is why stocks aren't appropriate for short-term financial growth.

Markets are volatile by nature; they go up and down, and investments need time to grow. Market volatility is an increasingly common condition that we have to live with. Investors should be aware of the fact that stocks in general (especially in turbulent markets) aren't suitable for short-term goals. Despite the fact that companies you're invested in may be fundamentally sound, all stock prices are subject to the gyrations of the marketplace and need time to trend upward.

Investing requires diligent work and research before putting your money in quality investments with a long-term perspective. Speculating is attempting to make a relatively quick profit by monitoring the short-term price movements of a particular investment. Investors seek to minimize risk, whereas speculators don't mind risk because it can also magnify profits. Speculating and investing have clear differences, but investors frequently become speculators and ultimately put themselves and their wealth at risk. Don't go there!

Understanding market risk is especially important for people who are tempted to put their nest eggs or emergency funds into volatile investments such as growth stocks (or mutual funds that invest in growth stocks, or similar aggressive investment vehicles). Remember, you can lose everything if you own stocks of companies that go out of business.

Inflation risk

Inflation is the artificial expansion of the quantity of money so that too much money is used in exchange for goods and services. To consumers, inflation shows up in the form of higher prices for goods and services. Inflation risk is also referred to as *purchasing power risk*. This term just means that your money doesn't buy as much as it used to. For example, a dollar that bought you a sandwich in 1980 barely bought you a candy bar a few years later. For you, the investor, this risk means that the value of your investment (a stock that doesn't appreciate much, or pay dividends for example) may not keep up with inflation.

Say you have money in a bank savings account currently earning 1 percent. This account has flexibility — if the market interest rate goes up, the rate you earn in your account goes up. Your account is safe from both financial risk and interest-rate risk. But what if inflation is running at 5 percent? At that point you're losing money.

Tax risk

Taxes (such as income tax or capital gains tax) don't affect your stock investment directly. Taxes can obviously affect how much of your money you get to keep. Because the entire point of stock investing is to build wealth, you need to understand that taxes take away a portion of the wealth that you're trying to build. Taxes can be risky because if you make the wrong move with your stocks (selling them at the wrong time, for example) you can end up paying higher taxes than you need to. Because Canadian tax laws change so frequently, tax risk is part of the risk-versus-return equation, as well.

It pays to gain knowledge about how the Canada Revenue Agency (CRA) rules can affect your wealth-building program before you make your investment decisions.

Political and governmental risks

If companies were fish, politics and government policies (such as taxes, interest rates, laws, and regulations) would be the pond. In the same way that fish die in a toxic or polluted pond, politics and government policies can kill companies. Of course, if you own stock in a company exposed to political and governmental risks, you need to be aware of these risks. For some companies, a single new regulation or law is enough to send them into bankruptcy. For other companies, a new law could help them increase sales and profits.

What if you invest in companies or industries that become political targets? You may want to consider selling them (you might always buy them back at a lower price later) or consider putting in stop-loss orders on the stock. For example, tobacco companies were the targets of political firestorms that battered their stock prices. Whether you agree or disagree with the political machinations of today is not the issue. As an investor, you have to ask yourself, "How does politics affect the market value and the current and future prospects of my chosen investment?"

Book III
Chapter 1

Building Wealth through Investing in Stocks

Taking the preceding point a step further, we'd like to remind you that politics and government have a direct and often negative impact on the economic environment. And one major pitfall for investors is that many misunderstand even basic economics. Considering all the examples we could find in recent years, we could write a book! Or . . . uh . . . simply add it to this book.

Personal risks

Frequently, the risk involved with investing in the stock market may not be directly involved with the investment or factors related to the investment; sometimes the risk is with the investor's circumstances.

Investors who don't have an emergency fund or a rainy-day fund sometimes find themselves confronted with large, sudden expenses they can't handle. You never know when your company may lay you off or when your basement may flood, leaving you with a huge repair bill. Car accidents, your health, emergency repairs, and other unforeseen events are part of life's bag of surprises — for anyone.

You probably won't get much comfort from knowing that stock losses are tax deductible (but only against stock gains) — a loss is a loss. However, you can avoid the kind of loss that results from prematurely having to sell your stocks if you maintain an emergency cash fund. A good place for your emergency cash fund is in either a bank savings account or a money market fund. Then you aren't forced to prematurely liquidate your stock investments to pay emergency bills.

Emotional risk

What does emotional risk have to do with stocks? Emotions are important risk considerations because the main decision makers are human beings. Logic and discipline are critical factors in investment success, but even the best investor can let emotions take over the reins of money management and cause losses. For stock investing, you're likely to be sidetracked by three main emotions: greed, fear, and love. You need to understand your emotions and what kinds of risk they can expose you to:

✦ **Greed:** The lure of the easy buck can easily turn healthy attitudes about growing wealth into unhealthy greed that blinds investors and discards common sense (such as investing for quick short-term gains in dubious hot stocks rather than doing your homework and buying stocks of solid companies with strong fundamentals and a long-term focus).

✦ **Fear:** Greed can be a problem, but fear is the other extreme. People who are fearful of loss frequently avoid suitable investments and end up settling for a low rate of return. If you have to succumb to one of these emotions, at least fear exposes you to less loss.

Also, keep in mind that fear is frequently a symptom of lack of knowledge about what's going on. If you see your stocks falling and don't understand why, fear will take over and you may act irrationally. When stock investors are affected by fear, the tendency is to sell their stocks and head for the exits and/or the life boats. Out of fear, inexperienced investors will sell good stocks if they see them go down temporarily (the "correction"). Experienced investors see that temporary down move as a good buying opportunity to add to their positions.

✦ **(Misplaced) love:** Stocks are dispassionate, inanimate vehicles, but people can look for love in the strangest places. Emotional risk occurs when investors fall in love with a stock and refuse to sell it, even when the stock is plummeting and shows all the symptoms of getting worse. Emotional risk also occurs when investors are drawn to bad investment choices just because they sound good, are popular, or are pushed by colleagues at work, family or friends. Love and attachment are great in relationships with people but can be horrible with investments. To deal with this emotion, investors have to deploy techniques that take the emotion out. For example, you can use brokerage orders (such as trailing stops and limit orders), which can automatically trigger buy and sell transactions and leave out some of the agonizing. Hey, disciplined investing may just become your new passion!

Minimizing Your Risk

Now, before you go crazy thinking that stock investing carries so much risk you may as well not get out of bed, take a breath. Minimizing your risk in stock investing is easier than you think. Although wealth building through the stock market doesn't take place without some amount of risk, you can practise the following tips to maximize your profits and still keep your money secure.

Gaining knowledge

Some people spend more time analyzing a restaurant menu to choose a $10 entrée than analyzing where to put their next $5,000. Lack of knowledge constitutes the greatest risk for new investors, but diminishing that risk starts with gaining knowledge. The more familiar you are with the stock market — how it works, factors that affect stock value, and so on — the better you can navigate around its pitfalls and maximize your profits. The same knowledge that enables you to grow your wealth also enables you to minimize your risk. Before you put your money anywhere, you want to know as much as you can.

Staying out until you get a little practice

If you don't understand stocks, don't invest! Yeah, we know this book is about stock investing, and we think that some measure of stock investing is a good idea for most people. But that doesn't mean you should be 100 percent invested 100 percent of the time. If you don't understand a particular stock (or don't understand stocks, period), stay away until you do understand. Instead, give yourself an imaginary sum of money, such as $100,000, give yourself reasons to invest, and just make believe (an exercise called "simulated stock investing or trading"). Pick a few stocks that you think will increase in value, track them for a while, and see how they perform. Begin to understand how the price of a stock goes up and down, and watch what happens to the stocks you choose when various events take place. As you find out more and more about stock investing, you get better and better at picking individual stocks, and you haven't risked — or lost — any money during your learning period.

A good place to do your imaginary investing is at websites such as Marketocracy (www.marketocracy.com) and Investopedia's simulator (http://simulator.investopedia.com). You can design a stock portfolio and track its performance with thousands of other investors to see how well you do.

Putting your financial house in order

Advice on what to do before you invest could fill a whole book all by itself. The bottom line is that you want to make sure you are, first and foremost, financially secure before you take the plunge into the stock market. If you're not sure about your financial security, look over your situation with a financial planner or an investment advisor.

You can do a few things to get your finances in order before you buy your first stock:

✦ **Have a cushion of money.** Set aside three to six months' worth of your gross living expenses somewhere safe, such as in a bank account or money market fund, in case you suddenly need cash for an emergency.

✦ **Reduce your debt.** Overindulging in debt was the worst personal economic problem for many Canadians in the late 1990s, and this has continued in recent years. When the U.S. housing bubble popped, millions of foreclosures were the result as homeowners piled on too much debt. In Canada, foreclosures and powers of sale have also increased, but not as dramatically as in the United States.

✦ **Make sure your job is as secure as you can make it.** Are you keeping your skills up to date? Is the company you work for strong and growing? Is the industry you work in strong and growing?

✦ **Make sure you have adequate insurance.** You need enough supplemental insurance to cover you and your family's needs in case of illness, death, disability, and so on. Although Canada's provincial health care plans cover many medical expenses, they may not be enough for certain types of illnesses.

✦ **Kick the tires.** Interview some investment advisers or financial planners whom you might consider hiring until you're confident to do it yourself.

Diversifying your investments

Diversification is a strategy for reducing risk by spreading your money across different investments. It's a fancy way of saying, "Don't put all your eggs in one basket." But how do you go about divvying up your money and distributing it among different investments? The easiest way to understand proper diversification may be to look at what you *shouldn't* do:

✦ **Don't put all your money in one stock.** Sure, if you choose wisely and select a hot stock you may make a bundle, but the odds are tremendously against you. Unless you're a real expert on a particular company, it's a good idea to have small portions of your money in several different stocks. As a general rule, the money you tie up in a single stock should be money you can do without.

✦ **Don't put all your money in one industry.** We know people who own several stocks, but the stocks are all in the same industry. Again, if you're an expert in that particular industry, it could work out. But just understand that you're not properly diversified. If a problem hits an entire industry, you may get hurt.

✦ **Don't put all your money in one type of investment.** Stocks may be a great investment, but you need to have money elsewhere too. Bonds, bank accounts, Treasury bills, real estate, and precious metals are perennial alternatives to complement your stock portfolio. Some of these alternatives can be found in mutual funds or exchange-traded funds (ETFs). An *exchange-traded fund* is a fund with a fixed portfolio of stocks or other securities that tracks a particular index or market sector but is traded like a stock. Check out Globe Investor (`www.globeinvestor.com/partners/free/etf/`) for more information about Canadian ETFs.

Okay, now that you know what you *shouldn't* do, what *should* you do? Until you become more knowledgeable, follow this advice:

✦ **Keep only 10 percent (or less) of your investment money in a single stock.**

✦ **Invest in four or five (and no more than ten) different stocks that are in different industries.** Which industries? Choose industries that offer products and services that have shown strong, growing demand. To make this decision, use your common sense (which isn't as common as it used to be). Think about the industries that people need no matter what happens in the general economy, such as food, energy, banking, communications, and other consumer necessities. The best start for your new portfolio might be companies of which you are a customer.

Weighing Risk against Return

How much risk is appropriate for you, and how do you handle it? Before you try to figure out what risks accompany your investment choices, analyze yourself. Here are some points to keep in mind when weighing risk versus return in your situation:

✦ **Your financial goal:** In five minutes with a financial calculator, you can easily see how much money you're going to need to become financially independent (presuming financial independence is your goal). Say that you need $500,000 in ten years for a worry-free retirement and that your financial assets (such as stocks, bonds, and so on) are currently worth $400,000. In this scenario, your assets need to grow by only 2.25 percent to hit your target. Getting investments that grow by 2.25 percent after tax and inflation safely is easy to do because that's a relatively low rate of return.

The important point is that you don't have to knock yourself out trying to double your money with risky, high-flying investments; some run-of-the-mill bank investments will do just fine. All too often, investors take on more risk than is necessary. Figure out what your financial goal is so that you know what kind of return you realistically need.

✦ **Your investor profile:** Are you nearing retirement, or are you fresh out of university? Your life situation matters when it comes to looking at risk versus return.

- If you're just beginning your working years, you can certainly tolerate greater risk than someone facing retirement. Even if you lose big time, you still have a long time to recoup your money and get back on track.

- However, if you're within five years of retirement, risky or aggressive investments can do much more harm than good. If you lose money, you don't have as much time to recoup your investment, and the odds are that you'll need the investment money (and its income-generating capacity) to cover your living expenses after you're no longer employed.

♦ **Asset allocation:** We never tell retirees to put a large portion of their retirement money into a high-tech stock or other volatile investment. But if they still want to speculate, we don't see a problem as long as they limit such investments to 5 percent of their total assets. As long as the bulk of their money is safe and sound in secure investments (such as Canada Savings Bonds), we can sleep well (knowing that *they* can sleep well!).

Asset allocation harkens back to diversification. For people in their 20s and 30s, having 75 percent of their money in a diversified portfolio of growth stocks (such as mid-cap and small-cap stocks) is acceptable. For people in their 60s and 70s, it's not acceptable. They may, instead, consider investing no more than 20 percent of their money in stocks (mid caps and large caps are preferable). Check with your financial adviser to find the right mix for your particular situation.

**Book III
Chapter 1**

**Building Wealth
through Investing in
Stocks**

Chapter 2: Gathering and Deciphering Stock Information

In This Chapter

✔ Using stock exchanges to get investment information

✔ Applying concepts from accounting and economics to your investing

✔ Deciphering stock tables

✔ Interpreting dividend news

✔ Navigating balance sheets

✔ Understanding cash flow statements

For the best approach to stock investing, you want to build your knowledge and find quality information first. Then buy stocks and make your fortunes more assuredly. Basically, before you buy stock, you need to know that the company you're investing in is

✦ Financially sound and growing

✦ Offering products and services that are in demand by consumers

✦ In a strong and growing industry (and general economy)

Where do you start and what kind of information do you want to acquire? Keep reading.

When you're ready to dive in and start investing in stocks, you first have to choose a broker. It's kind of like buying a car: You can do all the research in the world and know exactly what kind of car you want to buy; still, you need a venue to do the actual transaction. Similarly, when you want to buy stock, your task is to do all the research you can to select the company you want to invest in. Still, you need a broker to actually buy the stock, whether you buy over the phone or online. In this chapter, we introduce you to the intricacies of the investor/broker relationship.

Looking to Stock Exchanges for Answers

Before you invest in stocks, you need to be completely familiar with the basics of stock investing. At its most fundamental, stock investing is about using your money to buy a piece of a company that will give you value in the form of appreciation or income. Fortunately, many resources are available to help you find out about stock investing. Some of our favourite places are the stock exchanges themselves.

Stock exchanges are organized marketplaces for the buying and selling of stocks (and other securities). The Toronto Stock Exchange (TSX) and the New York Stock Exchange (NYSE) are the premier North American stock exchanges. They provide a framework for stock buyers and sellers to make their transactions. The TSX and NYSE make money not only from a piece of every transaction but also from fees (such as listing fees) charged to companies and brokers that are members of its exchanges.

The main exchanges for most North American stock investors are the NYSE, TSX, and NASDAQ. Many Canadians also buy smaller-cap stocks on the TSX Venture exchange (TSXV). These four exchanges encourage and inform people about stock investing. Because they benefit from increased popularity of stock investing and continued demand for stocks, they offer a wealth of free (or low-cost) resources and information for stock investors on their websites:

✦ New York Stock Exchange: www.nyse.com

✦ TSX and TSXV: www.tmx.com

✦ NASDAQ: www.nasdaq.com

Understanding Stocks and the Companies They Represent

Stocks represent ownership in companies. Before you buy individual stocks, you want to understand the companies whose stock you're considering and find out about their operations. It may sound like a daunting task, but you'll digest the point more easily when you realize that companies work very similarly to how you work. They make decisions on a day-to-day basis just as you do.

Think about how you grow and prosper as an individual or as a family, and you see the same issues with businesses and how they grow and prosper. Low earnings and high debt are examples of financial difficulties that can affect both Canadians and companies. You'll understand companies' finances when you take the time to pick up some information in two basic disciplines: accounting and economics. These two disciplines play a significant role in understanding the performance of a firm's stock.

Accounting for taste and a whole lot more

Accounting. Ugh! But face it: Accounting is the language of business, and believe it or not, you're already familiar with the most important accounting concepts. Just look at the following three essential principles:

✦ **Assets minus liabilities equals net worth.** In other words, take what you own (your assets), subtract what you owe (your liabilities), and the rest is yours (net worth)! Your own personal finances work the same way as Microsoft's (except yours have fewer zeros at the end). See Book 1, Chapter 1 to figure out how to calculate your own net worth.

A company's balance sheet shows you its net worth at a specific point in time (such as December 31). The net worth of a company is the bottom line of its asset and liability picture, and it tells you whether the company is *solvent* (has the ability to pay its debts without going out of business). The net worth of a successful company is regularly growing. To see whether your company is successful, compare its net worth with the net worth from the same point a year earlier. A firm that has a $4 million net worth on December 31, 2011, and a $5 million net worth on December 31, 2012, is doing well; its net worth has gone up 25 percent ($1 million) in one year.

✦ **Income less expenses equals net income.** In other words, take what you make (your income), subtract what you spend (your expenses), and the remainder is your *net income* (or net profit or net earnings — your gain).

A company's profitability (or its potential profitability) is the whole point of investing in its stock. As it profits, the business becomes more valuable, and in turn its stock price becomes more valuable. To discover a firm's net income, look at its income statement. Try to determine whether the company uses its gains wisely, either reinvesting them for continued growth, paying down debt, or paying dividends.

✦ **Do a comparative financial analysis.** That's a mouthful, but it's just a fancy way of saying how a company is doing now compared with something else (like a prior period or a similar company).

If you know that the company you're looking at had a net income of $50,000 for the year, you may ask, "Is that good or bad?" Obviously, making a net profit is good, but you also need to know whether it's good compared to something else. If the company had a net profit of $40,000 the year before, you know that the company's profitability is improving. But if a similar company had a net profit of $100,000 the year before and in the current year is making $50,000, then you may want to either avoid that company or see what (if anything) went wrong with it.

Accounting can be this simple. If you understand these three basic points, you're ahead of the curve (in stock investing as well as in your personal finances).

Understanding how economics affects stocks

Economics. Double ugh! No, you aren't required to understand "the inelasticity of demand aggregates" (thank heavens!) or "marginal utility" (say what?). But a working knowledge of basic economics is crucial (and we mean crucial) to your success and proficiency as a stock investor. The stock market and the economy are joined at the hip. The good (or bad) things that happen to one have a direct effect on the other.

Getting the hang of the basic concepts

Alas, many investors get lost on basic economic concepts (as do some so-called experts that you see on TV). We owe our personal investing success to our status as students of economics. Understanding basic economics helps us (and will help you) filter the financial news to separate relevant information from the irrelevant in order to make better investment decisions. Be aware of these important economic concepts:

✦ **Supply and demand:** How can anyone possibly think about economics without thinking of the ageless concept of supply and demand? *Supply and demand* can be simply stated as the relationship between what's available (the supply) and what people want and are willing to pay for (the demand). This equation is the main engine of economic activity and is extremely important for your stock investing analysis and decision-making process. Do you really want to buy stock in a company that makes porcelain busts of John Diefenbaker if you find out that the company has an oversupply and nobody wants to buy them anyway?

✦ **Cause and effect:** If you pick up a prominent news report and read, "Companies in the table industry are expecting plummeting sales," do you rush out and invest in companies that sell chairs or manufacture tablecloths? Considering cause and effect is an exercise in logical thinking, and believe us, logic is a major component of sound economic thought.

✦ **Economic effects from government actions:** Political and governmental actions have economic consequences. As a matter of fact, nothing (and we mean nothing!) has a greater effect on investing and economics than government. Government actions usually manifest themselves as taxes, laws, or regulations. They also can take on a more ominous appearance, such as war or the threat of war. Government can willfully (or even accidentally) cause a company to go bankrupt, disrupt an entire industry, or even cause a depression. It controls the money supply and the availability of credit. Government controls the structure but not the activity on the public securities markets.

Gaining insight from past mistakes

Because most investors ignored some basic observations about economics in the late 1990s, they subsequently lost trillions in their stock portfolios. During 2000–2012, the United States experienced the greatest expansion of total debt in history, coupled with a record expansion of the money supply. The Federal Reserve (or "the Fed"), the U.S. government's central bank, controls both. In Canada, government debt also increased in recent years, albeit less significantly. (In mid-2009 the Bank of Canada increased the money supply as well.) This growth of North American debt and U.S. money supply resulted in more consumer (and corporate) borrowing, spending, and investing. This activity hyperstimulated the stock market for over a decade, and caused stocks to rise until the stock market bubble popped in 2008.

At the same time the recent recession decimated portfolios, it also reminded people that the stock market is no ATM. Let's hope the lessons learned in 2008 won't be forgotten anytime soon. Here are a few things to always remember:

✦ Stocks are not a replacement for savings accounts. Always have some money in the bank or credit unions.

✦ Stocks should never occupy 100 percent of your investment funds.

✦ When anyone (including an expert) tells you that the economy will keep growing indefinitely, be skeptical and read diverse sources of information.

✦ If stocks do well in your portfolio, consider protecting your stocks (both your original investment and any gains) with stop-loss orders.

✦ Keep debt and expenses to a minimum.

✦ If the Canadian economy is booming, a decline is sure to follow as the ebb and flow of the economy's business cycle continues.

Reading (and Understanding) Stock Tables

The stock tables in major business publications such as *The Wall Street Journal* and *Investor's Business Daily* are loaded with information that can help you become a savvy investor — *if* you know how to interpret them. You need the information in the stock tables for more than selecting promising investment opportunities. You also need to consult the tables after you invest to monitor how your stocks are doing. The *National Post* (www. nationalpost.com) and *The Globe and Mail* (www.theglobeandmail. com) also produce stock tables for a selection of mostly Canadian equities in their print editions. As well, they let you check just about any stock (U.S. or Canadian) in their online editions.

**Book III
Chapter 2**

Gathering and
Deciphering Stock
Information

Looking at the stock tables without knowing what you're looking for or why you're looking is the equivalent of reading *War and Peace* backwards through a kaleidoscope — nothing makes sense. But we can help you make sense of it all (well, at least the stock tables!). Table 2–1 shows a sample stock table to refer to as you read the sections that follow.

Table 2–1		A Sample Stock Table						
52-Wk High	52-Wk Low	Name (Symbol)	Div	Vol	% Yield	P/E	Close	Net Chg
21.50	8.00	SkyHighCorp (SHC)		3,143		76	21.25	+.25
47.00	31.75	LowDownInc (LDI)	2.35	2,735	5.9	18	41.00	–.50
25.00	21.00	ValueNowInc (VNI)	1.00	1,894	4.5	12	22.00	+.10
83.00	33.00	DoinBadlyCorp (DBC)		7,601			33.50	–.75

Every newspaper's financial tables are a little different, but they give you basically the same information. This section, updated daily — and even more frequently online — is not the place to start your search for a good stock; it's usually where your search ends. The stock tables are the place to look when you own a stock or know what you want to buy and you're just checking to see the most recent price.

Each item gives you some clues about the current state of affairs for that particular company. The sections that follow describe each column to help you understand what you're looking at.

52-week high

The column in Table 2–1 labelled "52-Wk High" gives you the highest price that particular stock has reached in the most recent 52-week period. Knowing this price lets you gauge where the stock is now versus where it has been recently. SkyHighCorp's (SHC) stock has been as high as $21.50; its last (most recent) price is $21.25, the number listed in the "Close" column. (Flip to the "Close" section for more on understanding this information.) SkyHighCorp's stock is trading very high right now because it's hovering right near its overall 52-week-high figure.

Now, take a look at DoinBadlyCorp's (DBC) stock price. It seems to have tumbled big time. Its stock price has had a high in the past 52 weeks of $83, but it's currently trading at $33.50. Something just doesn't seem right here.

During the past 52 weeks, DBC's stock price fell dramatically. If you're thinking about investing in DBC, find out why the stock price fell. If the company is strong, it may be a good opportunity to buy stock at a lower price. If the company is having tough times, avoid it. In any case, research the firm and find out why its stock has declined.

52-week low

The column labelled "52-Wk Low" gives you the lowest price that particular stock reached in the most recent 52-week period. Again, this information is crucial to your ability to analyze stock over a period of time. Look at DBC in Table 2–1, and you can see that its current trading price of $33.50 is close to its 52-week low of $33.

Keep in mind that the high and low prices just give you a range of how far that particular stock's price has moved within the past 52 weeks. They could alert you that a stock has problems, or they could tell you that a stock's price has fallen enough to make it a bargain. Simply reading the 52-Wk High and 52-Wk Low columns isn't enough to determine which of those two scenarios is happening. They basically tell you to get more information before you commit your money.

Name and symbol

The "Name (Symbol)" column is the simplest in Table 2–1. It tells you the company name (usually abbreviated) and the stock symbol assigned to the company.

When you have your eye on a stock for potential purchase, get familiar with its symbol, also called a ticker. Knowing the symbol makes it easier for you to find your stock in the financial tables, which list stocks in alphabetical order by the company's name. Remembering the ticker will also help you quickly search for stock information online. Stock symbols are the language of stock investing, and you need to use them in all stock communications, from getting a stock quote at your broker's office to buying stock over the Internet. The Financial Post provides all symbols while the Report on Business does not show this courtesy.

Dividend

Dividends (shown under the "Div" column in Table 2–1) are basically payments to owners (shareholders). If a company pays a dividend, it's shown in the dividend column. The amount you see is the annual dividend quoted for one share of that stock. If you look at LowDownInc (LDI) in Table 2–1, you can see that you expect to get $2.35 as an annual dividend for each share of stock that you own. Companies usually pay the dividend in quarterly

**Book III
Chapter 2**

Gathering and
Deciphering Stock
Information

amounts. If I own 100 shares of LDI, the company pays me a quarterly dividend of $58.75 ($235 total per year) if there is no change to LDI's dividend declaration over the next four quarters. A healthy company strives to maintain or upgrade the dividend for shareholders from year to year. (We discuss additional dividend details later in this chapter.)

The dividend is very important to investors seeking income from their stock investment. For more about investing for income, see Chapter 1. Investors buy stock in companies that don't pay dividends primarily for growth. Also look at Chapter 1 for more information on growth stocks.

Volume

Normally, when you hear the word "volume" on the news, it refers to how much stock is bought and sold for the entire market: "Well, stocks were very active today. Trading volume at the Toronto Stock Exchange hit 350 million shares." Volume is certainly important to watch because the stocks that you're investing in are somewhere in that activity. For the "Vol" column in Table 2–1, though, the volume refers to the individual stock.

Volume tells you how many shares of that particular stock were traded that day. If only 100 shares are traded in a day, then the trading volume is 100. SHC had 3,143 shares change hands on the trading day represented in Table 2–1. Is that good or bad? Neither, really. The business news media generally mention volume for a particular stock only when it's unusually large. If a stock normally has a trading volume in the 5,000 to 10,000 range and all of a sudden it's at 87,000, then it's time to sit up and take notice. The Financial Post posts volume; Report on Business does not.

Keep in mind that a low trading volume for one stock may be a high trading volume for another stock. You can't necessarily compare one stock's volume against that of any other company. Large-cap stocks like Royal Bank or Goldcorp typically have trading volumes in the millions of shares almost every day, while less active, smaller stocks may have average trading volumes in far, far smaller numbers.

The main point to remember is that trading volume far in excess of that stock's normal range is a sign that something is going on with the stock. It may be negative or positive, but something newsworthy is happening with that company. If the news is positive, the increased volume is a result of more people buying the stock. If the news is negative, the increased volume is probably a result of more people selling the stock. What are typical events that cause increased trading volume? Some positive reasons include the following:

- ✦ **Good earnings reports:** The company announces good (or better-than-expected) earnings.

- ✦ **A new business deal:** The firm announces a favourable business deal, such as a joint venture, or lands a big client.

- ✦ **A new product or service:** The company's research and development department creates a potentially profitable new product.

- ✦ **Indirect benefits:** The business may benefit from a new development in the economy or from a new law passed by Parliament.

Some negative reasons for an unusually large fluctuation in trading volume for a particular stock include the following:

- ✦ **Bad earnings reports:** Profit is the lifeblood of a company. When its profits fall or disappear, you see more volume.

- ✦ **Governmental problems:** The stock is being targeted by federal or provincial government action, such as a lawsuit or a securities commission (Ontario Securities Commission, for example) probe.

- ✦ **Liability issues:** The media report that the company has a defective product or similar problem.

- ✦ **Financial problems:** Independent analysts report that the company's financial health is deteriorating.

Check out what's happening when you hear about heavier than usual volume (especially if you already own the stock).

Yield

In general, yield is a return on the money you invest. However, in the stock tables, *yield* ("Yield" in Table 2–1) is a reference to what percentage that particular dividend is to the stock price. Yield is most important to income investors. It's calculated by dividing the annual dividend by the last stock price. In Table 2–1, you can see that the yield *du jour* of ValueNowInc (VNI) is 4.5 percent (a dividend of $1 divided by the company's stock price of $22). Notice that many companies report no yield; because they have no dividends, their yield is zero.

Keep in mind that the yield reported in the financial pages changes daily as the stock price changes. Yield is always reported as if you're buying the stock that day. If you buy VNI on the day represented in Table 2–1, your yield is 4.5 percent. But what if VNI's stock price rises to $30 the following day? Investors who buy stock at $30 per share obtain a yield of just 3.3 percent (the dividend of $1 divided by the new stock price, $30). Of course, because you bought the stock at $22, you essentially locked in the prior yield of 4.5 percent. Lucky you. Pat yourself on the back.

P/E

The P/E ratio is the ratio between the price of the stock and the company's earnings. P/E ratios are widely followed and are important barometers of value in the world of stock investing. The P/E ratio (also called the "earnings multiple" or just "multiple") is frequently used to determine whether a stock is expensive (a good value). Value investors find P/E ratios to be essential to analyzing a stock as a potential investment. As a general rule, the P/E should be 10 to 20 for large-cap or income stocks. For growth stocks, a P/E no greater than 30 to 40 is preferable.

In the P/E ratios reported in stock tables, *price* refers to the last price of a stock. *Earnings* refers to the company's reported earnings per share as of the most recent four quarters. The P/E ratio is the price divided by the earnings. In Table 2–1, VNI has a reported P/E of 12, which is considered a low P/E. Notice how SHC has a relatively high P/E (76). This stock is considered rather pricey because you're paying a price equivalent to 76 times earnings. Also notice that DBC has no available P/E ratio. Usually this lack of a P/E ratio indicates that the company reported a loss in the most recent four quarters.

Close

The "Close" column tells you how trading ended for a particular stock when it last traded. In Table 2–1, LDI ended the most recent day of trading at $41. Some newspapers report the high and low for that day in addition to the stock's ending price for the day.

Net change

The information in the "Net Chg" column answers the question, "How did the stock price end today compared with its price at the end of the prior trading day?" Table 2–1 shows that SHC stock ended the trading day up 25 cents (at $21.25). This column tells you that SHC ended the prior day at $21. VNI ended the day at $22 (up 10 cents), so you can tell that the prior trading day it ended at $21.90.

Using News about Dividends

Reading and understanding the news about dividends is essential if you're an *income investor* (someone who invests in stocks as a means of generating regular income). The following sections explain some basics about dividends you should know.

You can find news and information on dividends in newspapers such as *The Globe and Mail, National Post, The Wall Street Journal, Investor's Business Daily,* and *Barron's.*

Looking at important dates

To understand how buying stocks that pay dividends can help you build wealth, you need to know how companies report and pay dividends. Some important dates in the life of a dividend are as follows:

✦ **Date of declaration:** This is the date when a company reports a quarterly dividend and the subsequent payment dates. On January 15, for example, a company may report that it is "pleased to announce a quarterly dividend of 50 cents per share to common shareholders of record as of February 10." That was easy. The date of declaration is really just the announcement date. If you buy the stock before, on, or after the date of declaration, it won't matter in regard to receiving the stock's quarterly dividend. The date that matters is the date of record (see that bullet later in this list).

✦ **Trade date:** This is the day you actually initiate the stock transaction (buying or selling). If you call up a broker (or contact her online) today to buy a particular stock, then today is the trade date, or the date on which you execute the trade. You don't own the stock on the trade date; it's just the day you put in the order. For an example, skip to the following section.

✦ **Settlement date:** This is the date on which the trade is finalized, which usually happens three business days after the date of execution. The closing date for stock is similar in concept to a real estate closing. On the closing date, you're officially the proud new owner (or happy seller) of the stock.

✦ **Date of record:** This is used to identify which shareholders qualify to receive the declared dividend. Because stock is bought and sold every day, how does the company know which investors to pay? The company establishes a cut-off date by declaring a date of record. All investors who are official shareholders as of the declared date of record receive the dividend on the payment date, even if they plan to sell the stock any time between the date of declaration and the date of record.

✦ **Ex-dividend date:** *Ex-dividend* means *without dividend.* Because it takes three days to process a stock purchase before you become an official owner of the stock, you have to qualify (that is, you have to own or buy the stock) *before* the three-day period. That three-day period is referred to as the "ex-dividend period." When you buy stock during this short time frame you aren't on the books of record, because the settlement date falls after the date of record. Read the next section to see the effect that the ex-dividend date can have on an investor.

✦ **Payment date:** The date on which a company issues and mails its dividend cheques to shareholders or deposits the money in the brokerage account where you hold your shares. (Finally!)

For typical dividends, the events in Table 2–2 happen four times per year.

Table 2–2	The Life of the Quarterly Dividend	
Event	**Sample Date**	**Comments**
Date of declaration	January 15	The date the company declares the quarterly dividend
Ex-dividend date	February 7	Starts the three-day period during which, if you buy the stock, you don't qualify for the dividend
Record date	February 10	The date by which you must be on the books of record to qualify for the dividend
Payment date	February 27	The date that payment is made (a dividend cheque is issued and mailed to shareholders who were on the books of record as of February 10)

Understanding why these dates matter

Three business days pass between the trade date and the settlement date. Three business days also pass between the ex-dividend date and the date of record. This information is important to know if you want to qualify to receive an upcoming dividend. Timing is important, and if you understand these dates, you know when to purchase stock and whether you qualify for a dividend.

As an example, say that you want to buy ValueNowInc (VNI) in time to qualify for the quarterly dividend of 25 cents per share. Assume that the date of record (the date by which you have to be an official owner of the stock) is February 10. You have to execute the trade (buy the stock) no later than February 7 to be assured of the dividend. If you execute the trade right on February 7, the closing date occurs three days later, on February 10 — just in time for the date of record.

But what if you execute the trade on February 8, a day later? Well, the trade's closing date is February 11, which occurs *after* the date of record. Because you aren't on the books as an official shareholder on the date of record, you aren't getting that quarterly dividend. In this example, the February 7–9 period is called the *ex-dividend period*.

Fortunately, for those people who buy the stock during this brief ex-dividend period, the stock actually trades at a slightly lower price to reflect the amount of the dividend. If you can't get the dividend, you may as well save on the stock purchase. How's that for a silver lining?

Gathering Data from SEDAR and EDGAROnline

In Canada, publicly traded companies are required to file business and financial information with provincial securities regulators. These reports are entered into a government-sponsored database called SEDAR — the System for Electronic Document Analysis and Retrieval (www.sedar.com).

Electronic filing with SEDAR is now a mandatory requirement for most public companies. The rules of who files what were established at the federal level by the Canadian Securities Administrators (CSA) regulatory body and are overseen by each provincial securities regulatory body. SEDAR is a link that enables enterprises to file securities documents and remit filing fees electronically. It saves them time and gives you, the Canadian investor, fast, easy, and free access to important information about companies (and mutual funds, as well).

In the United States, the peer site is called EDGAROnline (www.freeedgar.com). The EDGAROnline service is even more advanced than SEDAR. In addition to letting you access statutory filings, it also provides registered users with an e-mail alert every time a certain reporting firm files a document and links you to that document.

Individual investors can access downloadable data from both websites (EDGAROnline charges a fee but SEDAR is free). This means that you can download SEDAR and EDGAROnline reports to read later. The content available at these sites is critical to investors because it contains all significant financial, legal, and other types of statutory (mandatory) declarations that are important in the investment decision-making process. For example, financial statements tell you whether or not a company is fiscally fit. Legal matters (like big lawsuits) that are *material* (important enough to influence an investor's decision to buy or sell a stock) in nature can also be found at these sites. Any material changes, like a new senior executive appointment or a major shift in operations to China, would also be described in a filing in SEDAR or EDGAROnline.

Be aware that annual reports may include more than 50 pages, and they often exceed 100 pages. For example, Canadian and U.S. annual reports include financial statements with notes; supplementary data; wordy management discussions of financial conditions and operations results; business descriptions;

legal proceedings; shareholder voting matters; insider transactions; executive compensation; and leasing agreements. Fun stuff! So be selective about how much information you want — and need — to download.

The EDGAR database uses Google to search its archive. The more specific keywords you enter the better you'll find what you're looking for. Here are some of the different types of documents you may want to seek out:

✦ **Annual reports and filings (*10-K Reports* in EDGAR):** Annual reports that include shareholder information covering the firm's fiscal year

✦ **Quarterly financial statements (*10-Q Reports* in EDGAR):** Quarterly reports that include shareholder information for the company's last quarter

✦ **Notices of material changes (*8-K Reports* in EDGAR):** Special reports that are the result of a significant contract, lawsuit, or other material event

✦ **EDGAR S-1 registrations:** Forms required for businesses that want to offer stock to the public, often used for initial public offerings (IPOs); an S-3 registration is used to offer stock to the public in a secondary offering after an IPO

✦ **Notices of annual or special meetings (*14-A Forms* in EDGAR):** Information about annual general meetings (AGMs) and voting matters such as candidates seeking election to the board of directors, approval of the increase in authorized capital stock, and/or approval of a merger or acquisition

When you want to get big-picture information about a company, take a look at the reports that companies must file with SEDAR or EDGAROnline. By searching these repositories, you can find companies' balance sheets, income statements, and other related information. You can verify what others say and get a fuller picture of a company's activities and financial condition. All this information will help you make better investment decisions.

Reading the Income Statement

It comes as no surprise to you that business and economic activity are undertaken with the idea of generating a profit. *Profit* or *earnings* is simply the gross revenue of an enterprise, less the cost of producing that income, over a defined period of time. So much is made these days of earnings and earnings reports. Do you hear much about a company's cash balance, accumulated depreciation, or owner's equity on Canada's Business News Network or CNBC's *Mad Money* and other financial shows? Does everyone salivate four times a year for asset season?

Earnings are *the* driving force and key indicator of a company's progress and success. If earnings are growing, the financial press doesn't worry much about the other stuff. Conversely, serve up a couple of double faults on the earnings front, and everybody's all over asset impairment, write-offs, debt, weak cash positions, and the like.

Long-term stock price appreciation is based on the growth of a company's asset base and the owner's equity in that base. If a company is generating cash, and particularly if it earns it at a growing rate, that's a good thing. As Warren Buffett says, "If the business does well, the stock always follows." (We'd add that it *almost* always follows — in the stock market, as with life, no guarantees apply.)

Revenues

Revenues or sales are the monies a company is owed for providing goods or services to another party. In large companies, revenue recognition can be very complicated, and is one area that unethical managers like to manipulate. Revenue is also referred to as the *top line*.

In smaller companies, sales and revenues are straightforward. They represent accounting dollars generated for business products sold or services performed. (Remember, with accrual accounting it doesn't matter whether the company has been paid yet. If a sale meets accounting tests for recognition, the sale is put on the books even if the cash is received later.)

In many businesses, such as transportation or utilities, the top line may be called *revenues,* but it's the same thing. Occasionally, you will see an allowance for returns included that reduces the sales figure. If not, you can usually safely assume that returns have already been factored out and reduced the sales figure.

Cost of sales

A company's income statement shows how profitable a company's core operations are by indicating the revenue generated from sales of a product or service and then deducting the costs associated with the company's products or services. *Cost of sales* (COS) or *cost of goods sold* (COGS) relates directly to the sale of products or services. For manufacturers, this figure includes labour expenses, material costs, and overhead costs (for example, the portion of electricity costs that relates directly to the products sold). COS or COGS for companies selling goods is technically the beginning inventory, plus the cost of goods purchased or manufactured during some period, minus the ending inventory.

When a company uses the terms *costs* and *expenses* in its financial statements, what it really could be trying to say is that costs are incurred to produce products or render services and expenses are all the other stuff, like paying office rent and support staff.

COS is an important driver of business success. For all but a few companies with high intellectual property or service content, COS is the largest eater of the revenue pie. For example, the physical COS of Microsoft is tiny with respect to revenue, whereas a grocery store like Loblaws or a discount retailer like Walmart may see COS in the 70- to 80-percent range. Apples-to-apples comparisons are critical to effective analysis.

Gross margin

Gross margin, or *gross profit,* is the difference between a company's total sales and its cost of sales. It is the basic economic output of the business before additional overhead, marketing, and financing costs enter the picture. Gross profit takes on added meaning when taken as a percentage. This percentage — and trends in the percentage — speaks volumes for the health and direction of the business.

Selling, general, and administrative (SG&A)

A section of every income statement itemizes a series of expenses called *operating expenses.* These are the expenses other than COS, and other than interest and taxes. SG&A expense is one of these operating expenses.

SG&A expenses are operating costs associated with making sales, running the business, keeping headquarters, marketing, data processing, and administrating operations. These expenses are indirect in nature. No matter the business, any company incurs indirect costs, or the costs of doing business that aren't *directly* related to producing and selling individual units of product or service. Some call it "overhead"; however, SG&A expenses go a little beyond the traditional definition of overhead, and some overhead items we've seen are usually allocated to direct costs, or COS.

Many investors use SG&A as a barometer of management effectiveness — a solid management team keeps SG&A expenses in check. SG&A can mushroom into a vast slush fund and an internal corporate pork barrel that can easily get out of control. Be alert for excessive SG&A; the more the company keeps (in executive salaries, for example), the less the shareholder gets (in stock price growth and dividends). Like gross margin, looking at SG&A as a percentage is best.

Research and development (R&D)

This type of operating expense is common and essential in pharmaceutical and technology companies, which need to make ongoing investments in future products. R&D can also be rife with abuse; if a company wastes money, it can easily hide it in the R&D category. Because these investments occur long before products are produced, and because many of them never pan out into saleable products, companies are allowed by accounting rules to record most research and development (R&D) costs as a period expense.

Also note that companies without a significant R&D effort may not report it in a separate line. And in some financial statements, R&D is called *product development*.

Depreciation and amortization

Depreciation and amortization represent the accountant's assignment of the operating cost of a long-lived asset to specific business periods, or its estimated useful life. *Depreciation* is used when referring to physical fixed assets, and *amortization* is used when referring to intangible assets (such as goodwill, patents, and so forth). Some of you Canadian oil and mining investing bugs may run into the term *depletion:* a cost recovery for the exhaustion of natural resource assets.

In our experience, depreciation and amortization (operating) expenses show up in a wide variety of ways on the earnings statement. Sometimes you'll see a specific line in financial statements for depreciation expenses, especially for capital-intensive businesses.

Reserves

Reserves are operating expenses, or charges, taken in anticipation of events that are likely to negatively affect financial results. Reserves can be set aside to cushion companies from things such as doubtful accounts receivable or other bad debts. Reserves are sometimes taken during the good years and used in unprofitable years to smooth out the earnings numbers and make a company's operations seem more consistent than they really are.

Interest and taxes

Interest and taxes are the corporate world's equivalent of the proverbial sure things. So, not surprisingly, space is reserved for them on the earnings statement.

Companies invariably have some form of interest income or interest expense, and usually they have both. *Interest income* comes primarily from cash and short-term investments reflected on the balance sheet. *Interest expense* comes, again not surprisingly, from short- and long-term debt balances. Interest reporting is usually done as a *net interest* — that is, by combining interest income and expense into a net figure.

Taxes are quite complicated, just as they are for individuals, and the details go beyond the scope of this book. Normally an income-tax provision is recorded as a single line item on the earnings statement, although this consists of myriad federal, provincial, and local taxes put together.

You don't need to pay too much attention to taxes, but in today's economic climate you absolutely have to keep an eye on interest expenses. This is especially true for companies with high debt loads. These companies may be unable to make their debt payments (principal and/or interest), and may not be able to refinance their debt either.

Income from continuing operations

What results from netting out (deducting) interest and taxes from operating income is *income from continuing operations.* From this figure, you can get a good picture of company performance, not only from an operating perspective but also from a financial one. A close look at interest costs tells you, for instance, whether operating success (operating income) comes at a financial price (high interest expense). If operating income is low or declining and financing cost (interest) is large or increasing, look out below!

Income from continuing operations tells shareholders, in totality, what their investment return is after everyone, including the Canada Revenue Agency, is paid. Income from continuing operations is a good indicator of total business performance, but be aware of truly extraordinary events driving expenses or income.

Extraordinary items

Extraordinary items on an earnings statement are, according to accounting rules, to be tied to events that are atypical, irregular, and non-recurring. *Atypical* events aren't related to the usual activities of the business, and seldom occur. *Non-recurring* events aren't expected to occur again.

Extraordinary items commonly result from business closures (discontinued operations) or major restatements due to changes in accounting rules. They may result from debt restructurings or other complex financial transactions. They may result from layoffs and other employee transactions. Extraordinary items generally are *not* supposed to include asset write-downs (such as receivables, inventory, or intangibles), foreign currency gains or losses, or divestitures. They're not the elements described in our section about special items.

Our advice to you is to watch for extraordinary expenses that aren't so extraordinary. For example, companies that routinely have some kind of write-off every year or reporting period aren't doing as well as the investing community is being led to believe. If earnings are consistently $1 a share each quarter, with a consistent $4 write-off each year, the true value generated by the business is closer to zero than to four.

Also, *realized gains or losses* on investments are non-recurring items and ought to be segregated on the income statement if significant in amount. Some companies may try to create the impression that these are regular income sources by excluding them from extraordinary, unusual, or special items.

Impairments, investments, and other write-downs

When the value of an asset changes significantly in the eyes of management, a company can elect to take a write-down recognizing the change. The *write-down* shows up as a decrease in asset value on the balance sheet for the asset category involved and (usually) as a one-time operating expense somewhere on the earnings statement. The rules for when and how to take these write-downs are, shall we say, flexible. The rules for writing down investment losses are particularly complex and beyond the scope of this book. The good news is that write-downs are normally reported as a separate line and are well documented in the notes.

For you as a stock investor, knowing the detail or amount may not be as important as knowing the pattern. Are these write-downs really one-time adjustments, or does the company continually overinvest in unproductive assets? Are companies quick to recognize mistakes, or do they push the financial impact of mistakes into the financial statements of future periods, toward ultimate fiscal oblivion? Write-down behaviour provides insight into management behaviour and effectiveness as well as overall business consistency — and should not be ignored.

Common special items include restructuring charges, discontinued operations, and pension losses, and these are discussed below.

Restructuring charges

Restructuring charges from continuing operations are those expenses — such as employee layoffs, maintenance, or early lease terminations — that are incurred when a company closes down or mothballs facilities, or writes off impaired assets. Because these assets would have been used up in the process of creating operating revenues, charges for restructuring these assets are usually factored into the calculation of net income. Massive employee layoffs and plant closings, like we still see today, may indicate that the company does not expect future business activity to support current employee levels or the operation of plants, machinery, and equipment. Restructuring charges include real cash expenses, not just allocations of expense.

Some companies take what is called the *big bath*. They write off as much as they can now so that future earnings will look better through higher reported profits.

Discontinued operations

When a company ceases part of its operations, it has to report current results, but separately from operating results. This reporting enables investors to make better comparisons from period to period and creates a fairer representation of results.

Pension tension

After years of volatile and declining stock markets, many large pension plans are underfunded. Companies are now reporting pension losses instead of the gains they were accustomed to. These losses show up in a variety of forms, including special charges to earnings, cash flow, or equity, depending on the type of plan and the accounting rules involved. Although pension shortfalls may not be an immediate liquidity concern, they are often too large for investors to ignore. Keep an eye on pension expenses.

Net income

Sales less COS, less operating expenses, less interest and taxes, less or plus extraordinaries and special items, give you a company's *net income* (sometimes referred to as *net earnings,* or *income attributable to common shareholders,* or some similar phrase). Net income represents the final net earnings result of the business on an accounting — not necessarily a cash — basis.

Net earnings are usually divided by the number of shares outstanding to arrive at *earnings per share* — the common barometer seen in nearly all financial reports. Most analysts and investors focus on *diluted* earnings per share, which figure in outstanding employee stock options and other equity grants beyond the actual shares outstanding.

The Balance Sheet

The *balance sheet* can be a great indicator of the financial condition of a business. It is a snapshot of assets, liabilities, and what's left over at a point in time. It tells you about where the company has been and how well it did getting there.

Many investors and business analysts look closely for the following information in a balance sheet:

+ The absolute and relative size of the numbers

+ The makeup of assets, liabilities, and owner's equity

+ Trends

+ Valuation (assessing whether stated values reflect actual values)

Each of these examinations is done with an eye toward what the figure should be for a company in that line of business. A company such as Tim Hortons, which has frequent, small cash sales, shouldn't have a large accounts receivable balance. A retailer like Canadian Tire should have sizeable inventories, but they shouldn't be out of line for the industry and for the company's category. A semiconductor manufacturer like Zarlink Semiconductor has a large amount of capital equipment but should depreciate it aggressively to account for rapid technological change.

To determine whether balance-sheet numbers are in line, most analysts apply certain ratios to the numbers. Ratios serve to draw comparisons among companies, and among companies and their industry. By doing so, analysts detect whether a company's performance is better or worse than peers in its industry.

Cash and cash equivalents

For most businesses, cash is the best type of asset to have. With cash, no question exists about its value: Cash is cash! *Cash equivalents* are essentially cash. They're short-term marketable securities, such as treasury bills and commercial paper as well as bankers acceptances, with little to no price risk that can be converted to cash at a moment's notice.

Value investors — investors who look for undervalued companies — particularly like cash. Cash is security, and it forms the strongest part of the safety net that value investors seek. You should question a cash balance only if it appears excessive against the needs of the business. Also, take a look at the notes to the financial statements to make sure the marketable securities have not lost significant value and that they are, in fact, cash equivalents. Should a company put any extra cash to work in an investment or acquisition that might return more than the 3 or 4 percent it would get in a bank? And why isn't it being returned to shareholders as a dividend? Most companies don't retain that much cash, but occasionally it can become a red flag. Sometimes companies become the target of take-overs so the acquiring company can get its hands on the cash equivalents of the target company.

Accounts receivable

Accounts receivable represent funds that are owed to the business for products delivered or services performed. As individuals, everyone likes to be owed money — until we're owed *too much* money. The same attitude applies to corporations.

The type of industry that a company operates in dictates the amount of accounts receivable. Obviously a small-sale retailer such as Tim Hortons operates mostly on cash — you don't give them an IOU for those maple-dip donuts, do you? Most companies that sell directly to consumers have few accounts receivable.

Contrast this with companies that sell to other companies (business-to-business) or to distributors or retailers in the supply chain. Most of this business is done *on account,* meaning that first goods or services are delivered, and then invoices are sent. The billing process creates an accounts receivable that goes away only when the customer pays the bill. So suppliers to other businesses or distribution and sales channels often have significant accounts receivable.

How much of a company's asset base should be made up of accounts receivable? Current thinking suggests that cash businesses such as Tim Hortons have 5 percent or less of their asset base in accounts receivable. Traditional retailers and other business-to-consumer companies have 20 to 30 percent or more in receivables if they provide credit to customers through their own credit cards. Equipment manufacturers and other business-to-business companies sometimes carry receivables of 50 percent or more of their total assets.

For most business-to-business industries, accounts receivable are a part of doing business and, in a sense, a *cost* of doing business (cash is forgone to give the customer time to pay). The question is, "How much commitment to accounts receivable is necessary to support the business?" Be keenly aware of situations in which companies aren't collecting on their bills or are using accounts receivable to create credit incentives for otherwise questionable customers to buy their product.

To assign value to accounts receivable, pay attention to the following factors:

✦ **Size of accounts receivable relative to sales and other assets:** Is a company extending itself too much to sustain or grow the business? Industry comparisons and common sense dictate the answer.

✦ **Trends in accounts receivable:** Is a company continually owed more and more money, with potentially greater and greater exposure to non-payment? Look at a company's accounts-receivable history and compare the numbers to its sales figures.

✦ **Quality of accounts receivable:** Typically, most companies collect on more than 95 percent of their accounts-receivable balances, and thus they're almost as good as cash. But if accounts-receivable balances grow, and particularly if large reserves show up on the income statement (marked as "allowance for doubtful accounts" or some such), this is a red signal flare that no investor should miss. One of the problems that Nortel encountered was lending money to their customers who otherwise could not afford to buy Nortel's expensive products. We all know how that ended!

Some financial statements show notes receivable as a separate balance-sheet item under current assets. *Notes receivable* are essentially a special form of accounts receivable — a promissory note for a significant amount that's extended to a specific firm for a specific reason. For the most part, notes receivable should be treated as normal accounts receivable, but it might be worth a quick glance at the note-holder and the terms of the note to spot anything unusual.

Inventory

Inventory is all valued material procured by a business and resold, with or without added value, to a customer. *Retail inventory* consists of goods bought, warehoused, and sold through stores. *Manufacturing inventory* consists of raw material, work in process, and finished goods awaiting shipment.

For most companies, the key to successfully managing inventory is to match it as closely as possible to sales. That is, the faster that procured inventory can be processed and sold, the better. Money tied up in inventory is money that can't be invested elsewhere in the business — this is referred to as an *opportunity* cost of doing business.

Valuing inventory can be challenging. Companies don't provide much information about their inventories. The most information you'll normally get is a breakdown of how much inventory there was at the beginning of the year, how much inventory was purchased (or manufactured) during the year, and how much was left over at the end of the year. Little else is known about what those inventories really are, or about their real value. A warehouse of outdated computer processors probably carries a book inventory value, but the computers aren't worth much on the market.

Inventory valuation is further affected by accounting methods employed by a firm. The method affects both balance-sheet carrying value and cost recognition on the income statement.

You need to appraise inventory balances for economic value and efficiency of use. Look at the size of the asset in an absolute sense and relative to the size and sales of the business. Look for trends, favourable and unfavourable, in inventory balances. Look at competitors and industry standards. Where possible, look at inventory quality and past track records for inventory obsolescence and resulting write-offs. And then be conservative. It often makes sense to assign a value of 50 to 75 percent, sometimes less, to inventory values appearing on a balance sheet. The auditors could easily have dropped the ball when they counted and valued a client company's inventory!

Fixed assets

The balance sheet entry called *property, plant, and equipment* (PP&E) is pretty clear from the name. It refers to the fixed assets — land, buildings, machinery, fixtures, office and computer equipment, and similar items — owned by the firm for productive use. Depending on the industry, this line item may have a different name. Retail stores like Rona or Canadian Tire, for example, don't have many plants.

Valuation of PP&E can vary widely. The key to understanding PP&E value is to understand depreciation. *Depreciation* is an amount subtracted each year by accountants from an asset purchase price for normal wear and tear and technological obsolescence. Depreciation methods are discussed further later in this section, but for now all you need to know is that depreciation can affect underlying asset values substantially. Of course, the value of property, plant, and equipment can vary a lot by what it is, where it is, and how it's used. These factors, in turn, vary by industry and things specific to the company itself, such as its location.

Accountants have a variety of accepted methods for assigning depreciation dollars at their disposal. A detailed discussion of depreciation and depreciation methods is accounting stuff that's well beyond the scope of this book. But you may find it useful to recognize two major groupings of methods for assigning depreciation dollars: accelerated and straight-line depreciation.

The choice of depreciation methods is important. *Accelerated depreciation* allows greater deductions in the earlier years of the life of an asset, resulting in the most conservative PP&E asset valuations. It also results in the most conservative view of earnings and allows more room for future net earnings growth because you can assume that a greater portion of asset depreciation is behind you.

But some companies may deliberately prop up current earnings by employing *straight-line depreciation* methods, which spread the costs evenly over the life of an asset. Watch for companies switching over to straight-line from accelerated methods. Depreciation methods are disclosed in the notes section of the statements.

Depreciation is an accounting — not a cash — expense. No cheque is cut for depreciation. Instead, the cheque is cut when the asset is purchased. Depreciation is the leading difference between stated earnings and cash flows, and it can mean the difference between survival and failure for a company recording net income losses. Cash flow, unburdened by depreciation, may still be positive. But look out below. Cash consumed to keep a losing business afloat may not be available the next time a key piece of equipment needs to be replaced. Reporting methods that downplay depreciation or ignore it altogether, such as the *pro forma* reporting craze, indicate trouble.

Investments

Besides buying marketable securities that are easy to sell, many companies commit surplus cash to more substantial long-term investments. These company investments can serve many purposes: to achieve returns as any other investor would, to participate in the growth of a related or unrelated industry, or to eventually obtain control of another company. Long-term investments are harder to dispose of than marketable securities, but they can be very profitable during the holding period. Favourable tax treatment of Canadian dividends and gains makes investing in other Canadian companies more attractive still.

Investments can be valued in many ways, but ultimately they all boil down to historical cost or market valuation. Watch out for declining fair values and particularly for large *gross unrealized losses* — future write-offs and asset value impairment loom large. Gauge the size of investments on the balance sheet, look for details, and understand management's intent in making the investments.

Intangible assets

Asset valuation gets *really* fun for Canadian investors, and especially for value investors, when the discussion turns to intangibles, also sometimes referred to as *soft* assets. *Intangibles* are non-physical assets that are critical in acquiring and maintaining sales and producing a competitive edge. Intangibles include patents, copyrights, franchises, brand names, and trademarks. Also included is the all-encompassing *goodwill* often acquired when buying (and overpaying for) other companies. Goodwill is the premium paid over and above the net asset value (tangible and intangible assets minus liabilities) of a company. Such premiums are paid for various reasons, like to outbid another company in a takeover battle, or as a gesture of confidence in the future of the acquirer.

Placing a financial value on these ethereal and nebulous brand-related assets is difficult, but accountants seem to be able to pull it off. If a historical cost exists, accountants may carry the intangible at that cost. This is often the case with goodwill from company acquisitions or mergers.

The key to assessing intangible assets is to understand their carrying value and the amortization technique. Intangible assets should all be amortized, because patents expire, brand value may be diluted, and so forth. Goodwill from acquisitions most certainly — at least for now — must be amortized. Like depreciation, valuation depends heavily on the method of amortization.

Basically the same choice is available between straight-line and accelerated amortization, and the chosen method is disclosed somewhere in the financial-statement notes (refer to "Fixed assets" for the difference between accelerated and straight-line methods).

Intangibles are subject to a great deal of discretion in their accounting, and their sources and form can be numerous and highly variable from one company to the next. Cast a skeptical eye on large goodwill accounts in particular, especially if a company seems reluctant to write them off.

But with the advent of modern technology and marketing, the ideas of intellectual capital and brand equity are part of a company's value and cannot simply be ignored. In fact, for some companies, these intangibles may represent their greatest value. What is the value of the Bank of Nova Scotia without the Scotiabank brand name throughout the western hemisphere? Or the value of Microsoft without its lock on PC operating-system design? Such brands and locks often ultimately produce the best profit streams and best value. Contemporary stock investors need a clear understanding of intangible assets and should not just dismiss them in an offhand way.

Payables

Almost everyone, individuals or corporations, has *payables,* defined as money owed to others for products purchased or services rendered. The liability is created when the service or product arrives; a cash payment follows later to discharge the liability. Nearly all companies maintain a regular balance of current accounts payable, interest payable, and the like.

If payment is received in advance, as with a deposit, the unearned portion is tracked as a liability. Sometimes *contingent liabilities* may be recorded, as in warranty claims expected to be paid but not yet actualized.

You can do little with current liabilities except subtract them out from intrinsic company value. But also realize that current liabilities aren't necessarily a bad thing and that they can result in higher effective returns on ownership capital with relatively low cost and risk.

Long-term liabilities

Long-term corporate liabilities are really no different than those in personal finance: They represent contracted commitments to pay back a sum of money over time, with interest. For the individual, they come in the form of loans and mortgages; for the corporation, they occur more often in the form of tradeable notes and bonds. The result, however, is the same in both cases.

As for short-term liabilities, you don't need to look too closely at the amount or quality of these liabilities. Trends can be important, however. Relying increasingly on long-term debt may be a sign of trouble, especially these days. The company may not be making ends meet and may be having trouble raising capital in these tight credit markets, which is never a good sign.

In addition, a company that's constantly changing, restructuring, or otherwise tinkering with long-term debt may be sending tacit signals of trouble. The company may be seeking concessions from lenders behind the scenes. In any event, attention paid to this kind of activity diverts attention from the core business, which is not a good thing and should be a warning flag for value investors.

Excessive use of debt signals potential danger if things don't turn out the way a company expects them to. Leverage is a good thing when things are going a company's way. Debt financing can be used to produce more product for more markets — and, thus, more profit and, in the end, a bigger business. Return to owners is proportionately higher: Their investment stays the same while the returns grow. But, as everyone knows, this can work the other way. Stock investors don't like surprises, and a company with uncertain prospects and a lot of debt is very risky.

Again, factor in liabilities as a negative factor in company and stock valuation and look for unfavourable trends or the excessive use of long-term debt. Generally, liabilities don't require the close study that you might give to assets.

Owner's equity

Because you're contemplating making an investment in a company, isn't owner's equity the most important balance-sheet item? You and other investors are, in essence, either directly or indirectly contributing capital. This capital is in turn converted into an asset *and then* in turn converted into revenue and profit to produce a return to the owner. You're making a decision to allocate capital to a company that, for its part, tries to do the best job allocating capital to opportunities that produce the best return.

Owner's equity, or *book value,* is the sum of paid-in capital and retained earnings — assets (which can be valued and reported with a degree of latitude) minus liabilities (which occur at face value). Thus, book-value reporting is done with a degree of latitude. Value investors talk about three different book value measures:

- ✦ **Book value as owner's equity:** Total book assets minus liabilities
- ✦ **Tangible book value:** Total book value minus all or part of intangibles
- ✦ **Book value per share:** Accounting book value divided by the number of common shares outstanding

All three of these measures crop up in value-investing discussions and papers. Be alert, because sometimes they're used interchangeably.

Like liabilities, the equity portion of the balance sheet is critical to a company's functioning, but it really requires relatively little scrutiny on your part. We take you on a short tour but avoid the tedious discussions of classes of stock, par value, and the like that befuddle so many readers of financial stories. For this discussion, owner's equity consists of two things: paid-in capital — a fancy term for stock — and retained earnings.

Paid-in capital

Paid-in capital represents the total value paid into the company by its owners — its shareholders. It gets a little complicated with the discussion of par value and additional paid-in capital. Total paid-in capital represents capital actually paid into the company at initial or subsequent company stock sales and has nothing to do with market price or market value. In and of itself, you need pay little attention to this item.

Retained earnings

Retained earnings are profits from past operating periods that are retained or reinvested in the business. Technically speaking, company profits belong to the shareholders, but it becomes management's option to decide whether to actually pay them out. Typically, managers think that they can invest the money more effectively than their shareholders. Stock investors of all stripes are betting that they're right!

So long as a company's business is viable, shareholders probably want to see retained earnings as high as possible, and growing. It's a capital allocation game — the earnings are better suited to that company's purpose than anywhere else. By investing in the company, you've already decided that, so you may as well keep your money on the table.

So generally when it comes to retained earnings, more is better — especially if accompanied by a reasonable dividend policy in which management *is* sharing some of the spoils with the owners. On the other hand, watch for rapidly declining or, worse, negative retained-earnings balances. Negative retained earnings are almost a sure sign of trouble, usually brought on by asset values declining faster than expected, excessive debt, an overinflated stock offering price, or a combination of the three. As a value investor, you should view negative retained earnings as another bright-red signal flare.

The Statement of Cash Flows

Earlier, we mention the difference in timing between certain accounting transactions and related cash collections and disbursements. Build it and ship it this month and then record the revenue, even though cash payments may not arrive until months later. Buy and pay for a million-dollar machine today, but expense it over its production life through depreciation. Amortize a patent and never write a cheque at all.

These transactions and a host of others create differences between accounting earnings and cash measures of business activity. A business needs cash to operate. A business generating positive cash flow is much healthier than one that's bleeding cash and borrowing to stay afloat. Because of non-cash items, earnings statements don't give a complete cash picture. So stock investors look for a statement of cash flows as a standard part of the financial-statement package.

The statement of cash flows tracks cash obtained in, or used in, three separate kinds of business activity: operating, investing, and financing. It also tracks dividends paid to shareholders. It is a very important piece of the financial-statement puzzle.

Cash flow from operations

Similar to operating income, *cash flow from operations* tells you what cash is generated from, or *provided by,* normal business operation and what cash is consumed by, or *used for,* the business. ("Provided by" and "used for" are the terms used on the cash-flow statement.) Net income from continuing operations is thus the starting point.

To the net income, add (or subtract) the *adjustments to reconcile net income to operating cash flow.* Here is where you *add back* depreciation and amortization dollars; that is, dollars that came out of accounting income but had no corresponding cash payment. So far, so good.

Next comes *cash provided by (used for) current assets and current liabilities.* If this is familiar territory and you understand how increases in current assets and liabilities affect cash, it makes sense to you that an inventory increase consumed some cash. Increases in liabilities *provide* cash. Decreases in liabilities *use* cash. (This concept is easier to grasp: It's a single cash transaction to pay a bill.) Increases in current assets (other than cash) *use* cash. Decreases in assets (as in a net decrease in inventory) *provide* cash.

Cash flow from investing activities

Cash flow from operations tells what cash was generated in the normal course of business and by changes in current asset and liability (working capital) accounts on the balance sheet. But what about cash used to invest in the business? Or used to invest in other businesses? What about cash acquired by selling investments in other businesses? The second section of the statement of cash flow provides this information.

For most growing companies, cash flow from operations should absolutely be positive, but cash flow from investing activities is often negative. Why? Is this okay? Yes, because growing companies need more physical investments — property, plant, and equipment (PP&E) — to sustain growth. Generally, negative cash flows in PP&E suggest that the company is satisfied with its growth plan and feels that funds must be invested elsewhere for a maximum investment return.

"Free" cash flow

Free cash flow sounds like what we all want in our lives, eh? Positive cash flow, and it's free! Free cash flow is a good indication of what a company really has left over after meeting obligations, and thus the flow could theoretically return to shareholders.

Free cash flow is defined as net after-tax earnings, plus depreciation and amortization and other non-cash items, minus capital expenditures, minus (or plus) changes in working capital (current assets and liabilities). Earn income, pay for the costs of doing business, and then what's left over is yours to keep as an owner. Pretty simple. Many investors, especially value investors, use free cash flow as the basis for calculating intrinsic value.

Cash flow from financing activities

Investing activities tell what a firm does with cash to increase or decrease fixed assets and assets not directly related to operations. *Financing activities* tell where a firm has obtained capital in the form of cash to fund the business. Proceeds from the sale of company shares or bonds (long-term debt) are a *source* of cash. If a company pays off a bond issue or buys back its own stock, that's a *use* of cash for financing.

A consistent cash flow from financing activities indicates excessive dependence on credit or equity markets. Typically, this figure oscillates between negative and positive. A big negative spike reflects a big bond issue or stock sale. In such a case, check to see if the resulting cash is used for investments in the business (probably okay) or to make up for a shortfall in operating cash flow (probably not okay). If the generated cash flows straight to the cash balance, you should wonder why a company is selling shares or increasing debt just to increase cash, although often the reasons are difficult to know. Perhaps an acquisition? Perhaps something more troubling?

Chapter 3: Going for Brokers

In This Chapter

✔ Understanding what brokers do

✔ Differentiating investment advisers and discount brokers

✔ Selecting a broker

✔ Exploring the types of brokerage accounts

✔ Understanding brokerage orders

✔ Making sense of margin accounts

✔ Knowing the long and short of shorting

When you're ready to dive in and start investing in stocks, you first have to choose a broker. It's kind of like buying a car: You can do all the research in the world and know exactly what kind of car you want to buy; still, you need a venue to do the actual transaction. Similarly, when you want to buy stock, your task is to do all the research you can to select the company you want to invest in. Still, you need a broker to actually buy the stock, whether you buy over the phone or online. In this chapter, we introduce you to the intricacies of the investor/broker relationship.

Investment success isn't just about picking rising stocks; it's also about how you go about doing it. Frequently, investors think that good stock picking means doing your homework and then making that buy (or sell). However, you can take it a step further to maximize profits (or minimize losses). As a stock investor, you can take advantage of techniques and services available through your standard brokerage account. This chapter presents some of the best ways you can use these powerful techniques — useful whether you're buying or selling stock. In fact, if you retain nothing more from this chapter than the concept of *trailing stops* (see the section "Trailing stops"), you'll have gotten your money's worth. (Really!)

Just before the stock market bubble popped in 2008, many people (but not enough!) were warning that a bear market was on the way. Undoubtedly, it seemed like a time for caution. Canadian stock investors didn't have to believe it, but they could have (at the very least) used trailing stops and other techniques to ensure greater investing success. Investors who used stop-loss orders avoided the carnage of trillions of dollars in stock losses. In this chapter, we show you how to use these techniques to maximize your investing profit.

Defining the Broker's Role

The broker's primary role is to serve as the vehicle through which you either buy or sell stock. When we talk about brokers, we're referring to organizations such as TD Waterhouse, BMO InvestorLine, Scotia iTrade, and many others that can trade stock on your behalf. Brokers can also be individuals who work for such firms. Although you can buy some stocks directly from the company that issues them, to trade most stocks you still need a broker.

Brokers primarily buy and sell securities, such as stocks (keep in mind that the word *securities* refers to the world of financial or paper investments and that stocks are only a small part of that world). But they can also perform other tasks for you, including the following:

✦ **Providing advisory services:** Investors pay brokers a fee for investment advice. Customers also get access to the firm's research and underwriting of new securities.

✦ **Offering limited banking services:** Brokers can offer banking features like interest-bearing accounts, cheque writing, and direct deposit.

✦ **Brokering other securities:** Brokers can also trade bonds, mutual funds, options, exchange-traded funds, and other investments on your behalf.

Personal stockbrokers make their money from individual investors — like you — through various fees, including these:

✦ **Brokerage commissions:** These fees are for trading stocks and other securities.

✦ **Margin interest charges:** Interest is charged to investors for borrowing against their brokerage account for investment purposes.

✦ **Service charges:** These charges are for performing administrative tasks and other functions. Brokers charge fees to investors for administering Registered Retirement Savings Plans (RRSPs), Registered Education Saving Plans (RESPs), Tax Free Savings Accounts (TFSAs), for mailing stocks in certificate form, and for other special services.

The distinction between personal stockbrokers and institutional stockbrokers is important. Institutional brokers make money from institutions and companies through investment banking and securities placement fees (such as initial public offerings and secondary offerings), advisory services, and other broker services. Personal stockbrokers generally offer the same services to individuals and small businesses.

Distinguishing between Investment Advisers and Discount Brokers

Stockbrokers fall into two basic categories: investment advisers (sometimes known as full-service brokers) and discount brokers. The type you choose really depends on what type of investor you are. In a nutshell, investment advisers are suitable for investors who need some guidance. Discount brokers are better for those investors who are sufficiently confident and knowledgeable about stock investing to manage with minimal help.

Investment advisers

Investment advisers are just what the name indicates. They try to provide as many services as possible for investors who open accounts with them. When you open an account at a brokerage firm, a representative is assigned to your account. This representative may be called an *account executive,* a *registered rep,* or a *financial consultant* by the brokerage firm. This person usually has a securities licence and is knowledgeable about stocks in particular and investing in general, hence the name stockbroker.

Scotia McLeod, RBC Dominion Securities, Macquarie Private Wealth, and TD Waterhouse Private Investment Advice have many investment advisers. Of course, all brokerage houses now have full-feature websites to give you information about their services. Get as informed as possible before you open your full-service account. An investment adviser should be there to help make your fortune, not to help make you . . . uh . . . broker.

What they can do for you

Your investment adviser is responsible for assisting you, answering questions about your account and the securities in your portfolio, and transacting your buy and sell orders. Some things that investment advisers can do for you include:

✦ **Offer guidance and advice:** The greatest distinction between investment advisers and discount brokers is the personal attention you receive from your account rep. You get to be on a first-name basis with an investment adviser, and you disclose much information about your finances and financial goals. The rep is there to make recommendations about stocks and funds that are likely to be suitable for you.

✦ **Provide access to research:** Investment advisers can give you access to their investment research department, which can give you in-depth information and analysis on a particular company. This information can be very valuable, but be aware of the pitfalls.

✦ **Help you achieve your investment objectives:** Beyond advice on specific investments, a good rep gets to know you and your investment goals and *then* offers advice and answers your questions about how specific investments and strategies can help you accomplish your wealth-building goals.

✦ **Make investment decisions on your behalf:** Many investors don't want to be bothered when it comes to investment decisions. Investment advisers can actually make decisions for your account with your authorization. This service is fine, but insist they give you a reasonable explanation of their choices.

✦ **Offer non-investing advice:** A professional adviser can also assist you with reducing your debt and taxes while giving you sound financial planning strategies that can last a lifetime.

What to watch out for

Although investment advisers — with their seemingly limitless assistance — can make life easy for an investor, you need to remember some important points to avoid problems:

✦ **Advisers and account reps are still salespeople.** Most are honest; some are complete shills. No matter how well they treat you, they're still compensated based on their ability to produce revenue for the brokerage firm. They generate commissions and fees from you on behalf of the company. (In other words, they're paid to sell you things.)

✦ **Some advisers don't give clear reasons for their decisions.** Once again, whenever your rep makes a suggestion or recommendation be sure to ask why — and request a complete answer that includes the reasoning behind the recommendation. A good adviser is able to clearly explain the reasoning behind every suggestion. If you don't fully understand and agree with the advice, don't take it.

✦ **Investment advisers can be costly.** Working with an investment adviser costs more than working with a discount broker. Discount brokers are paid simply for performing the act of trading stocks for you. Investment advisers do that and more. Additionally, they provide advice and guidance. Because of that, investment advisers are more expensive (higher brokerage commissions and advisory fees). Also, most investment advisers expect you to invest at least $5,000 to $10,000 just to open an account.

✦ **Some brokers make bad decisions for you.** Handing over decision-making authority to your rep can be a possible negative because letting others make financial decisions for you is always dicey — especially when they're using *your* money. If they make poor investment choices that lose you money, you may not have any recourse because you authorized them to act on your behalf.

✦ **Many investment advisers engage in an activity called churning.** *Churning* is basically buying and selling stocks for the sole purpose of generating commissions. Churning is great for investment advisers but really hurts customers. If your account shows a lot of activity, definitely ask for justification. Commissions, especially those charged by investment advisers, can take a big bite out of your wealth. Don't tolerate churning or any other suspicious activity.

Discount brokers

Perhaps you don't need any hand holding from a broker. You know what you want, and you can make your own investment decisions. All you need is someone to transact your trades. In that case, go with a discount broker. They don't offer face-to-face advice — though many do provide research materials, analyst reports, and other tools to help you decide what to invest in. Discount brokers let you buy and sell through the Internet or by phone (automated or via a live representative who trades without providing advice).

Discount brokers, as the name implies, are cheaper to engage than investment advisers. Because you're advising yourself (or getting advice from third parties such as newsletters or independent advisers), you can save on the costs you incur when you pay for an investment adviser.

If you choose to work with a discount broker, you must know as much as possible about your personal goals and needs. You have a greater responsibility for conducting adequate research to make good stock selections. You must be prepared to accept the outcome, whatever that outcome may be.

What they can do for you

Discount brokers offer some significant advantages over investment advisers, such as

✦ **Lower cost:** This lower cost is usually the result of lower commissions, and it's the primary benefit of using discount brokers.

✦ **Unbiased service:** Discount brokers offer you the ability to just trade only. Because they don't offer advice, they have no vested interest in trying to sell you any particular stock.

✦ **Access to information:** Established discount brokers offer extensive educational and research materials at their offices or on their websites.

**Book III
Chapter 3**

Going for Brokers

What to watch out for

Of course, doing business with discount brokers also has its downside, including the following:

✦ **No guidance:** Because you've chosen a discount broker, you *know* not to expect guidance, but the broker should make this fact clear to you anyway. If you're a knowledgeable investor, the lack of advice is considered a positive thing — no interference.

✦ **Hidden fees:** Discount brokers may shout about their lower commissions, but commissions aren't their only way of making money. Many discount brokers charge extra for services that you may think are included, such as issuing a stock certificate, letting you access certain types of research, or mailing a statement. Ask whether they assess fees for maintaining RRSPs or fees for transferring stocks and other securities (such as bonds) in or out of your account. Find out what interest rates they charge for borrowing through brokerage accounts.

✦ **Padded prices:** Because discount brokers do not carry any inventory of stock or bonds, you will be vulnerable to paying more for your purchases and getting less for your sales due to the spread between bid and offer prices.

✦ **Minimal customer service:** If you deal with a discount brokerage firm, find out about its customer-service capability. If you can't transact business on its website, find out where you can call for assistance with your order.

Choosing a Broker

Look for a firm that's a member in good standing of IIROC — the Investment Industry Regulatory Organization of Canada (www.iiroc.ca). IIROC is Canada's self-regulatory organization, which oversees all member investment dealers. It also watches out for trading activity on debt and equity markets in Canada. IIROC sets regulatory and investment industry standards, tries to protect investor interests, and attempts to strengthen market integrity while maintaining smoothly operating capital markets.

In addition to performing the above "reference check," be sure to check out the provincial securities commissions. They have a national group that works toward making securities regulations consistent and standardized across Canada. This group is called the Canadian Securities Administrators

(CSA; www.securities-administrators.ca). Through the CSA, securities regulators from each of the ten provinces and three territories have teamed up to protect Canadian investors from "unfair, improper, or fraudulent practices" and to foster "fair and efficient capital markets."

However organized they are, provincial securities commissions possess nowhere near the power that's wielded by the more independent regulators of U.S. stock markets. As a result, options and remedies to the Canadian individual stock investor are very limited.

Before you choose a broker, you need to analyze and reassess your personal investing style. When you know yourself and the way you invest, you can proceed to finding the kind of broker that fits your needs. It's almost like choosing shoes: if you don't know your size, you can't get a proper fit. (And if you get it wrong, you can be in for a really uncomfortable future.)

When the time comes to choose a broker, keep the following points in mind:

✦ Match your investment style with an IIROC-member brokerage firm that charges the least amount of money for the services you're likely to use most frequently.

✦ Compare all the costs of buying, selling, and holding stocks and other securities through a broker. Don't look only at commissions; compare other costs, too, such as margin interest and other service charges.

✦ Contact a few firms before making your selection. Ask them if they are currently seeking accounts like yours. Ask for and call a few references to find out about the broker's strengths and weaknesses.

✦ Read articles that compare brokers in publications and newspapers such as *Canadian Business, The Globe and Mail*, and the *National Post*.

Your broker will influence your finances in a big way, so take the time to get to know your new financial friend to decide whether this is the right person for you.

The Canadian Investor Protection Fund (CIPF) is overseen by the Canadian investment industry and provides coverage for Canadians making investments through its members. It insures brokerage accounts similar to the way the Canada Deposit Insurance Corporation (CDIC) insures bank accounts. CIPF covers a customer's general accounts — up to $1,000,000 — for losses related to securities, commodity and futures contracts, segregated insurance funds, and cash balances. However, the amount of cash losses that you can claim as part of this limit is restricted, and other important coverage restrictions exist. Check out the CIPF website (www.cipf.ca) for full and detailed information. By the way — you aren't covered if the market corrects! When a market goes way higher or lower than it should, a natural tendency exists for stock indices to respond by falling or rising rapidly and settle into a more "normal" state.

Online Investing Services

Investing online has flourished for several reasons. Online investing, via a discount brokerage service (conventional or Internet-centric), lets you buy and sell stocks and other financial instruments using your personal computer and an Internet connection — in some cases, you can even invest using a mobile app. As we mention earlier, discount brokers provide most online broker services, but many investment advisers work for firms that support online services, as well. Several factors contribute to the popularity of online investing:

+ **Information aplenty:** The Internet provides quick and easy access to raw investment information (such as a stock quote) as well as refined information (such as a broker's analysis of a company, or other information services previously available only to investment professionals).

+ **Lower commission rates:** By eliminating the need for full-service brokers or advisers, online brokers can offer commission rates that are lower than offline brokers charge. For example, buying 500 shares of Potash Corporation through a traditional investment adviser could cost you about $100 in commissions. Online, the cost could be between $10 and $30, depending on the size of your assets and how frequently you trade. Easy account access is another reason for the popularity of online investing. Online brokers conveniently provide you with access to your account and the ability to place orders anytime and anywhere in Canada (or abroad) as long as you have an Internet connection.

+ **You're in charge:** Control of the investment process appeals to many investors. You can research a company, trade shares in it, monitor its progress, and chat with other shareholders in that company to hear their opinions.

Getting online trading services for less

As you may have guessed, no two online brokerage services are alike. Furthermore, individual brokerages may change their services and fees to keep pace with their competitors. To find the online broker that best meets your needs, you must investigate the prices, services, and features that various brokers offer.

Make certain that your brokerage doesn't charge you for services that are free elsewhere, or are hidden. Some hidden fees may include:

✦ Fees to close your account.

✦ Fees to withdraw funds from your trading account.

✦ Higher fees for accepting *odd-lot orders* (for example, orders that include increments of fewer than 100 shares).

Trading online at a discount

You can't measure broker service with a formula. You have to look at both financial and non-financial criteria.

Cost is one factor, as we just found out. Definitely look at how much each broker charges in commission at different volumes of trades. Also assess the quality of online trade execution by talking to others who use a service that you are considering. Are real-time quotes available? Is research material available? What is the overall ease of use of the service? Does the broker provide online screening tools?

Product selection is another important factor. You want to be able to trade things like guaranteed investment certificates (GICs), gold and silver certificates, federal and provincial bonds, futures, Canadian and foreign equities, and so on. A list of investment products to consider is provided later in this chapter.

Response time should be quick. Many online brokers boast trade execution times of a few seconds! Phone each firm to see how long it takes for the broker to respond. E-mail each broker under consideration with a few questions; ask for an application to be sent by mail. Again, evaluate the response time.

**Book III
Chapter 3**

Going for Brokers

Table 3–1 lists several discount brokerage services in Canada.

Table 3–1	You Can Trade at a Discount	
	Sample of Online Trade Fees	*Automated Telephone Trade Fee*
BMO InvestorLine 1-888-776-6886 www.bmoinvestorline.com	$29 for up to 29 trades a quarter; $9.95 for 30 trades or more	$29 for under $50,000 in assets; $9.95 for $50,000 in assets and above
CIBC Investor's Edge 1-800-567-3343 www.investorsedge.cibc.com	$28.95 for up to 1,000 shares; $9.95 for more than 30 trades a quarter; $6.95 for 150 plus trades a quarter	$35 plus a fee per share for Canadian stocks; $39 plus a fee per share for U.S. securities
Disnat 1-800-268-8471 www.disnat.com	$9.95 for 10 or more trades per month; $29 for under 10 trades per month	$35 plus a fee per share for Canadian stocks; $39 plus a fee per share for U.S. securities
HSBC InvestDirect 1-800-760-1180 www.investdirect.hsbc.ca/	$28.88 for up to 1,000 shares; $9.88 for 30 to 99 trades a quarter; $6.88 for 100 plus trades a quarter	$35 plus a fee per share for Canadian stocks; $39 plus a fee per share for U.S. securities
National Bank Direct Brokerage 1-800-363-3511 www.nbc.ca	$28.95 for up to 1,000 shares	$28.95 for up to 1,000 shares
Qtrade Financial Group 1-877-787-2330 www.qtrade.ca	$19 for up to 1,000 shares; $9.95 for 30 to 150 trades per quarter; $7 for 150 plus trades per quarter	Not available
RBC Direct Investing 1-800-769-2560 www.rbcdirectinvesting.com	$28.95 for up to 1,000 shares; $9.95 for 30 to 150 trades per quarter; $6.95 for 150 plus trades per quarter	$28.95 for up to 1,000 shares; $9.95 for 30 to 150 trades per quarter; $6.95 for 150 plus trades per quarter

	Sample of Online Trade Fees	*Automated Telephone Trade Fee*
Scotia iTRADE 1-888-872-3388 https://www.scotia itrade.com	$19.99 for up to 1,000 shares; $9.99 for 30 to 150 trades per quarter; $6.99 for 150 plus trades per quarter	Not available
ScotiaMcLeod Direct Investing 1-800-263-3430 www.scotiamcleod direct.com	$24.99 for up to 1,000 shares; $9.99 for 30 to 150 trades per quarter; $6.99 for 150 plus trades per quarter	Not available
TD Waterhouse 1-800-465-5463 www.tdwaterhouse.ca	$29 for up to 1,000 shares; $9.99 for 30 to 150 trades per quarter; $7.00 for 150 plus trades per quarter	$35 plus a fee per share for Canadian stocks; $39 plus a fee per share for U.S. securities

Checking out special features

Commission structures range widely from firm to firm because some Internet brokers include special or added features. When deciding which broker is best for you, factor in some or all of the features that we list in this section. First, consider whether each broker offers these features in your cash account:

✦ Confirmation of trades (via e-mail, phone, posted live to your accounts, or Canada Post)

✦ Consolidation of your money market, investment, and chequing and savings accounts

✦ Historical review of your trading activities

✦ Low minimum amount required to open an account

✦ Low or no fees with minimum equity balance

✦ Summary of your portfolio's value

Also, find out which of the following types of investments the broker enables you to trade:

+ Bonds (corporate, government, or municipal)
+ Canada and provincial savings bonds
+ Commercial paper
+ Government of Canada and U.S. Treasury bills
+ Guaranteed investment certificates (GICs)
+ Investment trusts
+ Mutual funds
+ Options
+ Precious metals
+ Stocks and preferred shares (foreign or domestic)
+ Treasury bills and bankers acceptances
+ Exchange traded funds (ETFs)
+ Limited partnerships
+ Flow-through shares
+ IPOs, treasury and secondary offerings

Finally, determine whether the brokerage offers the following analytical and research features:

+ Company profiles and breaking news
+ Economic forecasts
+ End-of-day prices automatically sent to you or updated in your accounts online
+ Real-time online quotes
+ Reports on insider trading and short positions
+ News on trading halts and merger announcements
+ Calendar of anticipated news releases

Opening your online brokerage account

Internet brokerage firms are basically cash-and-carry enterprises. They all require investors to open an account before trading — a process that takes a few days to two weeks to complete. Because most Canadian brokerages don't require minimum account balances, you can open an account with a nominal deposit. However, you can buy only so many shares of any of the banks or pipelines with $300 in your account!

When you place an order, your Internet broker withdraws money from your cash account to cover your trade. If you sell stock or receive a dividend, the Internet broker adds money to your cash account. All Internet brokers require that you complete an application form (which you can download online by following the instructions given at the website). The form will ask for your name, address, and social insurance number; your work history; and a personal cheque, certified cheque, or money order for the minimum amount (if any) needed to open an account. Canadian law requires all brokerages to have your signature on file. The Internet broker then verifies all the information on the form and opens your account. Investors are sent a personal identification number (PIN) by mail. After you receive your PIN, you're ready to begin trading.

Types of Brokerage Accounts

When you start investing in the stock market, you have to somehow *pay* for the stocks you buy. Most brokerage firms offer investors several different types of accounts, each serving a different purpose. We present three of the most common types in the following sections. The basic difference boils down to how particular brokers view your *creditworthiness* when it comes to trading securities. If your credit isn't great, your only choice is a cash account. If your credit is good, you can open either a cash account or a margin account. After you qualify for a margin account, you can (with additional approval) upgrade it to do options trades.

To open an account, you have to fill out an application and submit a cheque or money order for at least the minimum amount required to establish an account.

Cash accounts

A *cash account* means just what you think it means. You must deposit a sum of money along with the new account application to begin trading. The amount of your initial deposit varies from broker to broker. Although some brokers have a minimum of $10,000, others let you open an account for as little as $75. Once in a while you may see a broker offering cash accounts with no minimum deposit, usually as part of a promotion. Qualifying for a cash account is usually easy as long as you have cash and a pulse.

With a cash account, your money has to be deposited in the account before the settlement date for any trade you make. The settlement occurs three business days after the trade date. In other words, if you call your broker on Monday, October 10, and order 50 shares of CashLess Corp. at $20 per share, then on Thursday, October 13, you better have $1,000 in cash sitting in your account (plus commission). Otherwise, the purchase doesn't go through.

If you have cash in a brokerage account, see whether the broker will pay you interest on the uninvested cash in it, and how much. Some offer a service in which uninvested money earns money market rates.

Margin accounts

A *margin account* gives you the ability to borrow money against the securities in the account to buy more securities. Because you have the ability to borrow in a margin account, you have to be qualified and approved by the broker. After you're approved, this newfound credit gives you more leverage so that you can buy more securities or sell short.

Why use margin? "Margin" is to securities what "mortgage" is to real estate. You can buy real estate with 100 percent cash, but many times using borrowed funds makes sense because you may not have enough money or you prefer not to pay all cash. With margin, you could, for example, be able to buy $10,000 worth of securities with as little as $5,000 in cash (or securities owned) sitting in your account. This example assumes a 50-percent margin limit. The balance of the securities purchase is acquired using a loan (margin) from the brokerage firm.

For stock trading, the margin limit is usually 50 percent. (For very conservative stocks, the margin limit can be as high as 75 percent; ask your broker to inform you about margin limits on a stock-by-stock basis.) The interest rate that you pay varies depending on the broker, but most brokers generally charge a rate that's several points higher than their own borrowing rate.

Option accounts

An *option account* gives you all the capabilities of a margin account (which in turn also gives you the capabilities of a cash account) plus the ability to trade options on stocks and stock indexes. To upgrade your margin account to an options account, your Canadian broker must by law ask you to sign a statement that you're knowledgeable about options and familiar with the risks associated with them.

Options can be a very effective addition to a stock investor's array of wealth-building investment tools. A more comprehensive review of options is available in the book *Stock Options For Dummies* by Alan R. Simon (Wiley).

Checking Out Brokerage Orders

Orders you place with your stockbroker fit neatly into three categories:

✦ Time-related orders

✦ Condition-related orders

✦ Advanced orders

At the very least, get familiar with the first two types of orders. They're easy to implement, and they're invaluable tools for wealth building and (more importantly) wealth saving. Advanced orders usually are combinations of the first two types.

 Using a combination of orders helps you fine-tune your strategy so that you can maintain greater control over your investments. Speak with your broker about the different types of orders you can use to maximize the gains (or minimize the losses) from your stock investing activities. You also can read the broker's policies on stock orders at the brokerage website.

On the clock: Time-related orders

Time-related orders mean just that; the order has a time limit. Typically, you use these orders in conjunction with conditional orders. The two most common time-related orders are day orders and good-till-cancelled (GTC) orders.

Day order

A *day order* is an order to trade a stock that expires at the end of that particular trading day. If you tell your broker, "Buy BYOB Inc. at $37.50 and make it a day order," you mean that you want to purchase the stock at $37.50. But if the stock doesn't hit that price, your order expires at the end of the trading day unfilled. Why would you place such an order? Maybe BYOB is trading at $39, but you don't want to buy it at that price because you don't believe the stock is worth it. Consequently, you have no problem not getting the stock that day. Day orders also apply to selling stock.

When would you use day orders? It depends on your preferences and personal circumstances. We don't use day orders too often because few events cause us to say, "Gee, we'll just try to buy or sell between now and the end of today's trading action." However, you may feel that you don't want a specified order to linger beyond today's market action. Perhaps you want to test a price. ("I want to get rid of stock A at $39 to make a quick profit, but it's currently trading at $37.50. However, I may change my mind tomorrow.") A day order is the perfect strategy to use in this case.

If you make any trade and don't specify time with the order, most (if not all) brokers automatically treat it as a day order.

Good-till-cancelled (GTC)

A good-till-cancelled (GTC) order is the most commonly requested open order by investors. Although GTC orders are time-related, they're always tied to a condition, such as when the stock achieves a certain price. The GTC order means just what it says: The order stays in effect until it's transacted or until the investor cancels it. Although the order implies that it can run indefinitely, most Canadian brokers have a limit of 30 or 60 days (or more). By that time, either the broker allows the order to expire or contacts you to see whether you want to extend it. Ask about your broker's particular policy.

A GTC order is usually coupled with conditional or condition-related orders. For example, say you want to buy ASAP Corp. stock but you don't want to buy it at the current price of $48 per share. You've done your homework on the stock, including looking at the stock's price-to-earnings ratio, price-to-book ratio, and so on. So you say, "Hey, this stock isn't worth $48 per share. I'd only buy it at $36 per share." You think the stock would make a good addition to your portfolio, but not at the current market price. (It's over-priced or overvalued, according to your analysis.) How should you proceed? Your best bet is to ask your broker to do a "GTC order at $36." This request means that your broker will buy the shares if and when they hit the $36 mark (or until you cancel the order). Just make sure your account has the funds available to complete the transaction. Many brokers have a 90 day limit for GTC orders so that they are reviewed with clients who might not remember all their open orders.

GTC orders are very useful, so become familiar with your broker's policy on them. While you're at it, ask whether any fees apply. Many brokers don't charge for GTC orders because, if they happen to result in a trade order, they generate a normal commission just as any stock transaction does. Other brokers may charge a small fee.

To be successful with GTC orders, you need to know the following information:

+ **When you want to buy:** People have had a tendency to rush into buying a stock without giving some thought to what they could do to get more for their money. Some Canadians don't realize that the stock market can be a place for bargain-hunting consumers. If you're ready to buy a quality pair of socks for $16 in a department store but the sales clerk says that those same socks are going on sale tomorrow for only $8, what would you do — assuming that you're a cost-conscious consumer? Unless you're barefoot, you're probably better off waiting. The same point holds true with stocks.

Say you want to buy SOX Inc. at $26, but it's currently trading at $30. You think that $30 is too expensive, but you're happy to buy the stock at $26 or lower. However, you have no idea whether the stock will move to your desired price today, tomorrow, next week, or even next month (or maybe never). In this case, a GTC order is appropriate.

✦ **When you want to sell:** What if you bought some socks at a department store and then you discovered that they have holes (darn it!)? Wouldn't you want to get rid of them? Of course you would. If a stock's price starts to unravel, you want to be able to get rid of it, as well.

Perhaps you already own SOX (at $25, for instance) but are concerned that market conditions may drive the price lower. You're not certain which way the stock will move in the coming days and weeks. In this case, a GTC order to sell the stock at a specified price is a suitable strategy. Because the stock price is $25, you may want to place a GTC order to sell it if it falls to $22.50 to prevent further losses. Again, in this example, GTC is the time frame, and it accompanies a condition (sell when the stock hits $22.50).

At your command: Condition-related orders

A condition-related order means that the order is executed only when a certain condition is met. Conditional orders enhance your ability to buy stocks at a lower price, to sell at a better price, or to minimize potential losses. When stock markets become bearish or uncertain, conditional orders are highly recommended. A good example of a conditional order is a *limit order*. A limit order may say, "Buy Tim Hortons at $45." But if Tim Hortons isn't at $45 (this price is the condition), the order isn't executed.

Market orders

When you buy stock, the simplest type of order is a *market order* — an order to buy or sell a stock at the market's current best available price. It doesn't get any more basic than that.

Here's an example: Westjet is available at the market price of $10. When you call up your broker and instruct him to buy 100 shares "at the market," he'll implement the order for your account, and you pay $1,000 plus commission.

We say "current best available price" because the stock's price is constantly moving, and catching the best price can be a function of the broker's ability to process the stock purchase. For very active stocks, the price change can happen within seconds. It's not unheard of to have three brokers simultaneously place orders for the same stocks and get three different prices because of differences in the brokers' capabilities. (Some computers are faster than others.)

The advantage of a market order is that the transaction is processed immediately, and you get your stock without worrying about whether it hits a particular price. For example, if you buy Westjet with a market order, you know that by the end of that phone call (or website visit) you're assured of getting the stock. The disadvantage of a market order is that you can't control the price that you pay for the stock. Whether you're buying or selling your shares, you may not realize the exact price you expect (especially if you're buying a volatile stock — usually unpredictable because it has low trading volumes).

Market orders get finalized in the chronological order in which they're placed. Your price may change because the orders ahead of you in line caused the stock price to rise or fall based on the latest events.

Stop orders (also known as stop-loss orders)

A *stop order* (or *stop-loss order,* if you own the stock) is a condition-related order that instructs the broker to sell a particular stock only when the stock reaches a particular price. It acts like a trigger, and the stop order converts to a market order to sell the stock immediately.

The stop-loss order isn't designed to take advantage of small, short-term moves in the stock's price. It's meant to help you protect the bulk of your money when the market turns against your stock investment in a sudden manner.

Say that your Westjet stock rises to $20 per share, and you seek to protect your investment against a possible future market decline. A stop-loss order at $18 triggers your broker to sell the stock immediately if it falls to the $18 mark. In this example, if the stock suddenly drops to $17, it still triggers the stop-loss order, but the finalized sale price is $17. In a volatile market, you may not be able to sell at your precise stop-loss price. However, because the order automatically gets converted into a market order, the sale will be done, and you prevent further declines in the stock.

The main benefit of a stop-loss order is that it prevents a major decline in a stock that you own. It's a form of discipline that's important in investing because it minimizes potential losses. You may find it agonizing to sell a stock that has fallen. If you don't sell, however, your stock may continue to plummet as you keep holding on while hoping for a rebound in the price.

Most investors set a stop-loss amount at about 10 percent below the market value of a stock. This percentage gives the stock some room to fluctuate, which most stocks tend to do on a day-to-day basis.

Trailing stops

Trailing stops are an important technique in wealth preservation for seasoned stock investors, and they can be one of your key strategies in using stop-loss orders. A *trailing stop* is a stop-loss order that an investor actively manages by moving it up along with the stock's market price. The stop-loss order "trails" the stock price upward. As the stop-loss goes upward, it protects more and more of the stock's value from declining.

A real-life example may be the best way to help you understand trailing stops. Say you bought a stock at $25. As soon as you finished buying it, you immediately told your broker to put a stop-loss order at $22 and to make it a good-till-cancelled (GTC) order. Think of what you did. In effect, you placed an ongoing safety net under your stock. The stock can go as high as the sky, but if it should fall, the stock's price triggers a market order at $22. Your stock is automatically sold, minimizing your loss.

If your stock goes to $50 in a few months, you can call your broker, cancel the former stop-loss order at $22, and replace it with a new (higher) stop-loss order. You simply say, "Please put a new stop-loss order at $45 and make it a GTC order." This higher stop-loss price protects not only your original investment of $25 but also a big chunk of your profit, as well. As time goes by and the stock price climbs, you can continue to raise the stop-loss price and add GTC provisions. Now you know why it's called a trailing stop: It trails the stock price upward like a giant tail. All along the way, it protects more and more of your growing investment without limiting its upward movement.

William O'Neill, publisher and founder of *Investor's Business Daily,* advocates setting a trailing stop of 8 percent below your purchase price. That's his preference. Some investors who invest in very volatile stocks may put in trailing stops of 20 or 25 percent. Is a stop-loss order desirable or advisable in every situation? No. It depends on your level of experience, your investment goals, and the market environment. Still, stop-loss orders are appropriate in most cases, especially if the market seems uncertain (or if you do!).

A trailing stop is a stop-loss order that you actively manage. The stop-loss order is good-till-cancelled (GTC), and it constantly trails the stock's price as it moves up. To successfully implement trailing stops, keep the following points in mind:

✦ **Remember that brokers usually don't place trailing stops for you automatically.** In fact, they won't (or shouldn't) place any type of order without your consent. Deciding on the type of order to place is your responsibility. You can raise, lower, or cancel a trailing-stop order at will, but you need to monitor your investment when substantial moves occur to respond to the movement appropriately.

✦ **Change the stop-loss order when the stock price moves significantly.** Hopefully, you won't call your broker every time the stock moves 50 cents. Change the stop-loss order when the stock price moves about 10 percent. When you initially purchase the stock (say at $90), request that the broker place the stop-loss order at $81. When the stock moves to $100, cancel the $81 stop-loss order and replace it at $90. When the stock's price moves to $110, change the stop-loss order to $99, and so on.

✦ **Understand your broker's policy on GTC orders.** If your broker usually lets GTC orders expire after 30 or 60 days, be aware of it. You don't want to risk a sudden drop in your stock's price without the stop-loss order protection. If your broker's time limit is 60 days, note this so that you can renew the order for additional time.

✦ **Monitor your stock.** A trailing stop isn't a set-it-and-forget-it technique. Monitoring your investment is critical. Of course, if your investment falls, the stop-loss order prevents further loss. Should the stock price rise substantially, remember to adjust your trailing stop accordingly. Keep raising the safety net as the stock continues to rise. Part of monitoring the stock is knowing the beta, which you can read more about in the next section.

Using beta measurement

To be a successful investor, you need to understand the volatility of the particular stock you invest in. In stock market parlance, this volatility is also called the beta of a stock. *Beta* is a quantitative measure of the volatility of a given stock (and mutual funds and portfolios, too) relative to the overall market, usually the S&P 500 Index. Beta specifically measures the performance movement of a stock as the S&P moves 1 percent up or down. A beta measurement above 1 is more volatile than the overall market, while a beta below 1 is less volatile. Some stocks are relatively stable in their price movements; others jump around.

Because beta measures how volatile or unstable the stock's price is, it tends to be uttered in the same breath as "risk" — more volatility indicates more risk. Similarly, less volatility tends to mean less risk.

You can find a company's beta at websites that usually provide a lot of financial information, such as NASDAQ's website (www.nasdaq.com) or Yahoo! Finance (ca.finance.yahoo.com).

The beta is useful to know because it gives you a general idea of the stock's trading range. If a stock is currently priced at $50 and it typically trades in the $48–$52 range, a trailing stop at $49 doesn't make sense. In this case, your stock will probably be sold the same day you initiate the stop-loss order. If your stock is a volatile growth stock that could swing up and down by 10 percent, you should more logically set your stop-loss order at 15 percent below that day's price.

The stock of a large-cap company in a mature industry tends to have a low beta — one close to the overall market. Small- and mid-cap stocks in new or emerging industries tend to have greater volatility in their day-to-day price fluctuations; hence, they tend to have a high beta. (You can find out more about large-, small-, and mid-cap stocks in Chapter 1.)

Limit orders

A *limit order* is a very precise condition-related order, implying that a limit exists either on the buy or the sell side of the transaction. You want to buy (or sell) only at a specified price or better. Period. Limit orders work well for you if you're buying the stock, but they may not be good for you if you're selling the stock. Here's how it works in both instances:

✦ **When you're buying:** Just because you like a particular company and you want its stock, it doesn't mean you're willing to pay the current market price. Maybe you want to buy Westjet but the current market price of $20 per share isn't acceptable to you. You prefer to buy it at $16 because you think this price reflects its true market value. So what do you do? You tell your broker, "Buy Westjet with a limit order at $16." You also have to specify whether it's a day order (good for the day) or a GTC order (which we discussed earlier in this chapter).

What happens if the stock experiences great volatility? What if it drops to $16.01 and then suddenly drops again to $15.95 on the next move? Actually, nothing happens, you may be dismayed to hear. Because your order was limited to $16, it can be transacted only at $16, no more or less. The only way for this particular trade to occur is if the stock rises back to $16. However, if the price keeps dropping, then your limit order isn't transacted and it may expire or be cancelled.

On the other hand, many brokers, including TD Waterhouse, interpret the limit order as "Buy at this specific price or better." Presumably, if your limit order is to buy the stock at $10, you'll be just as happy if your broker buys that stock for you at $9.95. This way, if you don't get exactly $10 because the stock's price was volatile, you'll still get the stock at a lower price. Speak to your particular broker to be clear about their meaning of limit order.

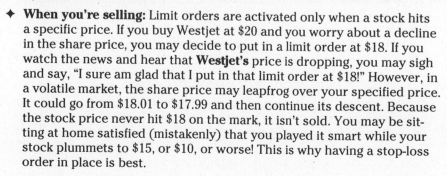

✦ **When you're selling:** Limit orders are activated only when a stock hits a specific price. If you buy Westjet at $20 and you worry about a decline in the share price, you may decide to put in a limit order at $18. If you watch the news and hear that **Westjet's** price is dropping, you may sigh and say, "I sure am glad that I put in that limit order at $18!" However, in a volatile market, the share price may leapfrog over your specified price. It could go from $18.01 to $17.99 and then continue its descent. Because the stock price never hit $18 on the mark, it isn't sold. You may be sitting at home satisfied (mistakenly) that you played it smart while your stock plummets to $15, or $10, or worse! This is why having a stop-loss order in place is best.

The joys of technology: Advanced orders

Brokers have added sophisticated capabilities to the existing repertoire of orders that are available for stock investors. One example is *advanced orders,* which provide investors with a way to use a combination of orders for more sophisticated trades. An example of an advanced order is something like, "Only sell stock B, and if it sells, use the proceeds to buy stock D." You get the idea. Check with your broker for details on this service. Examples of advanced orders include the following:

✦ **One order cancels another order:** This happens when you enter two orders simultaneously with the condition that if one order is executed, the second order is automatically cancelled.

✦ **One order triggers another order:** Here you submit an order, and if that order is filled another order is automatically submitted. Many brokers have different names for these types of orders, so ask them if they can provide such an order.

Other types of advanced orders are available, but you get the picture. Talk to your brokerage firm and find out what's available in your particular account. Investors need to know that today's technology allows them to have more power and control over the implementation of buying and selling transactions.

Pass the Margin, Please

As we said earlier, *margin* means buying securities, such as stocks, by using funds that you borrow from your broker. Buying stock on margin is similar to buying a condominium with a mortgage. If you buy a condominium at the purchase price of $100,000 and put 10 percent down, your equity (the part you own) is $10,000 and you borrow the remaining $90,000 with a mortgage. If the value of the condo rises to $120,000 and you sell (for simplicity's sake, we don't include closing costs in this example), you will have obviously made a profit of $20,000. The $20,000 gain on the property represents a gain of 20 percent on the purchase price of $100,000, but because your real investment was $10,000 (the down payment), your gain effectively works out to 200 percent (a gain of $20,000 on your initial investment of $10,000).

Examining marginal outcomes

Suppose you think that the stock for the company Manitoba Telecom Inc., currently at $40 per share, will go up in value. You want to buy 100 shares, but you have only $2,000. What can you do? If you're intent on buying 100 shares (versus simply buying the 50 shares that you have the cash for), you can borrow the additional $2,000 from your broker on margin. If you do that, what are the potential outcomes?

If the stock price goes up

This is the best outcome for you. If Manitoba Telecom goes to $50 per share, your investment will be worth $5,000 and your outstanding margin loan will be $2,000. If you sell, the total proceeds will pay off the loan and leave you with $3,000. Because your initial investment was $2,000, your profit is a solid 50 percent, because ultimately your $2,000 principal amount generated a $1,000 profit. (For the sake of this example, we leave out any charges such as commissions and interest paid on the margin loan.) However, if you pay the entire $4,000 upfront — without the margin loan — your $4,000 investment will generate a profit of $1,000, or 25 percent. Using margin, you double the return on your money.

Leverage, when used properly, is very profitable. However, it is still debt, so understand that you must pay it off eventually.

If the stock price fails to rise

If the stock goes nowhere, you still have to pay interest on that margin loan. If the stock pays dividends, this money can defray some of the cost of the margin loan. In other words, dividends can help you pay off what you borrow from the broker.

Having the stock neither rise nor fall may seem like a neutral situation, but you pay interest on your margin loan with each passing day. For this reason, margin trading can be a good consideration for conservative investors only if the stock pays a high dividend. Many times, a high dividend from $4,000 worth of stock can exceed the margin interest you have to pay on the $2,000 (50 percent) you borrow from the broker to buy that stock.

If the stock price goes down

If the stock price falls, buying on margin can work against you. What if Manitoba Telecom goes to $38 per share? The market value of 100 shares will be $3,800, but your equity will shrink to only $1,800 because you have to pay back your $2,000 margin loan. You're not exactly looking at a disaster at this point, but you'd better be careful, because the margin loan exceeds 50 percent of your stock investment. If it goes any lower, you may get the notorious *margin call*, when the broker actually contacts you to ask you to restore the ratio between the margin loan and the value of the securities. See the following section for information about appropriate debt-to-equity ratios.

Maintaining your balance

When you purchase stock on margin, you must maintain a balanced ratio of margin debt to equity of at least 50 percent. If the debt portion exceeds this limit, you'll be required to restore the ratio by depositing either more securities or more cash into your brokerage account. The additional securities you deposit can be transferred from another account.

If, for example, Manitoba Telecom falls to $28 per share, the margin loan portion exceeds 50 percent of the equity value in that stock — in this case, the market value of your stock is $2,800, but the margin loan is still at $2,000.

**Book III
Chapter 3**

Going for Brokers

The margin loan is a worrisome 71 percent of the market value ($2,000 ÷ $2,800 = 71 percent). Expect to get a call from your broker to put more securities or cash into the account to restore the 50 percent balance.

If you can't come up with more stock, other securities, or cash, the next step is to sell stock from the account and then to use the proceeds to pay off the margin loan. For you, it means realizing a capital loss — you lost money on your investment.

Margin, as you can see, can escalate your profits (on the upside), but magnify your losses (on the downside). If your stock plummets drastically, you can end up with a margin loan that exceeds the market value of the stock that you used the loan to purchase. In the bear market of 2000, many people were hurt by stock losses, and a large number of these losses were made worse because people didn't manage the responsibilities involved with margin trading.

If you buy stock on margin, use a disciplined approach. Be extra careful when using leverage, such as a margin loan, because it can backfire. Keep the following points in mind:

✦ **Have ample reserves of cash or marginable securities in your account.** Try to keep the margin ratio at 35 percent or less to minimize the chance of a margin call.

✦ **Consider using margin to buy stock in large companies that have a relatively stable price and pay a good dividend (if you're a beginner).** Some people buy income stocks that have dividend yields that exceed the margin interest rate, meaning that the stock ends up paying for its own margin loan. Just remember those stop orders.

✦ **Monitor your stocks constantly.** If the market turns against you, the result will be especially painful if you use margin.

✦ **Have a payback plan for your margin debt.** Margin loans against your investments mean that you're paying interest. Your ultimate goal is to make money, and paying too much interest can eat into your profits.

Book IV

Trials and Tribulations of Trading

The 5th Wave   By Rich Tennant

EARLY INVESTORS TRACKING A STOCK

©RICHTENNANT

Contents at a Glance

Chapter 1: Trying Out Trading: The Basics

In This Chapter

✔ **Knowing what trading involves**

✔ **Understanding the different markets and exchanges**

✔ **Recognizing different types of brokerage firms**

✔ **Making effective use of your computer**

Ask ten people to define trading and it's likely you'll hear ten definitions. "Trading is buying and selling stocks," your long-term-investing friend might say. "Dabbling in options and futures," says your financially savvy neighbour. Or maybe it's investing in an RRSP, or day trading 25 stocks every day. According to Investopedia.com, a site every investor should utilize, "In financial markets, trading. . .can mean performing a transaction that involves the selling and purchasing of a security."

In other words, trading can, technically, be all of the above. We've previously discussed mutual funds and stock investing, but now we go even further in depth on how to choose securities to trade. We'll discuss terms like price-to-earnings ratios, and we'll explain the differences between investing in equities and trading futures and options.

While not everything here will apply to the long-term investor — in the chapters of this Book we refer to trading in the context of short-term buying and selling — it will give you a better appreciation of how the stock market works. And the more you understand about the markets, the easier it will be to build your wealth.

Introducing the Broad Markets

You may think the foundation of the Canadian economy resides in Ottawa, where the Minister of Finance develops economic policy, or that the foundation of the United States economy resides inside the Capitol, where Democrats and Republicans argue over job growth and tax cuts. Nope. The continent's true economic centres are Bay Street and Wall Street, where billions of dollars change hands each and every day, thousands of companies are traded, and millions of people's lives are affected.

Stocks are not the only things sold in the broad financial markets. Every day, futures, options, and bonds also are traded. Although we focus on stock exchanges in this chapter, we first need to briefly explain each type of market.

Stock markets

The stocks of almost every major Canadian and U.S. corporation, and many major foreign corporations, are traded on stock exchanges in Canada and the United States every day — and none of the money involved in these trades goes directly into the companies being traded.

We won't get too into stocks here – we cover stocks in Book 3 – but in this chapter, we will focus on the four top stock exchanges in North America:

✦ The Toronto Stock Exchange (TSX)

✦ The New York Stock Exchange (NYSE)

✦ NASDAQ (the National Association of Securities Dealers Automated Quotation system)

✦ The American Stock Exchange (Amex)

We also introduce you to the evolving world of electronic communications networks (ECNs), on which you can trade stocks directly and thus bypass brokers.

Futures markets

Futures trading actually started in Japan in the 18th century to trade rice and silk. This trading instrument was first used in North America in the 1850s for trading grains and other agricultural entities. Basically, futures trading means establishing a financial contract in which you try to predict the future value of a commodity that must be delivered at a specific time in the future. (Yup, a working crystal ball would be very useful here.) This type of trading is done on a commodities exchange. The largest such exchange in North America today is the Chicago Mercantile Exchange. Commodities include any product that can be bought and sold. Oil, cotton, and minerals are just a few of the products sold on a commodities exchange.

Futures contracts must have a seller (usually the person producing the commodity — a farmer or oil refinery, for example) and a buyer (usually a company that actually uses the commodity). You also can speculate on either side of the contract, basically meaning:

✦ When you buy a futures contract, you're agreeing to buy a commodity that is not yet ready for sale or hasn't yet been produced at a set price at a specific time in the future.

✦ When you sell a futures contract, you're agreeing to provide a commodity that is not yet ready for sale or hasn't yet been produced at a set price at a specific time in the future.

The futures contract states the price at which you agree to pay for or sell a certain amount of this product when it's delivered at a specific future date. Although most futures contracts are based on a physical commodity, the highest-volume futures contracts are based on the future value of stock indices and other financially related futures.

Unless you're a commercial consumer who plans to use the commodity, you won't actually take delivery of or provide the commodity for which you're trading a futures contract. You'll more than likely sell the futures contract you bought before you actually have to accept the commodity from a commercial customer. Futures contracts are used as financial instruments by producers, consumers, and speculators. We cover those players and futures contracts in much greater depth in Chapter 5.

Bond markets

Bonds are actually loan instruments. Companies sell bonds to borrow cash. If you buy a bond, you're essentially holding a company's debt or the debt of a government entity. The company or government that issues the bond agrees to pay you a certain amount of interest for a specific period of time in exchange for the use of your money. The big difference between stocks and bonds is that bonds are *debt obligations* and stocks are *equity*. Shareholders actually own a share of the corporation. Bondholders lend money to the company with no right of ownership. Bonds, however, are considered safer, because if a company files bankruptcy, bondholders are paid before shareholders. Bonds are a safety net and not actually a part of the trading world for individual position traders, swing traders, and day traders. While a greater dollar volume of bonds is traded each day, the primary traders for this venue are large institutional traders. Many individuals will use short-term bonds and Treasury bills as a safe place to park their cash while waiting to enter a trading position.

Options markets

An *option* is a contract that gives the buyer the right, but not the obligation, either to buy or to sell the underlying asset upon which the option is based at a specified price on or before a specified date. Sometime before

**Book IV
Chapter 1**

**Trying Out Trading:
The Basics**

the option period expires, a purchaser of an option must decide whether to exercise the option and buy (or sell) the asset (most commonly stocks) at the target price. Options are also called *derivatives*. We talk more about this investment alternative in Chapter 5.

Reviewing Stock Exchanges

Most of this Book covers stock trading, so we obviously concentrate on how the key exchanges — TSX, NYSE, NASDAQ, and Amex — operate and how these operations impact your trading activity.

Toronto Stock Exchange (TSX) and other Canadian exchanges

Most securities in Canada trade on the Toronto Stock Exchange (TSX), which was established in 1852. The TSX is owned by the TMX Group, which also operates the TSX Venture Exchange for small new companies as well as the Montreal Exchange for derivatives trading. Fixed-income bonds, natural gas, crude oil, and electricity contracts also trade through the TMX Group. TSX is the seventh largest in the world by market capitalization.

A handful of electronic exchanges have taken some blue-chip stock trading business from the TSX because of improved technology and lower fees. Rivals include Alpha and Chi-X Canada, which operate as alternate trading systems (ATS). Pure trading is another ATS that is connected to the Canadian National Stock Exchange (CNSX), where shares of emerging companies are traded.

New York Stock Exchange (NYSE)

The U.S. stock market dates back to May 17, 1792, when 24 brokers signed an agreement under a buttonwood tree at what today is 58 Wall Street. From these meagre beginnings, the NYSE built itself into the largest stock exchange in the world, with many of the largest companies listed on the exchange.

Trading occurs on the floor of the exchange, with specialists and floor traders running the show. Today these specialists and floor traders work electronically, which first became possible when the exchange introduced electronic capabilities for trading in 2004. For traders, the new electronic trading capabilities are a more popular tool than working with specialists and floor traders. Electronic trading capabilities were enhanced when the NYSE merged with Archipelago Holdings in 2006. The exchange expanded its global trading capabilities after a merger with Euronext in 2007, which made trading in European stocks much easier.

You may not realize just how much the concept of supply and demand influences the trading price of a stock. Price swings of a stock frequently are caused by shifts in the supply of shares available for sale and the demand created by the number of buyers wanting to purchase available shares.

NASDAQ

NASDAQ, which used to stand for National Association of Securities Dealers Automated Quotations but now is just like any other proper name, is the fastest-growing stock market today and the second largest by capitalization in the world. The market was formed after an SEC study in the early 1960s concluded that the sale of over-the-counter (OTC) securities — in other words, securities that aren't traded on the existing stock exchanges — was fragmented and obscure. The report called for the automation of the OTC market and gave the responsibility for implementing that system to the National Association of Securities Dealers (NASD).

The NASD began construction of the NASDAQ system in 1968, and its first trades were made beginning February 8, 1971, when NASDAQ became the world's first electronic stock market. NASDAQ continues to be the world leader in volume trading per hour.

NASDAQ also continues to be the leader in electronic trading. Its system, called the NASDAQ Crossing Network, enables fully anonymous trade execution to minimize the market impact of trading.

Over-the-counter bulletin board stocks

Stocks that do not meet the minimum requirements to be listed on NASDAQ or other national securities exchanges are traded as *over-the-counter* or *bulletin-board* stocks. The OTC Bulletin Board (OTCBB) is a regulated quotation service that displays real-time quotes, last-sale prices, and volume information for the stocks traded as over-the-counter or bulletin-board. Generally fewer than two (and sometimes zero) market makers trade in these stocks, making buying and selling them more difficult.

Over-the-counter stocks are also traded on what is quaintly called the Pink Sheets — harkening back to a time when stock quotes were printed on pink coloured paper. Effectively little or no regulatory power exists over companies whose shares trade on the OTCBB or the Pink Sheets. Sadly, this is where many fraudulent penny stocks and their promoters have migrated from what used to be the Vancouver Stock Exchange, complete with its "penny dreadfuls." Five words of advice: Buyers beware; sellers be quick.

Book IV Chapter 1

Trying Out Trading: The Basics

NYSE Amex

When the NYSE moved indoors, some stocks still weren't good enough to be sold on the exchange. Those stocks were called *curb traders* and ultimately made up what became known as the American Stock Exchange (Amex), which moved indoors in 1921. Amex lists stocks that are smaller in size than those on the NYSE yet still have a national following. Many firms that first list on Amex work to meet the listing requirements of the NYSE and then switch over.

The Amex trading system was integrated into the NYSE trading system after the merger with the NYSE was completed in 2008. It is now called the NYSE Amex, and trades small-company stocks.

Electronic communications networks (ECNs)

Many traders look for ways to get around dealing with a traditional broker. Instead they access trades using a *direct-access broker.* We talk more about the differences in the next section of this chapter. A new system of electronic trading that is developing is called the *electronic communications network* (ECN).

ECNs enable buyers and sellers to meet electronically to execute trades. The trades are entered into the ECN systems by market makers at one of the exchanges or by an OTC market maker. Transactions are completed without a broker-dealer, saving users the cost of commissions normally charged for more traditional forms of trading.

Subscribers to ECNs include retail investors, institutional investors, market makers, and broker-dealers. ECNs are accessed through a custom terminal or by direct Internet connection. Orders are posted by the ECN for subscribers to view. The ECN then matches orders for execution. In most cases, buyers and sellers maintain their anonymity and do not list identifiable information in their buy or sell orders.

In the last few years ECNs have gone through consolidation, and only two independent ECNs are left. The two independent ECNs, Nomura's Instinet and Bloomberg Tradebook, primarily service the institutional marketplace. Archipelago now operates under the NYSE umbrella as NYSE Arca Options.

Choosing the Right Broker/Adviser for You

Before beginning a search for the right broker or adviser, you must first decide what type of trader you want to be and what services you need. If you want to be a position trader, or one who trades infrequently, your best bet is either a full-service investment adviser or a discount broker. The choice depends upon how independently you want to operate as a trader. If you want advice on your stock investing plans, you need to seek out a full-service adviser, but we don't always recommend this expensive option. Before risking your money on trading, however, you need to be comfortable enough with the language and mechanics of trading and how to conduct your own research.

Considering more than price

Your choice should be based on much more than who can offer you the cheapest price. Although price definitely is a factor in your selection, it's one of many factors you need to consider. The most important factors are the services your broker offers and how effective and efficient the broker is in carrying out those promised services. Look for brokers that offer smart and quick order routing capabilities, but steer clear of the ones that accept payment for order flow.

You may find an online broker that provides all the bells and whistles at the cheapest price, but if its systems break down at a critical trading moment and you're not able to implement your trades when you want to, those bells and whistles mean nothing, and not being able to rely on them can result in huge losses. Look for brokers that allow you to test drive a demo version of their order entry systems.

Doing a little research

If you expect to become an active and successful trader and want full access so you can trade electronically through the exchanges, you more than likely need to research direct-access brokers. If, however, you believe that your volume of trades per month will be lower than 50, you may want to consider a discount broker that offers access to ECNs. Basically, your choice comes down to the types of services and accounts you need and which broker offers the best mix for what you want to do and pay.

Research and compare ratings of brokers on the Internet. Try to find the annual rankings of online brokers done by *The Globe and Mail* every autumn. This survey has been published in the *Report On Business* section during the autumn since at least 2001.

The most recent survey ranked 13 online brokers in terms of their costs, tools, trading, customer satisfaction, account information, and websites. Be aware that 11 of the 13 discount brokers are owned by banks and credit unions. Due to this connection, you might consider using your own bank or credit union's online service for your trading. You might be able to drive a better bargain if you do your chequing, mortgage, line of credit, retirement savings, and credit cards at the same place you do your trading. Stay close to home until you're confident you know what you're doing, then seek the best service for your particular trading.

Norman Rothery has operated the Stingy Investor website since 1995, where he summarizes the choices in finding a good broker. As he points out it's often the qualitative aspects of the broker–client relationship that matter most (www.ndir.com).

You can find another review of discount brokers at Surviscor (www.surviscor.com), where sites are ranked by passive, serious, and active investors.

After narrowing down your choices, check out the disciplinary histories of the firms you're considering. You can do that by going to the website of the Canadian Securities Administrators (www.securities-administrators.ca) to find out what disciplinary actions (if any) have been taken by securities regulators. You might call your provincial regulator to be sure the specific dealer you're thinking about working with is licensed to do business in your province. This information can be crucial. If you work with an unlicensed dealer who goes out of business, you may not have any way of recovering lost funds even if an arbitrator or court rules in your favour.

Understanding how you'll be paying

After conducting your initial research into investment dealer firms and narrowing down your choices, be sure you understand how they are paid. You can find out by

✦ **Reviewing each firm's fee and commission schedule.** The schedules should include the fees or charges you're required to pay when opening the account and what you pay to maintain and close the account.

✦ **Finding out how your adviser is compensated if you're planning to work with a human being rather than trade online.** Many advisers receive higher compensation when they sell their firm's own products, so they may try to steer you toward them rather than another product that may be a better match for your trading objectives. Rarely are dealer products good trading vehicles.

One other level of protection that you need to check on is the dealer's membership in the Canadian Investor Protection Fund (CIPF). Although CIPF membership won't insure you against losses caused by market declines, the CIPF does give you some protection if your firm faces insolvency. You can find out more about the CIPF at www.cipf.ca. If you can't find your discount broker or investment adviser on the CIPF's current member list, then look elsewhere to do your trading.

Getting to Know the Rules

After you pick your dealer, you must be sure you know the trading rules. Although provincial law mandates margin requirements, sets trade settlement rules, and bans free riding (nope, we're not talking about horseback riding here), dealers sometimes have even more stringent rules for their clients. We review the provincial requirements here, but check with your dealer to find out any additional rules your chosen firm imposes.

Rules for stock trading fall under the jurisdiction of the provincial Securities Acts, and encompass margin accounts, securities transactions, credit extended based on securities, and other factors related to securities markets. We don't review all the specifics here, but instead home in on three key areas that impact your trading choices — margin requirements, settling trades, and free riding.

Margin requirements

The provincial Securities Acts specify how much you can borrow when you use a margin account to purchase new shares of stocks on margin. This *initial margin requirement* permits you to borrow up to 50 percent of the cost of shares trading over $5. For example, if you open a new margin account with a $10,000 cash deposit, you can buy up to $20,000 worth of stock. After your $20,000 purchase, your account will have a cash balance of $0, an equity balance of $10,000, and a margin balance of $10,000. At this time, all your equity is committed to this trade, so you cannot enter any new positions unless you deposit additional funds or securities. Some investment firms allow you to borrow 70 percent of the value of shares trading above $5, but only 20 percent of shares between $1.50 and $1.74 — it's a sliding scale for the cost of your loan to offset the risk of cheap shares.

If the stock price increases, your equity balance increases. If the stock price decreases, your equity balance decreases. In either case, your margin balance remains the same, $10,000. The only way to reduce the outstanding margin balance is to deposit extra cash or securities into your account or sell enough of the shares to get your margin back in balance.

When your stock price increases, your equity balance increases and you may use the increased equity as collateral to borrow additional money to buy additional shares. You may borrow up to the value of the increased equity balance. This will increase your margin balance.

However, if your equity balance decreases, so does the minimum equity position permitted in your account. Currently, the minimum is 25 percent of the total value of all margined securities. Some brokers may require more.

If the total value of the stock falls below $13,332, then the equity balance in your portfolio will be less than 25 percent of the total value. The math is simple: 25 percent of $13,332 is $3,333. Your cash balance is still $0 and your margin balance is still $10,000. Subtract $10,000 from $13,332 to determine your equity balance, which is $3,332. Your equity balance is less than 25 percent of your total account balance.

When this occurs, your broker will call and demand additional collateral to support the outstanding margin loan. This is a *margin call.* You may meet your margin call requirements by depositing more cash, or you may deposit fully paid, unmargined securities from another account. If you do not deposit additional collateral, your dealer is permitted to sell up to four times the amount of stock required to meet your margin call, and may sell any of the securities in your portfolio.

If you have more than a few positions, margin calculations become complex. It helps to think about it like this: When initiating a new position, you can never borrow more than half of the value of the position. To maintain sufficient collateral, your dealer will insist that the value of your stocks be more than enough to cover the loan. Therefore, if your equity balance falls below 25 percent of the total portfolio value, your adviser will ask for additional collateral in the form of a margin call.

As a day trader, you should seldom satisfy a margin call. Instead, close the offending position(s). It's possible that an extraordinary event may cause the value of your stocks to fall below the amount owed on your outstanding margin loan. If this happens, your dealer will close your positions, but you must still repay the debt. Unlike a cash account, you can lose more than 100 percent of the money you deposit into a margin account.

Not all stocks can be bought on margin, and neither can all stocks be used as collateral. If you want to trade on margin, be sure you understand the margin requirements imposed by your dealer. Some investment dealers require even stiffer requirements to maintain a margin account, especially if you trade low-priced volatile or lightly traded stocks. Find out even more about margin in Book 5, Chapter 5.

Settling trades

When you place an order to buy a stock, you must settle that transaction in three business days. This *settlement cycle* is known as *T+3.* The firm must receive your payment for any securities you buy no later than three days after the trade is executed. If you're selling a stock, it's probably being held in your account and will be taken out of that account on the day of settlement. Options and government securities trade on a *T+1* settlement cycle, which means these transactions settle the next trading day.

Free riding

No, we're not talking about hopping a train on the sly. *Free riding* in the stock-trading world can get you in a bunch of trouble, so keep reading. Basically it means that you must pay for a stock before you can sell it, and because it takes three days to settle a stock transaction, that means, in theory, you can buy a stock and then place an order to sell it before the stock purchase actually settles.

This is a cash account problem. Although many swing and day traders do turn around stock purchases and sales that quickly, they typically trade in a margin account and are able to sidestep the problem. Margin traders use the unsettled proceeds of a trade as collateral to borrow money until the trade is settled. Still, swing traders and day traders must have enough cash or buying power in their accounts to cover all purchases of stock.

Formally, in a cash account, a dealer may buy a security on your behalf — or sell a security — when either of the following applies:

✦ You have sufficient funds in the account.

✦ The firm accepts in good faith your agreement to make a full-cash payment for the security before you sell it.

If you do ever buy and sell a security before the settlement cycle (*T+3*) is complete — or even on the same day — and without sufficient cash in your account, an investment firm can make what is called an *intraday extension of credit* (a loan), but that exposes the firm to increased risks — especially the risk that you may overextend your financial resources and be unable to settle your trades. Most firms require active traders who buy and then sell securities within the settlement cycle to conduct those activities within a margin account.

If you take a free ride and haven't made some type of credit arrangement with your firm, it's likely to freeze your account for 90 days. During that 90-day period, the firm requires you to pay for any purchase on the date that you make the trade. In other words, you lose the option of settling your trades within three days. Some firms require you to have enough cash in your account to complete the transaction before you make the trade so you thus avoid even the risk of free riding.

Chapter 2: The Fundamentals: Economics and Stock Market Metrics

In This Chapter

✔ **Exploring business cycle basics**

✔ **Identifying economic ups and downs**

✔ **Deciphering economic indicators**

✔ **Interpreting income statements and balance sheets**

✔ **Understanding ratios, returns, and more**

*I*f we've learned anything over the last few years it's that *economics matters.* Terms like recession and inflation rarely came up in water-cooler chat before 2008, but now these topics are all anyone talks about. If you want to trade, invest, or simply build your wealth properly, you need to understand how economic cycles work.

Some traders might be thinking that because they use charts and technical analysis (which we discuss in Chapter 3 and in Book 5, Chapter 4) they don't have to worry about macroeconomic factors, market conditions, and fundamental factors. But taking the time to analyze the fundamentals of a stock puts you one step ahead of the trading crowd. Using fundamental analysis, you can determine how a stock's price compares with prices of similar companies based on earnings growth and other key factors, including business and economic conditions.

In this chapter we discuss important economic terms, and we'll show you how to properly read a company's income statement and balance sheet. If you're a technical trader it's still important to know how the fundamental guys think, and if you're a fundamental investor then the information contained here will help you decide which stocks are your must-haves and which ones are duds.

The Basics of the Business Cycle

The old adage "What goes up must come down" is as true for the economy as it is for any physical object. When a business cycle reaches its peak, nothing is wrong in the economic world; businesses and investors are making plenty of money and everyone is happy. Unfortunately, as we know all too well, the economy can't exist at its peak forever. In the same way that gravity eventually makes a rising object fall, a revved-up economy eventually reaches its high and begins to tumble.

The peak is only one of the four distinct parts of every business cycle — peak, recession, trough, and expansion/recovery. None of the four is designated as the beginning of a business cycle, but here are the portions of the business cycle that each represents:

✦ **Peak:** During a *peak,* the economy is humming along at full speed, with the gross domestic product (GDP — more about that later in the chapter) near its maximum output and employment levels near their all-time highs. Income and prices are increasing, and the risk of inflation is great, if it hasn't already set in. Businesses and investors are prospering and very happy.

✦ **Recession:** As the economy falls from its peak, employment levels begin to decline, production and output eventually decline, and wages and prices level off, but more than likely won't actually fall — unless the recession is a long, or "deep," one.

✦ **Trough:** When a recession bottoms out, the economy levels out into a period called the *trough*. If this period is prolonged it can become a depression, which is a severe and prolonged recession. The most recent depression in North America was in the late 1920s and early 1930s. Output and employment stagnate, waiting for the next expansion.

✦ **Expansion/recovery:** After the economy starts growing again, employment and output pick up. This period of expansion and recovery pulls the economy off the floor of the trough and points it back toward its next peak. During this period, employment, production, and output all see increases, and the economic situation again looks promising.

How do we know which part of the business cycle the economy is in? Officially, we don't usually find out until months after that part of the cycle has either started or ended.

The underlying process of the business cycle is of interest to analysts and traders. Statistics Canada's foray into this area has been well received by analysts over the years. Although no other organization has undertaken the work, it's worth noting that Statistics Canada is not providing "official" reference cycle dates in the sense that the results are beyond dispute or that StatsCan has a legislated requirement to do so.

In identifying the economy's ups and downs by determining the cyclical turning points, StatsCan allows a better understanding for policymakers and traders alike.

The peak of a business cycle occurs during the last month before some key economic indicators begin to fall. These indicators include employment, output, and new housing starts. We talk more about economic indicators and which of them are critical for traders to watch in the "Understanding Economic Indicators" section later in the chapter. However, because neither a recession nor a recovery can be declared until enough data are accumulated, finding a way around the time lag in official information is impossible.

Signals that the economy was weakening became clear to the markets as early as October 2007, when the major indices hit their peaks. Looking at an earlier business cycle, you can see the whole process. Just as in October 2007, clear signs the economy was headed toward a recession were seen as early as the spring of 2000, which is when the Nasdaq index hit its peak and began its downward spiral. The effects of the recession took a bit longer to hit the other major exchanges, but they started a downward trend by the summer of 2000. Just like in 2008, job losses had started mounting by mid-2000, and many economists already were sending alarms that the economy was headed into a recession.

Even though the National Bureau of Economic Research (NBER), the organization officially declares the peaks and troughs in America, announced the official beginning of that recession as March 21, 2001, and the official end of the trough and beginning of the recovery as November 2001, no significant recovery was seen in the markets until October 2002. Job growth remained anemic as of early 2004. The first sign of job growth was seen during the fourth quarter of 2003, after nearly three years of job losses. That economic expansion finally picked up steam, and ultimately lasted through 2007.

Identifying periods of economic growth and recession

Considering the type of lag time between events and official pronouncements from the NBER, we're sure you're wondering how you can determine which part of the cycle the economy is in and how you can use this information as a trader. Most economists attribute changing business cycles to disturbances in the economy. Growth spurts, for example, result from surges in private or public spending. One way public spending can surge is the building or upgrading of infrastructure, when government spending increases and companies in industries related to the construction effort prosper. They often need to increase hiring to fulfill government orders. Employees at these companies usually receive increases in their take-home pay and start spending that extra money. As consumer optimism increases, other companies must fulfill consumers' wants and needs, so production and output also increase in companies that are unrelated to the building of highways, schools, hospitals, hockey rinks, bridges, and other infrastructure projects.

Book IV
Chapter 2

The Fundamentals:
Economics and
Stock Market
Metrics

When these same factors work in reverse, the start of a recession is sure to follow. For example, a cut in government spending will likely result in layoffs at related industrial plants, reduced take-home pay, and finally declines in output and production to cope with reduced spending.

In addition to government spending, a decision by the Bank of Canada (BoC), and it's American counterpart, the Federal Reserve, to either raise or lower interest rates is another major disturbance to the economy. When interest rates rise, spending slows, and that can lead to a recession. When interest rates are cut, spending usually goes up, and that can aid in spurring an economic recovery.

Another school of economic thought disagrees with the notion that government policy or spending is responsible for changes in the business cycle. This second group of theorists believes that differences in productivity levels and consumer tastes are the primary forces driving the business cycle. From this point of view, only businesses and consumers can drive changes in the economic cycle. These economists don't believe that governmentally driven monetary or policy changes impact the cycle.

Which camp you believe is not critical; the key is picking up the signs of when the economy is in a recession and when it's in an expansion. Peaks and troughs are flat periods (periods where the high or low stays primarily even before moving in the opposite direction) and are impossible to identify until months after they end. As a trader, you can identify shifts in buying and spending behaviour by watching various economic indicators. By doing so, you can discover when the economy is in the early stages of a recovery or recession or if it's fully into a recession or recovery.

It's not very often that the economies of Canada and the United States are out of sync. Canada's companies did not warrant any American-style bailouts — well, except for the American automobile manufacturers in Ontario and the usual favours so often extended to Air Canada in Quebec. In fact, Canada's economy was so admired by foreign investors that our dollar reached — and passed — parity with the U.S. dollar while our interest rates were at all-time lows. The escalating value of our dollar can lead to deflation, but our international purchasing power is enhanced and we do not import as much inflation.

Perhaps the biggest compliment paid to how well Canada managed its monetary policy was to have our BoC Governor Mark Carney appointed as Chairman of the Financial Stability Board based in Basel, Switzerland. This international body includes all G-20 major economies as they strive to monitor our global financial system.

Relating bull markets and bear markets to the economy

You've probably heard the terms *bull market* and *bear market*. To understand what they mean, you first need to know how economic cycles affect the stock market. *Bulls* are people who believe that all is right with the world and the stock market is heading for an increase. They definitely think the economy is expanding. *Bears* are people who believe the economy is heading for a downturn, and stocks will either stagnate or go down. A *bull market* is a market in which a majority of stocks are increasing in value, and a *bear market* is a market in which a majority of stocks are decreasing. Bears definitely believe the economy is either in a recession or headed that way.

You can make money as a trader regardless of whether the bulls or the bears are right. The key: Identify the way the market is headed and then buy or sell into that trend. During a bear market, traders make their money by selling short, or taking advantage of falling prices (more about that in Chapter 4). Traders sell short by borrowing stock from their broker and then selling it with the hope of making a profit when the price falls.

Even during a bear market, some stocks offer opportunities for traders to make money, including oil and gas stocks and real estate investment trusts (REITs). (Find out more about REITs in Book 6, Chapter 1.) Some petroleum stocks and REITs pay higher dividends and, therefore, are most attractive when the rest of the market is falling or showing no growth potential. During a bull market, riding a stock through recovery but getting out before a fall is key.

Sector Rotation

In general, the markets are divided into sectors, and at any given time some of those sectors will be expanding, even during a bear market. Some traders are adept at rotating their investments from one sector to another that is more likely to benefit from the part of the business cycle driving the economy. This basic trading strategy is called *sector rotation*.

As a trader, you can take advantage of this knowledge by knowing which sectors are more likely to rise during the various parts of a market cycle. You need to buy into the sectors with stock prices that are likely to rise, or you can sell short the sectors in which prices are expected to fall.

Early recovery

You can spot an early recovery when consumer expectations and industrial production are beginning to rise while interest rates are bottoming out. That scenario was evident during a recent economic cycle discovered during the fall and early winter months of 2003. During the early stages of recovery, Sam Stovall, chief investment strategist for Standard & Poor's and a trading guru, found that industrial, basic industry, and energy sectors tend to take the lead.

Full recovery

When the economy has fully recovered, we start seeing signs that consumer expectations are falling and productivity levels and interest rates are flattening out. These factors were seen during the economy's recent period of full recovery leading up to the economic peak in December 2007. During that period, companies in the consumer staples and services sectors exhibited a tendency to take the lead, and interest rates had actually started to fall. As knowledgeable investors know, when that happens it's only a matter of time before a recession follows. The staples of life are needed even in times of recession, so the stocks of those companies tend to benefit.

Early recession

When the economy reaches the earliest part of a recession, consumer expectations fall more sharply and productivity levels start to drop. Interest rates also begin to drop. Most of the 217,200 Canadian job losses during the 2001 economic downturn occurred during late 2001 and early 2002. During 2001, the Bank of Canada cut interest rates nine times to try to ease the concerns about the upcoming recession. The BoC started to raise rates in 2002, but then lowered them in 2003 and again in 2008 during the mortgage crisis. At the end of 2011, the BoC's bank rate (the interest rate the BoC charges to banks) was 1.25 percent. Another key recession sign was the mounting job losses in 2008 and early 2009.

Utilities and finance-sector stocks are the most likely to see rising prices during the first part of a recession, because under those circumstances investors seek stocks that provide some safety (because owning them involves less risk) and pay higher dividends. Gold and other valuable mineral stocks also look good to investors seeking safety. Though the financial sector did not follow this pattern in the 2008 recession, it is still typical to see banks, insurance companies, and investment firms perform well during the early parts of a recession.

Full recession

Although it may not make much sense intuitively, during a full recession is when we first start seeing indications that consumer expectations are improving, which is shown by increased spending. However, industrial productivity remains flat, and businesses won't increase their production levels until they believe consumers actually are ready to spend again. Additionally, interest rates continue to drop, because both business and consumer spending are slow, so demand for the money weakens while competition for new credit customers grows among banks and other financial institutions. During a full recession, cyclical and technology stocks tend to lead the way. Investors look to safety during a recession, so companies that satisfy that need tend to do best.

Understanding Economic Indicators

The key to knowing where, as a trader, you are during the business cycle is watching the economic indicators. Every day you open your newspaper, you see at least one story about how the economy is doing based on various economic indicators. Popular indicators track employment, money supply, interest rates, housing starts, housing sales, production levels, purchasing statistics, consumer confidence, shipping, and many other factors that indicate how the economy is doing.

Economic indicators are useful to your trading. Some are definitely more useful than others. We don't have the space here to describe each of the indicators; instead, we focus on the ones that can provide you with the most help in making your trading decisions.

BoC and Fed watch: Understanding how interest rates affect markets

Watching the Governor of the Bank of Canada and the Federal Open Market Committee (FOMC) of the Federal Reserve (which includes the seven members of the Board of Governors, the president of the New York Federal Reserve Bank, and presidents of 4 of the other 11 Federal Reserve Banks) and tracking what they may or may not do to interest rates is almost a daily spectator sport in the business press. Although members of the FOMC meet only eight times per year, discussions about whether the Bank of Canada and the Federal Reserve will raise or lower interest rates serves as fodder for stories published on at least a weekly, if not daily, basis.

**Book IV
Chapter 2**

**The Fundamentals:
Economics and
Stock Market
Metrics**

The Canadian and U.S. economies tend to move in lockstep, so the perception is for monetary policy in both countries to go in the same direction. However, that has been less true since late 2000, when the Bank of Canada established eight pre-set dates per year to announce its key interest rate policy. This schedule is referred to as the BoC's *fixed announcement dates,* or fixed dates. In setting interest rates, Canada has recently tended to focus more closely on the inflation rate than the United States, which tends to be concerned with employment.

Because the Canadian economy is inextricably linked with the U.S., our manufacturing costs and output are structured around a Canadian dollar valued at a discount against the U.S. currency. The Canadian dollar is often perceived as a petro-currency by international investors: it fluctuates with oil and gas commodity prices. When the interest rate policy also starts to attract investors to Canada, the effect of a strong loonie is a struggle for our exporters. Higher interest rates and high energy prices causing a high currency exchange rate further increase the cost of our exports.

Therefore, Canadian interest rate policy is crafted with an eye to U.S. rate policy. Canada must be aware of U.S. interest rates in order to stay competitive with the potential of expanding exports to the United States. So that we are not totally dependent on our southern neighbour, we undertake regular trade missions to the growing markets across the Pacific.

The key reason for you to be concerned is that a change in interest rates can have a major impact on the economy and thus on how you make trades. An increase in rates is likely to slow down spending, which can lead to an overall economic slowdown. For the most part, when the BoC or the Fed raises interest rates, it's because the board believes the economy is overheated, which can fuel the risk of inflation. An increase in interest rates can reduce spending and thus ease overheating. If, on the other hand, the BoC or the Fed fears an economic downturn or is trying to fuel growth during a recession, the board frequently decides to cut interest rates to spur spending and growth.

Money supply

The money supply is a key number to watch, because growth in money supply can be a leading indicator of inflation in situations when the money supply is greater than the supply of goods. When more money than goods is around, prices are likely to rise. Commodities and money traders will want to keep close watch over these three aggregates — money supply, inflation, and goods and services.

Inflation rate

Several key economic indicators point us toward ways of identifying the risk of inflation. The primary overall indicator is GDP: a country's gross domestic product. (GDP is released quarterly by Statistics Canada; in the United States, the Department of Commerce's Bureau of Economic Analysis [BEA] tracks GDP.) You can also follow monthly trends by keeping your eye out for the Consumer Price Index, the Industrial Product Price Index, the Producer Price Index, and the Retail Trade Survey. We discuss the two main indicators, GDP and Consumer Price Index (CPI). Read about the rest in *Trading for Canadians for Dummies* (Wiley).

✦ **Gross domestic product (GDP)** represents the monetary value of goods produced during a specific period in the economy. GDP is released quarterly in three different versions. The first version, which includes advance data, is released at 8:30 a.m. on the last business day of January, April, July, and October for the previous quarter. Preliminary data are released a month later, and the final numbers are released a month after that. GDP is important to traders because it indicates the pace at which the economy is growing. In the GDP, you'll find numbers for consumer spending, private domestic investment, government or public spending, and net exports. Essentially, it includes all information about labour and property involving business activities inside the confines of Canada and the United States. If GDP fails to meet expectations set by the analysts or exceeds market expectations, stock prices will be affected at least temporarily. For a glimpse of what may be in store for the future, pay attention to the rate that inventories are increasing. It can be a leading indicator that growth is slowing or consumer demand is changing. Even though the final official numbers are released quarterly, the advance reports and preliminary reports give you a good indication of what to expect in the final numbers. Canadian GDP reports can be found at www40.statcan.gc.ca/l01/cst01/gdps04a-eng.htm. You can get full details about the American GDP reports at http://bea.gov/national/index.htm#gdp. You can track the release schedule for the GDP reports, as well as other government statistical reports, at http://bea.gov/national/index.htm. Often the report is posted at the Bureau of Economic Analysis early in the morning before the actual release and embargoed until the official release time, so as a trader you may be able to get a heads up before the news is actually reported by the press.

✦ **Consumer Price Index (CPI)** measures the cost of a representative basket of goods and services, including food, energy, housing, clothing, transportation, medical care, entertainment, and education. Each type of cost is weighted. For example, medical costs are weighted more highly in recent years because they are rising at a faster pace, especially as the current population ages. In addition to the broad CPI, a core rate is issued that excludes food, mortgage interest, and energy, which are considered more volatile. The core rate is an indicator you can watch for general price shifts. The financial markets, in general, look for a rate of increase in the range of 1 percent to 2 percent; anything higher may be a sign of inflation and can cause at least a temporary shock to stock prices. Any shock to stock prices obviously can be an opportunity for traders. CPI statistics are released in Canada by Statistics Canada at 7 a.m. ET around the 18th of each month. You can find CPI data at either

**Book IV
Chapter 2**

**The Fundamentals:
Economics and
Stock Market
Metrics**

www.statcan.gc.ca or www.bankofcanada.ca. This cost of living measure uses a shopping basket of about 600 goods and services used by most households. The American CPI is released by the U.S. Labor Department at 8:30 a.m. ET around the 15th of each month and reflects data from the previous month. You can track the U.S. CPI at the website of the U.S. Department of Labor's Bureau of Labor Statistics at www.bls.gov/cpi/home.htm.

Deflation

In addition to watching the economic indicators for inflation discussed in the previous section, traders also need to watch the numbers for signs of deflation. Serious concern about the possibility of deflation takes centre stage when prices start falling. *Deflation* occurs when a sustained period of falling prices takes place. The Great Depression of the 1930s was a classic period of deflation. Many economists believe that printing more money cures deflation, because (as we mention in the "Money supply" section) increases in the money supply normally lead to increases in prices when more money is around than goods to be purchased.

During periods of deflation, increasing the money supply isn't necessarily the answer. Some economists believe injecting more money into the economy is risky, especially when production capacity is in excess, and producers continue to produce goods even though prices are falling. In other economic situations, producers commonly stop producing when prices fall.

Jobless claims

The Labour Force Survey, another report from Statistics Canada (www.statscan.gc.ca), is one of the most important leading indicators to watch. This report is the first critical economic indicator released every month and frequently sets the expectations for the rest of the month's reports. For example, signs of a weak labour market reported in the Labour Force Survey usually are a strong indication of poor retail sales and other possible negative reports later in the month. The summary also breaks down data by industry, such as construction and manufacturing. For example, a significant drop in employment numbers for the construction sector is a strong sign that the housing starts report also will be negative.

This report can send shockwaves through the financial markets, especially if the numbers that are released vary greatly from expectations. Stock prices often fall whenever the report doesn't meet expectations or employment statistics show signs of weakness. On the other hand, stock prices can rise dramatically whenever the report indicates better than expected numbers. As is true with any shock to the market, changes in prices are temporary unless other indicators also exhibit the same trend or tendency.

The employment report can drive markets so strongly because its data are only a few days old. Because it is so timely, this report is widely recognized as the best indicator of unemployment and wage pressure. Rising unemployment can be an early sign of recession, while increased pressure on wages can be an early sign of inflation. The report also is a broad-based snapshot of the entire labour market, covering 50,000 Canadian households and every major industry.

Statistics Canada releases the report at 8:30 a.m. ET on the first Friday of each month with data for the previous month.

Consumer confidence

The Conference Board of Canada's survey of Canadian households has been ongoing since 1980. It measures consumers' level of optimism regarding current economic conditions. This index of consumer confidence is a crucial indicator of near-term sales for companies in the consumer product sector. It is constructed from responses to four attitudinal questions posed to random samples of Canadian households. Those surveyed are asked to give their views about their household's current and expected financial position and their short-term employment outlook. They are also asked to assess whether now is a good or a bad time to make a major purchase such as a house, car, or other big-ticket item. The Conference Board of Canada has revived the Help Wanted Index. Rather than major newspapers, the index tracks 79 job-posting websites throughout Canada. This leading indicator of employment level had been abandoned by Statistics Canada during early 2003 as it was deemed to have lost its predictive power. The index is published monthly at www.conferenceboard.ca.

Keeping an eye on consumer confidence in the United States is another way of casting a glance into the future of the market. When confidence is high, consumers are more likely to spend. The best overall index for monitoring American consumer confidence is the Consumer Confidence Index (CCI), which is put out by the Conference Board. This index is compiled through a sampling of 5,000 households and is widely respected as the most accurate indicator of consumer confidence.

Although minor changes in the CCI are not strongly indicative of a problem, major shifts can be a sign of choppy waters ahead. Most people who watch the CCI look for three- to six-month trends. The Fed, as an example, looks closely at consumer confidence when determining interest rate policy, which as you know can greatly affect stock prices. When confidence is trending lower, the Fed is more likely to lower interest rates. Stock markets love to hear about the Fed lowering interest rates. Confidence levels that are trending higher can be a warning of a pending inflationary period. A rapidly rising trend in consumer confidence can lead the Fed to raise interest rates to cut off inflation; moreover, a rise in interest rates can send stock prices lower.

**Book IV
Chapter 2**

**The Fundamentals:
Economics and
Stock Market
Metrics**

The Conference Board releases the CCI at 10 a.m. ET the last Tuesday of each month. The biggest weakness of this index is that it isn't based on actual spending data. Instead, it's a survey of planned spending. You can track the CCI online at www.conferenceboard.ca/topics/economics/Consumer_confidence.aspx.

Business activity

A number of key economic indicators can give you a good idea of what business is doing and how that information may impact the stock markets. Here are some key Canadian business indicators to watch. You can search online, or look at *Trading For Canadians For Dummies*, to find the similar American indicators.

✦ **The Ivey Purchasing Managers Index:** This index, sponsored by the Richard Ivey School of Business (University of Western Ontario) and the Purchasing Management Association of Canada (PMAC), shows month-to-month variation in economic activity.

The Ivey Purchasing Managers Index measures monthly changes in purchases as indicated by a panel of purchasing managers from across Canada. The 175 participants have been selected geographically and by sector to match the Canadian economy as a whole. The index includes both the public and private sectors. Index panel members indicate whether activity is higher than, the same as, or lower than the previous month across five categories: purchases, employment, inventories, supplier deliveries, and prices. The index is released at 10 a.m. ET on the third or fourth working day of each month at http://iveypmi.uwo.ca.

✦ **The Building Permits Survey for Canada:** This survey covers 2,400 municipalities representing 95 percent of the population. It provides an early indication of building activity. In addition to data on the number and value of building permits issued by Canadian municipalities, this publication provides information on the average value of dwellings, the number and value of mobile homes, and permits issued for building renovation. The value of planned construction activities shown in this release excludes engineering projects (such as waterworks, sewers, or culverts) and land. The Building Permits Survey is released by Statistics Canada on the fourth business day of each month at 8:30 a.m. ET and can be found at www.statcan.gc.ca.

✦ **Manufacturing Surveys:** The Canadian Monthly Survey of Manufacturing covers 21 industry groups that produce goods for both industrial and consumer use. The manufacturing sector's activity is monitored monthly and annually, as it accounts for a large part of Canada's gross domestic product. It's released by Statistics Canada around the 16th of each month at 8:30 a.m. ET and can be found at www.statcan.gc.ca.

Using the Data

You can see that plenty of data are available, but not all are relevant to the types of stocks you want to trade. Organizing your data collection and tracking the trends can make choosing economic signs and analyzing which part of the business cycle is driving the markets easier for you. We offer a few steps that can make this task much easier:

1. **Maintain a calendar of the release dates for the key economic indicators you decide to follow.**

   The markets may move in anticipation of these data, so if you know that a key economic indicator is about to be released, be sure to watch stock price trends for the possible impact the anticipated release may be having on the market.

2. **Know the parts of the economy that are most impacted by the economic indicators you're following.**

   For example, the GDP strongly suggests the path of economic growth, but PPI and CPI are strong measures of inflation.

3. **Know which economic indicators are most important to the market.**

   For example, in times of inflation, economic indicators that reveal key data regarding inflation are the biggest market movers. If the markets are worried about growth, the growth components of GDP and other indicators will have the greatest potential for moving the markets.

4. **Know what the market is expecting to see in the numbers.**

   The actual number is not as critical as whether that number was expected by the markets. Surprises are what move the markets.

5. **Know what parts of the economic indicator are important.**

   Newspapers may write headlines for shock value, but the parts of the index they cover may not be what are critical to your decision making. For example, traders know that food and energy components of the CPI are volatile, so the more important number to watch is the core CPI, which doesn't include food and energy. The news media may focus only on the more volatile number.

6. **Don't overreact to a newly announced economic indicator that didn't meet market expectations.**

   Indicators frequently are revised after they're initially issued. The difference may merely be related to a revision and not an indication of a shift in the business cycle. However, be sure to check information about revisions to the previous month and how those revisions have impacted the current month's trend.

Book IV Chapter 2

The Fundamentals: Economics and Stock Market Metrics

7. **Monitor the trends.**

   On your calendar, keep track of key components of each economic indicator that you watch. Follow the trends of the most important data components to get a good idea of where the business cycle is headed.

Keeping a tight watch on economic indicators is the best way for you to determine at what point the economy is in a new business cycle. Waiting for official pronouncements is much too late. By the time they're released, that phase of the cycle may be over and a new cycle may be driving the markets.

Understanding Stock Market Fundamentals

The income statement

The *income statement* is where a company periodically reports its revenues, costs, and net earnings or profit. It's basically a snapshot of how much a company is earning from its operations and any extraordinary earnings that may have impacted its bottom line during a specific period of time. From the income statement, you'll be able to determine the impact of taxes, interest, and depreciation on a company's earnings and to forecast earnings potential.

Every income statement has three key sections: revenue, expenses, and income. The revenue section includes all money taken into the company by selling its products or services minus any costs directly related to the sale of those products or services (called cost of goods sold). The expenses section includes all operating expenses for the company not directly related to sales, as well as expenses for depreciation (writing off the use of equipment and buildings — tangible assets), amortization (writing off the use of patents, copyrights, and other intellectual property or intangible assets such as goodwill), taxes, and interest.

The income section includes various calculations of income. Usually you'll find one calculation that shows income after operating expenses and before interest, taxes, depreciation, and amortization, called EBITDA. This will be followed by net income, which is the bottom line showing how much a company earned after all its costs and expenses were deducted. Public companies must file financial reports with the OSC and the SEC on a quarterly and annual basis. You can read any public company's financial reports at Canada's System for Electronic Document Analysis and Retrieval (SEDAR) (www.sedar.com) and at the EDGAR website (www.sec.gov/edgar.shtml) for American issuers.

A year's worth of figures won't show you much, so you need to look at the trends throughout a number of years to be able to forecast growth potential or assess how well a company is doing compared with its competitors.

Both quarterly and annual reports are important. Comparing a company's results on a quarter-to-quarter basis gives the trader an idea of how well the company is meeting analysts' expectations as well as the company's projections. Also, looking at, for example, results for the first quarter of 2011 versus the first quarter of 2012 you can see whether a company's earnings are increasing or decreasing in a similar market environment. While for some types of companies the first quarter is generally productive, other types of companies, such as retail stores, are dependent mostly on fourth-quarter holiday results, so you need to know what is expected in earnings for the various quarters. Quarterly results allow you to monitor results from similar time periods.

Annual statements give you a summary for the year. You can also compare current-year results to the results over a number of years to see at what rate the company is growing.

Revenues

The first line of any income statement includes the company's sales revenues. This number reflects all the sales that have been generated by the company before any costs are subtracted. Rather than go to all the trouble of showing their math — gross sales — any sales discounts, adjustments for returns, or other allowances = *net sales.* Most companies show only net sales on their income statements. From these figures, you want to see obvious signs of steady growth in revenues. A decrease in revenues from year to year is a red flag that indicates problems — it's probably not a good potential trading choice unless you're considering shorting the stock.

Cost of goods sold

The *cost of goods sold* (also known as cost of merchandise sold or cost of services sold, depending on the type of business) is an amount that shows the total costs directly related to selling a company's products or services. The costs included in this part of the revenue section include purchases, purchase discounts, and freight charges or other costs directly related to selling a product or service.

Gross margins

The gross margin or gross profit is the net result of subtracting the cost of goods sold from net sales. This figure shows you how much money a company is making directly from sales before considering other operating costs. The gross profit is the dollar figure calculated by subtracting costs of goods sold from net revenue. The gross margin is a ratio calculated by dividing gross profit by net revenue. Watching year-to-year trends in gross margins gives you a good idea of a company's profit growth potential from its key revenue sources.

Book IV
Chapter 2

The Fundamentals:
Economics and
Stock Market
Metrics

You can calculate a gross margin ratio by dividing a company's gross profit by its net sales:

Gross margin ratio = Gross profit ÷ Net sales

The *gross margin ratio,* expressed as a percentage, considers revenue from sales minus the costs directly involved in making those sales and is a good indicator of how well a company uses its production, purchasing, and distribution resources to earn a profit. The higher the percentage, the more efficient a company is at making its profit.

By comparing gross margin ratios among various companies within the same industry or business sector, you can get an idea of how efficient each company is at generating profits. Investors favour companies that are more efficient.

Expenses

The next section of the income statement shows the expenses of operating the business, including the sales costs and administrative costs of business operations. When comparing a company's year-to-year results, watch for signs of whether expenses are increasing faster than a company's gross profits — this can be an indication that a company is having a problem controlling its costs and won't bode well for future profit growth potential.

When you see expenses drop from one year to the next, while gross margins increase, that's usually a good sign and means a company likely has a good cost control program in place. The potential for growth in future profit margins is good.

Gross profits and expenses that rise at about the same rate are neither a significant positive nor negative sign. When that happens, the best way to get a reading on how a company is controlling its expenses is to compare its expenses with the expenses of other companies in similar businesses.

Interest payments

The interest payments portion of the expense section of an income statement gives you a view of a company's short-term financial health. Payments shown here include interest paid during the year on short- and long-term liabilities (more about those in the "Looking at debt" section later in this chapter). These payments are tax-deductible expenses, which help reduce a company's tax burden.

To determine a company's fiscal health, use the *interest expense number* and the earnings before interest and taxes (EBIT) number, which is usually shown on the income statement. If not, you can calculate it by subtracting interest and tax expenses from operating income (which will be gross profit minus expenses, also usually shown on the income statement). You can use this figure to determine whether the company is generating sufficient income to cover its interest payments using the interest coverage ratio. You can calculate the company's *interest coverage ratio* (expressed as a percentage, this ratio provides a clear-cut indicator of company's solvency) using this formula:

Interest coverage ratio = EBIT ÷ Interest expenses

Companies with high interest coverage ratios won't have any problems meeting their interest obligations, and their risk of insolvency (going belly up) is low. On the other hand, a low interest coverage ratio is a clear sign that a company has a problem and may face bankruptcy. Whether an interest coverage ratio tends to run high or low depends a great deal on the type of industry or business a company is in. Comparing the interest coverage ratios of several companies in the same industry or business is the best way to judge the value of the ratios.

Tax payments

Corporations are always looking to avoid taxes, just like you. The *income tax expense* figure on the income statement shows the total amount that a company paid in taxes. A corporation pays between 15 percent and 38 percent of its income in taxes, depending on its respective size; however, corporations have many more write-offs they can use to reduce their tax burdens than you have as an individual taxpayer. Most large corporations have teams of tax specialists who spend their days looking for ways to minimize taxes. When you're looking at tax payments, it's important to review how well the company you're interested in manages its tax burden compared with other similar companies.

Dividend payments

Companies sometimes pay a *dividend,* hopefully part of the company profits, for each share of common stock that an investor holds. This dividend is distributed to shareholders usually once every quarter after the company's board of directors reviews company profits and determines whether to pay and how much the dividend will be. Paying dividends is not a tax-deductible expense for companies that pay them. In the past, traders have preferred growth stocks that do not pay dividends. However, the way dividends are taxed in Canada may have altered the way traders view dividend-paying stocks. Dividends are more attractive, because the tax on dividends is reduced by the dividend tax credit applied to dividends received from Canadian companies.

Book IV
Chapter 2

The Fundamentals:
Economics and
Stock Market
Metrics

Testing profitability

You now can use the income statement to quickly check your company's profitability by using one or both of two ratios — the operating margin and net profit margin. The *operating margin* looks at profits from operations before interest and tax expenses, and the *net profit margin* considers earnings after the payment of those expenses.

We calculate operating margin using this formula:

Operating margin = Operating income ÷ Gross profit or net sales

We calculate net profit margin using this formula:

Net profit margin = Earnings after taxes ÷ Gross profit or net sales

Looking at Cash Flow

When you review income statements, you're looking at information based on accrual accounting. In *accrual accounting,* sales can be included when they're first contracted, even before revenue from them is collected. Sales made on credit are shown even if the company still needs to collect from the customer. Expenses are recorded as they're incurred and not necessarily as they're paid. However, the income statement definitely does not show a company's cash position. A company that's booking a high level of sales can have a stellar income statement but nevertheless be having trouble collecting from its customers, which may put that company in a cash-poor situation. That's why cash-flow statements are so important.

You can get an idea of your favourite company's actual cash flows from the adjustments shown on its *cash-flow statement.* The three sections to this statement are operating activities, investment activities, and financial activities. Cash-flow statements are filed with the OSC and the SEC along with income statements on a quarterly and annual basis.

Operating activities

Looking at cash flow from *operating activities* gives you a good picture of the cash that's available from a company's core business operations, including net income, depreciation and amortization, changes in accounts receivable, changes in inventory, and changes in other current liabilities and current assets. We talk more about these accounts in the "Scouring the Balance Sheet" section.

Calculating cash flow from operating activities includes adjustments to net income made by adding back items that were not actually cash expenditures but rather were required for reporting purposes. Depreciation is one such item. Similarly, expenses or income items that were reported for accrual purposes are subtracted out. For example, changes in accounts receivable are subtracted out, because they represent cash that has not been received. Conversely, changes in accounts payable represent payments that have not yet been made, so the cash still is on hand.

The bottom line: This section of a company's cash-flow statement shows actual *net cash from operations.*

Depreciation

For all companies, one of the largest adjustments to cash flow is depreciation. Depreciation reflects the dollar value placed on the annual use of an asset. For example, if a company's truck will be a useable asset for five years, then the cost of that truck is depreciated over that five-year period. For accounting purposes on its income statement, a company must use a method called *straight-line depreciation,* a method of calculating depreciation in which the company determines the actual useful life span of an asset and then divides the purchase price of that asset by that life span. Each year depreciation expenses are recorded for each asset using this straight-line method. Although no cash is actually paid out, the total amount of depreciation is added back to the cash-flow statement.

For tax purposes, companies can be more creative by writing off assets much more quickly and thus reducing their tax burdens at the same pace. One type of write-off enables a company to deduct the full cost of an asset during its first year of use. Other methods enable a company to depreciate assets sooner than the straight-line method. How a company depreciates its assets can have a major impact on how much that company pays in taxes.

Although you won't know how a company depreciated its assets by looking at its cash-flow statement, you will know the adjustment made for depreciation for cash purposes. Remember that depreciation is an expense that must be reported on an income statement, and not a cash outlay.

Financing activities

The financing activities section of a cash-flow statement shows any common stock that was issued or repurchased during the period the report reflects, and any new loan activity. The financial activities section gives you a good idea whether the company is having trouble meeting its daily operating needs and as a result is seeking outside cash. You won't, however, find that new financing always is bad. A company may be in the process of a major growth initiative and may be financing that growth by issuing new debt or common stock.

The bottom line: This section of the cash-flow statement shows a company's total cash flow from financing activities.

Book IV
Chapter 2

The Fundamentals:
Economics and
Stock Market
Metrics

Investment activity

This section of the cash-flow statement shows you how a company spends its money for growing long-term assets, such as new buildings or other new acquisitions, including major purchases of property, equipment, and other companies. It also shows you a company's sales of major assets or equity investments in other companies. Tracking investment activities gives investors a good idea of what major long-term capital planning activities have taken place during the period.

Scouring the Balance Sheet

The balance sheet gives you a snapshot of the company's assets and liabilities at a particular point in time. This differs from the income statement, which gives you operating results of a company during a particular period of time. A *balance sheet* has three sections, including

✦ An *assets* section that details everything the company owns.

✦ A *liabilities* section that details the company's debt or any other claims on the company's assets made by creditors.

✦ A *shareholder's equity* (also called owner's equity) section that lists all the claims made by owners or investors.

The balance sheet gets its name because the total assets of the company are supposed to equal the total claims against it — total liabilities plus total equity.

Assets and liabilities are listed on the balance sheet according to their *liquidity,* or how quickly and easily they can be converted into cash. Assets or liabilities that are more liquid appear first on the list, while the ones that are increasingly more difficult to convert to cash — long-term assets or liabilities — appear later. The asset section is divided into current assets (the ones that are used up in one year) and long-term assets (the ones whose life spans are longer than a year), as is the liabilities section — current liabilities and long-term liabilities.

Current assets include cash and other assets that can quickly and easily be converted into cash — marketable securities, money market investments, accounts receivables, and inventories. Long-term assets include holdings such as buildings, land, equipment, and sometimes goodwill. Similarly, on the liabilities side, current liabilities include any claims against assets that are due during the next 12 months, such as accounts payable and notes payable. Long-term liabilities are claims due in more than 12 months, such as mortgage or lease payables as well as bonds issued by the company.

Equity accounts include outstanding (remains on the market) preferred shares and/or common stocks and retained earnings. Retained earnings reflect the profits that are reinvested in the company rather than paid out as dividends to owners or shareholders.

Analyzing assets

In analyzing assets, two key ratios to look at are how quickly a company is collecting on its accounts receivable — the *accounts receivable turnover* — and how quickly inventory is sold — the *inventory turnover*.

A two-step process is used to find the accounts receivable turnover. First you must find out how quickly a company turns its accounts receivables into cash using this formula:

> Accounts receivable turnover = Sales on account ÷ Average accounts receivable balance

Then you need to find out how quickly a company collects on its accounts by dividing the accounts receivable turnover into 365 to find the average number of days it takes to collect on accounts.

Testing for inventory turnover uses a similar two-step process. First you must find out how quickly inventory turns over during the year using this formula:

> Inventory turnover ratio = Cost of goods sold ÷ Average inventory balance

Then you need to divide the inventory turnover ratio into 365 to find the average number of days it takes a company to turn over its inventory. Comparing these results for the companies you're considering can help you determine how well each company is handling the collection of its accounts receivable and the sale of its inventory. Obviously, the faster a company collects on accounts or sells its inventory, the better that company is doing in managing its assets. Compare companies in the same industry to determine how well a company is doing.

Whenever you see accounts receivable rising rapidly, and the number of days to collect on those accounts also is rising, consider it a red flag that signals cash problems likely lie ahead. Whenever you see inventory numbers rising, a company can be having a hard time selling its product — which also raises a red flag signalling problems ahead.

We're summarizing these two common ratios so that you know what they mean whenever you see them mentioned by analysts. As a trader, you aren't likely to take the time to do these calculations yourself.

Book IV
Chapter 2

The Fundamentals:
Economics and
Stock Market
Metrics

Looking at debt

When considering debt, or what a company owes, the two primary ratios you want to look at are the current ratio and acid, or quick, ratio. You can quickly calculate the *current ratio,* which tests whether a company can make its payments, by looking at the balance sheet and using this formula:

Current ratio = Current assets ÷ Current liabilities

Again, like the other ratios in this chapter, you must compare the ratio of one company to that of other companies in the same industry. A current ratio that's lower than most other companies in the industry can indicate the company is having a problem paying its short-term debts, which, in turn, is a strong sign that bankruptcy may be just around the corner. A current ratio that's significantly higher can be a bad sign too, because it can mean the company isn't using its assets efficiently. For these reasons, traders like to see companies with current ratios that are close to the industry average.

Luckily, you won't have to calculate current ratios, because they're easily found on any website that includes fundamental statistics

The acid test, or quick ratio, is almost the same as the current ratio; however, the key difference is that inventory value amounts are subtracted from current assets before dividing that result by current liabilities. Many financial institutions take this extra step because inventories aren't as easy to convert to cash. The acid test ratio is calculated by:

Acid test ratio = (Current assets − Inventory) ÷ Current liabilities

The acid test ratio is primarily of interest to financial institutions thinking about making a short-term loan to a company. They look for an acid test ratio of at least 1 to 1 before considering a company a good credit risk. Even though as a trader you're not likely to be in the business of making loans, a company that has problems getting short-term debt is likely to have problems meeting its short-term obligations. As the market recognizes the problem, the company's share price is likely to drop.

Reviewing goodwill

Goodwill is not a tangible asset but rather is usually collected through the years as companies are bought and sold. Goodwill reflects a competitive advantage, such as a strong brand or reputation. When one company buys another and pays more than the tangible assets are worth, the difference is added to the acquirer's balance sheet as goodwill. In other words, it's the premium in price that one company pays for another.

Determining Stock Valuations

By now the key question you're probably asking is, "How do I use all these data to decide how much I should pay for a stock?" Basically, the value of a stock is the amount buyers are willing to pay for the stock and the amount for which sellers are willing to sell the stock under current business conditions. The actual value of a stock shifts throughout the day and usually in a matter of seconds when the trading volume is high.

Fundamental analysis is one of the tools that investors and some traders use to analyze earnings, revenue growth, market share, and future business plans so they can determine the value of the stock and the price they're willing to pay for or sell it. Earnings and earnings growth are key factors and are considered a part of fundamental analysis. Common ratios used to determine a stock's value include the price to earnings multiple, or P/E ratio; price to book multiple, or price/book ratio; return on assets (ROA); and return on equity (ROE). We talk more about how these ratios are calculated in the sections that follow.

After considering all these data, investors decide whether a company's stock is undervalued or overvalued. Although past performance is no guarantee about a company's or stock's future success, fundamental analysts believe collecting and analyzing the appropriate data enables investors to make more of an educated guess about a stock's value.

Earnings

Using the income statement, we've talked extensively about a company's earnings. Remember the three types of earnings figures to consider are

✦ **Gross profit,** which is calculated after considering the direct costs related to sales

✦ **Operating income,** which shows a company's profit after subtracting operating expenses

✦ **Net income,** which is the bottom-line earnings after all expenses, taxes, and interest are subtracted

When you encounter discussions about earnings figures, be certain you know which types of earnings are being discussed for the stock you're eyeing. To be able to compare apples with apples, you must know that you're using the same type of earnings figures.

**Book IV
Chapter 2**

**The Fundamentals:
Economics and
Stock Market
Metrics**

Projected earnings growth rate

The projected earnings growth rate, which shows how quickly the company is expected to grow, isn't something you'll calculate. What you will find in the fundamental analysis for stocks are earnings growth rate projections made by industry analysts based on their analysis of a company's potential earnings. The earnings growth rate is included on all the websites that provide fundamental statistics. When looking for these data, be sure to check out the earnings growth rate potential at a number of those sites.

Figuring Your Ratios: Comparing One Company's Stock to Another

In this section, we show you how to calculate four key ratios — P/E, price/book, ROE, and ROA. Each of these ratios gives you just one more piece in the puzzle of determining how much you want to pay for a stock.

Price/earnings ratio

The *P/E ratio* is probably the one that's quoted more often in news stories. This ratio reflects a comparison of a stock's earnings with its share price. You calculate this ratio using this formula:

P/E ratio = Stock price ÷ Earnings per share

You'll probably find two types of P/E ratios for a stock. The *trailing P/E* is based on earnings reported in previous quarters, and the *forward P/E* is based on projected earnings. At Yahoo! Finance, the trailing P/E for Home Depot was 17.14, and its forward P/E, expectations as of November 11, 2011, was 14.20. Lowe's trailing P/E was 15.85, and its forward P/E, expectations as of November 11, 2011, was 13.28. Much difference exists in the trailing P/E ratios for Home Depot and Lowe's, but analysts seem to slightly favour Home Depot's with a higher forward P/E. Historically, market analysts believed a P/E ratio of 10 to 15 was reasonable. For a while, much higher P/Es were tolerated, but during the 2008 market conditions people drifted back to historical P/Es. When comparing companies, you can get a good idea of how the market values each stock by looking at its P/E ratio. While the P/E ratio is actually a percentage, it is rarely stated that way. However, you will sometimes hear it called a price multiple, because the P/E ratio represents how much you are paying for each dollar of a company's earnings.

Eyeing the most fundamental data of all

If we were allowed to choose only one piece of fundamental data to guide our trading, we'd choose the earnings growth rate (you'll sometimes see this called the EPS growth rate — EPS stands for earnings per share). You can use it as a quick summary of a company's performance. Evaluating the entire financial condition of a company isn't necessary when its earnings aren't up to par.

Price/book ratio

The *price/book ratio* compares the market's valuation of a company to the value that the company shows on its financial statements. The higher the ratio, the more the market is willing to pay for a company above its hard assets, which include its buildings, inventory, accounts receivable, and other clearly measurable assets. Companies are more than their measurable assets. Customer loyalty, the value of their locations, and other intangible assets add value to a company. Investors looking to buy based on value rather than growth are more likely to check out the price/book ratio. Price/book ratios are calculated using this formula:

Price/book ratio = Stock price ÷ (Book value – Total liabilities)

Return on assets

Return on assets (ROA) shows you how efficiently management uses the company's resources. ROA doesn't, however, show you how well the company is performing for its shareholders. To calculate return on assets, use this formula:

Return on assets = Earnings after taxes ÷ Total assets

Return on equity

Investors are more interested in *return on equity* (ROE), which measures how well a company is doing for its shareholders. This ratio measures how much profit management generates from resources provided by its shareholders. Investors look for companies with high ROEs that show signs of growth. You calculate ROE by using this formula:

Return on equity = Earnings after taxes ÷ Shareholder equity

**Book IV
Chapter 2**

**The Fundamentals:
Economics and
Stock Market
Metrics**

As a trader, you may not make your buy and sell decisions based on fundamental analysis, but collecting and having access to this information as part of your arsenal certainly helps you to make better and more informed stock choices. Knowing a company has strong fundamentals helps to back up what you're seeing in the technical analysis.

Chapter 3: Nearly Everything You Wanted to Know about Technical Analysis

In This Chapter

✔ **Understanding price charts**

✔ **Locating trends**

✔ **Minding the gaps**

✔ **Making the most of moving averages**

✔ **Making use of the MACD**

Investors and traders are always looking for an edge in forecasting stock prices to improve their trading results. The method of choice for many investors is *fundamental analysis,* which we describe in Chapter 2. For some traders, on the other hand, *technical analysis* — as described here, and in more depth in Book 5 — is the way to go.

Although some overlap exists between fundamental and technical analyses, you find dyed-in-the-wool, true believers in both camps, and they argue that their way is best, even going so far as to say the opposite way is worse than useless. For our money, the truth lies somewhere in between these two extremes.

In this chapter we cover the basics of charting (trust us — even just the basics is still a lot of information to take in). We'll show you how to draw price charts for a single stock, for an index such as the S&P/TSX Composite Index or the S&P 500, or for an exchange-traded fund. In addition, you'll find out how to identify trends and trading ranges and how to look for key transition points that often lead to good trading opportunities. You want to quickly identify the patterns we describe here when evaluating charts for your own trading.

After you read this chapter, flip to Book 5 on day trading, where we offer more complicated trading strategies such as head and shoulders. (No, it has nothing to do with the shampoo — check it out and you'll see what we're talking about.)

Why Technical Analysis?

Technical analysis is an excellent tool for managing your money, controlling your losses, and enabling your profits to run.

Even people who base their trades on fundamental factors can use chart analysis to help them time market entry and exit points and gauge price volatility and risk. Using technical analysis successfully means

- ✦ Being patient
- ✦ Finding out how to identify and use a small number of patterns and indicators
- ✦ Becoming proficient at finding these patterns and profitably trading on them
- ✦ Adding methodically to your tool kit to improve your trading results

Remember that no method is foolproof. Nothing ensures successful trades 100 percent of the time. But technical analysis is an excellent tool for improving your trading results.

Creating a Price Chart

Traders used to create their charts by hand. Today, however, many charting alternatives and options are available, including easy-to-use computer software and easily accessible Internet sites. You may, of course, still want to create charts by hand; that's something we encourage you to do — at least for a little while. Making your own charts is easy, a great way to discover charting concepts, and an excellent way of getting a feel for the markets.

A chart of stock prices shares characteristics with other charts with which you're probably familiar. These kinds of charts typically are made up of two axes; the *horizontal axis* represents time, and the *vertical axis* represents price. One unusual feature of a stock chart is that its vertical axis, the price axis, usually is shown on the right. The most current prices are shown on the right-hand side of the chart, and so are the newest trading signals. You always trade while those signals are on the right edge of a chart, so having the price axis closest to the most crucial part of the chart makes sense.

Creating a single price bar

Regardless of whether your chart is an *intraday chart* (showing fluctuations throughout a trading day) or a chart of daily or weekly prices, the format of the price bar is the same. Each bar represents the results for a single trading period. On a chart that provides daily information, for example, each bar represents the results for a single trading day.

Most stock-price bar charts show four important prices on each bar:

✦ **Open:** The price recorded for the first trade

✦ **High:** The highest price trade during the trading period

✦ **Low:** The lowest price trade during the trading period

✦ **Close:** The price recorded for the last trade

By convention, a daily bar chart shows trades for the Toronto Stock Exchange (TSX) and the New York Stock Exchange (NYSE) trading day — from 9:30 a.m. to 4:00 p.m. ET — but some charting packages include optional after-hours results (prices from trades that occur after the market closes) as part of each daily bar. Likewise, some charting packages omit the opening prices on intraday charts. The opening price on an intraday chart (almost) always is the same as the closing price for the previous bar, so omitting it is of little consequence. However, omitting the opening price on daily, weekly, and monthly charts diminishes the usefulness of the chart, so avoid charts that don't provide all four prices.

This identical format is used for all time periods. For example, an intraday chart may use 1-minute bars, where each bar spans all the prices for your stock that occur during trades over a full minute. Common time frames for stock price charts are

✦ **1-minute bars:** Each bar represents one minute of trading.

✦ **5-minute bars:** Each bar represents five minutes of trading.

✦ **10-minute bars:** Each bar represents ten minutes of trading.

✦ **15-minute bars:** Each bar represents 15 minutes of trading.

✦ **60-minute bars:** Each bar represents 60 minutes of trading.

✦ **Daily bars**: Each bar represents one full day of trading.

✦ **Weekly bars:** Each bar represents one week of trading.

✦ **Monthly bars:** Each bar represents one full month of trading.

In our own trading, we typically monitor weekly charts, daily charts, one or two intraday charts, and either 60-minute bars for stocks and exchange-traded funds or 5-minute bars for indices.

Measuring volume

In addition to prices, bar charts often show the volume, or the number of shares traded during the given time period represented by each bar. On a daily chart, trading volume shows the total number of shares traded throughout the day. By convention, the volume is shown as a separate bar graph and usually is shown directly underneath the price chart.

**Book IV
Chapter 3**

**Nearly Everything
You Wanted
to Know about
Technical Analysis**

Volume (the number of shares sold) is used as a confirming indicator. In other words, if a price bar shows bullish activity, that bullishness is confirmed by a higher-than-average trading volume. However, that bullish indication may diminish if trading volume is lower than average.

Volume also is used to gauge institutional participation in a stock. Significant trading volume often signals that large institutional investors — mutual funds, billionaires, pension funds, insurance companies, hedge funds, and others — are placing orders to buy or sell a stock. When prices rise and volume is strong, you usually can infer that institutions are accumulating positions in the stock. The reverse also is true. When prices fall and trading volume is high, large institutions may be liquidating positions, which is considered a bearish development.

Low-volume price changes are less meaningful, at least from a technical perspective, than high-volume changes. That's why technicians say, "Volume confirms price."

Identifying Trends

Identifying a trend is relatively straightforward. Instinctively, you know it when you see it. Visual techniques and calculated indicators both can be used to identify trend signals.

A steadily rising or falling stock is a *trending stock.* But if you watch stocks for any period of time, you know that they rarely go straight up or down. Instead, you see a stair-step effect in which a stock rises several steps and then falls back. Talking about a trend as a series of intermittent highs interrupted by intermittent lows makes good sense. So an *uptrend,* then, is a series of higher intermittent highs and higher intermittent lows. Conversely, a *downtrend* is a series of lower intermittent highs followed by lower intermittent lows.

Supporting and Resisting Trends

In an uptrend, as long as the pattern of higher highs and higher lows continues, you can say that the trend persists. The converse (lower highs and lower lows) is true in a downtrend. Unfortunately, you cannot say that breaks in these patterns signal the end of any trends.

Sometimes you see an uptrend pattern broken when the stock fails to reach a new high or when it makes a lower intermittent low. You may actually see several of these disconcerting lower lows, only to witness the resumption of a strong uptrend. As such, you need to anticipate these eventual hiccups as you plan your trading strategy, and you need tools to help you determine whether a stock is still trending or the trend has reached its end.

Drawing trend lines to show support

Trend lines are drawn underneath a trend, much as support lines are drawn underneath a trading range. And just like the support line, trend lines show areas of trading-range support that can be used to trigger short-term trading signals as you monitor the progress of a trend.

If you remember your days in geometry class, you'll recall that only two points are needed to define any line. Knowing which points to choose is the trick when drawing a trend line. You may, for example, choose to have the trend line touching two or more of the intermittent lows, or you may choose to draw the trend line based on the lowest closing prices between those intermittent lows.

Unfortunately, drawing trend lines is not a precise discipline, and no universal consensus exists for where and how to draw them. In fact, you're not likely to find any two traders drawing trend lines in exactly the same place for the same stock. Furthermore, you'll drive yourself crazy trying to touch all the important lows with your trend line.

Trend lines are drawn to fit historical data. That the trend rides atop the trend line is not surprising, given that you drew it that way. However, whether that trend line represents the actual trend or is able to generate reliable trading signals is constantly in doubt.

So many variables apply. You might, for example, draw the trend line on a traditional price scale as we've done here, but that trend line will look very different from one drawn on a log or semi-log scale that shows percentage price changes. It's hard to know which is the better choice. Also, trend lines are often drawn using the oldest historical data, but newer data are more relevant for generating trading signals. As such, constantly questioning your information and continually updating your trend line is a good habit to follow.

Watching the price bar cross below the trend line can be disturbing; it can signal the end of the trend, or it may mean that you need to redraw the trend lines. Unfortunately, when the stock price closes below the trend line you can't know whether the penetration represents the end of the trend or just another opportunity to redraw the trend line to conform to the newest price data.

**Book IV
Chapter 3**

Nearly Everything
You Wanted
to Know about
Technical Analysis

An alternative technique for drawing the trend line reduces the ambiguity just a bit. Instead of drawing the trend line from left to right, the way most people instinctively do, draw the trend line backward, or from right to left. Using the two most recent intermittent lows in the trend, draw the trend line backward as long as it is meaningful, then project the trend line toward the right. This approach has a couple of benefits:

✦ The slope of the trend line is more closely aligned with the most recent trading data, which usually are more relevant to your trading decisions.

✦ You'll resign yourself to the necessity of continually redrawing your trend lines based on the newest data.

Surfing channels

Traders use a *channel* to identify potential entry and exit points during a trend. Channel lines are formed when a line is drawn parallel with the trend line across a trend's intermittent highs. This *top channel line* is analogous to the resistance line in a trading range. The original trend line then becomes the *bottom channel line*.

Trending and channelling strategies

The strategies for using trend lines and channels are similar. When an uptrending stock approaches the trend line or the bottom channel line, short-term traders often see an opportunity to take a position in the direction of the dominant trend. As long as the stock's price does not fall through this support level, they will hold the position. Position traders, on the other hand, may use these same conditions to validate their existing positions as still viable. If, however, the stock closes below the trend line and remains below it for longer than a day or two, position traders *and* short-term traders must consider the possibility that the trend has reached its end. It's even possible that the trend has reversed.

It may seem perverse, but when an upwardly trending stock breaches the top channel line, it's not always good news. The stock may be overextended. At the very least, it's an indication to traders to pay close attention.

Trend lines and channels work better across longer periods of time. A stock price that violates a long-running, persistent trend or channel line on a weekly chart provides more meaningful guidance than when it breaches a support line on a daily chart or an intraday chart. In our experience, short-term trend lines add little information that isn't already present in the steady march of higher highs and higher lows.

When a stock breaks a short-term trend line, we believe it's best to step back one time increment to evaluate the situation. For example, if you're trading based primarily on daily chart data, display a weekly chart and examine the trend line and the series of intermittent highs and lows. If the march of higher highs and higher lows remains intact on the weekly chart, you may want to give your position a little room to work itself out. However, if a longer time frame shows a break in the pattern of higher highs and higher lows, consider exiting your position right away.

We use trend lines for guidance while trading, but rarely do we make decisions solely on the basis of a trend-line penetration. Although initiating short-term positions in the direction of the dominant trend is possible by using channels to enter and exit the position, doing so is very difficult, and few traders are able to engage in that practice profitably. Some traders even take this concept one step further by trying to take positions in opposition to the dominant trend as the stock price approaches the upper channel line. We believe trading in the direction opposite that of a dominant trend and a stock's fundamental picture is foolhardy and an excellent way to lose a substantial portion of your trading capital.

Bottom line: Trend lines and channels are additional tools you can use to monitor the progress of a stock price trend. They can be used to help identify trading opportunities, but we recommend they not be your primary method of determining entry and exit points.

Seeing Gaps

A *price gap* forms on a bar chart when the opening price of the current bar is above or below the closing price of the previous bar. Gaps occur mostly on daily charts, sometimes on weekly charts, and rarely on intraday charts. Depending on the circumstances, gaps can show continuation and reversal patterns, and they can signal an opportunity to enter or exit a position.

Some gaps are obvious and some are subtle. For example, if the opening price is above the previous close, but the low of the current bar is below the previous high, then those bars overlap and the gap is hard to spot. Many traders simply ignore that type of gap. If, however, the low of the current bar is obviously higher than the high of the previous bar, that will draw the attention of most traders. We discuss examples of obvious gaps in the following sections.

**Book IV
Chapter 3**

Nearly Everything
You Wanted
to Know about
Technical Analysis

Gaps are divided into several broad categories based on where the gap occurs. These categories determine your trading strategy and are discussed in the sections that follow.

Common gap

Gaps that occur within a trading range can be either a *common gap* or a *breakout gap*. If the gap occurs in the middle of the trading range, far from either the support or resistance level, it is a common gap. Common gaps occur frequently and are, well, rather common. They rarely provide meaningful trading opportunities. Ignoring them usually is the best policy.

Breakout or breakaway gap

When a stock price exceeds the high of a price range during a specific time frame or falls below the low during that same period and simultaneously forms a gap, traders describe that situation as a *breakout* or *breakaway gap*. A breakout gap often provides excellent trading signals to enter a new position, in the direction of the gap.

Continuation gap

A *continuation gap* is also known as a runaway gap or an acceleration gap. This type of gap occurs within an uptrend when the open price of the current bar is higher than the close price of the previous bar. If the low of the current bar is also obviously above the high of the previous bar, this gap usually indicates that the trend is very strong. Continuation gaps may also occur in downtrends. The defining characteristics are opposite those of the uptrend.

Some short-term traders may use a continuation gap as a signal to enter a position in the direction of the gap. Position traders may use this same signal to confirm that a current trade remains viable. You sometimes see a series of runaway gaps occur in close proximity to each other, and these gaps usually are a strong confirmation of the prevailing trend. However, continuation gaps also warrant caution, because they can turn into an exhaustion gap.

Exhaustion gap

Exhaustion gaps occur at or near the ends of strong trends. Unfortunately, the defining characteristics for an exhaustion gap are virtually identical to those for a continuation gap. Exhaustion gaps are often accompanied by very large volume, which is one clue that the gap may not be a continuation gap. Otherwise, distinguishing an exhaustion gap from a continuation gap is sometimes impossible, until the stock price changes direction. By that time, it is usually obvious that something is wrong with the trade and you should exit your position.

Island gap

An *island gap,* or an island reversal, forms when a trend changes direction. The pattern is actually two gaps that isolate either a single bar or a short series of bars from the dominant trend and the new trend. An island gap usually is a good indicator that the prior trend has been extinguished and can be used to signal an exit from an existing position. You may also use an island gap to initiate a new position, but only if the direction of the new trend aligns with the stock's underlying fundamental condition. Be sure to review the "Dealing with Failed Signals" section in this chapter before initiating any positions based on an island gap.

Waving Flags and Pennants

Flag and pennant patterns represent areas of consolidation on a trend chart. You've already encountered these patterns, just not by name. In a series of higher highs and higher lows, these patterns form the basis for the higher lows. In other words, the higher lows are made of flag and pennant patterns.

A *pennant pattern* looks like, well, a pennant. Support and resistance lines converge into a point forming what looks like a small pennant shape. A *flag pattern,* on the other hand, is bounded by parallel lines. All these patterns almost always fly counter to the prevailing trend, but the direction in which they're flying is not actually a requirement.

The key for each of these patterns is the breakout. If the breakout from the formation is in the direction of the established trend, then the trend continues. If not, it's possible that the trend is over.

Flags and pennants typically are associated with a trend, but you may also see these patterns within the confines of a trading range. A flag or pennant forming near the top of a trading range hints of an eventual breakout. The flag or pennant pattern shows the stock consolidating near the top of the trading range, and that suggests that selling pressure is diminishing and the stock is preparing to test the zone of resistance.

Book IV
Chapter 3

Nearly Everything
You Wanted
to Know about
Technical Analysis

Withstanding Retracements

A *retracement* occurs when a trending stock revisits recent prices. You've already seen many examples. When a stock makes a higher intermediate high and then a higher intermediate low, that is a retracement. A trading range can also be considered a retracement. You may hear a retracement called a price consolidation or a pullback, but the concept is the same.

Flags and pennants are relatively simple forms of retracement patterns. More complex retracements can occur within the confines of a trend, and like their simpler counterparts they don't actually signal the end of the trend. Unfortunately, complex retracements cause confusion and consternation for traders when they occur. Besides being difficult to anticipate, they send out conflicting signals to traders trying to make sense of which trading-plan adjustments are needed.

Three-step and five-step retracements

In an uptrend, you sometimes see breaks in the pattern of higher highs and higher lows when the stock price fails to reach a new high or makes a lower intermittent low. You may see several occurrences of these worrisome lower lows and lower highs happen one right after the other followed by a resumption of a strong uptrend.

You will see a couple of these benign multistep patterns frequently occur in the midst of a strong trend, so it's useful to watch for them. A *three-step retracement* makes at least one lower intermittent high and one lower intermittent low. A *five-step retracement* makes two lower highs and two lower lows. Multistep retracements also occur when a downtrending stock makes higher highs and higher lows.

Trust us when we tell you that situations like these are disconcerting whenever you're holding a position. They're not, however, absolute signals that a trend has reached its end. Knowing when a trend has ended, however, is nearly impossible, so you need a plan for dealing with it when it happens.

Where the multistep retracement occurs within a trend has some bearing on what plan you choose. If the stock price has just broken out of a long trading range and then falters, you may want to wait for a subsequent attempt to break out of the trading range, but closing the position is probably best. Look for trading opportunities elsewhere.

If a stock price starts what may be a three-step or a five-step retracement after a long period of trending, and your position is profitable, you may want to see how the retracement plays out. Absent any obvious sell signals, such as an island reversal or a downside breakout from a flag, pennant, or trading range formation, you can wait to see how the retracement resolves itself.

Checking out a chart that reflects a longer time frame can be helpful. For example, you can examine a weekly chart when the retracement occurs on the daily chart. If the trend shows no signs of faltering on the weekly chart, hold your position. If the stock recovers and heads higher, so much the better, but if it establishes another lower high and trades below its next lower low, it's time to exit.

Finally, considering fundamental factors before making your decision makes good sense. If a company's deteriorating financial situation is an underlying cause of the retracement, then exiting your position makes sense. You also need to be aware of the cycle the economy is in when making your decision. If the economy is approaching a turning point as your stock's technical situation deteriorates, getting out of the position usually is a good idea.

Dealing with subsequent trading ranges

A trading range or a cup and handle formation are also complex consolidation patterns. A trend that's interrupted by a period of range-bound trading may indicate either a pause before the trend resumes or the end of the trend. The only way of knowing which way the trend will go is to watch for the breakout. Unfortunately, you may be in for a long wait.

In the retracement pattern, you can make a valid argument interpreting the five-step retracement as a cup and handle formation. Technical analysis is an imprecise discipline, so you may encounter ambiguous situations like this. The results in this case were the same regardless of your interpretation. The stock broke out of its nine-week complex consolidation pattern and resumed its trend.

Breakouts that occur in the direction of the prevailing trend may indicate that the trend has farther to run, but they may also be a prelude to a failed breakout signal. Trading-range breakouts provide the strongest signals when they result in a change of direction from the previous trend.

Dealing with Failed Signals

All trading signals are subject to failure. Sometimes, things just don't work out as planned. However, even a failed signal provides additional information that you can use to revise your trading plans. In fact, sometimes the best trading signals are the direct result of a failed signal.

Trapping bulls and bears

Breakouts from trading ranges and cup and handle patterns sometimes fail. These failures happen to bullish and bearish signals, and when they fail it is called a *trap*. The two kinds of traps are

✦ *Bull traps,* which occur after an upside breakout. The stock breaks out of its trading range to the upside but then reverses back into the trading range and ultimately breaks out to the down side.

✦ *Bear traps,* which occur after a downside breakout. This opposite scenario to the bull trap often is very bullish. The stock reverses course and reenters the trading range. If a bear trap occurs within a trading range that's preceded by a long period of declining prices, it often represents an excellent buying opportunity, because it's a sign that selling pressure has evaporated in the stock, which thus is likely to attempt an upside breakout.

Whenever you see a potential bear trap taking place and the stock meets all of your fundamental criteria, you may want to enter a long position as soon as the stock price reenters the trading range.

Filling the gaps

A gap that's forming usually is interpreted as a signal that the prevailing trend will continue. If a stock reverses and retraces prices within the gap, we say that the gap has been filled. A gap that's filled negates the trading signal that it generated.

When dealing with a breakout gap, a stock price that falls back through the trading range resistance zone and fills the gap is likely to be a bearish development. Similarly, when a continuation gap is filled, you need to consider it a failed signal and exit your position. The same is true for an island gap. If prices trade back into the area of the isolated island, the trading signal has failed and you need to exit your position.

Deciding whether to reverse directions

A bear trap shows an example of where taking a position based on a failed signal makes sense. If, however, you already have a position and the signal fails, exiting your position is a wise choice — you're letting the market sort out its psychosis without risking your money.

You also need to consider economic and fundamental factors when deciding how to handle a failed signal. Acting on a contrary signal makes sense only when economic and fundamental conditions support the decision.

For example, if a bullish signal fails and becomes a bearish signal, selling a stock short makes sense only if it's fundamentally weak and the stock's sector is in decline. Conversely, if a bear trap occurs and generates a buy signal, taking a position in the stock makes sense only if its earnings are strong and growing, its sector is performing well, and the economy is on an upswing.

The Ins and Outs of Moving Averages

A *moving average* is a trading indicator that shows the direction and magnitude of a trend over a fixed period of time. Some traders call it a *price overlay,* because it's superimposed over the price data in a bar chart. Moving averages visually smooth out the data on a price chart to help make trend identification less subjective. All moving averages follow a stock's price trend but can't predict changes. They report only what has happened.

As its name implies, a *moving average* shows the average of a stock's up-and-down price movements during a specific period of time. A stock's daily closing price usually is the value being averaged, but any value on a price chart can be displayed as a moving average. Some traders, for example, prefer using the mid-point between daily high and low prices for the moving average calculation, but you can also use the opening, high, or low prices or any coincident value on a price chart, including volume.

You'll find that moving averages are used as indicators by themselves or in conjunction with other indicators. They are also the building blocks for other indicators and oscillators such as the moving average convergence divergence (MACD) invented by Gerald Appel in the 1960s. Before discussing how the MACD is used (see the section "Discovering MACD" in this chapter), we must explain moving averages and how they are calculated. In this section we describe two of the many types of moving averages.

Simple moving average

A simple moving average (SMA) is simple to calculate and simple to use. To calculate it, you add a number of prices together and then divide by the number of prices you added.

**Book IV
Chapter 3**

Nearly Everything
You Wanted
to Know about
Technical Analysis

If you're mathematically inclined, here's what the series looks like as an equation:

$$SMA = (P_{[1]} + P_{[2]} + P_{[3]} + \ldots P_{[N]}) \div N$$

Where: N is the number of periods in the SMA

$P_{[N]}$ is the price being averaged (usually the closing price)

Traders used to calculate SMAs by hand, but fortunately, computers now relieve traders from this rather mundane chore. The way you use a moving average in your trading is discussed in the next section.

Exponential moving average

Another commonly used moving average is the exponential moving average (EMA), which can be superimposed on a bar chart in the same manner as an SMA. The EMA is also used as the basis for other indicators, such as the MACD (moving average convergence divergence) indicator, which we discuss in the section "Discovering MACD" in this chapter.

Although the calculation for an EMA looks a bit daunting, in practice it's simple. In fact, it's easier to calculate than an SMA, and besides, your charting package will do it for you. Here are the calculations:

$$EMA_{[today]} = (Price_{[today]} \times K) + (EMA_{[yesterday]} \times (1 - K))$$

Where: N = The length of the EMA

$$K = 2 \div (N + 1)$$

$Price_{[today]}$ = The current closing price

$EMA_{[yesterday]}$ = The previous EMA value

$EMA_{[today]}$ = The now current EMA value

The start of the calculation is handled in one of two ways. You can either begin by creating a simple average of the first fixed number (N) of periods and use that value to seed the EMA calculation, or you can use the first data point (typically the closing price) as the seed and then calculate the EMA from that point forward. You'll see other traders handling it both ways, but the latter method makes more sense to us.

Comparing SMA and EMA

The SMA and EMA are used regularly by position and short-term traders alike. Each moving average has its strengths and weaknesses. Which one you choose is somewhat a matter of personal preference, but one probably is better suited than the other in several situations. As position traders, we use both. We use a relatively long-term SMA to help signal exit points, and we use EMAs whenever we rely on the MACD indicator (see "Discovering MACD" in this chapter).

Consistency

An SMA has the benefit of being consistently calculated from one charting package to the next. If you ask for a nine-period SMA, you can be certain that the result will be identical to every other nine-period SMA for the same stock during the same time period (as long as no errors have occurred in the price data — it's rare, but it happens).

Unfortunately, EMAs are not always consistent, because of the way the EMA is calculated — the starting point matters. In theory, you need to use all the price data available for any individual stock. In practice, however, that rarely is done. Some charting software packages enable you to specify how much data are used when calculating an EMA, but most Internet charting sites do not. The result: One charting vendor may calculate EMA values that are significantly different from the ones provided by another.

Discovering that you're basing your trading decisions on an inaccurate moving average is more than a bit disconcerting. This problem occurs with short-period calculations, but it is especially problematic for longer-term EMA calculations. Unfortunately, the only thing you can do is ask your chart supplier how much data it uses when calculating an EMA and then verify the resulting EMA by hand. Otherwise, you risk making trading decisions on faulty data. Also, if you use more than one charting package, make sure they both use the same method to calculate the EMA.

Reaction time

In general, short-term traders are more likely to employ EMA, but position traders are more inclined to use SMA. The EMA usually is closer to the current closing price, which tends to make it change direction faster than the SMA. As a result, an EMA is likely to be quicker in signalling short-term trend changes.

The SMA probably is the better indicator for identifying long-term changes in a trend. Unfortunately, those signals are likely to take more time to appear than the ones generated by a comparable EMA. The method used to calculate the SMA causes it to react to price changes a bit slower, and that's the tradeoff for getting a signal that is potentially more reliable.

Book IV
Chapter 3

Nearly Everything
You Wanted
to Know about
Technical Analysis

Sensitivity

An unfortunate result of the method of calculating an SMA is that every time you add a price, another price falls off the back end of the equation. In other words, each new SMA data point is affected by two prices, the most recent closing price and the oldest closing price in the calculation. Ideally, you want the most recent data having a greater influence on your indicators than the impact of older data. But in an SMA, the oldest price affects the newest SMA point with the same weight as the newest price.

EMA calculations eliminate that problem. Each data point affects the EMA only once. You never have to drop the oldest price as a new price is added. For that reason, the EMA has a much longer memory than the SMA. Every price ever used in calculating EMA has some small effect. As an added benefit, EMA calculations place additional weight on the most recent price.

To understand how this works, examine the role played by the *coefficient K* in an EMA calculation. In the earlier example showing a nine-period EMA, the value of K (the newest price) is 0.20, or 20 percent.

$$\text{For } N = 9; K = 2 / (N + 1) \rightarrow K = 2 / (9 + 1) = 2 / 10 = .20 = 20 \text{ percent}$$

This means every new price added to the calculation represents 20 percent of the value of the EMA, while all the previous data represent 80 percent of it. The implication: The oldest data always have an impact, but slowly fade away, and newer data have a greater influence on the EMA value and the placement of the EMA data point.

Notice also that as the EMA period, represented by N, grows larger, the value of K becomes smaller, which means that each new data point has less influence on the EMA as the period grows larger.

Interpreting and using moving averages

Traders use moving averages to trigger buy and sell signals. In general, when a moving average slopes upward, you can infer that the trend is up, and when the moving average slopes downward, the trend is down.

One simple mechanical strategy that some traders employ works like this:

+ Buy when the moving average slopes upward *and* the closing price crosses above the moving average.

+ Close the position when the price closes below the moving average.

+ Sell short when the moving average slopes downward *and* the closing price crosses below the moving average.

+ Close the short position when the price closes above the moving average.

Although simple crossover strategies like this are remarkably effective in some trending situations, they're equally ineffective in others. Many variables must be in alignment for this approach to work. For example, the stock must be trending, and the period for the moving average must be chosen carefully for the indicator to be effective. These trend-following systems fail miserably when a stock is range bound.

When a stock is range bound or in a retracement, it's difficult to know whether the buy and sell signals that the moving average crossover strategy generates are good entry or exit signals. Keeping an eye on these complex retracement patterns (which we discuss at length later in this chapter) helps you recognize that DIA may have entered a period of retracement — another way of saying the stock is trading within a range — in March and April 2007. You can't know for sure whether DIA will break out of its consolidation to the upside or the downside until after the breakout actually occurs.

From our perspective, waiting for the breakout causes you little, if any, harm. When DIA entered a retracement pattern in March 2007, the economic cycle appeared to be ascending and not ready to peak. Other traders, however, argue that you risk missed opportunities elsewhere when you're waiting on position in a range-bound stock to break out. Although that argument is valid, and favours action on the SMA sell signal, we're still inclined to wait for the breakout before deciding.

We normally want some sort of confirmation signal before entering or exiting any position in a stock or exchange-traded fund. For example, we might temper the buy signal in the simple mechanical strategy described earlier with a requirement that the stock price remains above its SMA for several days after the initial signal before entering a position. The same is true for the sell, or close, signal. You want the stock to close below the SMA for several days, or you'd like to see another coincident sell signal before exiting your position. We use a long-period SMA to provide one of several signals to exit from existing positions. For example, if the price closes below a relatively long-term moving average and remains below it for a couple of days, we use that signal to exit our position.

Support and resistance factors

In addition to their trend-following abilities, moving averages also tend to provide support and resistance in stock prices that are trending up or down. When a price is trending higher, you often see the stock trade down toward the moving average only to reverse course and head higher. The same is true in reverse for stock prices that are trending lower. You often see a downtrending stock move up toward its moving average before heading lower. The moving average acts as an area of resistance.

Book IV
Chapter 3

Nearly Everything You Wanted to Know about Technical Analysis

Uptrending DIA approached its 30-day moving average in mid-August, November, December, January, and February. After each lull, DIA headed higher. Short-term traders use these opportunities to enter positions in the direction of the dominant trend. When moving averages show a stock is trending higher by sloping upward, for example, short-term traders buy into a position when the stock price closes near or just below the moving average so they can ride the trend to sell at a higher price later on. Position traders also can use these signals as second-chance entry points whenever they miss the first breakout. This strategy is called *buying on a pullback*.

Deciding the moving average time frame

Perhaps the most difficult decision you have to make when creating a moving average is determining the length or period that best fits the situation. Regardless of whether you select an EMA or an SMA, shorter periods yield more signals but a greater percentage of those signals are false; longer moving-average periods yield fewer signals but a greater percentage of those signals are true. One hitch: Signals occur later in longer-term moving averages than they do in shorter-term ones.

In general, the shorter your trading horizon, the shorter the moving average you want to select. For us, a nine-period moving average is nearly useless. It generates too many signals that we have no intention of following. More isn't always better. We want our technical analysis tools to provide better signals, not more, because although getting good signals is important, avoiding bad signals is even more so.

To reiterate, we rarely use short-term moving averages to generate buy signals. Instead, we use a long-period SMA to monitor the health of a trend. Typically, we select either a 30-day or 50-day SMA, depending on the duration of the existing trend and prevailing economic conditions. If a trend has existed for a relatively long period of time, we choose the 50-day SMA as an exit indicator. However, if the economy appears to be nearing a peak, as described in Chapter 2, then we tend to tighten our exit procedures and shorten the SMA. See Chapter 4 for more on trading strategies and exit procedures.

Traders can fall into a trap when trying to fine-tune the moving average — or any indicator, for that matter — for a specific stock or situation. Logically, testing many different moving-average periods using historical data to find the one that generates the most profitable trades and the fewest losing trades seems right, and charting software packages enable you to do just that to your heart's content.

However, you'll soon discover that what worked when using historical data often fails miserably when trading real money in real time. We talk about this problem more in Chapter 4. For now, know that fine-tuning an indicator for a specific stock or index rarely has any predictive value and you must avoid it. You simply can't trade using historical data. You're better off settling on a moving-average period that satisfies the requirements for a great many situations, rather than trying to fine-tune the time frame of a moving average to fit each stock.

Understanding Stochastic Oscillators

The *stochastic oscillator* indicates momentum and attempts to show buying and selling pressure. This indicator compares current closing prices with the recent range of high to low prices and displays the results on a chart. Stochastic oscillator values cycle, or oscillate, between zero and 100 percent.

Calculating stochastic oscillators

The typical stochastic oscillator is measured across a 14-day period, but a different time frame can be specified. Here's the calculation:

%K = 100 × (closing price – lowest low (N)) ÷ (highest high (N) – lowest low (N))

%D = 3-period moving average of %K

Where: N is the number of periods used in the calculation (usually 14)

This calculation describes a fast stochastic. The names %K and %D, respectively, identify the stochastic oscillator and the signal line. We typically use a variation of this indicator that's called a slow stochastic. The slow stochastic oscillator calculation is

%K = 3-period moving average of (100 × (closing price – lowest low (N)) ÷ (highest high (N) – lowest low (N))

%D = 3-period moving average of %K

Where: N is the number of periods used in the calculation (usually 14)

In effect, the slow stochastic uses the %D value from the fast stochastic calculation as its starting point. Although the fast and slow stochastics look similar when plotted on a chart, the slow stochastic is smoother and less jumpy. It generates fewer and more reliable trading signals, but the signals appear more slowly than with the fast stochastic. ***Note:*** You will find that some charting packages permit you to specify different values for the moving-average period, and some even permit you to change from an SMA to an EMA.

Book IV
Chapter 3

Nearly Everything
You Wanted
to Know about
Technical Analysis

Interpreting stochastic oscillators

As we mention earlier, the stochastic oscillator cycles between zero and 100 percent. Readings of more than 80 percent imply an overbought condition. Readings of less than 20 percent are interpreted as an oversold condition. As with most indicators, an overbought condition can be resolved if a stock trades lower or enters a period of consolidation. Similarly, an oversold condition can be resolved if a stock trades higher or enters a period of consolidation.

Overbought and oversold conditions can persist for long periods of time; therefore, readings that stay above 80 percent or below 20 percent are not enough to generate trading signals. Instead, stochastic oscillator signals are generated

✦ When the stochastic oscillator moves from below to above 20 percent, triggering a buy signal

✦ When the stochastic oscillator moves from above to below 80 percent, triggering a sell signal

Some traders use a *stochastic oscillator crossover strategy,* where buy signals are triggered when %K crosses above %D and sell signals are triggered when %K crosses below %D. For our style of trading that generates too many signals, a very high percentage of which are false.

The stochastic oscillator is most useful when it's used in conjunction with other indicators. When a stock is trending, the stochastic oscillator is useful in finding entry points within a dominant trend. In an uptrend, for example, a buy signal that's generated when the stochastic oscillator moves from below to above 20 percent is likely to be a good one. The stochastic oscillator signals many overbought conditions within an uptrend and rarely generates useful sell signals. It also works well in trading-range situations, and you'll find short-term traders who use it to trigger buy and sell signals when a stock is in a trading range.

Discovering MACD

The *moving average convergence divergence indicator* (MACD) is a trend-following momentum indicator. MACD is designed to generate trend-following trading signals based on moving average crossovers while overcoming problems associated with many other trend-following indicators. MACD also acts as a momentum oscillator, showing when a trend is gaining strength or losing momentum as it cycles above and below a centre zero line. MACD is an excellent indicator and an integral part of our trading toolset.

Calculating MACD

Charting packages routinely calculate MACD for you, but knowing how this indicator is created is important for gaining a better understanding of how it works. The MACD calculation isn't complex; it's just three exponential moving averages. The steps are as follows:

1. Calculate a 12-period EMA (see the section on "Exponential moving average").

2. Calculate a 26-period EMA.

3. Subtract the 26-period EMA from the 12-period EMA to create the MACD line.

4. Use the resulting MACD line to calculate a 9-period EMA to create the signal line.

5. Plot the MACD as a solid line; plot the signal line as either a dashed or lighter-coloured line.

An additional indicator, the MACD histogram, is usually shown as part of the MACD. It uses a histogram to show the difference between the MACD line and the signal line. The histogram is plotted above the zero line when the MACD line is above the signal line, below the zero line when the signal line is above MACD, and at zero when they cross.

When using MACD, we prefer weekly charts. That's how the indicator was originally designed to be used, and for our style of trading a weekly MACD indicator provides more useful information about the strength and direction of a trend and potential trend reversals. You will find that other traders use this indicator for both longer and shorter periods as well.

Using MACD

MACD provides a remarkable amount of information in a concise format. It oscillates above and below a centre zero line and is a good indicator for showing the direction of the dominant trend, signalling

✦ An uptrend when the MACD line crosses above the centre line

✦ A downtrend when the MACD line crosses below the centre line

Some short-term traders use the signal line to trigger

✦ Buy signals when the MACD line crosses above the signal line

✦ Sell signals when the MACD line crosses below the signal line

**Book IV
Chapter 3**

Nearly Everything
You Wanted
to Know about
Technical Analysis

We don't, however, find that short-term technique to be very reliable because it generates too many false signals. Instead, we prefer using the position of the MACD line relative to the zero line as an indication that the stock has begun trending.

Divergences that occur in the same direction as the dominant trend are often useful for entering positions. However, a divergence that is counter to the dominant trend is less likely to be a reliable trading signal. For example, a bearish divergence in a dominant uptrend is rarely a good signal to enter a short position. This type of bearish divergence may, however, signal that the stock has entered, or is about to enter, a period of retracement.

Each time the MACD line crosses above or below the signal line suggests a potential change in the direction of the dominant trend. Although this is not an outright buy signal or sell signal, it does suggest a change may be in the wind. In the case of a bearish divergence, the best way to exploit that information is to monitor individual stocks and ETFs for weakness, and either close long positions when they deteriorate, or initiate new short positions as they present themselves.

Most charting packages enable you to fine-tune the MACD calculation. Many traders vary the 12-, 26-, and 9-week values. Although nothing is inherently wrong with this approach, you nevertheless risk the curve-fitting problem whenever you try to find parameters that give you better results for a specific stock. That said, Gerald Appel, the man who developed MACD, uses values different than the original 12, 26, and 9. He also uses different values to generate buy signals than he does to generate sell signals. So feel free to experiment and have fun after you gain some experience with the default parameters. Because MACD is prone to whipsaw (causing you to lose potential profit), many technicians now use MACD as a monitoring tool. Whipsaw is like whiplash caused by the violent jerk in the opposite direction when you get hit from behind. Traders can buy shares just before they fall in value or sell shares just before they go up in value by reading the MACD tealeaves too closely.

Revealing Relative Strength

Relative strength measures the performance of one stock against another, or, more commonly, against the performance of an index such as the S&P 500. The idea is to determine how the stock is performing compared with the broad market.

Unfortunately, you may run across another indicator with a similar name when working with your charting software. The other indicator is called the *relative strength index* (RSI) and it is something completely different from the relative strength discussed here. RSI is an oscillator that is used in a similar way as the stochastic oscillator described earlier. To keep the two separate, we suggest you call the RSI by its initials and use the phrase "relative strength" when you mean to compare the performance of a stock against a broad-based index or another stock.

Calculating relative strength

Among the many ways you can calculate relative strength is simply dividing the stock price by the index value and plotting the result, like this:

Relative strength No. 1 = Stock price ÷ Index value

Another technique compares the price of the stock during a given period of time against the index during the same period. Our preference is comparing percentage changes during the same period. The calculation looks like this:

Relative strength No. 2 = Percentage change in stock price ÷ Percentage change in index value

Either of these approaches, or any other that you may invent, can be plotted on a stock chart. Some Internet sites provide a relative strength capability; see www.stockcharts.com/charts/performance for an example. Unfortunately, if you're using a charting software package, you'll probably have to program it into your system by using its formula-editing capabilities.

Or, you can look it up. *Investor's Business Daily* has a proprietary calculation for relative strength that ranks stocks based on their six-month performance. It is a handy tool.

Book IV
Chapter 3

Nearly Everything
You Wanted
to Know about
Technical Analysis

Chapter 4: Money Management Techniques and Trading System Tips

---

In This Chapter

✔ Making successful trades (and cutting your losses)

✔ Managing your holdings

✔ Protecting your money

✔ Entering and exiting trades

✔ Getting to know the bid/ask spread, stop losses, and limit orders

✔ Avoid trading pitfalls

✔ Understanding trading systems

Now that you know how to pick your stocks, you're almost ready to trade. But we want to share a few more things before you hit the buy button. In this chapter we dig deeper into the technical analysis that most traders abide by. Most of this won't apply to the long-term investors who buy securities and hang on to them for a few years. It's the short-term traders — people who hold securities for between one day and a few months — who will get the most from the next several pages.

In this chapter we talk about money management strategies to help you minimize the damage of losses (you can't win them all). We also cover margin requirements, short selling, and developing a trading system. It's a lot of information, but it's a must read for anyone who wants to trade. Trust us, you're almost ready!

Identifying Important Characteristics of a Successful Trader

Successful traders share a common trait. You'll find that they all successfully manage their money. The critical points of successful money management may be difficult to implement, but they're easy to identify. They include

✦ Planning your trades carefully by identifying entry and exit points

✦ Minimizing losses by ruthlessly adhering to your stop-loss points

✦ Protecting your profits with trailing stops

✦ Exiting your position when the trend ends

When using technical analysis to make your trades, you won't get the lowest entry price or the highest exit price. That means you will always leave something on the table. The idea is identifying when a trend has begun, entering the position, and riding the trend until it ends.

Opening the Door to Successful Trading

Because your way to successful trading is disciplined money management, the key to opening that door to success is developing a plan for your trades and sticking to that plan, even if it goes against what your gut tells you. Sometimes you think you've picked what seems like the perfect stock, but then it just doesn't perform the way you expected.

Before entering that trade, you need to set an entry point, the price at which you'll enter a trade, and an exit point where you will exit the trade if it goes poorly. Don't deviate from your plan, even if it means accepting the fact that you made a mistake. We discuss setting entry and exit points later in the chapter.

Although it may be cliché, it's nevertheless true: Cut your losses short and let your profits run. In other words, fold (sell) when your losses first appear and hold as your profits continue to build.

Your most important money management goal is to get out of losing positions as quickly as possible. After taking normal up and down price fluctuations into consideration, you must develop a method of recognizing when a stock is not behaving the way you expected, and as a result be prepared to close a losing position before it consumes too much of your trading capital. Try to keep losses below 5 or 6 percent for any position. Or you could think in terms of your total trading capital and try to keep the loss from any single position below 1 or 2 percent. Unfortunately, achieving a balance between recognizing your losers and dumping them in time (knowing when to fold 'em) is more difficult than it sounds.

Managing Your Inventory

To be successful, you need to treat trading as a business and stocks as your business inventory. Just like any other business, you must carefully manage your inventory to succeed. Factors paramount to successful trading are:

✦ **Viewing trading as a business.** You trade to make money. Sometimes you pick the wrong stock and have to accept a loss. Losses are a part of any business. The key to good business planning is minimizing losses.

✦ **Overcoming the most common trader's dilemma.** Many traders get caught up in the moment, trying to defend their position even as it moves in the wrong direction. When your choices no longer make good business sense, you must quickly make cold, hard decisions and decisively act to cut losses short.

✦ **Approaching the solution to your trading dilemma as if it's a business problem to solve.** Sell when you stand the chance of making a healthy profit or when you must accept that you've made a mistake and it's time to move on. Select your entry and exit target points before you buy the first share.

Thinking of trading as a business

So, how do you start thinking of trading as a business? Conceptually, it's simple. Like any other business, traders have fixed costs; variable costs; finite amounts of working capital, assets, and liabilities; fickle customers (or fickle market conditions); fickle vendors (market conditions again); and inventory. Managing these business factors results in either profits or losses, and you, of course, want to maximize the profits and minimize the losses. The most important step you can take in treating trading as a business is thinking of the contents of your portfolio as your inventory. We go into more detail on how trading can be treated as a business in Book 5, Chapter 1.

Finding a better plan

Approaching the trader's dilemma as though it were a business problem for you to solve can be helpful. The business of women's fashions provides an analogy that will do so nicely. The fashion industry works in obvious cycles. For example, you see long-term cycles at work as hemlines rise and fall and even longer cycles as you witness periodic mysteries that cause Capri pants and bell-bottom trousers to appear and just as easily disappear. You also see shorter cycles as clothing for the current season is discounted to make way for the next season's fashions. These shorter seasonal cycles illustrate the day-to-day issues that traders face.

Picking stock for the seasons

As spring approaches, retailers stock up on colourful, lightweight merchandise. You may even see swimsuits before then for those lucky souls who head to the tropics to escape the frosty chill. Fall clothes start showing up in stores as summer heats up. Before summer is over, heavier-weight clothes, including a selection of winter coats, begin appearing on clothing racks.

Ideally, retailers try to sell all their winter coats — and all their bathing suits and spring outfits — before the next season arrives, but that rarely happens. Retailers often have unsold inventory as the end of the season approaches.

Cleaning out the stock

You can use a couple of alternatives for handling unsold seasonal inventory, but neither is pleasant. The retailer can store the merchandise until next year, but storage costs carry charges that eat into capital. The greatest cost of storing merchandise is the lost opportunity. The retailer's capital gets locked up in unsold merchandise and thus can't be used to buy current-season inventory that's more in demand. Making matters worse is the fact that fashions offer no guarantee they'll remain fashionable, so selling this year's inventory next year may be impossible.

Another alternative is marking down the price of merchandise beginning relatively early in the season and continuing to do so until all the merchandise is sold. This approach quickly

+ Frees up capital the retailer then can use to buy newer inventory
+ Stops the accrual of carrying charges
+ Clears out storage and display space
+ Avoids the risk that the merchandise will become worthless in the future

This solution is better, even though it sometimes means selling the merchandise below cost.

Clothiers buy inventory to sell it at a profit. They know their costs, and they determine the profits they want to earn from the sale of each item. Retailers try to earn as much profit as possible, but start cutting prices whenever sales don't happen quickly enough. Retailers cannot afford to fall in love with their winter coats. They need the space and capital for spring merchandise. They don't get choked up when it's time to sell.

Keeping your inventory current

Managing your trading business as if you were a retail merchant is a good idea. The cycle of economic expansion, peak, recession, and trough, as described in Chapter 2, is somewhat akin to the four seasons. Your stocks are your inventory. Their prices rise and are discounted in anticipation of the changing economic cycles. And your trading account is your working capital. Just like the retail merchant, your goal is to protect your principal — your working capital — so you can stay in business.

However, you may find that some factors differ. The stock market is, of course, a much more efficient pricing mechanism than the retail clothing industry. You can't set the price of merchandise; the market does it for you. You can take several approaches to keep your trading inventory current. Many traders use trend analysis and relative strength analysis to try to take positions in the best performing stocks and sectors. Some traders also track general market conditions, quarterly and annual OSC and SEC filings, company announcements, and key analysts' reports, as described in Chapter 2.

Protecting Your Principal

In the same way that retail merchants face the possibility of holding on to their stock of winter coats that may fall out of style, you can avoid the risk of owning a stock that falls out of favour with other investors and loses its value. By acting quickly when you see changes in the market, you can avoid losing a large chunk of your trading capital (or *principal*). As long as you get out of your position quickly, your trading capital won't be tied up in a losing stock position any longer, and you'll escape the losing trade with most of your cash intact. More importantly, you'll be able to trade another day.

It makes sense, of course, to hold on to a stock as long as its price is appreciating. However, being mindful of when your stock price begins to fall is important. You must have a plan for dealing with losing trades or deteriorating profits. Time to fold up the stock and get out!

If your goal is to keep trading for a long time, the only way to do that is to not lose too much money. This might seem patently obvious, but you would be surprised by how few investors, and even some traders, make capital preservation their highest priority. To avoid that mistake, it helps if you keep these important goals in mind as you trade:

**Book IV
Chapter 4**

**Money Management
Techniques and
Trading System Tips**

+ Protect your principal first.
+ Don't let a large profit turn into a small profit.
+ Don't let a small profit turn into a loss.
+ Don't let a small loss turn into a large loss.

Recovering from a large loss: It ain't easy

When thinking about protecting your principal, accept that taking a small loss is better than risking a larger one. You need to understand how badly (and quickly) things can go wrong, and how that can result in a loss of a huge chunk of your capital with little chance of recovering it. To illustrate, check out an example of the impact that large losses can have on your money.

Perhaps you bought XYZ stock for $10 per share. The stock falls to $9, representing a $1 loss. You've lost 10 percent of the original price of the stock. To recover from that loss the stock price must rise from $9 to $10, but notice that 10 percent of $9 is only 90 cents. In other words, your stock must gain more than 10 percent to recover from a 10 percent loss. Here's how to review the math using percentages.

To find the percentage loss, push the percent button on your calculator (or click it in a computer spreadsheet), or simply divide $1 by $10:

$$\$10 - \$9 = \$1 \rightarrow \$1 \div \$10 = 0.10 \rightarrow 0.10 \times 100 = 10\%$$

To find the percentage gain required to recover that $1 loss — again, notice that your stock is now a $9 stock and that 10 percent of $9 is only 90 cents, not $1 — divide $1 by $9:

$$\$1 \div \$9 = 0.1111 \rightarrow 0.1111 \times 100 = 11.11\%$$

In other words, your $9 stock needs to gain a little more than 11 percent to get back to even.

For losses of less than 10 percent, the required gain isn't significantly greater than the loss you've just experienced. But for larger losses, the problem grows unmanageably. Getting a stock to go up 5 or even 10 percent is hard enough. It seems irrational to hope for a stock that's fallen by 50 percent to quickly recover 100 percent, or for one that's fallen by 75 percent to ever recover 300 percent.

Selling quickly and avoiding large losses is a much better course. Otherwise, you'll be out of trading capital, and out of business, in a mighty quick hurry.

Setting a target price for handling losses

The most important concept of protecting your principal is accepting the fact that you made a mistake and moving on. Sell that loser. Don't let a small loss turn into a large one. Before entering a trade, make sure you set a target price that you're willing to initially pay for a stock, and set a target price for selling it if the trade results in a loss.

Setting a stop-loss price (or, as traders say, "setting your stop") is more akin to an art than a science. You can employ several techniques for determining your stop-loss price. One that others often advocate, but we don't recommend, is choosing a predetermined percentage loss as your stop-loss price. We think using technical analysis (see Chapter 3) to identify when a trade has failed is a better approach.

Why traders use percentages to describe results

Why do traders use percentages to describe their results? Because it's a simple way of accurately comparing the results of one trade with the results of another — as a percentage, a $1 gain on a $10 stock is identical to a $10 gain on a $100 stock. The price per share is not as important as the percentage gain (or loss) or the total gain (or loss). Look at it like this: If you have $1,000 in your trading account, you can buy 100 shares of a $10 stock, or you can buy 10 shares of a $100 stock. If the price of either stock rises by 10 percent, your account total is the same in either case — $1,100. A 10 percent rise in a $10 stock is $1. A 10 percent rise in a $100 stock is $10. But the total amount of money earned is the same in either scenario.

If you think in terms of percentage gains or losses, you can correctly compare the result of one trade with that of another. The actual price of a stock, and the actual number of points gained or lost, isn't as important as the size of the move in percentage terms. Although you can buy many more shares of the lower-priced stock, it's equally difficult for either stock to move 10 percent. If you think about it like this, you'll see that no reason exists to favour the lower-priced stock, even if you can buy more shares, over the higher-priced stock.

Understanding Your Risks

You need to look at the risks that traders face. The three general categories are market risks, investment risks, and trading risks.

Market risks

Market risks are pretty much out of your control. Of course you understand the risk that the markets are bound to rise and fall, but understanding the risks you face when they do helps you manage your money better. Three key risks that you can manage as a trader are

✦ **Inflation risk:** Although inflation is a risk that traders rarely consider, it nevertheless impacts people who are afraid to take risks. You definitely can't be a trader if you're afraid of taking risks. Basically, the risk that this factor poses is that your money won't grow fast enough to exceed the increases in costs that inflation causes. As you know, the basics — housing, clothing, energy expenses, and food — increase in price each year. By investing in monetary vehicles that don't keep pace with inflation, you actually end up losing money.

✦ **Marketability risk:** This factor relates to how liquid your investment is. If you're restricted from selling your investment when you want to do so, your target selling point won't mean much. For most stock traders, this factor isn't an issue, but if, for example, you choose to invest in a small company whose stock isn't traded on one of the major stock markets, you risk not being able to close your stock position when the time is right.

✦ **Currency translation risk:** Currency translation refers to disparities in trading stocks of companies in foreign countries. It's only a factor when you trade foreign stocks, because you then must be concerned with fluctuations between the values of your local currency and the currency in the country where the company is located. Even if the stock increases in price, you can still lose money based on the currency exchange rate. If the value of your currency rises against the other currency, your investment can be worth less when you convert it back.

Investment risks

Investment risks relate directly to how you invest your money and manage your entry and exit trades. Two critical risks you must manage are

✦ **Opportunity risk:** This kind of risk involves balancing your tradeoffs. When you trade, you establish a position that ties up money that otherwise can be used elsewhere. After you choose a stock and buy it, you lose the opportunity to buy something else that may strike your fancy, until you trade out of the first position. Essentially, you can miss other opportunities while your money's tied up in another position.

✦ **Concentration risk:** This kind of risk happens when you put too many eggs in one basket. You may think you've found that hot stock that's going to make you a millionaire, so you decide to invest a huge portion of your principal into that stock. By concentrating so much of your money on one investment, you also concentrate the risks associated with that investment and with the possibility of losing it all.

Trading risks

Risks that are unique to trading increase simultaneously with increases in trading volume. Swing traders and day traders often see a greater impact caused by these risks than do position traders, but everyone needs to be aware of these issues. See Chapter 5 and Book 5 for more information about swing trading and day trading, respectively. Risks associated with trading are

✦ **Slippage risk:** Hidden costs associated with every transaction are the focus of this risk factor. Every time you enter or exit a position, your account balance dwindles by a small amount. Every time you execute a trade, you subject yourself to the problem of buying at the ask price but selling at the bid price. The ask price is the lowest price available for the stock that you want. The bid price is the highest price someone is willing to pay for shares you own. Unfortunately, the bid price is always less than the ask price. Although you can mitigate bid/ask problems by using limit orders, doing so subjects you to the risk that your order won't get filled. The amounts for each trade may at first seem small, but as your trading volume increases, so do the amounts you lose to slippage. Trade only the stocks of the large, liquid companies so your bid/ask spread causes negligible slippage.

✦ **Poor execution risk:** This problem occurs whenever your investment adviser or discount broker has a difficult time filling your order, which can result from any number of factors including fast market conditions, poor availability of stock, or the absence of other buyers and sellers. The result is always the same: The price you expect is somewhat different than the price you actually receive. Although you can mitigate this problem to a degree by using limit orders, you still risk having the stock trade through your limit price and not getting your order filled at all. Ditto: trade large, liquid companies.

✦ **Gap risk:** This kind of risk comes into play whenever a break in trading occurs. Sometimes a stock opens at a price significantly higher or lower than its previous close, and sometimes a stock trades right through your exit price. For example, a stock may close at $25 a share today and open tomorrow morning at $20. If your planned exit price is $24, and you have a stop order in place, your order is likely to be filled at the opening price or worse. Price gaps created in this way occur most often at the open. And although relatively rare, a gap also can occur during the trading day whenever surprising news is reported or trading halts. We hope you have more nice gap profits than losses — they both occur regularly, so keep your spirit and optimism high.

Entering and Exiting Your Trade

When it's time to enter or exit a trade, you have to tell your discount broker or investment adviser what you want to do. To do that, you enter an *order* that tells the number of shares and the symbol (or at least the name) for the stock or security you're planning to trade. Your order also specifies the type of transaction you'd like to execute and how you'd like to handle your transaction. We discuss your choices for instructing how to handle your order in this section.

Before entering your trade order, you'll probably want to check for a stock quote. Ideally, your quote system provides information similar to what's explained below.

✦ **Description:** The symbol and name of the company.

✦ **Exchange:** The exchange on which the stock is traded.

✦ **Last Trade:** The last trade when the markets are open. (It will be the same as the close price when the markets are closed.)

✦ **Chg:** The change in price (+ or –) from the previous close.

✦ **Net Percentage Change:** The change in price expressed (+ or –) as a percentage difference between the previous close and the last trade.

✦ **Open:** The first trade of the day.

- ✦ **High:** The highest trade of the day.

- ✦ **Low:** The lowest trade of the day.

- ✦ **Previous Close:** The last trade for the previous day.

- ✦ **Bid:** The highest price to buy the stock.

- ✦ **Bid Size:** The number of shares at the bid price.

- ✦ **Ask (or Offer):** The lowest price to sell the stock.

- ✦ **Ask Size:** The number of shares at the ask price.

- ✦ **Close:** The last trade for the day.

- ✦ **Volume:** The number of shares traded.

- ✦ **P/E:** The price/earnings ratio (see Chapter 2).

- ✦ **EPS:** Earnings per share (see Chapter 2).

- ✦ **Last Ticks:** One or more symbols showing the direction of the last few trades in the stock. A plus sign or up arrow indicates a trade higher than the previous trade, or an *uptick*. A minus sign or down arrow indicates a trade less than the previous trade, or a *downtick*. And an equal sign or a dash indicates a trade at the same price as the previous trade.

- ✦ **Last Size:** The number of shares for the last trade.

Understanding bid and ask

A bit of background and a little history will help you understand the quote system. When you come to the stock market to buy some shares, you need to see what price sellers of those shares are *asking* you to pay — that's why the sell side is called the *ask*. When you come to the stock market to sell some shares, you need to see at what price buyers of those shares are *bidding* for your shares — hence, the buy side is called the *bid*.

In the bad ol' days each trader had a stockbroker, each stockbroker had a desk trader, each desk trader had a floor trader, and each floor trader had a market maker. So between a trader selling a stock and a trader buying a stock there were eight people all making a very good living. The market makers also kept the spread between their buying and selling prices way too wide. With the arrival of the Internet, many of those eight people are now driving taxis and waiting tables. Traders who agree on the price and volume at which they both want to trade the same stock no longer need all those intermediaries. Traders themselves have effectively become the market makers by setting the buying (bid) and selling (ask) prices themselves. Sometimes a market maker is needed to balance the buying and selling pressure when it gets out of hand. For most large capitalized public companies, their market makers are often spectators to the action.

A *market order* tells your broker to buy or sell at the current market price. This means that if you use a market order when buying, your order is likely to be filled at the ask price. When selling, your market order is likely to be filled at the bid price. Occasionally, your broker may be able to fill your order between the bid and ask prices — but never count on it, because it doesn't happen very often. Your order can, however, become the highest bid or the lowest ask, if you use a *limit order*. A limit order specifies the highest price you're willing to pay when buying or the lowest price you're willing to accept when selling. If you place your limit order between the current bid and ask prices, your order becomes either the best bid price if you're buying or the best asking price if you're selling. ***Note:*** You run the risk of having your order not executed at all when using a limit order if the current market price moves away from your limit price. Also, the TSX, NYSE, and Nasdaq each handle this a little differently. Your investment adviser can help you sort through the details if you encounter problems. Your online discount broker might not be so patient.

Understanding the spread

The *spread* is the difference between the bid and ask prices. It's sometimes referred to as the *inside spread,* which is the difference between the highest bid and the lowest ask. Back when stock prices were quoted in increments of eighths (12.5 cents) and quarters (25 cents), the minimum spread was either an eighth or a quarter. Today, with decimal pricing, the spreads tend to be tighter, and can be as low as a penny per share on actively traded stocks. Many of us veteran traders are pleased to see shares trading at prices ranging from $20 up to $200 with only a penny between bid and ask prices. Although the major exchanges do not support spreads less than one cent, the TSX and some ECNs (electronic communications networks; see Chapter 1) permit tighter spreads for a small number of securities. Canada was far quicker to adopt the very good idea of trading stocks priced in dollars and cents — unlike the New York Stock Exchange, which insisted on maintaining the units as one-eighth of a dollar (and 1/16 and 1/32 and even 1/64, if you can believe it!).

When you place a limit order within the spread, so that your limit price is between the current bid and ask prices, your order will usually become either the best bid if you're buying or the best ask if you're selling. This approach makes sense whenever the spread is particularly wide and the price isn't moving very fast. When the spread is narrow, using a market order is probably best — that is, as long as the market is open and the stock is widely traded with lots of volume.

The biggest problem with trying to squeeze a profit out of the inside spread is that prices move. Remember that stock quotes are only snapshots of current bid and ask prices. By the time your order reaches the market, these quotes can (and do) change. Even the fastest real-time quote systems lag a bit behind the market, so it's possible that the limit order you just entered between the spread is now outside the spread and won't be filled — and believe us when we say that can be disappointing.

Some markets, such as the OTCBB and the so-called Pink Sheets (see Chapter 1), do not allow traders to go inside the spread. Ridiculously, market makers are still able to ensure the spread is their nice little profit centre.

Devising an effective order-entry strategy

During trading hours, you can be reasonably confident that a market order will be filled at or near current market prices. But if you're like most people, you won't spend all your time watching the market. As such, you need another strategy for entering and exiting positions. You can use one or more of several alternative approaches to better control the terms and prices that you're willing to accept when your orders are placed in the hope of getting filled.

Using limit orders

If you're buying a stock, choose the maximum price you're willing to pay, and then pay no more. That means you can't use market orders to enter your positions. Instead, you can use limit orders, which enable you to set the highest price you're willing to pay for a stock, making that your *limit price*. If you're selling short, choose the lowest price at which you're willing to sell, and set that as your limit price.

Limit orders are effective for opening a position, but are problematic for exiting a position. For example, if you need to exit your position because the breakout has failed, you simply need to exit the position without trying to finesse the price. Failed trades recover infrequently, and they often get worse. You have no reason to be patient when things are going against you.

Similarly, whenever you have a profitable trade and you're trying to protect your profits, a limit order rarely is your best choice for exiting the position. You're better off exiting the position by using either a market order or a stop order after you've identified a reversal pattern.

Using stop orders and stop-limit orders to enter a trade

Traders normally talk about using stops for exiting or trading out of a position, but stops are also effective for opening a position. If you identify the stock you want prior to an actual breakout, you can enter a buy stop at a price above the breakout point. These orders can be entered on a GTC (good-till-cancelled) basis, so that even if the trading range lasts a while, your order is poised to trigger a transaction whenever the breakout occurs. Most investment dealers and discount brokers prefer to use "open" orders, which are good for about 90 days. The GTC status can be dangerous if not revisited often. You can read more about GTC orders in Book 3, Chapter 3.

Most firms limit the length of time orders can remain open to 90 days, so make sure you know your firm's GTC policies — and remember that Nasdaq doesn't have any provisions for handling stop orders. If you're trying to use stops when trading Nasdaq stocks, your broker or adviser has to provide the mechanism for triggering these trades when your stop price is hit. Make sure they can handle the stop orders you want to use.

The downside to this approach is obvious — you're unable to confirm the breakout. If the breakout fails, and you've triggered a buy order on the breakout, you now hold a position that's losing money.

Although we generally recommend waiting a few days to confirm the break-out, using this strategy at some times may be more appropriate than others. For example, if you're convinced the market is in a bull market phase, the stock's trading range is long and tight, and you can identify an obvious breakout, then entering a GTC buy stop order at a price that's a bit higher than the breakout price is probably okay. However, you need to be much more tentative when the market is only in a bullish transition or pullback phase, or when you're monitoring second and subsequent breakouts. When that's the case, make sure the breakout is confirmed — that means the stock remains above its breakout price for a bullish breakout — within a few days before entering your order. If you have any doubt, wait for confirmation.

Another problem with this approach is that after the stop price is reached, your order is triggered and it becomes a market order to buy or sell. You're in the exact situation you'd be in if you'd entered a market order while the market was closed. You have no control over the fill price after your stop is triggered.

For example, say the stock price gaps higher (Chapter 3) as it breaks out of its trading range and surpasses your stop price by two or three dollars. Your order is triggered and will likely be filled at a price that's much higher than your stop price, and much higher than you had anticipated. If the stock price falls below your fill price, you're now holding a losing position. The only way to avoid this problem is by using a stop-limit order, which means when your stop price triggers the release of your order, the order becomes a limit order rather than a market order and is filled only if the stock price pulls back below your limit price. Again, remember to confirm that your firm permits stop-limit orders on Nasdaq stocks.

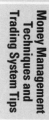

**Book IV
Chapter 4**

Money Management Techniques and Trading System Tips

You can also use a stop order or a stop-limit order to open a short position. You specify a sell stop or a sell stop-limit order, while designating your trade as a short sale. Again, you must confirm your firm supports these types of orders for Nasdaq stocks.

Using stop orders to exit positions

After your buy or sell order is filled, enter your stop-loss instructions. You need to protect your open positions and simultaneously stay clear of short-term traders trying to *run the stops*. Running the stops is a little game played by short-term traders where they try to find and execute open stop orders before driving the stock price in the other direction. It can be very lucrative for them and infuriating — not to mention expensive — for you. You can try to avoid being run over when they're running the stops by keeping your stop prices away from the most obvious location. For example, if a breakout occurs at $35.75, don't put your stop-loss one cent below at $35.74. Move down a few cents, to $35.69, or even $35.63, to stay away from the obvious stop-loss spots.

Entering orders after the market closes: Be careful

As long as you're entering your trades during market hours, using a market order is fine; however, if you're planning to check your charts each evening and then enter your trades before heading to work in the morning, you must use a different approach. Otherwise, you risk having your orders filled at prices that can differ significantly from the previous closing prices. To make matters worse, you may discover that your position is losing money soon after being filled.

Don't be surprised to discover that many traders trade this way. Because of their daily schedules, they analyze stock charts in the evening and enter orders before the markets open. Unfortunately, common breakout and reversal patterns cause many traders to react in a predictable fashion. When many traders enter buy orders for the same stock, a scarcity of that stock is likely to occur just after the market opens. Scarcity causes prices to rise, sometimes even dramatically, so that all those aftermarket orders are filled at prices significantly higher than the previous closing price. Making matters worse, after the buy orders are filled and buying pressure disappears, the stock price tumbles back toward the previous closing price.

Professional traders — including floor traders, market makers, day traders, and swing traders — exacerbate the problem even further. These short-term traders see the same fundamental and technical analysis signals that you see, and their goal is to profit from your enthusiasm, and perhaps your inexperience, as you try to open your position.

Another concern is automated algorithmic trading using computers programmed to enter orders like a robot. This is also known as *high-frequency trading* (HFT) or *black box trading*.

As a result, you need to think about the tactics these short-term traders employ before you enter any positions. When they see breakout or reversal patterns, short-term traders anticipate a flurry of buying activity in that stock, and they know that few people are going to be eager sellers when a stock breaks out of a trading range. Under those circumstances, the only way buyers can get an order filled is if they bid the price higher or accept whatever price is being asked for the stock. When that happens, the best asking price is going to be relatively high.

Someone will sell the stock to position traders, but only at a relatively high asking price. Short-term swing traders and day traders, who may not even own the stock, offer those asking prices, agreeing to provide the stock to the position traders as long as the buying pressure pushes the price of the stock upward. If the short-term traders don't own the stock, they must sell the shares short — in other words, they must borrow the stock before selling (see the section "Selling Stocks Short" in this chapter). After the short sellers absorb all that buying pressure the rally fades, the stock's price falls back toward the breakout price, and that's when short-term traders buy the stock (at prices lower than they sold it). So, they can cover their short positions — or, in other words, return the shares they borrowed to sell at higher prices to the position traders. How's that for taking a quick profit?

This scenario is at the heart of why being patient usually makes sense. By steering clear of these moments of buying pressure, you're more likely to get a much better fill, and you find out whether enough buying interest is present to keep the stock price above the breakout price. Being patient doesn't always work, of course. Sometimes buying pressure drives the price higher, forcing short sellers to cover at a loss, which in turn drives the price even higher, resulting in a *runaway stock*. When that does happen, you'll probably be left standing on the platform, watching the runaway stock as it leaves you behind. Fortunately, runaway stocks don't happen all that often. Thus, banking on runaway stocks is a poor tactic.

Our advice remains the same: Don't chase these breakout and runaway stocks. When the cycle exhausts itself, as it ultimately must, the stock returns to a more rational price and you can reevaluate whether your position continues to make sense. As a position trader, you can afford to be patient.

Selling Stocks Short

When you sell a stock short, you sell something you don't have first and buy it later with a goal of profiting from a falling stock price. To sell a stock short, you borrow shares so that you can sell them in the open market. Your firm gets those shares either from its own inventory or, more likely, from other clients. The proceeds of that sale go into your account. To close that position, you must buy the shares on the open market and return them to the firm. If the price you pay for the stock, or the *buy-to-cover price,* is less than your selling price, you've earned a profit on the short sale. Conversely, if the buy-to-cover price is higher, you've suffered a loss. Instead of buy low sell high, shorting is a case of sell high buy low.

Let's say you borrow 100 shares of Company X and sell the shares short for $100. When the price drops to $80, you buy the shares back (you might also say you covered the shorted shares) and return them. You sold the stock for $100, and bought it back for $80, netting a profit of $20. It's exactly the same profit as if you had purchased the stock for $80 first and sold it for $100 later. Conversely, say you borrow 100 shares of Company Y and sell them for $100. The stock price rises to $120, and you decide to cover your loss. You buy back the shares and pay $120, but you sold them for $100. You have lost $20 on this trade.

Some of the quirks unique to selling stocks short include

✦ **Paying dividends to the lender.** If the stocks pay a dividend during the time a short seller holds a position, short sellers pay the dividends on the ex-dividend date to the owners who loaned them the stocks. Short sellers need to keep the ex-dividend date in mind whenever shorting stocks.

✦ **Being forced to close a position.** Whenever the original owner sells the stocks you borrowed, your broker can *call away* the shorted shares, which means you're forced to return the borrowed shares by buying them on the open market at the current price. This happens rarely, and occurs only when no shares are available for shorting.

✦ **Mandating the execution of short sales from only a margin account.** Short sales must be executed in a margin account, because your firm loans you the stock to sell short, and charges you interest on any margin balance in the account.

✦ **Paying margin maintenance requirements.** Your firm can force you to close a short position if you're unable to satisfy maintenance margin requirements.

✦ **Having no or only minimal access to selling some stocks short.** Lightly traded stocks may be unavailable for selling short, and when they can be sold short, they may be more likely to be called away (which happens when the original owner sells the stock you borrowed and you are unable to borrow additional shares).

✦ **Restricting short sales on certain stocks.** You can't short a stock that's less than $5 per share, and you can't short initial public offerings (IPOs), usually for 30 days following the IPO. And, as we learned during the credit crisis, regulators can prohibit short selling on whole categories of stocks.

✦ **Limiting short selling to only stocks without a downtick.** The essence of the rule says you can't sell a stock short in a falling market. Although implemented a bit differently on various exchanges, the result is the same. Short sellers cannot easily pile into a falling stock. You cannot sell a stock short on a downtick. It must be at the last sale price or an uptick.

One unusual aspect of shorting is that it creates future buying pressure. Every shorted sale must eventually be covered, and that means every share that's been shorted has to be repurchased. Future buying pressure can cause the price of a heavily shorted stock to jump dramatically if all the short sellers simultaneously clamour to get out of their positions as the price rises, a situation called a *short squeeze.* You can find out how many others are shorting the stock by looking at short-interest statistics published twice monthly, effective the 15th and the end of each month, by the Toronto Stock Exchange and available at www.tsx.com as well as the *Financial Post* www.financialpost.com/markets. American short positions are in *Barron's* and *Investor's Business Daily* near the end of each month. From those statistics, you get some idea whether your short position is likely to be squeezed.

Understanding Trading Systems

A *trading system* is a collection of technical and fundamental analyses tools woven together to generate buy and sell signals. Trading systems often are built using common indicators, oscillators, and moving averages. You can combine these various technical analysis tools to create a virtually unlimited number of trading systems. For the new trader, the advantage to this approach is that you don't need to invent something new to create and personalize a workable system.

Although individual trading systems differ in many ways, thinking about them on the basis of a couple of broad characteristics is helpful. The first characteristic has to do with the two ways a trader interacts with the system. In this case, trading systems are one or the other of the following:

✦ **Discretionary trading systems:** A system that presents trading candidates for your consideration, but leaves the final trade execution decision to you.

✦ **Mechanical trading systems:** A computer-based system that automatically generates buy and sell signals that will always be traded.

**Book IV
Chapter 4**

Money Management
Techniques and
Trading System Tips

The other way to categorize a trading system is by how it treats trends in the markets. In this case, trading systems are one or the other of the following:

✦ **Trend-following trading systems:** A system that tries to identify trade entry and exit points for new or existing trends.

✦ **Countertrend trading systems:** A system that tries to identify trade entry and exit points by finding tops and bottoms.

Although these categorizations are not mutually exclusive — discretionary and mechanical systems, for example, can both be trend-following systems — each approach has adherents and detractors. We discuss the strengths and weaknesses of each type of system in the sections that follow.

As you read through our descriptions of the trading systems, understand that *no* system generates profits without any losing trades. Put another way, no system works in every situation. Keep that firmly in mind when you're developing ideas for and designing your personal trading system. Your goal needs to be designing a trading system that is useful to you across a large number of stocks and a large number of situations. Believe us when we say that you will run into trouble whenever you try to tailor a trading system to a specific stock. Additionally, try making your system work across long periods of time and across many different market conditions.

Discretionary systems

A *discretionary trading system* makes you an active participant in all phases of the trades you make and provides you with a great deal of leeway when making trading decisions. With this approach, evaluating the economic data, analyzing the broad market indices, determining which sectors are showing strength, and identifying high relative-strength stocks that are breaking out of long trading ranges and hoping to catch a new trend all are up to you. You make decisions based on what you see in charts and in fundamental economic data, and you enter and exit (buy and sell) positions based on that information.

A discretionary system requires a great deal of discipline, which can be a source of problems for some traders. This type of system works well for traders who are capable of making good decisions quickly under pressure. But discretionary systems may prove troublesome if you allow your emotions to wreak havoc with your ability to think clearly, act rationally, and make thoughtful trading decisions.

When emotions cloud your trading decisions, you may end up

✦ Overtrading

✦ Prematurely liquidating your positions

✦ Holding positions too long

✦ Anticipating trading signals in attempts to get better entry and exit prices

Another problem with discretionary systems is that they're difficult to test, which probably is their greatest drawback. System testing is useful, because it helps you understand situations in which an indicator works well and in which it fails. With a discretionary system you can test the indicators, but you cannot reliably test your discretion.

Controlling your emotions is so important to being a successful investor that one of Canada's largest mutual fund companies gave every investment adviser in the country a "stress control biofeedback card." Even more high-tech is the so-called EmoBracelet, developed by Royal Philips Electronics to limit the emotional response of traders. And the "trader's mood ring" was developed for Dutch bank ABN Amro, which is now owned by the governments of the United Kingdom and Holland.

Mechanical systems

A *mechanical system* addresses some of the problems that arise when using discretionary systems. Mechanical systems usually are computer-based programs that automatically generate buy and sell signals based on technical and/or fundamental data. You're expected to blindly follow the resulting trading signals. Some mechanical systems actually enter buy and sell orders directly into your account without your intervention.

If your greedy impulses or your fear of losing routinely cause you to make poor trading decisions, a mechanical system may be a better choice for you. An automated approach tends to reduce the stress and anxiety that arise when you have to make difficult decisions quickly. As such, you can make and execute trading decisions in a consistent, methodical way. A mechanical trading system also enables you to automatically include rigorous money management in your trading methodology.

Another benefit of the mechanical approach is having the ability to thoroughly test the system. Through testing you can confirm whether your trading system performs the way you expect it to and explore ways to improve your system before actually committing your trading capital. You can adjust and fine-tune your system after seeing the test results. Unfortunately, fine-tuning your system may lead to other problems. We discuss ways to avoid them in the "Identifying system optimization pitfalls" section in this chapter.

Trend-following systems

Trend following is favoured by many technicians for one simple reason: Trends offer excellent opportunities for profit. Unfortunately, the popularity of the trend-following approach is one of its weaknesses. Too many of these systems generate many similar buy and sell signals, which in turn makes outperforming the average trader difficult for any individual trend-following trader.

Even the best trend-following systems have a relatively large percentage of failed trades, primarily because they depend on several extremely profitable trades to make up for the large percentage of losing trades. If your trend-following system also is a discretionary system, your discretion (or lack of it) can cause you to miss a few of these profitable trades, and your overall results will suffer.

Trend-following systems typically are based on either moving averages or breakout patterns. Moving average–based trading systems are the most popular and can be quite profitable; however, they work only when a stock is trending. These trading systems depend on long-lasting trends to generate enough profit to outweigh a relatively large number of losing trades. In fact, the number of losing trades can easily outnumber winning trades with this trading system. When a stock is range bound (stuck in a specific price range), a moving-average system generates a large number of losing trades. Because of the large overall number of trades, this system often is accompanied by relatively high transaction and slippage costs (see the section "Accounting for slippage" in this chapter). Money management is critical when using a trend-following trading system.

You can make some adjustments to a trend-following system that may improve its performance. For example, you can insist that its trading signals be confirmed by another condition before actually entering any positions. If your system triggers a buy signal, for example, you may want to see whether the signal remains in effect for at least a day or two before entering a position. We show some examples of moving-average and breakout systems, along with some ideas to improve the performance of these systems, in the section "Developing and Testing Trading Systems."

Countertrend systems

For many traders, the quest to find a profitable countertrend trading system is all-consuming. *Countertrend systems* appear desirable because their goal is to buy low and sell high. These systems try to identify *inflection points,* or the moments when stocks change direction, so traders can take positions close to when they occur. This approach may work in a few narrowly defined situations, such as in a trading range or a trend channel, but it's likely to fail in a spectacular and expensive way if attempted on a broader scale.

The vast majority of trading systems follow market trends. Trend-following systems tend to outperform countertrend systems, especially for position traders. Swing traders and some day traders sometimes use a countertrend approach, but even then they usually do so in conjunction with a trend-following component.

Countertrend systems usually depend on oscillating indicators, reversal patterns, and channelling strategies to find turning points. Some countertrend systems also are based on cycle theory, and others are based on volatility, expansion, and contraction.

We discourage you from spending too much time evaluating countertrend systems, at least until you're confident in your ability to use trend-following systems to successfully make your trades. Countertrend systems generate a large volume of trades, and the more you trade the more you spend on commissions and fees, as well as bad fill prices known as *slippage.* These costs alone often swamp potentially profitable systems. Although a countertrend strategy can sometimes work profitably in a trading range or trend channel it's still risky, especially for a new trader.

Selecting System-Development Tools

Conceptually, you can use the back of an envelope to develop your trading-system ideas. However, most traders want some way of confirming that their newly designed systems can perform profitably before they commit real trading capital. That means you need a way to test your system, which further means using computer software to precisely define the system and evaluate its performance. Typically, this requires simulating trades by using historical data.

Regardless of whether you decide on a mechanical or a discretionary approach to trading, your system will benefit from testing. Although thoroughly testing a discretionary system is difficult, you can still test the component indicators to learn when they do and don't provide effective trading signals. To begin, you need a computer, development and testing software, and historical data.

Choosing system-development hardware

Doing the math that's required when testing your system can really slow down your computer, and it can generate a lot of data. Almost any computer will do the job when you're getting started, but if you end up testing many system ideas you definitely need a large amount of disk storage and a fast computer. The computer equipment required to run a proprietary trading platform, including products such as TradeStation or MetaStock, is usually enough for system development and testing.

**Book IV
Chapter 4**

Money Management
Techniques and
Trading System Tips

Selecting system-development software

Many trading system-development and testing products are on the market. Some proprietary trading platforms, such as TradeStation or MetaStock, include system-testing capabilities. Spreadsheet software, like Microsoft's Excel, also is useful for analyzing simple trading systems and for analyzing the results generated by specialized development and testing software.

Trading system-development and testing software

Consider the following criteria when evaluating your system-development and testing software:

✦ **All trading system-development and testing programs use some type of computer language to describe and test your system.** Some are terse and difficult to use, others are more intuitive. Traders with strong computer or programming skills have little problem mastering any of these languages, but others may struggle. Pay careful attention to this development language before selecting a system. Be certain you're actually able to use the system you choose.

✦ **You need to integrate your trading system with your stock charts.** Some system-development software requires you to actually write computer code that enables you to display your trading system and stock charts simultaneously. Avoid these systems if you're uncomfortable writing computer code.

✦ **The manner and effectiveness by which your system-development and testing software reports on how your trading system is performing is critical.** Some systems provide extremely detailed statistics about the performance of your trading systems. Others, however, list little more than the buy or sell signals. In general, more information is better.

✦ **Make sure your system-development and testing programs are capable of exporting the data they generate,** historical price data included, into a spreadsheet program for further analysis.

TradeStation is the gold-plated system-development platform. It has many built-in tools that make your development and testing job relatively easy. For those of you on tight budgets, one of the less-expensive alternatives you may want to consider is a charting and system-development program like AmiBroker (`www.amibroker.com`). Although flexible and powerful, AmiBroker isn't as feature-rich or as polished as TradeStation, and it requires significantly more effort on your part. For example, AmiBroker includes well-known technical-analysis indicators like moving averages and MACD (see Chapter 3), but the number of indicators included is a tiny subset compared with what TradeStation offers. Similarly, you have to use AmiBroker's formula language to create and enter any other indicators that you may be using.

Spreadsheet software

A spreadsheet program is another invaluable testing and analysis tool. Although a spreadsheet program can't do everything that a specialized system-development and testing program can do, it can add quite a bit of analysis horsepower to your system-development tool kit. You can actually code and test simple trading systems directly into the spreadsheet. You can also evaluate the results of your trading-system tests more thoroughly using the spreadsheet's built-in statistical and analysis functions.

You can, for example, copy the price data for a stock into your spreadsheet, calculate moving averages and other indicators, and then configure buy, sell, or sell-short signals. You can also export trading signals from your system-development program and import the results into your spreadsheet for further analysis.

One of our favourite spreadsheet projects is calculating the maximum favourable and unfavourable moves after our system has triggered a buy or sell signal. Simple to do, and it helps you understand the strengths and weaknesses of your trading system in great detail. You can see whether problems with your trading system might be solved by using different exit procedures or tighter (or looser) stop-loss points.

For example, although your entry signals may show promise, your exit signals may be causing you to leave a lot of money on the table. These situations are hard to see when you're working only with charts; however, they sometimes jump out when you're working with raw data during your spreadsheet analysis. You can find an example using this testing technique in the "Working with breakout trading systems" section in this chapter.

Some system-development programs provide a great deal of statistical analysis, so choosing among spreadsheet tools and system-development tools is a tradeoff between thoroughness and expediency. After you've been through the testing exercises a few times you get a feel for the strength of each approach. So it's likely that you'll decide to use both a system-development program and a spreadsheet program when creating and testing your new trading systems.

Developing and Testing Trading Systems

The ideas that you may want to include in your system development and testing are virtually limitless. Many new traders begin system testing by combining a few off-the-shelf indicators in an effort to obtain better trading results. Doing so is as good a place as any to begin.

However, we want to caution you to keep your systems simple enough that you can understand not only the system but also the result. Simplicity usually is better when trading, especially when you're first becoming familiar with the processes of system development and testing. We describe the process by looking at a couple of examples in the sections that follow.

Working with trend-following systems

Many trend-following systems use a moving average for their starting points. In this trend-following example the system is designed for position trading, which means we use a relatively long moving average. Short-selling won't be permitted with this simple system.

The first step is defining buy and sell rules for your initial testing. The actual code for defining these rules depends on your specific system-development package. Therefore, trading rules are described as generally as possible. The rules for an initial test may look like this:

✦ Buy at tomorrow's opening price when today's price crosses and closes above the 50-day exponential moving average (EMA).

✦ Sell at tomorrow's opening price when today's price crosses and closes below the 50-day EMA.

To test whether using a moving average as a starting point is a good idea in a trend-following system, apply these two rules to ten years of historical data for the stock or stocks of your choice. After testing theis idea, you find that this simple system works fairly well when stock prices are trending, but it's likely to trigger many losing trades when the prices of stocks are range bound. You can try to avoid these losing trades, and possibly improve your overall trading results, by filtering out trading-range situations. One way to accomplish that goal is by changing the buy rule to read: Buy at tomorrow's open when the following conditions are true:

✦ Today's closing price is above the 50-day EMA.

✦ The stock crossed above the 50-day EMA sometime during the last 5 days.

✦ Today's 50-day EMA is greater than the 50-day EMA from 5 days ago.

These added conditions serve as signal confirmation. When you test these rules you find they reduce the number of whipsaw trades for most stocks, but they're also likely to delay buy and sell signals on profitable trades and thus usually result in smaller profits on those trades. Yet this adjustment makes the overall system more profitable, because the number of losses is reduced.

You can find out whether other changes to your simple system actually can improve profitability. You may, for example, test different types of moving averages. Try, for example, a simple moving average instead of an exponential moving average (see Chapter 3 for the types of moving averages). Or you may want to try using different time frames for your moving average, such as 9-day, 25-day, or 100-day moving averages.

Identifying system optimization pitfalls

Most system-development and testing software comes equipped with a provision for system optimization that allows you to fine-tune the technical analysis tools used in your trading system. You can, for example, tell the system to find the time frame of the moving average that produces the highest profit for one stock, and then ask it to do the same thing for a different stock. Some systems enable you to test this factor simultaneously for many stocks.

Although something is alluring about using this approach, doing so is likely to cause you trouble. If you find, for example, that a 22-day moving average works best for one stock, a 37-day moving average works best for the next stock, and another stock performs best using a 74-day moving average, you're going to run into problems. The set of circumstances leading to these optimized results won't likely repeat in precisely the same way again. We can almost guarantee that whatever optimized parameters you may find for these moving averages won't be the optimal choices when trading real capital.

This is a simple example of a problem that is well-known to scientists and economists who build mathematic models to forecast future events. It's called curve fitting, because you're moulding your model to fit the historical data. You can expend quite a bit of effort fine-tuning a system to identify all the major trends and turning points in historical data for a particular stock, but that effort is not likely to result in future trading profits. In that case, your optimized system is more likely to cause a long string of losses rather than profits.

Testing a long moving average and comparing the results to a short moving average is fine, and so is testing a few points in between a long moving average and a short moving average. As long as you use this exercise to understand why short moving averages work best for short-term trades and why longer moving averages work better for traders with longer trading horizons, you'll be fine. Otherwise, you're probably moving into the realm of curve fitting and becoming frustrated with your actual trading results.

Testing with blind simulation

Blind simulation is a method for setting aside enough historical data so that you can test your system optimization results and avoid the problem of curve fitting. For example, you may test data from 1990 through 1999, and thus exclude data from 2000 through the present. After you've developed a system that looks good enough for you to base your trades on, you can then test your system against the data that were excluded. If the system performs as well with the excluded data as it did with the original test data, you may have a system worth trading. If it fails, you obviously need to rethink your system.

Another approach is choosing your historical data with extreme care. You can expect trend-following systems like a moving-average system to perform well during long, powerful trends. If your stock had a strong run-up during the long-lasting 1990s bull market, that kind of price data can skew your results, magically making any trend-following system appear profitable. Whether that success actually can be duplicated during a subsequent bull market, however, must first be thoroughly tested.

If the majority of your profits come from a single trade, or only a small number of trades, the system probably won't perform well when you begin trading real money. You may want to address this problem by excluding periods from your test data when your stock was doing exceptionally well or when the results of any trades were significantly more profitable than the average trade. This technique is a valid approach to eliminating the extraordinary results arising from extraordinary situations in your historical data. Using it should give you a better idea of your system's potential for generating real profits in the future.

Working with breakout trading systems

Similar to moving average–based systems, a breakout system can take many forms. You may already be familiar with the trading-range breakout system we describe in Chapter 3. To test a different approach, you can define a breakout system as follows:

✦ Buying at tomorrow's opening price when today's closing price is above the highest high price that occurred during the last 20 days.

✦ Selling at tomorrow's opening price when today's closing price is below the lowest low price that occurred over the last 20 days.

These trading rules are loosely based on the rules for *Donchian channels* (sometimes called *price channels*), which comprise a breakout system developed by Richard Donchian in the 1950s. Donchian was one of the early developers of trend-following trading systems.

A spreadsheet may be helpful for evaluating this system. You can, in fact, configure this system into a spreadsheet, include buy and sell signals, and perform analyses to determine how well the system performs. You also can use the spreadsheet to dig into the system's results to find out what works and what doesn't.

After you've downloaded your historical price data into a spreadsheet format, all you have to do is encode the formulas into the correct columns. If you're like most traders, the first thing you'll do is calculate some statistics about the system. For example, you can use spreadsheet functions to calculate the following:

✦ Total gain or loss for the system

✦ Average gain (the numerical average)

✦ Median gain (the middle result)

✦ Maximum gain for any single trade

✦ Maximum loss for any single trade

✦ Standard deviation

Then you can look at aggregate results to find out whether the system actually made money. In the case of the Donchian channel breakout system, initial results don't look promising. The system lost money during the entire test period.

If you're like most traders, your impulse is to discard the idea and move on to another. But with the Donchian channel breakout system, you need to dig a little deeper before you do. During the time frame of this test, the system triggered 30 trades, 18 of which were losing trades. However, 13 of those losing trades were profitable at some point during the process, and all the winning trades gave back a large part of the profits before the sell signal was triggered. In fact, many of the profitable trades gave back significantly more than half of the profits before the sell signal.

Accounting for slippage

Slippage is the term traders use to describe the costs of trading, which is made up of two components. The first is the actual transaction or commission cost for executing your trade. The second is more difficult to measure, because it's the sum of the cost of unfavourable fills. If, for example, you're planning to buy at tomorrow's opening price based on today's closing price, those two prices can be much different. An unfavourable fill is a cost of trading, and accounted for as slippage.

Most trading system-development packages have a provision for estimating slippage costs when testing your trading ideas using historical data. If you know your transaction costs, enter the exact amounts. Otherwise, estimate the transaction cost. You probably need to overestimate the cost of unfavourable fills, because it always seems to end up being worse in actual trading than most traders ever imagine. You may want to start with an estimate of 25 cents per share and adjust it as you gather data on your actual slippage costs.

Chapter 5: The Skinny on Swing Trading and Derivatives

In This Chapter

✔ Selecting stocks for swing trading

✔ Assessing the risks of swing trading

✔ Dealing with derivatives

✔ Getting the 411 on currency trading

*S*wing trading is a trading strategy that tries to take advantage of short-term opportunities in the market. It occupies the middle ground between position trading and day trading (for more on day trading, see Book 5). Swing traders use trend-following and countertrend strategies to participate in trading-range and trending stocks. This turbo-charged trading style requires an exceptional understanding of the inner workings of the markets and excellent analysis capabilities.

In this chapter, we discuss a few of the basic techniques used by swing traders along with the risks that are unique to the discipline. We also talk about the things swing traders trade, such as stocks, futures, options, and forex. We give you the ins and outs of each of these securities and explain how to properly trade them. When you've finished the following pages you may be ready to go — but it's a good idea to read the Book on day trading, which follows this chapter, for even more trading techniques.

Stock Selection Is Key

Swing trading is a *technical discipline*. Although no hard and fast rule applies, swing traders often trade in 1,000-share increments and usually limit the number of simultaneous positions to ten or fewer. A swing trade can last for as little as a few hours to as long as a few months, but typical swing trades span no more than a few weeks. On this kind of time scale, fundamental analysis has little impact on a stock's price movement; therefore, stock selections are made using technical analysis tools. Careful trade management is crucial to swing trading success.

Stock selection is even more important for swing trading than it is for position trading. When you're looking for a stock to move right away, you base your decisions on selection criteria that are different from when you're positioning for a move that may last for several weeks to several months. A few of the important selection criteria that swing traders use are

✦ **Volume and liquidity:** Swing traders typically focus on actively traded and relatively large stocks. The goal is finding stocks that are easy to buy, sell, and sell short. When trading time frames are short, you need to be able to execute your orders quickly. Unfortunately, stocks with the greatest liquidity and trading volumes are closely followed by the largest number of professional traders, which usually constrains the number of profitable swing trading opportunities, so swing traders often scout opportunities outside of the 25 or so stocks that have the highest trading volume and greatest liquidity.

✦ **Trending:** Trending stocks provide the best opportunity for swing-trading profits. You may use either the methods described in Chapter 3 for identifying trending stocks or the *average directional index* (ADX) indicator. This indicator has three components, the ADX reading, and two *directional movement indicators* — the +DMI and the –DMI. An ADX reading of more than 30 or so indicates a trending stock. A comparison of the two DMIs shows you whether the AMX is trending up or down. If the value of +DMI is larger than the value of –DMI, then the stock is trending higher. If the value of –DMI is larger than the value of +DMI, the stock is trending lower. The ADX indicator is included in most charting applications.

✦ **Volatility:** Swing traders depend on larger, or more volatile, short-term moves for profits. As a result, they want to trade stocks that have histories of making large moves in short periods of time. One popular approach to finding them is keeping an eye on the *average daily ranges,* or ADRs (not to be confused with *American depository receipts,* which are shares of foreign companies trading in the U.S. exchanges). ADRs are simple moving averages that track the day-to-day differences between an individual stock's daily high and low prices. If you're swing trading, you want stocks that show high ADRs. Volatility also can be measured using historical volatility, which is discussed in the "Trading volatility" section of this chapter.

✦ **Sector selection:** Just like position trading, swing traders try to trade stocks in the strongest sectors, and the weakest sectors are candidates for short sales. Use the techniques described in Chapter 4 to identify strong and weak sectors.

✦ **Tight spreads:** As a means of controlling slippage (see Chapter 4), you need to pay close attention to the difference between the bid and ask prices of the stocks you're considering as swing-trading prospects. Stocks with wide spreads make profitable swing trading difficult. Low-priced stocks rarely are good candidates for swing trading, because the spread, as a percentage of the stock price, is usually too wide.

Swing-Trading Strategies

Swing trading fluctuates between the use of trend-following and counter-trend strategies:

+ When a stock is trending strongly, swing traders primarily employ trend-following techniques, but may use countertrend techniques to fine-tune exit points.

+ When a stock is range bound, swing traders use countertrend methods to identify entry and exit points.

Trading trending stocks

Technical analysis patterns that we cover in Chapter 3 are all applicable to swing trading. Patterns repeat in all time frames. The difference is in how swing traders use and interpret these common patterns. Trend-following strategies are more aggressive for swing trading than they are for position trading. Although swing traders use some of the same indicators and patterns used by position traders, they often use them in different ways. We explain a few examples in the sections that follow.

Trading pullbacks

A *pullback* is another name for a consolidation within a trend. Consolidation patterns include flags and pennants, which we discuss in Chapter 3. Swing traders use daily charts and intraday charts — ranging from 1-minute bars to 60-minute bar charts — to identify the dominant short-term trend and any pullback patterns within the trend. They try to enter a position when the price of a targeted stock stops declining or pulling back, so they can capture the next move higher in the trend. Conceptually, pullback trading is simple, but in practice, it's trickier than it sounds.

After you identify a trending stock and find a flag or pennant pullback pattern by visually examining the daily charts, you must try to enter a position just as the pullback is ending. The classic setup is finding an orderly pullback in which the high of each bar on a chart of the pullback is lower than the previous one.

Entering a position is done by placing a buy-stop order. A buy-stop is like any stop order; when the price is hit, the order is executed. Entering a position to trade pullbacks is an iterative process, so it's best to use a day order instead of a GTC (good-till-cancelled; see Book 3, Chapter 3) order. Here are the steps:

✦ Select your buy-stop price so it's just above the intraday high price shown in the last bar of the chart.

✦ If the stock price trades above your buy-stop price, your order is executed. Otherwise, the order is cancelled at the end of the day.

✦ As long as you're still interested in this trade, adjust your buy-stop price to just above the intraday high of the most recent bar on the chart and reenter your order.

✦ After your order is filled, place a stop-loss order using a stop price just below the intraday low of the lowest bar in the pullback on the chart.

✦ As long as the trade is active, continue adjusting the stop price to be just below the intraday low of the most recent bar on the chart.

Surfing channels

Another trend-following approach to swing trading uses a channelling strategy to identify entry and exit points. After a channel is identified on the daily charts, channel lines are treated as lines of support and resistance.

After identifying support and resistance levels for a channelling stock, you can monitor its chart for reversals near the channel lines. As the stock price approaches the lower or *support channel line,* you have an opportunity to take a position in the direction of the trend. After entering a position, your stop-loss order is entered just below the support channel line. As the stock price approaches the upper or *resistance channel line,* that signals when to exit your position.

 You can use intraday charts to fine-tune this strategy. As a stock price falls toward its lower channel or support level, begin watching intraday charts for indications that the stock is changing direction and heading higher. If you see an intraday low near the location of the support channel line, followed by a higher high and a higher low, you can use that situation as an entry signal. After entering a long position, you place a stop-loss order just below the support channel line.

You hold this long position until it either is stopped out or the stock approaches its upper channel resistance level. Again, you need to monitor the intraday charts for hints of a change in direction and exit the trade whenever you see the reversal. After that, you wait for the stock to head back toward the lower channel line to initiate a new long trade.

Trading range-bound stocks

Unlike the typical position trader, a swing trader is more likely to use countertrend strategies (see Chapter 4) and actively participate when a stock is range bound. The swing trader tries to make trades based on price movements from the bottom to the top of the range and back down again. You can use either daily or weekly charts to identify the trading range.

Using intraday charts is another way to fine-tune your entry point. As the stock approaches the support line, you enter a position as soon as you see a reversal pattern on the intraday charts — for example, a higher high and a higher low, or a gap higher (Chapter 3).

You exit these kinds of positions when the stock reverses near its resistance line. You can then take a short position in the stock — using any of the entry techniques described earlier — or wait for the stock to return to the support line to initiate another long position.

If the stock breaks through its upper resistance level, you interpret that condition exactly the way a position trader does — a very bullish indication that the stock is likely beginning a new trend, immediately closing any open short positions and converting to a trend-following strategy (see the "Trading trending stocks" section).

Trading volatility

Swing traders try to trade stocks that move up and down more than average. To find these stocks, swing traders spend a great deal of effort measuring and analyzing volatility, usually in the form of historical volatility. Although the math required to calculate historical volatility is complex, the concept is simple. *Historical volatility* measures a stock's price movement. The faster it moves, the higher the historical volatility. Fortunately, many charting and analysis programs include a method for calculating historical volatility, so you don't have to program in the formula.

Historical volatility isn't concerned with the direction of a stock's price movement. A high historical volatility value doesn't reveal whether a stock's price is rising or falling. Although swing traders want to know that a stock trends in one direction or the other, they don't really care which direction. Downside movement is just as attractive as upside movement to the swing trader.

You can use historical volatility for swing trading in several different ways. One popular approach uses historical volatility for finding stocks that have been very volatile but currently are experiencing quiet periods. These temporarily quiet stocks often return to previous levels of historical volatility, and that presents a swing-trading opportunity. Swing traders identify these stocks by comparing measurements of historical volatility across longer and much shorter periods of time and expressing that comparison as a ratio. The ratio looks like this:

> Historical volatility ratio = Short-term historical volatility ÷ Long-term historical volatility

One common ratio compares a 6-day historical volatility with a 100-day historical volatility. Whenever the value of that ratio is less than 50 percent, the stock is a candidate for a swing-trading position.

After this stock takes a short low-volatility rest, it is likely to return to its historical level of volatility with a fast move. Remember that volatility tells you nothing about the direction of price movements, so to get around this limitation be sure to place buy and sell-short stop orders, respectively, above the high and below the low of the current bar. When the stock decides which way it will go, one of your stop orders will be filled and that should get you pointed in the right direction. Using more traditional technical analysis tools is another approach to evaluating a stock's current trend, so you can then trade in the direction of that trend.

Risks accompany both approaches. Using the first approach, the stock may take off in one direction and quickly reverse course, and you may end up holding a position with a highly volatile stock heading the wrong way. This same scenario also can happen with the second approach. Another potential problem occurs when the stock price gaps through your entry order, and your order may end up getting filled at a price that's significantly different than you expected.

Money management issues

Because of the short duration of each trade, swing trading generates a large volume of trades. Execution and slippage costs can be very high. Profits are relatively small when measured on each trade, so losses must be carefully controlled.

You need to adhere closely to the money management rules we discuss in Chapter 4. In addition, each swing trade must represent only a small percentage of your trading capital. Ten percent of your capital per trade is too much. Risking less than 5 percent — and perhaps as little as 2 percent — of your trading capital on any one swing trade is a more conservative approach. This approach is similar to the one used by professional traders. When profit potential is small don't take big risks, or you won't be a swing trader for long.

Using Options for Swing Trading

Stock options can be used as substitutes for the underlying stocks when swing trading. A *stock option* is a limited-duration contract that grants the *option buyer* the right to either buy or sell a stock for a fixed price. The *option seller,* usually called the *option writer* or the *option grantor,* is granting the right to the option buyer to either buy or sell a specific stock for a fixed price.

Each option represents 100 shares. A *call* is an option to buy 100 shares of a specified stock. The call buyer is acquiring a limited duration right to buy 100 shares from the option grantor at a fixed price, called the *strike price.* A *put* is an option to sell 100 shares. The put buyer is acquiring a limited duration right to sell 100 shares of a stock to the option grantor at the specified strike price. Options are discussed in more detail later in this chapter.

You can, for example, substitute a call option for a long stock position or a put option for a short stock position. You realize any profits by selling the options outright, or you can exercise an option and take possession of the shares. Swing traders, however, are more likely to sell the option than exercise it.

Although using options as stock substitutes has several advantages, it also has risks of its own. The primary advantage: An option costs far less than the underlying stock, which enables you to limit your risk to the price of the option.

Each option is a substitute for 100 shares or 100 shares of an exchange-traded fund. One call option, for example, gives you the ability to buy 100 shares at a fixed price for a certain length of time. As an example, assume that the QQQQ exchange-traded fund is trading at $27.10 per share. At the time of the example, you can buy one call option with a $27 strike price for $2.26 per share, or a total of $226, before transaction costs. That one option enables you to buy 100 shares of QQQQ for $27 before the option expires.

Say that the option in this example has approximately six weeks before expiration. Your option position is therefore profitable as long as the QQQQ exchange-traded fund trades above $29.26 (excluding transaction costs) before the expiration date. (We determined the break-even price by adding the $27 strike price to the $2.26 cost of the option, which totals $29.26.) Your risk is the price of the option. In other words, you can't lose any more than $2.26 per share, or $226, on this trade.

Unfortunately, option pricing is not as straightforward as stock pricing. The pricing example above is merely a snapshot that varies with changes in the price of the QQQQ exchange-traded fund. The following factors affect option prices:

✦ Options expire and their prices decay as the expiration date draws closer. This price decay is caused by the option's falling time value.

✦ The prices of current-month options decay at faster rates than longer-dated options.

✦ In percentage terms, *out-of-the-money* options often move at a faster rate than *in-the-money* options. (An option is said to be in-the-money if it has intrinsic value and out-of-the-money if it has no intrinsic value. For a call option, that means the price for the underlying stock is greater than the specified strike price. For a put, that means the price for the underlying stock is less than the strike price.) ***Note:*** Trading options that are far out of the money is rarely a good strategy.

✦ Volatility is a component of option pricing. Option prices rise and fall as the volatility of the stock rises and falls.

✦ Except in a few unusual circumstances, an option's price doesn't move in lockstep with the underlying stock's price. If a stock moves $1, the option, in general, moves some amount less than $1. The more an option is in-the-money, the closer the change in an option's price will be to the change in the underlying stock's price.

Another factor to consider when substituting options for stocks is that the option's *spread,* or the difference between the bid price and the ask price, is extremely wide when considered as a percentage of the option price.

Before you decide to substitute options for your stock trades, make sure you understand the option-pricing model. We discuss it in the following pages. And be careful you don't overtrade with options. If you normally buy 100 shares, then you need to buy only one option contract. Although the price of 10 option contracts may be attractive when compared with the price of the stock, 10 option contracts nevertheless represent 1,000. When buying options for 10 times the number of shares that you normally trade, you're increasing your exposure to risk by a factor of 10.

When trading options, you can't make money in as many ways as you can lose it. Being right on the stock's direction but still losing money on an option trade is possible because of pricing issues. That's why gaining an understanding of the option-pricing model is so important before you try to substitute an option for a stock. We discuss options more fully later in this chapter.

Getting a Grip on Swing-Trading Risks

Swing trading is risky and demands a great deal of time. As a swing trader, you must monitor the market during every trading hour. You also must be able to control your emotions so that you stay focused and trade within your plan.

Ask any swing trader; you're likely to hear that strict adherence to money management reduces risk. The counterargument is that swing trading exposes a great deal of capital to risk but makes only small profits. Some traders are able to swing trade profitably, but you need to realize that the odds are stacked against you. Only you can decide whether it's worth the effort.

Some argue that swing trading combines the worst aspects of position trading with the worst aspects of day trading. Like day trading, swing-trading profits are small and slippage costs are high. Swing-trading positions are held overnight, so swing traders can't take advantage of the special margin provisions that are available to day traders who close all positions by the end of the trading day.

More Than Stocks: Trading Derivatives

Derivatives are marketable instruments that over time acquire and relinquish value based on an underlying asset (see the section on "Options lingo" in this chapter), including such commodities as coffee or soybeans, bonds, energy prices, and even stocks. They are commonly used by commercial and institutional organizations to *hedge* against the risks of financial losses suffered by the underlying assets that they hold. Buying or selling a derivative, for example, can minimize your financial loss when a major change occurs in the price of an asset that you own. *Hedging* is a popular tactic used by growers, producers, portfolio managers, and users of the commodities.

The two basic and most common types of derivatives are contracts for options and for futures. Traders buy and sell them as a way to speculate on the direction that the volatile prices of underlying assets will take farther down the road. If their hunches are right and the prices move in the directions they expect, traders can make a significant profit. If, on the other hand, they're wrong, they can lose the amount they paid for the derivative — possibly even quite a bit more. Before we explain all the risks, we need to more accurately define futures and options.

Futures

Futures are legally binding contracts between two parties, one who agrees to buy and the other who agrees to sell an asset for a specific price at a specified time. The specific price is known as the *strike price*. The specified date is known as the *settlement date*. Futures were first used in the 18th century in Japan as a means of trading rice and silk, but they didn't appear in our markets until the 1850s, when futures markets were developed for buying and selling commodities such as wheat, cotton, and corn.

Futures contracts are one of the most volatile trading instruments. Prices can change rapidly, causing traders to face sudden and sometimes huge losses or gains. Futures contracts are traded based on the prices of underlying commodities, indices, bonds, and stocks. Most people who enter futures markets do not physically buy and sell the actual goods or underlying financial asset. A futures contract on pork bellies, for example, does not obligate you to fill your garage with bacon. Traders invest in futures contracts either to speculate on or to hedge the risks of the changing prices of the assets that they might or might not hold. A pig farmer uses a pork belly futures contract to hedge his swine breeding. A Saudi prince uses a pork belly futures contract to speculate on the price of bacon.

What's your position?

When people talk about futures, they're bound to say something about their positions. Here's what they mean:

✦ **Short positions:** The party in the contract who agrees to deliver the commodity, stock, or bond holds a short position. Traders who take short positions are expecting the price of the underlying commodities to go down.

✦ **Long positions:** The party in the contract who agrees to buy the commodity, stock, or bond in a futures contract holds a long position on the security. Traders who buy long positions are expecting the price of the underlying commodities to go up.

Making money using futures

Traders can make money from trading futures on the daily movements of the markets for the underlying commodities, stocks, bonds, or currencies involved in the contracts they trade.

For example, typical futures contracts for wheat are signed between wheat farmers and bread producers. On one side of this contract, farmers agree to sell a specific amount of the wheat they grow at a specific price and a specified time, and on the other side, producers agree to pay that price for the contracted amount of wheat to be delivered to them by the specified time. Farmers benefit by ensuring they can get a specific price or income from their wheat, and bread producers benefit by knowing how much they have to pay for the wheat they need to make the bread that they, in turn, sell to earn a living.

The value of that futures contract is adjusted daily. Assuming the farmer agreed in February to sell 10,000 bushels of wheat to the bread maker at $4 per bushel in July, and assuming that before the July settlement date the price of wheat rises to $5 per bushel, the farmer holding the futures contract has lost $1 per bushel of wheat, or $10,000. These types of price adjustments actually are calculated daily throughout the duration of the futures contract and that means the farmer's or bread maker's account is credited or debited as wheat prices fluctuate.

The farmer and bread maker will probably never actually exchange their goods. Instead, the obligations of the futures contract eventually are settled with cash. In this scenario, the bread maker will probably buy his wheat at the current price of $5 per bushel when he needs it, but because he speculated correctly on the price, it's only really costing him $40,000 (instead of $50,000 at the current market price) to buy the wheat. Although the bread maker pays $50,000 for 10,000 bushels of wheat, he has saved $10,000 because of the money he made on the wheat futures contract. The farmer, on the other hand, sells his wheat at $5 per bushel and gets $50,000 cash, but actually keeps only $40,000 because he has to cover his loss from the futures contract.

You can see from this example that futures contracts are actually financial positions. This financial position, or the buying and selling of futures contracts, is how traders speculate. If futures traders believe the price of wheat is rising, they buy futures contracts so they can benefit from the gain made by the price. But when the situation is reversed and the price of wheat drops to $3 per bushel, then the trader who buys can be on the losing side of that futures contract and be liable for a $10,000 loss. The cost of buying into a futures contract is called the *premium* paid for that contract, which is only a small percentage of the price of the actual commodity, stock, bond, or currency underlying the contract.

Commodities futures

People who buy commodities futures basically are agreeing to buy a certain amount of a commodity at a set price at a future date. Conversely, people who sell those same futures are agreeing to provide a certain amount of a commodity at the agreed-upon price by the agreed-upon time. Buyers or sellers can enter into futures contracts on many commodities, including farm products (pork bellies, wheat, corn, and soybeans), precious metals (gold, platinum, and silver), and many others.

Traders usually don't get directly involved as buyers and sellers of the actual commodities, because they get out of their futures contracts before the underlying commodities ever change hands. Instead, they're speculators, buying and/or selling futures contracts based on which way they think the commodity price is going to move. Speculation, as you know, is fraught with risk, and the reason the risk is so great is that a commodity contract controls a large amount of the commodity value compared with the relatively small price that it takes to buy or sell the contract. The result is extensive leverage, which means controlling a large position with only a small cash deposit. If the price moves in a direction that's the opposite of what the trader anticipates, he or she may have to take a huge loss to get out of the contract.

Index futures

Index futures are based on the expected direction of the value of indexes like the S&P/TSX Composite Index and the S&P 500 index. They can be the riskiest types of futures. No underlying commodities, stocks, or bonds ever change hands with these futures contracts. Any differences in these contracts must be settled with good ol' cold, hard cash. Leverage also is high on these types of futures. For example, the multiplier on the S&P/TSX 60 contract is $100 per each index point. A Dow Jones Industrial Average contract has a value that's 25 times the value of the underlying DJIA Index.

Smaller index futures contracts, known collectively as *e-minis,* or *mini futures,* are targeted at individual traders. These minicontracts are available for indexes such as the S&P/TSX and the Nasdaq 100. Their respective individual values range from 5 times to 100 times those of the underlying indices.

The Montreal Exchange (MX) — Canada's oldest exchange, founded in 1832 — has leadership in the financial derivatives market. It is the only foreign exchange authorized by the SEC to manage the technical operations of the Boston Option Exchange (BOX), which its parent company, TMX Group, owns. As well as the S&P/TSX Composite Index and the S&P/TSX 60, the Montreal Exchange also trades index futures in gold, energy, financials, and information technology sectors.

The S&P/TSX Composite mini futures contract, for example, is five times the value of the S&P/TSX Composite Index. In other words, if a trader takes a position in the S&P/TSX Composite mini futures contract, every time the underlying S&P/TSX Composite Index moves one point, the value of the S&P/TSX Composite mini futures contract changes by $5. Another way to think about this is that for every .25 point, the value of the S&P/TSX Composite mini futures contract changes by 5 cents. If you take a long position in the S&P/TSX Composite mini futures contract when the underlying index is at 1,000, and the index moves to 1,010, you have a $50 profit. The trader who took the other side of this trade, the short position, is in exactly the opposite position, losing $50.

Bond futures

The Montreal Exchange also offers bond futures based on the price of future delivery of a specific type of bond in a specific denomination at a specific interest rate on a specified date. Speculators basically are betting on whether the price of that bond goes up or down. Changes in interest rates have a big impact on the values of bonds. In general, when interest rates fall, bond prices go up, and when interest rates rise, bond prices go down. Speculators in bond futures basically enter positions based on whether interest rates will go up or down. For example, a speculator who thinks interest rates will go up sells contracts for the future delivery of bonds. If interest rates indeed go up as expected, the price for the underlying bonds goes down, and speculators can do one of two things:

✦ Buy the lower-priced bonds, and in turn earn a profit by selling them to the buyer to settle at the higher price named in the original futures contract.

✦ Close the contract to realize a profit.

Stock futures

Stock futures are contracts in which you agree to either deliver or purchase upon delivery 100 shares of a particular stock on or before a designated date in the future (known as the *expiration date*). For example, a trader who enters into a contract to buy 100 shares at $30 a share for a total of $3,000, and who expects the price of that stock to go up, can lock in the lower price and then buy the actual stock at that lower price on the settlement date or close the contract and realize a profit. Traders who enter into this type of contract generally must have about 20 percent of the cash value of 100 shares of the underlying stock in their futures accounts, so a trader in the earlier example would have to have $300 in a futures account.

Foreign currency futures

Future currency contracts are contracts that involve the future delivery of certain foreign currencies. We discuss these types of futures near the end of this chapter.

Yes, futures contracts are riskier than options, because you actually have to come up with the underlying commodity, bond, stock, or currency to satisfy the contract, sell the future at a loss before the settlement date, or pay the difference in cash to settle the contract. Futures are binding contracts that require you to fulfill the obligations specified in the contracts. Options are less risky because they're not an obligation to perform. Rather, they instead give the buyer of the option the right to exercise the option, but the buyer is not obligated to do so.

Options

Although futures have been available since the 1850s, it wasn't until 1975 when the old Montreal Stock Exchange became the first in North America to offer stock options for traders. In the United States options did not become available until 1982, when they were part of a government pilot program. The big advantage that options have over futures is that you buy the right to exercise the option, and yet you still can decide to allow the option to expire without ever exercising that right. When you let an option expire, you lose only the amount you paid for the option and not the full amount that otherwise can be lost in trading the underlying asset. Option sellers take the riskier stance, because they can lose the value of whatever asset they promised to sell or buy if the option buyer decides to exercise the option.

Options are financial contracts that give the buyer the right, but not the obligation, to buy or sell a particular asset at a predetermined date in the future at a specified price.

Options lingo

Trading in options has a language all its own, and you'll need to understand it before we get into the mechanics. Some key terms include:

+ **Puts:** A *put option* gives the buyer the right to sell a particular asset at a specified price at any time during the life of the option.

+ **Calls:** A *call option* gives the buyer the right to buy a particular asset at a specified price at any time during the life of the option.

+ **Option seller:** The person who writes or sells any option is called the *option seller* or *writer.* This seller (sometimes called an option grantor in the United States) must come up with the underlying asset promised in the option, even if doing so means a loss, whenever an option buyer decides to exercise an option. For example, if an option seller agrees to sell you 100 shares of ABC stock for $50 per share on or before May 1, and the stock price rises to $60 on April 20, then the seller must sell you that stock for $50 and take the $10-per-share loss. You get to sell ABC at the current price and reap the profit.

✦ **Covered calls:** If an option seller holds an *equivalent position,* or owns the same number of shares of the underlying asset that is offered in the call, this contract is considered a *covered call.* Options traders selling covered calls are trying to take advantage of a neutral or declining stock. If the option expires unexercised, the seller (writer) of the option keeps the premium. If, on the other hand, the buyer (holder) of the option exercises it, the stock must be delivered. However, because the option seller already owns the stock, the risk is limited. The opposite scenario is an *uncovered call,* which occurs when the seller sells a call for a stock that he or she doesn't own. The seller of an uncovered call is taking virtually unlimited risk.

✦ **Covered puts:** When the seller of a put option also has sold short an equivalent amount in the underlying security, then this option is considered a *covered put.* If the seller has neither established a short position in the underlying security nor deposited a corresponding amount of cash equal to the value of the put, then the put is called a *naked put.* The seller of a naked put also is taking virtually unlimited risk.

✦ **Option buyer:** The person who buys the option is called the option buyer or holder. If the option buyer buys the right to sell an asset at some time in the future, then he or she buys a put option. If the option buyer buys the right to purchase an asset at some time in the future, then he or she buys a call option. The most an option buyer can lose is the amount paid for the option contract.

✦ **Underlying asset:** An option is based on an underlying asset that can be bought or sold such as a futures contract or shares.

✦ **Premium:** The price paid for the option is called the *premium,* which is what the option holder pays to the option seller for the right to either buy or sell the underlying asset. Premiums for options are set by the open market. Option buyers must pay the premium plus a commission and fee.

✦ **Expiration date:** The *expiration date* is the last day that an option buyer can exercise the option. Options based on futures contracts usually expire one month before the settlement date of the underlying futures contract. After an option expires, the option holder no longer has any rights and the option has no value. So option buyers lose whatever premium they paid plus any commission and fee. In that case, the option is said to expire worthless, or out-of-the-money.

✦ **Exercise:** Option buyers can exercise their rights any time before the expiration date — if, that is, the option they purchased is an *American-style option. European-style options,* on the other hand, can be exercised only on their expiration dates. Exercising a call option means the option buyer buys the underlying asset at the price set in the option regardless of the current market price for the asset. Exercising a put option means the option buyer sells the underlying asset at the price set in the option.

An option buyer can always decide not to exercise the rights set forth in his or her option and simply let it expire. The option holder also can sell the option contract at its current market value.

✦ **Strike price:** The *strike price* is the price of the underlying asset at which the option can be exercised.

✦ **Offset:** If option buyers or sellers want to realize their profits or limit their losses, they can *offset* their option through a sale or purchase that also is called liquidating or closing an option. When an option is liquidated, no position is actually taken in the underlying asset. Offsetting is usually done on the same exchange where the trader first bought or sold the option. If he can sell the option for more than he bought it, then he will realize a profit. If she sells the option for less than she paid, then she will take a loss.

✦ **In-the-money:** An option is *in-the-money* when it's worthwhile to exercise the option and buy or sell the underlying asset. A call option is in-the-money when the market price for the underlying asset is above the strike price set in the option. A put option is in-the-money when the price for the underlying asset is lower than the strike price set in the option.

✦ **At-the-money:** An option is *at-the-money* when the strike price for the option is the same as the market price for the underlying asset.

✦ **Out-of-the-money:** An option is *out-of-the-money* when it's not worthwhile to exercise the option. A call option is out-of-the-money when the strike price is higher than the market price for the underlying asset. A put option is out-of-the-money when the strike price is less than the market price for the underlying asset.

Options pricing

The three factors affecting the price of an option premium are as follows:

✦ **Date of expiration:** As the option moves closer to its date of expiration, the value of the option declines, and that's why an option is considered a *wasting asset*. The more time you have until an option expires, the greater possibility you have for the option to reach the point of being in-the-money. Longer options therefore have higher premiums.

✦ **Strike price:** For out-of-the-money options, when the current market price moves more and more out-of-the-money and away from the strike price, the premium price gets lower and lower. The premium for an in-the-money option, on the other hand, rises in value if the underlying asset moves further into the money in relationship to the strike price.

✦ **Volatility:** The more volatility that's in the market for the underlying asset, or stock, the greater the chance that the option will become worthwhile to exercise. When the market for an asset is volatile, premiums for options on that asset are higher.

**Book IV
Chapter 5**

**The Skinny on
Swing Trading and
Derivatives**

When you get a quote for an option, you can choose from numerous strike prices and expiration dates that are available. When you're thinking about buying a call option, and its strike price is low and yet close to becoming worthwhile to exercise, the premium price (the price you pay for the option) will be much higher than for an option with a higher strike price. If you're thinking about buying a put option, then you'll pay more of a premium for an option with a high strike price than you will for one with a lower strike price.

Commissions vary greatly, so be certain you understand all the possible fees before initiating a trade. Some discount brokers charge commissions per trade, but others charge on the basis of a *round trip,* including both the purchase and the sale of the option. Some firms charge per-option transaction fees, while others charge on the basis of a percentage of the option premium that's usually subject to a minimum charge. Investment advisers can offer a flat management fee that allows option trading at large discounts.

Commission charges can have a major impact on whether you're able to earn a profit or have to suffer a loss on an option. A high commission charge reduces your potential for making a profit and can even drive what little profit you make into a loss. So be careful. Know what charges you have to pay and compare them with other discount brokers and investment advisers before you trade.

Options and futures are quoted with bid and ask prices just like stocks, and the spreads with options can grow pretty wide as a percentage of the option's premium — which in turn can have a significant impact on the profitability of your option position. The wider the spread, the harder it is for you to make a profit. As an option trader, you typically buy at the ask, the higher price, and sell at the bid, the lower price. That means any trade must recover the difference between the bid and the ask before you can earn a profit. As with stock trading, you can use a limit order to put your order between the bid and the ask, but no guarantee exists that your order will be filled. See Chapter 4 for more about bid/ask spreads.

Buying Options and Futures Contracts

All types of options and futures in Canada are traded on the Montreal Exchange. Some types of options can be traded on the NYSE and the Boston Option Exchange. The Chicago Board Options Exchange (CBOE) handles stock and several specialized futures options. You can trade stock options and some index options in a traditional investment account. Special risk release forms must be signed, but otherwise the account remains the same. Covered options and naked short positions require a margin account.

Opening an account

If you want to buy futures or options on futures, you must do so through an individual account that you open with a registered futures trading dealer.

You have the choice of opening either a discretionary account or a nondiscretionary account. A *discretionary account* is an account in which you sign a power of attorney over to your commodity trading adviser (CTA) so he or she can make trading decisions on your behalf. A *nondiscretionary account* is an account in which you make all the trading decisions. You also may want to consider trading through a commodity pool. When trading through a *commodity pool* you purchase a share or interest in a pool of other investors. Any profits or losses are shared proportionately by the members of the pool.

When you open an individual account, you need to make a deposit that amounts to a *margin payment* or *performance bond* for the options or futures you trade. This payment is relatively small compared to the size of your potential market position, and it gives you the opportunity to greatly leverage your money. Small changes in options and futures prices can result in large gains or large losses in relatively short periods of time.

Your futures trader calculates the values of the futures and option contracts in your account on a daily basis, and you need to maintain a margin level that's approximately 75 percent of the amount required when you originally enter your positions. If your holdings fall below that level you'll be asked to come up with the cash to restore your margin account to the initial level, a situation that's known as a *margin call* (see Chapter 1 of this Book for more on margins). If you can't meet the margin call in a reasonable period of time, which can be as little as an hour, your futures firm closes out enough of your positions to reduce your margin deficiency. If your positions are liquidated at a loss you can be held liable for that loss, which sometimes can be substantially more than your original margin deposit.

Custom-designed exchange-traded funds (ETFs) provide traders with many of the features of a futures contract. Traders also can trade options on ETFs — if they have the stomach for it — through the Montreal Exchange.

Calculating the price and making a buy

Before buying an option you first must calculate the break-even price; to do that you must know the option's strike price, the premium cost, and the commission or other transaction costs. With those three details in hand you can determine a break-even price for a call option using this formula:

Option strike price + Option premium costs + Commission and transaction fees = Break-even price

If you expect a stock price increase, you want to consider purchasing a call option, but if you expect a price decline, you want to consider purchasing a put option. In both scenarios, you need to check the fundamental and technical information you gathered on the underlying stock or asset, so you can be certain that any break-even prices you've calculated reasonably match what your analysis indicates.

Options for Getting Out of Options

After you buy an option, you have to decide how you want to opt out of that position. You can choose one of the following three alternatives:

✦ Offset the option

✦ Hold the option

✦ Exercise the option

Offsetting the option

You offset an option by liquidating your option position, usually in the same marketplace where you bought the option. If you want to get out of an option before its expiration date, you can try to sell it for whatever price you can get. Doing so either enables you to take your profits or reduces your potential loss by the amount you receive for the option. As long as you bought your option in an active market, other investors usually are willing to pay for the rights your option conveys. The key, of course, is how much they're willing to pay.

Your net profit or loss for this option is determined by the difference between what you originally pay in premiums, commissions, and other transaction costs minus the premium you receive when you liquidate the option after deducting commissions and other transaction costs.

Holding the option

If your option is not yet in-the-money but you still believe it may get there, you can continue to hold the option until the exercise date. If you're right, you can exercise the option before the expiration date or liquidate at a later date, which means to buy or sell the option before the expiration date at some time in the future. If you're wrong, you risk the possibility that you won't find a buyer or that you'll have to let the option expire and take a loss that is equal to the amount of the premium, commission, and transaction costs you paid. Some traders take an even more risky position by buying options that are deeply out-of-the-money for just pennies a share. Even if these options never grow any nearer to being in-the-money, as long as they move in the right direction the premiums will rise. Although we don't recommend using this strategy, profits can be made as long as you're able to sell the option before its expiration date.

Options decline in value as they get closer to their expiration dates, so if you think you've made a mistake and the market moves against your position, bite the bullet as soon as possible and try to liquidate your option to minimize your losses.

Exercising the option

You can exercise an option any time prior to its expiration date, as long as you're trading in American-style options. You don't have to wait until the exercise date to exercise an American-style option. (The Montreal Exchange has both European-style and American-style contract types depending on the instrument. Some option contracts sold in the United States are European-style, which can be exercised only on the expiration date.) Exercising an option means:

✦ Buying the underlying asset when you own a call

✦ Selling the underlying asset when you own a put

In general, call options are exercised only when the trader plans to hold the underlying asset, and put options are exercised only when the trader owns the underlying asset and wants to sell it. Option traders are more likely to realize any gains or losses by closing their option positions rather than exercising them.

The Risks of Trading Options and Futures

Trading in options and futures is risky business, and regulations governing those trades are stringent, even with regard to allowing you to open an account. Before opening an account for you, a firm must provide you with a disclosure document that describes the risks involved in trading futures and options contracts. The document gives you the opportunity to determine whether you have the experience and financial resources necessary to engage in option trading and whether option trading is appropriate for meeting your goals and objectives.

Topics that must be covered in the disclosure statement include the risks inherent in trading futures contracts or options and the effect that leveraging your account can have on potential losses or gains. The statement also must include warnings about trading futures in foreign markets, because those types of trades carry additional risks from fluctuations in currency exchange rates and differences in regulatory protection.

Commodities options and futures also can be risky, because many of the factors that affect their prices are totally unpredictable, such as the weather, labour strikes, inflation, foreign exchange rates, and governmental policies. Because positions in futures and options are so highly leveraged, even a small price movement against your position can result in at least the loss of your entire premium payment and possibly even much greater liability for additional losses.

After you begin trading options and futures, you can't close your account until all open positions are closed — if, that is, you're trading through an account with a commodities exchange. This restriction does not apply to options traded in an investment account. Any accruals on futures contracts are paid out daily. Any funds in your margin account that are beyond your required margin or account-opening requirements can be withdrawn, but other such funds have to remain in the account until all your positions are closed. Any restrictions on the withdrawal of your funds are stated in the original disclosure document. Be sure you understand those restrictions before committing your funds.

After opening your account, your firm usually mails or e-mails confirmation of all purchases and sales, a month-end summary of transactions that shows any gains or losses, and an evaluation of your open positions and current account values. You need to be able to get information from your firm on a daily basis after you begin to trade.

Futures traders must maintain adequate margin in their futures accounts by the process known as *marking-to-market*. At the end of each trading day, margin requirements are adjusted by the change in the price of the futures contracts.

Investment dealers are required to segregate any money you deposit in your account from the dealer's own funds. The amount segregated either increases or decreases depending on the success of your trades. Even when the firm segregates your funds, you still may not be able to get all your money back if the firm becomes insolvent and is unable to cover all the obligations to its customers unless the firm is a member of the Canadian Investor Protection Fund (CIPF) `www.cipf.ca`.

When problems with your dealer arise that you can't resolve without help, you do have dispute-resolution options. Before deciding how you want to proceed you must consider the costs involved, the length of time it may take to resolve the problem, and whether you want to contact an attorney. You can get more information about dispute resolution by contacting the Investment Industry Regulatory Organization of Canada (IIROC) at `www.iiroc.ca/English/Investors/MakingComplaint` or by calling 1-877-442-4322. Another useful website is `www.getsmarteraboutmoney.ca`, which is funded by the Ontario Securities Commission (OSC).

Minimizing Risks

In a nutshell, the best way to minimize the risks of derivatives trading is to take the time to find out as much as you can about the inherent risks of the derivatives you're trading and how others have dealt with them. The first step you can take is to check out the firms or individuals with whom you plan to trade. All firms and individuals that offer to trade options or futures must be registered with one of the members of the Canadian Securities Administrators (www.securities-administrators.ca). You can check out firms and individuals online at the IIROC website (www.iiroc.ca).

Next, be sure you're familiar with the firm's commission charges and how they're calculated. Compare the firm's quotes with those of other firms you're considering. Whenever a firm has unusually high commission charges, ask for a detailed explanation for the higher charges and what additional services justify the higher cost.

Always make sure you calculate the break-even price for any option you're thinking about purchasing, because you have to know at what point the option you're planning to buy will be profitable and whether the data you've collected justifies the option's premium costs.

You also need to understand the market for the underlying asset of the option or future you plan to buy and what can impact the market price of that asset. Be sure your expectations for the potential profits from the option or futures contract you choose are reasonable.

You don't ever want to buy an option without first coming to a full realization that you can lose the entire value of your trade. If you want to take the riskier position as an option seller, be sure you can accept the possibility that your losses may exceed the premium you initially received for the option. Option selling comes with the potential of unlimited losses, as does futures trading.

Just as with stock trading, you can limit your losses by carefully setting your risk limits before you start to trade. Don't let yourself get caught up in the emotions of futures and options trading. Develop a plan before you buy that first option or future and stick with that plan, and be sure to diversify your holdings not only by asset type but also by time of expiration.

After you determine how much capital you want to put into trading derivatives, make sure you know how much you can afford to lose on just one trade to be able to stay in business. You don't want to overexpose your cash position on one trade and risk the possibility that you won't have the money you need when the next opportunity comes along. By exposing your capital to a variety of markets, you also have a better chance that some of your trades will end up succeeding — how bad can that be?

Be wary of firms that lead you to believe you can make lots of money trading options or futures with very little risk. That's never true. If a firm is using high-pressure tactics to get you to trade that's a sure sign of a problem, so don't allow yourself to be rushed into a trading decision. If you aren't being given enough time to construct your own fundamental and technical analyses before you make a purchase, walk away from the deal.

**Book IV
Chapter 5**

**The Skinny on
Swing Trading and
Derivatives**

The risks associated with trading futures and options can be more than you initially paid for the trade, so be careful out there! We've given you an overview of the options and futures trading arena, but before you jump in be sure you get significantly more training.

Exploring the World of Foreign Currency Exchange

If you've ever travelled outside of Canada, you've probably traded in a foreign currency. Every time you travel you have to exchange your country's currency for the currency used in the country you're visiting. If you're a Canadian citizen shopping in England, and you see a sweater that you want for £100 (100 pounds — the pound is the currency in the United Kingdom), you'd need to know the exchange rate. In November 2011, for example, the rate was $1.6288 for one British pound. So a £100 sweater would cost you $162.88 in Canadian dollars.

We include this example here to show you how foreign currency exchange is used by the average shopper, but foreign currency traders trade much larger sums of money thousands of times a day. The majority of trades take place in three main centres of currency trading — the United Kingdom, the United States, and Hong Kong. The rest of the trading takes place primarily in Singapore, Switzerland, Japan, Germany, China, Canada, and Australia.

Currency trading is ongoing, 24 hours a day, with some countries just getting started as others are finishing up their business day. For example, when the trading day opens at 8 a.m. in London, the trading day is ending for Singapore and Hong Kong. When Toronto, Montreal, and New York open their trading doors, it's already 1 p.m. in London. Thus, traders must be alert around the clock, because a major event at an off hour anywhere in the world can shake the currency markets at any time. Pity poor Vancouver, San Francisco, and Los Angeles, the weakest links in the so-called 24-hour foreign exchange market that spans the globe.

Individual trades in the range of $200 million to $500 million are not uncommon. In fact, estimates indicate that quoted price changes occur as frequently as 20 times per minute, and the most active currency rates can change as many as 18,000 times in a single day, according to the U.S. Federal Reserve.

Types of currency traders

Traders can be grouped into one of four basic types — bankers, investment dealers, customers, and central banks. Each plays a different role in the foreign currency exchange market.

✦ **Bankers, banks, and other financial institutions** do the lion's share of trading. They make profits buying and selling currency with each other. Approximately two-thirds of all forex transactions involve banks dealing directly with each other.

✦ **Investment dealers** sometimes act as intermediaries between the banks, helping them — or other traders looking for a good deal — find out where they can get the best currency trade. Buyers and sellers like working through investment dealers, because they can trade anonymously through intermediaries. Dealers make profits on currency exchanges by charging a spread for the transactions they arrange.

✦ **Customers,** which primarily are major companies, trade currency so they can operate globally or invest internationally. For example, if a Canadian car manufacturer buys parts from a manufacturer in Japan, then the Canadian car manufacturer needs to buy and pay for the parts in Japanese yen. Companies that trade currencies regularly have their own trading desks, while others conduct their currency trading through dealers or banks.

✦ **Central banks,** like the Bank of Canada (BoC) and the U.S. Federal Reserve, which act on behalf of their governments, sometimes participate in the forex market to influence the value of the currencies of their respective countries. For example, if the Bank of Canada believes the dollar is weak, it may buy dollars and even encourage central banks of other countries to do the same in the forex market, to boost, or increase, the value of the dollar. This policy has not been used by the BoC for a long time.

Why currency changes in value

Among the many factors that impact the value of a nation's currency are

✦ Interest rates

✦ Business cycles

✦ Political developments

✦ Changes in tax laws

✦ Stock market news

✦ Inflationary expectations

✦ International investment patterns

✦ Policies adopted by governments and central banks

✦ Employment levels

Traders must monitor all these potential factors so they can stay on top of political or economic changes that impact the value of the currencies they hold. Currency trading, like other forms of trading, is affected by the basic economic principle of supply and demand. When a whole bunch of one type of currency is available for sale, the market can be flooded with it, and the price of that currency drops. When the supply of currency is low and the demand for it is high, then the value of that currency rises. Governments may try to influence the value of their respective currencies by flooding the market whenever they want the value to fall or making the supply scarce (by buying their own currency) whenever they hope the value of their currencies might rise.

What traders do

Currency traders look for a currency that offers the highest return with the lowest risk. For example, if a nation's financial instruments, such as stocks and bonds, offer high rates of return with relatively low risk, then traders who are foreign to that nation want to buy that currency, thus increasing the demand. Currency is also in demand when its country is going through a growth segment in its business cycle highlighted by stable prices and a wide range of goods and services available for sale. Forex traders who speculate on currencies to earn their keep look for specific signs to indicate when exchange rates may change, including the following:

✦ **Political instability:** Unrest in a country drives up demand for currency in safer markets, such as Canadian dollars, as speculators race to find safe havens. The U.S. dollar used to be the world's safe haven of choice; not so since its recent credit crunch troubles. In fact, during 2009 fifteen of the world's currencies rose in value against the once-mighty U.S. dollar. Only the Japanese yen slipped against the American dollar.

✦ **Rising interest rates:** Higher interest rates encourage offshore investments in countries where local investors are seeking better rates of return than they can get at home.

✦ **Economic reforms:** Economic reforms in developing countries may help improve their currencies. As a result, investors see new opportunities for investing in the currencies of those successfully developing countries.

Traders try to predict these moves in advance, so they can get in or out of a currency before others. Correctly guessing where a currency is going and taking a position in that currency at the beginning of the trend can mean huge profits for a trader. Traders make money either by buying the currency at a lower price and then selling it later at a higher price, or by selling their currencies of other countries at higher prices before they have time to react negatively. After the markets for their original holdings fall, they simply reestablish positions at bargain prices.

When a trader purchases a large amount of a particular currency, then he or she is *long the currency*. Conversely, when a trader sells a large amount of a currency, then he or she is *short the currency*.

The forex market is dominated by four currencies, which account for 80 percent of the market — the U.S. dollar, the euro, the Japanese yen, and the British pound. These currencies always are liquid, which makes finding someone willing to buy or sell any of them easy for traders. Other currencies are not as liquid, and as is true with the stocks of small companies, you're sometimes unable to find any buyers or sellers when you're ready to trade for the currency of a smaller country. Currencies of developing countries are softest, usually facing lower demand than the currencies of developed countries. Soft currencies at times can be difficult to convert.

Understanding Money Jargon

The world of foreign currency exchange has a unique language of its own. Prices are quoted two ways, meaning that when one trader talks price with another, they state their respective prices in terms of what *exchange rate* they'll pay to buy it and what they'll take when selling it. Bid and ask price differences, or *spreads,* usually are stated in *pips* or hundredths of a currency unit. Spreads normally are no more than ten pips.

Pips are the smallest incremental price movement permitted in the currency market. Although most transactions deal in thousands or millions of dollars, yen, euro, or other currencies — and a one-cent spread can equal thousands of dollars — most currency price quotes nevertheless are extended out four decimals (1.5432, for example). Many times traders quote only the last two digits, or the small numbers, such as 32 exchange for 22, because the incremental changes are so small only the last two digits matter.

As a trader, you need to think in terms of the host currency when receiving a quote for *direct exchange,* which would be an exchange based on the value of the host country's currency. Quotes for *indirect exchange* are just the opposite. They're based on the foreign currency for which you are seeking a trade rather than on the host currency. For example, if you're in Canada and receive an indirect price quote, you'd be getting a price based on buying a set amount of foreign currency in exchange for Canadian dollars. Most exchanges take place on the interbank market — currency exchanges among the world's banks — and are based on the U.S. dollar. The one exception to the rule is the British pound sterling.

Traders use three different types of trades to exchange currency. They're known as spot, forward, and options transactions.

Spot transactions

Spot transactions account for about a third of all forex transactions and involve trades in which two traders agree on an exchange rate and then trade currencies based on that rate. These transactions usually start with one trader calling another and asking for a price on a particular type of currency without specifying whether he or she wants to buy or sell. The trader on the receiving end of the call gives the caller a two-way price — one if he or she wants to buy and another if he or she wants to sell. If they agree to do business, the two exchange their respective currencies.

Forward transactions

Forward transactions are used when traders want to buy or sell currency at some agreed-upon forward date. A buyer and a seller set an exchange rate for the transaction, and the transaction occurs at the set price at the appointed time regardless of what the current market price is for the currencies. Forward transactions can be only a few days or even years in the future, although most futures contracts are for 30, 60, or 90 days. The two types of forward transactions are futures and swaps.

✦ **Futures:** *Futures* are forward transactions that have standard contract sizes and maturity dates. These types of transactions are traded on an exchange set up for this purpose.

✦ **Swaps:** A *swap,* the more common type of forward transaction, is a private contract through which two parties exchange currencies for a specific length of time and then agree to reverse the transaction at a later date, which is set at the time of the initial contract.

The risk that traders take in using forward transactions is that market rates can change, turning the contract to which they've just agreed into a losing trade. They still have to fulfill the contract at the fixed price, because after the contract is signed the price cannot be revised.

Companies that place orders for imported products from foreign firms usually use this type of transaction so they can lock in an exchange rate at some time in the future when their orders are ready. Companies placing these orders don't want to lay out the cash upfront to exchange currencies, but they nevertheless want to be able to budget set amounts for their purchases. As such, they'd rather risk missing a better rate for the currency exchange in the future than a major shift in the price of the product (perhaps brought on by a currency shock) that's going to end up costing them much more than they intended to pay.

Options

Option contracts were added to the forex world to give traders a bit more flexibility than a forward transaction affords them. Like forward transactions, the owner of an option contract has the right to either buy or sell a specified amount of foreign currency at a specified rate up to a specified date. The big difference with option contracts is that traders who hold a contract are not obligated to fulfill the transaction. They can, instead, simply decide to let it expire.

Option buyers have to pay for the right to buy or sell these transactions on or before a specified date. The set price at which the currencies are exchanged is called the *strike price.* When the date for the exchange arrives, the option holder determines whether the strike price is favourable. If it is, the option owner completes the transaction and earns a profit. If it isn't favourable, the option owner allows the option to expire and absorbs the cost of purchasing the original option, which is less of a loss than actually exchanging the currencies. The two types of options currency traders deal with are

✦ **Call options,** to buy currency at some set price in the future

✦ **Put options,** to sell currency at some set price in the future.

For example, suppose a trader purchases a six-month call option on one million euros at an exchange rate of 1.39 dollars to the euro. During that six-month period, the trader can (has the option to) either purchase the euros at the $1.39 rate, buy them at market rate, or do nothing at all. As market rates for currencies fluctuate, options in those currencies can be sold and resold many times before the expiration date. Companies operating overseas use options as insurance against major unfavourable market shifts in the exchange rate and thus avoid locking their companies into guaranteed exchanges.

Trades are made using various currency symbols that are similar to stocks when seeking price quotes. You can find current exchange rates — and symbols — for most major currencies online at the Universal Currency Converter (www.xe.com/).

How Money Markets Work

The currency exchange market is made up of about 2,000 dealer institutions that are particularly active in foreign currency exchanges. Most of the players are commercial or investment banks that are geographically dispersed in the key financial centres around the world. Among these 2,000 dealers, around 100 to 200 members carry on the core trading and market-making activities. Major players are fewer still.

As of May 2011, three British banks, a German bank, a Swiss bank, and two American banks commanded 65 percent of the overall volume of currencies traded. When a dealer buys a Canadian dollar, regardless of where in the world the transaction takes place, the actual deposit is located either directly in a Canadian bank or in a claim of a foreign bank on a dollar deposit located in Canada. The same is true of the currency of any other country.

Different countries, different rules

The actual infrastructures of the various currency markets and how they operate are determined by each separate nation. Each country enforces its own laws, banking regulations, accounting rules, and tax codes. The method of payment and the settlement system also are determined separately by each country. But yikes, doesn't that mean you have to know a lot about international monetary laws to be able to trade? Yup. Especially if you want to be successful.

Luckily, considerable global cooperation exists among exchange regulators, which minimizes differences and helps protect forex traders from fraud and abuse. Governments around the world reach agreements, or *memoranda of understanding* (MOUs), with most other major nations that have active currency exchanges, and these MOUs form a method of cooperation between regulatory and enforcement authorities across international borders that combats fraud and other illegal practices that can harm customers or threaten market integrity.

If you plan to become involved in foreign currency exchange, be sure to bone up on your knowledge of the company you're dealing with and find information about recently exposed scams and other illegal activities. You certainly don't want to get caught up in a fraudulent deal and lose all your money. Some very nasty scams have involved so-called "offshore currency trading."

The almighty (U.S.) dollar

Despite its large decline during 2008–2009, the U.S. dollar still is the most widely traded currency. The euro and the U.S. dollar are the two currencies that are involved in more than 85 percent of all global foreign exchange transactions. The U.S. dollar wears many hats, serving as an investment currency in many capital markets, a reserve currency for many central banks, a transaction currency for many commodity trades, an invoice currency for many contracts, and a currency of intervention used by countries that want to influence the values of their own currencies.

Due to the ups and downs of the U.S. dollar, and especially the steep declines we saw during and after the recession, China and some of the oil-exporting countries (such as Venezuela and Iran) have voiced concerns about its default status as the currency of choice. So far it's lots of talk, and we don't know of any major purchases for which U.S. dollars have been refused. Vendors of commodities priced in U.S. dollars have been asking for more and more U.S. dollars to complete their transactions as the U.S. dollar continues to decline. The last Middle East oil producer to export its oil in euros rather than dollars was Iraq's Saddam Hussein. A few months later the Americans and British troops invaded.

The currency in China is the yuan, which is fixed or "pegged" to the U.S. dollar. President Obama wants China to dismantle the currency peg and let the value rise against the U.S. dollar. A rising yuan would assist Canada's export industries looking for Asian markets to replace our dependence on American consumers.

Due to this friction over the value of the U.S. dollar, some executives at the International Monetary Fund (IMF) say the days of the almighty U.S. dollar as the global benchmark are numbered.

Organized exchanges

The money market is largely unregulated as a *defined market.* By that, we mean that a commercial bank in Canada or the United States doesn't need any special authorization to trade or deal in foreign currencies. Securities and investment firms don't need special permission from the OSC or any other regulatory body to carry out foreign exchange activities.

Transactions can be carried out based on whatever terms the law permits and using whatever provisions are acceptable to the two parties, subject to the commercial law governing business transactions. Of course that means the money market can be the closest thing to the Wild West you'll find in some parts of the trading world. Almost anything goes. Institutions that participate are not inspected specifically for their exchange practices, but regulatory authorities nevertheless look into trading systems as part of their regular examinations of financial institutions, just to be sure they're operating under the country's commercial banking or securities laws. They're also inspected in order to prevent laundering of drug money, proceeds of crime, or terrorist financing.

Although no official rules or restrictions govern the hours or conditions of trading on this over-the-counter (OTC) market in the United States, trading conventions developed mostly by market participants are in place in Canada.

The currency exchange market is mostly accounted for by the Big Five chartered banks in Canada, including spot transactions, forwards, and swaps. If you're new to forex trading, starting out is much safer with a large bank, where you can trade currency futures and certain currency options.

Many forex trading websites might prove to be for use at your own peril.

The Risks of the World Money Market

Leverage, or margin, which means borrowing money to trade, is the number-one risk to your portfolio when trading in money markets. Success on the foreign currency market means having to trade in large sums, because profits are made at differences of only fractions of a cent or pips. Banks or dealers determine the leverage they want to offer you, but you might not find strict regulations like the ones that govern stock margin accounts.

After you're approved for trading, you're given a set amount or allowance on which you can trade on margin. A common starting allowance for trading on margin is 5 percent (see Chapter 4 for more about margins), which means that if you put $100,000 in the bank, you're allowed to execute transactions of up to $2 million. As you gain success with more experience, that margin may be lowered to 1 percent, which means you'd be allowed to trade as much as $10 million on your $100,000 deposit — but you'll be liable for all your losses and your costs of borrowing.

When trading at those high margin levels, even a minor mistake can wipe out your entire deposit.

The most conservative of banks require *full margin,* meaning you have to deposit $1 million to be able to trade $1 million. Be sure you understand the leverage you're being offered and the loss potential you face if your trade goes sour. Just imagine starting with $100,000, which you can use to trade $2 million, and then losing half of that trading maximum with trades that have gone sour. You could end up $900,000 in the hole. Sure, lots of traders can come up with that, no problem. In reality, as long as you stick to trading the major currencies drastic price changes that end up in that type of loss are possible but unlikely — but a loss of 10 to 20 percent of your holding in a matter of minutes can happen. Only trading in third-world currencies could result in losses of the million-dollar magnitude described here, and only if there was a major uprising in the country and the price of its currency dropped dramatically — like what sadly has happened in Zimbabwe!

Types of risk

You also face a number of different kinds of risk, including market risk, exchange risk, interest rate risk, counterparty risk, volatility risk, liquidity risk, and country risk.

Market risk

All traders and investors face market risk. Basically, *market risk* comprises changes in price that adversely impact your trade or investment. Market risk is in play from the moment you enter into a foreign currency position until the moment you exit it. The foreign exchange rate can change any time during that period, so when you're dealing in foreign currency, two key factors can impact the price of the currency — exchange risk and interest rate risk.

Exchange risk

Foreign exchange traders take on exchange risk the moment they buy or sell a foreign currency. Every time you take on a new foreign exchange position, regardless of whether it's through a spot, forward, future, or option transaction, you're immediately exposed to the potential that the exchange rate will move against your position, making it worth less than when you bought it. In only a matter of seconds, a profitable transaction can turn into an unprofitable one.

Interest rate risk

Foreign exchange positions can change in value not only because of the exchange rate but also because of the currency's underlying interest rate. Whenever a country's central bank (think Bank of Canada) raises or lowers the underlying interest rate for its currency, the impact on any positions you're holding in that country's currency can be major.

Counterparty risk

In the currency trading world, a *counterparty* is the other entity involved in a transaction — a bank or banker, a dealer, or another trader. When you buy a currency option or execute a forward transaction, you risk the possibility that the counterparty to your transaction won't be able to meet his, her, or its obligations.

Note: When you buy the option through an exchange rather than directly from the counterparty, this risk is not a factor. When that happens you run into additional replacement costs, because you're forced to enter into another currency transaction to meet your own foreign currency needs. The key to avoiding this kind of risk is entering into contracts with known institutions that have high credit ratings. Additionally, you need to investigate whether the counterparty with which you're trading has had any problems with regulators, insolvency, or questions of ethical conduct.

When evaluating a company, first consider its credit risk. You can find credit rankings for many major banks at the Standard & Poor's website (www. standardandpoors.com). You can research a company's creditworthiness by investigating the requirements and standards it uses when providing credit to its customers. Companies that provide easy credit to their customers run a greater risk of not being able to meet their obligations. Conversely, companies with higher margin limits definitely are safer to do business with when you're entering into a contract.

Volatility risk

Volatility risk relates to the possibility of rapidly changing exchange rates that can impact your positions in foreign currencies. As we mentioned earlier, currency prices can change thousands of times per day. Options on currencies are valued according to volatility and underlying changes in the prices of the respective currencies. If a trader sees an increase of 100 percent in volatility, or a doubling of volatility, then the price of the option can increase 5 percent to 10 percent. If you're trading on credit, which is highly likely, your bank or dealer can reevaluate the credit it's extending to you whenever it sees a dramatic increase in the volatility of your holdings.

Liquidity risk

Liquidity risk is not a major factor if you're trading in the more commonly traded currencies, but if you decide to trade in less active currencies it can become a factor when you're unable to sell a currency you hold at the express time you want the sale to take place, especially when the market for that currency is not active — such as the hours when Toronto is closed and Hong Kong is not yet open. You can avoid liquidity risk by buying currency options or futures on an exchange.

Country risk

Country risks come in several different varieties, all of which you need to consider whenever you trade in foreign currencies. Among those aspects are

✦ **Political risk:** This variety relates to the political stability of the country in whose currency you're trading. We have seen recent seizures of commercial assets by some nations. For example, Venezuela took control of its oil industry by seizing assets of non-Venezuelan oil companies. American and European governments have seized control of automotive and financial companies. If you trade in currencies of countries that are at risk of possible *destabilization,* the currency you buy can become worthless if the country changes political leaders.

✦ **Regulation risk:** This variety relates to what can happen after you establish a position in a country's currency. Its government can change its regulations, and in effect put restraints on the ownership established by your position in the currency and by the position of your counterparty — and that can get messy.

✦ **Legal risk:** This variety relates to which country has jurisdiction to rule on a contract if your counterparty happens to default. Unfavourable contract law in the host country of your counterparty can end up determining that the contract is invalid or illegal, and you can lose your position. Be sure you understand from whom you're buying and under which country's laws any disputes will be settled. Be certain you understand contract law in the country of the counterparty with whom you're trading.

✦ **Holiday risk:** This variety relates to the possibility that the country in whose currency you're trading has different religious, political, or government holidays that can shut down trading in that currency right when you need the money. Be sure you know the holiday schedules for the countries in whose currencies you trade.

Seeking risk protection

Although trading in foreign currencies often is called the modern-day Wild West, forces are in place that can help you minimize the risks — provided you take advantage of them and trade within their boundaries. The primary monitors of foreign currency trading are the world's central banks. They monitor the flow of money between countries and the balance of payments between governments and banking institutions. Regulatory authorities exist in most major currency markets, but if you decide to do business with a non-banking institution you're transacting your business in unprotected waters outside the safe harbour of regulatory oversight and must do so under the often fateful guise of caveat emptor — let the buyer beware.

Internationally, the Bank for International Settlement (BIS; www.bis.org) is the leading independent agency for evaluating foreign exchange trading institutions on a global basis. BIS created risk-weighted evaluation and capital requirements for institutions that trade in foreign currencies and money market transactions. Be certain that any institution with which you plan to conduct trades meets BIS standards.

A number of common clearing systems assist with the transfer of foreign currencies. The two best-known ones are the Clearing House Interbank Payments System, or CHIPS, and the Society for Worldwide Interbank Financial Telecommunication, or SWIFT. Be sure you're using one of these systems when you trade, because they code transactions to avoid defaults and help you identify the creditworthiness of transactions.

If you're trading in foreign currency futures your risks are much less, because the futures industry is highly regulated. Clearinghouses for futures are efficient, and futures transactions usually are cleared hourly or in some cases even minute-by-minute.

Book V

Delving into Day Trading

The 5th Wave — By Rich Tennant

"She had a great first week day trading. We're hoping for another so she can buy the matching desk."

Contents at a Glance

Chapter 1: Making a Day Trade of It

In This Chapter

- ✔ Understanding what day trading is
- ✔ Treating day trading as a business
- ✔ Delving into day trading basics
- ✔ Recognizing types of securities and knowing how to trade them
- ✔ Differentiating among investing, trading, and gambling

What Is Day Trading?

A number of market-savvy Canadians aren't content with just investing in GICs, bonds, and stocks for the long term. They want to see immediate returns. Those who act on this desire are called active or day traders — by definition they usually hold securities for no more than 24 hours, though some hang on to their investments for a few weeks or months.

Day trading is not for the faint of heart. You're watching tiny movements in the markets and using complicated charts and strategies to help make buying and selling decisions. Often, you get the same shot of adrenaline trading as you do gambling — in fact, many say trading is no different than putting all your dough on black. Although it's true that you're trying to make money off the markets, trading is not investing. To put it simply: investing is long-term, trading is short-term.

Still, people do exist who have built significant wealth making daily trades. The next five chapters delve into the world of day trading. We explain how you can trade with less risk of losing your shirt and offer some strategies that traders around the world employ.

Day Trading Is Work. . .A Lot of Work

Day trading is sometimes presented as a profitable hobby. Anyone who buys a day trading DVD course via infomercial can make money easily in just a few hours a week, right? Well, no. Day trading is a job. It can be a full-time job or a part-time job, but it requires the same commitment to working regular hours and the same dedication to learning a craft and honing skills as any other job.

The best traders have plans for their business and for their trades. They know in advance how they want to trade and what they expect to do when they face the market. They may find themselves deviating from their plans at times, due to luck or circumstance or changing markets, but in those cases at least they understand why they are trying something else.

Failing to plan is planning to fail. And if you can't remember that right now, don't worry. We repeat it several times.

Here's another reason for planning: Trading comes in many flavours, and many of those who call themselves day traders are actually doing other things with their money. If you know in advance what you want to do, you'll be less likely to panic or follow fads. You'll be in a better position to take advantage of opportunities in a way that suits your personality, trading skills, and goals. And that's why much of this chapter is devoted to planning.

Planning Your Trading Business

The day trader is an entrepreneur who has started a small business that trades in securities in hopes of making a return. You'll get your business off to a good start if you have a plan for what you want to do and how you're going to do it. That way, you know what your goals are and what you need to do to achieve them.

You can find a lot of sample business plans in books and on the Internet, but most of them are not appropriate for a trader. A typical business plan is designed not only to guide the business, but also to attract outside financing. Unless you're going to take in partners or borrow money from an outside source, your day trading business plan is for you only. No executive summary and no pages of projections needed.

So what do you need instead? How about a list of your goals and a plan for what you will trade, what your hours will be, what equipment you'll need, and how much to invest in the business?

Setting your goals

The first thing you need in your plan is a list of your goals, both short term and long term. Here is a sample list to get you started:

✦ Where do you want to be in the next three months, six months, nine months, a year, three years, five years, and ten years?

✦ How many days a year do you want to trade?

✦ What do you need to know to trade better?

✦ How much do you want to make?

✦ What will you do with your profits?

✦ How will you reward yourself when you hit your goals?

Be as specific as possible when you think about what you want to do with your trading business, and don't worry if your business goals overlap with your personal goals. When you're in business for yourself, the two often mix.

You might be tempted to say, "I want to make as much money as I possibly can," and forget the rest, but that's not a goal that's quantifiable. If you don't know that you've reached your goal, how can you go on to set new ones? And if you don't meet your goal, how will you know how to make changes?

Picking the markets

There are so many different securities and derivatives that you can day trade! Sure, you want to trade anything that makes money for you, but what on Earth is that? Each market has its own nuances, so if you flit from futures to forex (foreign exchange), you might be courting disaster. That's another reason why you need a plan. If you know what markets you want to trade, you'll have a better sense of what research services you'll need, what ongoing training you might want to consider, and how to evaluate your performance.

Later on in this chapter we cover different asset classes. For now, Table 1–1 gives a little cheat sheet that covers those that are most popular with day traders. Think about your chosen markets in the same way: What do you want to trade, where will you trade it, what is the risk and return, and what are some of the characteristics that make this market attractive to you?

And what do zero sum, leverage, and upward bias mean? Well, *zero sum* means that for every winner, there is a loser. No net gain exists in the market. *Leverage* is the use of borrowed money, which increases potential return and also increases risk. *Upward bias* means that in the long run, the market is expected to increase in price, but that doesn't mean it will go up on any given day that you are trading.

Table 1–1		Popular Things for Day Traders to Trade	
Item	*Exchange*	*Risk/Reward*	*Characteristics*
Stock index futures	MX, CME	Zero sum/ leverage	Benefits from movements of broad markets
Treasury bond futures	CBT	Zero sum/ leverage	Best way for day traders to play the bond market
Foreign exchange	OTC	Zero sum/ leverage	Markets open all day, every day, except Sunday
Commodities	CBT, CME	Zero sum/ leverage	An agricultural market liquid enough for day traders
Large-cap stocks	TSX, NYSE	Upward bias	Good stocks for day trading, large and volatile

Key: TSX = Toronto Stock Exchange, MX = Montreal Exchange, CME = Chicago Mercantile Exchange, CBT = Chicago Board of Trade, OTC = Over the counter, NYSE = New York Stock Exchange

The characteristics of the different markets and assets will affect both your business plan and your trading plan. The business plan should include information on what you will trade and why, as well as on what you hope to learn to trade in the future. The trading plan looks at what you want to trade each day and why, so that you can channel your efforts.

Many day traders work in a few different markets, depending on their temperament and trading conditions, but successful traders have narrowed down the few markets where they want to concentrate their efforts. Start slowly, working just one or two different securities, but consider adding new markets as your experience and trading capital grow.

Fixing hours, vacation, and sick leave

The markets are open more or less continuously. Although many exchanges have set trading hours, there are traders working after hours who are willing to sell if you want to buy. Some markets, such as foreign exchange, take only the briefest of breaks over the course of a week. This gives day traders incredible flexibility — no matter what hours and what days are best for you to trade, you can find something that works for you. If you are sharpest in the evenings, you might be better off trading Asian currencies, because those markets are active when you are. Of course, this can be a disadvantage, because no one is setting limits for you. Few markets are great places to trade every hour of every day.

If you want to, you can trade almost all the time. But you probably don't want to. To keep your sanity, maintain your perspective, and have a life outside of your trading, you should set regular hours and stick to them. In your business plan, determine when you're going to trade, how often you're going to take a vacation, how many sick days you'll give yourself, and how you'll know to take a day off. One of the joys of self-employment is that you can take time off when you need to, so give yourself that little perk in your business plan.

Trading is a stressful business. You need to take time off to clear your head, and you'll probably find that working while sick is a sure-fire route to losses. Build in some sick time and vacation time — and read Chapter 3 for more information on how to manage the stress of the markets.

Getting yourself set up

Part of your business plan should cover where you work and what equipment you need. What can you afford now, and what is on your wish list? Do you have enough computing equipment, the right Internet connection, and a working filing system? This is part of your plan for getting your business underway, so put some thought into your infrastructure.

And yes, this is important. You don't want to lose a day of trading because your computer has crashed, nor do you want to be stuck with an open position because your Internet service provider has a temporary outage. And you certainly don't want to lose your concentration because you're trying to work in the family room while other members of your household are playing video games.

Investing in your business

You won't have the time and money to do everything you want to do in your trading business, so part of your business plan should include a list of things that you want to add over time. A key part of that is continuous improvement: No matter how good a trader you are now, you can always be better. Furthermore, the markets are always changing. New products come to market, new trading regulations are passed, and new technologies appear. You will always need to absorb new things, and part of your business plan should consider that. Ask yourself

✦ What percentage of your time and trade gains will go into expanding your knowledge of trading?

✦ Do you want to do that by taking seminars or by allocating the time to simulation testing?

✦ What upgrades will you make to your trading equipment?

✦ How are you going to set yourself up to stay in trading for the long haul?

It takes money to make money — another cliché. It doesn't mean that you should spend money willy-nilly on any nifty gadget or fancy video seminar that comes your way. Instead, it means that an ongoing, thoughtful investment in your trading business will pay off in a greater likelihood of long-run success.

Evaluating and revising your plan

One component of your business plan should be a plan for revising it. Things are going to change. You may be more or less successful than you hope, market conditions may change on you, and you may simply find out more about how you trade best. That's why you should set a plan for updating your business plan to reflect where you are and where you want to be as you go along. At least once a year, and more often if you feel the need for a change, go through your business plan and revise it to reflect where you are now. What are your new goals? What are your new investment plans? What are you doing right, and what needs to change?

Business plans are living documents. Use your plan to run your trading business; as your business runs, use the results to update your plan. You can keep the old ones around to show you how much progress you have made, if you're so inclined.

Planning Your Trades

A good trader has a plan. She knows what she wants to trade and how to trade it. She knows what her limits are before she places the order. She's not afraid to take a loss now in order to prevent a bigger loss in the future, and she's willing to sit out the market if nothing is happening that day. Her plan gives her the discipline to protect her capital so that she has money in her account to profit when the opportunities present themselves.

In this section, we cover the components of trade planning. When you start trading, you'll probably write notes to set up a trading plan for each day that covers what you expect for the day, what trades you hope to make, and what your profit goals and loss limit are. As you develop experience, trade planning may become innate. You develop the discipline to trade according to plan, without needing to write it all down — although you might find it useful to tape a list of the day's expected announcements to your monitor.

Like a business plan, a trading plan is flexible. The markets don't know what you've planned, and you'll probably end up deviating on more than one occasion. The key thing is knowing *why* you deviated: Was it because of the information that you saw when you were looking at your screen, or was it because you became panicky?

What do you want to trade?

The first step in your trading plan should also be addressed in your business plan: What is it that you want to trade? Many traders work in more than one market, and each market is a little different. Some trade different products simultaneously, whereas others choose one for the day and work only on that.

You need to figure out which markets give you the best chance of getting a profit that day. It's going to be different. Some days, no trades will be good for you in one market. If you're too antsy for that, then find another market to keep you busy so that you don't trade just to stay awake. (Of course, many traders report that the big money opportunities are in the slower, less glamorous markets.)

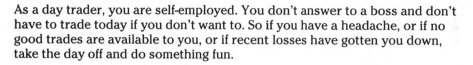

As a day trader, you are self-employed. You don't answer to a boss and don't have to trade today if you don't want to. So if you have a headache, or if no good trades are available to you, or if recent losses have gotten you down, take the day off and do something fun.

How do you want to trade it?

Figuring out how to trade an asset involves a lot of considerations: What is your mood today? What will other traders be reacting to today? How much risk do you want to take? How much money do you want to commit? This is the nitty-gritty stage of trade planning that can help you manage your market day better.

Starting the day with a morning review

Before you start trading, take some time to determine where your head is relative to the market. Is today a day that you can concentrate? Are there things happening in your life that might distract you, are you coming down with the flu, or were you out too late last night? Or are you raring to go, ready to take on whatever the day brings? Your mindset should influence how aggressively you want to trade and how much risk you want to take. You have to pay attention to do well in the markets, but you also have to know when to hang back during the day's activities. For example, many traders find that their strategies work best at certain times of the day, such as at the open or before major news announcements.

Think about what people will be reacting to. Go through the newspapers and check the online newswires to gather information. Then figure out the answers to these questions:

✦ Are there big news announcements scheduled for today? At what time? Do you want to trade ahead of the news or want to wait and see what the market does?

✦ Did something happen overnight? Will that affect trading on the open, or is it already in the markets? Do you want to trade on the open or wait?

✦ What are the other people who trade the same future, commodity, stock, or currency that you do worried about today? How are they likely to respond? Do you want to go with the market or strike a contrary position?

For a handy list of expected news announcements on any given trading day, check out www.tradethenews.com (you'll need to sign up to access their calendar). For Canadian company news, visit CNW Group at www.newswire.ca and review the day's press releases.

Drawing up a sample order

After you have a sense of how you're going to tackle the day, you want to determine how much you're going to trade. The key considerations are the following:

✦ Do you want to be long or short? That is, do you want to bet that the asset you're trading is going up in price or down?

✦ Do you want to borrow money? If so, how much? Borrowing — also known as *margin* or *leverage* — increases your potential return as well as your risk. (We discuss margin and short selling in Chapter 5.)

Some contracts, such as futures, have built-in leverage. As soon as you decide to trade them, you are borrowing money.

✦ How much money do you want to trade — in dollars, and as a percentage of your total account size?

After you have those items detailed, you're in good shape to get started for the day.

Figuring out when to buy and when to sell

After you get insight into what the day might be like and how much money you want to allocate to the markets, your next step is to figure out when you will buy and when you will sell.

The very best traders aren't selling trading advice; they're already retired. Everyone else is figuring it out as they go along, with varying degrees of success.

Many traders rely on *technical analysis,* which involves looking at patterns in charts of the price and volume changes. We discuss technical analysis in Chapter 4. Other traders look at news and price information as the market changes, rather than looking at price patterns, and that's discussed in Chapter 4 too. Still others care only about very short-term price discrepancies, covered in Chapter 5. But the most important thing, no matter what approach you prefer, is that you *backtest* and simulate your trading before you commit real dollars. That way, you have a better sense of how you'll react in real market conditions.

Setting profit goals

When you trade, you want to have a realistic idea how much money you can make. What's a fair profit? Do you want to ride a winning position until the end of the day or do you want to get out quickly when you've made enough money to compensate for your risk? No one answer to this question exists, because so much depends on market conditions and your trading style. In this section we give some guidelines that can help you determine what's best for you.

But first, we take a detour and define all the different terms for profits that you might come across.

The language of money

Profits are discussed differently in different markets, and you may as well have the right lingo when you write your plan:

✦ **Pennies:** Stocks trade in decimal form, so each price movement is worth at least a penny — one cent. It's an obvious way to measure a profit.

✦ **Pips:** A *pip* is the smallest unit of currency that can be traded. In foreign exchange markets (forex), a pip is generally equal to one one-hundredth of a cent. If the value of the euro moves from $1.2934 to $1.2935, it has moved a pip.

Do not confuse a pip in the forex market with an investment scheme known as *PIP*, sometimes called People in Profit or Pure Investor. (The fraud also operates as *HYIP*, for High Yield Investment Program.) PIP has been promoted as a trading system with a guaranteed daily return, but it's really a pyramid scheme that takes money from participants and returns little or nothing. You can get more information from the U.S. Securities and Exchange Commission's website, www.sec.gov/divisions/enforce/primebank.shtml.

✦ **Points:** A *point* is a single percentage. A penny is a point, as is a 1 percent change in a bond price. A related number, a *basis point,* is a percent of a percent, or .0001.

✦ **Teenies:** Many securities, especially bonds and derivatives on them, trade in increments of ⅛ of a dollar. Half of an eighth is a sixteenth, also known as a *teeny*.

✦ **Ticks:** A *tick* is the smallest trading increment in a futures contract. It varies from product to product. How much it works out to be depends on the contract structure. For the S&P/TSX Composite Index Mini Futures (SCF), one tick value equals five index points, and each index point represents $5. That means the tick value is equal to $25. The value of an SCF futures contract is calculated by multiplying the current level of the contract by the tick value. On the Chicago Mercantile Exchange's E-Mini S&P 500 contract a tick is equal to US$12.50, calculated as a 0.25 change in the underlying S&P 500 index multiplied by a US$50 multiplier. A tick on a Chicago Board of Trade E-Mini soybean contract is US$1.25, calculated as ⅛ cent on a bushel of soybeans in a contract covering 1,000 bushels. You can get information on the tick size of contracts that interest you on the website of the offering exchange.

No one ever lost money taking a profit, as the cliché goes. (The trading business is rife with clichés, if you haven't noticed.) The newer you are to day trading, the more sense it makes to be conservative. Close your positions and end your day when you reach a target profit — and then make note of what happens afterward. Can you afford to hold on to your positions longer in order to make a greater profit?

Thinking about profits

Your profit goals can be sliced and diced a few different ways. The first is the *gain per trade,* on both a percentage basis and an absolute basis. The second is the *gain per day,* also on both a percentage basis and an absolute basis. What do you have to do to reach these goals? How many successful trades will you have to make? Do you have the capital to do that? And what is right for the trade you're making right now, regardless of what your longer-term goals are?

Setting limits on your trades

It's a good idea to set a *loss limit* along with a profit goal.

For example, many futures traders have a rule to risk two ticks in pursuit of three ticks. That means they'll sell a position as soon as it loses two ticks in value, and they'll also sell a position as soon as it gains three ticks in value. And for anything in between? Well, they close out their positions at the end of the day, so whatever happens happens.

Even traders who do not have a rule like that often set a limit on how much they will lose per trade. Other traders use computer programs to guide their buys and their sells, so they need to sell their positions automatically. Brokers make this easy by giving customers the choice of a stop order or a limit order to protect their positions.

You want to limit your loss per trade *as well as* your loss per day. If today is not a good one, close up shop, take a break, and come back fresh tomorrow.

Stop orders

A *stop order,* also known as a *stop loss order,* is an order to sell a security at the market price as soon as it hits a predetermined level. If you want to make sure you sell a block of stock when it falls below $30 per share, for example, you could enter a stop order at $30 (telling your broker "Sell Stop 30"). As soon as the stock hits $30 the broker sells it, even if the price goes to $29 or $31 before all the stock is sold.

Limit orders

A *limit order* is an order to buy or sell a security at a specific price or better: lower than the current price for the buy order, higher than the specific price for a sell order. If you want to make sure you sell a block of stock when it reaches $30 per share, for example, you could enter a limit order at $30 (telling your broker "Sell Limit 30"). As soon as the stock hits $30, the broker sells it, as long as the price stays at $30 or higher. If the price goes even a penny below $30, the limit is no longer enforced. After all, no buyers are going to want to pay an above-market price just so you can get your order filled all the way!

Stop limit orders

A *stop limit* order is a combination of a stop order and a limit order. It tells the broker to buy or sell at a specific price or better, but only after the price reaches a given stop price. If you want to make sure you sell a block of stock when it falls below $30 per share, but you do not want to sell it if it starts to go back up, for example, you could enter a stop order at $29 — the price is usually set lower than your stop price — with a limit of $31 (telling your broker "Sell 29 Limit 31"). As soon as the stock hits $29, the broker sells it as long as the price stays under $31. If the price goes above $31, the order is no longer enforced. The price range where this order will be executed is very small. Stop limit orders aren't typically used as a trading strategy, but it can come in handy if there's a sudden drop in the market like we saw with the "flash crash" on May 6, 2010. On that day the market fell, for reasons not fully understood, by 600 points and then minutes later shot back up. A stop limit order may have prevented your stocks from falling.

Are you confused? Well, the differences may be confusing, but understanding them is important to helping you manage your risks. That's why Table 1–2 is a handy breakout of the different types of orders.

Table 1–2		Different Types of Orders	

Buy Orders

	Stop Order	Limit Order	Stop Limit Order
Order instructions	Buy Stop 30	Buy Limit 30	Buy Stop 30 Limit 31
Market Price ($)	**Action after the stock hits $30**		
28.50	Buy	Buy	Buy
29.00	Buy	Buy	Buy
29.50	Buy	Buy	Buy
30.00	Buy	Buy	Buy
30.50	Buy	Nothing	Buy
31.00	Buy	Nothing	Nothing
31.50	Buy	Nothing	Nothing

Sell Orders

	Stop Order	Limit Order	Stop Limit Order
Order Instructions	Sell Stop 30	Sell Limit 30	Sell Stop 30 Limit 29
Market Price ($)	**Action after the stock hits $30**		
28.50	Sell	Nothing	Nothing
29.00	Sell	Nothing	Sell
29.50	Sell	Nothing	Sell
30.00	Sell	Sell	Sell
30.50	Sell	Sell	Sell
31.00	Sell	Sell	Sell
31.50	Sell	Sell	Sell

What if the trade goes wrong?

No matter how in tune you feel with the market, no matter how good your track record, and no matter how disciplined you are with setting stops, stuff is going to happen. Just as you can make more money than you plan to, you can also *lose* a lot more. If you're going to day trade, you have to accept that you'll have some really bad days.

So what do you do? You suck it up, take the loss, and get on with your life.

Yes, the market may have blown past your stops. That happens sometimes, and it's hard to watch real dollars disappear into someone else's account, someone you will never know. Still, close your position and just remember that tomorrow is another day with another chance to do better.

Don't hold in hopes of making up a loss. The market doesn't know what you own, and it won't reward your loyalty and best hopes.

After you take the loss and clear your head, see if you can learn something for next time. Sometimes a loss can teach you valuable lessons that make you a smarter, more disciplined trader in the long run.

Closing Out Your Position

By definition, day traders hold their investment positions only for a single day. This is important for a few reasons:

✦ Closing out daily reduces your risk of something happening overnight.

✦ Margin rates — the interest rates paid on money borrowed for trading — are low and in some cases zero for day traders, but the rates go up on overnight balances.

✦ It's good trade discipline that can keep you from making expensive mistakes.

But like all rules, the single-day rule can be broken and probably should be broken sometimes. In this section, we cover a few longer-term trading strategies you may want to add to your trading business on occasion.

Swing trading: Holding for days

Swing trading involves holding a position for several days. Some swing traders hold overnight, whereas others hold for days or even months. The longer time period gives more time for a position to work out, which is especially important if it is based on news events or if it requires taking a position contrary to the current market sentiment. Although swing trading gives traders more options for making a profit, it carries some risks because the position could turn against you while you're away from the markets.

A tradeoff always exists between risk and return. When you take more risk, you do so in the hopes of getting a greater return. But when you look for a way to increase return, remember that you will have to take on more risk to do it.

Swing trading requires paying attention to some basic fundamentals and news flow. (We discuss fundamental research in Chapter 4.) It's also a good choice for people who have the discipline to go to bed at night instead of waiting up and watching their position in hopes that nothing goes wrong.

Position trading: Holding for weeks

A *position trader* holds a stake in a stock or a commodity for several weeks and possibly even for months. This person is attracted to the short-term price opportunities, but he also believes that he can make more money holding the stake for a long enough period of time to see business fundamentals play out. This increases the risk and the potential return, because a lot more can happen over months than minutes.

Maxims and Clichés That Guide and Mislead Traders

In this section, we cover a few of the many maxims traders use to think about their trading, such as

✦ The stock doesn't know you own it.

✦ Failing to plan is planning to fail.

✦ Your first loss is your best loss.

You'll hear a lot more out there.

Clichés are useful shorthand for important rules that can help you plan your trading. But they can also mislead you because some are really obvious — too obvious to act on effectively. (Yes, everyone knows that you make money by buying low and selling high, but how do you tell what low is and high is?) Here's a run-through of some you'll come across in your trading career, along with our take on what they mean.

Pigs get fat, hogs get slaughtered

Trading is pure capitalism, and people do it for one primary reason: to make money. Sure, a ton of economic benefits come from having well-functioning capital markets, such as better price prediction, risk management, and capital formation. But a day trader just wants to make money.

However, get too greedy and you're likely to get stupid. You start taking too much risk, deviating too much from your strategy, and getting careless about dealing with your losses. Good traders know when it's time to take a profit and move on to the next trade.

This is also a good example of an obvious but tough-to-follow maxim. When are you crossing from being a happy little piggy to a big fat greedy hog that's about to be turned into a pork belly? Just know that if you're deviating from your trading plan because things are going so great, you might be headed for some trouble.

In a bear market, the money returns to its rightful owners

A *bull* market is one that charges ahead; a *bear* market is one that does poorly. Many people think they're trading geniuses because they make money when the entire market is going up. It was easy to make money day trading just about any stock in 2009, when the market recovered from near economic collapse, but it wasn't so easy the year before when the frighteningly out-of-control financial crisis began. It's when the markets turn negative that those people who really understand trading and who know how to manage risk will be able to stay in until things get better, possibly even making nice profits along the way.

The corollary cliché for this is, "Don't confuse brains with a bull market." When things are going well, watch out for overconfidence. It might be time to update your business and trading plans, but it's not time to cast them aside.

The trend is your friend

When you day trade, you need to make money fast. You don't have the luxury of waiting for your unique, contrary theory to play out. An investor may be buying a stock in the hopes of holding it for decades, but a trader needs things to work now.

Given the short-term nature of the market, the short-term sentiment is going to trump long-term fundamentals. People trading today may be wrong about the direction of foreign exchange, interest rates, or share prices, but if you're closing out your positions tonight, you need to work with the information in the market *today*.

In the short run, traders who fight the market lose money.

Two problems exist with *The trend is your friend*. The first is that by the time you identify a trend, it may be over. Second, there are times when it makes sense to go against the herd, because you can collect when everyone else realizes their mistakes. This is where the psychology of trading comes into play. Are you a good enough judge of human behaviour to know when the trend is right and when it's not?

Buy the rumour, sell the news

Markets react to information. That's ultimately what drives supply and demand. Although the market tends to react quickly to information, it can overreact, too. Lots of gossip gets traded in the markets as everyone looks to get the information they need in order to gain an advantage in the markets. And despite such things as confidentiality agreements and insider-trading laws, many rumours turn out to be true.

These rumours are often attached to such news events as corporate earnings. For whatever reason — good news, analyst research, a popular product — traders might believe that the company will report good quarterly earnings per share. That's the rumour. If you buy on the rumour, you can take advantage of the price appreciation as the story gets more play.

When the earnings are actually announced, one of two things will happen:

✦ They will be as good as or better than rumoured, and the price will go up. The trader can sell into that and make a profit.

✦ They will be worse than rumoured, everyone will sell on the bad news, and the trader will want to sell to get out of the loss.

Of course, if the rumour is *bad,* you want to do the opposite: sell on the rumour, and buy on the news. For more information on *short selling* — selling securities in hopes that they fall in price — turn to Chapter 5.

The problem with *Buy the rumour, sell the news* is that rumours are often wrong, and there may be more opportunities to buy on bad news when other traders are panicking, thus driving prices down for a few minutes before sanity sets in. But it's one of those rules that everyone talks about, whether or not they actually follow it.

Cut your losses and ride your winners

We mention in this chapter that you need to cut your losses before they drag you down. No matter how much it hurts and no matter how much you believe you're right, you need to close out a losing position and move on.

But the opposite is not necessarily true. Although good traders tend to be disciplined about selling winning positions, they don't use stops and limits as rigorously on the upside as they might on the downside. They're likely to stick with a profit and see how high it goes before closing out a position.

Note that this conflicts a little with *Pigs get fat, hogs get slaughtered.* (Trading maxims can be so contradictory!) To prevent overconfidence and sloppiness from greed, ride your winners *within reason.* If your general discipline is to risk three ticks on a futures contract in order to make five, and a contract goes up six ticks before you can close it out, you might want to stick with it. But if you also close out at the end of every day, don't give in to the temptation of keeping that position open just because it's still going up. Keep to your overall discipline.

You're only as good as your last trade

The markets churn on every day with little regard for why everyone trading right now is there. Prices go up and down to match the supply and the demand at any given moment, which may have nothing to do with the actual long-term worth of an item being traded. And it certainly has nothing to do with how much you really, really want the trade to work out.

One of the biggest enemies of good traders is overconfidence. Especially after a nice run of winning trades, a trader can get caught up in the euphoria and believe that he finally has the secret to successful trading under control. While he's checking the real estate listings for that beachfront estate in Maui, BAM! The next trade is a disaster.

Does that mean that the trader is a disaster, too? No, it just means that the markets won this time around.

Most day traders are working in zero-sum markets, which means that for every winner there is a loser. Hence, not everyone can make money every day. The challenge is to maintain an even keel so as not to be distracted by confidence when the trading is going well or by fear when the trading is going poorly. The next trade is a new trade.

What Makes a Good Day Trading Asset?

In academic terms, the universe of investable assets includes just about anything you can buy at one price and sell at another, potentially higher price. That means artwork and collectibles, real estate, and private companies would all be considered to be investable assets.

Day traders have a much smaller group of assets to work with. It's not realistic to expect a quick one-day profit on price changes in real estate. Online auctions for collectible items take place over days, not minutes. If you're going to day trade, you want to find assets that trade easily, several times a day, in recognized markets. In other words, you want *liquidity*. As an individual trading your own account, you want assets that can be purchased with relatively low capital commitments. And finally, you may want to use *leverage* — borrowed money — to improve your return (discussed in more detail in Chapter 5), so you want to look for assets that can be purchased using other people's money.

Liquidity

Liquidity is the ability to buy or sell an asset in large quantity without affecting the price levels. Day traders look for *liquid assets* so they can move in and out of the market quickly without disrupting price levels. Otherwise, they may not be able to buy at a good price or sell when they want.

At the most basic level, financial markets are driven by supply and demand. The more of an asset supplied in the market, the lower the price; the more of an asset that people demand, the higher the price. In a perfect market, the amount of supply and demand is matched so that prices don't change. This happens if a high volume of people are trading, so that their supply and demand is constantly matched, or if a very low frequency of trades are happening, so that the price never changes.

You may be thinking, Wait, don't I want big price changes so that I can make money quickly? Yes, you want price changes in the market, but you don't want to be the one causing them. The less liquid a market is, the more likely your buying and selling is going to affect market prices, and the smaller your profit will be.

Volume

Volume is the total amount of a security that trades in a given time period. The greater the volume, the more buyers and sellers are interested in the security, and the easier it is to get in there and buy and sell without affecting the price.

Day traders also look at the relationship between volume and price. This is an important technical indicator, discussed in more detail in Chapter 4. The simple version is this:

✦ High volume with no change in price levels means an equal match between buyers and sellers.

✦ High volume with rising prices means more buyers than sellers, so the price will continue going up.

✦ High volume with falling prices means more sellers than buyers, so the price will keep going down.

Frequency

Another measure of liquidity is *frequency*, or how often a security trades. Some assets, like stock market futures, trade constantly, from the moment the market opens until the very last trade of the day, and then continue into overnight trading. Others, like agricultural commodities, trade only during market hours or only during certain times of the year. Other securities, like stocks, trade frequently, but the volume rises and falls at regular intervals related to such things as *options expiration* (the date at which options on the stock expire).

The more frequently a security trades, the more opportunities you'll have to identify the short-term profit opportunities that make day trading possible.

Volatility, standard deviation, and variance

The *volatility* of a security is how much the price varies over a period of time. It tells you how much prices fluctuate and thus how likely you are to be able to take advantage of that. For example, if a security has an average price of $5 but trades anywhere between $1 and $14, it will be more volatile than one with an average price of $5 that trades between $4 and $6.

One standard measure of volatility and risk is *standard deviation,* which is how much any given price quote varies from a security's average price. The math is shown below (we're sure you're dying to see it), but you can calculate it with most spreadsheet programs and many trading platforms. N is the number of price quotes, x_i is any one price quote, and the funky "X" with the line over it is the average of all the prices over time.

$$\sigma = \sqrt{\frac{1}{N}\sum_{i=1}^{N}\left(x_i - \bar{x}\right)^2}$$

For each of the prices, you calculate the difference between it and the average value. So if the average price is $5, and the closing price today is $8, the difference would be $3. (More likely, the research service that you use would calculate the difference for you; read more about research services in Chapter 7 of *Day Trading For Canadians For Dummies,* published by Wiley.)

After you have all the differences between the prices and the average, you find the square of these differences. If the difference for one day's price is $8, then the square would be $64. You add up all the squared differences over the period of time that you're looking at and then find the average of them. That number is called the *variance,* or σ^2. Finally, calculate the square root of the variance, and you have the standard deviation.

The higher the standard deviation, the higher the volatility; the higher the volatility, the more a security's price is going to fluctuate, and the more profit — and loss — opportunities exist for a day trader.

Standard deviation is also a measure of risk that can be used to evaluate your trading performance; we discuss that use of the measure in Chapter 11 in the full *Day Trading For Canadians For Dummies* book.

Capital requirements

You don't necessarily need a lot of money to begin day trading, but you do need a lot of money to buy certain securities. Stocks generally trade in *round lots,* which are orders of at least 100 shares. If you want to buy a stock worth $40 per share, you need $4,000 in your account. Your broker will probably let you borrow half of that money, but you still need to come up with the other $2,000.

Options and futures trade by contract, and one contract represents some unit of the underlying security. For example, in the options market, one contract is good for 100 shares of the stock. These contracts also trade in round lots of 100 contracts per order.

No one will stop you from buying a smaller amount than the usual round lot in any given security, but you'll probably pay a high commission and get worse execution for your order. Because the returns on each trade tend to be small anyway, don't take up day trading until you have enough money to trade your target asset effectively. Otherwise, you'll pay too much to your broker without getting much for yourself.

Bonds do not trade in fractional amounts; they trade on a per-bond basis, and each bond has a face value of $1,000. Some trade for more or less than that, depending on how the bond's interest rate differs from the market rate of interest, but the $1,000 is a good number to keep in mind when thinking about capital requirements. Many dealers have a minimum order of 10 bonds, though, so a minimum order would be $10,000.

Marginability

Most day traders make money through a large volume of small profits. One way to increase the profit per trade is to use borrowed money in order to buy more shares, more contracts, or more bonds. *Margin* is money in your account that you borrow against, and almost all brokers will be happy to arrange a margin loan for you, especially if you're going to use the money to make more trades and generate more commissions for the brokerage firm. In Chapter 5, we discuss how margin is used within an investment strategy. Here, though, you want to think about how margin affects your choice of assets for day trading.

Generally, a stock or bond account must hold 50 percent of the purchase price of securities when you borrow the money. So if you want to buy $100 worth of something on margin, you need to have $50 in your account. The price of those securities can go down, but if they go down so much that the account now holds only 30 percent of the value of the loan, you'll get a margin call.

In Canada, margin requirements for each security are set by the Canadian regulators, though brokerage firms sometimes set their own, higher amounts. No rules limit the maximum amount of money you can borrow, but the brokerage firms will lose a lot of money if you don't pay them back. That's why they may set a limit on the loan. Each firm has its own rules, so check with your broker on how they set their margin requirements.

You probably think that the 1929 crash was responsible for the Great Depression of the 1930s, right? Think again. Most economic historians believe that the crash was a distraction. Instead, the real problem was that interest rates fell so rapidly that banks refused to lend money, while prices fell so low that companies had no incentive to produce. It's a situation known as *deflation,* and it's relatively rare, but it is devastating when it occurs.

Most stocks and bonds are marginable (able to be purchased on margin), and IIROC allows traders to borrow up to 70 percent — you have to put at least 30 percent down — of their value. But not all securities are marginable. Stocks priced below $5 per share, those traded on America's OTC Bulletin Board or Pink Sheets, and those in newly public companies often cannot be borrowed against or purchased on margin. Your brokerage firm should have a list of securities that are not eligible for margin.

If leverage is going to be part of your day trading strategy, be sure the assets you plan to trade are marginable.

Securities and How They Trade

In the financial markets people buy and sell securities every day, but just what are they buying or selling? *Securities* are financial instruments. In the olden days, they were pieces of paper, but now they are electronic entries that represent a legal claim on some type of underlying asset. This asset may be a business, if the security is a stock, or it may be a loan to a government or a corporation, if the security is a bond. In this section, we cover different types of securities that day traders are likely to run across and tell you what you need to jump into the fray.

In practice, *asset* and *security* are synonyms, and *derivative* is considered to be a type of asset or security. But to be precise, these three are not the same:

✦ An asset is a physical item. Examples include most companies, a house, or gold bullion.

✦ A security is a contract that gives someone the right of ownership of the asset, such as a share of stock, a bond, a promissory note, a loan.

✦ A derivative is a contract that draws its value from the price of a security.

Stocks

A *stock,* also called an *equity,* is a security that represents a fractional interest in the ownership of a company. Buy one share of Microsoft, and you're an owner of the company, just as Bill Gates is. He may own a much larger share of the total business, but you both have a stake in it. Shareholders elect a board of directors to represent their interests in how the company is managed. Each share is a vote, so good luck getting Bill Gates kicked off Microsoft's board.

A share of stock has *limited liability*. That means you can lose all your investment, but no more than that. If the company files for bankruptcy, the creditors cannot come after the shareholders for the money they are owed.

Some companies pay their shareholders a dividend, which is a cash payment usually made out of firm profits. Because day traders hold stock for really short periods of time, they don't normally collect dividends.

How stocks trade

Stocks are priced based on a single share, and most brokerage firms charge commissions on a per-share basis. Despite this per-share pricing, stocks are almost always traded in round lots of 100 shares. The supply and demand for a given stock is driven by the company's expected performance.

A stock's price is quoted with a *bid* and an *ask*.

✦ The bid is the price at which other buyers will buy the stock from you if you're selling.

✦ The ask is the price at which other sellers will to sell you if you're the one buying.

Bid ask prices on Canadian exchanges are a centralized quote — they represent the best bid and ask prices from all participants on the market. In the U.S. it's the broker who sets the bid ask price — and often profits off the spread — but in Canada quotes are posted for everyone to see regardless of broker.

Here's an example of a price quote:

```
MSFT $27.70 $27.71
```

That's a quote for Microsoft (ticker symbol: MSFT on the Nasdaq). The bid is listed first: $27.70; the ask is $27.71. That's the smallest spread you'll ever see! The spread here is so small because Microsoft is a liquid stock, and no big news events at the moment might change the balance of buyers and sellers.

If your American trading buddy is talking about how his broker takes a cut of the spread, don't panic and wonder why you haven't noticed those same fees. In Canada brokers make money off commission — it's unlikely they're taking a percentage of the spread.

We tend to use the words *broker* and *dealer* interchangeably, but a difference does exist. A broker simply matches buyers and sellers of securities, whereas a dealer buys and sells securities out of its own account. Almost all brokerage firms are both brokers and dealers.

Bonds

A *bond* is a loan. The bond buyer gives the bond issuer money. The bond issuer promises to pay interest on a regular basis. The regular coupon payments are why bonds are often called *fixed income investments.* Bond issuers repay the money borrowed — the principal — on a predetermined date, known as the *maturity.* Bonds generally have a maturity of more than ten years; shorter-term bonds are usually referred to as *notes,* and bonds that will mature within a year of issuance are usually referred to as *bills.* Most bonds in North America are issued by corporations (corporate bonds) or by the federal and provincial governments (called government bonds in Canada and Treasury bonds in the States). Some local governments in the U.S. also issue municipal bonds, but that's much less common in Canada.

The interest payments on a bond are called *coupons.* You've probably seen "car for sale" or "apartment for rent" signs with little slips of paper carrying a phone number or e-mail address cut into the bottom. If you're interested in the car or the apartment, you can rip off the slip and contact the advertiser later. Bonds used to look the same. The bond buyer would receive one large certificate good for the principal, with a lot of smaller certificates, called coupons, attached. When a payment was due, the owner would cut off the matching coupon and deposit it in the bank. (Some old novels refer to rich people as "coupon clippers," meaning that their sole labour in life was to cut out their bond coupons and cash them in. Nowadays, bond payments are handled electronically, so the modern coupon clipper is a bargain hunter looking for an extra 50 cents off a jar of peanut butter.)

Over the years, enterprising financiers realized that some investors needed regular payments, but others wanted to receive a single sum at a future date. So they separated the coupons from the principal. The principal payment, known as a *zero-coupon bond,* is sold to one investor, while the coupons, called *strips,* are sold to another investor. The borrower makes the payments just like with a regular bond. (Regular bonds, by the way, are sometimes called *plain vanilla.*)

The borrower who wants to make a series of payments with no lump-sum principal repayment would issue an *amortizing* bond to return principal and interest on a regular basis. If you think about a typical mortgage, the borrower makes a regular payment of both principal and interest. This way, the amount owed gets smaller over time so that the borrower does not have to come up with a large principal repayment at maturity.

Other borrowers would prefer to make a single payment at maturity, so they issue *discount bonds.* The purchase price is the principal reduced by the amount of interest that otherwise would be paid.

If a company goes bankrupt, the bondholders get paid before the shareholders. In some bankruptcies, the bondholders take over the business, leaving the current shareholders with nothing.

How bonds trade

Bonds often trade as single bonds, with a face value of $1,000, although some brokers will only take on minimum orders of ten bonds. They don't trade as frequently as stocks do because most bond investors are looking for steady income, so they hold their bonds until maturity. Bonds have less risk than stocks, so they show less price volatility. The value of a bond is mostly determined by the level of interest rates in the economy. As rates go up, bond prices go down; when rates go down, bond prices go up. Bond prices are also affected by how likely the loan is to be repaid. If traders don't think that the bond issuer will pay up, then the bond price will fall.

Generally speaking, only corporate (and municipal in the U.S.) bonds have repayment risk. It's possible that the U.S. government could default, but that's unlikely as long as it can print money. Most international government bonds have similarly low default risk, but some countries *have* defaulted — and there are some that, thanks to the financial crisis, are on the verge of default. The most notable default was Russia, which refused to print money to repay its debts in the summer of 1998. This caused huge turmoil in the world's financial markets, including the collapse of a major hedge fund, Long-Term Capital Management.

The global financial crisis also put many countries at risk, especially in Europe. In 2010 fears spread that Greece would default on its loans after Standard & Poor's — a U.S.-based company that rates borrowers — downgraded the country's debt rating to junk bond status. That sent stock markets plunging and spread fear that other financially strapped European countries, like Spain and Portugal, would default too. So, as you can see, just because a bond is issued by a government doesn't mean your investment is guaranteed.

In the past, investment banks and governments would sell new bonds directly to institutional investors, like pension plans or mutual funds. Now, anyone can buy bonds — but because they are usually purchased in large quantities, it's possible that a retail investor would buy a few bonds to complement her stocks. Traders, though, have more access to the bond market thanks to their broker. The broker will buy hundreds of thousands of dollars in bonds (or much more) and then sell them piecemeal to traders. Most bonds trade over-the-counter, meaning dealers trade them among themselves rather than on an organized exchange.

A bond price quote looks like this:

```
3 3/4 Mar 12 n 99:28 99:29
```

This is a U.S. Treasury note maturing in March 2012 carrying an interest rate of 3.75 percent. Similar to stocks, the numbers right after the "n" (for *note*) list the bid and ask. The first number is the bid, and it's the price at which the dealer will buy the bond from you if you're selling. The second number is the ask, and it's the price the dealer will charge you if you're buying. The difference is the spread, and that's the dealer's profit.

But wait, there's more: corporate bonds trade in eighths of a percentage point, and government bonds trade in 32nds. The bid of 99:28 means that the bond's bid price is 99 $\frac{28}{32}$ percent of the face value of $1,000, or $998.75.

Why on Earth do bonds trade in eighths or fractions of eighths? Do traders just like to show off their math skills? No, it goes back to before the American Revolution. The dominant currency in most of the Americas then was the Spanish doubloon, a large gold coin that could be cut into fractions to make trade easier. Like a pie, it would be cut into eight equal pieces, so prices throughout the colonies were often set in eighths. (In Robert Louis Stevenson's book *Treasure Island,* the parrot keeps squawking "Pieces of eight! Pieces of eight!" This is why.)

The fractional pricing convention carried over to North American securities markets, and has persisted because it guarantees dealers a bigger spread than pricing in decimals. After all, $\frac{1}{32}$ of a dollar is more than $\frac{1}{100}$. U.S. and Canadian stocks were priced in sixteenths until 2001. You'll notice a difference between the U.S. and Canadian bond markets though. If you're purchasing an American bond it will be priced using the old convention, but buy a Canadian bond and you'll be dealing in decimals.

Most bonds are not suitable for day traders. Only government bonds have enough consistent trading volume to attract a day trader. Because of the capital required to trade and the relatively low liquidity of many types of bonds, many traders prefer to use *futures* to bet on interest rates. We discuss futures later in this chapter.

Exchange-traded funds (ETFs)

Exchange-traded funds are a cross between mutual funds and stocks, and they offer a great way for day traders to get exposure to market segments that might otherwise be difficult to trade. A money management firm buys a group of assets — stocks, bonds, or others — and then lists shares that trade on the market. (One of the largest organizers of exchange-traded funds is iShares, www.ishares.com.) In most cases, the purchased assets are designed to mimic the performance of an index, and investors know what those assets are before they purchase shares in the fund.

Exchange-traded funds are available on the big market indexes, like the S&P/TSX Composite Index, the S&P/TSX 60, the S&P 500, and the Dow Jones Industrial Average. They are available in a variety of domestic bond indexes, international stock indexes, foreign currencies, and commodities.

How exchange-traded funds trade

For day traders, the advantage of exchange-traded funds is that they can be bought and sold just like stocks. Customers place orders, usually in round lots, through their brokerage firms. The price quotes come in decimals and include a spread for the dealer.

Cash and currency

Cash is king, as they say. It's money that's readily available in your day trading account to buy more securities. For the most part, the interest rate on cash is very low, but if you're closing out your positions every night, you'll always have a cash balance in your brokerage account. The firm will probably pay you a little interest on it, so it will contribute to your total return.

For day traders, money market accounts are boring. Instead, of seeking a reliable return, traders find more excitement in trading cash as foreign currency. Every day, trillions (yes, that's trillions with a *t*) of dollars are exchanged, creating opportunities to make money as the exchange rates change. Currency is a bigger, more liquid market than the U.S. stock and bond markets combined. It's often referred to as the *forex* market, short for *foreign exchange*.

How currency trades

The exchange rate is the price of money. It tells you how many dollars it takes to buy yen, pounds, or euros. The price that people are willing to pay for a currency depends on the investment opportunities, business opportunities, and perceived safety in each nation. If American businesses see great opportunities in Thailand, for example, they'll have to trade their dollars for baht in order to pay rent, buy supplies, and hire workers there. This will increase the demand for baht relative to the dollar, and it will cause the baht to go up in price relative to the dollar.

Exchange rates are quoted on a bid-ask basis, just as are bonds and stocks. A quote might look like this:

CADJPY 78.47 78.50

This is the exchange rate for converting the Canadian dollar into Japanese yen. The bid price of 78.47 is the amount of yen that a dealer would give you if you wanted to sell a dollar and buy yen. The ask price of 78.50 is the amount of yen the dealer would charge you if you wanted to buy a dollar and sell yen. The difference is the dealer's profit, and perhaps, you'll be charged a commission, too.

Note that with currency, you're a buyer and a seller at the same time. This can increase the profit opportunities, but it can also increase your risk.

Day traders can trade currencies directly at current exchange rates, which is known as *trading in the spot market*. They can also use currency exchange traded funds or currency futures to profit from the changing prices of money.

How the Canadian dollar is traded

The most common currency transaction is the euro against the U.S. dollar, mainly because Europe is one of the largest trading blocs in the world and a lot of business is done between those two countries. But Canadians often trade the loonie against the greenback for two reasons: America's our biggest trading partner, and it's just what we know. You can, of course, trade the Canadian dollar against any other currency too.

Beginners may want to stick to the Canada–U.S. relationship, simply because most news outlets in the Great White North report on currency fluctuations relative to the American buck. Understanding how to trade the loonie against the yen takes a bit more work.

Commodities and How They Trade

Commodities are basic, interchangeable goods sold in bulk and used to make other goods. Examples include oil, gold, wheat, and lumber. Commodities are popular with investors as a hedge against inflation and uncertainty. Stock prices can go to zero, but people still need to eat! Although commodity prices usually tend to increase at the same rate as in the overall economy, so they maintain their real (inflation-adjusted) value, they can also be susceptible to short-term changes in supply and demand. A cold winter increases demand for oil, a dry summer reduces production of wheat, and a civil war could disrupt access to platinum mines.

Day traders aren't going to buy commodities outright — if you really want to haul bushels of grain around all day, you can do that without taking on the risks of day trading. (You'd get more exercise, too.) Instead, day traders who want to play with commodities can look to other investments. The most popular way is to buy futures contracts, which change in price with the underlying commodity. Increasingly, many trade commodities through exchange-traded funds that are based on the value of an underlying basket of commodities.

Derivatives and How They Trade

Derivatives are financial contracts that draw their value from the value of an underlying asset, security, or index. For example, an S&P/TSX 60 futures contract would give the buyer a cash payment based on the price of the S&P/TSX 60 index on the day that the contract expires. The contract's value thus depends on where the index is trading. You're trading not the index itself, but rather a contract with a value derived from the price of the index. The index value changes all the time, so day traders have lots of opportunities to buy and sell.

Types of derivatives

Day traders are likely to come across three types of derivatives. Options and futures trade on dedicated derivatives exchanges, whereas warrants trade on stock exchanges.

Options

An *option* is a contract that gives the holder the right, but not the obligation, to buy or sell the underlying asset at an agreed-upon price at an agreed-upon date in the future. An option that gives you the right to buy is a *call,* and one that gives you the right to sell is a *put.* A call is most valuable if the stock price is going up, whereas a put has more value if the stock price is going down.

Here's one way to remember the difference: you *call up* your friend to *put down* your enemy.

For example, a RIM 2011 Mar 22.50 call gives you the right to buy Research in Motion at $22.50 per share at the expiration date on the third Friday in March, 2011. (Did you know that Research in Motion gave the world the Blackberry? Clever, huh?) If RIM is trading above $22.50, you can exercise the option and make a quick profit. If it's selling below $22.50 you could buy the stock cheaper in the open market, so the option would be worthless.

You can find great information on options, including online tutorials, on the Montreal Exchange's website, www.m-x.ca. For an American perspective visit the Chicago Board Options Exchange's website, www.cboe.com.

Futures

A *futures* contract gives one the obligation to buy a set quantity of the underlying asset at a set price and a set future date. These started in the agricultural industry because they allowed farmers and food processors to lock in their prices early in the growing season, reducing the amount of uncertainty in their businesses. Futures have now been applied to many different assets, ranging from pork bellies (which really do trade — they are used to make bacon) to currency values. A simple example is a locked-in home mortgage rate; the borrower knows the rate that will be applied before the sale is closed and the loan is finalized. Day traders use futures to trade commodities without having to handle the actual assets.

Most futures contracts are closed out with cash before the settlement date. Financial contracts — futures on currencies, interest rates, or market index values — can only be closed out with cash. Commodity contracts may be settled with the physical items, but almost all are settled with cash. No one hauls a side of beef onto the floor of the Chicago Board of Trade!

Warrants

A *warrant* is similar to an option, but it's issued by the company rather than sold on an organized exchange. (After they are issued, warrants trade similarly to stocks.) A warrant gives the holder the right to buy more shares in the company at an agreed-upon price in the future.

A cousin of the warrant is the *convertible bond,* which is debt issued by the company. The company pays interest on the bond, and the bondholder has the right to exchange it for stock, depending on where interest rates and the stock price are. Convertibles trade on the stock exchanges.

Contract for difference (CFD)

A *contract for difference* allows traders to get exposure to an underlying asset, such as a share, index, currency, or commodity, without actually owning the asset itself. Because you don't own the asset commissions are often less — CMC Markets, one of the main CFD brokers, charges $5 for buying a contract on a stock; if you bought the actual stock through a discount broker you'd pay anywhere between $7 and $20.

CFDs are similar to futures contracts, but they have no fixed expiry date or contract size. A trader makes money depending on what the difference is between the initial contract price and the time the CFD is sold.

Investing vs. Trading vs. Gambling

As we mention at the beginning of this chapter, trading and investing are different. Trading and gambling are different too, but only if you follow the instructions in this book. Here's a more in-depth explanation on the differences.

Investing

Investing is the process of putting money at risk in order to get a return. It's the raw material of capitalism. It's the way that businesses get started, roads get built, and explorations get financed. It's how our economy matches people who have too much money, at least during part of their lives, with people who need it in order to grow society's capabilities.

Investing is heady stuff. And it's very much focused on the long term. Good investors do a lot of research before committing their money, because they know that it will take a long time to see a payoff. That's okay with them. Investors often invest in things that are out of favour, because they know that with time others will recognize the value and respond in kind.

One of the best investors of all time is Warren Buffett, Chief Executive Office of Berkshire Hathaway. His annual letters to shareholders offer great insight. You can read them at `www.berkshirehathaway.com/letters/letters.html`.

What's the difference between investing and saving? When you save, you take no risk. Your compensation is low — it's just enough to cover the time value of money. Generally, the return on savings equals inflation and no more. In fact, a lot of banks pay a lot less than the inflation rate on a federally insured savings account, meaning that you're paying the bank to use your money.

In contrast to investing, day trading moves fast. Day traders react only to what's on the screen: no time to do research, and the market is always right when you are day trading. You don't have two months or two years to wait for the fundamentals to work out and the rest of Wall Street to see how smart you were. You have today. And if you can't live with that, you shouldn't be day trading.

Trading

Trading is the act of buying and selling securities. All investors trade, because they need to buy and sell their investments. But to investors, trading is a rare transaction, and they get more value from finding a good opportunity, buying it cheap, and selling it at a much higher price sometime in the future. But traders are not investors.

Traders look to take advantage of short-term price discrepancies in the market. In general, they don't take a lot of risk on each trade, so they don't get a lot of return on each trade, either. Traders act quickly. They look at what the market is telling them and then respond. They know that many of their trades will not work out, but as long as more than half work, they'll be okay. They don't do a lot of in-depth research on the securities they trade, but they know the normal price and volume patterns well enough that they can recognize potential profit opportunities.

Trading keeps markets efficient, because it creates the short-term supply and demand that eliminates small price discrepancies. It also creates a lot of stress for traders, who must react in the here and now. Traders give up the luxury of time in exchange for a quick profit.

Gambling

A *gambler* puts up money in the hopes of a payoff if a random event occurs. The odds are always against the gambler and in favour of the house, but people like to gamble because they like to hope that if they hit it lucky, their return will be as large as their loss is likely.

Some gamblers believe that the odds can be beaten, but they are wrong. (Certain card games are more games of skill than gambling, assuming you can find a casino that will play under standard rules. Yeah, you can count cards when playing blackjack with your friends, but it's a lot harder in a professionally run casino.) They get excited about the potential for a big win and get caught up in the glamour of the casino, and soon the odds go to work and drain away their stakes.

A *fair lottery* takes place when the expected payoff is higher than the odds of playing. You won't find it at most casinos, although sometimes the odds in a sports book or horse race favour the bettor, at least in the short term. A more common example takes place in lotteries when the jackpots roll over to astronomical amounts. Canadian lotteries don't get high enough to fit this description, but if you're travelling through the States you may want to pick up a multi-state Mega Millions ticket.

Trading is not gambling, but traders who are not paying attention to their strategy and its performance can cross over into gambling. They can view the blips on their computer screen as a game. They can start making trades without any regard for the risk and return characteristics. They can start believing that how they do things affects the trade. And pretty soon, they are using the securities market as a giant casino, using trading techniques that have odds as bad as any slot machine.

Chapter 2: Regulations and Taxes

In This Chapter

⯈ Understanding who all these regulators are, anyway

⯈ Acing Canadian tax law 101

⯈ Differentiating earned income and capital gains

⯈ Trading in RRSPs, RRIFs, RESPs, and TFSAs

*W*hether you're building wealth through investing or trading, it's important to know the ins and outs of regulation and tax law. It may not be the most exciting stuff, but the more you know about how the markets work and what the taxman wants from you, the better.

One reason why the markets work so well is that they are regulated. That may seem like an oxymoron: Isn't capitalism all about free trade, unfettered by any rules from nannying bureaucrats? Ah, but for capitalism to work, people on both sides of a trade need to know that the terms will be enforced. They need to know that the money is in their account and safe from theft. And they need to know that no one has an unfair advantage. *Regulation* creates the trust that makes markets function.

Who Regulates What?

In Canada, financial markets get regulatory oversight from various bodies, but most of the rules come from the provincial security commissions, such as the Ontario Securities Commission (OSC) and the Investment Industry Regulatory Organization of Canada (IIROC). Both have similar goals: to ensure that investors and traders have adequate information to make decisions, and to prevent fraud and abuse.

Unlike in the United States, which has the Securities and Exchange Commission, Canada has no national regulator. IIROC governs dealers (the institutions whose trading software you're using) across the country, and the securities commissions enforce the provincial Securities Act and Commodity Futures Act. The commissions' mandate, says the OSC's website, is to protect investors from "unfair, improper or fraudulent practices and to foster fair and efficient capital markets and confidence in capital markets."

Both IIROC and Canada's other self-regulatory organization, the Mutual Fund Dealers Association (MFDA), which oversees dealers who sell only mutual funds, police their own members, but the former self-regulatory organization (SRO) does a lot more. IIROC regulates the TSX, the Canadian National Stock Exchange, and various alternative trading systems such as Bloomberg Tradebook and Omega ATS.

When it comes to equity exchanges, IIROC's main job is to make sure nothing fishy is happening. The organization monitors trading activity and can place halts or delays if market integrity is compromised. It also enforces Universal Market Integrity Rules — the rules in Canada that govern trading.

IIROC also monitors how securities are traded in order to look for patterns that might point to market manipulation or insider trading. It works with brokerage firms to make sure they know who their customers are and that they have systems in place to make certain these customers play by the rules.

Because the stock and corporate bond markets are the most popular markets and have a relatively large number of relatively small issuers, regulators are active and visible. Not just one government is issuing currency — a whole bunch of companies issue shares of stock. When it turns out that one of these companies has fraudulent numbers the headlines erupt, and suddenly everyone cares about what the regulators are up to. That's just the first layer in regulating this market.

As we write this, serious talk is happening in the hallowed halls of the Legislature about creating a single national securities regulator in Canada, much like the SEC in the United States. Governments have been debating the question of whether Canada needs one for decades, so the chances of it happening soon are slim. However, if you're reading this book a few years after its publication date, be aware that some of what we've written here may be obsolete. Canada is the only decent country in the world without a single national securities regulator.

Provincial securities commissions

Each province has its own agency to ensure the markets work efficiently. Although rules may vary, they all share a common goal: to keep capital markets safe from fraud. Each commission governs its own jurisdiction, but they do work together. The commissions also work with the SEC or other governing bodies when fraud crosses country borders.

The provincial securities commissions have various functions, including:

✦ Regulating provincial capital markets by enforcing the provincial Securities Act and, depending on where, the Commodity Futures Act. The commissions ensure that any companies that have securities listed on exchanges in their jurisdiction report their financial information accurately and on time, so that investors can determine whether investing in the company makes sense for them

✦ Working with various stakeholders — retail investors, pensions funds, dealers, advisers, stock exchanges, alternative trading systems, SROs, and more — in ensuring compliance, investor protection, and keeping fair and efficient markets.

✦ Prosecuting firms and individuals who violate securities law. Although the commissions spend a lot of time investigating allegations of misconduct, they hold hearings over takeover bids and other regulatory issues, too.

Investment Industry Regulatory Organization of Canada (IIROC)

www.iiroc.ca

IIROC is a relatively new organization. It was created in 2008 when the Investment Dealers Association and Market Regulation Services merged. The IDA was an SRO that oversaw Canadian dealers, and MRS provided regulation services for Canadian markets. The union has brought better oversight to the industry, making it more difficult for nefarious crooks to take advantage of investors.

The new SRO oversees investment dealers in Canada that trade stocks, bonds, mutual funds, options, forex (foreign exchange), and other securities. It also looks after trading activity on debt and equity markets. It has more than 200 member firms, with about 28,000 people who are registered to sell securities. IIROC administers background checks and licensing exams, regulates securities trading and monitors how firms comply, and provides information for investors so that they are better informed about the investing process.

IIROC also requires advisers to know as much as they can about their clients, via Know Your Client forms. This includes determining whether an investment strategy is suitable for them. We discuss suitability later in this chapter under "Are you suitable for day trading?" — for now, just know that it's an IIROC function.

The first thing a day trader should do is check IIROC and MFDA's media release pages and the security commissions' registration sites. Every time a disciplinary hearing against a firm or adviser takes place, the progress of the proceedings is posted on the site. Find out whether the firm you want to trade with has violated any regulations. The security commissions' registrations sites allow you to type in the name of a person or firm and see whether they are in fact registered, what category they're registered in, and if any conditions were attached to that registration. These tools help ensure you're not dealing with a criminal.

Mutual Fund Dealers Association of Canada (MFDA)

www.mfda.ca

Unlike IIROC, which oversees dealers who trade stocks and bonds, the MFDA represents members who work only with mutual funds. Despite operating under its own set of rules, it shares many of the same goals as IIROC. It regulates operations, standards, and business conduct of its members and tries to improve investor protection. It can fine members for violating rules, and works with authorities when criminal charges are laid.

The MFDA represents about 130 firms and almost 74,000 advisers, with about $303 billion in assets under administration. It's highly unlikely the brokerage firm you use will be an MFDA member. Because you're trading more than just mutual funds, you'll be working in an IIROC environment.

The exchanges

It wasn't long ago that each major city had its own exchange. But through mergers and an agreement that Toronto would host a central stock exchange, the TSX became the main exchange in the country. However, depending on what you trade, the TSX is not the only game in town — you'll also find the Toronto Venture Exchange (TSXV), the Montreal Exchange (MX), and other exchanges and alternative trading systems.

Canada's main exchanges are owned by the TMX Group. It oversees the TSX, the TSXV, the MX, the Natural Gas Exchange (NGX), the Boston Options Exchange (BOX), and a few others. The group has outsourced its regulation duties of the TSX and TSXV to IIROC, and the others regulate trading activity in-house.

Brokerage Basics for Firm and Customer

No matter how they are regulated, brokers and futures commission merchants have to know who their customers are and what they are up to. That leads to some basic regulations about suitability and money laundering — and extra paperwork for you. Don't be too annoyed by all the paperwork you have to fill out to open an account, though — your brokerage firm has even more.

Are you suitable for day trading?

Brokerage firms have to make sure the activity surrounding their customers is appropriate. The firms need to know their customers and be sure that any recommendations are suitable. When it comes to day trading, firms want to be sure their customers are dealing with *risk capital* — money they can afford to lose. They also want to be sure that their customers understand the risks they are taking. Depending on the firm, and what you're trying to do, you might have to submit financial statements, sign a stack of disclosures, and verify that you have had previous trading experience.

It's no one's business but your own, of course, except that the regulators want to make sure that firm employees aren't talking customers into taking on risks they should not be taking. Sure, you can lie about it. You can tell the broker you don't *need* the $25,000 you're putting in your account, even if that's the money paying for your kidney dialysis. But when it's gone, you can't say you didn't know about the risks involved.

Staying out of the money Laundromat

Money laundering is a way to receive money acquired from illegal activities. Your average drug dealer, Mafia hit man, or corrupt politician doesn't accept credit cards, but he really doesn't want to keep lots of cash in his house. How can he collect interest on his money if it's locked in a safe in his closet? And besides, his friends are an unsavory sort. Can he trust them to stay away from his cache? If this criminal fellow takes all that cash to the bank, those pesky bankers will start asking a lot of questions, because they know that most people pursuing legitimate business activities get paid through cheques or electronic direct deposit.

Hence, the felon with funds will look for a way to make it appear that the money is legitimate. It happens in all sorts of ways, ranging from making lots of small cash deposits to engaging in complicated series of financial trades and money transfers, especially between countries, that become difficult for investigators to trace. Sometimes these transactions look a lot like day trading, and that means that legitimate brokerage firms opening day trade accounts should be paying attention to who their customers are.

Fighting money laundering took on urgency after the September 11, 2001 attacks, because it was clear that someone somewhere had given some bad people a lot of cash to fund the preparation and execution of their deadly mission. Several nations increased their oversight of financial activities during the aftermath of the strikes on the World Trade Center and Pentagon. That's why one piece of paperwork from your broker will be the anti–money laundering disclosure. The Financial Transactions Reports Analysis Centre of Canada (FINTRAC) is the government body that looks after money laundering activities, but brokers track this as well. If they suspect a trader is laundering money they'll report it to FINTRAC, which will then investigate.

In order for your brokerage firm to verify that it knows who its customers are and where their money came from, you'll probably have to provide the following when you open a brokerage account:

✦ Your name

✦ Date of birth

✦ Street address

✦ Place of business

✦ Social Insurance Number

✦ Driver's licence and passport

✦ Copies of financial statements

Rules for day traders

Here's the problem for regulators: Many day traders lose money, and those losses can be magnified by the use of *leverage strategies* (trading with borrowed money, meaning that you can lose more money than you have in the quest for large profits). If the customer who lost the money can't pay up, then the broker is on the hook. If too many customers lose money beyond what the broker can absorb, then the losses ripple through the financial system, and that's not good.

IIROC has a long list of rules that its member firms have to meet in order to stay in business. The organization sets margin requirements and, depending on the type of account, the requirements are stricter to reflect the greater risk. You can read through all the rules by visiting this link: www.iiroc.ca/English/ComplianceSurveillance/RuleBook/Pages/UMIR.aspx.

The rules set by IIROC are minimum requirements. Brokerage firms are free to set higher limits for account size and borrowing in order to manage their own risks better.

Tax reporting

If you're a long-term investor receiving dividends, your online broker will send you a slip at the end of the year detailing how much income you've made. Traders will also receive tax forms if they received dividends or interest income — this mostly applies to people who hold overnight positions. Brokers will also send out a summary of trades to help track capital gains and losses. We cover tax issues below.

Money laundering: Al Capone or Watergate?

Although some believe that the term *money laundry* dates back to Al Capone's attempts to evade taxes by owning laundries — businesses that had a large number of small cash transactions — the U.S. Federal Reserve Board says the term didn't come into use until the Watergate scandal, when Nixon's campaign staff had to hide the money used to pay the people who broke into his opponent's psychiatrist's office.

Hot Tips and Insider Trading

The regulations are very clear for things about suitability and money laundering. You get a bunch of forms, you read them, you sign them, you present documentation, and everyone is happy. The rules that keep the markets functioning are clear and easy to follow.

Another set of rules also keeps markets functioning — namely, that no one has an unfair information advantage. If you knew about big merger announcements, interest rate decisions by the Bank of Canada, or a new sugar substitute that would eliminate demand for corn syrup, you could make a lot of money in the stock market, trading options on interest rate futures, or playing in the grain futures market.

Insider trading is a broad term. Any non-public information that a reasonable person would consider when deciding whether to buy or sell a security could apply, and that's a pretty vague standard — especially because the whole purpose of research is to combine bits of immaterial information together to make investment decisions.

Day traders can be susceptible to hot tips, because they are buying and selling so quickly. If these hot tips are actually inside information, though, the trader can become liable. If you get great information from someone who is in a position to know — an officer, a director, a lawyer, an investment banker — you may be looking at stiff penalties. According to the Canada Business Corporations Act, courts can assess civil penalties of "any measure of damages it considers relevant in the circumstances." A criminal conviction can land someone in jail for up to ten years.

Insider trading is difficult to prove, so federal regulators use other tools to punish those it suspects of making improper profits. In the United States, Martha Stewart wasn't sent to prison on insider trading charges; she was charged with obstructing justice by lying to investigators about what happened.

Whenever a big announcement is made, such as a merger, the exchanges go back and review trading for several days before to see whether any unusual activities occurred in relevant securities and derivatives. Then they start tracing them back to the traders involved through the brokerage firms to see whether it was coincidence or part of a pattern.

The bottom line is this: You may never come across inside information. But if a tip seems too good to be true, it probably is — so be careful.

Tax Issues for Traders and Investors

Think trading and investing returns come without a catch? Think again, because the CRA has plenty of ways to catch you come April 30. Both day trading and investing involve strategies that can generate both high returns and high tax liabilities, which can eat away at your total return if you're not careful. Depending on how you file, not all of your expenses are deductible. And, even more troubling for traders, the CRA could classify your activities in a way that may really hurt your bottom line.

Taxes themselves aren't necessarily bad, because somehow we have to pay for things like roads and schools and health care. But taxes can be devastating to your personal finances if you haven't planned for them. You need to consider the tax implications of your trading strategy right from the start and keep careful records so that you're ready.

Tax issues are complex and change frequently. Check the most recent federal regulations at www.cra-arc.gc.ca and work with an accountant or tax expert who has experience in these matters. This chapter is just a guide. We're reasonably social folks and all, but we're not going on an audit with you.

Are You a Trader or an Investor?

In Chapter 1, we cover the differences between investing, trading, and gambling. Day traders aren't investing — they're looking to take advantage of short-term price movements, not to take a stake in a business for the long term. At least that's how the CRA looks at it. The taxman will brand you a trader if you meet some (not necessarily all) of the following criteria:

✦ You have a history of "extensive buying and selling" of securities. The CRA doesn't explain what extensive means, but if you're selling hundreds of securities a year — like most day traders do — it's likely you'll be considered a trader.

✦ You own securities for a short period of time. Again, no specific timeframe applies, but you can assume they're talking days, not years.

✦ You know a thing or two about or have experience in the securities markets.

✦ Trading makes up a part of your regular business activities.

✦ You spend a "substantial" amount of time studying markets and looking into potential purchases.

✦ You primarily buy on margin or use another type of debt.

✦ You've made it known that you're a trader, or are willing to purchase securities.

✦ The shares you purchase are speculative or non-dividend-paying investments.

Even if you trade part-time, have other employment, or are new to the day trading game, the CRA could define you as a trader — and therefore will be expecting a heftier tax bill at the end of the year.

Those who qualify as traders enjoy deductions that regular investors don't. You might qualify as a trader for some of your activities and as an investor for others. If this looks to be the case you need to keep detailed records to separate your trades, and you should use different brokerage accounts to make the difference clear from the day you open the position.

In political economies, taxation serves two purposes. The first is to raise money for the government. The second is to encourage people to do things that the elected officials who amend the tax code want them to do. Much of the investing tax code is intended to promote the formation and growth of wealth and savings. The intention of short-term day trading isn't to do that — it's so people can make heaps of money in an exciting, high-pressure environment (often from the comfort of home), instead of toiling at a nine-to-five job. So, if you qualify as a trader, the CRA will tax you as though it's your job. Instead of paying the financially preferable capital gains tax, you'll be paying tax on your total income earned.

Legally, if you day trade you have to file income tax as though it's your full-time job. Capital gains taxes will not apply. However, lots of traders try to push the boundaries and file capital gains taxes rather than income tax until they're told otherwise, an approach we don't advocate. Talk to your tax adviser about how you should file and the consequences of filing incorrectly.

Hiring a Tax Adviser

You don't have to hire someone to do your taxes, but you probably should. If you're claiming capital gains, day trading will generate a lot of separate transactions to track, and the tax laws are tricky. Mistakes can end up costing you your entire trading profit.

Do yourself a favour and find a tax expert. You can talk to other traders, get references from the attorneys and accountants you work with now, or even do Internet searches to find people who understand both CRA regulations and the unique needs of people who frequently buy and sell securities, whether or not the CRA calls them traders.

Anyone can represent clients before the CRA in audits, collections, or appeals, but it's a good idea to hire an accountant, or someone who knows a lot about tax and, preferably, investing.

Questions to ask a prospective adviser

After you identify a few prospective candidates to prepare your taxes, talk to them and ask them questions about their experience. Because you're supposed to claim your day trading profits as earned income, there really isn't anything special your tax expert needs to do beyond knowing what to deduct. The main goal is to find someone who can help you determine what you owe in taxes and not one penny more.

You'll feel more comfortable with your tax preparer if *you* have an understanding of the issues at stake. Even if you are hiring someone — and you should — keep reading this chapter for more in-depth references on taxes and trading.

Some things you should ask a potential tax preparer include the following:

✦ What investors and traders have you worked with? For how long?

✦ Who will be preparing my return? How involved will you be?

✦ What's your audit record? Why have your clients been audited? What happened on the audit?

✦ What are your fees?

It is illegal for tax preparers to base their fees on the size of your tax refund.

You still want to do it yourself?

It's possible for traders to do their own taxes, especially if they're claiming earned income. If you are comfortable with tax forms, you might be able to do this yourself. You need a few things: the proper CRA forms and, if you're not classifying yourself as a full-time trader, tax preparation software that can handle investment income.

The CRA website, www.cra-arc.gc.ca, is a treasure trove of tax information. All the regulations, publications, forms, and explanations are there, and some of it is even in plain English. It's so vast and detailed that you will probably be overwhelmed; get back at the CRA by calling them up and asking them to explain it all to you.

The primary section that covers the tax implications of trading and other investing activities is the Income Tax Interpretation Bulletin IT-479R, "Transactions in Securities." To find this document, go to the CRA's website and type IT-479R into the search bar. Click on the first result, and voilà.

Tax preparation software

Those who do their own taxes know that tax prep software is a godsend, and it's even more valuable for those do-it-yourselfers who trade a lot. The software fills out the forms, automatically adds and subtracts, and even catches typographical errors. In many cases, it can download data straight from your brokerage account, making data entry really simple.

Some of the big brands, such as TurboTax, are set up to import and manage investment data, but if you're making regular and frequent trades you may want to shell out the close to $1,000 it costs to purchase something like TJPS Software, which offers a range of trading-related functions.

What Is Income, Anyway?

Income seems like a straightforward concept, but not much about taxation is straightforward. To the CRA, income falls into different categories, with different tax rates, different allowed deductions, and different forms to fill out. In this section we cover income definitions you'll run into as a day trader.

Earned income

Earned income includes wages, salaries, bonuses, net rental income, and tips. It's money that you make on the job. If day trading is your only occupation — and even if it isn't — your earnings could be considered earned income. This means that day traders will have to pay tax based on their personal income tax rate.

Canada has both federal and provincial tax rates — the latter varies by province, but the former is consistent for all Canadians. In the federal system, you're taxed:

+ 15 percent on the first $41,544 of taxable income

+ 22 percent on the next $41,544 of taxable income

+ 26 percent on the next $45,712 of taxable income

+ 29 percent of taxable income over $128,800

Got that? To put it another way, if you fall into the highest tax bracket, about 29 percent of your yearly earnings will go to the federal government. You will also pay provincial tax which could bring you into the 46 percent tax bracket. (***Note:*** these numbers are 2011 amounts — the rates can change from year to year.)

Provincial tax rates vary from province to province. To find out how much you'll be taxed, go to www.cra-arc.gc.ca/tx/ndvdls/fq/txrts-eng.html, scroll halfway down the page, and find your province.

Most traders are self-employed, which means you can deduct expenses and reduce your income's dollar figure. That could bump you into a lower bracket and therefore you'll pay less tax.

The big benefit of claiming your gains as income is that, if you lose money, you can apply those losses against all sources of income or any profits down the road. So, if you have a part-time job, those losses will help bring down your tax bill leaving more money in your pocket. The CRA allows you to apply losses against income earned for the last three years, or carry them forward indefinitely.

 Keep your long-term investments separate from your day trading income — if you don't, the CRA could assume all your investing is related to trading. And that is bad news. The tax treatment for investments is different than work income, so if the CRA thinks all your investing, including that mutual fund you've held for 20 years, is related to day trading, all your gains could be taxed at the marginal tax rate.

 Being a day trader once meant you didn't have access to employment insurance benefits. That's not the case anymore. Starting January 31, 2010, traders who pay income tax can apply for maternity, parental, sickness, and compassionate care benefits. You have to opt in to this yourself — and decide whether you want to send even more money to the taxman. Visit CRA's website to find out more.

Capital gains and losses

A *capital gain* is the profit you make when you buy low and sell high, and that's the aim of day trading. The opposite of a capital gain is a *capital loss,* which happens when you sell an asset for less than you paid for it. Investors can offset some of their capital gains with some of their capital losses to reduce their tax burden.

Those who trade frequently and can avoid having their gains classified as earned income will have many capital gains and losses. Day traders get tripped up by capital gain and loss problems all the time, so when designing your trading strategy think long and hard about how to ease the pain taxes might cause.

 The financial world is filled with horror stories of people who thought they found a clever angle on making big profits, only to discover at tax time that their tax liability was greater than their profit. That's why properly tracking gains and losses is a must. It's not easy. The price difference of every trade you make needs to be accounted for, so create an Excel spreadsheet or use Write-Up, a comprehensive computer program offered by TJPS Software (www.tjpssoftware.com).

Tax treatment

Day traders want to pay taxes on capital gains, rather than earned income, because only half of a capital gain is taxed. If you make $1,000 on a trade, and it's being taxed as income, the entire gain will be subject to tax. If you're paying capital gains you'd pay only tax — at your marginal tax rate — on $500. See why the CRA wants day trading profits to be taxed as income?

If you lose money on a trade you can claim capital losses. It's similar to applying losses against earned income, but you can only use half of the amount you lose, rather than the entire price tag of the loss. Capital losses would be applied against gains, which can reduce your total tax bill. Capital losses can be carried back three years or used indefinitely in the future.

Now's a good time to remind you, again, that the CRA frowns upon traders who claim capital gains instead of earned income. If you meet the criteria of a trader, which we list earlier in the chapter, you're supposed to claim your earnings as income — just as you would if you worked in a cubicle shuffling papers.

Covering your basis

Capital gains and losses are calculated using a security's adjusted cost base (ACB) in Canada or cost *basis* in United States tax law, which may or may not be the same as the price that you paid for it or sold it at. Some expenses, such as commissions, are added to the cost of the security, and that can reduce the amount of your taxable gain or increase the amount of your deductible loss.

For example, if you bought 100 shares of stock at $50 per share and a $0.03 per share commission, your basis would be $5,003 — the $5,000 you paid for the stock and the $3.00 you paid in commission.

Tracking Your Investment Expenses

Day traders have expenses. They buy computer equipment, subscribe to research services, pay trading commissions, and hire accountants to prepare their taxes. It adds up, and the tax code recognizes that. That's why day traders who pay personal income tax can deduct many of their costs from their income taxes. In this section, we go through some of what you can deduct.

You'll make your life much easier if you keep track of your expenses as you incur them. You can do this in a notebook, in a spreadsheet, or through personal finance software such as Quicken or UFile.

Day traders who try to get around paying personal income tax don't have nearly as many expensing opportunities. That's one of the benefits of treating your day trading activities as a regular job.

Deductible investment-related expenses

You can deduct expenses as long as they are considered to be ordinary, necessary, and used to produce or collect income, manage property held for producing income, and directly related to the taxable income produced.

Investment counsel and advice

The CRA allows you to deduct fees paid for counsel and advice about investments that produce taxable income. This includes books, magazines, newspapers, and research services that help you refine your trading strategy. It also includes anything you might pay for investment advisory services, such as trade coaching or analysis.

Investment interest

If you borrow money as part of your strategy, and most day traders do, you can deduct the interest paid on those loans. In most cases this is *margin interest* (see Chapters 1 and 5 for more information on margin), and for most day traders it is relatively small because few day traders borrow money for more than a few hours at a time.

If you borrow money against your account for anything other than income-producing activities, you can't deduct the interest. And yes, most brokerage firms let you take out margin for your own general spending, as a way to let you stay in the market and still get cash.

You can deduct expenses only if day trading is your day job and you're getting taxed on earned income. Again, paying income tax, rather than capital gains tax, will allow you to claim all that good stuff we mentioned. Sure, you may have to pay more in tax than if you just paid gains, but, as a consolation, you can write off a lot more — and you don't have to worry about being reprimanded by the CRA!

Commissions

If you're a day trader paying income, you can deduct commissions come tax time. However, if you're paying capital gains, you're out of luck. We know, it's disappointing, but that's life. (Well, at least the way CRA wants life to be.) Again, if you really want to deduct those extra fees, claim your profits as income.

Other qualified expenses

Office expenses

If you do your day trading from an outside office, you can deduct the rent and related expenses. You can deduct the expenses of a home office, too, as long as you use it regularly and for business. Your trading room can be used as the guest room, but you need to figure out how many hours you use it for business. According to the CRA, calculate how many hours in a day you use the room and divide that by 24. Multiply the number by your business-related home expenses. Deduct that number.

You can also deduct certain office expenses for equipment and supplies used in your business; just use the same formula above to determine how much of your computers, desks, chairs, and the like you can write off. (If it's an office chair that's used only for work, you can write off the entire amount. If it's a love seat that doubles as a work chair, you can claim only part of it.)

To get the deduction you have to spend the money first, and your expenses don't reduce your taxes dollar-for-dollar. If you're in the 46 percent tax bracket, then each dollar you spend on qualified expenses reduces your taxes by $0.46. In other words, don't go crazy at the office supply store just because you get a tax deduction. It may be helpful to think of deductible expenses as discounts, because in the end that's more or less what they are.

Clerical, legal, and accounting fees

You might use the services of a lawyer to help you get set up, and you will almost definitely want to use an accountant who understands investment expenses to prepare your income tax returns each year. The good news is you can deduct attorney and accounting fees related to your income. If your trading operation gets big enough that you hire clerical or bookkeeping help to keep track of all those trade confirmations, you can deduct that cost, too.

Safe deposit box rent

Have a safe deposit box down at the bank? You can deduct the rent on it if you store any investment-related documents. If you also keep jewellery that you inherited and never wear or other personal items in the same box, you can deduct only part of the rent.

Paying Taxes All Year

If you have been an employee for years and years, all of your tax liabilities would have been covered by your payroll tax deductions. The CRA likes it best that way, because then it gets money all year 'round. And really, the easier it is to pay, the more likely you are to do it.

People who are self-employed don't get the luxury of having their tax bill taken care of by someone else. To ensure you have squirrelled away enough for the CRA, estimate your tax liability for the year, divide it by 12, and put aside a portion of your profits every month. Nothing's worse than having to pay tax and not having the money at the end of the year. (It's tempting, but don't buy a new plasma TV with what's supposed to be the government's money.)

In your first two years as a day trader you won't be forced to pay in instalments, but after that, and if you're making over $30,000 annually, the government will require you to send in a cheque four times a year. The CRA bases the amount on what you've made the prior two years; if you end up owing less you'll get money back, and if you owe more your final cheque will make up the difference.

Estimated taxes are paid via Form INNS3, also known as the Installment Remittance Voucher. Fortunately, they're due on a nice, even, quarterly schedule: the 15th of March, June, September, and December.

Using Your RRSP, RRIF, and RESP

Much of the tax hassle associated with day trading is eliminated if you trade through a self-directed Registered Retirement Savings Plan, or RRSP. (Find out more about RRSPs, RRIFs, and RESPs in Book 1, Chapter 3.) Most brokerage firms can set them up for you and handle the necessary paperwork. You're allowed to contribute 18 percent of your previous year's earned income up to a maximum of $22,970 for 2012 and $23,820 for 2013. If you didn't use up all your room the year before, you can carry it forward indefinitely. That means if you haven't used an RRSP before you could deposit a lot of cash or securities in kind.

When you put money into the registered account you'll get a tax deduction, which can be nice if you've made a lot of money that year. However, if you want to take cash out you'll be taxed at your marginal rate (refer to the section "What Is Income, Anyway?" in this chapter for more). That's why most people wait until they're 71 to withdraw — the older you are, the lower your earned income is likely to be. So it's not a good idea to use an RRSP if you need immediate access to your money.

What's different about day trading in an RRSP is that capital gains and losses don't apply. You don't have to pay any tax on the investments. You're asked to pay the taxman only on the amount you remove from the account. Again, if you can hang on to the money until you retire (though day trading is not a good retirement strategy) then you'll pay a lot less tax. You're also not allowed to trade on margin in an RRSP (see Chapter 5 for more on leverage), and you can't participate in *naked call options* (when an investor sells a call option without owning the security) or *short selling* (selling a security you don't own and buying the stock back at a lower price). The CRA considers it carrying on a business activity inside an RRSP, which is a no-no. The same is basically true for Registered Retirement Income Funds (RRIFs) and Registered Education Savings Plans (RESPs).

Do your bulk of trading in an unregistered account so you can have quick access to money without incurring the withdrawal taxes that come with investing in an RRSP.

Trading within a Tax-Free Savings Account

On January 1, 2009, the federal government introduced a new savings vehicle for Canadians called the Tax-Free Savings Account (TFSA). The idea is to get more people saving money. You're allowed to put $5,000 into the account each year and remove it tax free at any time. The room also accumulates by $5,000 each year, so if you didn't deposit anything in 2009 you could put in $10,000 in 2010, and so on. The TFSA is meant for long-term investors — you'd put your cash in a corporate bond or a mutual fund, in the TFSA account, and let it grow. You might withdraw it if you wanted to buy a car or house, because you can take it out without incurring a tax penalty.

The TFSA is similar to an RRSP, except you don't get a tax break when you deposit money into the account and you don't get taxed when you remove it.

The best part is that none of capital gains, interest income, or dividends are taxed in a TFSA. That's good news for traders who claim gains or income. However, you can't claim losses — not so good if you're losing money. Your initial deposit also can't exceed your contribution room, so this is not the place to make a $100,000 trade. If you do put more in the account than your allotted amount — $5,000 per year — 100 percent of the profits from the extra cash will go to the taxman.

Like an RRSP, you can't participate in naked call options or short selling and you can't take advantage of margin in a TFSA. Use this as a secondary account, not your primary one.

Chapter 3: Managing Stress and Your Positions

In This Chapter

- ✔ Finding out how to control your emotions
- ✔ Understanding trading plans and why you need one
- ✔ Figuring out your expected return
- ✔ Exploring the many styles of money management
- ✔ Knowing how money management can affect returns

*D*ay trading can be a ruthless business. Some days, you don't find any trades worth making. Other days, you find trades, but they don't work out the way you want them to. And some days, too many good trades come along, more than you can possibly make, and so you watch profitable opportunities slip away. When you're working with real money, it can be too much to take.

In a money management or brokerage firm, traders have tremendous camaraderie. They are working for the same employer and need to stick together to blow off the stress. What do you do at home, though? How do *you* keep from panicking, getting depressed, or otherwise letting this business hurt your profits and hurt you?

If you're going to day trade, you need to understand the very real physical and psychological stresses that the market pushes on its participants. In this chapter, we offer some information and advice that can help you avoid a crisis. Investors are also wise to heed the information here. When markets are in flux, as we saw during the recession and in the years after, you might get the same night sweats and panicky feelings as many day traders do. Learn how to keep your emotions in check and you'll coast through the volatile times.

First, the Cautionary Tales

Trader lore is loaded with stories of people who flamed out in spectacular and destructive ways. People who work on trading desks or on trading floors tell tales of colleagues who went down hard, walked off the desk, broke down in the pit, or died at the trading post. They can rattle off lists of colleagues who are alcoholics, who suffered bitter divorces, who committed suicide. Even though day traders usually work by themselves, stories of their self-destructive behaviour abound.

Sure, many day traders lead pleasant lives and suffer no more problems than any other person. That's because they have perspective, balance, and the right personality for the business. Know what can go wrong, because it can help you keep in the right.

Jesse Livermore

Jesse Livermore is sometimes considered to be the father of day trading. He's the subject of the 1923 book *Reminiscences of a Stock Operator* by Edwin Le*fè*vre a classic book about trading. Livermore was born in 1877 and started trading stocks when he was in his teens. He claimed to have made $1,000 when he was 15, which may not seem like much, except that he was very young and price levels were a little different in 1892. (That $1,000 would be worth over $20,000 in today's dollars.) He made huge fortunes betting against the market in 1907 and again in 1929, and he managed to lose it all both times. By 1934 he was broke and depressed. He attempted suicide in 1935 and succeeded in 1940.

Mark Barton

Mark Barton lost $105,000 day trading and he snapped. On July 27, 1999, he bludgeoned his wife and two children to death. Then he went to the downtown Atlanta offices of Momentum Securities, a brokerage firm that specialized in working with day traders. He had an appointment to deliver $50,000 so that he could cover his losses and start trading again. Instead, he took out a gun, opened fire, and killed four people. He then went to the offices of All-Tech Investment Group, another day trading firm where he had an account, and killed another five people. Barton killed himself before he was arrested. This case is one of the worst workplace massacres in the United States, and it did as much as the 2000 meltdown in Nasdaq technology stocks to reduce the enthusiasm for day trading.

Anecdotal suicides, divorces, alcoholism

Because not that many people day trade consistently, not a lot of good demographic studies have been conducted on just how many day traders end up abusing drugs and alcohol, getting divorced or becoming estranged from friends, and turning to suicide. The anecdotal evidence is pretty strong, though. People in the securities business face high pressure and real dollar losses every day they go to work. Their performance is constantly judged by the market, and it doesn't grade on a curve. If you spend even a few minutes talking to people in the business, you hear horror stories. Ann C. Logue, co-author of *Day Trading For Canadians For Dummies* (Wiley), personally knows a trader who set fire to his house, killing his 90-year-old mother in the process, to get the insurance proceeds to cover his financial shortfalls. (He's currently doing a 190-year sentence.)

Don't be the person who finally gives researchers enough critical mass to report on day trader self-destruction. Stress is a real part of day trading, and not all day traders handle it well. If you know what you're up against and prepare for it, you'll be better off than many.

Controlling Your Emotions

The key to successful day trading is controlling your emotions. After all, the stock doesn't know that you own it, as equity traders like to say, so it isn't going to perform well just because you want it to. This can be infuriating, especially when you're going through a draw-down of your capital. Those losses look mighty personal.

Traditional financial theory is based on the idea that traders are rational. In practice, however, most of them are not. In fact, traders and investors are often irrational in completely predictable ways, which has given birth to a new area of study called *behavioural finance*. It's a hot area generating Nobel Prize winners, and it may eventually help people incorporate measures of investor behaviour into buy and sell decisions.

You have to figure out a way to manage your reactions to the market, or you shouldn't be a day trader. Day traders talk about their enemies being fear and greed. If you panic, you'll no longer be trading to win, but trading not to lose. The distinction is important: If your goal is not to lose, you won't take appropriate risk, and you won't be able to respond quickly to what the market is telling you.

This is all much easier said than done. Human beings are emotional creatures, constantly reacting (and sometimes overreacting) to everything that is happening in their lives. Knowing the emotions that affect trading and having some ways to manage them can greatly improve your overall performance.

The big five emotions

When it comes to trading — and investing — five big emotions can take over and mess up your strategy and your returns. At this point in your life, you may already know whether you have tendencies toward some of them. If so, trading can exacerbate them. If you've never experienced them, you might for the first time. Here's a list and some descriptions so that you know what you're up against and can plan accordingly. We include some tips that can help, but if you are really in the throes of an emotional crisis that affects your trading, you should seek out professional help.

Anxiety

Anxiety is the anticipation of things going wrong, and it often includes a physical response: perspiration, clenched jaw, tense muscles, heart palpitations. Anxious people worry, agonize, overanalyze, and generally stress out. And then they avoid whatever it is that makes them upset. That means that a trader might not make an obvious trade, but instead hesitate and miss a market move. He might hold on to a losing position too long because he's worried about the effect that selling it will have on his portfolio. He becomes too nervous to trade according to his plan, and his performance suffers.

One way to fight trading anxiety is to concentrate on following the trading plan, not on making a set amount of money. That way, following the plan becomes more automatic, and you spend less time worrying about what can go wrong.

Boredom

Brace yourself for an ugly truth about day trading: It can be really dull. In an eight-hour trading session, you might spend seven and a half hours waiting for the right opening. A flurry of trades, and it's all over. To keep yourself entertained, you might start making bad trades, spending too much time in chat rooms, or letting your mind wander away from the task at hand. None of those things is conducive to profitable trading.

If you're really bored and tempted to do something stupid, close out your positions and take a break. Going for a walk or quitting early can clear your head and help you focus when you get back. Remember, day traders work for themselves, and one of the benefits of that is no boss to find out you knocked off early. Take advantage of that!

Depression

Depression is a severe downturn in your mood, especially one that causes you to feel inadequate and lose interest in things you used to like. Although everyone is susceptible to depression, the ups and downs of the market can make traders particularly vulnerable. At best, depression can make it hard for a trader to face a day with the market. At worst, it can lead to alcoholism, alienation, and even suicide.

If you think you might be depressed, check out the handy quiz at www.depressionhurts.ca/en/symptomchecklist.aspx. Or better yet, go to your doctor.

Fear

Fear is one of the worst emotional enemies of the day trader. Instead of trying to make money, the fearful trader is trying hard not to lose it. She is so afraid of failing that she limits herself, doesn't take appropriate risk, and questions her trading system so much that she no longer follows it, no matter how well it worked for her in the past.

By the way, it isn't just failure that traders fear. Many fear success, sometimes for deep-seated psychological reasons that we are in no position to address. A trader who fears success may think that if she succeeds, her friends will treat her differently, her relatives will try to take her money, and that she will become someone she doesn't want to be.

One way to limit fear is to have a plan for the trading business. Before you start trading, take some time — maybe half a day — to sit down and think about what you want, what will happen to you if you get it, and what will happen to you if you don't. For example, if you lose your trading capital, then you'll have to live on your walk-away fund (see later in this chapter) until you find another job. If you make a lot of money, then you can pay off your mortgage and your friends will be none the wiser.

Greed

Greed seems like a silly thing to have on this list. After all, isn't the whole purpose of day trading to make money? This isn't charity, this is capitalism at its purest. Ah, but there's a popular saying in the finance world: "Pigs get fat, but hogs get slaughtered."

Traders who get greedy start to do stupid things. They don't think through what they are doing and stop following their trading plans. They hold positions too long in the hope of eking out a return and sometimes they make rash trades that look an awful lot like gambling. The greedy trader loses all discipline and eventually loses quite a bit of money.

If your goal is simply to make more and more money, you might have a problem with greed. Sure, everyone wants to make more, but give some thought to the difference between your *need-to-make number* (enough to cover your costs and your basic living expenses) and your *want-to-make number* (enough to cover costs, basic expenses, and extras that are important to you). If you know what those numbers are, you're well on your way to preventing the problem.

Limit orders, which automatically close out positions when they hit set prices, are one way to force discipline in the face of greed. You can read more about limit orders in Chapter 1.

Having an outlet

Successful day traders have a life outside of the markets. They close out their positions, shut off their monitors, and go do something else with the rest of the day. That's the whole idea behind day trading.

The problem is that a market is always open somewhere. Traders can work overnight, after hours, and even on the weekends and sometimes move the action to exchanges in other parts of the world. Without something to mark a beginning and an end to your trading day, and without other things happening in your life, the market can consume you in a way that's simply not healthy.

So as you plan your life as a day trader, think about what else you're going to do with your days. Exercise, meditation, socializing, and having outside interests are key to maintaining balance and staying focused on the market when you have to be.

Support systems

There's a veritable industry of support for traders, and it's easy to tap into. Many day traders find that reading books, hiring a coach, or finding other day traders helps them get through the day.

Books

A library-full of books have been written on the psychology of trading itself. In addition, many traders rely on other self-help and history books for inspiration and ideas. (Possibly every trader we've ever known owns a copy of Sun Tzu's *The Art of War,* which is about military strategies and tactics. They find that it helps them prepare their minds to face the market, or at least gives them something interesting to talk about.)

Counselling and coaching

Because it takes a lot of mental toughness to handle big losses — and big gains — many traders find professional support. They use counsellors, psychologists, or life coaches to help them deal with the challenges of the market and understand their reactions to it. You can ask other traders or your doctor for a referral, or check the online directory at *Psychology Today*'s website, `http://therapists.psychologytoday.com` (you'll find many Canadian therapists there), or the International Coach Federation, `www.coachfederation.org`. When interviewing coaches or counsellors, ask whether they have experience with traders or others who work in finance.

Many day trading training and brokerage firms also offer coaching services that specialize in helping people learn and follow day trading strategies. Some day traders find these people to be invaluable, whereas others find they are just glorified salespeople.

Some day trading coaches may be more interested in selling you specific trading strategies rather than helping you manage your own system. Check references and find out what other forms of compensation the coach receives before you sign up.

Finding other traders

To offset the loneliness of trading alone, many day traders choose to work out of trading rooms operated by brokerage firms (see Chapter 6 in *Day Trading For Canadians For Dummies*) or join organizations where they will meet other traders. These may be formal or informal groups where traders can socialize, learn new things, or just commiserate.

Many day traders get together through social networks, which we discuss in more detail later in this chapter. These groups are less formal, more anonymous, and sometimes more destructive than supportive.

Most day traders lose money and give up their first year. You may find that spending too much time with other traders is more depressing than supportive.

Your walk-away money

A lot of traders have a secret that gets them through the worst of the markets. It's something called *walk-away money,* although traders sometimes use more colourful language to describe it. It's enough money that they can walk away from trading and do something else.

And just exactly how much is it? Well, it varies from person to person, but having enough money to pay three months' worth of expenses on hand and in cash is a good place to start. If you know that you can pay the mortgage and buy the groceries even if you don't make money trading today, you'll be better able to avoid desperate trading. You won't have to be greedy, and you won't have to live in fear.

The more money in your walk-away fund, the better. Then you have more time to investigate alternative careers should day trading prove not to be your thing, and you can relax more when you face the market every day.

Most day traders quit after a year or so. There's nothing wrong with deciding to move on and try something else. If you have some money saved, then you're in a better position to control when you stop trading and what you do next.

If all your trading capital is gone, you might be tempted to tap your walk-away fund to stay in the game. *Don't.* That's exactly the time when you should use your walk-away money to, yes, *walk away,* if only for a short time to clear your head and rethink your strategies. Otherwise, your trading losses may become financial ruin.

Importance of a Trading Plan

You read about trading plans in Chapter 1, but it's worth repeating that a plan is so important to maintaining the discipline that leads to trading success. You have to know what you're doing, and how to recognize entry and exit points, and then go and do it.

In this section, we cover how you can use a trading plan to manage stress and give you a few tips for sticking to your trading plan even as the markets sometimes move against you.

Problems following direction

Was that written on all your report cards? We hope not. A good, tested trading plan sets out market patterns that work often enough that you can make good trading profits. But some people have trouble following their plan, and that leads to stressful mistakes.

Prevent choking!

In sports lingo, an athlete who *chokes* starts playing so carefully that he or she looks like a beginner. This is often caused by overthinking — by being so afraid of failure that the mind slows and breaks down the play step by step. It's not pretty to watch a contender choke during a championship game. The fans want to see a good match.

Anyone in a high-performance situation can choke. When a trader chokes, he seems to be following the plan, but it's no longer automatic. Trading becomes so slow and deliberative that obvious trades get missed.

The more you trust your plan, the less likely you are to choke. Has it been tested? Are there parts that you can automate? In Chapter 11 of *Day Trading For Canadians For Dummies* we offer some ideas on how to measure a trading plan's performance before you start to trade with the plan.

Reducing panic

Panic occurs when you just stop thinking. Your most basic survival instincts take over, even when they are totally uncalled for. You're losing money? You start to trade more and more, off-plan, in a desperate gamble to win it back. You're making money? You close out all your trades right now so that you can't possibly lose, even if your plan tells you to hold your positions. When you panic, you can't think straight, and you can't follow your plan.

One problem is that when your positions are down, and you seem to be losing money, you really should be buying and sticking it out so that you can make money later. That's tough to do and requires a lot of discipline. With experience traders learn to avoid panic.

You're probably going to have more than a few losing trades when you get started. It's a good idea to keep a trading diary where you write down the reasons behind every trade you made. (See *Day Trading For Canadians For Dummies* for more details.) The notes help you remember what it felt like to lose money. Can you handle it emotionally? If losing upsets you too much, you might not be cut out for day trading. You can't trade with a clear head when you're bogged down with negative thoughts.

Confidence versus ego

Day trading requires a lot of confidence, because you *are* going to lose money and you *are* going to get beaten up some days. You have to not only remain confident in the face of adversity, but also be careful you don't cross from confidence into an inflated ego. The more your trading success and failure become part of your personal identity, the more trouble you are going to have.

What's the difference between confidence and ego? It's "I'm smart enough to figure out what the market is telling me" versus "I'm smarter than the market." The difference is crucial to your success.

Revising and troubleshooting your trading plan

Strong discipline is key to success in trading, but only if you're disciplined in following the right system. If your trading method is flawed, then sticking to it is going to hurt you. If something isn't working, don't get mad at the system; take some responsibility and make some changes.

How do you figure out whether your trading system is right and what changes to make? Go through your trading diary and ask yourself some questions:

✦ Why did you choose this system? What is the market telling you about it? Is it telling you that the system works if you follow it, or is it telling you that something is wrong with the underlying assumptions?

What works for someone else might not work for you. There's no flaw in admitting that you made a mistake and that you need to make a change.

✦ Were your mistakes because you followed the plan, or because you didn't?

✦ What part of the system is causing the trouble? Are you having trouble identifying entry points or exit points? Or are you stuck when it comes time to enter the trade, causing you to miss a point? Or is it that the trades your system identifies never seem to work out?

When you know where the problem is, you can change it.

✦ Can you improve your trade efficiency? Is there a way to reduce the number of mistakes? Would automating some or all of your trading help?

One way to get your confidence back while still staying in the market is to trade in very small amounts so that your profits and losses don't really matter. Trade 100 shares, not 1,000 shares. You give up the upside for a time, but you can also get out of the cycle of greed and fear that has destroyed many a trader.

Managing Your Money and Positions

The first three chapters of the day trading part of this book are designed to give you ideas about whether to day trade at all, what you want to trade, and how you want to trade it. That leaves one remaining issue: how much of your money to put on the line each time you trade. Risk too much, and you can be put out of business when you lose your capital. Risk too little, and you can be put of out business because you can't make enough money to cover your costs and time.

Over time, many academic theorists and experienced traders have developed different systems of money management designed to help traders, investors, and even gamblers manage their money in order to maximize return while protecting capital. In this chapter, we explain how some of the better-known systems work so that you can figure out how to best apply them to your own trading.

Some of the material in the latter half of this chapter is related to *leverage,* which is borrowing money to trade. Leverage can dramatically increase the money that you have available to trade as well as the risk and return profile of the trades that you make, so it affects how you manage your money. Flip to Chapter 14 in *Day Trading For Canadians For Dummies* for more information on leverage and why you might want to use it.

What's Your Expected Return?

Before you can figure out how to manage your money, you need to figure out how much money you can expect to make. This is your *expected return,* although some traders prefer the word *expectancy.* You start by laying out your trading system and testing it (described in Chapter 11 of *Day Trading For Canadians For Dummies*). You're looking for four numbers:

+ How many of your trades are losers?

+ What's the typical percentage loss on a losing trade?

+ How many of your trades are winners?

+ What's the typical percentage gain on a winning trade?

Say you determine that 40 percent of the time a trade loses, and it loses 1 percent. Sixty percent of the time the trade wins, and winning trades are up 1.5 percent. With these numbers, you can calculate your per-trade expected return, like this:

```
% of losing trades × loss on losing trades + % of winning
    trades × gain on winning trades = expected return
```

Which, in this example, works out to be:

```
.40 × −.01 + .60 × .015 = −.004 + .009 = .005
```

On average, then, you would expect to earn a half-percent on every trade you make. Make enough trades with enough money, and it adds up.

You're more likely to make more money when you have a high expectation of winning trades and when you expect those winners to perform well. As long as some probability of loss exists, you stand to lose money.

The Probability of Ruin

Expected return is the happy number. It's how much money you can expect to make if you stay in the trading game. And it has a counterpart that is not so happy but is at least as important: the *probability of ruin*.

As long as you face some probability of loss, no matter how small, some probability exists that you can lose everything when you are trading. How much you can lose depends on how large each trade is relative to your account, the likelihood of each trade having a loss, and the size of the losses as they occur.

Figure 3-1 shows the math for finding R, the probability of ruin.

Figure 3-1:
How to calculate the probability of ruin.

$$R = \left[\frac{(1 - A)}{1 + A} \right]^{c}$$

A is the advantage on each trade in Figure 3-1. That's the difference between the percentage of winning trades and the percentage of losing trades. In the expected-return example we discuss earlier, trades win 60 percent of the time and lose 40 percent of the time. In that case, the trader's advantage would be:

```
60% - 40% = 20%
```

C is the number of trades in an account. Assume we're dividing the account into ten equal parts, with the plan of making ten trades today. The probability of ruin today is 1.7 percent (Figure 3-2).

Figure 3-2:
An example of the risk of ruin calculation.

$$1.7\% = \left[\frac{(1 - .20)}{1 + .20}\right]^{10}$$

Now, 1.7 percent isn't a high likelihood of ruin, but it's not zero, either. It could happen. If your advantage is smaller, if the expected loss is larger, or if the number of trades is fewer, then the likelihood becomes even higher.

Figure 3-3 shows you the relationship between the trader's advantage, number of trades, and the corresponding probability of ruin, rounded to the nearest percentage.

Probability of Ruin

Figure 3-3:
Adding trader's advantage to the mix.

Trader's Advantage	Number of Trades									
	1	2	3	4	5	6	7	8	9	10
2%	96%	92%	89%	85%	82%	79%	76%	73%	70%	67%
4%	92%	85%	79%	73%	67%	62%	57%	53%	49%	45%
6%	89%	79%	70%	62%	55%	49%	43%	38%	34%	30%
8%	85%	73%	62%	53%	45%	38%	33%	28%	24%	20%
10%	82%	67%	55%	45%	37%	30%	25%	20%	16%	13%
12%	79%	62%	49%	38%	30%	24%	18%	15%	11%	9%
14%	75%	57%	43%	32%	24%	18%	14%	10%	8%	6%
16%	72%	52%	38%	27%	20%	14%	10%	8%	5%	4%
18%	69%	48%	34%	23%	16%	11%	8%	5%	4%	3%
20%	67%	44%	30%	20%	13%	9%	6%	4%	3%	2%

The bigger the edge and the more trades you can make, the lower your probability of ruin. Now, this model is a simplification in that it assumes a losing trade goes to zero, and that's not always the case. In fact, if you use stops (automatic buy and sell orders, described in Chapter 1), you should never have a trade go to zero. But you can see steady erosion in your account that will make it harder for you to make money. Hence, probability of ruin is a useful calculation that shows whether you will lose money in the long run.

The more trades you can make with your account, the lower your probability of ruin. That's why money management is a key part of risk management.

Why Size Matters

As long as some chance of losing all your money exists, you want to avoid betting all of it on any one trade. But as long as you have a chance of making money, you want enough exposure to a winning trade so that you can post good profits. How do you figure it out?

Later in this chapter, we describe some of the different money management systems that traders use to figure out how much money to risk per trade. But first we want to explain the logic behind a money management system, so that you understand why you need one. That way, you can better manage your funds and improve the dollar returns to your trading.

Valuing volatility

Expected return gives you an idea of how much you can get from a trade on average, but it doesn't tell you how much that return might vary from trade to trade. The average of 9, 10, and 11 is 10; the average of –90, 10, and 100 is also 10. The first number series is a lot narrower than the second. The wider the range of returns a strategy has, the more *volatile* it is.

We can measure volatility in several ways. One common way is *standard deviation,* which tells you how much your actual return is likely to differ from what you expect to get. (We provide a detailed explanation of the standard deviation calculation in *Day Trading For Canadians For Dummies.*) The higher the standard deviation, the more volatile, and riskier, the strategy.

In the derivatives markets, volatility is measured by a group of numbers known as the Greeks: delta, gamma, vega, and theta. They're based on calculus.

✦ **Delta** is a ratio that tells you how much the option or future changes in price when the underlying security or market index changes in price. Delta changes over time.

✦ **Gamma** is the rate of change on delta. That's because a derivative's delta will be higher when it is close to the expiration date, for example, than when the expiration date is farther away.

✦ **Vega** is the amount that the derivative would change in price if the underlying security became 1 percent more volatile.

✦ **Theta** is the amount that a derivative's price declines as it gets closer to the day of expiration.

Day traders seek out more volatile securities, because they offer more opportunities to make money during any given day. That means they have to have ways to minimize the damage that might occur, while being able to capitalize on the upward swings. Money management can help with that.

Staying in the market

You have only a limited amount of money to trade. Whether it's $1,000 or $1,000,000, when it's gone, you're out. The problem is that you can have a long string of losing trades before the markets go in a direction that favours you and your system.

Say you trade 100 percent of your account. If you have one trade that goes down 100 percent, then you have nothing. If you divide your account into ten parts, then you can have ten total losers before you're out. If you start with ten equal parts and double each time you lose, you can be out after four losing trades.

The riskier your trading strategy, the more thought you need to put into money management. Otherwise, you can find yourself out of the market in no time.

On the other hand, if you divide your account into 100 portions, then you can endure 100 losing trades. If you trade fractions of your account, then you can keep going infinitely, or at least until you get down to a level that's too low to place a minimum order. (That's the philosophy behind the Kelly criterion, described later in this chapter.) Money management can keep you in the game longer, and that will give you more opportunities to place winning trades.

Considering opportunity costs

Opportunity cost is the value you give up because you choose to do something else. In trading, each dollar you commit to one trade is a dollar that you cannot commit to another trade. Thus, each dollar you trade carries some opportunity cost, and good traders seek to minimize this cost. During the course of the trading day, you may see several great trades, and some opportunities will show up before you're ready to close out a different trade.

If you've committed all your capital to one trade, you will miss out on the second. That alone is a good reason to keep some money on the table each time you trade.

Money Management Styles

Over the years, traders have developed many different ways to manage their money. Some of these are rooted in superstition, but most are based on different statistical probability theories. The underlying idea is to never place all of your money in a single trade; rather, put in an amount that is appropriate given the level of volatility. Otherwise, you risk losing everything too soon.

Calculating position size under many of these formulas is tricky stuff. That's why brokerage firms and trading software packages often include money management calculators. Check Book 4, Chapter 3 for more information on brokers, and Chapter 7 in *Day Trading For Canadians For Dummies* for more on the different software and research services.

This is only a sample of some methods. We talk about some other ones in *Day Trading For Canadians For Dummies*. Keep in mind that none is suitable to all markets all the time. Folks trading both options and stocks may want to use one system for option trades and another for stock trades. If that's your situation, you have one big money management decision to make before you begin: how much money to allocate to each market.

Fixed fractional

Fixed fractional trading assumes you want to limit each trade to a set portion of your total account, often between 2 and 10 percent. Within that range, you'd trade a larger percentage of money in less risky trades and stay toward the smaller end of the scale for more risky trades. (In other words, it's not all that "fixed" — but no one asked us to pick a name for the system.)

The fixed fractional equation is shown in Figure 3-4.

Figure 3-4: The equation for calculating fixed fractional trade proportions.

$$N = f\left(\frac{equity}{|trade\ risk|}\right)$$

N is the number of contracts or shares of stock you should trade, *f* is the fixed fraction of your account that you have decided to trade, *equity* is the value of your total account, and *trade risk* is the amount of money you could lose on the transaction. Because trade risk is a negative number, you need to convert it to a positive number to make the equation work. Those vertical bars in the equation (| |) are the sign for absolute value, and that means you convert the number between them to a positive number.

This means that if you've decided to limit each trade to 10 percent of your account, you have a $20,000 account, and the risk of loss is –$3,500, your trade should be what is shown in Figure 3-5.

$$0.57 = .10\left(\frac{20{,}000}{|-3500|}\right)$$

Of course, you probably can't trade .57 of a contract, so in this case you would have to round up to one.

Fixed ratio

The *fixed ratio* money management system is used in trading options and futures. It was developed by a trader named Ryan Jones, who wrote a book about it. In order to find the optimal number of options or futures contracts to trade, N, you use the equation shown in Figure 3-6.

$$N = 0.05\left(\sqrt{1 + 8\left(P/\Delta\right)} + 1\right)$$

N is the number of contracts or shares of stock that you should trade, P is your accumulated profit to date, and the triangle, delta, is the dollar amount that you would need before you could trade a second contract or another lot of stock. (This is *not* the same delta measure discussed previously, which is a measure of volatility.)

For example, the minimum margin for the Chicago Mercantile Exchange E-Mini S&P 500 futures contract, which gives you exposure to the Standard & Poor's 500 stock index, is $3,500. Until you have another $3,500 in your account, you can't trade a second contract. If you are using fixed ratio money management to trade this future, your delta will be $3,500.

If your delta is $3,500, and you have $10,000 in account profits, you should trade 1.2 contracts (see Figure 3-7). In reality, that means you can trade only one contract or two contracts, nothing in between. That's one of the imperfections of most money management systems.

Figure 3-7:
An example using the fixed ratio calculation.

$$1.2 = 0.05\left(\sqrt{1 + 8\left(10{,}000/3500\right)} + 1\right)$$

The idea behind fixed ratio trading is to help you increase your exposure to the market while protecting your accumulated profits.

Kelly criterion

The Kelly criterion emerged from statistical work done at Bell Laboratories in the 1950s. The goal was to figure out the best ways to manage signal–noise issues in long-distance telephone communications. Very quickly the mathematicians who worked on it saw its applications to gambling, and in no time the formula took off.

To calculate the ideal percentage of your portfolio to put at risk, you need to know what percentage of your trades are expected to win as well as the return from a winning trade and the ratio performance of winning trades to losing trades. The shorthand that many traders use for the Kelly criterion is *edge divided by odds,* and in practice the formula looks like this:

```
Kelly % = W - [(1 - W) / R]
```

W is the percentage of winning trades, and R is the ratio of the average gain of the winning trades relative to the average loss of the losing trades.

Earlier in the chapter, we had an example of a system that loses 40 percent of the time with a loss of 1 percent and that wins 60 percent of the time with a gain of 1.5 percent. Plugging that into the Kelly formula, the right percentage to trade is .60 – [(1 – .60)/(.015/.01)], or 33.3 percent.

As long as you limit your trades to no more than 33 percent of your capital, you should never run out of money. The problem, of course, is that if you have a long string of losses, you could find yourself with too little money to execute a trade. Many traders use a "half-Kelly" strategy, limiting each trade to half the amount indicated by the Kelly criterion as a way to keep the trading account from shrinking too quickly. They are especially likely to do this if the Kelly criterion generates a number greater than about 20 percent, as in this example.

Martingale

The *martingale* style of money management is common with serious casino gamblers, and many traders apply it as well. It's designed to improve the amount of money you can earn in a game that has even odds. Most casino odds favour the house (roulette wheels used to be evenly black and red, but casinos found that they could make more money if they inserted a green slice for zero, thus throwing off the odds). Day trading, on the other hand, is a zero-sum game, especially in the options and futures markets. This means that for every winner there is a loser, so the odds of any one trade being successful are even. The martingale system is designed to work in any market where the odds are even or in your favour.

Under the martingale strategy, you start with a set amount per trade, say $2,000. If your trade succeeds, you trade another $2,000. If your trade loses, you double your next order (after you close or limit the first trade) so that you can win back your loss. (You may have heard gamblers talk about *doubling down* — this is what they are doing.)

Under the martingale system, you will always come out ahead as long as you have an infinite amount of money to trade. The problem is that you can run out of money before you have a trade that works. The market, on the other hand, has almost infinite resources because of the huge volume of participants coming and going all over the world. That means you have an enormous disadvantage. As long as you have a disadvantage, thoughtful money management is critical.

How Money Management Affects Your Return

It's one thing to describe why you need money management, but it's more fun to show you how it works. And because we love making spreadsheets (we all need a hobby, right?), we pulled one together to show you how different ways of managing your money might affect your return.

In Figure 3-2, we started with the expected return assumptions that we used in the earlier example: 40 percent of the time a trade loses, and it loses 1 percent. Sixty percent of the time the trade wins, and winning trades are up 1.5 percent. In Figure 3-8, she picks a hypothetical account of $20,000 and sets up mock trades using these expected return numbers. Figure 3-8 compares the performance of martingale and Kelly money management to betting the whole account each time.

You may notice in Figure 3-8 that you end up with the most money from trading the entire account. That doesn't mean you always get the most money this way, just that that's how the numbers worked out in this case, given the 60/40 win ratio and a 3/2 winning size/losing size ratio. (Keep in mind that if you were using a Kelly or martingale system, you'd probably be doing something with the rest of the account rather than just letting it sit there.)

Martingale: Starting with 10% and Doubling Losses

	Performance	Intial Account Value	% Traded	Amount Traded	Ending Account Value	% Change
Trade 1	1.5%	$ 20,000	10%	$ 2,000	$ 20,030	
Trade 2	1.5%	$ 20,030		$ 2,000	$ 20,060	
Trade 3	-1.0%	$ 20,060		$ 2,000	$ 20,040	
Trade 4	-1.0%	$ 20,040		$ 4,000	$ 20,000	
Trade 5	1.5%	$ 20,000		$ 8,000	$ 20,120	
Trade 6	1.5%	$ 20,120		$ 2,000	$ 20,150	
Trade 7	-1.0%	$ 20,150		$ 2,000	$ 20,130	
Trade 8	-1.0%	$ 20,130		$ 4,000	$ 20,090	
Trade 9	1.5%	$ 20,090		$ 8,000	$ 20,210	
Trade 10	1.5%	$ 20,210		$ 2,000	$ 20,240	1.20%

Kelly: Trading 33%

	Performance	Intial Account Value	% Traded	Amount Traded	Ending Account Value	
Trade 1	1.5%	$ 20,000	33%	$ 6,660	$ 20,100	
Trade 2	1.5%	$ 20,100	33%	$ 6,693	$ 20,200	
Trade 3	-1.0%	$ 20,200	33%	$ 6,727	$ 20,133	
Trade 4	-1.0%	$ 20,133	33%	$ 6,704	$ 20,066	
Trade 5	1.5%	$ 20,066	33%	$ 6,682	$ 20,166	
Trade 6	1.5%	$ 20,166	33%	$ 6,715	$ 20,267	
Trade 7	-1.0%	$ 20,267	33%	$ 6,749	$ 20,199	
Trade 8	-1.0%	$ 20,199	33%	$ 6,726	$ 20,132	
Trade 9	1.5%	$ 20,132	33%	$ 6,704	$ 20,233	
Trade 10	1.5%	$ 20,233	33%	$ 6,738	$ 20,334	1.67%

Betting Everything

	Performance	Intial Account Value	% Traded	Amount Traded	Ending Account Value	
Trade 1	1.5%	$ 20,000	100%	$ 20,000	$ 20,300	
Trade 2	1.5%	$ 20,300	100%	$ 20,300	$ 20,605	
Trade 3	-1.0%	$ 20,605	100%	$ 20,605	$ 20,398	
Trade 4	-1.0%	$ 20,398	100%	$ 20,398	$ 20,194	
Trade 5	1.5%	$ 20,194	100%	$ 20,194	$ 20,497	
Trade 6	1.5%	$ 20,497	100%	$ 20,497	$ 20,805	
Trade 7	-1.0%	$ 20,805	100%	$ 20,805	$ 20,597	
Trade 8	-1.0%	$ 20,597	100%	$ 20,597	$ 20,391	
Trade 9	1.5%	$ 20,391	100%	$ 20,391	$ 20,697	
Trade 10	1.5%	$ 20,697	100%	$ 20,697	$ 21,007	5.04%

Figure 3-8:
How money
management
affects your
return.

WARNING!

This is just an example, applying some different strategies to different hypothetical returns. We're not recommending any one system over another. The best system for you depends on what assets you are trading, your personal trading style, and how much money you have to trade.

Planning for Your Profits

In addition to determining how much to trade each time you place an order, you need a plan for what to do with the profits that accumulate in your account. That's as much a part of money management as calculating your probability of ruin and determining trade size.

Are you going to add the money to your account and trade it as before? Leverage your profits by trading them more aggressively than your core account? Pull money out and put it into long-term investments? Or a combination of the three?

Compounding interest

Compound interest is a simple concept: Every time you get a return, that return goes into your account. You keep earning a return on it, which increases your account size some more. You keep earning a return on your return, and soon the numbers get to be pretty big. (Find out more in Book 1, Chapter 1.)

In order to benefit from that compounding, many traders add their profits back into their accounts and keep trading them, in order to build account size. Although day traders earn little to no interest (which is compensation for loaning out money — say, by buying bonds), the basic principle holds: By returning profits to the trading account to generate even more profits, the account should grow over time.

This practice of keeping profits in the account to trade makes a lot of sense for smaller traders who want to build their accounts and take more significant positions over time.

Pyramiding power

Pyramiding involves taking trading profits and borrowing heavily against them to generate even more profits. Traders usually do this during the day, using unrealized profits in trades that are not yet closed as collateral for loans used to establish new positions. If the new positions are profitable, the trader can keep borrowing until it's time to close everything at the end of the day.

This works great as long as the markets are moving in the right direction. If all the positions in the pyramid remain profitable, you can make a lot of money during the course of the day. But if one of those positions turns against you, the structure collapses and you end up with a call on your margin. Figure 3-9 starts with an initial trade of $2,000 and assumes a return of 10 percent on each transaction — not realistic, necessarily, but it makes for a nice chart. If the profits from each trade are used as collateral for borrowing, and if that 10 percent return holds all day, then the trader can make 17 percent by pyramiding those gains. If a reversal hits before the end of the trading session and the positions lose 10 percent, then pyramiding magnifies the losses — assuming your broker would let you keep borrowing. After all, the borrowed money has to be repaid regardless of what happens in the market.

Pyramiding magnifies returns
Assume that you need to maintain 25% margin

	Initial Trade Equity	Amount Borrowed	Total Trade Size	Profit at 10% Return
First trade	$ 2,000	$ -	$ 2,000	$ 200
Second trade	$ 200	$ 600	$ 800	$ 80
Third trade	$ 80	$ 240	$ 320	$ 32
Fourth trade	$ 32	$ 96	$ 128	$ 13
Fifth trade	$ 13	$ 38	$ 51	$ 5
Sixth trade	$ 5	$ 15	$ 20	$ 2
Return on initial $2000 trade:	$ 332			
Percentage return:	17%			

... And pyramiding magnifies losses

	Initial Trade Equity	Amount Borrowed	Total Trade Size	Profit at 10% Return
First trade	$ 2,000	$ -	$ 2,000	$ (200)
Second trade	$ 200	$ 600	$ 800	$ (80)
Third trade	$ 80	$ 240	$ 320	$ (32)
Fourth trade	$ 32	$ 96	$ 128	$ (13)
Fifth trade	$ 13	$ 38	$ 51	$ (5)
Sixth trade	$ 5	$ 15	$ 20	$ (2)
Return on initial $2000 trade:	$ (332)			
Percentage return:	-17%			

Figure 3-9:
Pyramiding
magnifies
returns and
losses.

Pyramiding is not related to a *pyramid scheme*. In trading terms, pyramiding is a way to borrow against your profits to generate even bigger profits. A pyramid scheme is a fraud that requires participants to recruit new members, and fees paid by the new members go to the older ones. Eventually, the pyramid collapses because it gets too difficult to recruit new members, and those at the bottom get nothing.

Some investment frauds have been structured as pyramid schemes, so be wary of deals that sound fabulous and also require you to recruit others.

Pyramiding increases your trading risk, but also your expected return. It's a useful way to grow a portion of your trading account, especially when the market is favouring your trading system. It's a good technique for a medium-sized account that would have enough money left over to stay in the market if a pyramid were to collapse on you.

Regular withdrawals

Because day trading can be so risky, many traders look to diversify their total financial risk. One way to do this is to pull money out of the trading account to put into a less volatile long-term investment. Many traders routinely pull out a percentage of their profits and put that money into government bonds, a low-risk mutual fund, or real estate. None of these investments is as glamorous or exciting as day trading, but that's the point: Trading is hard work, and anyone can lose money any day, no matter how big their account is or how much money they have made so far. By moving some money out, a trader can build a cushion for a bad trading stretch, prepare for retirement, and have some money to walk away for a short period or even forever. That can greatly reduce the stress and the fear that go with trading.

The larger the account, the easier it is to pull money out, but even smaller traders should consider taking 5 or 10 percent of each quarter's profits and moving them into another type of investment. If you don't trust yourself to do it, many brokerage firms can set up automatic withdrawal plans that zap money from your trading account over to a stock or bond mutual fund.

Chapter 4: Using Fundamental and Technical Analysis

In This Chapter

✔ Researching markets and trades

✔ Using technical analysis to forecast prices

✔ Gleaning information from the charts

✔ Getting a handle on market psychology

✔ Assessing the mood of the markets

✔ Understanding market anomalies and traps

In some ways, day trading is easy. Open up an account with a brokerage firm and off you go, buying and selling securities! But how are you going to know when to buy and when to sell? That's not a simple matter. Most day traders fail because it's easy to place the order, but hard to know if the order is the right one.

Traders use different research systems to evaluate the market. They have access to tools that can help them figure out when a security is likely to go up in price and when it is likely to go down.

Research systems fall into two categories: fundamental and technical. *Fundamental* research looks at the specific factors that affect a security's value. What's the relationship between the trade deficit and futures on two-year Treasury notes? What's the prediction for summer rainfall in Saskatchewan, and how will that affect December wheat futures? How dependent is a company on new products to generate earnings growth?

Technical research, on the other hand, looks at the supply and demand for the security itself. Are people buying more and more shares? Is the price going up as they buy more, or does the price go up just a little bit? Does it seem like everyone who is likely to buy has already bought, and what does that mean for the future price?

Anyone with a surefire system has already made a fortune and retired to a private island in a tropical climate. He or she is too busy enjoying drinks with umbrellas in them to share that surefire trading system with you.

Research Techniques Used in Day Trading

Day traders need to make decisions fast, and they need to have a framework for doing so. That's why they rely on research. But what kind? Most day traders rely heavily on *technical research,* which is an analysis of charts formed by price patterns to measure the relative supply and demand for the security. But some use fundamental analysis to help inform their decisions, too.

What direction is your research?

Securities are affected by matters specific to each type and by huge global macroeconomic factors that affect every security in different ways. Some traders prefer to think of the big picture first, whereas others start small. And some use a combination of the two approaches. Neither is better; each is simply a different perspective on what's happening in the markets.

Top-down research

With a *top-down* approach, the trader looks at the big economic factors: interest rates, exchange rates, government policies, and the like. How will these things affect a particular sector or security? Is this a good time to buy stocks or short interest rate futures? The top-down approach can help evaluate the prices in big market sectors, and it can also help determine what factors are affecting trading in a subsector. You don't have to trade stock market index futures to know that the outlook for the overall stock market will have an effect on the trading of any specific company's stock.

Bottom-up research

Bottom-up analysis looks at the specific performance of the asset. It looks at the company's prospects and then works backward to figure out how it will get there. What has to happen for a company's stock price to go up 20 percent? What earnings does it have to report, what types of buyers have to materialize, and what else has to happen in the economy?

Fundamental research

Day traders do very little fundamental research. Sure, they know that demand for ethanol affects corn prices, but they really want to know what the price will do right now relative to where the price was a few minutes ago. How a proposed farm bill might affect ethanol prices in six years doesn't figure into day trade, though. Knowing a little bit about the fundamentals — those basic facts that affect the supply and demand for a security in all markets — can help the day trader respond better to news events. It can also give you a better feel for when *swing trading* (holding a position for several days) will generate a better profit than closing out every night. But knowing a lot can drag a day trader down.

Fundamental analysis can actually *hurt* you in day trading, because you may start making decisions for the wrong reasons. If you know too much about the fundamentals, you might start considering long-term outlooks instead of short-term activity. For example, someone may buy an S&P/TSX Composite Index ETF for their RRSP because they believe that in the long run, the market will go up. That doesn't mean people should trade S&P/TSX Composite Index Mini Futures today, because there can be a lot of zigzagging between right now and the arrival of the long-run price appreciation.

Fundamental research falls into two main categories: top-down and bottom-up. As we mention earlier, top-down starts with broad economic considerations and then looks at how those will affect a specific security. Bottom-up looks at specific securities and then determines whether those are good buys or sells right now.

If you love the very idea of fundamental research, then day trading is probably not for you. Day trading requires quick responses to price changes, not a careful understanding of accounting methods and business trends. A little fundamental analysis can be helpful in day trading, but a lot can slow you down.

Technical analysis

Information about the price, time, and volume of a security's trading can be plotted on a chart. The plots form patterns that can be analyzed to show what happened. How did the supply and demand for a security change, and why? And what does that mean for future supply and demand? Technical analysis is based on the premise that securities prices move in trends, and that those trends repeat themselves over time. Therefore, a trader who can recognize a trend on the charts can determine where prices are most likely to go until some unforeseen event comes along that creates a new trend.

The basic element of technical analysis is a *bar*, which shows you the open, high, low, and close price of a security for a given day. It looks like Figure 4-1.

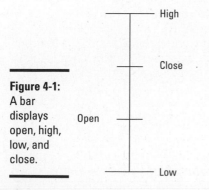

Figure 4-1:
A bar displays open, high, low, and close.

In most markets, every day generates a new *bar* (many traders talk about bars instead of days, and they aren't talking about where they go after work). A collection of bars, with all their different open, high, low, and close points, is put together into a larger *chart*. Often, a plot of the volume for each bar runs underneath, with the result looking like Figure 4-2.

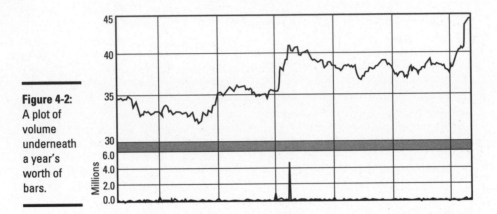

Figure 4-2: A plot of volume underneath a year's worth of bars.

Many patterns formed in the charts are associated with future price moves. Technical analysts thus spend a lot of time looking at the charts to see whether they can predict what will happen. Many software packages send traders signals when certain technical patterns occur, so that the traders can place orders accordingly.

Technical analysis is a way to measure the supply and demand in the market. It's a tool for analyzing the markets, not predicting them. If it were that easy, everyone would be able to make money in the markets.

Price changes

Market observers debate *market efficiency* all the time. In an efficient market, all information about a security is already included in the security's price, so no point exists to doing any research at all. Few market participants are willing to go that far, but they concede the point that the price is the single most important summary of information about a company. That means that technical analysis, looking at how the price changes over time, is a way of learning about whether a security's prospects are improving or getting worse.

Volume changes

The basic bar shows how price changed during the day, but adding *volume* information tells the other part of the story: how much of a security was demanded at that price. If demand is going up, then more people want the security, so they are willing to pay more for it. The price tells traders what the market knows; the volume tells them how many people in the market know it.

How to Use Technical Analysis

Technical analysis helps day traders identify changes in the supply and demand for a security that may lead to profitable price changes ahead. It gives traders a way to talk about and think about the market so that they can be more effective.

Charts are generated by most brokerage firm quote systems, sometimes with the help of additional software that automatically marks the chart with trendlines. That's because a technical trader is looking for those trendlines. Is the security going up in price, and is that trend going to continue? That's the information a trader needs before placing an order to buy or sell.

One interesting aspect of technical analysis is that the basics hold no matter what market you are looking at. Technical analysis can help you monitor trends in the stock market, the bond market, the commodity market, and the currency market. Anywhere people try to match their supply and their demand to make a market, technical analysis can be used to show how well they're doing it.

Finding trends

A technical analyst usually starts off by looking at a chart and drawing lines that show the overall direction of the price bars for the period in question. Rather than plot the graph on paper or print out the screen, she probably uses software to draw the lines. Figure 4-3 shows what this basic analysis looks like.

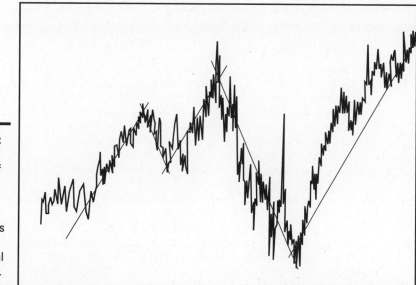

Figure 4-3:
Basic
analysis of
trends in
price bar
changes
draws lines
showing
the general
movement.

With the basic trendlines in place, the trader can start thinking about how the trends have played out so far and what might happen next.

Here's the thing about trends: Sometimes it's good to follow, and sometimes it's good to deviate. Remember when you were a kid, and you wanted to do something that all your friends were doing? And your mother would invariably say, "If all your friends jumped off of a bridge, would you have to jump off, too?"

Well, Mom, guess what? If the bridge was on fire, if the escape routes were blocked by angry mobs, if the water were just a few metres down, yes, we just might jump off the bridge like everyone else. Likewise, if someone was paying us good money to jump, and we knew we weren't likely to get hurt on the way down, we'd be over the railing in a flash. Sometimes it's good to be a follower.

But if our friends were idiots, if there were no fire and no angry mob, and if we couldn't swim, we might not be so hasty.

Trend following is like those mythical childhood friends on that mythical hometown bridge. Sometimes, you should join the crowd. Other times, it's best to deviate.

Draw those trendlines!

The most basic *trendline* is a line that shows the general direction of the trend. And that's a good start, but it doesn't tell you all you need to know. The next step is to take out your ruler, or set your software, to find the trendlines that connect the highs and the lows. That will create a channel that tells you the *support level* — the trendline for the lows — and the *resistance level* — the trendline for the highs. Unless something happens to change the trend, securities tend to move within the channel, so extending the line into the future can give you a sense of where the security is likely to trade. Figure 4-4 shows you an example.

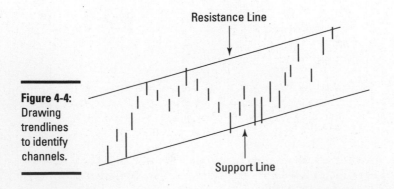

Figure 4-4:
Drawing trendlines to identify channels.

Resistance Line

Support Line

When a security hits its support level, it is usually seen as relatively cheap — so that's a good time to buy. When a security hits its resistance level, it is usually seen as relatively expensive, so that's a good time to sell. Some day traders find that simply moving between buying at the support and selling at the resistance can be a profitable strategy, at least until something happens that changes those two levels.

Calculating indicators

In addition to drawing lines, technical analysts use their calculators — or have their software make calculations — to come up with different *indicators*. These are numbers that are used to gauge performance. The following is a list of some common indicators, with definitions.

Pivot points

A *pivot point* is the average of the high, low, and close price for the day. If the next day's price closes above the pivot point, that sets a new support level, and if the next day's price is below the pivot point, that sets a new resistance level. Hence, calculating pivot points and how they change might indicate new upper and lower stops for your trading. (You can read more about using stops in Chapter 1.)

For markets that are open more or less continuously, such as foreign exchange (dealing in currencies), the close price is set arbitrarily. The usual custom in Canada and the United States is to use the price at 4:00 p.m. Eastern time, which is the closing time for the Toronto Stock Exchange and the New York Stock Exchange.

Moving averages

Looking at all those little open-high-low-close lines on a chart will give your bifocals a workout. To make the trend easier to spot, traders calculate a *moving average*. It's calculated by averaging the closing prices for a given time period. Some traders prefer to look at the last 5 days, some at the last 60 days. Every day, the latest price is added, and the oldest price is dropped to make that day's calculation. Given the wonders of modern computing technology, it's easy to pull up moving averages for almost any time period you want. The average for each day is then plotted against the price chart to show how the trend is changing over time. Figure 4-5 shows an example of a 10-day moving average chart.

Traders use the moving average line to look for crossovers, convergences, and divergences. A *crossover* occurs whenever the price crosses the moving average line. Usually, it's a good idea to buy when the price crosses above the moving average line and to sell when the price crosses below it.

To use *convergence* and *divergence* in analysis, the trader looks at moving averages from different time periods, such as 5 days, 10 days, and 20 days. Figure 4-6 shows what it looks like.

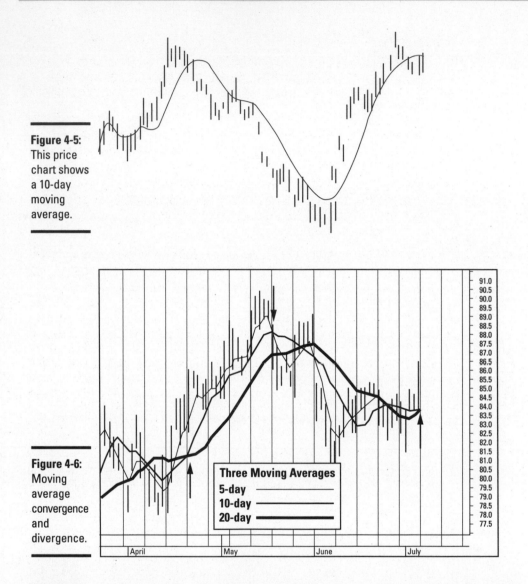

Figure 4-5:
This price chart shows a 10-day moving average.

Figure 4-6:
Moving average convergence and divergence.

When two or three of the moving average lines converge (come together), it means the trend may be ending. That often makes it a good time to buy if the trend has been down — and a good time to sell if the trend has been up. If two or three of the moving average lines split up and diverge, that means the trend is likely to continue. It's probably a good time to buy if the trend is up and sell if the trend is down.

A moving average is a lagging indicator. It sums up trading activity in the last 5, 10, 30, or 60 days. That means that the line will smooth out changes in the trend that may affect future prices.

Trends move in phases

Price trends tend to move in cycles that can be seen on the charts or observed in market behaviour. Knowing the phases of a trend can help you better evaluate what's happening. Here is a summary of some phases of a trend:

✦ **Accumulation:** This is the first part of the trend, where traders get excited about a security and its prospects. They start new positions or add to existing ones.

✦ **Main phase (also called continuation):** Here, the trend moves along nicely, with no unusual price action. The highs get higher on an uptrend, and the lows get lower on a downtrend. A trader might make money, but not big money, following the trend here.

✦ **Consolidation (also called congestion):** This is a sideways market. The security stays within the trend, but without hitting higher highs or lower lows. It just stays within the trading range. A consolidation phase is good for scalpers, who make a large volume of trades in search of very small profits. It can be boring for everyone else.

✦ **Retracement (also called correction or pullback):** This is a secondary trend, a short-term pullback away from the main trend to the support level. Retracements create buying opportunities, but they can also kill day traders who are following the trend.

✦ **Distribution:** In the distribution phase, traders don't think that the security can go up in price any more. Hence, they tend to sell in large volume.

✦ **Reversal:** This is the point where the trend changes. It's time to sell if you had been following an uptrend and buy if you had been following a downtrend. Many reversals follow classic patterns, which are discussed later in this chapter.

Those ever-changing trends

Although technical traders look to follow trends, they also look for situations where the trend changes so that they can find new profit opportunities. In general, day traders are going to follow trends, and swing traders — those who hold securities for a few days or even weeks — are going to be more interested in identifying changes that may play out over time.

Momentum

Following the trend is great, but if the trend is moving quickly you want to know so that you can get ahead of it. If the rate of change on the trend is going up, then rising prices are likely to occur.

To calculate *momentum,* take today's closing price for a security, divide that by the closing price ten days ago, and then multiply by 100. This gives you a *momentum indicator.* If the price didn't go anywhere, the momentum indicator will be 100. If the price went up, the indicator will be greater than 100. And if it went down, it will be less than 100. In technical analysis, trends are usually expected to continue, so a security with a momentum indicator above 100 is expected to keep going up, all else being equal.

But it's that "all else being equal" that's the sticky part. Technical analysts usually track momentum indicators over time to see if the positive momentum is, itself, a trend. In fact, momentum indicators are a good confirmation of the underlying trend.

Momentum is a leading technical indicator. It tells you what is likely to happen in the future, not what has happened in the past.

Momentum trading is usually done with some attention to the fundamentals. When key business fundamentals such as sales or profits are accelerating at the same time that the security is going up in price, the momentum is likely to continue for some time. You can read more about momentum trading and investing in *Day Trading For Canadians For Dummies.*

Finding breakouts

A *breakout* occurs when a security price passes through and stays above — or below — the resistance or support line, which creates a new trend with new support and resistance levels. A one-time breakout may just be an anomaly, what technicians sometimes call a *false breakout,* but pay attention to two or more breakouts. Figure 4-7 shows what breakouts look like.

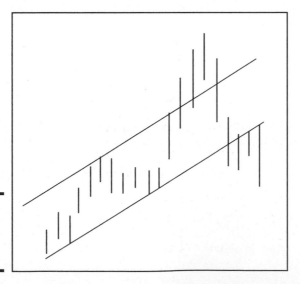

Figure 4-7:
A breakout
indicates a
new trend.

When a true breakout occurs, a new trend starts. That means an upward breakout will be accompanied by rising prices, and a downward breakout will be accompanied by falling prices.

With a false breakout, some traders buy or sell thinking that the trend will continue, see that it doesn't, and then turn around and reverse their positions at a loss.

A false breakout can cause those misled traders to wreak havoc for a day or two of trading. This is where the ability to size up the intelligence of the other traders in the market can come in handy.

Good technical analysts look at several different indicators in order to see whether a change in trend is real or just one of those things that goes away quickly as the old trend resumes.

Reading the Charts

How long does it take to find the trend? How long does it take for the trend to play out? When do you act on it? Do you have minutes, hours, or days to act?

Because markets tend to move in cycles, technical analysts look for patterns in the price charts that give them an indication of how long any particular trend may last. In this section, we show you some of the common patterns that day traders look for when they do technical analysis. Alas, some are obvious only in hindsight, but knowing what the patterns mean can help you make better forecasts of where a security price should go.

This is just an introduction to some of the better-known (and cleverly named) patterns. Technical analysts look for many others, and you really need a book on the subject to understand them all. Check out the Appendix in the complete *Day Trading For Canadians For Dummies* book for more information on technical analysis so that you can get a feel for how you can apply it to your trading style.

Waving your pennants and flags

Pennants and *flags* are chart patterns that show retracements, which are short-term deviations from the main trend. With a retracement, no breakout comes from the support or resistance level, but the security isn't following the trend, either.

Figure 4-8 shows a pennant. Notice how the support and resistance lines of the pennant (which occur within the support and resistance lines of a much larger trend) converge almost to a point.

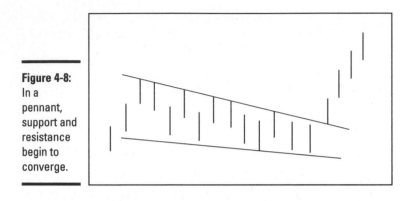

Figure 4-8:
In a pennant, support and resistance begin to converge.

Figure 4-9, by contrast, is a flag. The main difference between a flag and a pennant is that the flag's support and resistance lines are parallel.

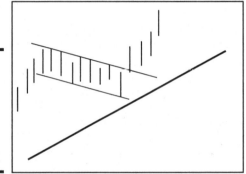

Figure 4-9:
A flag, like a pennant, usually indicates falling volume.

Pennants and flags are usually found in the middle of the main phase of a trend, and they seem to last for two weeks before going back to the trend-line. They are almost always accompanied by falling volume. In fact, if the trading volume isn't falling, you're probably looking at a *reversal* — a change in trend — rather than a retracement.

Not just for the shower: Head and shoulders

The *head and shoulders* formation is a series of three peaks within a price chart. The peaks on the left and right (the shoulders) should be relatively smaller than the peak in the centre (the head). The shoulders connect at a price known as the neckline, and when the right shoulder formation is reached, the price plunges down.

The head and shoulders is one of the most bearish technical patterns, and it looks like Figure 4-10.

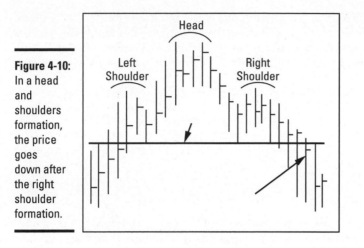

Figure 4-10:
In a head
and
shoulders
formation,
the price
goes
down after
the right
shoulder
formation.

The head and shoulders formation seems to result from traders holding out for a last high after a security has had a long price run. At some point, though, the trend changes, because nothing grows forever. And when the trend changes, the prices fall.

An upside-down head and shoulders sometimes appears at the end of a downtrend, and it signals that the security is about to increase in price.

Drinking from a cup and handle

When a security hits a peak in price and falls, sometimes because of bad news, it can stay low for a while. But eventually, the bad news works itself out, the underlying fundamentals improve, and it becomes time to buy again. The technical analyst sees this play out in a *cup and handle* formation, and Figure 4-11 shows you what it looks like.

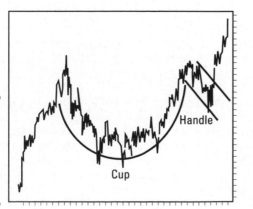

Figure 4-11:
A cup and
handle
formation is
a long-term
trend.

The handle forms as those who bought at the old high and who felt burned by the decline take their money and get out. But other traders, who do not have the same history with the security, recognize that the price will probably resume going up now that those old sellers are out of the market.

A cup and handle formation generally shows up over a long period of trading — sometimes as long as a year — so many subtrends will occur during that time. A day trader will likely care more about those day-to-day changes than the underlying trend taking place. Still, if you see that cup formation and the hint of a handle, it's a sign that the security will probably start to rise in price.

Mind the gap

Gaps are breaks in prices that show up all the time, usually when some news event takes place between trading sessions that causes an adjustment in prices and volume. Whether it's an acquisition, a product line disappointment, or a war that broke out overnight, the news is significant enough to change the trend, and that's why traders pay attention when they see gaps.

A gap is a break between two bars, and Figure 4-12 shows what one looks like:

Figure 4-12: A gap down often means it's time to sell.

Gap

Gaps are usually great signals. If a security gaps up at the open, that usually means that a strong uptrend is beginning, so it's time to buy. Likewise, if it gaps down, that's often the start of a downtrend, so it's better to sell.

Day traders can get sucked into a gap, a situation known as a *gap and crap* (or gap and *trap,* if you prefer more genteel language). When the security goes up in price, many traders view that as a great time to sell, so the day trader who buys on the gap up immediately gets slammed by all the selling pressure. Some day traders prefer to wait at least 30 minutes before trading on an opening gap, while others rely on their knowledge of the buyers and sellers in a given market to decide what to do.

Grab your pitchforks!

A *pitchfork* is sometimes called an *Andrews pitchfork* after Alan Andrews, the technical analyst who popularized it. It identifies long-run support and resistance levels for subtrends by creating a channel around the main trendline. Figure 4-13 shows what it looks like.

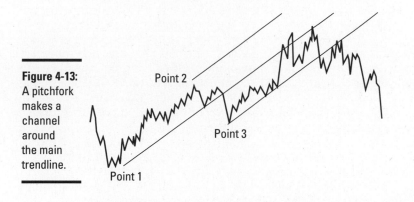

Figure 4-13:
A pitchfork makes a channel around the main trendline.

Point 2

Point 3

Point 1

The upper fork shows the resistance level for upward subtrends, and the lower fork shows the support level for lower subtrends. The middle line forms a support and a resistance line, depending on which side trading takes place. If the price crosses above the mid-line, it can be expected to go no higher than the highest line. Likewise, if it crosses below the mid-line, it can be expected to go no lower than the lowest line.

Pitfalls of Technical Analysis

A lot of people make a lot of money selling services to day traders. They produce videos, organize seminars, and (ahem) write books to tell you how to be a success. But in the financial world, success is a combination of luck, skill, and smarts.

Before you commit wholeheartedly to any particular school of research, and before you plunk down a lot of money for some "proven" system demonstrated on an infomercial, think about who you are and what you're trying to do. Despite all the books and all the seminars and all the business-school debates, every form of research has its drawbacks. Keep them in mind as you develop your day trading business plan.

If it's obvious, no opportunity exists

Many day trading systems work much of the time. For example, a security gaps up, meaning that due to positive news or high demand, the price jumps from one trade to the next (refer to Figure 4-12 for a gap formation). This is good, and the security is likely to keep going up. So you buy the security;

you make money. Bingo! But here's the thing: Everyone is looking at that gap, everyone is assuming that the stock will go up, so everyone will buy and that will bid up the security. Double bingo! The profit opportunity is gone. So maybe you're better off going short? Or avoiding the situation entirely? Who knows! And that's the problem. Looking for obvious patterns like gaps tells you a lot about what is happening in the market, but only your own judgment and experience can tell you what the next move should be.

Reverse-reverse psychology

Sitcoms always revert to tired formulas. The smart kid brags about how he or she will dominate a talent or quiz show and then panics on the big day. The two people who can't stand each other will get a horrible sickness that requires them to be quarantined — in the same hospital ward. The teenage son can't believe what fabulous soup his mother made, and it turns out she was brewing a homemade cleaning solution.

Or how about this one: The kids want to do something that the parents don't approve of. The parents try reverse psychology. "Go to the party, kids, have fun!" they say, thinking that the kids will not want to do anything their parents approve of. The kids, knowing that the parents are trying to pull the reverse psychology, decide to play along with reverse-reverse psychology. "Don't worry, we'll stay home!" they say — and then sneak out. Hilarity ensues.

Technical analysis is a useful way to gauge market psychology. But when trying to determine the mood of the market, it's really easy to start overanalyzing and working yourself into a knot. Should you follow the trend or trade against it? But if everyone trades against it, would you be better off following it?

Instead of puzzling over what's really going on, develop a system that you trust. Do that through backtesting, simulation, and performance analysis. *Day Trading For Canadians For Dummies* has plenty of advice on how to do this. The more confident you feel in how you should react given a market situation, the better your trading will be.

The random walk with an upward bias

Under the efficient markets theory, all information is already included in a security's price. Until new information comes into the market the prices move in a random pattern, so any security is as likely to do as well as any other. In some markets, like the stock market, this random path has an upward bias, meaning that as long as the economy is growing, companies should perform well, too; therefore, the movement is more likely to be upward than downward, but the magnitude of the movement is random.

If price movements are random, some people are going to win and some are going to lose, no matter what systems they use to pick securities. If price movements are random with an upward bias, then more people are going to win than lose, no matter what systems they use to pick securities. Some of those who win are going to tout their system, even though it was really random chance that led to their success.

Technical analysis is a useful way to measure the relative supply and demand in the market, and that in turn is a way to gauge the psychology of those who are trading. But it's not perfect. Before you plunk down a lot of money to learn a complex trading system or to subscribe to a newsletter offering a can't-miss method of trading, ask yourself whether the person selling it is smart or just lucky. A good system gives you discipline and a way to think about the market relative to your trading style. A bad system costs a lot of money and may have worked for a brief moment in the past, with no relevance to current conditions.

Understanding How the Markets Work

Day traders put their research to work through a range of different strategies. All strategies have two things in common: They are designed to make money, and they are designed to work in a single day. And the best ones help traders cut through the psychology of the market.

Although some trading is handled through automatic algorithms and other programs that place orders whenever certain conditions occur, the vast majority of trading takes place between human beings who want to make money, in markets where short-term profit potentials can be very small. As much as they want to be dispassionate, traders are going to get sucked into hope, fear, and greed: the three emotions that ruin people every day. To complicate matters, many markets, such as options and futures, are zero-sum markets, meaning that there is a loser for every winner. Some markets, such as the stock market, have a positive bias, meaning that there are more winners than losers in the long run — but that doesn't mean that will be the case today.

With thin profit potential and so much emotional upheaval, it can be tough to make money in the long run. This chapter might help. In it, we cover some common day trading strategies, and we discuss some of the cold analysis that goes into figuring out the psychology of the markets.

The Psychology of the Markets

For every buyer, there is a seller. There has to be, or no transaction will take place. The price changes to reach the point where the buyer is willing to buy the security and the seller is willing to part with it. This is basic supply and demand. The financial markets are more efficient at matching supply and demand than almost any other market out there. There are no racks of unsold sweaters at the end of the season, no hot model cars that can't be purchased at any price, no long lines to get a table. The prices change to match the demand, and those who want to pay the price — or receive the price — are going to make a trade.

Despite this ruthless capitalistic efficiency underlying trading, the markets are also dominated by human emotion and psychology. All the buyers and all the sellers are looking at the same information, but reaching different conclusions. A seller exists for every buyer, so the trader looking to buy needs to know why the seller is willing to make a deal.

And why would someone be on the other side of your trade?

✦ **The other person may have a different time horizon.** For example, long-term investors might sell on bad news that changes a security's outlook. A short-term trader might not care about the long-term outlet, if the selling in the morning is overdone, creating an opportunity to buy now and sell at a higher price in the afternoon.

✦ **The other person may have a different risk profile.** A conservative investor might not want to own shares in a company that's being acquired by a high-flying technology company. That investor will sell, and someone with more interest in growth will be buying.

✦ **The other person may be engaging in wishful thinking, or acting out of fear, or trading from sheer greed.**

✦ **You may be engaging in wishful thinking, acting out of fear, or trading from sheer greed.**

It's highly unlikely that you're smarter than everyone else trading, but you might be more rational and disciplined. In the long run, controlling your emotions and sticking to your limits will make you more money than if you are smart but can't control your trading. And if you happen to be both disciplined and smart, you might do very well.

Betting on the buy side

Every market participant has his or her own set of reasons and rationales for placing an order today. In general, though, it's safe to say that although many reasons exist to sell — to pay taxes, generate cash for university tuition, or meet a pension obligation, among many others — there's only one reason to buy: You think the security is going up in price.

For that reason alone, traders often pay more attention to what is happening to buy orders than to sell orders. They look at the number of buy orders coming in, how large they are, and at what price to get a sense of who out there is projecting a profit. We cover volume and price indicators in more detail later in the chapter.

Because there are so many good reasons to sell but only one good reason to buy, it can take a long time for the market to recognize bearish (pessimistic) sentiment indicators. Even if you see that prices should start to go down in the near future, you have to consider that the market today can be very different from what you see coming up. And day traders only have today.

The projection trap

If you started reading at the beginning of this chapter, you would have noticed that it's possible to see what you want to see in some price charts. And if you thought a little about fundamental analysis, you might have realized that it's just as easy to interpret information the way you want to, too. Instead of looking objectively at what the market is telling them, some traders see what they want to see. That's one reason why it's so important to know your system and use your limits. Information in Chapters 1 and 3 can help you with both.

The best traders are able to figure out the psychology of the market almost by instinct. They can't necessarily explain what they do — which makes it hard for someone trying to learn from them. But they can tell you this much: If you can rationally determine why the person on the other side of the trade is trading, you can be in a better position to make money and avoid the big mistakes brought on by hope, fear, and greed.

Measuring the Mood of the Market

For decades, most traders were rooted on the floors of the exchanges. They had a good sense of the mood of the market because they could pick up the mood of the people in the pits with them. They often knew their fellow traders well enough to know how good they were or the needs of the people they were working for. It made for a clubby atmosphere, despite all the shouting and arm waving. It wasn't the most efficient way to trade big volume, but it allowed traders to read the minds of those around them.

And now, almost all trading is electronic, and not all those old floor traders have been able to make the transition. Some find that unless they can watch the behaviour of other traders and hear the emotions in their voices, they can't gauge what's happening in the markets.

Other professional traders, who work for brokerage firms or fund companies, trade electronically, but along long tables (known as trading desks) where they sit next to colleagues trading similar securities. Even though everyone is trading off a screen, they share a mood and thus a sense of what's happening out there. Some day traders can replicate this by setting up shop at a trading arcade, a business that operates trading desks for day traders (you can read more about them in *Day Trading For Canadians For*

Dummies). However, most traders are working alone at home, with nothing but the information on their screens to tell them what's happening in the market.

There are ways to figure out what's happening, even just looking at the screen, and some of these may work for you. These include price, volume, and volatility indicators, and you're in the right place to find out more about them.

As we mention in Chapter 3, some traders rely on Internet chat rooms or social media networks to help them measure market sentiment. This can be risky. Some Internet users are smart people who are willing to share their perspectives on the market, but many are novice traders who have no good information to share, or they're people who are trying to manipulate the market in their favour. Do your due diligence when it comes to online sources before you start participating.

Pinpointing with price indicators

In an efficient market, all information about a security is included in its price. If the price is high and going up, then the fundamentals are doing well. If the price is low and going lower, then something's not good. And everything in between means something else.

The change in a security's price gives you a first cut of information. Price changes can be analyzed in other ways to help you know when to buy or when to sell.

Momentum

Momentum, which we discuss in detail in *Day Trading For Canadians For Dummies,* is the rate at which a security's price is increasing (or decreasing). If momentum is strong and positive, then the security will show both higher highs and higher lows. People want to buy it for whatever reason, and the price reflects that. Likewise, momentum can be strong and negative, and negative momentum is marked with lower highs and lower lows. No one seems interested in buying, and that keeps dragging the price down.

The exact amount of momentum that a security has can be measured with indicators known as *momentum oscillators.* A classic momentum oscillator starts with the moving average, which is the average of the closing prices for a past time period, say the last ten trading days. Then the change in each day's moving average is plotted below the price line. When the oscillator is positive, traders say that the security is *overbought;* when it is negative, they say that the security is *oversold.* Figure 4-14 shows a momentum oscillator plotted below a price line.

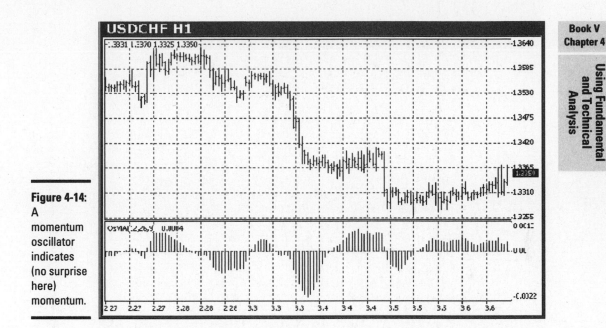

Figure 4-14:
A momentum oscillator indicates (no surprise here) momentum.

If a momentum oscillator shows that a security is overbought (when it's above the centre line), that means too many people own it relative to the remaining demand in the market, and some of them will start selling. Remember, some of these people have perfectly good reasons for selling that may have nothing to do with the underlying fundamentals of the security, but they are going to sell anyway, and that will bring the price down. Traders who see that a security is overbought will want to sell in advance of those people.

If a momentum oscillator shows that a security is oversold (when the line is below the centre line), it means the security is probably too cheap. Everyone who wanted to get out has gotten out, and now it may be a bargain. When the buyers who see the profit opportunity jump in, the price will go up.

The trend is your friend . . . until the end. Although great reasons exist to follow price trends, remember that they all end, so you still need to pay attention to your money management and your stops, no matter how strong a trend seems to be.

Given that most trends end, or at least zig and zag along the way, some traders look for securities that fit what they call the *1–2–3–4 criterion*. If a security goes up in price for three consecutive days, then it's likely to go down on the fourth day. Likewise, if a security has fallen in price for three days in a row, it's likely to be up on day four. Be sure to run some simulations — which you can do on most trading sites — to see whether this works for a market that interests you.

Trading on the tick

A *tick* is an upward or downward price change. For some securities, such as futures contracts, the tick size is defined as part of the contract. For others, such as stocks, a tick can be anywhere from a penny to infinity (at least in theory).

You can also calculate the tick indicator for the market as a whole. (In fact, most quotation systems calculate the market tick for you.) This is the total number of securities in that market that traded up on the last trade, minus the number that traded down on the last trade. If the tick is a positive number, that's good — that means the market as a whole has a lot of buying interest. Although any given security might not do as well, a positive tick shows that most people in the market have a positive perspective right now.

By contrast, a negative tick shows that most people in the market are watching prices fall. Sure, some prices are going up, but there are more unhappy people than happy ones (assuming that most people are trading on the long side, meaning that they make money when prices go up, not down). This shows negative sentiment in the market right now.

Tracking the trin

Trin is short for *trading indicator,* and it's another measure of market sentiment based on how many prices have gone up relative to how many have gone down. Most quotation systems will pull up the trin for a given market, but you can also calculate it on your own. The math looks like Figure 4-15.

The numerator is based on the tick: the number of securities that went up divided by (not less) the number that went down. The denominator includes the volume: the number of shares or contracts that traded for those securities that went up, divided by the number of securities traded for those that went down in price. This tells you just how strongly buyers supported the securities that were going up and just how much selling pressure faced those securities that went down.

Figure 4-15:
Calculating the trading indicator (the trin) can give you a measure of market sentiment.

$$\frac{\dfrac{advances}{declines}}{\dfrac{advance\ volume}{decline\ volume}}$$

Measuring the Mood of the Market **455**

Book V
Chapter 4

Using Fundamental
and Technical
Analysis

If the trin is less than 1.00, that usually means a lot of buyers are taking securities up in price, and that's positive. If the trin is above 1.00, then the sellers are acting more strongly, and that indicates a lot of negative sentiment in the market.

Volume

The trin indicator looks at price in conjunction with volume. That makes this a good time to introduce volume indicators.

Volume tells you how much trading is taking place in the market. How excited are people about the current price? Do they see this as a great opportunity to buy or to sell? Are they selling fast, to get out now, or are they taking a more leisurely approach to the market these days? This information is carried in the volume of the trading, and it's an important adjunct to the information you see in the prices. Volume tells you whether enough support exists to maintain price trends, or if price trends are likely to change soon.

Force index

The *force index* gives you a sense of the strength of a trend. It starts with information from prices — namely, if the closing price today is higher than the closing price yesterday that's positive for the security. And that means that if today's closing price is lower than yesterday's, the force is generally negative. Then that price information is combined with volume information. The more volume that goes with that price change, the stronger that positive or negative force.

Although many quotation systems will calculate force for you, you can do it yourself, too. For each trading day,

```
Force index = volume × (today's moving average - yesterday's
    moving average)
```

In other words, the force index simply scales the moving average momentum oscillator (discussed above) for the amount of volume that accompanies that price change. That way, the trader has a sense of just how overbought or oversold the security is any particular day.

On-balance volume

The *on-balance volume* is a running total of the amount of trading in a security. To calculate it, first look at today's closing price relative to yesterday's. If today's close is higher than yesterday's, then add today's volume to yesterday's on-balance volume. If today's closing price is less than yesterday's, then subtract today's volume from yesterday's total. And if today's close is the same as yesterday's, don't do anything: Today's balance is the same as yesterday's.

Many traders track on-balance volume over time, and here's why: A change in volume signals a change in demand. That might not show up in price right away if enough buyers exist to absorb volume from sellers. But if still more buyers are out there, then the price is going to go up. Hence, the volume from even small day-to-day increases in price needs to be added up over time. If the volume keeps going up, then at some point prices are going to have to go up to meet the demand.

On the downside, the volume from small price declines will add up, too. Over time, it may show very little pent-up interest, indicating that prices could languish for some time.

Many traders look to on-balance volume to gauge the behaviour of so-called *smart money,* such as pension funds, hedge funds, and mutual fund companies. Unlike individual investors, these big institutional accounts tend to trade on fundamentals rather than emotion. They tend to start buying a security at the point where the dumb money is tired of owning it, so their early buying may show big volume with little price change. But as the institutions keep buying, the price will have to go up to get the smarter individuals and the early institutions to part with their shares.

Open interest

Open interest has a different meaning in the stock market than in the options and futures markets, but in both cases it gives traders useful information about demand.

In the stock market, open interest is the number of buy orders submitted before the market opens. If the open interest is high, people are ready to add shares to their positions or initiate new positions, and that in turn means the stock is likely to go up in price on the demand.

In the options and futures markets, open interest is the number of contracts at the end of every day that have not been exercised, closed out, or allowed to expire. Day traders won't have open interest, because by definition, day traders close out at the end of every day. But some traders will keep open interest, either because they think that their position has the ability to increase in profitability or because they are hedging another transaction and need to keep that options or futures position in place. If open interest in a contract is increasing, then new money is coming into the market and prices are likely to continue to go up. This is especially true if volume is increasing at about the same rate as open interest. On the other hand, if open interest is falling, then people are closing out their positions because they no longer see a profit potential, and prices are likely to fall.

Volatility

The *volatility* of a security is a measure of how much it tends to go up or down in a given time period. The more volatile the security, the more the price will fluctuate. Most day traders prefer volatile securities, because that creates more opportunities to make a profit in a short amount of time. But volatility can make it tougher to gauge market sentiment. If a security is volatile, the mood can change quickly. What looked like a profit opportunity at the market open might be gone by lunchtime — and back again before the close.

Average true range

The *average true range* is a measure of volatility that's commonly used in commodity markets, but some stock traders use it, too. Many quotation systems calculate it automatically, but if you want to do it yourself, start with finding each day's *true range*. This is the greatest of

✦ The most recent high less the most recent low.

✦ The absolute value of the most recent high less the previous close.

✦ The absolute value of the most recent low less the previous close.

Calculate those three numbers, then take the highest of them and average it with the true range for the past 14 days.

Each day's true range number shows you just how much the security swung between the high and the low, or how much the high or the low that day varied from the previous day's close. It's a measure of how much volatility occurred each day. When averaged over time, it shows how much volatility takes place over time. The higher the average true range, the more volatile a security is.

Beta

Beta is the *covariance* (that is, the statistical measure of how much two variables move together) of a stock relative to the rest of the market. The number comes from the capital assets pricing model, which is an equation used in academic circles to model the performance of securities. Traders don't use the capital asset pricing model, but they often talk about beta to evaluate the volatility of stocks and options.

What does beta mean?

✦ A beta of more than one means that the security moves at a faster rate than the market. You would buy high betas if you think the market is going up, but not if the market is going down.

✦ A beta of less than one means that the security moves more slowly than the market. This is good if you want less risk than the market.

✦ A beta of exactly one means that the security moves at the same rate as the market.

✦ A negative beta means that the security moves in the opposite direction of the market. The easiest way to get a negative beta security is to *short* (borrow and then sell) a positive beta security.

MVX

MVX is short for the Montreal Exchange's Implied Volatility Index. The calculation of it is complex, but it is available on quotation systems and on the exchange's website at www.m-x.ca/indicesmx_mvx_en.php.

The MVX is based on the implied volatility of options on the iShares of the Canadian S&P/TSX 60 Fund (XIU), which are traded on the Montreal Exchange. Because the XIU's value is based on Canada's equity benchmark — S&P/TSX 60 Index — the MVX is a good way to determine investor sentiment for the entire Canadian equity market. The greater the volatility, the more uncertainty investors have, and the more options that show great volatility, the more widespread the concern is within the market. Some would consider the MVX to be a gauge of market fear. The greater the MVX, the more bearish the outlook for the markets in general.

Traders can use the MVX to help them value options and futures on the market indexes. The MVX can also be used to help confirm bullish or bearish sentiment that shows up in other market signals, such as the tick or the on-balance volume measures described earlier.

VIX

VIX stands for the Chicago Board Options Exchange Volatility Index. It works the same way as the MVX, but it gauges sentiment in the American markets. It's available on many quotation systems and on the exchange's website at www.cboe.com/micro/vix/introduction.aspx.

The VIX is based on the implied volatility of options on stocks included in the S&P 500 Index and, like the MVX, if the index is high that means more risk exists in the market.

In addition to the VIX, the exchange also tracks the *VXN* (volatility on the Nasdaq 100 Index) and the *VXD* (volatility on the Dow Jones Industrial Average).

Volatility ratio

The *volatility ratio* tells traders what the implied volatility of a security is relative to the recent historical volatility. It shows whether the security is expected to be more or less volatile right now than it has been in the past, and it's widely used in option markets. The first calculation required is the *implied volatility,* which is backed out using the Black-Scholes model, an academic model for valuing options. (As a point of interest, Nobel Prize winner Myron Scoles was born in Timmins, Ontario, and graduated from Hamilton's McMaster University.) When you plug in time until expiration, interest rates, dividends, stock price, and strike price to the model, the implied volatility is the volatility number that then generates the current option price. (You don't have to do this yourself, because most quotation systems generate implied volatility for you.)

After you have the implied volatility, you can compare it to the historical volatility of the option, which tells you just how much the price changed over the last 20 or 90 days. If the implied volatility is greater than the statistical volatility, the market may be overestimating the uncertainty in the prices, and the options may be overvalued. And, if the implied volatility is much less than the statistical volatility, the market may be underestimating uncertainty, so the options may be undervalued.

Measuring Money Flows

Money flows tell you how much money is going into or out of a market. They are another set of indicators that tell you where the market sentiment is right now and where it might be going soon. They combine features of price and volume indicators to help traders gauge the market. Although amounts spent to buy and sell have to match — otherwise, no market would exist — the enthusiasm of the buyers and the anxiousness of the sellers shows up in the volume traded and the direction of the price change. Just how hard was it for the buyers to get the sellers to part with their positions? And, how hard will it be to get them to part with their positions tomorrow? That's the information contained in money flow indicators.

The most basic money flow indicator is closing price multiplied by the number of shares traded. If the closing price was higher than the closing price yesterday, then the number is positive; if the closing price today was lower than the price yesterday, then the number is negative.

Accumulation/distribution index

In trading terms, *accumulation* is controlled buying, and *distribution* is controlled selling. This is the kind of buying and selling that doesn't lead to big changes in securities prices, and it's usually because the action was planned. No one accumulates or distributes a security in a state of panic.

But even when the buying and selling activity isn't driven by madcap rushes in and out of positions, it's still important to know whether, on balance, the buyers or the sellers have the slight predominance in the market, because that may affect the direction of the price in the near future. For example, if a security has been in an upward trend, but more and more down days are occurring with increasing volume, that means that the sellers are starting to dominate the trading and that the price trend is likely to go down.

Here's the equation:

```
Accumulation/distribution = ((Close - Low) - (High - Close))
    / (High - Low) × Period's volume
```

Some traders look at accumulation/distribution from day to day, whereas others prefer to look at it for a week or even a month's worth of trading.

Money flow ratio and money flow index

Money flow is closing price multiplied by the number of shares traded. That basic statistic can be manipulated in strange and wonderful ways to generate new statistics carrying even more information about whether the markets are likely to have more buying pressure or more selling pressure in the future.

The first is the *money flow ratio.* This is simply the total money flow for those days where prices were up from the prior day (days with positive money flow), divided by the total money flow for those days where prices were down from the prior day (days with negative money flow). Day traders tend to calculate money flow ratios for short time periods, such as a week or ten days, while swing traders and investors tend to care about longer time periods, like a month or even four months of trading.

The money flow ratio is sometimes converted into the *money flow index,* which can be used as a single indicator or tracked relative to prices for a given period of time. This equation looks like Figure 4-16.

Figure 4-16:
This equation figures out the money flow index.

$$MFI = 100 - \frac{100}{1 + money\ ratio}$$

If the money flow index is more than 80, the security is usually considered to be overbought — meaning that the buyers are done buying, and the sellers will put downward pressure on prices. If the money flow index is less than

20, then the security is usually considered to be oversold, and the buyers will soon take over and drive prices up. In between, the money flow index can help clarify information from other market indicators.

Short interest ratios

Short selling is a way to make money if a security falls in price. In the options and futures markets, one simply agrees to sell a contract to someone else. In the stock and bond markets, it's a little more complicated. The short seller borrows stocks or bonds through the brokerage firm, and then sells them. Ideally, the price will fall, and then the trader can buy back the stocks or bonds at the lower price to repay the loan. The trader keeps the difference between the price where the security was sold and the price where the security was repurchased. (The process is described in more detail in Chapter 5.)

People take the short side of a position for only one reason: They think that prices are going to go down. They may want to hedge against this, or they may want to make a big profit if it happens. In the stock market in particular, monitoring the rate of short selling can give clues to investor expectations and future market direction.

The New York Stock Exchange and Nasdaq report the short interest in stocks listed with them. The data are updated monthly, as it can take a while for brokerage firms to sort out exactly how many shares have been shorted and then report those data to the exchanges. The resulting number, the *short interest ratio,* tells the number of shares that have been shorted, the percentage change from the month before, the average daily trading volume in the same month, and the number of days of trading at the average volume that it would take to cover the short positions.

Traders can get similar data for the Toronto Stock Exchange. Twice a month the exchange generates a Short Position Report for the top 20 largest consolidated short positions. The PDF document includes the total number of shares shorted and the net change from previous report. You can get to these reports from the Stock Market News section on the TMX website (www.tmx.com).

The loans that enable short selling have to be repaid. If the lender asks for them back, or if prices go up so that the position starts to lose money, the trader is going to have to buy shares in order to make repayment. The harder it is to get the right number of shares in the market, the more desperate the trader will become, and the higher prices will go.

An increase in short interest shows that investors are becoming nervous about a stock. However, given that short interest is not calculated frequently, the number would probably not give a trader a lot of information about the prospects for the company itself. This doesn't mean short interest doesn't carry a lot of useful information for traders. It does. If the short interest is high, then the security price is likely to go up when all the people who are short need to buy back stock. Likewise, if short interest is low, little buying pressure will occur in the near future.

High short interest, along with other bullish indicators, is a sign that prices are more likely to go up than down in the near future.

Information Cropping Up During the Trading Day

Technical analysis and all the indicators discussed in this chapter offer useful information about what's happening in the markets, but there's one problem: Because so many of those indicators are based on closing prices and closing volume, they aren't much use during the trading day. And, in fact, many traders read through the information in the morning before the open to sort out what is likely to happen and what the mood of the market is likely to be, but then they have to recalibrate their gauge of the market as information comes to them during the trading day. That information doesn't show up on charts or in neat numerical indicators until the day ends. But several sources of information are updated while the market is open to give a trader a sense of what's happening at any given time.

Price, time, and sales

The most important information for a trader is the current price of the security, how often and in what volume it has been trading, and how much the price has moved from the last trade. This is the most basic real-time information out there, and it's readily available through a brokerage firm's quotation screens.

In *Day Trading For Canadians For Dummies,* we discuss the different quotation services that traders can obtain from their brokerage firms. Although your broker may charge you more to get more detailed quotes, it's worth it for most trading strategies. Knowing how the price is moving can give you a sense of whether the general mood of the market is being confirmed or contradicted. That can help you place more profitable trades.

Order book

High-level price quote data, such as that available through TMX Datalinx, Nasdaq Level II, or Nasdaq TotalView, include information on who is placing orders and just how large those orders are. (Refer to Chapter 6 in the full *Day Trading For Canadians For Dummies* book to see what this looks like.) The book gives you key data, because it gives you a sense of how smart the other buyers and sellers are. Are they day traders just trying not to be killed? Or are they institutions that have done a lot of research and are under a lot of performance pressure? Sure, day traders are often very right and institutions are often very wrong, but the information you see in the order book can help you sense whether people are trading on information or on emotion.

An additional piece of information from the order book can help you figure out what's happening in the market now — namely, the presence of an *order imbalance*. An order imbalance means that the number of buyers and sellers don't match. This often happens during the open, because some traders prefer to place orders before the market opens, whereas others prefer to wait until after the open. These imbalances tend to be small and clear up quickly. However, if a major news event takes place, or a great deal of fear is present in the market, large imbalances can occur during the trading day. These can be disruptive, and in some cases the exchange stops trading until news is disseminated and enough new orders are placed to balance out the orders.

News flows

Although much of the discussion in this chapter has been about the information contained in price, volume, and other trade data, the actual information that comes from news releases is at least as important.

Much of the news is regularly scheduled and much predicted: corporate earnings, Bank of Canada rate announcements, unemployment rates, housing starts, and the like. When this information comes in, traders want to know how the actual results compare with what was expected, and how this fits with the overall bullish or bearish sentiment of the market.

The second type of news is the unscheduled breaking event, such as corporate takeovers, horrible storms, or other happenings that were not expected and that take more time for the market to digest. That's in part because these events have the ability to change trends rather than play out against them. In some cases, the markets will halt trading to allow this information to disseminate; in others, traders have to react quickly based on what they know now and what they suspect will happen in the near future.

Chapter 5: Leverage and Arbitrage

In This Chapter

✔ Taking an in-depth look at leverage

✔ Managing margin

✔ Assessing arbitrage

Taking Other People's Money to Make Money

The dollars you make from trading depend on two things: your percentage return on your trades and the dollars you have to start out with. If you double your money but only have a $1,000 account, then you are left with $2,000. If you get a 10 percent return but have a $1,000,000 account, then you make $100,000. Which would you rather have? (Yes, we know, you'd rather double your money with the $1,000,000 account. But we didn't give you that choice, alas.)

The point is that the more money you have to trade, the more dollars you can generate, even if the return on the trade itself is small. If you have $500,000 and borrow $500,000 more, then your 10 percent return will give you $100,000 to take home, not $50,000. You have doubled the dollars returned to you by doubling the money you used to place the trades, not by doubling the performance of the trade itself. Clever, huh?

Leverage gives you more money to trade. That helps you generate more dollars for your account — or lose more dollars, if you aren't careful or have a string of reversals.

When you borrow money or shares of stock, you have to pay it back, no matter what happens. That's why borrowing can be risky.

Why leverage is important in short-term trading

Day traders and other short-term traders aren't looking to make big money on any single trade. Instead, the goal is to make small money on a whole bunch of trades. Unfortunately, it can be hard for all those little trades to add up to something big. That's why many day traders turn to leverage. They either borrow money or stock from their brokerage firm, or they trade securities that have built-in leverage, such as futures and foreign exchange.

The fine print on margin agreements

Leverage adds risk not only to your own account, but also to the entire financial system — just ask Greece. If everyone borrowed money and then some big market catastrophe happened no one would be able to repay their loans, and those who lent the money would go bust, too.

As a result, an incredible amount of oversight goes with leverage strategies. The Investment Industry Regulatory Organization of Canada (IIROC) regulates how much money a trader can borrow. Many brokerage firms have even stricter rules in place as part of their risk management.

This means you have about as much flexibility when you borrow from your broker in order to buy and sell securities as you would have if you borrowed from your friendly neighbourhood loan shark to play a high-stakes poker game. Meaning: not much. Margin loans are highly regulated, and you must meet the broker's terms. If you fail to repay the loan, your positions will be sold from underneath you. If you try to borrow too much, you will be cut off. No amount of begging and pleading will help you.

Your brokerage firm makes you sign a margin agreement, which says that you understand the risks and limits of your activities. You probably can't have a margin account unless you meet a minimum account size, usually between $5,000 and $10,000, and the amount you can borrow depends on the size of your account. Generally, a large-cap stock account must hold 30 percent of the purchase price of securities when you borrow the money. A mid-cap stock requires minimum margin of 50 percent; you have to have 75 percent of the purchase price to borrow money for small-cap or penny stocks. The price of those securities can go down, but if they go down below the value of the loan, you'll get a margin call. (Some brokers will call in loans faster than others; their policies are disclosed in their margin agreements.)

Brokerage firms handle margin trades all the time. You do the paperwork once, when you sign a margin agreement. Each time you place an order, you're asked if you are making the trade with cash or on margin. Click the "Margin" box, and you've just borrowed money. It's that easy.

Managing margin calls

If the value of your account starts falling, and it looks like it is falling below the 30 percent minimum margin requirement (this depends on the security you're trading), you'll get a *margin call*. Your broker will call you and ask you to deposit more money or securities in your account. If you can't do that, the broker will start selling your securities to close out the loan. And if you don't have enough to pay off the loan, the broker will close your account and put a lien, which is a claim on your assets, against you.

Most brokerage firms have risk-management limits in place, so you'll probably get plenty of warning before you get a margin call or see your account closed out. After all, neither you nor your brokerage firm wants to lose money. Just keep in mind that it's a possibility.

Some brokerage firms advertise that, as a service to you, they will close out your account as soon as you lose the amount in it, to keep you from losing more money. It's as much a service to the brokerage as it is to you, but it's an example of the built-in risk management that firms have to limit risks to everyone.

Margin bargains for day traders only

Day traders are often able to avoid margin calls because they borrow money for such short periods of time. Good day traders look for small market moves and cut their losses early on, which minimizes the risk of using other people's money. And, by definition, day traders close out their positions every night.

Lots to Discover about Leverage

Leverage is the use of borrowed money to increase returns. Day traders use it a lot to get bigger returns from relatively small price changes in the underlying securities. And as long as they consistently close out their positions at the end of the day, day traders can borrow more money and pay less interest than people who hold securities for a longer term.

The process of borrowing works differently in different markets. In the stock and bond markets, it's straightforward: You just tell your broker you're borrowing before you place the order. In the options and futures markets, you're buying and selling contracts that have leverage built into them. You don't borrow money outright, but you can control a lot of value in your account for relatively little money down.

In stock and bond markets

Leverage is straightforward for buyers of stocks and bonds: You simply click the box marked "Margin" when you place your order, and the brokerage firm loans you money. Then, when the security goes up in price, you get a greater percentage return because you've been able to buy more for your money. Of course, that also increases your potential losses.

Figure 5-1 shows how it works. The trader borrows money to buy 400 shares of SuperCorp. If the stock goes up 4 percent, she makes 8 percent. Whoohooo! But if the stock goes down 4 percent, she still has to repay the loan at full dollar value, so she ends up losing 8 percent. That's not so good.

A trader buys $10,000 of SuperCorp with $5,000 of her own cash and a $5,000 loan
SuperCorp trades at $25/share, so the trader purchases a total of 400 shares.
The trader closes out at the end of the day, so no interest is charged.
What happens as the stock price changes?

	Ending Price	Ending Value	Loan Value	Net Equity	Trader's Rate of Return	% Change in Stock Price
Figure 5-1: An example of trading stocks on margin.	$ 26.00	$ 10,400	$ 5,000	$ 5,400	8%	4%
	$ 25.50	$ 10,200	$ 5,000	$ 5,200	4%	2%
	$ 25.00	$ 10,000	$ 5,000	$ 5,000	0%	0%
	$ 24.50	$ 9,800	$ 5,000	$ 4,800	-4%	-2%
	$ 24.00	$ 9,600	$ 5,000	$ 4,600	-8%	-4%

REMEMBER

If you hold your margin position overnight or longer, you'll have to start
paying interest. That will cut into your returns or increase your losses.

In options markets

An *option* gives you the right, but not the obligation, to buy or sell a stock
or other item at a set price when the contract expires. A *call option* gives
you the right to buy, so you would buy a call when you think the underlying
asset is going up. A *put option* gives you the right to sell, so you would buy a
put when you think the underlying asset is going down. By trading an option,
you get exposure to changes in the price of the underlying security without
actually buying the security itself. That's the source of the leverage in the
market.

A day trader might use options to get an exposure to price changes in a
stock for a lot less money than it would cost to buy the stock itself. Suppose
a call option is *deeply in-the-money.* That means that its *strike price,* the price
that you would be able to buy the stock at if you exercised the option, is
far below the current stock price. If this happens, the obvious thing is for
the option price to be set at the difference between the current stock price
and the strike price, and that's more or less what happens (more in theory,
less in practice). When the stock price changes, the option price changes
at almost exactly the same amount. This means that you can buy the price
performance of the stock at a discount, the discount being the strike price of
the stock.

Figure 5-2 shows the performance-boosting leverage from this strategy. The
trader buys call options with an exercise price of $10 on a stock trading at
$25. The option price changes the same amount that the stock price does,
but the call holder gets a greater percentage return than the stock holder.

Figure 5-2:
What happens to the option value when the stock price changes?

A trader buys deep in-the-money call options on SuperCorp. The exercise price is $10, and the stock is trading at $25.

Stock Price	Initial Option Price	Exercise (Strike) Price	New Option Price	Stock Price Change	Option Price Change
$ 26.00	$ 15.00	$ 10.00	$ 16.00	4%	7%
$ 25.50	$ 15.00	$ 10.00	$ 15.50	2%	3%
$ 25.00	$ 15.00	$ 10.00	$ 15.00	0%	0%
$ 24.50	$ 15.00	$ 10.00	$ 14.50	-2%	-3%
$ 24.00	$ 15.00	$ 10.00	$ 14.00	-4%	-7%

Many other options strategies that day traders can use exist, but a discussion of them goes beyond the scope of this book.

In futures trading

A *futures* contract gives you the obligation to buy or sell an underlying financial or agricultural commodity, assuming you still hold the contract at the expiration date. That underlying product ranges from the value of Treasury bonds to barrels of oil and heads of cattle, and you're only putting money down now when you purchase the contract. You don't have to come up with the full amount until the contract comes due — and almost all options and futures traders close out their trades long before the contract expiration date. Here we talk about how leverage works in the futures market.

Although most options and futures contracts settle with cash long before the due date, contract holders have the right to hold them until the due date and, in the case of options on common stock and agricultural derivatives, demand physical delivery. It's rare, but the commodity exchanges have systems in place for determining the transport, specifications, and delivery of grain, cattle, or ethanol. One advantage of day trading is that you close out the same day, without ever even thinking about the fine print of physical delivery.

Because *derivatives* have built-in leverage that allows a trader to have big market exposure for relatively few dollars upfront, they've become popular with day traders. Figure 5-3 shows how it works. Here, a trader is buying the Chicago Mercantile Exchange's E-Mini S&P 500 futures contract, which gives traders exposure to the performance of the Standard & Poor's 500 Index, a standard measure of the stock performance of a diversified list of 500 large American companies. The futures contract trades at 50 times the value of the index, rounded to the nearest $0.25. The minimum margin that a trader must put down on the contract is $3,500. Each $0.25 change in the index leads to a $12.50 ($0.25 × 50) change in the value of the contract, and that $12.50 is added to or subtracted from the $3,500 margin.

Figure 5-3:
Margin
and the
derivatives
trade with
built-in
leverage.

A day trader buys a Chicago Mercantile Exchange E-Mini S&P 500 futures contract.
The contract price is $50 x the index level. To buy it, the trader must post margin of $3,500

Initial Index Value	Ending Index Value	Multiplier	Initial Contract Value	Contract Value	Value Change in Dollars	Value Change in Percent	Initial Margin	Ending Margin	Percent Change in Margin
1,457.50	1,458.50	$ 50.00	$ 72,875.00	$ 72,925.00	$ 50.00	0.07%	$ 3,500.00	$ 3,550.00	1.43%
1,457.50	1,458.00	$ 50.00	$ 72,875.00	$ 72,900.00	$ 25.00	0.03%	$ 3,500.00	$ 3,525.00	0.71%
1,457.50	1,457.50	$ 50.00	$ 72,875.00	$ 72,875.00	$ -	0.00%	$ 3,500.00	$ 3,500.00	0.00%
1,457.50	1,457.00	$ 50.00	$ 72,875.00	$ 72,850.00	$ (25.00)	-0.03%	$ 3,500.00	$ 3,475.00	-0.71%
1,457.50	1,456.50	$ 50.00	$ 72,875.00	$ 72,825.00	$ (50.00)	-0.07%	$ 3,500.00	$ 3,450.00	-1.43%

Some exchanges use the term *margin,* and others prefer to use *performance bond.* Either way, it's the same thing: money you put in upfront to ensure you can meet the contract terms when it comes due. If you hold the contract overnight, your account is adjusted up or down to reflect the day's profits. If it gets too low, you're asked to add more money.

In foreign exchange

The *foreign exchange,* or *forex,* market is driven by leverage. Exchange rates tend to move slowly, by as little as a tenth or even a hundredth of a penny a day. And the markets are so huge that it's easier to hedge risk. You might have trouble borrowing shares of stock to short them, but you should have no trouble ever borrowing Japanese yen or other currencies of the world's largest countries. In order to get a big return, forex traders almost always borrow huge amounts of money.

In the stock market, day traders can generally borrow up to three times the amount of cash and securities held in their accounts. Forex trading is also regulated by IIROC. Although some offshore brokers will allow traders to borrow 400 times the amount in their accounts, legitimate Canadian firms will let people borrow only about 20 times (you'll need to put up between 3 percent and 5 percent of a trade).

Forex trading allows for more borrowing than stock trading because the market is open 24/7. This means trading systems can sell a position any time, day or night, before the account goes under margin and the trader loses money. Less risk of squandering big bucks exists, so brokers offer more leverage. Because stock markets are only open for trading during business hours, there is a chance share prices could decline in the middle of the night. That adds risk; hence a higher margin requirement.

The reason why a forex firm wants to hedge its risks against its day trading customers is that most day traders lose money. The firms know that if they bet against the aggregate trades held by their customers, they'll probably come out ahead. Don't trade in forex or any other market until you've worked out a strategy and practised it, so that you can avoid becoming a statistic. *Day Trading For Canadians For Dummies* has information on testing and evaluating trading strategies.

An exchange rate is just the price of money. If the Canadian dollar–American dollar rate is 1.0121, that means one loonie will buy US$1.01.

Borrowing in Your Trading Business

Leverage is only part of the borrowing involved in your day trading business. Like any business owner, sometimes you need more cash than your business generates. Other times, you see expansion opportunities that require more money than you have on hand. In this section, we discuss why and how day traders can borrow money over and above leveraged trading.

Margin loans for cash flow

If day trading is your job, then you face a constant pressure: How do you cover the costs of living while keeping enough money in the market to trade? One way to do this is to have another source of income — from savings, a spouse, or a job that doesn't overlap with market hours. Other day traders take money out of their trading account.

If the market hasn't been cooperative, then there might not be enough to take out of the account while still having enough capital to trade. One option is to arrange a margin loan through a brokerage firm. The firm will let you take out a loan against the securities that you hold. You can spend the money any way you like, but you will be charged interest — and you will have to repay it. Still, it's a good option to have, because day trade earnings tend to be erratic.

Borrowing for trading capital

Some day traders use a double layer of leverage: They borrow the money to set up their trading accounts and then they borrow money for their trading strategies. If the market cooperates this can be a great way to make money, but if not you could end up owing a lot of people money that you don't have.

If you want to take the risk, though, you have a few resources to turn to other than your relatives: You can borrow against your house, use your credit cards, or find a trading firm that will give you some money to work with.

Borrowing against your house

Yes, you can use a mortgage or a home equity line of credit to get the money for your day trading activities. In general, this carries low interest rates because your house is your collateral, but the loan might be tax deductible, only if you have structured it the proper way. This can be dangerous so get professional advice. This can be a relatively low-cost way to pull value stored in your house for use in trading. The risk? If you can't pay back the loan, you can lose your residence. Just don't borrow against your car, too, as you'll need a place to live when the bank evicts you.

Putting it on the card

The business world is filled with people who started businesses using credit cards. And you can do that. If you have even halfway decent credit, credit card companies are happy to lend you all the money you want.

Naturally, they charge you a mighty high rate of interest, one that even the sharpest traders will have trouble covering from their returns. If the only way you can raise the capital for day trading is through your credit card, consider waiting a few years and saving your money before taking the plunge. Because day trading income can be erratic, you may end up using your credit cards to cover your living expenses some months. You may want to save your credit for that rather than dedicate it directly for your day trading.

Risk capital from an arcade

Trading arcades, also called prop firms, are office spaces where traders can rent space. These are usually located in major cities, though there are a lot less of them than there used to be. Some trading arcades offer more than just desk space. Some have training programs, whereas others give promising traders some capital to trade in exchange for a cut of the profits. This may be an option for you to consider if you are new to day trading and want to put more money to work than you currently have available.

Assessing Risks and Returns from Leverage

Leverage introduces risk to your day trading, and that can give you greatly increased returns. Most day traders use leverage, at least part of the time, in order to make their trading activities pay off in cold, hard cash. The challenge is to use leverage responsibly. In Chapter 3 we go into money management in detail, but here we cover the two issues most related to leverage: losing your money, and losing your nerve. Understanding those risks can help you determine how much leverage you should take, and how often you can take it.

Losing your money

Losing money is obvious. Leverage magnifies your returns, but it also magnifies your risks. Any borrowings have to be repaid regardless. If you buy or sell a futures or options contract, you are legally obligated to perform, even if you have lost money. That can be really hard. Day trading is risky in large part because of the amount of leverage used. If you don't feel comfortable with that, you may want to use little or no leverage, especially when you are new to day trading or when you are starting to work a new trading strategy.

Losing your nerve

The basic risk and return of your underlying strategy isn't affected by leverage. If you expect that your system will work about 60 percent of the time, then that should hold no matter how much money is at stake or where that money came from. However, it's likely that it does make a difference to you on some subconscious level if you have borrowed the money.

Trading is very much a game of nerves. If you hesitate to make a trade, cut a loss, or otherwise follow your strategy, you're going to run into trouble.

Say you are trading futures and decide that you'll accept three downticks before selling, and will look for five upticks before selling. This means you are willing to accept some loss, cut it if it gets out of hand, and then be disciplined about taking gains when you get them. This strategy keeps a lid on your losses while forcing some discipline on your gains.

Now, suppose you're dealing with lots and lots of leverage. Suddenly, those downticks become too real to you — it's money you don't have. Next thing you know, you accept only two downticks before closing out. But this keeps you from getting winners. Then you decide to ride with your winners, and suddenly you aren't taking profits fast enough, and your positions move against you. Your fear of loss is making you sloppy. That's why many traders find it better to borrow less money and stick to their system, rather than borrow the maximum allowed and let that knowledge cloud their judgment.

Lenders can lose their nerve, too. Your brokerage firm might close your account because of losses, even though waiting just a little longer might turn a losing position into a profit. In *Day Trading For Canadians For Dummies,* we talk a bit about Long-Term Capital Management, a fund that was shut by lenders worried about not being repaid. Some evidence exists that if the fund had been allowed to borrow more money, it would have turned a big profit in 1998. (Read the full *Day Trading* book, or search for Long-Term Capital Management on the web to find out more.)

The World of Arbitrage

Day traders work fast, looking to make lots of little profits during a single day. *Arbitrage* is a trading strategy that looks to make profits from small discrepancies in securities prices. The word *arbitrage* itself comes from the French word for judgment; a person who does arbitrage is an *arbitrageur,* or *arb* for short. The idea is that the arbitrageur arbitrates among the prices in the market to reach one final level.

In theory, arbitrage is riskless. It's illogical for the same asset to trade at different prices, so eventually the two prices must converge. The person who buys at the lower price and sells at the higher one will make money with no risk. The challenge is that everyone is looking for these easy profits, so there may not be many of them out there. Good arbitrageurs have a paradoxical mix of patience, to wait for the right opportunity, and impatience, to place the trade the instant the opportunity appears. If you have the fortitude to watch the market, or if you are willing to have software do it for you, you'll probably find enough good arbitrage opportunities to keep you busy.

True arbitrage involves buying and selling the same security, and many day traders use arbitrage as their primary investment strategy. They may use high levels of leverage to boost returns. Other traders follow trading strategies involving similar, but not identical, securities. These fall under the category of *risk arbitrage*. In this part of the chapter, we cover the terms and strategies used by day traders who engage in arbitrage. We discuss the basics of arbitrage and how it can be put to good use by a patient trader. We outline the tools you can use to profit from price differences among similar securities. Finally, we list the many types of arbitrage you might want to include in your arsenal of trading strategies.

Obeying the Law of One Price

The key to success in any investment is buying low and selling high. But what's low? And what's high? Who knows!

In the financial markets, the general assumption is that, at least in the short run, the market price is the right price. Only investors, those patient, long-suffering accounting nerds willing to hold investments for years, will see deviations between the market price and the true worth of an investment. For everyone else, especially day traders, what you see is what you get.

Under the *law of one price,* the same asset has the same value everywhere. If markets allow for easy trading — and the financial markets certainly do — then any price discrepancies will be short-lived because traders will immediately step in to buy at the low price and sell at the high price.

Punishing violators of the law

But what happens if what you see in Toronto is not what you see in New York? What happens if you notice that futures prices are not tracking movements in the underlying asset? How about if you see that the stock of every company in an industry has reacted to a news event except one?

Well, then, you have an opportunity to make money, but you'd better act fast — other people will probably see it, too. What you do is simple: You sell as much of the high-priced asset in the high-priced market as you can, borrowing shares if you need to, and then you immediately turn around and buy the low-priced asset in the low-priced market.

Think of the markets as a scale, and you, the arbitrageur, must bring fairness to them. When the markets are out of balance, you take from the high-priced market (the heavier side of the scale) and return it to the low-priced market (the lighter side) until both even out at a price in between.

If you start with a high price of $8 and a low price of $6, and then buy at $6 and sell at $8, your maximum profit is $2 — with no risk. Until the point where the two assets balance at $7, you can make a profit on the difference between them.

Of course, most price differences are on the order of pennies, not dollars, but if you can find enough of these little pricing errors and trade them in size, you can make good money.

Understanding arbitrage and market efficiency

The law of one price holds as long as markets are efficient. Market efficiency is a controversial topic in finance. In academic theory, markets are perfectly efficient, and arbitrage simply isn't possible. That makes a lot of sense if you are testing different assumptions about how the markets would work in a perfect world. A long-term investor would say that markets are inefficient in the short run but perfectly efficient in the long run, so they believe that if they do their research now, the rest of the world will eventually come around, allowing them to make good money.

Traders are in between. The market price and volume are pretty much all the information they have to go on. It may be irrational, but that doesn't matter today. The only thing a trader wants to know is whether an opportunity to make money is available given what's going on right now.

In the academic world, market efficiency comes in three flavours, with no form allowing for arbitrage:

+ **Strong form:** Everything, even inside information known only to company executives, is reflected in the security's price.

+ **Semi-strong form:** Prices include all public information, so it may be possible to profit from insider trading.

+ **Weak form:** Prices reflect all historical information, so research that uncovers new trends may be beneficial.

Those efficient-market true believers are convinced that arbitrage is imaginary, because someone would've noticed a price difference between markets already and immediately acted to close it off. But who are those mysterious someones? They are day traders! Even the most devout efficient-markets adherent would, if pressed, admit that day traders perform a valuable service in the name of market efficiency.

Those with a less-rigid view of market activity admit that arbitrage opportunities exist, but that they are few and far between. A trader who expects to make money from arbitrage had better pay close attention to the markets to act quickly when a moment happens. And, we'd say this is the case for most arbitrage strategies open to day traders.

Finally, those who don't believe in market efficiency believe that market prices are usually out of sync with asset values. They do research in hopes of learning things that other people don't know. This mindset favours investors more than traders, because it can take time for these price discrepancies to work themselves out.

Because arbitrage requires traders to work fast, it tends to work best for those traders who are willing and able to automate their trading. If you are comfortable with programming and relying on software to do your work, arbitrage might be a great strategy for you.

Scalping for Profits

The law of one price is all well and good, but prices change constantly during the day. They go up a little bit, they go down a little bit, they move every time an order is placed. A way exists for traders to profit from those movements. It's not exactly arbitrage, it's *scalping*. Especially active in commodities markets, scalpers look to take advantage of changes in a security's *bid–ask spread*. That's the difference between the price that a broker will buy a security for from those who want to sell it (the *bid*) and the price that the broker will charge those who want to buy it (the *ask* — also called the *offer* in some markets).

In normal trading, the bid–ask spread tends to be more or less steady over time because the usual flow of supply and demand stays in balance. After all, under market efficiency everyone has the same information, so their trading is consistent and allows the broker-dealers to generate a steady profit.

Sometimes, however, the spread is a little wider or narrower than normal, not because of a change in the information in the market, but because of short-term imbalances in supply and demand.

A basic scalping strategy looks like this:

+ If the spread between the bid and the ask is wider than usual, then the ask is higher and the bid is lower than it should be. That's because slightly more people want to buy than sell, so the brokers charge the buyers higher prices. The scalper uses this as a sign to sell.

✦ If the spread between the bid and the ask is narrower than usual, then the ask is lower and the bid is higher than it would normally be. That happens if there are slightly more sellers than buyers, and the broker wants to find buyers to pick up the slack. The scalper would be in there buying — and hoping that the selling pressure is short lived.

The scalper has to work quickly to make many small trades. He might buy at $20.25, sell at $20.50, and buy again at $20.30. He has to have a low *trade cost structure* in place or else he'll pay out all his profits and more to the broker. He also has to be sure that the price changes aren't driven by real information, because that will make market prices too volatile to make scalping profitable. Scalping is "picking up nickels in front of a steamroller," some traders say, because of the risk of focusing on small price changes when bigger changes are underway.

Many day traders rely heavily on scalping, especially on slow market days. Because each trade carries a transaction cost (discussed in the next section), it can contribute to more costs than profits. Done right, though, it's a nice way to make some steady profits.

Scalping, as defined here, is perfectly legal. However, the word is also sometimes used to describe some illegal activities, such as promoting a security in public and then selling it in private.

Those Pesky Transaction Costs

Pure arbitrage works best in a world where trading is free. In reality, it costs good money to trade. Sometimes you might notice a price discrepancy that seems to last forever. You can't work it because the profit wouldn't cover your costs. And you know what? That may be true for everyone else out there.

In the real world, trading costs money. Consider all the costs of getting started: buying equipment, paying for Internet access, learning how to trade. Then there are the costs of doing business that vary with each transaction: commissions, fees, interest, the bid–ask spread, and taxes. You don't make a profit on a trade unless it covers those costs.

Even if you work with a broker that charges little or no commission, and even if your broker charges no interest on day trading margin (loans against your securities account), you can bet that your broker is making money off you. That broker's profit is showing up in the spread and the speed of execution, so a cost to arbitrage that must be covered still exists, even on a seemingly free account. Trust us, brokerage firms are in business to make money, whether or not their customers do.

Add up those trading costs, and you can find yourself in a frustrating situation: You can see the opportunity right there staring you in the face, but you can't take it. It either sits there, taunting you, or gets picked off by a trader who has lower costs than you do.

On the other hand, if you know what your costs are, you can avoid unprofitable opportunities. Don't consider your fixed costs, like your office and your equipment. Those expenses don't change with any given trade. (Yes, you have to cover them in the long run to stay in business, but you can ignore them in the short run.) Instead, figure out how much money you give to your broker on any given trade, on a per order, per share, or per contract basis. Write that number down on a sticky note, and put it on your monitor so that you remember what you have to clear before you risk a trade. Just don't get so fixated on covering your costs that you avoid exiting trades at the right time.

Risk Arbitrage and Its Tools

In its purest form, arbitrage is riskless because the purchase of an asset in one market and the sale of the asset in another happen simultaneously — you just let those profits flow right into your account. It is possible to do this, but not often. No day trader who pursues only riskless arbitrage stays in business long.

Return is a function of risk. The more risk you take, the greater the return you expect to make.

Because so few opportunities for true arbitrage exist, most day traders looking at arbitrage strategies actually practise *risk arbitrage*. Like true arbitrage, risk arbitrage attempts to generate profits from price discrepancies; but, like the name says, risk arbitrage involves taking some risk. Yes, you buy one security and sell another in risk arbitrage, but it's not always the same security and not always at the same time. For example, a day trader might buy the stock of an acquisition target and sell the stock of an acquirer in the hopes of making a profit as the deal nears the closing date.

Risk arbitrage usually involves strategies that unfold over time — possibly hours, but usually days or weeks. Pursuing these strategies puts you into the world of swing trading (described in Chapter 1), which carries a little more risk than day trading.

In risk arbitrage, a trader is buying and selling similar securities. Much of the risk draws from the fact that the securities are not identical, so the law of one price isn't absolute. Nevertheless, it forms the guiding principle, which is this: If you have two different ways to buy the same thing, then the prices of each purchase should be proportional. If they are not, then an opportunity exists to make money. And what day trader doesn't want to make money?

Arbitrageurs use a mix of different assets and techniques to create these different ways of buying the same thing. In this section we describe some of their favourites.

Derivatives

Derivatives are options, futures, and related financial contracts that draw or derive their value from the value of something else, such as the price of a stock index or the current cost of corn. They offer a lower-cost, lower-obligation method of getting exposure to certain price changes. In the case of agricultural and energy commodities, derivatives are the only practical way for a day trader to own them. Because they are so closely tied to the value of the underlying security, derivatives form a useful "almost, but not quite" asset for traders looking for arbitrage situations. A trader may see a price discrepancy between the derivative and the underlying asset, thus noticing a profitable trading opportunity.

Using a derivative in tandem with its underlying security, traders can construct a range of risk arbitrage trades (and you can read more about them later in this section). For example, a trader looking to set up arbitrage on a merger could trade options on the stocks of the buying and selling companies rather than trading the stocks themselves. More arbitrage opportunities means a greater likelihood of making a low-risk profit.

Levering with leverage

We've already covered leverage in detail, but we're bringing it up again here. It's the process of borrowing money to trade in order to increase potential returns. The more money the trader borrows, the greater the return on capital that she can earn. Leverage is commonly used by day traders, because most trades with a one-day time horizon carry low returns unless they are magnified through borrowing.

That magic of magnification becomes especially important in arbitrage, because the price discrepancies between securities tend to be really small. The primary way to get a bigger return is to borrow money to do it.

However, leverage has a downside: Along with improving returns, it increases risk. Because even risk arbitrage strategies tend to have low risk, this may be acceptable. Just remember that you have to repay all borrowed money, no matter what happens to prices.

Short selling

Short selling, which we discussed above, creates another set of alternatives for setting up an arbitrage trade. Short selling allows a day trader to profit when a security's price goes down. Instead of buying low and then selling high, the trader sells high first and then buys back low. The short seller goes to her broker, borrows the security that she thinks will decline in price, sells it, and then buys it back in the market later so that she has the shares to repay the loan. (It all happens electronically, no office visits required!) Assuming she's right and the price does indeed fall, she pockets the difference between the price where she sold the security and the price where she bought it back. Of course, that difference is her loss if the price goes up instead of down.

By adding short selling to the bag of tricks, an arbitrageur can find a lot more ways to profit from a price discrepancy in the market. New combinations of cheap and expensive assets — and more ways to trade them — give a day trader more opportunities to make trades during the day.

The opposite of *short* is *long.* When a trader holds a security, he's said to be long.

Synthetic securities

Feeling creative? Well, then, consider creating *synthetic securities* when looking for arbitrage opportunities. A synthetic security is a combination of assets that have the same profit-and-loss profile as another asset or group of assets. For example, a stock is a combination of a *put option,* which has value if the stock goes down in price, and a *call option,* which has value if the stock goes up in price. By thinking up ways to mimic the behaviour of an asset through a synthetic security, a day trader can find more ways for an asset to be cheaper in one market than in another, leading to more potential arbitrage opportunities.

A typical arbitrage transaction involving a synthetic security involves shorting the real security and then buying a package of derivatives that match its risk and return.

Many of the risk arbitrage techniques covered later in this chapter involve the creation of synthetic securities.

Complex arbitrage trading strategies require more testing and simulation trading and may possibly involve losses while you fine-tune your methods. Be sure you feel comfortable with your trading method before you commit big time and big dollars to it.

An Array of Arbitrages

The tools of arbitrage — derivatives, leverage, short selling, synthetic securities — can be used in all sorts of ways to generate potentially profitable trades, and that's what we cover in this section of the chapter. Most day traders who decide to do arbitrage will pick a few strategies to follow. After all, it's hard enough to spot these opportunities; the trader who tries to do too much is the trader who will soon be looking for a new job. Armed with the information here, you can decide whether an arbitrage strategy matches your approach to the market so that you can make it your own.

The varieties of arbitrage transactions are listed here in alphabetical order. It's not exhaustive; plenty of other ways to exploit price differences in the market exist, but some involve more time than a day trader is willing to commit. We've put them in alphabetical order. Some are more complex than others, some generate more opportunities than others, and some work best if you are willing to swing trade (hold for a few days) rather than day trade (close out all positions at the end of the day).

Many arbitrage strategies work best in combination with other strategies, such as news-driven trading (discussed in Chapter 4). For example, it might take a news announcement to cause people to pay attention to a company's stock so that enough trading activity happens that day to close a price gap. If you know about the pricing problem ahead of time, you can swoop in and make the arbitrage that day.

Other types of arbitrage certainly do exist out there. Wherever people pay close attention to the markets and price changes, they find small price differences to turn into large, low-risk profits. If you think you've found an arbitrage strategy not listed here, by all means, go and test it and see if it will work for you.

Capital structure arbitrage

Companies issue securities in order to finance their business, and investment bankers are in the business of helping them do just that. Some companies are nice and simple. Microsoft, for example, uses only stock for financing and has only one class of stock. Others are far more complicated, using mixtures of different classes of stock and different issues of debt to finance the growth. TD Bank, for example, has one class of common stock and several different, preferred share securities for its parent company and its finance subsidiary.

The way that a company is financed is its *capital structure,* and capital structure arbitrage looks for inappropriate price differences among all the different classes of stock and debt outstanding. Although all securities tied to the same business should trade in a similar fashion, they don't always, and that creates opportunities.

Say, for example, that SuperTech Company has two classes of stock, one on its core business and one that tracks the performance of its nanotechnology subsidiary. (A *tracking stock* is a corporate finance gimmick that goes in and out of style; it's stock on a subsidiary that is controlled by the parent company.) The parent company still has exposure to the nanotechnology subsidiary, but that is not reflected in its stock price. One day, the nanotechnology subsidiary announces great earnings, and the stock goes way up, but

SuperTech stock doesn't move even though it benefits. The capital structure arbitrageur immediately shorts the nanotech subsidiary tracking stock and buys the parent company stock (matching the size of the long and short positions so that they move up and down in tandem), waiting for people to realize that the discrepancy is there.

Convertible arbitrage

As part of designing their capital structure, some companies issue *convertible bonds* (sometimes called a *convertible debenture*) or *convertible preferred stock*. These securities are a cross between stocks and bonds. Like an ordinary bond, convertibles pay regular income to those who hold them (interest for convertible bonds and dividends for convertible preferred stock), but they also act a little like stock because the holders have the right to exchange the convertible security for ordinary common stock.

For example: a $1,000 convertible bond pays 7.5 percent interest and is convertible into 25 shares of stock. If the stock is less than $40 per share, the convertible holder will prefer to cash the interest or dividend cheques coming from the 7.5 percent convertible bond. If the company's stock trades above $40, the convertible holder would make more money giving up the income in order to get the stock cheap. Because of the benefit of conversion, the interest rate on a convertible security is usually below that on a regular corporate bond.

Because a convertible security carries a built-in option to convert to the underlying stock, it generally trades in line with the stock. If the convertible's price gets too high or too low, then an arbitrage opportunity presents itself.

Consider this case: A day trader notices that a convertible bond is selling at a lower price than it should be, given the current level of interest rates and the price of the company's common stock. So, he buys the convertibles and sells the common stock short. When the stock's price moves back into line, he collects a profit from at least one and maybe both sides of the trade.

Fixed income and interest rate arbitrage

Fixed income securities are bonds, notes, and related securities that give their owners a regular interest payment. They are popular with conservative investors, especially retirees, who want to generate a regular income from the quarterly interest payments. They are considered to be safe, predictable, long-run investments, but they can fluctuate wildly in the short term, which makes them attractive to arbitrageurs.

Interest rates are the price of money, and so they affect the value of many kinds of securities. Fixed-income securities have a great deal of interest-rate exposure, because they pay out interest. Some stocks have interest-rate exposure, too. Trading in foreign exchange is an attempt to profit from the changing price of one currency relative to another, and that's usually a function of the difference in interest rates between the two countries. Derivatives have a regular expiration schedule, so they have some time value, and that's measured through interest rates.

With so many different assets affected by changes in interest rates, arbitrageurs pay attention. With *fixed-income arbitrage,* the trader breaks out the following:

✦ The time value of money

✦ The level of risk in the economy

✦ The likelihood of repayment

✦ The inflation-rate effects on different securities

If one of the numbers is out of whack, the trader constructs and executes an arbitrage trade to profit from it.

It's rarely practical for a day trader to buy bonds outright. Instead, day traders looking at fixed income arbitrage and other interest-rate-sensitive strategies usually rely on interest rate futures, offered by the Montreal Exchange or the Chicago Board of Trade.

How would this work? Think of a day trader monitoring interest rates on Canadian government bonds. He notices that two-year bonds are trading at a higher yield than expected — especially relative to five-year bonds. He sells futures on the two-year bonds and then buys futures on the five-year bonds. When the difference between the two rates falls back where it should be, the futures trade will turn a profit.

Index arbitrage

Market observers talk a lot about the performance of the Canadian S&P/TSX Composite Index, or the S&P 500 Index and the Dow Jones Industrial Average, the two main American markets. These are *market indices,* designed to represent the activity of the market, and are widely published for market observers to follow. The performance of the index is based on the performance of a group of securities, ranging from all of the TSX's large companies, currently about 250 companies, (S&P/TSX Composite Index) to the TSX's 60 largest companies (S&P/TSX 60).

Sure, an arbitrageur could buy all the stocks, and some hedge funds exist to do just that. But very few people can do that. Instead, they get exposure to index performance through the many different securities based on the indices. Buy-and-hold mutual fund investors can buy funds that hold all the same stocks in the same proportion as the index. Those with shorter-term profits in mind can buy exchange-traded funds, which are baskets of stocks listed on organized exchanges, or they can trade futures and options on the indices.

Garbitrage

Traders get sloppy when an exciting merger is announced. If one company in an industry gets taken over, the stock in all the companies in the industry will go up, often for no good reason. Some get so carried away that they buy the wrong stock entirely, usually because of confusion over ticker symbols. If GAP Stores, ticker symbol GPS, were to be taken over, chances are good that the stock in Great Atlantic and Pacific Tea Company — operator of the A&P grocery stores, ticker symbol GAP — would also go up. Such bad trading is known as *garbitrage*.

Arbitrageurs love the idea of an asset — like an index — that has lots of different securities based on its value. That creates lots of opportunities for mispricing. Unless the index, the futures, the options, and the exchange-traded funds are all in line, some canny day trader can step in and make some money.

For example, suppose the S&P/TSX 60 futures contract is looking mighty cheap relative to the price of the S&P/TSX 60 Index. A trader can short an exchange-traded fund on the index and then buy futures contracts to profit from the difference.

Merger arbitrage

Every day, companies get bought and sold, and that creates arbitrage opportunities. In fact, one of the better-known arbitrage strategies out there is *merger arbitrage,* in which traders try to profit from the change in stock prices after a merger has been announced. It starts by looking at the following details in the merger announcement:

+ The name of the acquiring company
+ The name of the company being taken over (and no matter what PR people say, no mergers occur between equals)
+ The price of the transaction
+ The currency and securities (cash, stock, preferred shares, debt)
+ The date the merger is expected to close
+ Financing to pay for the take-over

Until the date that the merger actually closes, which may be different from the date in the merger announcement, any and every one of the announced details can change. The acquiring company may learn new information about the target company and change its mind. A third company might jump in and make an offer for more money. The shareholders may agree to support the deal only if they get cash instead of stock. The government might intervene to block the deal. All that drama creates opportunity, both for traders looking for one-day opportunities and for those willing to hold a position until the merger closing date.

Consider this example. Say that Major Bancorp offers to buy Downtown Bank for $50 per share in cash. Major Bancorp's shares will probably fall in price, because its shareholders will be concerned that the merger will be a lot of expense and trouble. Downtown Bank's shares will go up in price, but not all the way to $50, because its shareholders know that some risk exists the deal won't go through. An arbitrageur would short Major Bancorp and buy Downtown Bank to profit from the concerns. If Overseas Banque decides to step in, then it might be a profitable idea to buy Major Bancorp and short Overseas Banque. (If another bidder steps in and places a higher offer for Downtown Bank, then the whole arbitrage unravels — hence, the risk.)

Option arbitrage

Options form the basis of many arbitrage strategies, especially for those day traders who work the stock market. Many types of options are available, even on the same security. The two main categories are *puts,* which bet on the underlying security price falling, and *calls,* which bet on the underlying security price rising. Puts and calls on the same security come in many different strike prices, depending on where you want to bet the price goes. Some options, known as *American options,* can be cashed in at any time between the date of issue and the expiration date, and you can exercise others, known as *European options,* only at the expiration date. (To complicate matters, American and European options can be issued anywhere.) With all those choices, a few price discrepancies are bound to arise for the alert arbitrageur.

Maybe a day trader notices that on a day when a company has a big announcement, the options exchanges seem to be assuming a slightly higher price for the stock than where the stock is actually trading. He decides to buy the underlying stock as well as a put; he also sells a call with the same strike price and expiration date as the put. This creates a synthetic security that has the same payoff as shorting the security, meaning that the trader has pulled off a riskless arbitrage transaction. He effectively bought the security cheap in the stock market and sold it at a higher price in the options market.

Pairs trading

Pairs trading, which involves buying a cheap stock and shorting an expensive stock in the same industry group, is popular with many people who day trade stocks. (It was also the core of traditional hedge-fund investing, although very few hedge funds rely on it nowadays.)

A pairs trader watches an industry group and looks for situations where one company seems to be doing especially well or one is doing especially poorly. That would most likely indicate a problem in the way people are pricing the industry, because in general what's good for one company is good for all of them. A pairs trader would pay particular attention to news events that seem to affect all but one or two companies in the same industry. If one of them appears to be overvalued relative to the others, the pairs trader shorts the pricey stock and buys the cheapest one.

The pairs trader isn't dealing with identical assets, of course, so the simultaneous purchase and sale is a lot riskier than it would be in true arbitrage. Sometimes, one stock is more expensive and one is much cheaper than the rest of the industry for very good reason. Good pairs traders are willing to do a little fundamental research (see Chapter 4) so they can avoid being short the winner and being long the loser in an industry undergoing big changes.

Book VI

Reviewing Real Estate Investing

The 5th Wave · By Rich Tennant

"I know renovations can add to a property's value, but don't you think this might be a little excessive?"

Contents at a Glance

Chapter 1: Introducing Real Estate Investing

In This Chapter

- Looking at real estate investments
- Exploring residential properties
- Checking out commercial and industrial properties
- Considering condos
- Reviewing recreational properties
- Investigating undeveloped land
- Seeking out syndicates
- Tucking into real estate investment trusts

Real estate is everywhere: the apartment or house you call home, the mall where you go shopping for groceries and clothes, and the office where you work. Even the park where you take your kids and walk your dog is property with potential investment value. But like any other investment, real estate has its risks, too. Remember the old saying "land rich, cash poor"? The expression summarizes the very real wealth that exists in land but also the financial dangers land ownership poses if you don't have a strategy. What kind of real estate interests you most? Have you considered the skills — and weaknesses — you bring to your role as an investor? Building wealth through real estate investing means becoming land rich in order to become cash rich, too. You want to do it right!

In this chapter, we discuss the various opportunities awaiting you as an investor, and some of the risks real estate carries. We look at some of the considerations you should bear in mind as you're sizing up the different investment tools available. Finally, we investigate how real estate can fit into a long-term financial plan, and the implications that it can have for your retirement and your estate.

Investigating Real Estate Investing

So what's the big deal about real estate, anyhow? Why is everyone from the government honchos who manage the Canada Pension Plan right on down to your Uncle Ed buying property? In this section, we check out the advantages of real estate and compare property relative to other kinds of investments you may consider as part of your portfolio.

Discovering the opportunities

Statistics from the Canadian Real Estate Association indicate that residential real estate has increased in value by an average of more than 5 percent a year over the past 30 years. While there have been some significant dips during that period, and not every property will make the same gains in every year or from city to city, the trend is unmistakable: The long-term potential for the appreciation of your real estate investment can be tremendous if you manage to structure your properties properly. And several reasons bolster our argument that an investment in real estate makes sense. We outline them below.

Leverage opportunities

Leverage is all about using a small amount of your own money and letting someone else's cash do the rest of the work. Because real estate provides the loan's *security,* a guarantee of repayment if you're unable to pay off the loan, the risk can be low if things go right for you. If you run into financial trouble and your *creditors,* the people who've loaned you cash, demand immediate repayment and call your loan, your property could be subject to proceedings that lead to its sale. Providing the property sells for more than the amount owing, you stand to emerge relatively unscathed. The nature of forced sale of your property depends on the province and the mortgage documents you have signed. For example, in Ontario the power of sale process does not require court approval, whereas in some other provinces the foreclosure and property sale process requires the court to be involved throughout.

Equity opportunities

By paying down a mortgage, you're paying down the liability value of the property and making its value your own. Real estate is therefore unlike many other investments because it gives you a chance to build *equity* — your share of the property's net worth at the time of purchase — over the course of the investment rather than invest everything upfront and hope for the best. Given the chance for an appreciation in the value of your property while you're making those payments, that's a significant advantage over other forms of investments where leverage is not involved

Beware of negative equity! Although real estate is a convenient means of building equity (and that's a good thing), a drop in the market can bring destruction and result in *negative equity,* a situation in which the market value of a property is less than the mortgage it secures. This typically happens when an investment is financed with too much debt, a condition known as being overleveraged, and was a common scenario in the United States following 2006 as interest rates on certain types of sub-prime mortgages began increasing and saddling buyers with payments they couldn't afford. It has also been an issue in a minority of cases in Canada. To some investors, negative cash flow is more relevant than negative equity. In this scenario, the investor would consider negative equity an unrealized loss that over time could turn into positive equity as the market improves. Leveraging is the key to successful investing, not overleveraging. The latter concept implies excessive risk taking, which for many investors would not be a prudent investment business model.

Be careful because real estate is the major cause of families going bankrupt.

Return opportunities

That's return on money, not the chances you'll return alive from a property! But you'll probably do that, too, and get to enjoy the benefits of a net return of as much as 150 percent annually on your investment. How do we figure that? Simply put, the return is calculated on your investment.

If you buy a $200,000 property with a $20,000 down payment and the property increases in value by half over five years, the increase in equity is $100,000. That amounts to approximately $75,000 after the government taxes the appreciation in the property's value, or *capital gain.* This would represent a return of 375 percent over five years, or at least 75 percent annually on your original investment of $20,000. Given that the debt you incurred to buy the property would have decreased over the course of the five years, and provided leasing allowed you to see income from the property, you would enjoy an even greater return on your investment.

Tax opportunities

Real estate offers several tax advantages for you as an investor, especially if you've developed an investment strategy that accounts for taxes. Taxes erode the return you'll see on investments yielding a fixed return, such as bank accounts, bonds, and guaranteed investment certificates (GICs), but not Tax-Free Savings Accounts (TFSAs). Stocks and other equities put your principal at risk. Leveraged real estate investments, however, often are subject to a reduced tax rate. The tax advantages range from tax-free capital gains on your principal residence to savings as great as 50 percent on taxes levied on capital gains from investment properties. You might also be able to deduct investment expenses and write off any depreciation in property values.

Hedge opportunities

No, we're not suggesting you hide from your creditors in a bush! The kind of hedging we're talking about means taking shelter from the effects of inflation, which works to erode your buying power. The rate of inflation varies from month to month, year to year, and even country to country. But real estate typically appreciates at a rate three to five percentage points above the inflation rate. So if inflation is running at 3 percent, look for your investment in real estate to appreciate at 6 to 8 percent. If you choose wisely, your investment stands a good chance of increasing at a rate greater than that of inflation, as Figure 1–1 shows.

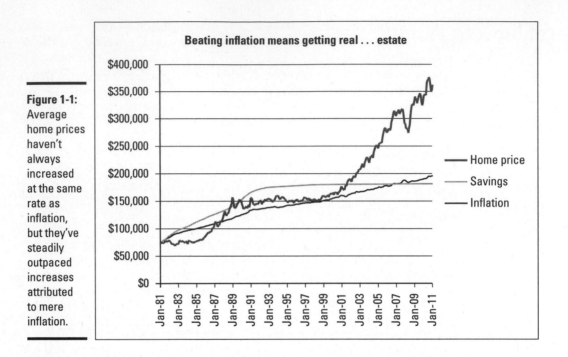

Beating inflation means getting real . . . estate

— Home price
— Savings
— Inflation

Figure 1-1:
Average home prices haven't always increased at the same rate as inflation, but they've steadily outpaced increases attributed to mere inflation.

You're paying off your mortgage in dollars that reflect inflation, also known as *real dollars*. So, although the value of your mortgage will diminish over time, you will typically enjoy a higher income thanks to salary increases or rental revenue increases that will help make your mortgage more affordable to carry over the long term.

Flexibility opportunities

Real estate offers a variety of investment options that give you flexibility in terms of how much attention they demand and the amount of risk you'll bear. By investing in just one property rather than several, or in partnership with family or friends, you can limit (or increase) your involvement to the level that suits you. Be warned when investing with family because blood and money often do not mix well. Make sure all your co-ownership documents are sound.

Learning opportunities

Most investments entail some sort of learning process. Real estate is no different. Prior involvement in buying property, such as a home, may make it easier, but don't underestimate the need to learn about the particular dynamics of investing in real property. Real estate investment also offers opportunities to learn about the community issues and economic trends at work in neighbourhoods. And, if you're game for the role of landlord, you'll also have a chance to improve your people-management skills.

Homing In on Residential

Buying a home is typically the first major real estate purchase you'll make. But if you've never considered your home as the starting point for an investment portfolio, why not? Even tycoons need somewhere to lay their heads, and finding a home for yourself is a convenient way to explore and hone the skills you'll need to tackle more complex deals as an investor.

Home-buying is a chance to practise the basic acquisition skills you'll need to select and secure properties. If you decide to rent out a suite in your condominium, townhouse, or house, you'll be able to test your management and human relations skills, as well as other joys of being a landlord. And, of course, home ownership brings regular opportunities to familiarize yourself with the hands-on maintenance that makes up the practical side of managing a real estate investment.

Investing begins at home

For many, the family home has a venerable position worth more than its weight in gold. Making money on it is the last thing some people consider doing — but more than one homeowner has been delighted to find that his home has appreciated in value, bringing him a sizeable nest-egg just in time for retirement. For families who have occupied the same home for several decades, the original investment can deliver a return in both happy memories and hard cash.

Buying a home with the added motive of seeing it double as an investment property will intensify the importance of many of these issues. You'll be scouting features that not only are desirable to your family as occupants but also could appeal to potential tenants. You'll also be conscious of points that could help the home fetch a higher resale value when it comes time to sell.

Rent out a suite, pay down a mortgage

Tenants aren't called "mortgage-helpers" for nothing. Homeowners looking to build equity in their property can do so far faster if they have rental income feeding into their cash flow than by going it alone. Tenants also help a mortgage out in another way: Most mortgage companies will factor rental revenue into the value of a home when calculating the amount of a mortgage you can obtain when you're buying.

Tenants can help you pay off a mortgage faster, whether it's for your primary residence or a full-fledged rental property. Figure 1–2 shows why tenants can give you something to rave about — at least from a financial perspective.

Take the example of a $125,000 bungalow with a finished basement (separate entrance, of course) in Charlottetown. Renting the basement to a student at University of Prince Edward Island for $500 a month would give you enough to add an extra $100 a week to your mortgage payments. Assuming an average interest rate of 6 percent over a standard 25-year term, those extra payments could reduce the length of your mortgage by 11 years and save you just over $37,300 in interest.

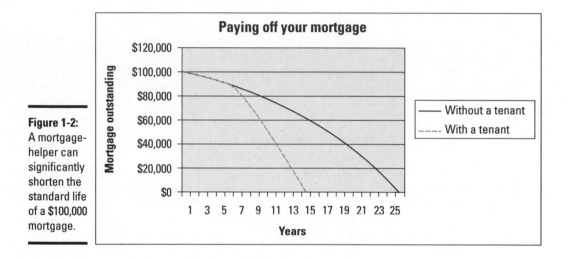

Figure 1-2:
A mortgage-helper can significantly shorten the standard life of a $100,000 mortgage.

Being a landlord isn't for everyone, however. Renting a suite in your home to a tenant, even temporarily, not only gives you some extra cash to put toward the mortgage, but also gives you a good idea of whether you want to become a full-time landlord on a larger property or multiple properties.

A shifting rental market is one of the major risks to renting a suite in your home. This is particularly true in smaller college or university towns, where you may be able to count on only eight months of rental income a year. Should demand for rental accommodation slacken, you may lose your ability to levy rents adequate to service your mortgage.

Modifying your home for rental purposes (so long as local bylaws allow, of course) will affect your insurance coverage, so for peace of mind make sure your policy protects you with additional coverage. Insist that tenants obtain their own home insurance and provide you with a copy. You need to be sure you're covered in case a fire starts in the rental suite and your own property is consumed.

Managing tenants

Even the best tenants and properties require attention. From maintenance you might otherwise ignore, to keeping track of and collecting rent, you have to keep on top of issues that you wouldn't have to watch if you were just counting on your property to rise in value rather than generate revenue. Knowing some of the scenarios that could arise will help you prepare and be a more confident landlord — and a more successful investor! Right now it's worth emphasizing the importance of having a rental agreement, especially if you're renting a suite in your primary residence.

To cut off potential problems at the pass, ask prospective tenants to complete a tenancy application form soliciting information such as rental history, names of previous landlords and other references, and the right to do a credit bureau investigation.

Rental contracts should include the following:

+ The number of permanent residents allowed in the unit

+ The term of the lease — whether month-to-month, renewable after a year, or reverting to month-to-month after an initial term (usually a year)

+ Whether or not pets and smoking are allowed

+ The damage deposit and grounds for its return or retention.

Managing property

Your ability to attract tenants and charge a higher rent will increase with the quality of the suite you offer. Be prepared to make modest, ongoing investments in the suite that will allow you to maximize the rent you can reasonably expect a tenant to pay. Painting the suite may enable you to charge a higher rent that will more than pay for the paint job over the course of the tenancy. Getting in the habit of investing in regular maintenance and upgrades in your own home will prepare you for the economics of managing a stand-alone residential investment.

Securing Commercial and Industrial Properties

Commercial and industrial properties are not the most glamorous investments, but if they pass muster with the Canada Pension Plan and other institutional investors, why not with you? Buying an office building or warehouse is more complex than buying the average home, but with leases typically running for years at a time, you stand a good chance of enjoying a more stable cash flow than you would from residential properties. The trick is finding the opportunities, especially if you're just starting out. Although anyone can relate to residential housing, investing in commercial and industrial properties requires preparation and the help of experienced advisers.

**Book VI
Chapter 1**

Introducing Real
Estate Investing

Hunting commercial properties

What the Multiple Listing Service (www.realtor.ca) is for residential real estate, ICX (www.icx.ca) is for non-residential properties. It is one of several services that can help you locate commercial and industrial properties. The larger commercial real estate listing firms also publish their listings, not all of which are necessarily linked to the MLS system. Don't forget to check out the various media that publish real estate listings, whether targeted specifically to real estate investors, such as Western Investor (www.western investor.com), or trade publications for specific industries. A wide range of print and electronic resources exist to help you uncover opportunities.

However high the standards you have for residential real estate, houses are relatively simple propositions when it comes to market influences. By contrast, commercial and industrial properties are subject to diverse factors and influences rooted in economic trends. People shop in only so many places, and only so much office space is required in each community. And warehouses? They're not quite as numerous as coffee shops.

Still, opportunities exist to do well by commercial and industrial properties, which are home to the businesses that can be the lifeblood of communities. However, this is generally not a viable option for investors with less than $50,000 to invest.

Assessing classes

Several classes of commercial and industrial real estate exist, with the most recognizable being retail, office, and industrial, each with a different level of liquidity, based on the performance of the local economy and the shifting measure known as investor confidence:

✦ **Retail:** The humble shop front is a mainstay of main streets everywhere. But often a private landlord will own the building, which may or may not have some residential units above. Indeed, a mixed-use building in a smaller town can provide your portfolio with a measure of diversity by giving you a stake in two asset classes at once. Many large urban centres feature retail units within condo developments. The retail units are sold off like the apartments above, and at comparable prices. Providing you can find a tenant who will meet the needs of the surrounding neighbourhood — this often requires some skill, rooted in a knowledge of the neighbourhood and an ability to devise a lease package that will attract the right tenants — you will be able to reap the benefits of their success.

Small community-oriented plazas with just a few shops can also provide a steady income and, in the right location, appreciation in value if resold for redevelopment.

Retail units also work well if you need premises for your own business. Just as you buy a home rather than rent an apartment so you can build equity in your own property rather than someone else's, buying commercial space can be a good long-term investment. Car dealerships are typical examples; some auto dealers make more money off the lots from which they sell cars than from the cars themselves. Depending on your business, you may be able to operate out of a piece of property that will make you more money than your business ever does.

✦ **Office:** Office space is a type of real estate few businesses can do without. Similar to residential, it's available in both stand-alone buildings and larger developments ranging from condo developments to business parks.

Despite exposure to shifts in the economy, office properties generally allow you to implement longer-term leases than are typically possible on other forms of real estate. Businesses value long-term arrangements to ensure the stability of their own operations, and you can use that fact to stabilize your investment portfolio.

Although it's worth noting that vacancies are often higher than for residential real estate, remember that you'll also be able to charge a higher rent, and contract for increases over the life of a lease.

✦ **Industrial:** The workhorses of the real estate sector, industrial properties are probably the least glamorous assets you'll encounter. Bare-bones construction makes them functional rather than fashionable, designed as they are to serve the needs of manufacturers, distributors, or any grab-bag of blue-collar uses. But the basic service they provide also makes them stable investments with a good potential for return.

Know what your tenants are doing with the industrial space you're leasing! The activities of some tenants raise the risk of soil contamination, which could negate any return rents hand you and even land you in debt or, worse, legal trouble.

Assessing liquidity

A property's *liquidity* — its ability to be sold — is more important in assessing the long-term potential of non-residential assets than homes and apartments. But it is also more complex to determine, depending on your familiarity with the several factors at play. Most residential buyers, for example, don't examine trends in a specific industry to determine where to buy a home. But you'll want to study the demand for retail space in a community if you're buying a strip mall, or examine commodity price trends if you've been offered a warehouse previously used by the forest sector. Are you up for the challenge?

An asset's liquidity is a function of its attractiveness and appeal to investors, perhaps even more than market cycles (which we discuss in Chapter 3). An asset in Montreal, for example, will tend to have greater liquidity than a property in Corner Brook — not because Corner Brook is a bad place to invest, but because Montreal is a larger centre with a more diverse economy and, in short, more opportunities for the use of the property. Properties that can deliver a greater return than more expensive assets will also enjoy healthy liquidity, regardless of how the broader market is faring.

The greater the future demand for a property, the better your chance of seeing a return when the time comes to sell — whether that's next year or five years away. Factors to take into account include

✦ The property's proximity to properties used by similar or complementary businesses

✦ Prospects for the growth of the sector the property serves

✦ The economic strength of the community in which the property is located

✦ The property's proximity to transportation networks that may enhance its appeal to users in a sector other than that of the current user

For example, a port is a good location for a warehouse, but an office building located nowhere near other offices might be a hard sell to potential tenants and therefore future buyers.

Laying Into Condos

Condos (short for condominium), also known as strata-titled units in British Columbia and co-proprietorships in Quebec, are more than just apartments. Although residential condos (both apartments and townhomes) are the best-known form of this type of real estate, it also encompasses commercial and hotel properties. Residential condos are the primary form, however, with commercial and hotel units available in smaller numbers. When people talk of condos, they almost always mean residential.

Because condo units are generally subject to the building council's regulations, condos carry some of the perils of joint ownership. Condo bylaws occasionally limit activities allowed in suites, including the ability to rent units. You need to check the bylaws before you make any commitment. There could be some provinces that permit condo rentals as a right. Because provincial legislation can change at any time, you need to do your due diligence research in advance. Read the provincial legislation online, and check with a condo lawyer. Condo fees have the potential to vary, with special levies possible for maintenance and repairs. Just because a problem didn't affect your suite, the mere fact that it happened in the building at all may subject you to these levies and diminish the value of your unit.

Investing in residential condos

Residential condos are popular investments. Vancouver, which boasts one of Canada's most active condo markets, has seen as many as half the units in some new buildings sold to investors. That's an important statistic, but not great news if you're planning to rent a unit in that kind of situation. Investors who purchase a unit with the intention of renting it out want to know they have a reasonable hope of finding tenants, something that's more difficult to do when several landlords are competing for the same limited number of prospects.

On the other hand, condos can be an attractive alternative to standard rental accommodation. And this raises the potential for them to command a higher rent than other forms of residential rentals. Barring a glut of similar product, and providing your unit is in an appropriate neighbourhood, condos can be an affordable means for you to claim a slice of the rental market.

Because condos are run by a council which are often very amateur because many members are volunteer neighbours, make sure you know what the rules allow before you buy. Some buildings limit suites available for rental, others limit the kinds of improvements that can be made or whether pets are allowed. Other issues to consider include management fees and the potential for upcoming expenses, which are usually shared among the owners. Ask to see the minutes of the council meetings and view other records associated with the building's operation and management.

Investing in commercial condos

Retail, office, and industrial condos are relatively few in number. The usual precautions regarding investment in the condo class aside, guidelines for investing in these properties are similar to those for other forms of commercial property.

Owner-occupiers reap the most advantages of owning a commercial condo, however. Some of the benefits include

✦ **Fixed business costs:** Because you own the commercial space, you aren't subject to rising rents. Although operating costs may fluctuate based on condo fees, as a member of the building council you have some input into what those fees will be.

✦ **Tax advantages:** The standard business-related advantages of occupying property you own hold true for condo units, including opportunities to deduct depreciation and business expenses associated with the unit.

✦ **Appreciation in value:** Like any other investment, you also reap the benefit from any appreciation in property value — the reason you became an investor in the first place!

Dreaming of Recreational Properties

Recreational properties are more than a cottage at the lake for an investor. From fractional ownership to islands with development potential, the opportunities available are wide-ranging and far-flung. And, as a type of property hit hardest by the slowdown in real estate when development financing tightened at the end of the 2000s, many offer opportunities for investors seeking lower-priced units that will let them capitalize on the coming wave of baby boomer retirees.

Should you have the chance to sell either your principal residence or recreational property, you have the option of naming one of the two properties as your principal residence. Generally, this is the one with the largest capital gain; as your principal residence it would not be subject to capital gains tax. The other property would be subject to capital gains tax. Talk to your accountant!

Cottages and cabins

Cottages and cabins are a simple form of recreational property with the same potential to appreciate in value as any other residential asset. Renovations and the possible renting out of cottages provide the opportunity to boost value and provide cash flow on an ongoing basis. When compared to other forms of recreational real estate, this is probably the one most familiar to people and easily understood.

Many cottages come with an acreage that provides recreational opportunities. The acreage itself may be a good investment if you have the foresight (and good fortune) to buy in the path of urban development. Calgary is a good example of a city that has swallowed up many smaller communities in the course of its growth, turning countless former retreats from city life into part of the city itself — and handing the former owners of the properties a windfall to boot.

Fractional ownership

Fractional ownership, as the name implies, gives you an equity share in a property — usually a resort-style development — with rights to access it in proportion to your share. For example, if you own 10 to 25 percent of a property, you have rights to use it 10 to 25 percent of the time.

Unlike a time share, in which you purchase only rights to use the property in proportion to your interest, a fractional ownership purchase puts your name on the title deed, along with those of the other owners. The owners generally have an agreement outlining the procedure for selling interest in the property. To avoid any misunderstandings or conflict, make sure you have a proper legal structure and appropriate documentation of the arrangement.

One of the draws of fractional ownership is that your unit is often in a rental pool when you're not using it. Even if that option isn't offered, you may be able to rent it yourself. You need to have your real estate lawyer read the unit contract before any commitment. Either way, you'll get to enjoy some income in addition to having a getaway for your own use.

Most fractional ownerships of residential properties where the owner is registered on the land title as a fractional owner tend to be from ¼ to ⅒. It could have a higher fraction, but that is not the norm. In most cases, based on the per unit cost of the fraction, the actual aggregate purchase value of the "investment" could be valued many times more than the actual market value.

Resorts by the suite

Earlier in this chapter we talk about condo developments in the context of hotels. Many resort properties offer similar investment opportunities. Like fractional ownership arrangements, these allow owners to acquire a stake in a property that's more affordable than if they had full ownership.

Developers have pursued these types of developments because they reduce the risk of proceeding with construction. You benefit from access to the suite for set periods of time each year, as well as proceeds from the net profits of the suite's operation.

Some overseas resort projects undertaken by or marketed to Canadians may seem like attractive opportunities, but be sure to thoroughly investigate the risks. We briefly discussed cross-border investing above, but resort properties are worth special scrutiny — most people want a vacation property that's a slice of heaven rather than a taste of, er, the other place. Moreover, local factors may complicate development of a project you're considering solely based on the plans. Be sure you understand what safeguards exist for investors, and know your exit strategy.

Developing a Taste for Raw Land

Just because something hasn't been built on a piece of property doesn't mean the property's worthless. Sometimes the value has yet to be realized. As a *land banker,* someone who buys up properties for the value of the land alone, you can be the first to realize a value from property that will be in demand in the future. The future purchaser may be another investor, an individual who wants to build a home, or even a developer with visions of a subdivision. The land you bank doesn't have to be in the city, either; it can just as easily be in a rural community with a growing residential population.

Raw land is good if you're an investor with a long-term plan. The downside of land banking is the chance you'll find yourself waiting a long time before the value of the land increases enough to make it worth selling.

Staking your claim

You may feel like an old-time prospector when you first buy a piece of raw land. It might not pan out for you, regardless of your gut feeling. But for the low price at which you can buy undeveloped land in many parts of Canada, raw land is frequently a gamble worth taking. Whether you're in the city or the countryside, several alternatives can help you make good on your investment.

Choosing a locale, as with every other real estate purchase, requires research into the area's current conditions and future prospects. Because the return you're looking for probably requires the development of the property into something new, your attitude should be similar to that of a renovator: Look for a site with the potential to be popular, and one that is showing signs of a turnaround. For a rural community, the clues might lie in proximity to an urban centre, and demographic trends such as an influx of retirees or younger couples.

Try to find the best fit between the land you purchase and what your research tells you is fuelling the long-term potential of the surrounding community. You want to be where the action is, so that you can benefit from the potential future interest in your site.

Raw land comes with just as many responsibilities as any other property. You have to make sure your property conforms to any local bylaws, especially with regards to appearance and cleanliness. You don't want it to become a liability, and you will be liable if hazards exist on it that could bring others to harm. You also want to ensure it meets environmental conditions, so that you don't find yourself with a nasty surprise when the time comes to sell.

Goin' country or swingin' in the city?

Development often follows a relentless pace. The patch of grass where you played as a kid has become a block of town houses. As a real estate investor you may not want to lose what was, but you can't help thinking of what's to come.

This country wouldn't have any cities had someone not first put up a house and begun developing undeveloped land. Because the cost of urban property is often quite high, opportunities to secure vacant lots are sometimes most frequent in rural communities. British Columbia and Ontario considered the trend so significant that legislation in these two provinces limits the use of farmland.

Vacant lots in urban settings are subject to far more variables, including the use of surrounding properties, local zoning, and carrying costs (especially property taxes). You must often be prepared to hold land for a long time before you see a return. Often, the payoff comes from having a property someone else needs to pursue a development. Through strategic buying, a small investment can deliver a decent return relative to the time spent managing it.

This is true in small towns as well as cities. A small town won't always be small, especially if it is adjacent to a growing city. Calgary is a good example of a city that's grown, absorbing smaller communities in its path. Had you owned a parcel of land in some of those communities when they were outside the city, you might be enjoying a wealthy retirement today.

Banking on land

Rather than holding a single lot, you may have the opportunity to acquire a large tract of land. As a land banker you may add to this tract, or wait patiently to sell it either in whole or in part to a developer. Although land bankers typically deal with residential land, some bank land for other uses.

The main risk to banking land is that you're not receiving any income from it, unless you've been able to lease it to a farmer for grazing purposes, or otherwise make use of it. At the same time, you have to pay taxes and other carrying costs until you see a return. Knowing how long you can afford to carry the property is key to planning its eventual sale.

Deciding to build

Because you won't see a significant return on your investment in raw land until it's developed, it's important to plan potential uses for the property. What kind of development promises the greatest payoff? Are you willing to do it yourself? If not, are you willing to *joint-venture,* or partner, with a fellow investor or developer? Perhaps, in rare cases, you will be able to see a return by merely holding the land and selling it at a profit.

Becoming a developer

You're not likely to become a developer with your first piece of property, unless you're undertaking renovations. But if you've got the cash to fund development, why not add value to part or all of the land you've been acquiring? This can include everything from a single building on a rural acreage to an urban in-fill project that takes a sliver of land to a higher and better use.

Partnering with others

Sometimes it can pay to enter into an arrangement with a partner that allows you to reap a return from the development of your land. Perhaps you supply the land alone, or commit to arranging the servicing; perhaps you do more, such as undertake rezoning that poises it for development. Whatever the arrangement, this can allow you to see a better return than you would by selling off the raw land to an eager developer.

A partnership could also speed the sale of the land if your hopes for the area where you bought haven't quite come true. One developer we know had a tract of land subdivided for sale as development lots for single-family homes. But the lots weren't selling. So the developer approached a home builder who designed custom homes on the lots. The partnership added value to the land, allowing the developer to sell the lots for much more than the market value of the bare land, and the home builder was able to make a few sales, too.

Holding out for a gain

Occasionally, the land you've assembled and patiently held will yield a return without any improvement at all. This can happen when development happens on surrounding properties and the prospects for your property become brighter by association. Or perhaps the land itself is suitable for a particular use, such as growing grapes rather than apples, and the price of vineyard land is rising. You'll be able to take advantage of the shift.

Needless to say, if you're planning to hold land, you should have a long-term plan that supports that objective.

Howdy, Partners: Buying into Syndicates

Syndicates, in which money from investors supports a property's acquisition for investment purposes, have a checkered past. Reforms to the regulations governing them have boosted their favour among investors who have an appetite for real estate but no desire to actually own or manage property themselves.

Syndicated properties offer several benefits, including potentially a lower degree of risk because the syndicator rigorously scrutinizes properties before investors join the syndicate. Syndicated properties also typically offer a higher return to investors than comparable properties investors manage themselves because they enjoy the attention of a dedicated management team.

Syndication generally occurs through investment firms charged with selling the investment to clients. The investment managers at such firms are similar to those who manage equities, insofar as they're alert to trends in the investment world and determined to manage assets for the best return possible.

Gaining strength in numbers

The benefit of syndicates is that you're not alone. The acquisition of the property is through a partnership, meaning your share is one of several.

You pay for the limited risk the investment entails because the syndicator takes a cut of the proceeds on the property's sale, and the profits are shared with other investors. Among the benefits you enjoy are capital appreciation and even deferred taxes. As with any service for which you pay, however, shop around and find an investment and management team with which you feel comfortable.

Knowing the risks

Syndicates aren't risk-free. You run the chance an investment may not work out. But the advantage is that you're not the one taking the initial hit. Thanks to securities regulations, even if you lose your shirt, you're not likely to lose your pants as well. The partnership syndicating investment in the property is legally bound to live up to its obligations to investors.

Before anteing up your hard-earned cash, however, speak with your tax accountant, financial planner, or lawyer for their opinions on the investment and the safeguards it provides.

Researching Real Estate Investment Trusts

Real estate investment trusts (REITs) have gained popularity in recent years for the regular dividends they promise from the ongoing operation of their assets — by definition, real estate. Like syndicates, they offer an efficient means of investing in real estate while avoiding direct ownership of property.

What's the excitement about?

Like public companies, *income trusts* are traded on the stock exchanges. Shares in the company are known as *units,* which can fluctuate in value but which entitle their holders to a share in the distributable income flowing from the business of the trust. For real estate investment trusts (REITs), that business is the operation of the various buildings in its portfolio. These can include apartment buildings, seniors' care facilities, shopping centres, office buildings, hotels, or any other class of real estate in which the REIT chooses to invest.

Trust units trade on the stock exchanges like stocks but are different. Although stocks represent an ownership stake in the company that issues them, trust units entitle holders to distributions from the business or businesses that deliver their profits to the trust.

The range of REITs in Canada offers investors opportunities to invest in most classes of real estate. The low degree of risk (beyond fluctuations in market value) makes them a good choice for conservative investors who want a stake in the real estate market.

Choosing an asset type

The constraints of the trust structure eliminate some of the guesswork you'll have to do as you weigh the merits of the various REITs. Regardless of the asset classes in which REITs are invested, they're limited to paying unitholders out of their taxable earnings, and are accountable to their unitholders for distributions that aren't made.

Searching for the perfect trust is as simple as opening the business pages of your daily newspaper or browsing the Internet. Searching the terms *investment trust, REIT,* and even *income fund* and *income trust* presents you with several options. You can then investigate the trusts that interest you via more online searching, looking up financial statements on SEDAR (www. sedar.com) if they're Canadian, or consulting your investment adviser.

Regardless of the trust structure, the assets managed by the operating business of the trust are subject to the same forces that apply to every other building in their class. Multi-family residential properties tend to have stable incomes, for example. Hotel REITs operate in a more volatile environment and will tend to see greater fluctuations in the returns they can deliver. Shopping centres also offer a measure of stability, but will provide a return that reflects the strength of the retail sector.

Don't take the word *trust* literally! The trust's assets remain subject to the trends influencing the sector in which they operate. These trends will have an impact on their operations, profitability, and, in turn, the amount of the distributions you receive. In extreme cases, if the operating business of the trust performs poorly, a distribution may not land in your lap at all. On the other hand, as witnessed when stock markets dove in late 2008, an otherwise solid REIT may be discounted by the market regardless of how well its real estate is performing, because the units of the REIT are seen as just one more equity.

Reading financial statements

To get a better grasp of what the trust in which you're considering investing is all about, one of the most important things you can do is crack open its books. Thanks to SEDAR (www.sedar.com), an electronic database handling the filings of all public companies in Canada, this is relatively easy to do. SEDAR, which stands for System for Electronic Document Analysis and Retrieval, logs quarterly financial statements, annual reports, annual information forms, and all other public documents issued by the various real estate investment trusts that operate in Canada.

Studying the statements SEDAR collects gives you some insight into the performance of a trust, any issues it may have faced, and how its executives handled them. Don't neglect the notes to the financial statements, which can harbour extra information not expressly stated in the formal part of the quarterly and annual reports! Before you even glance at a trust's financial statements, have a look at the annual information form. It provides an overview of the trust's business, its development, and observations on the risks to the operating business from which it receives the profits.

Understanding the operation of a given trust can be invaluable in helping you decide whether to buy units in the trust, or to opt for one involved in an asset class more to your taste.

Chapter 2: Figuring Out Financing

In This Chapter

✓ Identifying sources of financing

✓ Deciding whether to partner up, and with whom

✓ Understanding the difference between variable and fixed-rate financing

✓ Choosing and obtaining a mortgage

✓ Getting the low-down on insurance

✓ Sorting out payment schedules

Remember when you were a kid and saw something you really liked? If you didn't have enough money, your parents probably told you to save up, or maybe shovel the neighbour's driveway for the extra cash.

Being a real estate investor is kind of like that. But because most of the things you want to buy are a whole lot more expensive than what you can afford with a single paycheque, it helps to have a strategy that employs less labour-intensive ways than shovelling driveways to get you the cash you need (lucky you). In this chapter, we discuss some of the ways you can optimize your saving strategies, as well as scrape together your own cash before approaching banks, private lenders, and other sources of capital.

We also cover finding, and cultivating, workable partnerships. Because many of the sources we discuss are friends and family, we also offer some tips on making sure you stay on good terms with them. Just because they're family doesn't mean you should be any less professional with them. Nor should they expect anything other than professional behaviour from you.

Identifying Resources

So, how much cash do you have to play with, anyway? And how are you going to use it to fund your real estate purchase? Tapping a mix of resources is just as important as investing in a diverse range of assets. Reducing your reliance on a single source of investment funds limits the chance you will be caught short if that source of financing dries up. Cultivating other sources may also create opportunities for funding future investments as you grow your portfolio.

Resources fall into three categories:

✦ *Liquid,* such as savings in your piggy bank, credit union, or bank account, which you can access and pour into alternative investments relatively easily

✦ *Illiquid,* which aren't easily converted to cash you can use to fund other types of investment and typically include long-term, locked-in investments or investments whose risk inhibits conversion

✦ *Vaporous* (okay, *vaporous* isn't a legitimate financial term but it fits!), which are difficult to pin down until they take the form of liquid resources; they usually come from other sources on request.

Typically, you want to supplement any liquid resources you're ready to invest with illiquid resources converted for the purposes of the investment you're about to make. Shortfalls in your own resources can be made up with funds from others who are game to support your investment: friends, family, or even strangers.

Social capital is just as important as financial capital. Some cultures avoid financial institutions in favour of cooperating among themselves, and some of them have enjoyed huge success in the real estate market. Don't underestimate the value of your social connections when assessing your own investment abilities. We go into further detail on this topic in the section of this chapter that deals with tapping friends and acquaintances for financing. You may even wish to establish a formal partnership with your supporters, an option we discuss elsewhere in this chapter.

Liquid: Savings

Savings and other liquid resources typically account for no more than one-third of a balanced investment portfolio. Whether you're working with an old-fashioned bank account or a low-risk, income-oriented mutual fund, you've got cash on hand.

The advantage of liquid resources is that they're available in the event of unexpected circumstances such as job loss, emergency travel, or medical expenses. But compared to other investments, they're probably not advancing your personal wealth to any extent. Fortunately, they're available when an investment opportunity comes around.

Depending on your investment strategy, however, you may not have a lot of liquid resources sitting around waiting for an investment opportunity. Perhaps you haven't had a lot of cash to play with and have kept most of your available resources in relatively liquid forms. More aggressive investors tend to have less in liquid resources.

Savings and other low-risk investments don't offer high returns and tend to grow slowly if they grow at all after considering income tax and inflation. Some low-risk investments lose value over the long term in exchange for a greater degree of liquidity.

TIP

Limit the amount of cash you keep in liquid investments to make the most of these vehicles. Restricting yourself to three months' worth of expenses frees up more cash for investment in higher-yielding options that may offer better returns, building the amount you're able to invest in less time.

TIP

Savings don't include just the money you set aside, however. Although putting aside a specific amount each month is a good plan, don't forget to review your spending habits and look for savings in your day-to-day expenses. Most of us have heard (and maybe even taken) the advice to cut down on expenses such as that daily hit of java, but don't forget that unused gym membership, public transit rather than a car (if possible), and even reading material from the public library rather than the bookstore. (One old codger we know of made a fortune in real estate but never bought his own copy of the newspaper!)

Illiquid: Long-term investments

Planning is critical if you hope to use long-term investments to finance a real estate purchase. Whether you're waiting for market conditions to improve before you cash out, or simply waiting for a bond or guaranteed investment certificate (GIC) to mature, planning can help ensure your illiquid investments meld together to provide you with the cash you need when you need it for other purposes.

The challenge you face highlights the need for a diverse investment portfolio. We're not talking just diversity of investment types but diversity of liquidity. Although the latest darling of the stock market may have spectacular growth potential, you want to be sure you can cash out at an appropriate time. A stable stock may offer a lower return but ensure you get to see the gains it has made since you bought it. With the advice of a financial planner or investment adviser, consider a mix of stock types and set goals for the ongoing sale of shares that will allow you to secure the greatest gains possible for your ultimate goal of real estate investment.

Similarly, if you favour bonds and other fixed-term investments, make sure they mature on a regular basis rather than all at once. Known as *laddering*, spacing maturity dates limits your exposure to changes in interest rates. You also have an opportunity to top up your investments or shift them into either higher-yielding vehicles or more liquid forms for investing in property.

Some registered retirement savings plans (RRSPs) as well as some registered education savings plans (RESPs) are sometimes illiquid if they've been designed as tax deferral plans with a long-term investment timeline. While first-time homebuyers can tap them for a home purchase — a home which may also have a rental suite — a property investor can't withdraw the funds without incurring a penalty. Withdrawals will be considered part of your annual income, and will potentially boost your personal rate of income tax. That would be a bad thing if, say, it boosted you into the highest tax bracket. However, you may be able to remove a judicious portion to complement the other assets you're allocating to a real estate investment. Just beware of the tax implications, and consult with your advisers. Many forms of real estate investments are designed to be held within registered tax deferral plans such as RRSPs, RESPs, and even registered retirement income funds (RRIFs).

Something you want to minimize — and if at all possible completely avoid — are penalties and fees for early redemption or transfers. Good planning should limit the risk of paying too much for sound management of your investments. Tax implications may also accompany the redemption of shares, so consult your accountant for advice on how to minimize taxes as you line up your resources to invest in real estate.

Tax-Free Savings Accounts (TFSAs) are an emerging but convenient alternative to RRSPs when it comes to building — and tapping — funds for property investment. Although the income placed in an RRSP is sheltered from taxes until withdrawal, TFSA funds are never taxed. The growth of TFSA funds is free of tax, however. Depending on the options your financial institution offers, you may be able to grow your TFSA deposits faster — and more cheaply — than if they were in a standard fixed-term investment or RRSP. Further information on TFSAs is available at `www.tfsa.gc.ca`.

A financial planner or investment adviser can advise you on balancing your short-term and long-term needs, and identifying the resources you should keep in liquid, short-term investments and less liquid, higher-yielding long-term investments. Financial planners are important people to have on your advisory team, and this is just one of the reasons why!

Tallying cash

Determining the amount of cash you have available at any given time for real estate investment depends largely on your having a clear financial plan in place and sticking to it. No formula exists, as the amount you have depends wholly on your risk or debt comfort level, your goals and priorities, your borrowing leverage from a lender or through a mortgage broker, the possibility that the seller could carry you in terms of a mortgage (vendo take-back financing), your family connections and borrowing abilities through them, and your creativity and initiative. However, we have some tips on elements of your spending and saving habits you may want to monitor, assess, and update on an ongoing basis:

- The amount of cash you need and want for a down payment

- Your disposable income, net after tax

- ✔ The maximum personal line of credit that you can get from your lender

- ✔ Additional sources of income that might be available to you, such as working a second job, working overtime, or starting a part-time home-based business on the side

- ✔ Money your family or relatives may be prepared to lend you, or possibly invest with you in real estate, and the amount, their expectations for the investment, and any restrictions

- ✔ How much RRSP borrowing room exists for a first-time home buyer, if that is applicable for you and your partner

- ✔ Your credit rating (set out a plan to improve it if required)

- ✔ A pre-approved mortgage for the maximum amount possible and to be held for the maximum length of time possible (say, 90–120 days)

- ✔ The amount of rental revenue you could obtain from a property through a basement suite as well as the rest of the house to maximum revenue for mortgage eligibility purposes, if that's the investment scenario you're interested in

- ✔ The members of your investment group and why they would be assets (if you are thinking of group investing); also look at developing such a group of people with a clear investment plan in writing so that you can exploit purchase opportunities

Vaporous: Friends and family

Other people's money may be as important to the success of your investment as your own, but don't forget the people you see every day. You may not have told people you're thinking about investing in real estate, but they may not have told you *they're* thinking about it, either!

A shortfall in your own resources and a desire to not involve an institutional lender, for whatever reason, may make a friend or other acquaintance a good source of funding. That's especially true if they're also looking for investment opportunities. A casual conversation may be an effective way of broaching your need for capital and gauging a friend's interest, but having a plan ready to discuss won't hurt. To reflect a professional approach, be able to tell potential investors:

- ✦ What you need, and for how long

- ✦ Why you need it

- ✦ The way you hope their participation will benefit them

A realistic and confident attitude about the amount you need, and willingness to offer a competitive return (either through interest payments, a share of the cash flow if it's an income-producing property, or a stake in the property itself that will deliver a return when you decide to sell the property — see also the section on partnership in this chapter) bolsters your ability to secure the support you need. Setting a realistic time frame for the investment will also give your potential financier the information required to decide whether to buy in.

Family matters

Jordan recently moved to Halifax and was enthusiastic about buying a property in a part of the city that was beginning to see a lot of redevelopment. The upside was good, and he wanted to get in early. He found a property with a two-bedroom suite in the basement and planned to renovate and find tenants for the upstairs. He would live in the basement with Kim, his partner. Jordan's parents agreed to provide a $50,000 loan toward the purchase and renovation of the house, but didn't insist on a written agreement outlining the terms. After all, Jordan had always been a responsible person and this was a way of helping him out.

But, after a year of renovations and a few months of renting the upstairs portion, Kim and Jordan broke up. She went to a lawyer and brought a claim forward arguing that because she had helped make monthly payments and contributed to renovations and maintenance of the property, she was entitled to half the equity in the house.

Because there was nothing in writing proving that the money from Jordan's parents was a loan, and there was no mortgage securing the funds, the cash was accounted as a gift. After much legal haggling, Jordan and Kim reached an out-of-court settlement for $25,000 (not to mention legal fees). Proper documentation could have avoided the mess that resulted, and ensured that all parties benefitted, at least financially, from the break-up.

Because you're approaching someone you know, be sure to limit the potential for personal conflict by having a legal agreement in place that safeguards interests on all sides. Don't let the convenience of tapping a friend for the cash you need become a source of bad feeling. You want the deal to be a winning prospect for all concerned. By the same token, don't promise something you can't deliver.

Some people make a habit of treating their family differently than they treat their friends. Ironically, that sometimes means worse rather than better. However, we feel strongly that you should treat everyone with whom you do business in a professional manner. That's especially true of family, because the close relationship and trust you have with them is more in jeopardy where money's involved.

Although family members can help boost your own resources, and even provide expertise when it comes to real estate investing, make sure you manage the relationship properly. This includes everything from the moment you raise the possibility, through any challenges or difficulties you face, right up to the time you cash out and distribute the proceeds of the investment.

Approaching family to invest in your next real estate venture doesn't always have to be an option of last resort. In several situations it's more than just a convenient idea, it's good business sense, too:

✦ When a family member has the cash you need to close a deal

♦ When a family member has not only cash but also expertise that can help you develop your investment portfolio as well as your investing skills

♦ When a family member is willing to become a full partner and meets the criteria you would set for any other business partner

Don't let the ties that bind blind you to professional practice. Make sure you have a formal contract outlining the terms of loans and any other support that family members provide, and the benefit to them of the arrangement. Don't take the support of family for granted, unless you wish to invite resentment. Honour your agreement as you would that with any other lender.

Working with Professional Financial Partners

Given all the cautions we've issued about working with family, maybe you would prefer to turn to professional or institutional financiers, the folks for whom real estate financing is as natural as breathing. Even if you've enlisted the help of family and friends, you may need a little extra cash to round out your financial backing. The options are many, from financial institutions such as a bank or credit union to independent-minded career investors looking for opportunities to invest their loose cash.

Regardless of whether you seek institutional or independent financiers, shop around. Services and rates vary among financial institutions, and even among branches of the same institution. You want to be sure you're getting not just the best deal, but also the best service for your purposes.

Private lenders, who may be friends of friends or contacts you'll discover in the process of networking, require particular caution to ensure that the deal is fair and equitable for all concerned. Even if they're hoping the purposes to which you're putting their cash brings them a return, you want to make sure interest is reasonable for the purposes and that you're being treated fairly.

Squaring accounts

Getting the best deal from a financial partner, and ensuring the best treatment possible, demands attention to the three *R*'s: rates, results, and references.

Rates

Of course, if you need additional cash to close a deal, you want to receive it for the lowest possible price. The benchmark interest rate is known as the *prime rate,* which banks give to their best customers. You can find both current and historical rates on the Bank of Canada website (www.bankof-canada.ca). Comparing interest rates, and the terms of mortgages, is vital. Some bargaining room exists if you're looking for a better rate or terms, so muster whatever persuasive skills and goodwill you can in an effort to reach an arrangement that works for you.

Other lenders typically charge a higher interest rate than the major financial institutions, but the persuasion can also help you secure a better deal from them.

Results

After you've identified lenders offering the best rates on the financing you need, have a look at the results they've been able to secure for others. You can tell a lender by the company it keeps, and institutional lenders are generally happy to tell you who they've done business with and the deals they've made happen. It's to their credit if they've played a role in a landmark transaction, and it works in your favour if they know the kind of deal you want to do, whether it's a simple house purchase or a land transaction.

References

References are invaluable whenever you're investigating a partnership. That's especially so when it comes to lenders, as their integrity is vital to the success of your venture.

Check with others who've done business with the lender you're considering. What was their experience, especially in terms of service? Was the lender responsive and easy to work with? Knowing the experience of others may bring to light issues that didn't appear in either your preliminary investigation or the documentation they provided.

Run a credit check of your potential financial partner. You probably don't have to worry about a major financial institution or credit union, but if you're considering receiving financing from an individual or small business, you should check their credentials and financials. A search of provincial court records, for example, may turn up information that steers you to safer partners. Most provincial courts have searchable databases of judgments (or decisions) available online.

Recognizing danger

It usually happens in only the most desperate of cases, but lenders may want to charge interest at levels approaching the maximum rate allowed by law (60 percent in many jurisdictions). That's hardly competitive with prime! Though 60 percent and under isn't legally considered *usury* (the practice of charging an exorbitant rate of interest), in these days of cheap capital it's close, and brings to mind Dante's reservation of a special place in Hell for usurers.

More common dangers include inflexible agreements and the lack of adequate leeway for yourself, especially if you run into cash flow difficulties or other circumstances that temporarily prevent you from meeting obligations. References from other investors who have worked with the lender should clear up any concerns in this area.

For a beginning investor, a prudent investment strategy is important. A more sophisticated and experienced investor might feel comfortable with paying a high rate of interest if they look at the overall investment potential and return on investment. For example, an experienced investor might be less concerned about the rate of interest than whether the loan can be paid back at any time without penalty. In this scenario, a savvy investor might feel comfortable about paying 20 percent interest, for example, if there is a realistic prospect of obtaining a 200 percent return on investment within a relatively short period of time.

Understanding How Mortgages Work

Mortgages aren't the sort of thing you laugh about. When people talk about adult responsibilities the mortgage is omnipresent, on the list alongside kids and credit cards.

So, how do mortgages come to be? How do they work? The borrower, also called the *mortgagor,* mortgages property — say, a building, land, and other real assets — in exchange for the cash needed to purchase the property and gain title. A mortgage document filed against the title of the property in the appropriate provincial land registry provides security to the lender against other creditors the borrower may have.

When you take out a mortgage to buy a house or property, the mortgage is in effect until you pay it off. If you fail to make your payments, you're in *default* (see the section "Default: Don't go there") and responsible for a debt typically satisfied through *foreclosure.* Foreclosure proceedings terminate your legal right to the property, which is typically sold through a court-ordered sale with the proceeds going toward satisfying the outstanding debt. In the event the borrower defaults on the mortgage, the lender (or *mortgagee*) is first in line to receive any proceeds from the sale of the mortgaged property. Property taxes and unpaid strata fees can come in priority before even the first mortgages.

Properties in Ontario are often subject to power-of-sale proceedings. Written into the mortgage agreement, the power-of-sale clause allows a lender to step in without resorting to the courts in order to protect its financial interest in a property. It's typically a shorter process than a foreclosure proceeding and satisfies the lender's claims faster. The owner maintains title to the property in a power-of-sale proceeding and receives any excess equity the sale generates. By contrast, a foreclosure proceeding strips the owner of title to the property and grants the lender sole rights to sale proceeds.

Since title remains with the owner, the lender must get a market assessment and appraisal of the property prior to sale to ensure the property is sold at market value. A lender that fails to secure the best possible value for the property may be subject to a lawsuit from the former owner, who has a right to seek compensation for the difference between the sale proceeds and the market value that should have been had.

Of the two different ways that a property could be sold on mortgage default, it varies depending on the province. The judicial foreclosure process occurs in six provinces — B.C., Alberta, Manitoba, Saskatchewan, Quebec, and Nova Scotia. The power of sale process occurs in four provinces — Ontario, Newfoundland and Labrador, New Brunswick, and PEI.

Discharge, or satisfaction of the terms of the mortgage, must occur before a new owner can claim title to the mortgaged property. Typically, the seller's lawyer is responsible for making sure this happens.

Mortgages typically run for a fixed period of time, during which the property owner makes regular payments of a fixed sum. Because a mortgage represents debt, regular payments ensure that the value of a mortgage decreases over time, building *equity,* which is the difference between mortgage and other claims against a property and the net proceeds from the property.

The regular payments include the *principal* of the mortgage, the amount actually loaned to you for the purchase, as well as *interest,* the amount you're charged for the use of the money. The time during which you make payments to repay the loan is the *amortization* period. We consider these concepts in greater detail in the next sections.

Mortgages are subject to both federal and provincial regulations, but they're registered in the land registry office of the province in which the borrower has mortgaged property. Although the laws governing mortgages may differ from province to province and in the territories, the mortgages themselves function in pretty much the same way.

For specific information regarding the mortgage registration and enforcement laws in your province or territory, consult your local land registry office or the lawyer you've chosen to handle your purchase.

Interest

Interest is the price a lender charges for you to use the money. The lender may charge interest at a rate that remains *fixed* for the term of the mortgage (for six months to ten years), or a *variable* rate that fluctuates in tandem with a base rate the lender sets. The monthly payments will vary as the interest shifts. (We get into more detail about these different types of mortgages later in this chapter, in the section "Exploring the Types of Mortgages.")

Mortgages, like bonds and other fixed-term investments, may bear *compound interest* — that is, interest charged on interest owing. When interest compounds, the amount of money you pay in interest charges increases.

Mortgage agreements must contain a statement explaining how the lender calculates interest. Mortgage interest traditionally compounds every six months.

The initial rate quoted for a mortgage is called a *nominal rate,* and the *effective rate* is the actual rate of interest you're paying. For example, a mortgage that quotes a nominal rate of 6 percent has an effective rate of interest of 6 percent when compounded yearly, 6.1 percent when compounded semiannually, and 6.17 percent when compounded monthly.

Variable-rate mortgages often compound interest monthly, reflecting monthly fluctuations in interest rates. Taking this into account when you're scouting mortgages is important in deciding the term of the mortgage, and whether you want a variable-term mortgage at all. (See "Choosing between Fixed or Variable Mortgages" later in this chapter for more.)

Amortization

Amortization is the length of time over which the regular (usually monthly) payments are calculated. The calculation assumes that you will pay off the mortgage by the end of the period. The standard amortization period is 25 years, although you may have the option of a 5-, 7-, 10-, 15-, or 20-year amortization period and even 30-year options.

The advantage of a shorter amortization period is the savings on interest; a longer amortization period may allow payments that suit your monthly budget but require you to spend more servicing the debt. The drawback, of course, is a lower net return on your investment.

Assuming a $50,000 mortgage and an interest rate of 6 percent (interest being compounded semiannually), Table 2–1 indicates the standard monthly mortgage payments for various amortization periods.

Table 2–1	Amortization and Payments			
	Amortization period in years			
Payment	*10*	*15*	*20*	*25*
Monthly payment of principal and interest	$553.26	$419.95	$356.10	$319.91
Total of mortgage payments over the amortization period	$66,390.31	$75,558.58	$85,461.45	$95,968.63

Exploring the Types of Mortgages

Far from being homogeneous creatures, mortgages come in many forms to meet the diverse needs of property purchasers. A conventional mortgage satisfies the needs of most residential property purchasers, but knowing the alternatives may suggest means for you to structure a deal that suits your particular situation.

A glance at the various types of mortgages reveals straightforward, conventional mortgages for single or multiple properties, arrangements that reflect the circumstances of a particular property, and options for those who would rather avoid institutional lenders or who have special needs. Approximately 95 percent of all mortgages are of the conventional or high-ratio forms; the others we discuss are available for the specific purposes described.

Though the conventional route may be familiar to you, some forms of mortgage may be better suited to certain properties than others. Examine the pros and cons of each type of mortgage and become familiar with the benefits and risks they present.

Conventional mortgage

Conventional mortgages are loans representing no more than 80 percent of a property's appraised value or purchase price, whichever is less. The federal National Housing Act requires insurance for mortgages for loans greater than 80 percent, a measure that protects lenders in the case of default. Purchasers who seek a conventional mortgage must provide at least 20 percent of a property's purchase price through a *down payment* or other means, such as a vendor take-back mortgage. The major financial institutions generally offer conventional mortgages.

The benefits of a conventional mortgage include allowing you to secure a property in exchange for regular payments and few additional costs compared to mortgages that require insurance or charge a higher rate of interest. Moreover, by putting down at least 20 percent of the property's value you've generally insulated yourself against the phenomenon of *negative equity,* in which your mortgage outweighs the property value. If you've analyzed your cash flow to ensure it matches the financing and operating costs of the property, you've also minimized the major risk of a conventional mortgage — being unable to make the payments.

Should the property, or your own circumstances, not fit with the lender's policies, you may either have to get mortgage insurance or seek an alternative source of funding (we discuss some of the options in the "Securing a Mortgage" section later in this chapter).

High-ratio mortgage

A high-ratio mortgage provides financing for between 80 and 95 percent of a property's value. Because they carry a greater risk, federal law requires that high-ratio mortgages be insured. The insurance is designed to protect the lender, encouraging lenders to provide financing when they might otherwise consider the risk of the loan too great. The two major providers of mortgage insurance in Canada are the Canada Mortgage and Housing Corporation (www.cmhc.ca), a federal Crown corporation, and Genworth Financial Canada (www.genworth.ca), the largest private mortgage insurer in the country with approximately 20 percent of the current market. Canada Guaranty Mortgage Insurance (www.canadaguaranty.ca), formerly known as AIG, also handles a small volume.

**Book VI
Chapter 2**

**Figuring Out
Financing**

The two different options available for high-ratio mortgage insurance provide the public with a competitive marketplace and prevent the federal government from monopolizing the business. The private insurer provides additional competitive options that CMHC does not.

Both conventional and high-ratio mortgages may offer the option of extending or compressing your repayment schedule; for example, an accelerated biweekly schedule can reduce interest charges by reducing the principal faster. On the other hand, CMHC and Genworth have adjusted their rules to allow an amortization period of 30 years. (There was a 35-year amortization period, but the Canadian government, to help protect against a U.S.-style housing meltdown, got rid of it in March 2011.) The longer term reduces monthly payments — but because the debt decreases more slowly, interest charges will be greater than with a conventional mortgage. Investigate the bite that extra interest will take out of your ultimate return.

You require a high-ratio or insured mortgage if you're unable to provide 20 percent of a property's purchase price. A high-ratio mortgage and insurance is good when you need a hand getting into the market, but it also lays a greater burden on you — your monthly payments are generally higher and you will consequently pay more interest to service the loan. These two factors make such a mortgage a more costly proposition.

High-ratio mortgages are available from most major financial institutions, but your specific circumstances determine the exact amount of financing a lender provides. Check with your realtor and lender or mortgage broker regarding any conditions that may affect whether a high-ratio mortgage is the only — or best — option for you.

Condominium mortgage

Condos are eligible for conventional mortgages, but because purchasers also enjoy an interest in the common elements of the development special conditions apply. This interest is considered *undivided* — that is, the condo owner shares an equal right to the common elements of the property (such as the grounds, rec centre, swimming pool, and other amenities) with every other unit owner in the condo development.

The lender requires the borrower to comply with all the terms of the bylaws, rules, and regulations of the condominium corporation. Any default on the borrower's part will constitute default under the mortgage. Also, if the borrower doesn't pay the appropriate portion of maintenance costs of the common elements, the lender is entitled to pay the costs on behalf of the borrower and add these onto the principal amount outstanding on the mortgage, with interest charged to this amount.

In the case of default, the lender has a right to use the unit owner's vote or consent in the condo corporation. This protects the lender's interest in the property subject to the mortgage. Though the lender doesn't usually vote on any and all decisions in normal circumstances, the lender can require the borrower to provide notice of all condominium corporation meetings and is entitled to receive copies of all minutes and information the council gives to owners.

In short, condo purchasers face greater pressure to comply with the terms of their purchases than home buyers who purchase single-family houses.

Leasehold mortgage

Leasehold mortgages allow the person who holds an interest in land to use it for a fixed period of time. An agreement between the landlord, who owns the property, and the owner of the leasehold interest, or tenant, sets out the terms and conditions of the relationship. The leaseholder can sell only the right to use the land for the time remaining on the lease — subject, of course, to the conditions of the lease.

Mortgages for property on leased land are always for a term less than that of the lease, and are therefore in a class of their own. Normally, a lender won't grant mortgages for such properties unless the lease runs significantly longer than that of the mortgage, because the lender may have to sell the property if the borrower defaults. The longer the time on the lease, the better the chance of selling the property.

For example, if a condo is on leasehold land with a 99-year lease and 85 years remain on the lease from the end of the mortgage, the lender has a good chance of selling the property. On the other hand, if the lease runs 30 years and 5 years remain after the scheduled end of the mortgage, the lender will likely consider the risk too high.

Buyers typically want an assurance of the terms of leased property when they buy. The last thing most property owners want is to see the terms of a lease change, possibly increasing the cost of the land on which their buildings sit. Five or ten years is rarely long enough to reassure potential purchasers that a property will have the value they saw in it when the time comes to sell.

Blanket mortgage

Blanket mortgages, in which several properties come under a single mortgage, are cozy arrangements — at least for the lender. A blanket mortgage provides the lender with additional property as security, enabling a borrower to access more money than the lender would typically provide on the basis of a single property. In the event of default, the lender could proceed against one or several of the properties in order to get sufficient funds to satisfy the outstanding debt.

When one of the properties covered under a blanket mortgage sells, all or a portion (for example, half or three-quarters) of the purchase price of the property has to be paid to the lender to reduce the blanket mortgage. The payment is a condition for the lender's releasing the encumbrance on the individual property. After that, the lender releases the portion of the blanket mortgage that was filed on that property in order for the purchaser of the property to place his own mortgage.

Blanket mortgages are an efficient means of mortgaging several lower-value properties within your portfolio with a view to consolidating their value through the purchase of a more valuable asset. This is an attractive means of trading up if you've gotten a foothold in the market with several low-value properties. For example, an investor with three apartment properties valued at $1 million apiece may secure a blanket mortgage that facilitates the purchase of a $4 million apartment block with a greater number of units in an up-and-coming neighbourhood. The new purchase promises not only greater cash flow in the short term, but if the property values in the neighbourhood rise, the investor could be sitting on a property worth more than those initial three apartment buildings ever were.

Collateral mortgage

Collateral mortgages, in practical terms, provide lenders with a form of backup protection for loans filed against property. Rather than the mortgage agreement itself serving as the main security for the loan, the security is typically a *promissory note* (a legal agreement regarding the loan signed by both the lender and borrower), personal guarantee, or the assignment of some other form of security. Discharge of the collateral mortgage occurs when the borrower fulfils the terms of the promissory note.

A collateral mortgage resembles a conventional mortgage, with the difference that a subsequent buyer can't assume it when a property sells. This makes the collateral mortgage a common option for raising funds for purposes other than purchasing property, such as home improvements or other investments.

Builder's promotional mortgage

To encourage buyers of new homes, a builder may offer mortgage packages arranged through the lender that's financing the project. For example, the builder's lender could offer buyers a mortgage at half a percentage point less than the posted rate for a mortgage and include all legal costs for transferring title and doing the mortgage work. The arrangement provides more business for the builder's lender, which could result in a better deal on project financing for the builder. The builder may even receive a commission for sending business the lender's way.

When it comes to a builder's mortgage, beware! Ask a mortgage broker if you can get a better deal. If a builder has arranged with its lender to offer a half-point discount on a mortgage complete with legal costs, you're probably going to be able to find an institutional lender that can offer to cover your legal costs as well as reduce your interest rate by a full point. When a builder offers a special mortgage, it has made arrangements with the lender to subsidize the discounted or incentive cost of the mortgage by paying the lender for its calculated loss. Conversely, the lender may have a deal with the builder that if the lender gets more than 50 percent of the mortgage business — say, a minimum of 200 out of 400 condos for sale — it will absorb the discounted mortgage. Another reality is that it might just be a one- or two-year mortgage with a discount. If you want a longer mortgage than that, you would pay extra for the additional years.

Make sure you obtain legal advice to ensure the terms of the mortgage meet your requirements. You may want to investigate the option of renegotiating the mortgage from the builder's lender at a future date should your needs change.

Construction mortgage

A *construction mortgage* is actually a line of credit secured by a mortgage on a property under development. You must provide documentation for the construction, including the contractor's detailed costing estimate, building plans, and other information including permits. After the mortgage is approved, the lender provides a document for you to sign that sets out the terms of the mortgage, including a schedule of advances up to an approved amount that will cover each stage of construction. The lender will want confirmation from the builder or contractor when each stage completes before release of the next payment.

The close scrutiny to which a lender subjects a construction mortgage aims to ensure that you manage construction smoothly and don't invite claims against the project. The property should remain free of *liens,* claims that could prevent the lender from retrieving the full value of its loan. The lender registers the mortgage on the property where the construction is taking place and may even register it against your current residence to ensure sufficient security in case of default. When construction completes, the lender converts the construction mortgage to a conventional mortgage.

Vendor mortgage

A *vendor mortgage* is one in which the party selling a property (the vendor) offers to lend part of the purchase price to the prospective buyer. This is useful if you require assistance securing institutional financing, because the vendor can supplement the cash you need for a down payment. For example, if you don't have enough funds to provide a 20 percent down payment, the vendor may provide 15 percent of the purchase price in an arrangement that would effectively serve as a second mortgage on the property. You would only need a down payment of 5 percent.

The vendor may also offer a mortgage with a lower interest rate than what institutional lenders are offering. The arrangement may help you buy the property, but beware of drawbacks. In some cases, the vendor may boost the price of the property to make up for the discounted rate of interest; in others, the discount may last for a short period of time, after which you need to secure a regular mortgage. The arrangement has advantages if you need some help buying a property before other financing becomes available, but it may be false economy.

Assumed mortgage

An *assumed* mortgage is one that already exists — for which you *assume* responsibility to repay. (Not one that you just *think* is there.) This can save you and your vendor legal fees and disbursements for registering the mortgage, among other expenses. Whenever you assume an existing mortgage, make sure your lawyer obtains a statement that shows the principal balance outstanding, the method of paying taxes, the remaining term on the mortgage, and a copy of the mortgage that shows other features such as prepayment privileges and insurance requirements.

Place some qualifications on the assumability of any mortgage you seek, if you agree to its assumability. If you're the vendor, qualifications allow you to check out the creditworthiness and debt-servicing ability of the owner assuming your mortgage so that you can be sure the new owner is a good risk.

Should the person assuming your mortgage default, you might find yourself on the hook for their unfortunate circumstances if your name is on the mortgage document. You can avoid this scenario by obtaining a statement from the lender that the lender will not hold you liable under the mortgage agreement after the new property owner assumes the mortgage. Have your lawyer review the document to ensure your interests are properly protected.

Second and subsequent mortgages

Second and subsequent loans rank lower in priority when it comes to payment than those registered before them, so they typically bear a greater rate of interest that reflects their riskier nature. The risk stems from the hierarchy of repayment for the various mortgages. For example, a $200,000 property may have, say, three mortgages: one of $125,000 at 5 percent; $75,000 at 7 percent; and $20,000 at 10 percent. But the largest mortgage doesn't carry the most risk to the lender — the smallest one does. When the property sells, the proceeds pay the outstanding property taxes, then unpaid strata fees (if any), then the first mortgage, then the second mortgage, and so on. Repayment of the third mortgage happens only after the others are satisfied. Should the sale price cover only the first two mortgages, the third lender could be out of luck.

Second and subsequent mortgages sometimes supplement the financing obtained through the first mortgage, and typically represent up to 80 percent of the value or purchase price of the property that secures them, whichever is lower. Some mortgage brokers, among other lenders, offer second mortgages for 90 percent and even higher of the purchase price or appraised value (again, whichever is lower).

If a borrower can obtain sufficient financing to buy a property with only a first mortgage, that is the best option, because the rate is the lowest. However, the lender may only lend up to 80 percent of the financing, and the borrower needs to find an additional 15 percent because he wants to make a minimal down payment of 5 percent and borrow the remaining 95 percent.

Or you may want a second mortgage because you're buying from someone whose mortgage you can assume and that mortgage is 2 percent lower than the prevailing rate. To make up the shortfall on the purchase price, you would need to get more financing, which, after the mortgage is registered, would constitute a second mortgage. If you required more money still, you might have yet another mortgage registered, which would constitute a third mortgage in the security lineup ranking.

When your second mortgage has a term longer than your first mortgage, make sure you have a postponement clause in the agreement governing the second mortgage. A postponement clause enables you to automatically renew or replace the first mortgage when it becomes due, if you wish to do so, without having to obtain permission from the second mortgage lender. The clause ensures that the mortgage you renew or replace continues to rank ahead of the existing second mortgage in order of priority.

Keep an eye on the value of the property you're mortgaging and the size of the debt you're carrying. All that cash may look good right now, but if you need to sell a mortgaged property make sure you can discharge in full the mortgages registered against it. Talk to your accountant or financial planner to ensure you're not loading yourself down with more debt than you can handle.

Choosing between Fixed or Variable Mortgages

The difference between fixed and variable mortgages is similar to the difference between relationships — and, yes, sometimes the terms are even the same. You can have a fixed, or closed mortgage, in which you're the faithful partner of one debt for the long term (well, at least as long as you've agreed to it). Or, you can have a variable, or open, mortgage that leaves you subject to each new rate that comes along, and offers you more options if want to pay it off and get out. The choice is yours. This section outlines the advantages — and disadvantages — of each option.

Fixed-rate mortgages

The fixed-rate mortgage is the most popular form of mortgage in Canada because it offers stability, a characteristic that appeals to Canada's long-established commitment to "peace, order, and good government." A stable, fixed-rate mortgage means regular payments of fixed amounts, and a time-table for renegotiation.

An investor who wants to stabilize his or her costs, or be insulated from fluctuations in interest rates over the course of the term, should consider a fixed-rate mortgage. Just remember that the drawbacks include being unable to take advantage of lower borrowing costs should interest rates drop.

As an investor, if your investment plan is to have a long-term hold for the property — say, 7 or 10 years — and the interest rate is attractively low, you may prefer to lock in a fixed-term mortgage so you can budget accordingly. On the other hand, if you are not sure how long you intend to hold the property, or the interest rates are high, you may prefer to have a variable-rate mortgage to give you flexibility. It all depends on your plan and your circumstances.

Traditionally, lenders imposed a higher qualification threshold on borrowers to ensure they will be able to bear the burden of the debt over the course of the full term. This has helped safeguard the interests of lenders and borrowers alike, playing no small part in the stability of the Canadian mortgage market — and perhaps Canada's economic well-being to boot. This changed in early 2010, however, when new rules came into effect that applied the qualification criteria set forth for five-year fixed-term mortgages to all mortgages, both fixed-rate loans of less than five years and variable-rate mortgages.

Variable-rate mortgages

Fixed-rate mortgages offer a stable interest rate for the term of the mortgage. But if you're caught in a cycle of declining interest rates, you're not likely to want to lock in at a rate that's bound to be much lower within weeks of your locking in. Enter the variable- or floating-rate mortgage.

The interest on a variable-rate mortgage is adjusted according to an index, such as the Bank of Canada prime rate, but at certain intervals and with a limit on the amount of interest. Many lenders allow you to set the terms such that you can quickly convert your variable-rate mortgage into a fixed-term mortgage if you think interest rates are about to rise.

The impact of rising interest rates may not be seen in all cases. You may have agreed to pay a set amount each month under the terms of the mortgage agreement, but an upward variation in interest rates means you'll pay down the principal less quickly, leaving you with more debt than you expected at the end of the term. Moreover, if you wait too long to convert the mortgage, you may lose out on favourable rates on fixed-rate mortgages.

Some variable-rate mortgages may compound interest monthly. This could boost the total interest you pay compared to a mortgage with a higher but fixed rate of interest.

Variable-rate mortgages typically have required borrowers to meet a lower threshold, but this changed in 2010 when the federal government required borrowers seeking variable-rate mortgages to meet the same criteria as fixed-rate borrowers. A variable-rate mortgage can save an investor money if he or she has the interest and time to monitor the mortgage marketplace, so that he or she can lock in to a fixed-term rate if variable rates start to increase beyond his or her comfort level.

Another option that may help investors *hedge,* or protect themselves, against changes in interest rates is through a blended mortgage format. A *blended* mortgage combines a fixed-rate mortgage and a variable-rate mortgage. The smaller portion is usually subject to a variable-rate loan, which can ideally be converted or paid off more easily in the event of an adverse change in interest rates or sudden windfall of cash. A blended mortgage will often save hundreds if not thousands of dollars in interest.

Determining Your Mortgage Limit

Regardless of how you finance your real estate purchase, you need to know how large a mortgage you can take on. Why over- or underestimate your abilities when you can get some hard facts? First, calculate the size of mortgage for which you're eligible; next, consider strategies for stretching your limits.

Calculating your limits

Different lenders have different criteria for approving the amount of mortgage they're willing to grant, but you can ballpark what you're eligible to receive by calculating your *gross debt-service ratio* and the *total debt-service ratio.*

The gross debt-service ratio is the total of your monthly mortgage principal, interest, and taxes divided by your monthly income. Typically, you want to use 30 percent of your gross income to pay the mortgage principal, interest, and taxes. The total debt-service ratio is higher, usually 35 to 40 percent of your gross monthly income, though this varies among lenders. The calculation is the same as for the gross debt-service ratio except it includes not just your mortgage payments, interest, and taxes, but also all other debts you're carrying.

Stretching your limits

To boost the amount of mortgage you're eligible to carry, a key strategy is to demonstrate to lenders that you're able to service the debt you want to carry. Two ways to do this include finding a property generating a stable cash flow, and finding a mortgage charging a lower interest rate:

✦ **Cash flow:** A home with a rental suite provides a regular cash flow that most lenders will factor into your debt-service ratio, allowing you to carry a larger mortgage. This is also a useful option when you've got your eye on a piece of raw land with future development potential. You may be able to secure greater financing if you can lease the property to a local farmer or demonstrate that a woodlot on the property is able to generate regular income.

✦ **Working with interest:** A mortgage broker can help you source a mortgage with the best interest rate and mortgage terms possible. This is especially useful if you're seeking a lower rate that allows you to carry more debt. Be sure to plan for a possible rise in interest rates that could jeopardize your ability to carry the remaining debt when it comes time to renegotiate the mortgage. Similarly, if you have a variable-rate mortgage, be sure to monitor the market so you can quickly convert your mortgage into a fixed-term mortgage for budget purposes if rates begin to rise (we discuss variable-rate mortgages elsewhere in this chapter).

Securing a Mortgage

Our goal in this section is to outline the financing options available to you. We cover the various types of institutional and non-institutional lenders available, as well as the standard criteria they look for. We also discuss mortgage brokers, what they can offer, and how to select one.

Banks, credit unions, and brokers

Two main sources of financing are available for property purchases:

✦ **Institutional lenders,** which include banks, trust companies, and credit unions, all of which are subject to government regulations.

✦ **Non-institutional lenders,** which are a wider-ranging lot, including everyone from mortgage brokers to partners, friends, and family.

Mortgage brokers are also subject to government legislation, setting them apart from most other non-institutional lenders, but like other non-institutional lenders they're often willing to refer you to lenders who agree to take on greater levels of risk.

As with any other business relationship, your time shopping around to find a match that's right for you is well spent. You may already have a relationship with a particular financial institution but the branch you deal with may not have the expertise you need. A competitor may offer a better interest rate, or offer to advance an amount that broadens the range of properties you can consider. You can afford to put your interests first when selecting a lender; the research you do can only help improve your ability to negotiate a deal that serves your needs.

Tough negotiation pays off, and sometimes isn't that tough to pull off. Ask what incentives are available to attract your business, and whether the lender can offer a discount from the rate posted at the door. Try to achieve a one-point reduction in the posted rate. Cite your history with the lender if you do most of your financial business there, or mention that you're comparing rates; the mortgage business is competitive, so a lender will strive to keep you as a customer, especially if it's a credit where you have your chequing account and your credit card and your spouse's RRSP as well as your children's RESPs.

Consider obtaining a credit report on yourself. This is usually free, and lets you see whether any elements in your credit history are likely to make a lender nervous. It also assures you that lenders are receiving accurate information about your credit. (For more on credit reports, see *Real Estate Investing For Canadians For Dummies.*)

What lenders require

Knowing what lenders require, and being prepared to deliver it, can go a long way toward securing the best possible mortgage in the shortest possible time. Of course, you won't have control over all parts of the process, but do what you can to make the best impression and negotiate the rest to secure a workable deal.

During the one to five days it takes to approve a mortgage for the winning investment you're about to make, a lender investigates two key areas: your potential purchase, and you, the borrower.

Getting to know the property

The most important aspect of the property to the lender is its ability to serve as collateral. If you get the loan needed to buy the property and the lender eventually has to sell the property to recover the loan, the lender wants to make sure the property is valuable enough to cover the outstanding debt.

When you apply for a mortgage, provide a copy of the agreement of purchase and sale, the basic document that will become the sales contract when the deal closes. An appraisal, usually at your expense, provides the information the lender needs to both verify the description in the sales agreement and determine the property's future market potential. A recent property tax assessment is also very useful for your lender to see.

Thanks to the vast stores of information available about property transactions, appraisals are a much simpler process today than they once were. However, the basic criteria factoring into the valuation remain the same:

**Book VI
Chapter 2**

**Figuring Out
Financing**

✦ Location

✦ Previous selling price

✦ Current condition of the property and the surrounding neighbourhood

✦ Structural engineer or inspector's report

✦ Available services, infrastructure, and amenities

✦ Comparative sales in the area

Because lenders typically prefer a more conservative valuation, the bank settles for a lower valuation than necessary. This may decrease the size of the mortgage the lender is willing to give, but it also invites you to make a case for yourself.

A lender could refuse to provide a mortgage following an appraisal, but if so, you'd probably be wise to get out of the deal. For example, the appraisal may say the property you want to buy is only worth about 80 percent of what you've agreed to pay for it, or that significant problems exist with the property, all of which could put the lender's security at unacceptable risk.

Getting to know yourself

Character and capacity for debt are the two criteria lenders take into account when deciding whether to grant you a mortgage. The two factors are unique yet in many ways interdependent. Your capacity for debt will indicate how much debt you can realistically handle, while your character will give the lender an idea of how you're likely to handle that debt under different circumstances.

Character and capacity for debt made headlines in Canada in early 2010 when the federal government announced changes to make the criteria for five-year, fixed-term mortgages the baseline for all mortgages — both those of less than five years and the traditionally more flexible variable-rate products. Regulators in Ottawa wanted to make sure borrowers could handle real estate debt in the face of a potential rise in interest rates. They also wanted to prevent eager bankers from inducing a U.S.–style housing meltdown north of the border.

The main verification of your character the lender seeks to ensure you can handle a mortgage is a credit check. The lender also wants to know your employment history, and the stability of the sector in which you work. A letter from your employer (if you have one) that confirms your position, length of time with the employer, and salary is important. If you're self-employed, be ready to provide copies of your financial statements and/or tax assessments for the past three years. Historically, self-employed individuals have been considered higher risks than those with conventional employment, but this attitude is steadily changing.

The greater stability you can demonstrate in both your credit and employment history, the better you appear to a potential lender. Be ready to make a forceful case for yourself, and negotiate the best possible mortgage!

Some lenders will work with you to identify the various payments you would make on a mortgage at varying interest rates. This not only is important in determining your ability to service a variable-rate mortgage, but also helps you plan and strategize for potential interest rate increases at the end of your term. If your lender doesn't offer this service, talk with your accountant to get a better handle on how changes in interest rates might affect your ability to service your mortgage.

Calculating your total debt-service ratio will give you an idea of how much debt you can handle, and the size of mortgage a lender may be willing to grant. To secure a mortgage that allows you to consider the broadest range of properties, back up your case with an accurate statement of your assets and liabilities and detail the exact financing (and sources) you intend to supply. Identify strategies, such as renting a suite, that may convince the lender you can support a larger mortgage than usual for that particular property. Perhaps a well off family member will co-sign for your loan.

Presenting a sound financial plan developed with the help of your accountant or financial planner could help make your case stronger and sway the lender in your favour. Don't forget to seek the help of these advisers!

A relatively simple way to determine the amount of mortgage available to you is to consult the mortgage calculators available on the sites of the Canada Mortgage and Housing Corporation (www.cmhc.ca) and Genworth Financial Canada (www.genworth.ca). The calculators will be able to provide customized calculations for your personal situation. Still having trouble? Contact the mortgage rep at your bank or credit union, or a mortgage broker, and request the information you're looking for. You usually receive it at no cost or obligation.

Selecting a mortgage broker

Traditionally, when people couldn't secure mortgages through institutional lenders, they turned to mortgage brokers — who, for a slightly higher interest rate, would match them with the funds they needed.

Today, a mortgage broker remains an intermediary between those who want money and those who have money to provide. This could include traditional mortgage lenders, as well as private lenders, pension funds, and insurance companies, which lend money for residential mortgages. If a mortgage brokerage is large enough, it may also lend money, but generally brokers, well, broker other people's money.

Mortgage brokers enjoy a booming business thanks to their ability to tap into a broad range of financing sources, from the conventional to the unconventional. Mortgage brokers frequently get the best discounted rates from lenders due to the volume of business they command. Some common sources of funds include:

✦ Banks, trust companies, and credit unions

✦ Canada Mortgage and Housing Corp. (CMHC)

✦ Private and union-sponsored pension funds

✦ Real estate syndication funds

✦ Insurance companies and private lenders

The process of selecting a mortgage broker is pretty much the same as for selecting any other type of lender. References from friends and associates may help make the decision easier and, as always, it pays to compare. Mortgage brokers generally charge a fee of between 1 and 5 percent for their services, based on the standard lending criteria as well as the difficulty and urgency of your particular situation. Normally, mortgage brokers receive a referral fee from the lender for your business and you aren't responsible for the payment. However, if you are having difficulty raising the funds you need, for example, or are involved in commercial real estate, there are normally mortgage broker fees that you would pay if they can arrange financing.

We recommend the use of mortgage brokers in all cases for many different reasons. It will save you time and money: Time running around doing your own comparison shopping, and money because mortgage brokers can submit your request to multiple lenders who will give their best rate within the competitive marketplace. Mortgage brokers are in the mortgage money business. That is all they do. They know which lenders are anxious to lend money at any given time, and the incentives that will be offered to make a deal. Also, mortgage brokers get a referral fee from the lender, so you don't pay for the service. The lender is glad to pay a referral fee to the mortgage broker as a cost of marketing in a highly competitive money-lending environment.

**Book VI
Chapter 2**

**Figuring Out
Financing**

The mortgage broker you choose should be a member of the Canadian Association of Accredited Mortgage Professionals (www.caamp.org). Its membership handles 90 percent of mortgages in Canada. Many of its members hold the association-backed Accredited Mortgage Professional (AMP) designation, introduced in 2004.

Checking Out Insurance

Three types of insurance are critical elements of mortgages. The first two offer you protection; the other protects your property. All three protect your lender from potential loss. We explore the two types in detail in the following sections.

Insuring your mortgage

Mortgage insurance protects you from circumstances that may lead to your defaulting on your mortgage obligations, and also ensures that whoever has loaned you money for your property purchase gets paid in the event circumstances prevent you from doing so. Mortgage insurance is a requirement whenever the down payment provided for the mortgage is less than 20 percent of the purchase price (for more about high-ratio mortgages, see the section "High-ratio mortgage" in this chapter). The insurance fee runs between 1.75 and 2.75 percent of the amount of the mortgage. You may pay it in a single payment, or pay it alongside your mortgage.

Mortgage insurance is just for high-ratio mortgages. In the past it was available only through the federal Crown corporation CMHC (Canada Mortgage and Housing Corporation), but now consumers can also obtain it through the private sector. The largest private company, Genworth Financial Canada, has a significant market share but CMHC is the principal insurer.

Genworth follows the same federal guidelines as CMHC in most cases, but could have some flexibility in certain situations. Compare the two supplier options to find the best fit for your needs.

Mortgage life insurance serves a similar purpose to mortgage insurance but kicks in only when you die. Mortgage life insurance guarantees that the lender will receive full payment of the mortgage in the event of your death, leaving your property mortgage-free to your estate or designated heirs.

Be prepared for a mortgage lender to try to up-sell you on the benefits of a mortgage life insurance policy. From a risk management, business, and estate planning viewpoint, obvious benefits to your peace of mind come with knowing your mortgage will be cleared off in the event of your death. However, if you like the idea of insurance protection you also have a more flexible option to consider.

Ensuring a good deal

Trying to get the best possible deal on your insurance policies? Insurance premiums vary from policy to policy and situation to situation. The rate you pay will reflect the insurance company's assessment of the risks you face, such as the age of the property, location, crime statistics for the area, and other factors. Always compare and get written quotes from at least three insurance brokers for any type of insurance you are considering. Also, ask about obtaining discounts, each of which could range from 5 to 10 percent off the original premium. You could use several of them, but most insurance companies don't allow the aggregate amount of discounts to exceed 50 percent of the original premium. Common types of discounts given for property insurance coverage may be available if you have

✔ No claims in the previous five years, or at all

✔ A mortgage-free discount

✔ Three or more years' standing as a client

✔ A Block Watch or similar volunteer monitoring program in your community

✔ Eligibility for an age-related discount for property owners over the age of 65, and sometimes as young as 50

✔ A new home ten years old or less (this may result in a depreciated premium discount based on the home's age)

✔ A monitored fire and burglar alarm in place

✔ Local alarm systems (not monitored)

✔ Different types of insurance products with the same insurance company or broker (may result in a multi-line discount)

Personal term life insurance from a general insurer can often do the trick for less money. Payable to your estate on your death, it guarantees your estate sufficient funds to pay off your mortgage. Talk to your financial planner and insurance broker about the kind of policy that best serves you and your real estate investment strategy. One of the benefits of carrying your own term life insurance is that it is portable, and not connected directly to your mortgage. So if you subsequently become uninsurable for some reason, at least you know you have a term insurance policy for the future. Term insurance is a very competitive marketplace, so premium rates are attractive.

You may also wish to consider critical illness insurance, which provides income in the event you are unable to work. Because we hope your properties will be generating cash flow that supports them, rather than requiring you to cover their operating expenses out of your own pocket, this kind of insurance is not likely to be a high priority for you.

Insuring the property

Because the property that secures a mortgage is the lender's basis for advancing cash in the first place, the last thing you — or the lender — want to see is that building damaged or destroyed. Most mortgages therefore require that you insure your property against fire. The insurance policy must show that the mortgagee is first in line in case of a claim.

Because the lender's interest in protecting your property is significant, the insurance policy typically includes a clause allowing the lender to pay the premium in the event you don't. The lender also typically has the right to augment the amount of coverage on the property.

Should the lender act in your stead, you may find the extra premiums part of the principal of your mortgage. You'll also pay interest on the payments, something you wouldn't have done had you made the payments or taken the coverage yourself.

Some of the major types of insurance designed to safeguard your property, above and beyond whatever your lender might require, include property insurance (which typically includes clauses for fire and other calamities), title insurance, and, in the case of new homes, new home warranty packages that offer coverage during the initial years of the property's existence.

Property insurance

Property insurance, the basic coverage that property owners have for a variety of protections, covers claims after you take ownership of a property. It generally includes fire, theft, and liability insurance (which protects you from any lawsuits for injury to those who enter on or into your property). Depending on where you live, you may also want to have earthquake or flood insurance. If you are on a known flood plain, you may not be able to obtain insurance — or, if you do, it could have high premiums, high deductibles, and only partial damage recovery.

Speak to at least three insurance brokers, and obtain comparative quotes in writing. Read the fine print — it reveals the exact coverage you receive along with any exclusions, limitations, and deductibles. If you don't clearly understand the document, speak to various brokers and then obtain advice from a lawyer who specializes in insurance law. You can normally obtain a free or nominal-cost initial consultation by checking with your provincial lawyer referral service, provided by the provincial law society or provincial branch of the Canadian Bar Association.

Being on a flood plain may not be a disaster waiting to happen, but finding out the local fire service is a skeleton crew of volunteers is a different story. Depending on the risks of your particular situation, and the chance of what insurers like to call "an event" occurring in your particular circumstance, you may find yourself facing limited coverage or no coverage at all. If insurance is granted, the broker may require a higher deductible or greater premium. Consult your insurance broker to see what coverage is available, and whether the coverage is sufficient to satisfy your concerns.

Just because the property of your dreams wasn't eligible for a certain level of coverage when you first bought it doesn't mean it won't get coverage in the future. Any time you reduce an insurance risk you can go back to the insurer and request a re-evaluation and argue for reduced premiums.

Deficiencies discovered during due diligence may be small hurdles you can overcome as you improve the property and make it a more valuable — and insurable — asset.

Title insurance

Title insurance protects a buyer against defects and errors in a property's *title* — the owner's right to a property. The insurance provides coverage from the time you take title until you sell your property. Title insurance will cover the legal fees incurred in defending your ownership of the property, as well as your actual financial losses.

Problems with title can include

+ Competing claims of ownership or interest in the property

+ Survey errors that pre-date your acquiring an interest in the property, resulting in your not receiving what you were told you were receiving in purchasing the property

+ Outstanding building code issues that render a building on the property non-conforming under municipal bylaws

+ Liens and other encumbrances, such as discharged mortgages that remain on title

+ New liens that arrive on your title unknown to you due to identity theft

The cost of resolving many of these issues falls on the shoulders of the new owner, but title insurance provides coverage against such claims. Many companies in Canada provide title insurance; one of the largest is First Canadian Title (www.firstcanadiantitle.com).

Some investors use title insurance to reduce the legal costs associated with closing a deal. Traditionally, lawyers would search a title prior to a property purchase closing. Today, all major financial institutions accept title insurance in place of a title survey demonstrating the prospective purchaser's clear title. However, a full search as part of the due diligence process will provide genuine security that title is indeed clear and free of encumbrances.

New home warranty programs

Several private, third-party warranty programs exist across Canada for new homes. New home warranties — as the name implies — insure new homes against defects for up to ten years. All new homes must carry insurance of some form, usually offered by the developer as part of the sale package.

Although most buyers wouldn't expect defects in new homes, insurance is a useful protection against unforeseen problems. Some builders include the warranty coverage premium in the purchase price, others require the buyer to pay for it upfront, and still others split the cost 50/50 with the buyer. If you are buying a two- or three-year-old home that is still covered by the original home warranty protection, you will want to check on the terms of the coverage and make sure you understand them, or ask questions during the due diligence period to satisfy yourself. Be sure to get everything in writing in case you need to reference the terms and verify coverage. Make sure the remaining time for home warranty protection is transferable to you as the new owner.

Resident builder homes, residences built by the future occupant, are among the several types of housing exempted from new home warranty coverage. Beware of homes developed by erstwhile resident builders offered to you directly. They may not have the coverage they legally require, which may not only cause headaches for you, but also leave you on the hook for repairs should a defect emerge.

Scheduling Payments

Strategies for managing your mortgage, and especially its ultimate cost to you, focus on the *amortization schedule* — that is, the schedule determining how quickly you pay off the mortgage.

You may plan to sell a property before paying the mortgage on it in full. Because you're likely to have a mortgage on one property or another as long as you're a real estate investor, however, you should focus on building equity in your properties. The greater the equity you build in a property, the greater the wealth you'll be able to recoup when you sell the property. Scheduling payments that let you build equity quickly and efficiently will play a key role in your success.

Make a date: Payment schedules

Mortgage payments occur within two types of arrangements, open and closed systems. Most mortgages take the form of a *closed mortgage,* which defines payments for the term of the mortgage and levies a penalty on advance payments. A standard closed mortgage usually requests three months' interest in the event you sell the property before paying off the mortgage. The lender may waive the penalty if the purchaser takes out a new mortgage with the same lender.

An *open mortgage* allows you to boost payments of the principal at any time, and allows you to pay the mortgage in full at any time with no penalty or extra charge. In exchange for this flexibility, which can limit the amount a lender sees in interest, open mortgages often charge a higher interest rate.

The actual mortgage payments occur at regular intervals regardless of whether the mortgage is open or closed. These range from weekly to monthly and annually. The more frequent your payments, the lower the amount of interest you pay. (We discuss this in more detail in the following section.)

Mortgage payments themselves are blended to include both principal and interest. The payments are traditionally a set amount calculated assuming monthly payments. However, variations in payments may occur. We mention the idea of balloon payments in *Real Estate Investing For Canadians For Dummies,* in the context of a strategy that allows you to defer interest payments, and variable-rate mortgages, in which the mix of principal and interest in your set payment fluctuates on a monthly basis, or in some cases more frequently than that. Check beforehand.

You may choose to negotiate with your lender a graduated payment schedule. *Graduated payments* are lower at the beginning of the term of the mortgage and increase over time, so that payments at the end of the mortgage's term are considerably higher. This is a useful arrangement for revenue-generating properties, or if you expect your ability to pay down the mortgage will increase over time.

The risk of a graduated payment strategy is that you could find yourself paying more interest than you had expected if interest rates rise and you have the greatest amount of payments yet to make. You also build equity in the property at a slower rate than if you make set payments throughout or larger payments at the beginning of the term.

As often as possible: Payment frequency

The amount of interest you pay on a given mortgage depends in part on the frequency of your mortgage payments. Table 2–2 shows the difference in interest payments per thousand dollars of mortgage when interest compounds semiannually during the payment period. Comparing the difference in interest costs between paying every two weeks (bi-weekly, or 26 times a year) and twice a month (or 24 times a year) gives a glimpse of the kind of savings you can enjoy — at a 5 percent interest rate, the difference is 16 cents per thousand dollars of mortgage, or $16 per $100,000. By the end of the year, and the end of the term, this represents money in your pocket you'd be crazy not to take.

The more frequently you make payments, the more frequently the lender gets its principal debt reduced; therefore, less interest is charged to you.

Table 2–2	Tallying Interest Payments			
Interest rate %	*Weekly $*	*Every two weeks $*	*Twice a month $*	*Monthly $*
3.50	$0.67	$1.33	$1.44	$2.90
4.00	$0.76	$1.52	$1.65	$3.31
4.50	$0.85	$1.71	$1.86	$3.72
5.00	$0.95	$1.90	$2.06	$4.12
5.50	$1.04	$2.08	$2.26	$4.53
6.00	$1.13	$2.27	$2.47	$4.94
6.50	$1.23	$2.46	$2.67	$5.34
7.00	$1.32	$2.64	$2.87	$5.75
7.50	$1.41	$2.83	$3.07	$6.15
8.00	$1.51	$3.01	$3.27	$6.56

On the other hand, if your cash flow makes monthly payments more convenient, then swallowing the extra interest cost is the price you pay for convenience.

Whether or not you want to pay your mortgage more frequently is a strategic investment decision. If you are a homeowner, you want to pay down your principal residence debt as soon as possible. You want to become mortgage-free, and you cannot write off your interest, so you're paying off your mortgage with after-tax income.

However, as an investor, it's a different situation. You can write off your mortgage interest against rental revenue, and you may prefer to have lower monthly mortgage payments so that your monthly rental revenue services your expenses. You reduce your mortgage payments by paying less frequently — say, monthly rather than weekly — and having a longer amortization period — say, 30 years rather than 20 years. In this investment scenario, your motivation could be to carry the property payments comfortably, look to obtaining positive monthly cash flow, enjoy appreciation over time, and maximize market demand to provide you with a capital gain when you sell the property in an optimal market.

Opening doors: Prepayment privileges

Most closed mortgages have a prepayment feature that allows you to pay off the mortgage faster than you initially thought possible.

Prepayment privileges create a mortgage that's a cross between an open and a closed mortgage, permitting prepayment at specific stages and in a certain manner. For example, a prepayment feature may allow you to prepay between 10 percent and 20 percent on the principal amount of the mortgage each year. This would allow you to prepay up to a certain amount, giving you a useful measure of flexibility while assuring the lender you're going to be paying down the mortgage for some time to come. You may also have the option of increasing the amount of your monthly payment once a year.

Table 2–3 shows the savings you can achieve based on a $50,000 mortgage at a 6 percent interest rate, with interest compounded semiannually.

Table 2–3	Prepayment or Increased Payment Savings		
	Standard mort-gage 25-year amortization	*10% annual increase in mortgage payment*	*10% annual prepayment of principal*
Mortgage repaid in months	300	164	97
Total interest charged	$45,968.63	$29,504.54	$14,060.22
Interest savings vs. standard 25-year mortgage	N/A	$16,464.09	$31,908.41

Exercising your prepayment privileges can save you an incredible amount of interest while reducing the amortization period and building the equity in your investment. Make sure you completely understand your prepayment options, as they could save you a lot of money.

Default: Don't go there

Sometimes even the best strategies fall apart, especially if you've taken on too much debt (as happened to some investors during the real estate boom of the last decade) or interest rates rise faster than you expect and you're caught short when the time comes to negotiate the loan. Any number of factors may derail your plans to repay your mortgage, and you may find yourself entering a state of *default*. Technically, default occurs when your payment isn't received within 30 days of the due date (a period in which you're considered to be in *arrears,* or behind in your payments). Defaulting on a mortgage has potentially serious consequences. If you're consistently late, you could jeopardize your credit rating, your ability to renew your mortgage, and even your ability to obtain mortgages in the future.

Lenders are typically generous about grace periods before they consider legal action, often allowing mortgage payments to fall three to six months behind before commencing legal action. At any given time, approximately 0.3 percent to 0.5 percent of all mortgages in Canada are three months in arrears. How quickly a lender intervenes to protect its interest will depend on the circumstances and how effectively you have communicated the reasons for the lack of payment (for example, reduced income, sickness or injury, or a family breakup). A lender usually commences foreclosure or sale proceedings only if the property is at risk and you have failed to communicate the reasons; generally the lender will try to work things out with you first.

Renegotiating and Refinancing

When the term of your mortgage ends, usually six months to ten years after negotiation, you have the option to *renegotiate* it or seek *refinancing*. Renegotiating allows you to continue to work within the framework of an existing mortgage. Refinancing gives you the chance to consolidate debts and perhaps tap the equity that's accumulated since you acquired the property. Both offer opportunities to further your investment goals.

When to renegotiate

Renegotiation can help you achieve a better deal, or tailor your existing agreement to more closely meet your needs. Renegotiation is an attractive option if significant changes appear in the lending environment between the beginning and end of your mortgage term:

✦ **Changing lending environments:** Renegotiating makes sense if interest rates have fallen over the course of the previous term and you want to reduce the cost of servicing your debt, freeing up more cash to put toward paying down the principal of your mortgage. Conversely, if interest rates have increased, and your income allows it, you may wish to boost the amount of your monthly payments to shorten the amortization period.

✦ **Changing personal circumstances:** Changes in your personal circumstances may also prompt you to renegotiate your mortgage. Regardless of what interest rates have done, changes in household income may allow you to boost the amount you pay to your mortgage each month. Or perhaps you find yourself worse off financially than you were when you first negotiated the mortgage. Renegotiating can extend the amortization period to accommodate your straitened circumstances.

Adjusting the length of the term of your mortgage may also accommodate current or pending changes in either the lending environment or your own circumstances. A falling interest rate may prompt you to renegotiate for shorter periods, whereas a short-term mortgage may tide you over temporary changes in your personal finances or help you prepare for a possible sale of the property.

Renegotiating your mortgage is as simple as talking to your lender. Well, not quite, as there may be different qualification standards to meet given your circumstances or the demands of the bank, but starting the conversation is simple. Your lender may levy a penalty if you're trying to get out of a closed mortgage, but if the savings make sense you'll be ahead in the long run. And ahead is where you want to be.

Why refinancing can make sense

Refinancing is the strategy of paying off an existing mortgage with the proceeds from a new mortgage. It can help you rejig your mortgage payments to better suit your circumstances as well as access equity for maintenance, upgrades, or a down payment on a new property. Whereas renegotiation adjusts the terms of the mortgage, refinancing lets you reapply for a mortgage on the same property.

Refinancing is a good move if interest rates have decreased, as you will be able to service a greater debt, potentially secure a larger mortgage, and pay less interest per month than you would otherwise. It also makes sense if you've experienced a significant improvement in your gross debt-to-service ratio, for similar reasons. Changes that allow you to access, and service, a greater amount of financing will potentially benefit your ability to invest in better-quality properties.

On the other hand, refinancing may not be such a wise move if changes in the value of your property and your personal financial situation conspire to limit your ability to borrow. You may find yourself able to access a greater volume of debt but facing a longer amortization period that costs you in terms of interest payments. Speak with your mortgage broker and, if you wish, your accountant and financial planner before you refinance, to ensure you are doing what's best for your long-term investment success.

Splitting your mortgage into fixed-rate and variable-rate components — a blended mortgage, which we talk about earlier in this chapter — may make sense during a refinancing (or renegotiation), especially if you need to tap accumulated equity to address a short-term need. The fixed-term portion will typically have tighter repayment rules, whereas the variable-rate portion (or a line of credit) may allow lump-sum payments that allow you to pay it off when the need for cash is over. We discuss fixed- and variable-rate mortgages at greater length in the "Understanding How Mortgages Work" section of this chapter.

A property is not a bank machine! The equity accumulated in a property is not free cash; it comes at the cost of the interest you'll pay under the terms of the refinancing. The pitfalls of tapping too much equity in properties were demonstrated during the housing bust that hit many parts of the world in 2007. Always remember to check your ability to carry the new debt you're seeking under the terms of a refinancing, lest you enter a state of default.

Chapter 3: Scouting Properties: Where to Look and What to Look For

In This Chapter

✔ Identifying the best time to buy

✔ Choosing your ideal market

✔ Finding the right property for you

✔ Assessing a property's potential

✔ Doing your due diligence

*F*inding the right property takes skill, luck, and a whole lot of intuition. But the hard work of scouting properties will give you the gut feelings you need to make the hard decisions successful real estate investors make. This chapter is something of a scout's handbook, and we can't help but advise, "Be prepared!"

We discuss everything about finding properties, from the big picture down to the specific property. We tackle some of the basic issues in Chapter 1, but in this chapter we get into the nitty-gritty of sizing up the conditions in specific markets, neighbourhoods, and even the property you're looking at investing in. We can't know the specifics of every situation you have to choose from, of course, but we hope we can provide some useful examples and guidelines.

Assessing Current Market Cycles

The wild ride real estate markets have taken in the past five years highlights the need to be savvy to the direction a cycle is moving. You don't want to be jumping in on the downside thinking it's a temporary correction, only to be dragged down. And you don't want to miss the low point of a particular market.

This section walks you through an analysis of market cycles as they apply to the process of purchasing a property. Three main steps go into assessing the current market cycle: conducting research, analyzing the facts you've found, and making a decision.

Research: Doing your homework

The first step is to figure out what type of market you're in. Is it a *buyer's market,* with plenty of product to choose from? Or a *seller's market,* with rising prices and limited supply? Or are conditions stable, reflecting a relatively *balanced market*?

Knowing where to find basic information — and when to dig for more — is an important skill for researching market cycles. In this section, we give you the pointers you need to be an effective market analyst!

Tracking interest rates

Higher interest rates are probably not something you appreciate, but the cautious lenders financing your investment certainly will! The lower the interest rate charged on a mortgage, the greater the incentive for you to borrow to buy a property – if values are attractive. Don't overpay just because money is cheap.

The primary source of information on interest rates is the Bank of Canada (www.bankofcanada.ca), the Ottawa-based central bank that lending institutions across Canada pay attention to when setting their own interest rates. Find out more about how interest rates are determined in Chapter 2, Book 4.

Though we don't recommend trying to second-guess interest rates, a close look at past rates, current trends, and the projections of the various banks should indicate whether rates are set to rise, plateau, or fall. By gauging trends in interest rates against various other factors such as the health of the economy, you can make your own call as to whether financing will be more or less expensive in future and whether you should select a variable or fixed-rate mortgage. Interest-rate trends also indicate whether you should buy now, wait a few months when financing might be cheaper, or sell while low rates are creating opportunities for buyers to hop into the market. With interest rates so low now during 2012, it's difficult to see them getting any lower. So studying property values will be vital rather than worrying about interest rates.

Rising rates may make financing more expensive but they can sometimes create opportunities for buyers by putting pressure on owners who have overleveraged their portfolio. Selling when buyers are active can provide financing you can use to purchase properties when debt-burdened owners have to unload assets.

Determining property taxes

Property taxes may seem like fixed costs but they are important considerations for investors. A booming market with rising sale values pushes up assessors' valuations of properties. A slack market, by contrast, could see property values fall. This has a direct impact on the annual tax assessment, not only in the coming year, but often in the three years following the change in value. Taxes levied on a property will affect the return you see as an investor, and possibly your financing costs.

Different investors have different expectations and projections for their profit margins. Most investors want a *double return,* that is, a positive cash flow for a rental revenue stream, and a capital gain over the original purchase price. Traditionally, real estate has gone up an average of about 5 percent a year for the past 30 years. However, that figure can be higher or lower depending on the real estate cycle, location, type of property, and other factors. Most investors would like to see equity in their properties increasing at least 5 percent a year.

This will affect municipal property taxes, which are the primary revenue source for towns and cities. Residential property taxes are often just a small percent of annual assessed value, but those few percentage points will eat into your cash flow. Knowing which way property taxes are likely to head in a particular market will help you determine the kind of cash flow you'll need to get from the property to cover costs, as well as the long-term drag on your return.

Capital gains are another consideration. If your property gains an average of 10 percent a year in value over ten years, the property will double in value. If you buy it for $100,000, and sell it for $200,000, you have a $100,000 gain in your original investment. You are taxed by the Canada Revenue Agency on 50 percent of your gain. In this example, that means you could keep $50,000 tax-free, and pay tax on the remaining $50,000. At the top marginal tax rate of approximately 50 percent, you would pay approximately $25,000 tax. At the end of the day, you could keep $75,000 of your original $100,000 gain, after tax.

If your original purchase price was $100,000, that would mean a 75-percent return over ten years, or an average of 7.5 percent a year non-compounded. But you'll also have to factor in positive cash flow from rental income to determine your actual return less expenses such as property tax and mortgage interest.

On the other hand, maybe you just put down 10 percent and borrowed the other 90 percent on a mortgage. Therefore, you actually received a 75 percent return on your original personal resource down payment of $10,000 over ten years. The reason is that your original $10,000-down "investment" resulted in a $75,000 net gain, or an average of $7,500 a year on your original $10,000, or a 75 percent return per year. Better than obtaining, say, a 3 percent return on a term deposit that is taxed as investment income in your hands in that taxation year. Depending on your tax bracket you could pay 30 percent or more on that interest income, meaning that net after tax you actually received only about two-thirds of your interest, or 2 percent in the example given.

Property tax assessment records are available through municipal offices or provincial assessment authorities. You will also find explanations of trends in the annual reports of the municipality in which you hope to buy. Often, local media cover trends in property taxation, providing you with insights into overall municipal approaches to setting tax rates (in some provinces, the provincial government sets the rates).

Be sure to discuss the impact of property taxation policies on your investment with an appraiser, who is often able to coordinate appeals on any assessments you consider out of line with the reality of your holding. Given the range of factors that affect the value of a property, and its performance in any given market, you should understand how property taxes will influence your own cash flow as well as the property's appeal to future investors. Assessments that indicate opportunities for investment can easily rise after investors move in, improve the properties, and improve the tone of the surrounding neighbourhood.

Reviewing leasing conditions

Fully leased properties with long-term tenants make for great investments from a revenue perspective, but a close look at the tenant mix may reveal nothing more than a good tease. The last thing you want to do is enter a market on the basis of an apparently healthy lease market, only to find that leasing activity is actually declining and taking property prices with it.

Fortunately, several sources can help you investigate the current and long-term history and prospects for local leasing markets. If you're looking at residential rental properties, have a gander at the annual rental housing market survey the Canada Mortgage and Housing Corp. (www.cmhc.ca) produces. Commercial brokerages such as Colliers International (www.colliers.com) prepare similar reports on a quarterly basis for commercial and industrial markets. Retail leasing reports are also available from the big brokerages, but high rates of turnover make these more difficult to produce.

Knowing where vacancies stand in your market, and the rents tenants are paying for their spaces, will indicate investment opportunities and reflect landlords' capital requirements. High vacancies may indicate buying opportunities as existing owners may want to sell out because of cash flow pressures; alternatively, low vacancies may make assets attractive to purchasers, resulting in a vendor's market as buyers compete for assets.

A good leasing market doesn't necessarily mean a good investment market. Conversely, high vacancies won't always prompt landlords to sell. Still, knowing rental conditions can help you build an argument for investing in particular locales and devising a negotiating strategy that will win over vendors.

Gauging consumer confidence

Buyers' confidence in markets is as changeable as the markets themselves. The two, after all, have an intimate relationship. Confident investors contribute to a strong market, while conservative investors limit the volume of activity taking place in the market.

But short of doing psychological assessments of a random sampling of active investors, how can you gauge the level of confidence in the market? Let others skilled in the art research it for you, of course!

The Conference Board of Canada (www.conferenceboard.ca) is just one of the organizations that issues business and consumer confidence surveys. For a fee, the Board provides detailed analyses for specific regions. Newspapers also record perceptions of where markets are heading. The information gleaned from these sources, like interest-rate projections, can help you gauge whether markets are in for a boom or a downturn.

Rising consumer confidence may indicate an increased willingness to invest in real estate. As an investor, you may consider preparing your residential property for sale to the potential buyers, or perhaps you'll opt to buy before the market heats up. On the other hand, falling confidence in the market may signal purchase opportunities as people retrench in anticipation of harder times.

Consumer confidence is less definite than monetary policy and interest rates, and relies on a good grasp of the current economic climate. Unforeseen events can put the kibosh on existing predictions, so although we recommend consulting assessments of the market's mood, know that the mood is just that — a mood. It won't necessarily obey scientific laws.

Considering local planning activities

Urban planning activities have a peripheral influence on market cycles but may play a role in spurring demand in local areas. Including a glance at urban planning initiatives in the areas where you're considering investing is therefore a good plan!

Here's how planning has an influence: An area that has languished at the bottom of the local market cycle may find itself at the top of a council's priority list because of public concern over its status or the potential for improvement if it is rezoned for certain purposes. A community planning process may identify certain goals and uses for the area. Perhaps planners will propose development incentives. A combination of these factors may spark a rush into the area.

Knowing the pressures coming to bear on specific neighbourhoods, and where these areas rank in the city's planning priorities, will give you clues to where the market in these areas is likely to go in the future. This gives you an advantage over other investors, potentially allowing you to get in when the market is low and sell when the market is high. Conversely, if an area is set for rezoning, you want to be aware that the market for properties with uses allowed under the previous zoning is about to collapse.

Analyzing thoroughly: Tallying the variables

Making sense of the information you glean through your research into market conditions and perceptions of the market may seem like voodoo. And, to be fair, seeing the big picture takes a good deal of intuition. Of course, we face similar decisions. To make life easier for you, we offer a chart in the sidebar "Sizing up the cycle" that will help you determine where the market sits and what your course of action should be. Find the set of criteria that come closest to what you've discovered about the market, and gauge how you should respond!

The decision: Trust your gut

Whether you're buying or selling, don't make your decision lightly. Consult your long-term investment plan and take stock of what your advisers are saying. Knowing when you're ready to sell is as important as knowing when you're ready to invest. (We discuss selling a property in Chapter 4.) Though you may consider selling a handful of properties in your portfolio, the range of properties you can buy is typically larger. Knowing whether the market is at the right point for a purchase, however, is just one aspect of your investment decision.

Few markets are uniform, after all. Even an unfavourable market can harbour good investments. Finding the good deals in difficult circumstances is part of the challenge — and joy — of investing in real estate.

X Marks the Spot: Identifying a Target Market

Throwing a dart at a list or map showing the areas where market conditions are favourable is one way of identifying a target market for investing, but we hope you'll put a bit more effort than that into your decision. A number of factors may sway you in favour of (or against) a particular locale, particularly in the wake of the dramatic boom-bust-recovery cycle that swept through Canada between 2005 and 2009. The landscape can change rapidly, and although stable, long-term areas may not see much change in their appeal (or lack thereof), market changes often create new opportunities for investors in marginal or transitional areas.

We explore some of the considerations you'll want to take into account when you're narrowing down your list of potential neighbourhoods for investment. We want you to keep the fundamentals of the local market in mind, looking past the fads to the actual investment potential of the area.

Sizing up the cycle

To make your job of determining market conditions a bit easier, we've put together a table that assembles various variables and suggests an appropriate action based on the variables most prevalent in your corner of the market. Of course, determining a market's character is hardly an exact science, but this table should help you put circumstances into perspective.

	A	*B*	*C*	*D*
Values	Depressed	Increasing	Increasing	Declining
Rents	Low	Increasing	Increasing	Declining
Vacancy level	High	Beginning to decrease	Low	Increasing
Occupancy level	Low	Increasing	High	Decreasing
New construction	Very little	Increasing	Booming	Slowing
Profit margins	Low	Improving	Widest	Decline
Investor confidence	Low	Negative to neutral	Positive	Slightly negative
Media coverage	Negative and pessimistic	Positive and encouraging	Positive and optimistic	Negative and pessimistic
Action	Buy	Second best time to buy	Sell	Be cautious

Of course, your perception and affinity for a particular neighbourhood may count more than the hard financial stats. To ensure your investment balances financial wisdom with personal feeling, find out what conditions on the ground are really like.

Separating the fads from the fundamentals

Successful real estate investment requires that you know what you're buying and trust that it's going to deliver a return. Remember the old joke about diplomacy being the skill of telling someone to go to Hell in a way that they actually look forward to the trip? Real estate marketing can be a lot like that; a marketer will sell you a piece of Hell and you'll enjoy the heat and other amenities!

Although the marketing of new developments tends to focus on lifestyle and neighbourhood options, you may look at other aspects of the property and be wondering whether that development is really so great. The hottest new neighbourhood under development or redevelopment may not fit your investment strategy, no matter what advantages the marketers tout.

Points to consider when comparing a property in a hot neighbourhood to one in a locale generally considered less favourable include not only their price, but also their potential for appreciation, maintenance costs, and cash flow:

✦ **Price** is an important factor when stacking up properties, and especially when gauging the relative merits of two properties whose neighbourhoods differ in quality. Check whether the list price of each property is within area norms, and whether either of the two is undervalued. A market correction may create opportunities to buy undervalued properties simply because the original owners have become skittish and want out. An undervalued asset in a good neighbourhood is a wise bet, but steer clear of an overpriced home in an undervalued neighbourhood because you'll have less room for long-term appreciation while the rest of the neighbourhood catches up with your property's value (or the property's value may actually fall in line with the rest of the neighbourhood).

✦ **Potential for appreciation** will indicate the return you can expect on your investment. The greater the potential for appreciation, the better the investment. Consult an appraiser for a prognosis on the kind of return you can expect on the various properties you're considering. (We talk more about working with appraisers in Chapter 4.)

✦ **Potential maintenance costs** could cut into your margins, especially in a less-favourable neighbourhood. We're not talking only about deferred maintenance that's contributed to the lower asking price of the property and greater potential for appreciation; we're talking about the ongoing maintenance associated with graffiti, litter, vandalism, overgrown grounds and the like. You may be able to make something of the property, but will you be able to *keep* that something?

✦ **Potential for cash flow** could moderate your enthusiasm for that high-end asset if you find tenants hard to come by. Depending on your investment strategy, it may be better for you to invest in a more modest property with solid cash flow potential than a trophy few can afford to rent from you. On the other hand, if you have a chance to pick up two residential properties, and can swing the financing, you may opt to live in one and rent the other — effectively having *two* slices of cake and eating them too. (Just be sure you know which piece is sweeter.) Also be careful to arrange your financing so you maximize your income tax deductions every year. Ask your accountant to explain to you the difference between good debt and bad debt.

Getting to know markets and neighbourhoods

Bearing in mind the fundamentals of sound investing, part of your job as a diligent investor is to familiarize yourself with the neighbourhoods you're targeting for investment. There are several ways to do this, from research to walkabouts, and a number of factors to consider.

We recommend identifying three neighbourhoods, based on your research into market conditions, that could serve as investment opportunities. This will allow you to see how each compares with the others, tally up their relative advantages and disadvantages, and generally get a feel for which neighbourhood you're most comfortable with.

Basic factors to consider before you even visit a neighbourhood relate to its age, its character, and its unique mix of properties and infrastructure.

Book VI
Chapter 3

Scouting Properties:
Where to Look and
What to Look For

Sizing up age

Older neighbourhoods either are well-to-do and established, or show their age. The good news is that a neighbourhood with an aging stock of properties with rock-bottom values can offer great value. You may be able to renovate the property and make it into something people want, either as tenants or owners. On the other hand, an established neighbourhood with good-quality homes may offer few opportunities for you to enter the market.

A new neighbourhood may be the hottest place for some investors, but it also has the potential for surprises. Where an established neighbourhood has a reputation, a new neighbourhood has yet to prove itself. The quality of the homes may be good and the infrastructure may be there, but what will it become?

Sizing up character

The kind of neighbourhood character we're talking about isn't necessarily the vibe you'll pick up during a stroll down the street. Rather, it's the mix of people actually in the neighbourhood, the ages and income levels, and education and employment indicators. These factors are worth considering because they contribute to the kind of tenant you attract, and also how the locale maintains itself.

For example, an upper-income neighbourhood in a suburb with a growing working-class population may have a prime piece of real estate to offer. Buying the upper-end property hoping to lease suites to workers or students may not be the best idea because the rents you'll have to charge to make ends meet on the property probably won't match what the workers and students are able to pay. Chances are the better opportunity will lie in an asset that can provide affordable housing to the growing population of workers.

We don't recommend a snobby attitude in selecting properties, but as an investor you should consider what serves the market. Paying attention to the demographics and overall character of a neighbourhood helps you find an asset that's the right fit, not only with your own goals but also with those of the people to whom you hope to lease.

Sizing up the mix

The right mix of properties in a neighbourhood ensures a match made in heaven between the kind of property you want to own and the needs of any tenants you hope to secure.

Perhaps you've got a penchant for a small industrial building. The three mid-size bays inside are perfect for light industrial users. But a glance at the uses of surrounding properties indicates that it's nowhere near any amenities, and neighbouring properties don't really complement the kind of users you hope to secure. However good a deal it is, and whatever the future growth potential of the industrial area where it's situated, chances are the small industrial users you're looking for may not want to lease the premises. Therefore it won't suit their needs, and the investment won't live up to your expectations.

Amenities are key to supporting the needs of the users you hope to attract to a revenue-producing property. Several electronic resources allow you to gauge the potential of a neighbourhood before you even see it; some real estate listings offer 360-degree views and video tours of the surrounding neighbourhood, for example, while Google (not to mention many municipalities) provides satellite and street-level views of your potential neighbourhood that give a sense of the area's layout (a simple Web search will pull up others).

Honing your vision

You wouldn't buy a car without kicking the tires, so it makes sense to take a walkabout in each area where you're considering investing. Testing your response to these neighbourhoods gives you a sense of how others are likely to respond to them.

To become familiar with a potential neighbourhood, pay it a few visits at various times of day and night. Give yourself a chance to experience it as a driver, a pedestrian, and a transit user. Are traffic patterns unusual? Is it walkable? Are transit connections frequent, smooth, or a hassle? Your experience of these aspects of the community may give you an understanding of why a neighbourhood is hot or not, and may point you to areas within the neighbourhood that are more convenient places to be than others.

Keeping watch

Having an extra pair of eyes scouting properties is a great help when you're looking for a good investment. And who better to ask than a real estate agent, especially one with access to databases such as the Multiple Listing Service (www.mls.ca) for residential properties or ICX (www.icx.ca) for commercial properties?

Take Dan, for example. An experienced real estate investor, Dan regularly buys properties that need some tender loving care. He fixes them up, puts them back on the market, and reaps a profit. To do that, Dan has a long-standing professional relationship with his agent, Pam. Dan sets out the type of property he's interested in buying, the location he wants to buy in, and the price he's prepared to pay.

Pam monitors new listings as soon as they're listed, getting the low-down on them even before they've officially hit the MLS site. When a property comes up that meets Dan's requirements, she gets in touch with Dan. Dan quickly checks the properties, and before the market is fully aware of the listing he puts in his offer.

Knowing what you want and developing a relationship with a listing agent who's able to connect you with properties that meet those criteria can give you an edge over other buyers. The properties Dan scouts need lots of work and typically list for the value of the lot, so he faces a limited number of competitors. Still, without his relationship with Pam, he wouldn't have been as successful as he has been in finding the best deals possible.

A walkabout is a more intensive way for you to gauge several of the factors we discuss in this section. Keep your eyes open for the following:

✦ **The fabric of the neighbourhood:** This includes the condition of the properties and landscaping. The better the condition of the neighbourhood, the more attractive it will be to potential tenants and the less risk to the condition and value of your own property.

✦ **Local businesses and amenities:** These are important indicators of your fortunes in the neighbourhood. A handful of local businesses serving up staples and a few pleasures is a good sign. Communities that lack a decent grocery store and other basic shops stand to be less favoured by potential tenants and future buyers.

✦ **Street vibe:** This is a significant factor in making a neighbourhood a place people want to be. Good traffic flows, people who chat with one another, maybe even street-side decorations are all signs of a vibrant neighbourhood. On the other hand, desolate streets where the windows of the homes have bars may not send the right message to people you're trying to interest in your property.

✦ **Noise and environmental factors:** These affect different people in different ways. Unless you're investing in commercial or industrial property, chances are you won't want to buy something on the flight path to the local airport.

Be sure to consider the full range of factors at play in the neighbourhoods you're considering! A personal visit may help you make sense of issues local newspapers have raised about the area, or may temper the impressions you've received from others who claim to know what's going on.

Consulting the locals

One of the best things you can do as a potential investor in a neighbourhood is to get to know the locals. This gives you a feel for the area, as well as local concerns and attitudes, and furthers your understanding of the community. You may even discover information about the property you're looking at that may encourage you — or prompt you to think twice about the investment you were hoping to make.

Opportunities for meeting locals abound. Buy a paper and chat up the person who serves you. Stop in to the local coffee shop (if there is one), listen to the chatter, and maybe strike up a conversation with the people at the neighbouring table. You may not be good at small talk, but even chatting about the weather can create an opportunity to hear what people are saying about the market.

Building relationships with locals is something you can never begin too early. This is especially true if you plan a major development of a property or are considering a rezoning. Cultivating an open relationship with members of the community will help bring them onside with your plans. The goodwill you foster by participating in the community as either a home-owner or business operator is invaluable.

Selecting a Property

The property you're seeking in the locale you've chosen may not be simple to find. You have to look for it, or have your broker do so. After you've selected a neighbourhood in which to invest, you'll want to pull out newspapers, log on to websites such as the Multiple Listing Service (www.mls.ca) for residential property or ICX (www.icx.ca) for commercial and industrial properties, and keep your eyes open.

Facets of the property to consider include its location, the availability of amenities and services, and the property's potential for appreciation. The criteria are largely refinements of the principles that have allowed you to narrow your search to a handful of properties. By now you should know what you want!

Home sweet home

A house which is your home draws out a lot of emotion, regardless of whether you're the owner-occupant or simply a tenant with the option of moving out if it gets on your nerves. You have a lot more conditions you want to satisfy when you're looking for a chunk of residential real estate than, say, a retail unit. Your standards are especially high if you're also planning on living in the house. Any tenants you welcome into the building are there because they've chosen to rent from you and can move on if the place isn't what they expect, but you're going to be stuck with the place as the primary occupant and user. So be selfish and put your own interests first!

First off, consider where you want to live. Price, affordability, and availability each play a role in determining where you buy, but your own idea of what makes a livable neighbourhood also factors into your decision. Being practical won't hurt; what appeals to you may appeal to tenants or future buyers. Being able to tout a feature of your neighbourhood that has been of particular value to you will help the sales pitch you'll make to the next purchaser.

You have many factors to consider when selecting a home, whether for your own use or as an investment. Here are a few questions to ask yourself:

+ **What is the neighbourhood like?** A thriving neighbourhood promises to be a great place to live, whereas one where not much is going on could make for dull evenings and weekends. Or, the run-down nature of some of the buildings could mean more excitement happens than you really care to know about. These factors won't just affect your quality of life as a resident, either; they could be indicative of long-term trends that will either make it easier or more difficult for you to sell your property in the future.

+ **What are traffic flows like?** The local highway may be a great feature if you do a lot of commuting, but you don't necessarily want to be living next door to it. Consider, too, the potential health impacts from living next door to a major traffic artery. These factors could limit the resale value of your property, but convenient access to transportation networks could be an asset for some buyers. Research the traffic patterns and impact on property values in any area in which you're considering buying.

+ **What community amenities are within a 10-kilometre radius?** Nearby schools, places of worship, parks and recreation facilities, transit, and shopping can be points in the favour of residential real estate. The closer your property is to amenities, the more you're able to offer others. The higher value of a location can pay itself back if you approach the purchase as an investment rather than simply your own home.

+ **What does municipal zoning allow for the property?** Favourable zoning can open the door to enhancements that can affect the value of your property. Depending on your neighbourhood, changes may be in the works that will either increase the value of your property or diminish it. Researching what the city plans for a particular residential neighbourhood is an important part of analyzing a property.

✦ **What are property tax rates like?** Taxes are one of the few certain things in life, so make sure you study which direction residential property taxes are heading before you buy. Rates typically differ from city to city, so you may be able to find a property comparable to one you like in a municipality that levies a higher tax rate on homeowners, and thus end up paying less tax.

✦ **What are the prospects for an increase in property value?** Regardless of where you buy, try to make sure your home has potential to appreciate in value! Some of the basic market research you'll undertake to determine a location (which we discuss in "Separating the fads from the fundamentals") can help you make this call.

✦ **What are condo fees and building regulations like?** Don't forget to take condo fees and bylaws passed by the building council into account when you're looking at condominiums. Be sure to review building council minutes prior to buying to become aware of any ongoing issues. (We also discuss investing in condos in Chapter 1.)

Having chosen a neighbourhood in which to buy, scout potential homes using the Internet. Here are a few sites to check out:

✦ The Canadian Real Estate Association maintains the Multiple Listing Service (MLS) site, which boasts the majority of residential listings across Canada (www.mls.ca). This will give you an idea of the homes available for purchase in a given area, after which you can approach a Realtor to assist your search. You can identify several potential Realtors through listings on the MLS site.

✦ Independent agents also exist who can offer insights and connections regarding the area where you hope to buy. You need to find someone with the experience and skills to serve your needs and with whom you can work — so look around.

✦ A number of services also exist that give owner-vendors a venue for pitching their properties, such as PropertyGuys.com and ForSalebyOwner.ca. Although we encourage you to use a real estate agent in your various transactions, it's worth remembering that not all people will. You may find a deal on one of these sites that, given some skillful negotiating, will hand you a bargain.

In addition, you can find listings of court-ordered sales (a process we discuss in *Real Estate Investing For Canadians For Dummies*), either at the local courthouse or through services that collect such data and distribute it for a fee. You may be able to find these listings on the Web, but as often as not vendors facing foreclosure are actively trying to avoid the circumstance and working with brokers who will be able to tip you off to potential opportunities in your locale.

Accommodating tenants

A home isn't a good investment if you can't achieve a return on it. Although appreciation over time is one means of achieving this goal, sharing your home with a tenant provides an ongoing cash flow. To ensure your experience with a tenant has the best chance of success, you want to make sure the home you buy has certain features.

Ideally, if the previous owner of the home has had tenants, you'll be able to judge the property on its features as both a residence and a rental property. Though you may need to make adjustments to the layout, the structure itself should be flexible enough to accommodate some key features:

✦ Dividing walls, to ensure a more complete separation of your living area from the tenant's

✦ Potential for sharing laundry facilities and other amenities, which could eliminate your need to set up a separate laundry area for tenants

✦ Wiring and circuitry necessary for the installation of a fridge, stove, and other appliances as well as cable television and internet access

✦ Shared or separate front doors, back doors, and parking

These features make the space less hassle for you to adapt for rental use, and create a more desirable space for potential renters.

Dividing walls are just one element that helps ensure a happy co-existence between your family and your tenants. A separate entrance is a primary consideration; this will give the tenants a feel of privacy and decrease the chance their comings and goings will disturb you. But if you're buying a two- or three-bedroom condo and want to rent a room, you may want to put a higher priority on having an extra washroom as well as adequate sound-proofing.

Buying a home located close to a major public transit route will enhance your chance of securing a tenant. A parking spot is another attractive feature.

Not all municipalities allow secondary suites, so be sure to check the legality of having tenants before you buy! Some jurisdictions will turn a blind eye to tenants, but you invite a range of hassles by not complying with the letter of the law. For peace of mind check what local bylaws have to say, and speak to your lawyer.

Attracting purchasers

Gauging future demand for housing in your neighbourhood is difficult, but you can take steps that will position your home to be attractive to potential purchasers in 5, 10, or even 20 years. Some of these will be reasons that you're attracted to the home yourself, such as proximity to schools, parks, shopping areas, transportation, and other amenities. But looking at the locale is also worthwhile:

✦ Is it close to major institutional employers with ongoing employment needs, such as a hospital or university?

✦ What is the potential of the home to be adapted for other uses, say rental to tenants, home office use, or the like?

✦ Does it have the potential to appeal to buyers completely different from yourself?

✦ Does the local zoning allow expansion or redevelopment of the home? You may not be interested in doing this, but the possibility might attract a future owner.

Location, location, location

Okay, "location, location, location" is a time-worn phrase, but it makes sense! And what would a book that includes real estate be without it? A property's location isn't something to take lightly, given the potential impact on appeal to tenants, your cash flow, and potential resale value.

Appealing to tenants

Many of us, at one time or another, have had a landlord who's baffled us. The rent was good, but property conditions were such that we didn't have to wonder why we were the ones living in the suite rather than the owner!

Now that you're a landlord, why do the same thing to your tenants? As we discuss in the previous section, choosing a property that's in a location where you would want to live yourself makes sense even if you *don't* live there. That's because lots of other people probably would look forward to finding the place you've found. A decent neighbourhood makes for happy tenants, which makes for stable cash flow and, ultimately, a better return on your investment. (We cover the value amenities can add to a property's location in the section "Amenities and services" in this chapter.)

A property that's attractive to tenants is better than a utilitarian rental property with no cachet at all. Chances are you'll also be able to charge higher rents, potentially securing yourself a long-term advantage that beats buying a larger property in a less attractive neighbourhood commanding lower rents.

Cashing in

The quality of the neighbourhood will affect not only how long tenants stay and the rents they're willing to pay, but also the cash flow the property generates. You'll be able to charge tenants higher rents for suites in well-located properties, and you'll likely face lower operating expenses.

Though you may pay closer attention to the overall appearance of a property that's surrounded by attractive neighbours, the quality of the tenant that a better-groomed property attracts helps your investment property deliver a return. You'll find it easier to secure better-quality tenants — that is, tenants who respect your property — who reduce your maintenance costs. This ensures better margins on the rents you're able to charge. Also one of your tenants may be able to make you an offer for the place that you simply can't refuse. How nice is that?

Trading up

Future buyers will have an interest in the property you've bought if it is in a better-quality location. The chances for appreciation increase if the fortunes of the surrounding area are also on the upswing.

Even if the locale seems to be facing a downturn, a better-quality asset will tend to lose less of its value than one in a poor location in a poor neighbourhood.

Amenities and services

The kinds of amenities and services you hope to have near your investment property vary. Users of residential properties want something different from tenants of commercial and industrial properties. When identifying amenities available to users of the property you're considering buying, you're generally safe to look in a 10-kilometre radius around the property.

Residential

Standard residential amenities include schools, places of worship, parks and recreation facilities, transit links, and shopping areas. The closer a property is to a greater selection of amenities, the more you'll be able to command in rent.

Amenities are also increasingly important to resort properties, with those who want to get away from it all not wanting to leave their urban comforts behind. Ensure that the resort property into which you're buying is well-served with amenities suited to the recreational user.

Commercial

Commercial properties, such as office and retail buildings, have their own unique set of needs. Depending on the size and kind of workforce, selling points can include proximity to recreational amenities and shopping facilities as well as food service. Postal outlets and business supply and service centres are also important.

Infrastructure such as parking areas, proximity to main commuting routes, and transit services can also enhance the value of the assets in which you're looking to invest.

Industrial

Connections to transportation infrastructure are among the most important amenities you can provide industrial users. Because these properties are typically where items are made, stored, and distributed, it's important that users have ready access to roads, and even rail and port connections. In many areas of Canada, quick access to the U.S. border is also a consideration.

Like commercial users, industrial tenants appreciate proximity to food service and retail outlets.

Looking to the future

Here's a startling revelation: No one can predict the future. But based on the amount of research you've put into finding a property, we bet you'll be able to take an educated guess at what the future holds for the ones you're considering buying. Because the main success of your investment will be in its appreciation, you want to make sure the property itself stands to gain in value. You should also have some confidence that the prospects for the surrounding neighbourhood are good.

Looking in

The future prospects for your investment in and of itself depend on the quality of the building and overall market conditions.

We discuss the various ways to gauge a property's inherent value in Chapter 4, but it's worth pointing out here that your property should be structurally sound. A building with potential for adaptation will also have stronger potential to appreciate in value in future years, as residential and other requirements change. The greater the number of uses to which a future owner can put a property, the greater the chances that it will retain its value, and even become a more valuable asset.

The overall market conditions are something over which you have little control. A glance at the history of the property's value should indicate whether or not it has seen a steady appreciation, or whether it has suffered depreciation in the past. Researching the causes for past fluctuations in value may not reveal the potential for appreciation or depreciation, but such research will indicate whether any unusual circumstances were behind the fluctuations.

Looking out

The surrounding neighbourhood can sometimes work to lower or raise the value of your property. Although your property is a passive player in the phenomenon, any increase or decrease in the quality of the community could have an impact.

As an investor, aim to find a property in a stable neighbourhood with potential for appreciation. Recognizing the warning signs that could indicate the start of a downward trend in value is a skill that should prompt you to sell the property — or stay away from it if you thought it might be a good purchase.

Appraising Properties

When you buy a property, the lender typically wants to have an independent professional appraisal done to make sure the property is worth what is being paid for it. This has implications in terms of protecting the mortgage security on the property. Normally the lender will pay the cost of the appraisal, which averages about $300 to $400. Sometimes the lender will pass that cost on to you.

A basic appraisal is a pretty simple matter of comparing recent sale prices for comparable assets and extrapolating a value based on what the market is likely willing to pay for the asset. Thanks to the wealth of information available in databases these days, the job is so simple that most residential appraisals are now computer-generated. This might be expedient when you're looking for a loan, and may even work to your advantage. But as an investor you want to make sure the values measure up to your standards — not a machine's.

A good appraisal is really more complex than a simple comparison. It takes into account a variety of factors, from the construction value of a property to the sale value to intangible factors such as location, future uses, and all-round potential. In this section, we discuss some of the basic types of appraisals, and how you can use professional appraisers to your advantage when scouting properties.

Understanding appraisals

You may not always understand how an appraiser reaches a specific value, but knowing the basic methods appraisers use can help you understand something of the rationale for their calculations.

Here are four primary methods of appraising investment properties:

✦ **Market comparison,** or the traditional point-in-time valuation, by which an appraiser compares several benchmark sales and determines a value for the property you're considering

✦ **Cost comparison,** involving comparison of a property's market value against the cost of buying the lot and constructing a similar building

✦ **Income comparison,** a common method to evaluate the relative merits of income-producing properties as well as attempt to gauge the maximum an investor would pay for a property

✦ **Internal rate of return,** which gives a measure of the annual rate of return an investor can see from a property

The several kinds of appraisal aren't mutually exclusive. Often, it helps to have a couple of different perspectives on the potential value of the asset you're considering. You'll then get a sense of how to make the most of properties others may consider poor investments.

Comparing values

To compare values, you need other values. Circumstances most conducive to the market comparison approach to appraisals are those in which properties are numerous and sales are frequent. During the downturn of 2008 and 2009, it was difficult to get comparative sale values in some neighbourhoods, and for some types of properties. Condominiums, single-family houses, and raw land are the most common types of properties for which to use the market comparison method.

No two properties are alike, of course. Variables include age, location, layout, size, features, and overall quality. Conditions in the market at the time of sale also influence value (the values would never change, otherwise). Special features of the property and the property's location — anything that makes it more or less desirable in the market — also factor into its appraised value.

Because market comparison relies on the existence of similar properties for comparison purposes, you may find yourself caught out by a lack of suitable properties. The motivations of the vendors of the properties are difficult to gauge, too, meaning the prices of the properties you select as benchmarks may not accurately reflect a fair value.

When sales of comparable properties aren't available to check the value of the property you're considering — whether because of a lack of sales in the immediate area or the unique character of the property you're examining — take a look at the sales history of the property and the price it last sold for. Stack that up against recent listings in the area — the agent you work with should be able to provide two or three years' worth of listings for the purposes of comparison — and what market reports are saying about the area's future. This should allow you to determine the amount you're willing to pay for a property with a sense of its future potential.

Comparing costs

You may be looking for a home to renovate, but comparing the cost of buying an older property and renovating to the cost of building anew may make you think twice. A cost comparison will help you see what the difference is, and may even give you the tools you need to negotiate a better price than the one you're offered for the property.

To compare costs, estimate the cost of developing a new building relative to the one already on the property. Determine the value of the existing building, taking into account depreciation. Because the land value is stable, you won't need to concern yourself with this; simply compare the value of the existing building to the cost of building anew. If the replacement cost is above market value, or above the list price plus any renovations or maintenance you plan, the investment is probably a good one.

To ensure you've made an accurate comparison, seek an appraiser's assistance when calculating depreciation. In addition, construction costs vary depending on location, supply and demand, and inflation. Consult an appraiser to be sure your calculations aren't misleading you. (After all, appraisers do their job professionally, and even the most talented amateurs can make mistakes!)

Renovations often increase the value of a home (see our discussion of the advantages of renovations in Chapter 4). Buying the undervalued property and renovating it increases the chance the future value can repay you handsomely.

Comparing incomes

As the moniker *comparing incomes* suggests, this method is primarily useful in comparing the relative value of revenue properties. Other means of appraising the property's value are important too, but the potential of the property to generate revenue and pay for itself is key if you're buying a property as an income-producing investment.

Comparing the net income of properties indicates not only how the properties stack up against one another in terms of income generation, but also how many years they'll take to pay for themselves. Although you may not hold them this long, the ratio you get is important as a comparable, and it will also indicate how much an investor would be willing to pay for your property.

You can determine the net income of a property by simply looking at its financial history — that is, the annual rental income less all the expenses — to identify either positive cash flow (money into your pocket) or negative cash flow (money *out of* your pocket). Typical expenses include property tax, insurance, mortgage interest, maintenance, repairs, and possibly utilities depending on whether you pass that cost on to the tenants or absorb it yourself. After you know whether the property is generating cash or losing it, you can compare the net profit or loss with other properties to determine which property has the most favourable net revenue profit before income tax.

A $1 million property with an annual net income of $100,000 would take ten years to pay for itself. But if your investment strategy pins you to a seven-year payback time frame, you may want to find a comparable property that generates more income or a smaller, less expensive property for which you can achieve higher rents.

Some investors assess the value of a property based on gross income, but this is an inaccurate method because it doesn't reflect operating expenses. Expenses may vary, and unless the assessment looks at the net income, the true value (inclusive of margins) isn't known.

Comparing returns

The *internal rate of return* (IRR) is a measure of how much a property will return an investor annually on the investment made. It differs from the investor's actual return, which reflects the equity less any debts and sales-related expenses.

An internal rate of return of 25 percent, for example, represents the return an income property delivers on the initial down payment. An $800,000 rental property purchased with an initial investment of $200,000, for example, would boast a 25-percent internal rate of return if the projected net cash flow from the property and the anticipated net sale proceeds averaged 25 percent of the initial investment.

An internal rate of return of 25 percent doesn't reflect the income you're likely to see from the property in each year of ownership! Considering the internal rate of return and ignoring the actual cash flow isn't a good idea. You may find yourself counting on a return far better than what you'll actually enjoy. Nevertheless, the higher the rate of return touted, the better the investment promises to be. (The key word here is *promises* — like a promising relationship, it could go either way.)

The IRR doesn't reflect inflation. Ideally, you want an IRR that exceeds the rate of inflation. To compare the actual IRR of various properties, you should adjust the IRR for inflation. Calculate the IRR for a given period, then subtract the real (or, more likely, forecast) IRR for the same period. The current inflation rate is available from the Bank of Canada (www.bankofcanada.ca), which also offers a calculator to show the impact of inflation on your

investments (www.bankofcanada.ca/en/rates/investment.html).
Because an IRR is only an estimate of the expected return on your investment capital, consult your tax adviser regarding specific implications for
your situation.

Seeking professional advice

What do you do with an appraiser after you've found one? Here are a few
ideas:

✦ **Determine the most appropriate purchase price for a property:** An
appraiser's expertise in comparing property values can assist you in
determining how much you should pay for a particular property. You
can use some of the insights the appraiser offers regarding the property
as you negotiate the purchase price of your investment.

✦ **Develop a strategy for increasing the amount of mortgage financing
available to you:** An appraiser's assessment of a property's value may
flag opportunities for you to develop the property. You may be able
to use these to argue for a larger mortgage than you may otherwise
receive, as in the case of a residence to which you hope to add a rental
suite.

✦ **Appeal your tax assessment:** An appraiser's knowledge of the value of
your property and the rationale for the appraisal can help you craft solid
arguments if you need to appeal your property tax assessment. This is a
lucrative segment of many appraisers' business.

✦ **Determine future potential of the property:** An understanding of zoning
and other municipal policies that can influence a property's potential
enables some appraisers to provide insights into how you can make
better use of a property. The improvements can help increase the property's value or at least safeguard its value in the event that market conditions seem set to change.

✦ **Identify investors with an interest in purchasing your property:**
Knowing what makes a property valuable allows an appraiser to suggest target markets for your property, based on its various attributes,
including the value assigned to it. Read more about selling a property in
Chapter 4.

Of course, these are just some of the ways in which appraisers can assist
you. You may use any of these and other services appraisers provide as you
hone your portfolio and investing strategy.

Assessing Potential

Potential, by its definition, is something not yet realized. It is a power yet to be exercised. The potential of a property depends on several factors, from the fabric of the building itself to operating expenses and demand in the market for that kind of property.

To ensure the potential of the property you're considering buying is worth the listing price — and to rein in your own enthusiasm for the property itself — set some goals. Goals may be both personal and financial, and include operating expenses, potential return as an income-producing property and eventual sales offering, and perhaps even a redevelopment opportunity.

Operating expenses

Running a standard apartment building in Canada isn't cheap. Rents usually come in at just over double the expenses, which account for between 35 and 45 percent of gross income. Although expenses vary, this is a good rule of thumb. A vendor who suggests expenses are any more or any less may be toying with the facts.

Ask for records and documentation from the current owner for all the expenses, including property taxes, utility costs, maintenance costs, and insurance. That is a good starting point. Your mortgage costs could be less or more than the current owner's, but you're now in a position to estimate the expenses. What was the current owner getting for rental income? Was it a realistic price or considerably under what the marketplace would pay?

You don't need to contract someone else to obtain this information if you can obtain it yourself. However, you need to discuss the information with your accountant, to determine whether the investment will work for you. This is important for three reasons:

✦ You receive confirmation of the operating expenses, and are better able to understand how the building will fit into your portfolio, what rents you may want to charge, and so forth.

✦ You have insight into what a fair price for the asset should be, and better grounds for negotiating with the vendor.

✦ An audit is a way to identify areas that may benefit from upgrades and improvements, expenses that you'll want to bear in mind as you negotiate a price for the property but which could make the property more efficient and valuable over the course of your ownership.

An investment property with potential should have reasonable operating expenses. Knowing what these include, and how your management of the property will compare to the previous owner's, will indicate the property's potential to provide a decent return.

The fewer multiples of the net income — that is, rents collected less expenses — required to match the property's purchase price, the better the investment. The more efficient the property's operation, the lower the expenses (see *Real Estate Investing For Canadians For Dummies* for more on this topic). Professional advisers will help you draft a strategy for reducing expenses and making the most of your property!

Cap rates

When you purchase a revenue property, it will have what's known as a *cap rate*. Cap rates are similar to an annual rate of return, insofar as they are measures of the potential cash flow you can expect from the property. In short, the cap rate assumes a property is worth a multiple of its annual net operating income.

Cap rates often drop when markets are strong because more buyers are willing to pay higher amounts for the available assets. The greater the purchase price, the less favourable the net operating income is as a return. The cap rate is important to take into account when assessing a property's potential, because knowing where the cap rate is heading will give you an idea of demand for the asset you're considering buying and what kind of a return you're likely to see on it. Cap rates are hardly a sexy topic, but they're a common indicator of a property's merit.

For example, a cap rate of 6 percent on a $4 million office block indicates that the building annually returns $240,000 in net income to the owner. Had the owner paid $4.5 million or $5 million for the property, the cap rate (and return) would be less.

Compression in cap rates means markets are peaking and generally signal a shift to a sellers' market. You may wish to hold off buying until cap rates loosen. Ideally, you want to buy when cap rates are higher, because you'll enjoy greater ongoing yields. Should cap rates rise, however — whether because rents in the market improve or because demand for investment properties decreases — you will enjoy an advantage when it comes time to sell because the property may look better to potential purchasers who see that current rents are generating a decent return on the property at its current value. Your read of the market cycle will help you determine where cap rates are heading.

You might have bought that $4 million office block at a 6 percent cap rate, and began enjoying $240,000 in annual net income. But over the course of your first two years of ownership, the value rises to $6 million. You're still receiving $240,000 because of the lease agreements that are in place, but the cap rate has dropped to 4 percent. For the property to be as appealing to a potential purchaser as it was to you, either the value of the property would have to drop (bang! there goes your appreciation), or you'll need to find ways to boost the property's net income by $80,000 to $360,000. Looking for tips? Chapter 4 discusses ways to build property value.

Good neighbourhoods, bad buildings

One indicator of a building's potential is its neighbourhood. You probably wouldn't buy property in a neighbourhood that was heading for a tailspin, because the chances of finding someone to take it off your hands when you want to sell would be pretty slim.

Opportunities await investors who invest in lower-quality buildings in good neighbourhoods, however. Such properties have a potential to deliver steady returns based on the need for affordable product in good locations. Whether you're targeting the apartment or office market, smart management can make a winner out of a building that would otherwise be a loser.

A building may be lower quality for several reasons, including age, decor, maintenance issues, and layout. To make the most of such properties, look closely at what neighbouring buildings have to offer and attempt to match these offerings as much as possible in your own property. This may require you to make some cosmetic improvements, or tweak your marketing strategy.

Living it up

A lack of affordable housing in many better-off neighbourhoods creates opportunities for investors willing to maintain a property that is appealing without being extravagant. Some tenants, including students and young couples, are interested in affordable housing with quirks that make the property memorable, though not necessarily appealing to those able to afford a better-quality apartment.

Making the most of down-market apartments involves basic maintenance. The premises should be clean, the fabric of the building sound, and the apartment should exhibit an overall character that distinguishes it from others on the market. This will allow you to serve a niche market for housing, not with an *ex*clusive property but one that is more *in*clusive. The approach opens up a wider pool of tenants for you, an advantage when times get tough.

Operating costs may be higher for a down-market apartment building unless you make upgrades that ensure the building is energy efficient and won't require constant attention. Regularly inspect the premises to ensure it isn't costing you money to operate.

Renovations versus redevelopment

Gauging the potential of renovating a building versus redeveloping the site is worth doing when you're buying an older property, or one in need of maintenance. Most buildings have a useful lifetime after which it is more economical to demolish them and start over than renovate them. Unless, that is, you enjoy renovating properties and making something new out of them.

We discuss the calculations required to assess the relative cost of buying as opposed to redevelopment in this chapter under cost-comparison appraisals. Both renovations and redevelopment have their complications as well as benefits:

✦ **Complications** associated with renovations include the need to respect the existing structural elements of the building, potentially raising the cost of the project. You may also need to satisfy municipal requirements with respect to permitting and zoning, or building code issues if the building is old enough to require upgrades to bring it in line with current construction standards. Redevelopment, on the other hand, may make sense financially but could leave you with less than when you began if municipal development guidelines allow you to develop a smaller building on the site than currently exists.

✦ **Benefits** of renovating a property include a chance to redefine and reinterpret the existing structure, perhaps making the inner space more flexible and contemporary. You also have an opportunity to upgrade internal systems and create a building that's more efficient to operate. The result could be a building that's worth far more than the old one ever was or could be.

An analysis of the potential a renovation or complete redevelopment has to deliver a return in terms of cash flow, future sales value, and mere convenience will help you to decide whether the expense is worthwhile.

Understanding Due Diligence

Due diligence is unlike the appraisal process because it doesn't concern itself with value so much as with the facts regarding a property. The facts may include the appraised value, but they also include the stated condition of the property, whether or not clear title is available, and so forth.

Your job as a real estate investor is to make sure that everything the vendor has said about a property is in fact correct. Performing your due diligence also gives you a chance to satisfy your curiosity on matters that might not be critical, but which could help you gauge the true value of the investment you're about to make.

A careful eye is one of the attributes a good investor brings to real estate transactions. During the due diligence process, you have an opportunity to take a second look at what you think you know about the property, but also at any underlying factors that may create problems.

Buyers typically conduct due diligence after securing a property through a deposit or some other consideration that confirms their genuine interest in completing the transaction (we discuss the sale in Chapter 4). Because it occurs late in the process, buyers generally have enough knowledge about the property to be sure that it's right for them. Whether the due diligence bears that out, however, is another story. Consider due diligence as the final opportunity to review a purchase: Speak now or forever hold your peace!

The due diligence process can last as long as you please. The more complex the deal, the longer it lasts. For a simple purchase, such as a house, it can be as little as 24 hours. For an office tower or industrial building, the due diligence can last months. The less complex the deal, the greater the vendor's expectation of a short turnaround time. You won't find many single-family homes subject to weeks of due diligence!

Due diligence is an important step in the purchase process because it allows for the investigation of issues raised in *subject clauses,* or conditions, in the purchase agreement. These can ensure the deal closes smoothly. If you have lingering doubts about the appraised value of the property, or the prospects for the neighbourhood, due diligence can allow you to conduct further investigation of the property's value and potential. You may also wish to use the time to research the environmental quality of the site (if fears of contamination arise) or to double-check that no *liens* (outstanding legal claims) against the property or other issues, formally known as *encumbrances,* exist that could place you at risk if you buy.

To protect yourself, you can include many of the most contentious issues that could prevent the sale of the property in the subject clauses of the offer to purchase. Should due diligence uncover a significant problem, the subject clauses can give you an exit from the deal. We discuss subject clauses at greater length in *Real Estate Investing For Canadians For Dummies.*

Generally, due diligence is a means to limit your risk and cut any losses you could suffer when you purchase a property. Due diligence is a priority in three specific areas, which we cover in the following sections.

Sizing up the property

Making sure the property you're about to buy is a good investment is one of the main goals of due diligence. The central part of any real estate deal, the property, should live up to the expectations you have for it. Have you been told the basement doesn't leak during the spring thaw? Call in a specialist to do an assessment. Not sure whether the back portion can accommodate that renovation you're planning? Now's the time to check. (We include additional information regarding property inspections later in this chapter.)

Confirming the facts about a property, and its potential, can save you from several costly disappointments:

✦ You'll know that facts such as square footage are correct as well as the survey boundaries of the lot.

✦ You won't overestimate the property's ability to serve as an investment property.

✦ You'll know how the property will perform under various environmental conditions.

✦ You won't make the investment with unrealistic expectations.

Book VI Chapter 3

Scouting Properties: Where to Look and What to Look For

You may also be pleased to find that the property has more potential, or is even more suitable for your purposes, than you'd originally imagined. Either way, becoming more familiar with a property will allow you to avoid unexpected losses and enjoy greater clout in negotiating financing. This is especially true if you see an opportunity to increase the cash flow possible from the property, and have a plan for maximizing its revenue-producing potential. Lenders will often take the potential cash flow into account when they gauge your ability to service a debt.

Sizing up the vendor

Due diligence is also important in giving you a clearer picture of a property's vendor. We're not necessarily talking personal information here, but rather their reasons for selling and any reasons why you might want to be wary of what they're offering. In short, due diligence is an opportunity to shed further light on what the vendor brings to the table, aside from an asset that interests you.

Becoming familiar with the vendor is important, because circumstances that aren't readily apparent may be behind the sale. These include several factors that could influence the asking price. Should you dig up information about the vendor that doesn't quite match what you've been told, you might want to seek legal counsel in case there's potential for fraud.

Suspicious about a vendor? Checking a vendor's credit rating through Equifax (www.equifax.ca) may tip you off to potential dangers of the sale. Also make sure that every last bit of information in the offer to purchase is correct — down to the vendor's name and company (if included). Inconsistencies can indicate a potential problem.

Sizing up the deal

Due diligence is part of closing the deal, but the deal itself also requires scrutiny.

Two particular areas of interest to you are the financial and legal aspects. Double-crunch the numbers to make sure they work and fit in with your worst-case scenario for your portfolio. Make sure numbers such as the appraised value, potential return, and similar elements mesh with official figures.

Legal considerations include making sure you can secure clear title to the property, and that no competing claims to it exist. Verify that any renovations you have planned are in accordance with municipal bylaws.

Consult with your advisers to ensure the deal meets with their approval. They have the skills to examine the deal in greater depth than you can, and you should involve them as necessary throughout the due diligence process.

Inspecting a Property

A basic part of any due diligence related to real estate is the property inspection. Professional inspectors are available from several fields. Depending on their expertise, they may be able to provide either a general inspection or an in-depth examination and assessment of particular parts of the property.

We flag elements to which you may want to pay particular attention or ask for greater detail, and provide tips that may make it easier for you to determine which parts of a given property require the closest inspection. We also discuss inspection reports, and occasions when you should seek professional advice regarding the results of the inspection.

What to watch for

Depending on the age, type, and size of a property, a professional property inspector will spend a few hours or several days examining the property. The inspection should take into account the material integrity and soundness of a building and how the material integrity and soundness equip the building to withstand a major event such as a flood, fire, or earthquake. The inspection will often be visual, but a trained inspector will be able to flag particular areas for investigation by engineers or other professionals.

The focus of the inspection will centre on three main points:

✦ The building itself

✦ Site conditions

✦ Servicing and infrastructure

Keeping watch

Some of the features a property inspector will watch for are common to several types of real estate; others are pertinent to just one or two. Obviously you won't get an inspection report on an elevator shaft for that suburban bungalow you're buying to rent out, but the elevator might be on the list if you're buying a four-storey apartment property.

To give you an idea of things to watch for, here are a few categories that a property inspector assesses:

✔ **Driveway:** Condition of the concrete or asphalt; slope; potential for water and debris accumulation

✔ **Walkways:** Condition of the concrete or paving stones

✔ **Roof:** Slope and type of covering; condition of the flashing around chimney and vents; presence of skylights

✔ **Attic:** Condition; evidence of leaking; insulation extent and type

✔ **Laundry area:** Condition of the laundry tub and machine hook-ups; presence of electrical outlets and number

✔ **Garage:** Overall condition; type of firewall and condition; electrical outlets; presence of leaks and other factors that may affect overall maintenance

✔ **Interior rooms:** Overall condition; type and quality of floor coverings, wall coverings, and ceiling; assessment of plumbing, venting, and electrical systems; assessment of toilets, sinks, shower stall, and tubs

✔ **Basement:** Presence of cracked walls, sloped floor, and condensation; condition of windows and other means of access; presence of smoke detectors and sump pumps; type of electrical outlets

These three elements all play into the future value and potential risks you face if investing in the property.

The cost of an inspection reflects the time required to conduct it and prepare a report, but generally ranges from $300 to more than $1,000 for a residential property. If you're considering a commercial property, the cost will be much higher. Older and larger properties often take more time, resulting in more expensive reports, as more problems are typically present. The qualifications and expertise of the inspector, as well as demand in the market, also factor into pricing. The number of variables means some negotiation on price is possible, but make sure you obtain a written quote in advance.

Make a point of you or your realtor being present during the property inspection, to see exactly what was inspected. Some inspectors photograph areas of concern and include the images in their reports, a useful service if you're unable to accompany the inspector during the inspection. Being able to ask questions specific to the potential troubles is important. Your questions combined with the inspector's observations and experience may reveal issues that will make you want to run away from the deal as quickly as possible! When speaking to the inspector, take notes and ask questions regarding the possible cost of repairing any problems found.

Finding a property inspector

Buyers who have been burned will advise you not to turn to your Realtor for advice on a property inspector (the agent and the inspector could be in cahoots). Do your own legwork, beginning your search for an accredited property inspector with the Canadian Association of Home & Property Inspectors (www.cahpi.ca). Selecting a qualified inspector is as important as picking advisers. The CAHPI site is a fountain of useful information on property inspection, and features a directory of association members across Canada. Provincial associations are also good sources of potential inspectors. These include the following:

Canadian Association of Home & Property
Inspectors British Columbia
#5 - 3304 Appaloosa Road
Kelowna, BC V1V 2W5
Tel: 250-491-3979
Web: www.cahpi.bc.ca

Canadian Association of Home & Property
Inspectors Alberta
P.O. Box 27039, Tuscany RPO
Calgary, AB T3L 2Y1
Tel: 800-351-9993
Web: www.cahpi-alberta.com

Canadian Association of Home & Property
Inspectors Saskatchewan
P.O. Box 20025
RPO Cornwall Centre
Regina, SK S4P 4J7
Tel: 866-546-7888
Web: www.cahpi-sk.com

Ontario Association of Home Inspectors
1515 Matheson Blvd. East, Suite 205
Toronto, ON L4W 2P5
Tel: 416-256-0960
Web: www.oahi.com

Quebec Association of Building Inspectors
5–7777, Louis H. Lafontaine
Anjou, QC H1K 4E4
Tel: 514-352-2427
Web: www.aibq.qc.ca

CAHPI-Atlantic
3045 Robie Street, #257
Halifax, NS B3K 4P6
Tel: 888-748-2244
Web: www.cahpi-atl.com

The building council minutes for a condominium property should include reports from inspections the building council commissioned on any part of the property. These reports may flag areas that you'll want an inspector to investigate in any report you commission prior to your purchase.

The structure itself: Building confidence

A building inspection will tell you what's right about a building and what's wrong. The inspector you employ should inspect every accessible part of a building, including the following:

- ✦ Interior
- ✦ Exterior
- ✦ Attic area and roof
- ✦ Basement and crawl spaces

Particular buildings may have other specific areas worth inspecting. A condo building may have a parkade the inspector will examine, to flag any issues that may lead to charges owners will have to bear. A commercial or industrial property might have interior stairwells or hallways that require special attention. Feel free to request an inspection of an area that concerns or interests you. You want to make sure you're comfortable with every aspect of the building, and its suitability for the uses you have in mind, before you buy.

Site conditions: Grounding the deal

Site considerations such as drainage also demand consideration from an inspector, as these could factor into the future value of the property if a disaster strikes or you want to undertake a significant renovation or addition to the existing structure.

The property inspector will commonly assess the following:

- ✦ Garage, carport, and garden shed
- ✦ Steps, paths, and driveway
- ✦ Retaining walls separate from the building itself
- ✦ Fencing
- ✦ Septic field
- ✦ Surface water drainage and storm-water runoff

Certain areas of your site may concern you even before you receive the property report. These may fall outside the inspector's expertise or demand the attention of an accredited professional. Advice or a second opinion from an engineer, lawyer, or other consultant simply helps further your knowledge and comfort with the decision you eventually make regarding the property.

Servicing and infrastructure: Serving it right

Consider investigating the servicing (such as sewer, water drainage, electricity, cable, propane gas, and so on) provided to your property. Age, capacity, and maintenance history are factors worth taking into account as you consider whether disruptions in the operation of your property are likely.

Although you may not have to bear the cost of repairing damage to municipal infrastructure, being without key services is extremely inconvenient.

You can check with the building department of City Hall as to what types of municipal utilities or servicing are currently available, and if not, when they will be available, if at all, and what projected costs there might be for users.

Privately delivered utilities such as telephone and Internet connections are worth factoring in, too. More and more areas enjoy high-speed access, but it's still far from universal. The level of Internet service in a particular area may affect how you use the property or position it to potential tenants.

Inspection reports

Any given property report has the potential to deliver good, middling, or just plain bad news. As you read the report — typically a point-by-point assessment of the property that can run from just a few pages to hundreds of pages in length — focus on areas of particular interest to you and future buyers. These include the following:

✦ **Reason for the inspection:** This is a vital element because it indicates whether the inspection was routine or if a specific concern prompted it. A report conducted as part of due diligence generally counts as a routine report.

✦ **Areas not inspected:** As well as outlining the areas of the property that were inspected, the inspector will flag areas the inspection didn't cover. Perhaps the areas were inaccessible, or some obstacle prevented an examination. You may need to hire a specialist to investigate these areas if the inspector considers it beneficial. Some specialists you may need to consider include electricians, plumbers, painters, drywallers, mechanical contractors, and pest control and extermination specialists.

✦ **A summary of the property's condition:** The summary is the heart of a property report. It will detail both the good and the bad of the property.

✦ **A list of significant problems:** Problems flagged in the summary may require varying levels of attention. The inspector will detail the most urgent. Factor these into your negotiating strategy and your decision to purchase the property. Serious problems may prompt you to decline the purchase altogether.

Chapter 4: Closing the Deal

In This Chapter

✔ Getting the deal that works for you

✔ Signing the papers

✔ Building property value

✔ Preparing the property for sale

After you find a property you think will be a good investment, you've got to make it your own. In this chapter, we talk about negotiating a deal that fits your investment goals and closes as quickly and as smoothly as possible.

Because each transaction is as different as the people involved, we can't offer you the secret formula for the perfect deal. Instead, we walk you through a range of strategies that are good to have in your back pocket when you're at the negotiating table. (Knowing a few negotiating strategies will also prove helpful if you ever decide to sell your property, something we discuss later in this chapter.)

Negotiating a deal successfully is just one part of closing on your new purchase, however. To make sure your investment gets off to a good start, you need to clear away the financial and legal details. You also need to make sure the appropriate people are paid for their roles in the transaction. We guide you through the finer points of the purchase, and offer a checklist to help make sure you dot your *i*'s and cross your *t*'s. We also tell you what you need to know about becoming a full-fledged owner as you prepare to manage your investment and enhance its value.

Getting the Deal You Want

Finally! You're itching to own and you know that you've found the place you've been looking for. It's time to play *Let's Make a Deal,* a game that — for you — has three rounds:

✦ Offer

✦ Evaluation

✦ ACCEPTANCE — YOU WIN! — OR REJECTION — PLAY AGAIN! — OR COUNTEROFFER — not so quick, mate!

In this section we walk you through each stage, explaining the ins and outs of the process and offering tips to help you get the best deal possible.

Even though you may feel tempted to pretend you're a ruthless real estate mogul, you will reap more rewards through gracious deal-making at every stage of the negotiation process. Deals that work well for you and the vendor may lead to future deals and business relationships. Be serious and professional, but not unreasonable in negotiations.

Making an offer

In real estate, an offer is a formal document written up by the prospective buyer's realtor and passed to the vendor's realtor or real estate agent. It may all seem mighty impersonal, but you have a lot of influence over how the deal proceeds.

Being straightforward is one of the ground rules. Even if you're playing your cards close to your chest, every purchase offer requires a few basic elements:

✦ **Who is offering to buy the property:** Are you buying the property as an individual, a partnership, or a corporation? (We discuss the various types of ownership in Chapter 1.)

Be completely clear about who you are. Opening the door to an *assignee,* someone who could take over your position in the deal, may benefit you by allowing you to step back and enjoy an interest in the deal but not necessarily a front seat. Think twice about doing this, however, as the move could potentially create confusion about who the purchaser actually is. Similarly, clearly stating that you're bidding through a corporation may prevent you from bearing personal liability for legal claims if the deal falls through.

✦ **What amount you're willing to pay:** This amount should reflect everything you know about the market, the neighbourhood, and the seller's motivations. Knowledge of the market and a gutsy willingness to pay top dollar will ensure you have the attitude needed to outwit competing bidders for the property.

Offer the lowest reasonable price but make sure it's just that — reasonable. Low-balling could turn off the vendor, and may make you seem less than serious about doing a deal. By the same token, be ambitious and start with the ideal price and terms as determined by the market research you've done. The vendor, depending on the rationale for the sale, may find your lower bid attractive. Don't anticipate rejection; if the vendor counteroffers, you enjoy an opportunity to exact concessions. Concessions reflect the nitty-gritty of negotiating.

✦ **Any clauses you want to impose:** Your offer will come with strings attached, in the form of subject clauses. These are conditions you choose to place upon the vendor that will have to be fulfilled if your offer is to move to completion. State a specific date by which the clause has to be fulfilled, as well as the person whom the clause benefits (this also allows them to waive the condition if they choose). Setting conditions on the deal ensures you get the property you want and can also give you extra negotiating room. Some common clauses in your interest that you might write into the deal include:

- **Confirmation of financing:** You may need time to arrange a mortgage, or may plan to use proceeds from the sale of another property or investments to finance your new purchase. This clause will give you time to make sure you have the funds required, as well as reducing your risk should you not be able to secure the financing you hoped to get.

- **Deposit funds:** Your offer should state what happens to any deposit you place on the property to secure your interest. Ideally, your deposit should be sitting in an interest-bearing account, with interest accruing to you in trust until the deal closes. Should the deal fail to complete, you want to ensure you get your deposit back with the interest it was earning.

- **Conveyance of free title:** You want to be sure title to the property you're buying is clear; that is, free of any outstanding legal claims. Ensuring that's the case is typically the responsibility of the vendor. This condition should state what has to be done, and whose responsibility it is, and establish the deadline for clearing the title. A lack of clear title could limit your ability to make the most of your investment. It may require more time to clear the title of one property than another, but you'll want to set a time limit if you can't wait for title to be cleared. Some properties have too many claims upon them to make them worth your while, and a clause requiring free title will allow you to exit negotiations if that's the case.

- **Satisfactory inspections:** You may want to seek a second opinion about the property you're hoping to invest in, whether it's from your business partner, spouse, or an engineer. They may have expertise and insights you don't have. A structural engineer may notice weaknesses in the building that could save you headaches as a manager. Whatever the reason, make sure you set aside enough time to get the opinions you need to make an informed decision about your purchase.

- **Resolution of site conditions:** A growing area of concern for many purchasers is the legacy of a site's previous uses. You may want to stipulate that the vendor remediate site conditions, such as landscaping, so that the site approximates its original condition. Soil contamination is a more serious concern that could leave you liable to claims from the owners of neighbouring properties, so it's in your interest to make sure the vendor removes unwanted or dangerous materials (such as asbestos or urea formaldehyde foam insulation) from the site prior to the deal closing.

**Book VI
Chapter 4**

Closing the Deal

Condo (strata) units and apartment buildings may require special clauses. For instance, you may want the right to check out an apartment building owner's books to be sure that the building's cash flow is everything you think it is. Or in the case of a condo, you may want to subject the deal to information in the minutes of the strata council and engineers' reports on the integrity of the unit and building. This information could strengthen your bargaining position, allowing you to suggest a lower price than the vendor is asking. The minutes could also alert you to potential structural problems that may need repairs in the future. Knowing the potential dangers helps you make a decision so future assessments, if any, aren't a complete surprise.

The vendor may also stipulate certain conditions that you'll want to take into account:

✦ **Removal of conditions in the event of a backup offer:** The vendor may receive a competing bid that seems more attractive. To ensure the vendor has a free hand in the other negotiations, she will ask that you remove your conditions within a set period of time (usually 72 hours).

✦ **Confirmation of vendor take-back mortgage:** The vendor may have financed the last deal for the property you're interested in through a mortgage broker. To ensure the financing can be paid off through the proceeds from your purchase of the property, the vendor may ask for time to arrange this with the mortgage broker.

✦ **Deposit funds:** Just as you want to make sure your deposit is secure, the vendor wants to make sure the funds you deposited go toward the purchase price after the deal completes. The vendor will stipulate that they're nonrefundable and payable after all your conditions have been met.

✦ **Credit check:** Of course, you're an honest dealer. But the vendor may want to make sure that's the case, especially if she wants to pay off a debt with your payment for a property. Give her time to confirm your creditworthiness, so she's confident that you're her best offer.

✦ **Legal review:** You may want to make sure that you're buying a solid investment, but the vendor will also want to make sure you're offering a legitimate deal. Make sure you give the vendor as much time as you need yourself to make sure the deal is up to snuff and doesn't include legal loopholes or traps.

✦ **Expiry date:** Set a time limit for the evaluation period, usually a minimum of 24 hours, but for more complex deals you might extend it to three or four months. If you're considering purchasing urban land or a commercial property, it may sit under contract for months while due diligence proceeds. Make sure you have enough time to satisfy yourself and close the deal properly. Too short a time frame and you may not be able to satisfy your questions about what you're buying; too long, and the vendor may question your motives.

✦ **Closing date:** When do you want this all wrapped up? After your offer is accepted, you need a final date that gives both parties enough time to complete any outstanding due diligence and necessary paperwork. The date should respect both your desire to take possession and the needs of the vendor.

The various elements in the offer to purchase are important, not only because they will become the basis for the purchase contract if your offer is accepted, but also because you want to make sure they give the negotiations the momentum that helps you and the vendor to reach a satisfying deal.

Evaluating the bid

What are you waiting for? After you've submitted your offer, the vendor will evaluate it and eventually respond with outright acceptance or rejection, or a counteroffer and/or an offer to discuss. While you're waiting for the vendor's response, however, stay cool, but be collected. You'll be doing your own due diligence, enjoying a perfect opportunity to do research that strengthens your negotiating position. The information that you gather in fulfillment of the subject clauses (see above) can help you in the event that you have to respond to a vendor's counteroffer.

Hot markets raise the potential for competing bids, often several on a single property. Don't let your guard down! A willingness to make a better offer, based on both your research and the advice of your advisers, is key to gracious — and professional — negotiating. Your bid shouldn't be so far out of line with the state of the market that you lose credibility, but the early stages of a hot market can see significant appreciation in a property's value during the sales process. Outbidding a competitor, then selling the property further on in the cycle, may net you a healthy profit.

Finding acceptance

Like the moments just before the contents of the sealed envelope are revealed at the Oscars, the time waiting for the vendor's answer is filled with anticipation. But having kept on top of the market and having addressed your concerns about the property during the vendor's evaluation period, you'll be ready to handle counteroffers and maybe even exact concessions from the vendor.

Of course, if your offer is accepted, then you're ready to move on with closing the deal and becoming an owner. But if your offer is rejected, you may want to consider submitting an amended offer that addresses the vendor's concerns. Similarly, if the vendor thinks the prospect of a deal exists, he will counteroffer and set a deadline for acceptance, rather than simply reject your offer and walk away.

Planning to rent? Think ahead!

Nancy was about to buy her first house in an up-and-coming neighbourhood in Toronto. A single professional, Nancy knew the list price was in her range but she also knew having a tenant would help her job of making the payments that much easier. After Nancy took possession of the house, she searched for a tenant, and wasn't able to find one for three months — three months in which Nancy wasn't seeing rental income that she had been counting on.

Had Nancy been more experienced, she would have made advertising for tenants a condition of her purchase offer. The clause could have allowed her, in agreement with the vendors, to advertise and show the property to potential tenants. The clause would have given Nancy a head start on renting in what was admittedly a tough market. An abundance of rental properties meant that anyone interested in moving would have to give their existing landlord a full month's notice or end up paying double rent. Nancy bought the house early in the month, so the earliest that any prospective tenant could give notice and be able to move in would be approximately two months after she closed the deal.

Alternatively, Nancy could have included a clause in her offer that set the closing date four days before the start of the month in which she planned to rent the property. This would have been another way for Nancy to avoid losing three months' rental income.

Trying again

A counteroffer will test your negotiating skills. Ask your Realtor exactly why your offer was rejected. If you don't ask the question, you won't know the answer. Perhaps the vendor has discovered something about you in the course of the evaluation period that he feels he can use to leverage concessions from you. Perhaps the vendor knows a better offer than yours is in the offing and wants to see how far you're willing to go to secure the property. It helps to be able to provide an argument for the competitiveness of your offer. And whatever the circumstances of the counteroffer, be candid but professional as you hammer out a deal that satisfies both you and the vendor.

When there's a need to counteroffer, and price is an issue, don't immediately counteroffer a large price increase unless you know that it is in line with the vendor's expectations. Small price increases that become smaller as you approach the maximum price you're willing to pay may help wear down the other agent and seller, who won't want to waste time haggling. Of course, just beware that you don't lose the sale by frustrating the life out of the vendor. You may be able to divert attention from a lower price than the vendor might be willing to accept by focusing negotiations around issues like chattels (something we discuss under "Tallying the costs" in this chapter) and closing date.

Dotting i's, Crossing t's: Financial and Legal Paperwork

Closing can be within a few days of making an offer for a residential property or several months away for a complex transaction. Various changes may have taken place in the market or in financing conditions since the sale, but now's the time to get your papers in order and become an owner.

Wading through the legalese

Your advisers should be able to help you wade through the legalese on the various documents, but here are a few tips that will help you prepare. The most important document is the offer to purchase, as it will become the sale agreement if your offer is accepted. It sets out the terms and conditions between the parties and will become legally binding on the satisfaction of any subject clauses.

All contracts must be in writing to have legal effect. Although you may make verbal agreements, always make sure all agreements relating to the purchase are set down in the offer to purchase, and ultimately the sale agreement. That includes any withdrawal of your offer, which you have a right to do at any point prior to acceptance. But remember, if your offer has been accepted and signed prior to receipt of your withdrawal, a binding contract has occurred.

Tallying the costs

The offer to purchase will include a few financial figures in addition to the sale price of the property you hope to acquire. Keeping track of these figures could play an important role in structuring the deal. We discuss the figures of interest in the following sections.

Paying down the purchase

The cash deposit required to secure the property for you while the purchase completes is an important element of the contract. It usually takes the form of a cash deposit equal to 5 to 10 percent of the purchase price. The deposit makes the sale agreement binding, and in competitive situations may be increased to demonstrate sincere interest. Alternatively, it may be a token amount — we've heard of deposits of as little as 1 percent being made.

Make sure your deposit money goes into a lawyer's or real estate agent's trust account, where it is protected by provincial legislation. Never give your deposit funds to an individual or company that is not a lawyer or licensed real estate agent. Also, make sure your deposit is in an interest-bearing trust account with interest to your credit between the deposit date and closing date or when the funds are returned to you.

Make any purchase offer conditional on various requirements being met to your satisfaction. For example, subject to your financing, home inspection satisfactory to you, review of the condo corporation's financial statements and minutes over the previous two years, and whatever other conditions you care to impose. If your conditions are not met, and a deal isn't reached, you automatically get all your deposit monies back. If you place a deposit and remove all conditions and then change your mind and don't complete the deal, you could lose your deposit monies, plus be sued for any financial shortfall the vendor could suffer if they can't sell the property for the same price or more to someone else. Obtain legal advice on your rights in advance if you are considering trying to get out of a deal in this type of situation.

Though it is in your interest to offer the smallest possible deposit so that you don't tie up any more money than needed, it is sometimes worth laying down a bit extra to make it clear that you're serious about closing the deal.

Consult a lawyer if you opt to withdraw an offer or proceed with rescission of a signed contract. Several provinces have a rescission period that allows the parties to back out of a deal without penalty, but you may wish to incorporate such a clause in your offer to purchase. This could help avoid litigation regarding non-performance of an agreement to purchase or actions seeking damages for your failure to buy the property.

Court action is costly, however. Costs are currently between 25 and 40 percent of the damages awarded, meaning you need to take a good look at what you're actually going to gain from the time and stress involved in launching a lawsuit. (We discuss liability and court action in *Real Estate Investing For Canadians For Dummies [Wiley].*)

Chatting about chattels

Chattels include the moveable elements of a property. Occasionally, however, doorknobs and chandeliers also feature in the list of a property's chattels. Because tax implications are associated with the value of the property attributed to the land, the property, and the chattels, clearly stating what the chattels include is important.

Defining what each of these categories comprises is also a good idea. Chattels can be particularly contentious. A chattel is moveable, but items such as doorknobs and chandeliers that you might assume to be fixtures can be treated as chattels. Generally, fixtures aren't named in the agreement and are considered part of the purchase price. But to avoid future legal difficulties, it's worth stating that all fixtures are included except those specifically excluded in the agreement. You should also include a clause listing chattels.

Some properties have a history, a location, or a reputation that deserves a value in its own right. This is particularly true of commercial properties, less usually of residential properties. The value of this component, known as *goodwill,* should also feature in the offer to purchase. This relates specifically to the allocation of value when buying a property for tax purposes. For example, you could allocate W amount for the market value of the land, X amount for the depreciated value of the building, Y amount for any chattels (such as furniture) included in the building, and Z amount for "goodwill" — the long history of being leased to good, long-term tenants that make the revenue stream more attractive (and valuable to you as an investor).

The purchaser and vendor can enjoy tax benefits depending on the allocation of values to W, X, Y, and Z. For example, based on tax advice you could negotiate a lower overall sale price for the commercial building to the purchaser, in exchange for a higher value on the land, because the land could have capital gains tax savings. We know an investor who has a professional accountant review his purchase offer. One of the accountant's strengths is analyzing the tax implications of real estate investments. He usually encourages our investor friend to negotiate chattels separately from the property itself, to allow for extra leeway when it comes to calculating profits.

Offering a rewarding fee

Any commission owing on the sale of the property, usually a percentage of the purchase price, should appear in the contract to purchase. The contract should also indicate to whom the commission is owing. We talk more about this in the next section.

Paying the piper (and everyone else)

Closing a sale requires paying not only the vendor, but also the various advisers and professionals who've helped you make the investment.

The vendor, not the purchaser, pays the commission owing to the Realtor. If you use a "buyer broker," this realtor splits the sales commission according to an agreed-upon formula. The vendor and the realtor will negotiate the commission in advance and confirm it in writing in the listing agreement. The amount of the commission paid is negotiable, and can vary considerably depending on the circumstances.

The fee for legal services required to transfer title of the property and doing the mortgage documentation is also negotiable. You should comparison shop in a competitive marketplace because pricing is frequently negotiable. The standard fee range could be from .25 to .50 percent of the purchase price for transfer of title and mortgage legal services, but it could be higher or lower based on various factors. Taxes and disbursements (out-of-pocket expenses) are extra, of course. Have a fixed quote for all the legal fees confirmed in advance in writing to avoid any confusion. The quotes also make it easier for you to cost out the transaction!

Some property investors take a particular interest in watching every penny they spend when buying or selling a property. The attention given to each deal allows maximum net after-tax profit (with the help of an accountant, of course). One strategy is to use the same real estate agent to both buy and sell properties. The solid relationship allows investors to negotiate an attractive commission on all deals.

You also have to take several taxes into account:

✦ Sales taxes, provincial taxes, and the harmonized sales tax (HST) in some provinces and the federal goods and services tax (GST) in others, are applicable to chattels (making it important to factor the value assigned chattels into the purchase offer).

✦ Though HST or GST isn't charged on resale homes, it may be owing on substantial improvements to a property.

✦ Provincial property purchase tax, or land transfer tax, which varies from province to province, will also be due.

Many provinces have harmonized sales taxes (HST), which combine the federal GST with the provincial sales tax. Although a combined tax shocks buyers when it's first introduced, Atlantic Canada has been living with it since 1996 and it didn't dampen sales activity when property boomed a decade later. The tax is applied the same way as the GST to closing costs, although a rebate may exist for homes priced below a certain level.

Building Property Value

Appreciation of property, and in turn your portfolio, doesn't have to be a spectator sport. Developing a strategy that allows your properties to rise beyond their natural value in a market is part of wise management.

Strategies either can involve hands-on involvement or be part of the general management of the property. For example, the decisions to invest in maintenance or even do a complete overhaul of the property are examples of strategic decisions that can boost the property's value. On the other hand, improving the tenant mix, raising rents, and giving tenants greater responsibility for utilities and services (topics we discuss as part of "Managing Expenses," later in this chapter) are management strategies that involve taking a look at your books to see what can improve the property's performance.

We could remind you to check with your accountant (never a bad thing), but keep in mind as well that consulting firms exist that can help you devise a strategy to boost your property's value and overall performance. Many appraisers also handle this kind of work, so talk to your local chapter of the Appraisal Institute of Canada (`www.aicanada.ca`) for references. The real estate firm you deal with may also know consultants with the expertise you're seeking. A simple Internet search for "real estate consultant" brings up people with diverse skills, so finding a consultant who can serve your needs may require networking until you find the one who's right for you.

Ongoing maintenance

Maintenance expenses factor on the return you file with the Canada Revenue Agency, so it makes sense to understand how they'll affect the amount of tax you pay now and in the future.

One of the most important distinctions your accountant will make when it comes to investing in maintenance is the difference between

✦ Current expenses, which you can write off for the tax year in which they're made

✦ Capital expenses, which you must deduct through the capital cost allowance for depreciation

Your accountant can tell you the dollar threshold at which a simple expense becomes a capital expense. Knowing the basic distinction between the two allows you to schedule maintenance and renovations in a way that delivers the best return on your investment through write-offs and the like.

Current expenses

Current expenses are the minor costs of operating a business. In the case of an investment property, they can include

✦ Mortgage interest

✦ Phone charges

✦ Advertising

✦ Cleaning and maintenance supplies

✦ Maintenance and landscaping services

✦ Property insurance and taxes

✦ Utilities

Major equipment purchases and direct investment in the property itself, such as renovations, are capital expenses.

Book VI
Chapter 4

Closing the Deal

Typically, current expenses are inescapable. Although you can economize on various operational costs, items like property insurance are annual costs that are difficult to avoid. You either have them or you don't. By the same token, greater control over current expenses will give you a better handle on your overall cash flow.

Knowing where your cash is going — and when — helps you assess your cash flow. Analysis of your spending habits could prompt you to economize in some areas and boost spending in others. Accounting software packages can help you crunch the numbers.

Scheduling regular payments so that you aren't hit with a load of expenses at any one time can help you achieve a stable cash flow with fewer strains and hiccups. No sense letting bills pile up only to deal with them later, or to leave yourself open to a massive run on your bank account. Paying all your bills at once may be a cathartic experience — and we won't deprive you of it if that's the case — but paying your bills gradually allows you to develop your savings steadily and brings greater discipline to your investing habits.

Current expenses are great when tax time comes around because you can use them to offset income earned. Although you have to pay for them out of cash flow, in the case of a rental suite in your home the expenses related to the operation of the rental suite may completely offset the income you derive from the suite. This may sound like a bad thing, but considering the rental suite is in your primary residence, the result is actually a more economical residence for you!

Even if expenses don't completely offset taxes owing, they reduce what you have to pay even as they make your investment property that much more viable to operate. Not claiming current expenses is the easiest way to leave money on the table at tax time.

Keep accurate records of expenses related to your investment property. If you don't you'll risk missing out on deductions you're entitled to claim, which could hurt your investment's bottom line significantly.

Not all current expenses are eligible for deduction, however. Be especially careful if any of the expenses you hope to claim have a personal component, and consult with your accountant to be sure the expenses you're claiming are legit. Claiming deductions the taxman later disallows will increase the taxes you owe, but also raises the risk you'll be paying interest on unpaid taxes — a potentially hefty amount if the deduction is disallowed several years after you file the return.

Recouping sales taxes

Building value in your property may mean boosting cash flow through charges for services, such as rental of amenity or fitness rooms, laundry facilities, and parking. Some service charges may allow you to charge GST/HST, which you could register to do — and then be eligible to set those charges against the GST/HST you're paying out for supplies needed to operate or maintain the building. This reduces the amount of tax you're paying by creating an income stream that generates some of the tax dollars you owe, and perhaps revenue from the services you're offering will cover the rest.

Those service charges will also make your balance sheet more appealing to future purchasers, because your property will be seen as generating greater revenues than comparable properties whose owners haven't taken advantage of the revenue opportunities. On the other hand, make sure you aren't seen as a grasping, penny-pinching individual by your tenants. Your property might well be seen as more expensive to potential tenants unless you're providing value for the money you're taking in.

A market that's leaning in the buyer's favour may require you to do more to a property in order to sell it than you had expected. Ongoing maintenance helps you show the property at its best. Fresh paint, new siding, and even landscaping each help your property make a better impression on buyers and potentially boost the return it delivers. And, you may be able to deduct the entire cost as a current business expense on that year's tax return. (Not the siding, however — read the section on capital expenses below for what doesn't qualify as a current expense.)

Capital expenses

Capital expenses include major expenditures for the structural improvement of a property, such as new siding, windows, and insulation, as well as major equipment purchases. Your accountant can provide the most current information on what qualifies as a capital expense.

The investments you make in a property help enhance its value to potential purchasers. Regular upgrades ensure the property is in a condition to sell no matter when an opportunity arises. A poor market typically presents the best time to invest in your property, however, for two reasons:

✦ **Low tenant demand:** A market that's seeing little interest in the kind of property you've got because of low demand from tenants offers an opportunity to invest in upgrades because you may be disturbing or displacing fewer tenants. Similarly, a building hit with higher-than-usual vacancies is a chance for you to make improvements that could attract new tenants, or to reassess the current tenant mix and reposition the property to target a new kind of tenant.

✦ **Potential for appreciation:** A buyer's market is a great time to prepare for a seller's market. Upgrading at a low point in the market cycle may allow you to make cost-effective improvements that could better position your property to take advantage of an improvement in the market when it happens. The greater the appreciation, the better the return on your investment.

Adding to the value of your assets during a poorer period in the market increases their ability to provide leverage for purchases in the future. A general upswing in the market will tend to raise the value of all properties. You'll be glad you enhanced your equity in a property when the price was low.

By definition, you can't claim capital expenses in a single swoop; you can only deduct them gradually in accordance with the rules of the capital cost allowance. Making a huge capital investment in the hope of writing it off in the first year will result in an unpleasant surprise come tax time. You'll end up paying more tax than you had expected, and have less money with which to do it, crunching your cash flow.

Capital expenses help ensure a property remains a good investment, above and beyond the everyday maintenance you have to do as a landlord. Thanks to depreciation rules, capital expenses provide ongoing opportunities for deductions that promise to offset your investment income from the property for years at a time.

On the other hand, strategically deferring capital expenditures can allow you to make investments in a property at a time when the capital expense will do you the most good. For example, when cash flows are tight, upgrading a property can offer a significant first-year deduction against limited rental income, reducing the tax payments required of you. As income improves, partly (we hope) due to the upgrades, you'll have more cash to pay an increasing amount of tax but still be able to claim a significant amount of capital expenses.

Reserving capital for improvements may also allow you to diversify your investment portfolio. It pays to consult with your accountant on a proper strategy for deferring maintenance. If the roof's leaking, no sense painting your building just because it's looking a bit drab. Although both could improve the appeal of the property, the roof is clearly a more urgent matter than the paint job.

As with current expenses, it pays to make regular capital investments both to ensure the property is always in tip-top shape, and also to prevent the hit to your cash flow.

Renovating for fun and profit

For some, renovating properties and reselling them is a way of life. When it comes to revenue-generating investment properties, however, you may have other considerations.

An established tenant base may make renovations difficult, for example, or perhaps you've just bought the property and are trying to stabilize its cash flow before undertaking major improvements. Perhaps the market is hot enough that improvements aren't required to keep tenants. Any mix of reasons may factor into your decision to renovate or postpone such improvements.

Before undertaking a renovation, make sure what you're proposing works out in terms of payback (see Table 4–1 for an idea of the scale of benefit you can expect from some common procedures). It doesn't make sense to undertake a renovation that allows, for example, a rental suite in your home if the cost is going to outweigh the rental income or resale value of the home. Talk to your accountant and other advisers for their opinion on the situation before you undertake a renovation project.

Table 4–1	Recovery on Renovation Costs		
Renovation project	*Recovery on resale*	*Renovation project*	*Recovery on resale*
Adding a full bath	96%	Adding insulation	65%
Adding a fireplace	94%	Adding a room	62%
Remodelling kitchen (minor)	79%	Re-roofing	61%
Remodelling kitchen (major)	70%	Adding a wood deck	60%
Remodelling bathroom	69%	Adding a greenhouse	56%
Adding a skylight	68%	Replacing windows, doors	55%
Adding new siding	67%	Adding a swimming pool	39%

Substantial renovations — those involving 90 percent or more of the building — may be eligible for tax rebates. (This typically excludes minor additions such as a porch, sunroom, family room or bedroom, or the construction of more than one room.) The Canada Revenue Agency allows you to claim a rebate on GST/HST paid on costs related to the purchase of the land and construction, providing the fair market value of the home after the renovation is $450,000 or less (this amount may change, so be sure to check with the Canada Revenue Agency). Keep in mind that you won't be able to sell the remade home without charging GST/HST, however, as the substantial renovations you've completed put the property in the same class as a new home.

Doing renovations to your primary residence is a good way to boost the resale value of your home — added value on which you don't have to pay capital gains tax. And if the renovation is of a property other than your primary residence that you've been using for rental income, renovation expenses reduce the taxable capital gains you'll realize when the property sells.

Take a rental property, for example: When a renovated property sells, renovation costs are tallied with the property's original purchase price and the sum is subtracted from the sale proceeds. What's left over is the capital gain, which is taxed at 50 percent. For a $150,000 home renovated at a cost of $25,000, the sum is $175,000. But if proceeds from the property's sale total $200,000, you've realized a capital gain of $25,000 — half of which you have to hand over to the government. This may sound bad, but if the renovations weren't taken into account you would be paying capital gains on $50,000!

Managing Expenses

Given the number of current and capital expenditures you potentially face as a landlord, the strategy you draft for your property should seek to effectively manage — ideally, minimize — the money flowing out as well as maximize the money coming in.

Every property has its costs, so a key decision you need to make as owner and operator of a property is who will pay for the cost of running the property. If you're the primary user, you won't have a lot of other people willing to cover costs stemming from your use. But if you lease out the building to tenants, you have opportunities to share costs and thereby increase your margins.

In this section, we discuss opportunities for you to lower operating costs, explore which items you can manage alone, and identify expenses that you can legitimately ask tenants and building users to cover. We also discuss other opportunities to make good on expenses through savvy tax filings and wise negotiating when the time comes to sell a property.

Distributing costs

The skill of knowing where to cut costs and how to spend wisely goes by the old-fashioned name of prudence. And it's a virtue, especially when you're confronted with many costs and perhaps too little time to assess them all as much as you would like. A prudent investor (that's you) knows which costs to watch, which ones to cut, and which ones to pass along to others. Your goal should be to allocate costs in a way that makes the most sense for everyone, without shirking your duties as landlord (we discuss some of these in Chapter 1).

For example, many landlords pay for heat and hot water, but leave electricity to their tenants. Why? Although different tenants have different comfort levels when it comes to heating, it doesn't make sense for every unit to have its own heating system. At least with electricity, a separate meter can track energy consumption. Heating is a lot more difficult to track, unless of course the radiators run off electricity.

What to watch

A simple assessment of your building can highlight the various expenses it faces each month, or on an annual basis. For example, property taxes and insurance, utilities, and garbage pickup are hefty charges that require attention. Maintenance, repairs, and landscaping (including snow removal) have to be addressed. Although some of the costs are fixed for the long term (which can be as little as a year), others crop up in the regular running of a property. Tenancy legislation typically requires you to cover the replacement cost of anything that was in the suite when the tenant moved in that later breaks down, whereas the tenant has to cover the cost of repairs (hence the safeguard of damage deposits). Landlords are legally on the hook to replace items they've provided in the suite that wear out, but most tenants won't call their landlord if a light bulb blows or similar small items need replacing.

Damage is another matter, which is why *damage deposits* — typically a half-month's rent that covers damage a tenant may inflict on leased premises — exist. The laws governing landlord–tenant relations in your province set some basic ground rules for these, so familiarize yourself with them. Most jurisdictions also have free booklets in lay language explaining these types of things. The information is typically available online through your provincial government website.

Due diligence prior to your purchase should provide a clear picture of the average annual expenses associated with the property. This information, combined with a consultation with your accountant, should highlight areas where you may want to make changes. Perhaps you'll decide to pass along some of the costs to your tenants, or a review of your expenses may flag areas where you're spending more money than necessary and need to economize.

What to absorb

Typically, the more an expense applies to tenants as a whole or the common cost of operating your property, the more reasonable it is for you to cover it. For example, garbage collection is usually handled on a per-building basis rather than tenant by tenant. It makes sense for you to cover the costs associated with garbage collection, but electricity, gas, cable television, telephone, and high-speed Internet are items best left to the individual.

Making it clear that the rent you're asking covers certain utilities may make your suite more attractive to potential tenants who don't want to deal with bills. You may even be able to charge a premium for the suite. Make sure you're stating a competitive rate for the utilities, however. Don't, for example, argue that the apartment is $750 a month and utilities $50 a month when a standard electricity bill in your area is typically closer to $25 a month.

Just because you pay upfront for utilities and the like doesn't mean you have to actually bear the cost! Tallying your average monthly operating expenses and dividing the total by the number of tenants in your building is, after all, one way of determining the rent to charge. The expenses should work out on a per-suite basis to something less than the average annual rent in your area. If not, you need to either seriously question the viability of the investment, or make upgrades that allow you to charge more.

What to pass on

Of course you can pass along the entire cost of operating a building to tenants, but it isn't usually advisable. The tenant of a suite in your basement is unlikely to be willing to pay a rent that reflects the sum of your property taxes, utilities, and other expenses. Similarly, if you've invested in a strip mall with five bays of varying sizes, you may want to divide garbage collection fees equally but pro-rate property taxes according to unit size.

Key items to pass along to tenants directly are regular, recurring metered utilities such as hydro and natural gas. Unless you're able to track the consumption of utilities on a per-suite basis, however, handing the responsibility to just one tenant is probably not a good idea. Living in a duplex, the natural gas, which powers the hot water tank, can be cut off because a neighbour didn't pay the bill. The mistake of one causes distress to many. The situation can take several hours to resolve, embarrassing the landlord and prompting tenants to think owning their own home might not be such a bad thing.

Natural gas-fired fireplaces are appealing, but not everyone is as attentive to them as they should be. Unregulated use can end up consuming a great deal of natural gas. The result is that many property developers are ensuring each suite has control and responsibility for natural gas consumption. This prevents individual building users and tenants generally from bearing the cost of someone else's profligacy.

Determining how much gets passed along may be part of the bargaining process with prospective tenants, particularly if you're a landlord with commercial property. You may have a basic asking rent in mind, but by negotiating other elements of the lease you may be able to secure a deal landing you a long-term tenant and stable revenues.

Recouping expenses

Developing a strategy for recouping expenses has something to do with passing along costs, but it also has to do with tax planning and knowing something about the marketing of your property. You may not be able to recoup every cost immediately, but knowing the opportunities can help you plan to take advantage of opportunities when they come up in the future.

Book VI
Chapter 4

Closing the Deal

From tenants

Typically the go-to people when expenses rise, many landlords opt not to raise rents on existing tenants and instead look to boost income received from new tenants.

On the one hand, limitations typically apply to increases made to rent during the tenancy term, but the usual limitations on rent increases don't apply when a lease is negotiated afresh. The new lease agreement allows you to boost rents immediately to reflect current costs.

 Minor upgrades to units can justify a rent increase beyond that which current expenses indicate you should charge. By increasing your margins, you make the property a better investment with an operating income that's more desirable to future owners of the property. They'll want, after all, to get a piece of the pie you've been enjoying.

From the taxman

Seeking higher rents from tenants boosts your income, but structuring your expenses strategically allows you to offset a fair amount of your income.

 More important, your accountant can advise you on tax mitigation strategies that may allow you to recoup cash during the ownership of the property and on its sale. We're not tax experts, so we leave it to those in the know to steer you in the right direction.

From purchasers

Negotiating a good deal for a property whether you're a buyer (see Chapter 3) or a seller (see the next section in this chapter) should include attention to the operating expenses and the investment a property requires to keep it in top shape.

An owner who's worked hard to bring down a property's operating costs through sound management and investments in its operations may ask a prospective buyer for more than the property alone is worth. As a vendor, being able to tell the story of the property, where it's come from and how much its performance has improved, can significantly boost the return. A buyer, on the other hand, may argue for a discount that reflects shortcomings in a property.

Being in both positions — both as the buyer negotiating a discount and the vendor talking up the price of a property to reflect your achievements — is where you want to be. Recouping the costs associated with a property from the time you purchase it is part of the strategic buying and selling investors have a chance to do.

Knowing When to Sell

Just as you can increase your potential gain by buying when the market's low, you can improve your return by selling as the market's rising. Gauging when your returns are as good as they're going to get is difficult, however. (We discuss market cycles in Chapter 3 — check it out if you need a few tips.)

An investment not only helps you to make more of your resources in the present, but also promises to help you do more in the future. Many investors invest with a view to funding their retirement, so devising a disposition strategy that helps achieve your financial goals is integral to the financial plan you develop.

Major reasons for disposing of assets include rebalancing your portfolio in favour of more liquid or higher-yielding investments, and securing funds for retirement or in accordance with your estate plan.

A standard strategy is regular renewal of your portfolio, either through maintaining existing assets or trading up to new or higher-yielding properties. Consider the strategy of pyramiding. Not to be confused with pyramid schemes, *pyramiding* involves the purchase of one or two select assets on a regular basis and the sale of others, ensuring that your portfolio constantly renews itself and doesn't become stale. Pyramiding also provides an opportunity to review your investments and assess how your financial plan is helping you achieve the goals you've established.

When you're looking to sell, you may face some added incentives to move a property that could affect your judgment of what constitutes a good return. These include the following:

✦ The desire for a prompt sale, for personal or business reasons

✦ A need for proceeds to finance other investments

✦ An inability to finance repairs or improvements to the property

✦ A slowing market that could make it difficult to sell a property in the future

Striking a realistic balance between your needs and the state of the market improves your chances of securing a return that satisfies you.

Gauging your needs

Here's our best advice when it comes to selling an investment property: *Know your goals.* These may dictate your willingness to accept a range of offers, the degree of variation you'll accept, and how far you're willing to go to strike a deal. Your goals may also help you feel comfortable accepting less for the property than you might otherwise, if, say, exiting a sour partnership is the priority.

For example, if you're selling a piece of property to finance a new business venture, you may wish to sell only so much as will garner you the amount you need. Or, if you're selling an entire property and that isn't enough, you may want to consider a more creative deal structure. You may own a property that's also a business, such as a bed-and-breakfast or a gift shop. You may consider selling the property but striking a deal that allows you to stay on as manager until you've recouped the amount you hoped to secure.

The urgency of your needs may also prompt you to accelerate a sale, taking a lower price for a property than you might have hoped because a better opportunity awaits or the cash flow on the operation isn't panning out for you. Divesting yourself of the property may deliver a better return than holding it till you receive a better offer. Cutting your loss of sleep over a bad investment sometimes means taking a loss on the financial side.

Include the tax implications of any capital gains possible from a sale in your marketing plans. Strive to sell properties on which you expect significant capital gains in a year where you have seen significant losses on other investments. The losses offset the capital gains on real estate investments, ensuring even bad investments deliver a benefit.

Some investors quibble over the list price for a property they want to sell only to have the market drop in the meantime, rendering the discussion of the list price moot and guaranteeing that nobody gets what they want — not the folks who want to sell high, and not the folks who want to sell immediately. Everyone loses when it comes to the closing price, and we won't even mention the added stress.

Waiting out the market

When the market's not in your favour, as a seller, you can take several steps to make the most of your time (and investment). Here are a few suggestions:

✔ Boost the so-called "curb appeal" of the property through inexpensive steps such as painting, minor landscaping, and the like to improve its appeal to prospective buyers.

✔ The small improvements may allow you to increase rents over the normal annual increase limit. This ensures that you maximize the cash flow from the property before you sell. You're responsible for making sure you're getting the most revenue from the property you can, while you've got the opportunity!

✔ Look for ways to decrease expenses on the property. For example, maybe you can arrange for the tenant to cut the lawn or do other maintenance work for a reduction in rent, which would cost you less money than if you paid an outside contractor to do the ongoing work.

✔ Reduce your debt-servicing costs if possible. For example, your mortgage may be coming up for renewal. Negotiate the lowest possible mortgage rate with a mortgage broker, taking out a long-term mortgage at the more favourable rate and extending your amortization period to 30 years to reduce your monthly payments.

✔ Monitor trends and surveys to get a sense of when the market appears to be going up again, and be ready to sell.

Gauging the market

As we discuss in the previous section, your circumstances may dictate that you can't wait until a market turns favourable to turn over your property. Ideally, you want to sell during a *seller's market,* when buyers are plentiful in relation to the supply of available properties and prices are rising with demand.

The cyclical nature of the real estate market means a seller's market won't always exist, however. Gauging when to enter the market takes research, something we discuss in Chapter 3, but if you're serious about selling you may want to test the waters to see what the market will bear. An appraiser can help you judge the several market factors that could come to bear on your property, and the realtor you enlist to handle the sale can flag the property to potential buyers and see if any bite. Any offers received during these preliminary forays into the market could go firm.

Regardless of when you go to market with a property, whether it's a case of soft-pedalling it or a full-on market blitz to find a buyer, don't forget to be professional. Bringing a property to market too often can give it a well-worn scent that doesn't wash with buyers. In fact, you may need to rinse off the scent of disinterest before a sale actually takes place! If that's the case, be prepared to give the property a dramatic facelift, or, more simply, wait till the market's forgotten its previous inability to sell.

If you're unsure about market conditions, it probably makes sense to bring a property to market gradually. That doesn't mean moving it closer to the street or selling it one brick at a time; rather, it's a question of building interest in the property before you begin marketing it in earnest. You might opt for a bit of gentle marketing, for instance, treating the initial offers seriously so that potential buyers have the sense you know what you want. This helps to discreetly build momentum around a property until a deal actually comes together. People may talk about how long it took the property to sell, but they won't be able to gainsay your discretion and handling of the deal.

Managing the Sale

Securing a great deal for a property is just as complicated for the seller as the buyer. Although the vendor holds the right to reject any purchase offer, the only offers coming forward are what the market is willing to pay.

Given these conditions, managing a sale is just as important to the vendor as negotiating skills are to a potential purchaser. The vendor can position the property and spark demand for it if buyers respond to the narrative woven around the property and the basic fundamentals of the property are strong.

In this section, we explore the sale process from the perspective of the vendor (that's you) and tell you how to achieve the best deal possible from your real estate — even when you're cutting losses because the property or the surrounding neighbourhood is experiencing a downturn.

Becoming a vendor

You may have spent your entire investment career buying properties. Now the time has come to sell. Making the transition to a vendor requires turning the tables and being as respectful, yet hard-nosed, with buyers as you were with the people who sold you the properties.

We advise against buying a property without the assistance of a realtor. Naturally, here we advise against selling without a realtor's assistance. A realtor's expertise can save you a lot of time, stress, market exposure, potential legal difficulties, and a host of other troubles.

Avoiding personal exposure in the market may be one of the best reasons to work with a realtor. A realtor helps shield you from excessive scrutiny, especially if you're trying to sell a less-than-desirable property in your portfolio. A healthy measure of anonymity may also be an advantage as you review and assess offers.

On the other hand, the deal may be such that a face-to-face meeting benefits the negotiations. Your realtor can screen offers and select the candidates most likely to buy from you.

Whatever the case, maintain an open attitude even when working through a realtor. Your negotiating style sets the tone for the discussions. Your mission as vendor is to move the property, not hold it forever.

Preparing the property

Buyers may have the burden of due diligence, but as vendor, you've got the challenge of preparing the property to look its best. You may be able to contract out elements of this to *stagers,* consultants that transform properties to look better to a target market, but the ultimate decisions are yours. The real estate firm with which you're dealing may have people in-house who can help you stage your home; or your community may have one of the growing number of firms that focus on home staging. Some home stagers are represented by the Canadian ReDesigners Association (`www.canadian redesignersassociation.org`).

Preparing to sell a property involves three basic steps:

1. Research the market, particularly comparing similar properties

2. Identify the property's prime selling points, and the value you believe these add to the property

3. Enhance the property's appearance and appeal to potential purchasers

Researching the market

Knowing the kinds of properties available in a given neighbourhood or market area helps you position your property to prospective buyers. The research isn't much different from what you would do as a buyer, only this time you're looking at the market from a vendor's perspective.

You may have a one-of-a-kind home, a piece of land in a locale where others have sold for an elevated price, or a commercial property in an area that's booming. Or, recent sales information and a conversation with your Realtor may prompt you to downgrade your expectations of your property's worth.

Knowing the features of your property that will appeal to the typical buyer for your area is also important. Research the following to develop an argument why a given buyer should snap up your property:

✦ **Demographics,** which may have changed since you purchased the property and bear re-examination

✦ **Site conditions** may make renovation or redevelopment of the property an option for the next owner

✦ **Buyers** scouting properties in your area may require you to position your property in such a way that it appeals to their interests, motivations, and investment goals, and allows you to achieve an appropriate return.

Getting the scoop on these elements is key to meeting the market — and your buyers — where they're at.

Identifying selling points

The features of your property that appealed to you or worked for users may not strike a chord with the next owner, but they're what you know. Use the aspects of which you're most proud as starting points for the pitch to prospective buyers that you'll craft with the agent selling your property. Your agent may know what's appealing to the current market, but you know your property better than your realtor and can provide a list of advantages. These talking points help the realtor frame the property for potential buyers.

Your inventory of selling features should include recent improvements and any major renovations or upgrades that support the asking price. Recent landscaping, a new furnace or heating system, or even new carpeting all deserve a mention. Don't forget to mention intangible improvements too. A reversal in a rental property's stagnant occupancy rate indicates a significant improvement in overall cash flow that highlights how you have enhanced the property's stature since purchasing it.

Neighbourhood amenities such as transportation links, shopping centres, and public amenities including schools, parks, and playgrounds warrant a reference. In short, anything highlighting a property's worth helps your realtor weave a compelling narrative to attract potential buyers.

Grooming the property

We've all seen sad-sack properties with lots of potential that somehow just don't grab us. You don't want your property to come across the same way. To improve the "curb appeal" of your property, make it as attractive as possible. Inside and outside, the home should appeal to the prospective buyer — enough to command a decent price in short order.

Knowing the kind of buyer to whom a property most likely appeals is only part of your focus in making an appropriate presentation. Getting rid of unnecessary possessions that detract from a sale is also effective. Many people like their surroundings to be filled with familiar items, no matter how unattractive or impractical, and they underestimate how unappealing their personal effects are to complete strangers. The decor and detritus of your life could be a complete turnoff to buyers.

Rather than getting rid of personal effects completely, simply remove them during the sales period and keep them in storage until the sale is complete. (Although if the sales process has also inspired you to cull your stuff, we won't discourage you!)

Working with buyers

Buyers negotiate to get the most possible for the lowest reasonable price. This gives them a better chance at seeing some appreciation in their investment. By that same token, you're aiming for the greatest possible return on your property; negotiate with that aim in mind.

The two meet in mutual respect for the other's objectives. Specifically, focus your negotiations on the following:

✦ Price

✦ Conditions

✦ Benefits like chattels, upgrades, and goodwill

Pricing it right

A common strategy is to price a property slightly higher than what you hope to receive. This forces the buyer to meet your terms with an offer, usually less than your asking price, that should come near the real value of the property. A buyer willing to pay the asking price without questions is a sign you've either priced the property too low, or are extremely fortunate.

Buyers, especially in a *buyer's market* offering lots of choice to relatively few buyers, have a keen eye to pricing. You could defer a sale if the offers you're seeing aren't what you want, but you may not have the luxury of time.

To improve your chance of selling the property, gain as much exposure for the property as possible so that competition increases sufficiently to warrant a higher price. One of the key things you want to ask the real estate agent you select to market your property is what sort of marketing he can do for you. Write details of the marketing plan into the listing agreement. An effective plan may make a difference in how you optimize the curb appeal of your property, what price you ask, how quickly the property sells, and what you eventually sell for.

Be sure to weigh the cost of a marketing blitz for your property against the higher value you hope to get from a property. Any exposure should have a payoff in the form of a faster sale, or greater sales proceeds.

Conditions: Clause for thought

A buyer's offer to purchase may include various subject clauses, points to be resolved before the deal goes firm and closes. Asking for a few clauses of your own gives you some leverage in the deal. These may include the following:

✦ **Removal of conditions in the event of a backup offer:** You may wish to keep your hands free in case a more attractive, competing bid emerges following receipt of an initial purchase offer. The standard time stated in such clauses is usually 72 hours. The clause stipulates the removal of conditions from the initial bid in the event a more favourable bid comes forward.

✦ **Legal review:** Your lawyer should review any real estate deal you enter, whether it's a purchase or sale. Ask for enough time to thoroughly review the purchaser's offer, and then in some cases follow up any specific concerns.

✦ **Timeline:** Set a time limit for the evaluation of the deal, usually a minimum of 24 hours but sometimes as much as four months. You want to be able to satisfy any outstanding issues and be able to close the deal properly. When you accept a purchase offer, you'll also need to set a closing date. Requesting more time may give you greater opportunity to ensure a deal is the best one possible, but if the market is hot, you may opt to set a specific day and time for receiving offers. This creates an auction-like atmosphere, and prospective buyers know they need to offer their best price or risk losing the deal. A slower market allows for a more balanced approach and a longer time frame for reviewing offers and making counteroffers, sometimes up to two weeks.

We discuss subject clauses at greater length under "Making an offer" in this chapter.

Counting the benefits

Weaving a good story about a property is one way to support a relatively high asking price (note that by "weaving" we don't mean "making up"), but you can also point to several aspects of a property that support its claimed value:

✦ **Chattels:** The goods that are ancillary to the property itself are often assigned a value that is negotiable aside from any buildings and lands included in the deal. The greater the perceived value of these, the greater the price you can ask for the property.

✦ **Upgrades:** We discuss elsewhere in this chapter the importance of touting the improvements you've made to a property. The asking price should reflect these; highlight them as needed among the reasons why the property is worth the tremendous (yet very reasonable) amount you're seeking.

✦ **Goodwill:** Perhaps your property is a landmark apartment block on a prime corner. Perhaps the property has heritage status. You can sometimes assign a value to the importance of a property that pure market forces don't reflect. Knowledge of a property's history and importance boosts your chances of making a viable argument for its goodwill value.

Capitalizing on each of these elements allows you to boost the return a property delivers. You won't be able to claim each of them every time, but being familiar with their contribution to property value allows you to argue more effectively for a higher price.

Closing the deal

We discuss the legal requirements of closing a deal earlier in this chapter. Yet from a vendor's point of view, closing costs are a primary consideration in completing a successful investment. Miscalculate the costs and years of hard work could suffer a significant blow.

A primary concern is *prepayment costs,* a penalty charged for prepaying a *closed,* or locked-in, mortgage (we discuss closed mortgages and prepayment penalties in Chapter 2). The purchaser's assumption of your mortgage would save you from these charges, but you need to discuss any such arrangements during negotiations for the property.

For example, if five years are left on a mortgage's seven-year term and interest rates had decreased 3 percent from the rate on your mortgage, your decision to prepay the whole amount would leave the lender short in terms of lost interest revenue. The penalty in this scenario is normally the difference between your mortgage rate and the prevailing market rate for the balance of the term, or three months' interest (whichever is more). For an $800,000 locked-in mortgage bearing interest at a rate three percentage points above the rate when you decide to repay, you would find yourself paying a $24,000 penalty (that is, $800,000 \times 0.03$). But you could avoid the penalty if the buyer agreed to assume the mortgage.

When someone assumes the mortgage you originally secured, obtain a release from your lender in case the new buyer defaults on the mortgage. Otherwise, you could be held responsible for the balance of your original mortgage.

Make sure the proceeds from the deal are taxed as little as possible. Your accountant can advise you on potential tax mitigation strategies prior to closing the deal. In fact, such strategies should form part of your investment strategy, given their importance to your portfolio's bottom line.

Index

Numerics

A

B

C

M

N

O

Q

R

S

BUSINESS & PERSONAL FINANCE

978-1-118-13346-0   978-0-470-73684-5

Also available:
- 76 Tips For Investing in an Uncertain Economy For Canadians For Dummies 978-0-470-16099-2
- Bookkeeping For Canadians For Dummies 978-0-470-73762-0
- Business Plans For Canadians For Dummies 978-0-470-15420-5
- Canadian Small Business Kit For Dummies 978-0-470-93652-8

- Investing For Canadians For Dummies 978-0-470-16029-9
- Personal Finance For Canadians For Dummies 978-0-470-67988-3
- Trading For Canadians For Dummies 978-0-470-67744-5
- Wills & Estate Planning For Canadians For Dummies 978-0-470-67657-8

EDUCATION, HISTORY & REFERENCE

978-0-7645-2498-1   978-0-470-46244-7

Also available:
- Algebra For Dummies 978-0-7645-5325-7
- Art History For Dummies 978-0-470-09910-0
- Canadian History For Dummies 978-0-470-83656-9
- Chemistry For Dummies 978-0-7645-5430-8

- English Grammar For Dummies 978-0-470-54664-2
- French For Dummies 978-0-7645-5193-2
- Statistics For Dummies 978-0-7645-5423-0
- The Canadian GED For Dummies 978-0-470-68091-9
- World History For Dummies 978-0-470-44654-6

FOOD, HOME, & MUSIC

978-0-7645-9904-0   978-0-470-67895-4

Also available:
- 30-Minute Meals For Dummies 978-0-7645-2589-6
- Bartending For Dummies 978-0-470-05056-9
- Brain Games For Dummies 978-0-470-37378-1
- Diabetes Cookbook For Canadians For Dummies 978-0-470-16028-2

- Gluten-Free Cooking For Dummies 978-0-470-17810-2
- Home Improvement All-in-One Desk Reference For Dummies 978-0-7645-5680-7
- Violin For Dummies 978-0-470-83838-9
- Wine For Dummies 978-0-470-04579-4

Available wherever books are sold. For more information or to order direct: U.S. customers visit www.dummies.com or call 1-877-762-2974. U.K. customers visit www.wileyeurope.com or call 0800 243407. Canadian customers visit www.wiley.ca or call 1-800-567-4797.

GARDENING

978-0-470-58161-2

978-0-470-57705-9

Also available:
- Gardening Basics For Dummies 978-0-470-03749-2
- Organic Gardening For Dummies 978-0-470-43067-5
- Sustainable Landscaping For Dummies 978-0-470-41149-0
- Vegetable Gardening For Dummies 978-0-470-49870-5

GREEN/SUSTAINABLE

978-0-470-84098-6

978-0-470-59678-4

Also available:
- Alternative Energy For Dummies 978-0-470-43062-0
- Energy Efficient Homes For Dummies 978-0-470-37602-7
- Green Building & Remodelling For Dummies 978-0-470-17559-0
- Green Cleaning For Dummies 978-0-470-39106-8
- Green Your Home All-in-One For Dummies 978-0-470-59678-4

HEALTH & SELF-HELP

978-0-471-77383-2

978-0-470-16036-7

Also available:
- Borderline Personality Disorder For Dummies 978-0-470-46653-7
- Breast Cancer For Dummies 978-0-7645-2482-0
- Cognitive Behavioural Therapy For Dummies 978-0-470-01838-5
- Diabetes For Canadians For Dummies 978-0-
- Emotional Intelligence For Dummies 978-0-470-15732-9
- Healthy Aging For Dummies 978-0-470-14975-1
- Neuro-linguistic Programming For Dummies 978-0-7645-7028-5
- Understanding Autism For Dummies 978-0-7645-2547-6

HOBBIES & CRAFTS

978-0-470-28747-7   978-0-470-29112-2

Also available:
- Crochet Patterns For Dummies
  97-0-470-04555-8
- Digital Scrapbooking For Dummies
  978-0-7645-8419-0
- Knitting Patterns For Dummies
  978-0-470-04556-5

- Oil Painting For Dummies
  978-0-470-18230-7
- Quilting For Dummies
  978-0-7645-9799-2
- Sewing For Dummies
  978-0-7645-6847-3
- Word Searches For Dummies
  978-0-470-45366-7

HOME & BUSINESS COMPUTER BASICS

978-0-470-49743-2   978-0-470-48953-6

Also available:
- Office 2010 All-in-One Desk
  Reference For Dummies
  978-0-470-49748-7
- Pay Per Click Search Engine
  Marketing For Dummies
  978-0-471-75494-7

- Search Engine Marketing For
  Dummies 978-0-471-97998-2
- Web Analytics For Dummies
  978-0-470-09824-0
- Word 2010 For Dummies
  978-0-470-48772-3

INTERNET & DIGITAL MEDIA

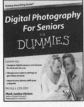 

978-0-470-44417-7   978-0-470-39062-7

Also available:
- Blogging For Dummies
  978-0-471-77084-8
- MySpace For Dummies
  978-0-470-09529-4

- The Internet For Dummies
  978-0-470-12174-0
- Twitter For Dummies
  978-0-470-47991-9
- YouTube For Dummies
  978-0-470-14925-6

MACINTOSH

978-0-470-27817-8   978-0-470-58027-1

Also available:
- iMac For Dummies
  978-0-470-13386-6
- iPod Touch For Dummies
  978-0-470-50530-4
- iPod & iTunes For Dummies
  978-0-470-39062-7

- MacBook For Dummies
  978-0-470-27816-1
- Macs For Seniors For Dummies
  978-0-470-43779-7
- Mac OS X Snow Leopard All-in-One
  Desk Reference For Dummies
  978-0-470-43541-0

PETS

978-0-470-60029-0   978-0-7645-5267-0

Also available:
- Cats For Dummies
  978-0-7645-5275-5
- Ferrets For Dummies
  978-0-470-13943-1

- Horses For Dummies
  978-0-7645-9797-8
- Kittens For Dummies
  978-0-7645-4150-6
- Puppies For Dummies
  978-1-118-11755-2

SPORTS & FITNESS

978-0-471-76871-5   978-0-470-73855-9

Also available:
- Exercise Balls For Dummies
  978-0-7645-5623-4
- Coaching Volleyball For Dummies
  978-0-470-46469-4
- Curling For Dummies
  978-0-470-83828-0
- Fitness For Dummies
  978-0-7645-7851-9

- Mixed Martial Arts For Dummies
  978-0-470-39071-9
- Sports Psychology For Dummies
  978-0-470-67659-2
- Ten Minute Tone-Ups For Dummies
  978-0-7645-7207-4
- Wilderness Survival For Dummies
  978-0-470-45306-3
- Yoga with Weights For Dummies
  978-0-471-74937-0